DETECTING
ACCOUNTING FRAUD

DETECTING ACCOUNTING FRAUD

ANALYSIS AND ETHICS

Cecil W. Jackson
University of Southern California

PEARSON

Boston Columbus Indianapolis New York San Francisco Upper Saddle River
Amsterdam Cape Town Dubai London Madrid Milan Munich Paris Montréal Toronto
Delhi Mexico City São Paulo Sydney Hong Kong Seoul Singapore Taipei Tokyo

Editor in Chief: Donna Battista
Acquisitions Editor: Lacey Vitetta
Editorial Project Manager: Nicole Sam
Editorial Assistant: Christine Donovan
Director of Marketing: Maggie Moylan
Marketing Manager: Alison Haskins
Team Lead, Project Management: Jeff Holcomb
Senior Production Project Manager: Liz Napolitano
Manager, Rights & Permissions: Michael Joyce
Rights & Permissions Coordinator: Samantha Graham
Senior Manufacturing Buyer: Carol Melville

Cover Designer: Laura Gardner
Cover Art: background graphic: Mark Bernard/ Shutterstock; main image: Maxim Kazmin/Fotolia
Full-Service Project Management: GEX Publishing Services
Composition: GEX Publishing Services
Printer/Binder: Edwards Brothers Malloy/ State Street
Cover Printer: Lehigh-Phoenix Color/Hagerstown
Typeface: Palatino 10/12

Library of Congress Cataloging-in-Publication Data
Jackson, Cecil Wilfrid.
 Detecting accounting fraud : analysis and ethics / Cecil W. Jackson, University of Southern California.
   pages cm
 ISBN 978-0-13-307860-2 (pbk.)
  1. Accounting fraud--United States. 2. Corporations--Accounting--Corrupt practices--United States.
  3. Corporations--Accounting--Law and legislation--United States. I. Title.
 HF5686.C7J263 2015
 658.4′73--dc23
                          2013041593

10 9 8 7 6 5 4 3 2

ISBN 10: 0-13-307860-4
ISBN 13: 978-0-13-307860-2

To my family:
Sandra, Kate, and David

BRIEF CONTENTS

CONTENTS

PREFACE

ABOUT THE BOOK

Accounting fraud, or the manipulation of financial statements, has become an increasingly serious issue over the last two decades, leading to the collapse of ostensibly solid companies, exacerbating a serious global recession, and resulting in an acute lack of confidence in financial markets and in the accuracy of financial statements. This book provides an informative and invaluable analysis of the **Top 20 Methods of Fictitious Financial Reporting** that lists the most frequently used methods of overstating earnings and assets and understating debt in financial statements. The book also presents a detailed examination of the main **Signals** indicating possible fictitious reporting in financial statements. Taking the viewpoint that no book on accounting fraud would be complete without an examination of the breakdown in ethics that underlies the fraud, this text examines the three major **Theories of Ethics**, as well as ethical decision-making models that are applicable to the business world in general and to students of accounting in particular.

Detecting Accounting Fraud: Analysis and Ethics takes the following **eight-step case-study approach**:

1. Identifies the accounting fraud or method of fictitious financial reporting utilized by a specific, real-world company.
2. Presents background information about the company and its key executives.
3. Describes the fraud or scheme in detail, referencing the company's financial statements as well as primary documents such as Accounting and Auditing Releases, Litigation Releases, SEC Complaints, and Bankruptcy Reports.
4. Explains how a particular accounting scheme or fraud leads to specific signals in the company's financial statements indicating that these financial statements have been manipulated.
5. Asks students to address relevant ethical issues in the "Ethics at Work" sections throughout the book.
6. Provides short, end-of-chapter questions to ascertain that students have understood the material.
7. Provides in-depth discussion questions and exercises to encourage a more comprehensive grasp of the material.
8. Presents a new, real-world case study of another company that perpetrated an accounting fraud or scheme similar to that discussed earlier in the chapter. Students are provided with extracts from this new company's financial statements, as well as relevant excerpts from original documents such as Litigation Releases and Complaints. Students are then given the opportunity to identify signals in this company's financial statements indicating how the company has manipulated its financial statements.

Intended Audience

This book has been written for instructors and students of undergraduate and graduate courses to be used in the following areas:

- Accounting Fraud (in business schools, MBA programs, and law schools)
- Accounting Ethics and Business Ethics
- Financial Accounting Case Studies
- Auditing (in business schools and MBA programs)

Distinguishing Features of *Detecting Accounting Fraud: Analysis and Ethics*

- In addition to analyzing the more well-known case studies (Sunbeam, WorldCom, and Countrywide), the book presents a number of new and unusual real-world case studies for students to examine. These include companies such as Beazer Homes, Peregrine Systems, Buca, Inc., and TierOne Bank.
- The book is written in a lively and engaging style, with interesting background information on many of the companies and their executives.
- The material is well organized and complex material is presented in a logical, easy-to-follow manner as the chapters systematically examine the *Top 20 Methods of Fictitious Financial Reporting.*
- The book concludes with a useful Appendix summarizing the *Top 25 Signals Indicating Possible Fictitious Reporting in Financial Statements.*
- Students are presented with a variety of original, primary documents (or relevant extracts from such documents), adding a high level of authenticity to the real-world cases covered in the text.
- Students are given the opportunity to examine the ethical dimensions (or lack thereof) of a variety of the case studies.
- The wide range of end-of-chapter assignments provides students with ample opportunity to apply what they have learned.
- The new case studies presented at the end of the chapters give students the valuable opportunity to examine original documents and look for evidence of accounting manipulation in a real-world company.
- The book features an extensive list of references for each chapter, inviting further research and reading on the various topics covered.

INSTRUCTOR SUPPLEMENTS

Instructor's Solutions Manual: The Instructor's Solutions Manual provides both thought-provoking responses to all the open-ended questions and clear, concise solutions to the broad range of accounting issues and numerical questions presented in the text. To assist the instructor in guiding student discussions on ethical issues, the manual presents a range of comprehensive responses to all the questions in the Ethics at Work sections. It also contains answers to all the True/False, Fill-in-the-Blank, and Multiple Choice Questions in each chapter. It offers suggested responses to all the Discussion Questions, as well as detailed answers to all the Short-Answer Questions and Case Study Questions.

PowerPoint Presentations: Complete PowerPoint presentations are provided for each chapter. Instructors may download and use each presentation as is or customize the slides. Each presentation allows instructors to offer an interactive presentation using colorful graphics, outlines of chapter material, and graphical explanations of difficult topics.

Both the Instructor's Solutions Manual and the PowerPoint presentations are available online at www.pearsonhighered.com/irc.

ACKNOWLEDGMENTS

It certainly "takes a village" to write a book, and this book could not have been written without the encouragement and support of many. Thanks to the Leventhal School of Accounting and the Marshall School of Business at the University of Southern California and to the many undergraduate and graduate students who have taken my classes on detecting accounting fraud over the years and have provided valuable feedback on the material presented in this text.

Thank you to the following reviewers, whose comments helped to shape the final manuscript: Richard G. Brody, University of New Mexico; Jim Cali, Southern Illinois University – Carbondale; Judith M. Clark, The University of Northwestern Ohio; Dr. Marina Grau, Houston Community College-Southwest; Venkataraman Iyer, University of North Carolina at Greensboro; Jacquelyne L. Lewis, North Carolina Wesleyan College; and Timothy A. Weiss, University of Northwestern Ohio.

A warm thank-you to the people at Pearson for their various and invaluable contributions to this project: to Sari Orlansky for initiating the venture; to Stephanie Wall for bringing me on board; to Donna Battista for her guidance; to Lacey Vitetta, Nicole Sam, Liz Napolitano, and Christine Donovan, thank you for successfully and expertly steering the project through the complex publication process. To Linda Harrison, the development editor, thanks for the helpful and insightful feedback. To Kelly Morrison at GEX Publishing Services, many thanks for navigating this book through production so efficiently.

To Christine Burdick-Bell who, in spite of her demanding schedule, is always available to answer a question or give valuable feedback on the text, I am sincerely grateful.

To my daughter Kate—Ph.D. student and budding ethicist—thank you for your significant contributions to the chapter on "Ethics at Work" and for the assignments and suggested solutions to accompany that chapter.

To my wife, Sandra, thank you for keeping track of everything and keeping everything on track! You brought your expertise to every step of the process, and I could not have completed this book without you.

ABOUT THE AUTHOR

Cecil Jackson, Professor of Clinical Accounting in the Leventhal School of Accounting at the University of Southern California, teaches courses on detecting accounting fraud and on managerial accounting for the MBA program as well as the graduate and under-graduate accounting programs. Dr. Jackson developed Leventhal's highly regarded course on "Detecting Fraudulent Financial Reporting."

Cecil Jackson's previous book, *Business Fairy Tales: Grim Realities of Fictitious Financial Reporting* (2006) received favorable reviews from publications such as *Barrons*, *The CPA Journal*, *Investor's Business Daily*, the *Motley Fool*, and *The Accounting Review*.

Dr. Jackson has appeared on a number of business news shows, including *Bloomberg Television*, *The Street.Com*, and *CNN*. He has worked for two leading public accounting firms and qualified as both a CPA and Chartered Accountant. Dr. Jackson has won several awards for his teaching and is a respected speaker and consultant on aggressive financial reporting issues. In May 2010, he was awarded the prestigious Evan C. Thompson Teaching and Learning Innovation Award by the Marshall School of Business. In May 2012, he was voted one of the best professors in the Marshall School of Business and received the Golden Apple Award.

DETECTING ACCOUNTING FRAUD

CHAPTER 1

Introduction to the Problem of Accounting Fraud

Learning Objectives

After studying this chapter, you should be able to:

- Identify the elements of accounting fraud.
- Recognize the pervasiveness of accounting fraud.
- Identify the major financial gatekeepers in corporate governance.
- Explain the main elements of Sarbanes-Oxley reform.
- Explain the main elements of Dodd-Frank reform.
- Identify the top 20 methods used to manipulate financial statements.

CHAPTER OUTLINE

- What Is Accounting Fraud?
- Accounting Fraud at the Turn of the Millennium
- The Sarbanes-Oxley Act of 2002
- Accounting Fraud and the Financial Crisis of 2008
- The Dodd-Frank Act of 2010
- The Top 20 Methods of Fictitious Financial Reporting
- Assignments

Although gold dust is precious, when it gets in your eyes it obstructs
your vision.

—His-Tang Chih Tsang, Chinese Zen Master

In July 2010, in the wake of the mortgage crisis and financial tsunami that had hit the United States in 2008, Mary L. Schapiro, then chairman of the United States Securities and Exchange Commission (SEC), described the vast damage caused by the financial crisis and went on to point out: "One of the fundamental requirements for rational investing and efficient capital formation is the availability of high quality information. One of our core functions is collecting and making publicly available financial and other relevant information from public companies." The health of our markets—and the very foundation of our financial system—relies on the production and accessibility of this "high quality" financial information.

Unfortunately, as a review of the last 15 years reveals, the financial information from a variety of public companies that were once regarded as mainstays of the U.S. economy was naïvely misleading at best and blatantly fraudulent at worst. Numerous executives have been exposed in cases of greed and betrayal, of blatant duplicity and moral bankruptcy. Central to almost every case discussed in this book is the fact that these corporate executives manipulated financial statements—or encouraged others to tamper with financial statement disclosures—and misled those who trusted them.

WHAT IS ACCOUNTING FRAUD?

Before addressing *accounting fraud*, it is helpful to briefly examine the concept of *fraud* in general. Defining *fraud* is a complex legal exercise, and definitions may differ from state to state, from federal courts to state courts, and from criminal cases to civil cases. This discussion addresses the issue in broad terms and is not meant to be taken as legal advice. The Association of Certified Fraud Examiners describes fraud as follows:

> In practice, fraud embraces all the multifarious means that human ingenuity can devise for one person to gain an advantage over another by false suggestion or suppression of the truth. No final, invariable rule can be laid down in defining fraud—according to *Black's Law Dictionary*, the act of fraud includes surprise, trick, cunning, and a range of unfair ways by which people are cheated. The only boundaries are those that limit human knavery. (*The Fraud Trial*, 2011, p. 6)

According to Lawrence and Wells (2004), "Under common law, three elements are required to prove fraud: a material false statement made with an intent to deceive ..., a victim's reliance on the statement and damages." The Federal Bureau of Investigation (FBI) defines *fraud* as follows: "The intentional perversion of the truth for the purpose of inducing another person or other entity in reliance upon it to part with something of value or to surrender a legal right" (*www.fbi.gov*).

Accounting fraud (also sometimes called "corporate fraud[1]" or "financial reporting fraud") is a particular type of fraud that involves the manipulation of financial statements. In its report on *Deterring and Detecting Financial Reporting Fraud* (2010), the Center for Audit Quality defines *financial reporting fraud* as "a material misrepresentation resulting from an intentional failure to report financial information in accordance with generally accepted accounting principles" (p. i).

For criminal fraud cases, the burden of proof (or level of proof) required is generally higher than for civil fraud cases: "For civil cases that burden is a 'preponderance of evidence.' In criminal fraud the standard is 'beyond a reasonable doubt'" (Lawrence & Wells, 2004). For this reason, many cases of accounting fraud are tried in civil court or result in civil actions such as SEC enforcement actions.

Civil Accounting Fraud

The Enforcement Division of the SEC publishes "financial reporting related enforcement actions concerning civil lawsuits brought by the Commission in federal court and notices and orders concerning the institution and/or settlement of administrative proceedings" ("Accounting and Auditing Enforcement Releases"). The SEC issues its findings in the form of an Accounting and Auditing Enforcement Release (AAER) or a Litigation Release (LR) or both. In an AAER or LR, the SEC describes how a company has allegedly infringed securities law. The SEC will usually accept an "Offer of Settlement," and the respondents agree to the "Order Instituting Public Administrative and Cease and Desist Proceedings." The respondents generally do not admit or deny the findings.

After the Sarbanes-Oxley (SOX) Act was passed in 2002, SEC enforcement actions increased from 598 in fiscal year 2002 (Dickey, Sturc, & Van Lobels Sels, 2003) to 679 actions in fiscal 2003. The next few years saw a slowdown in cases, until the financial crisis hit the economy to cause another upswing in enforcement actions. As can be seen in Figure 1.1 (below), the SEC's Enforcement Actions cover a range of financial violations, such as insider trading, market manipulation, and securities offering violations in addition to financial fraud/issuer disclosure violations. The category of "Financial Fraud/Issuer Disclosure" (i.e., accounting fraud) involves violations related to financial statements and financial disclosures released by "issuers" of financial statements. These are the types of violations that we examine in this text.

The crisis of 2008 shifted the focus of SEC enforcement investigations and actions away from accounting and issuer disclosure violations for a few years. According to an article in The *Wall Street Journal*, it is expected that

---

[1] While not all corporate fraud is accounting fraud, accounting fraud is the most prevalent and most damaging form of corporate fraud. ("Financial Crimes Report," 2011. *www.fbi.gov*)

FIGURE 1.1	Year-by-Year SEC Enforcement Statistics									
Enforcement Actions by Fiscal Year	2003	2004	2005	2006	2007	2008	2009	2010	2011	2012
Broker-Dealer	137	140	94	75	89	67	109	70	112	134
Delinquent Filings	n/a	n/a	n/a	91	52	113	92	106	121	127
FCPA[2]	n/a	n/a	n/a	n/a	n/a	n/a	n/a	n/a	20*	15
Financial Fraud/ Issuer Disclosure	199	179	185	138	219	154	143	126	89**	79
Insider Trading	50	42	50	46	47	61	37	53	57	58
Investment Adviser/ Investment Co.	72	90	97	87	79	87	76	113	146	147
Market Manipulation	32	39	46	27	36	53	39	34	35	46
Securities Offering	109	99	60	61	68	115	141	144	124	89
Other	80	50	98	49	65	21	27	35	31	39
Total Enforcement Actions	**679**	**639**	**630**	**574**	**655**	**671**	**664**	**681**	**735**	**734**

* Prior to FY 2011, FCPA was not a distinct category and FCPA actions were classified as Issuer Reporting and Disclosure.

** Prior to FY 2011, this category was reported as Issuer Reporting and Disclosure and included FCPA actions, which are now tracked separately from Financial Fraud/Issuer Disclosure actions.

Source: *www.sec.gov/news/newsroom/images/enfstats.pdf*

new SEC Chairman Mary Jo White, who assumed leadership of the SEC in April 2013, will be more likely to shift SEC focus back to accounting fraud in future years (Eaglesham, May 27, 2013). A recent article in *Accounting Today* agrees that the SEC's emphasis will move from fraud on "Wall Street to Main Street" (Cohn, 2013).

Criminal Accounting Fraud

Sometimes, a company may also be pursued by the Department of Justice and the Federal Bureau of Investigation (FBI) and charged with criminal fraud. Since 2010, the FBI has had special agents "embedded at the SEC" to swiftly isolate securities and corporate frauds and initiate criminal investigations where necessary (Mueller, 2012). Most of the criminal corporate fraud investigated by the Financial Crimes Section (FCS) of the FBI involves financial reporting fraud:

> The majority of corporate fraud cases pursued by the FBI involve accounting schemes designed to deceive investors, auditors, and analysts about the true

---

[2] Foreign Corrupt Practices Act.

financial condition of a corporation or business entity. Through the manipulation of financial data, the share price, or other valuation measurements of a corporation, financial performance may remain artificially inflated based on fictitious performance indicators provided to the investing public. In addition to significant financial losses to investors, corporate fraud has the potential to cause immeasurable damage to the U.S. economy and investor confidence. ("Financial Crimes Report," 2011)

The number of corporate fraud cases pursued by the FBI has grown steadily since 2007. At the end of its 2011 fiscal year, the FBI was investigating 726 cases of corporate fraud in the United States (Figure 1.2).

The Extent of Accounting Fraud

While there is some debate concerning the extent of corporate fraud, in their study "How Pervasive Is Corporate Fraud?" (2013), Dyck, Morse, and Zingales posit that there is an "iceberg" of corporate fraud and falsified financial statements that remains undetected and that the iceberg is "3 times bigger under the water than above the water" (p. 4).

In addition, accounting-related litigation is on the upswing. According to a recent Cornerstone Research article, "In 2012, the proportion of securities class action settlements involving accounting allegations increased to almost 70 percent from less than 50 percent in 2011" (qtd. in Wilczynski, 2013).

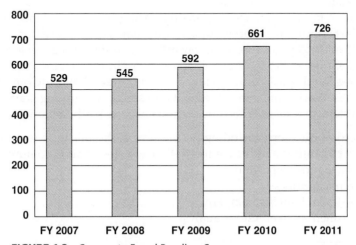

FIGURE 1.2   Corporate Fraud Pending Cases

Source: "Financial Crimes Report to the Public: Fiscal Years 2010–2011." (October 1, 2009–September 30, 2011). Federal Bureau of Investigation. *www.fbi.gov*

Increasingly, corporate frauds are also being exposed through the relatively new Dodd-Frank Whistleblower Program. According to the SEC, in 2012, the most frequent whistleblower complaints "related to corporate disclosures and financials" ("SEC Receives …," 2012). Clearly, in spite of increased regulations, accounting fraud remains a serious and persistent problem.

ACCOUNTING FRAUD AT THE TURN OF THE MILLENNIUM

At the turn of the millennium, the nation's attention was focused on the dangers of fictitious financial reports and the shortcomings of the financial reporting system as a result of the spectacular business and financial reporting failures of Enron and WorldCom.

Enron and WorldCom

In an Amended Complaint (May 1, 2003) charging Enron executives with fraud, the Deputy Director of the Enforcement Division of the SEC, Linda Chatman Thomsen, declared:

> At a point when Enron's touted groundbreaking broadband technology was little more than a concept—and its business model was not commercially viable—these defendants played important roles in perpetuating the fairy tale that Enron was capable of spinning straw—or more appropriately, fiber—into gold.

Within weeks of the beginning of Enron's meltdown in mid-October 2001, employees had lost over a billion dollars' worth of Enron stock in their 401(k) plans, stockholders had lost billions of dollars as the stock price fell from $60 per share to below $1, and debt holders were about to lose more than $3.9 billion that Enron owed them. On December 3, 2001, about 4,000 of Enron's employees were given notice to leave the company on the same day.

Unfortunately, Enron's accounting fraud was just one more case in an all-too-frequent litany of falsified financial reports that had grown in incidence over the 1990s and into the 21st century, when accounting fraud seemed to reach pandemic proportions. WorldCom's bankruptcy was soon to follow in 2002, and staggeringly, it topped Enron's[3].

In his *First Interim Report* (2002), Richard Thornburgh, WorldCom's Bankruptcy Examiner, presented a list of the gatekeepers who failed WorldCom. Thornburgh found failure by WorldCom's management and senior accounting staff and its internal control system, as well as failed checks and balances by the following gatekeepers:

- The board of directors, including general oversight failure as well as failures by the audit committee and the compensation and stock option committee
- The internal audit department
- The external auditors
- The investment banking company
- The investment banker's stock analyst

---

[3]However, six years later, in September 2008, Lehman Brothers became the largest bankruptcy in U.S. history and Washington Mutual became the second largest. WorldCom dropped to third place, and Enron's bankruptcy fell to sixth on the list (Ovide, 2011).

What gatekeeping checks and balances were in place in the financial reporting environment at that time? Why did these checks and balances fail? What were the factors that led to such widespread allegations of accounting fraud?

Stock Options

Because management has ultimate responsibility for the preparation of a company's financial statements, it is not surprising that the huge rise in the incidence of fraudulent financial reporting enforcement actions at the turn of the millennium was associated with huge increases in incentives for management to present financial statements that overstated earnings. Time and time again, the SEC's AAERs alleged that management orchestrated frauds to meet Wall Street analysts' earnings expectations. In most cases, senior management compensation agreements included stock options that would provide significant additional remuneration if analysts' earnings expectations were met.

Former SEC chairman Arthur Levitt (2002) told of the losing battle that he fought when he tried to pass measures that he believed would cool the dramatic increase in the granting of stock options as a major form of executive compensation. As SEC chairman, Levitt had seen firsthand the temptations created by massive options grants. Levitt thought that if companies had to expense the value of stock options given to executives as compensation, the decrease in earnings reported in the income statement would dampen shareholders' willingness to agree to awarding stock options as an ever-increasing form of executive compensation.

By 2001, a troubling 80 percent of top management compensation "was in the form of stock options" (Levitt, 2002, p. 111). In an article by Byrne, Lavelle, Byrnes, and Vickers in May 2002, *Business Week* reported that in 2001, "CEOs of large corporations made 411 times as much as the average factory worker." This was up dramatically from the 1970s when CEOs had earned only about 20 times more than average workers (Weissmann, 2013). With the lure of tantalizing riches from stock options, many top executives could not resist the temptation to present financial statements that satisfied Wall Street's earnings expectations.

External Auditors

At the same time that stock options were growing rapidly as a component of executive compensation, Levitt was also fighting a losing battle against another growing trend that concerned him. External auditors were collecting ever-escalating consulting fees from the same clients for whom they performed "independent" audits. At the beginning of 2002, an article in *Business Week* confirmed that consulting fees for external auditors were spiraling: "That accountants have become increasingly dependent on consulting is clear.... In 1993, 31% of the industry's fees came from consulting. By 1999, that had jumped to 51%." It may be a matter of debate whether keeping the audit client because of the audit fees alone was enough to make some auditors compromise their audits or whether the double incentive of consulting fees was a deciding force. However, the high number of SEC enforcement actions revealed too many auditors who either accepted scope limitations on their audits—such as not demanding full access to the entire general ledger and not issuing a disclaimer or qualified report on the financial statements—or who knowingly yielded to incorrect financial statements. Clearly, many auditors could not take the increased pressure from management who stood to gain significantly from fraudulent financial reports. *Business Week* summed it up as follows: "Still, in many people's minds the rising importance of consulting has contributed to a decline in auditor skepticism. It simply looks bad to have Andersen earning more on consulting to Enron than on auditing." (Quotes from Nanette Byrnes et al., 2002)

Together with condemnation for accepting increasing consulting fees from audit clients, the auditing environment faced other tough criticisms at the time of the colossal reporting failures. The self-policing practices of the auditing profession came under scrutiny. Since 1977, the Public Oversight Board (POB) had been responsible for monitoring audit independence and quality. However, this board did not have the power to subpoena, nor did it have any real power to punish wrongdoers, and with the onslaught of accounting frauds, the American Institute of CPAs (AICPA) came to loggerheads with the oversight board. The board ceased to exist in May 2002.[4] The AICPA also had a peer review system, but "no Big Five[5] firm [had] ever failed a review" (Nanette Byrnes et al., 2002). Regrettably, the oversight division lacked the weapons to protect its domain.

Furthermore, as scrutiny of the Enron failure showed, independent auditors would frequently leave the auditing profession and join the staff of a company that they had audited. Clearly, there was often too much familiarity and camaraderie between a former employee of an audit firm and the external auditors, making it difficult for the external auditors to remain entirely independent.

Finally, audit firms usually audited the same companies year after year, developing friendships with management, growing complacent, and sometimes dropping their guard. Mandatory rotation of auditors could have prevented them from losing their independence in at least two ways: First, the forced rotation would have precluded the audit firms from building too much familiarity. Second, knowing that a new firm would be arriving the following year and reviewing the work papers and the client's financial statements would have been an added incentive for external auditors to resist management's pressure to compromise their audits.

Boards of Directors

In attempting to address yet another corporate governance concern, Levitt (2002) focused his attention on both chummy and absentee members of companies' boards of directors. In his book *Take on the Street*, Levitt discussed the many directors who lacked independence, as well as those directors who were indifferent and had no interest in company activities. Levitt also observed that there were too many "inside" directors who were company employees and that there were too few "outside" directors.

---

[4] The POB was replaced by the Public Company Accounting Oversight Board (PCAOB), which was created by the SOX Act of 2002.

[5] The Big Five became the Big Four after the collapse of Arthur Andersen in 2002.

Further, he pointed out that too many "outside" directors apparently lacked independence in the sense that they were either friends or relatives of the company's CEO, were associated with competing businesses, or had been involved in business transactions with the corporation and had earned lucrative fees. All of these situations could, and often did, influence a director's autonomy in overseeing the direction of the company. Levitt (2002) described some of the responsibilities of a board of directors:

> One of its responsibilities is to advise the CEO and the top executive team with impartial common sense and various kinds of expertise. The board should meet regularly to discuss such issues as the ongoing health of the business, the current management team and its performance, the compensation of the top executives, and the future outlook of the company. (pp. 207–208)

Typical of many boards in the late 1990s and into the new millennium, WorldCom's board was criticized by the Bankruptcy Examiner for not monitoring the outrageous, unfocused growth of WorldCom. In addition, the board's compensation committee came under scrutiny for its "generosity" to the CEO, Bernard Ebbers. The audit committee of WorldCom's board of directors was scrutinized for its lax supervision of accounting issues.

Investment Bankers

Thornburgh, WorldCom's Bankruptcy Examiner, also criticized WorldCom's investment banker, Salomon Smith Barney (SSB), and its star analyst, Jack Grubman. Thornburgh described SSB's distribution of coveted "Friends of the Company" IPO shares to Ebbers, WorldCom's CEO. Thornburgh then revealed the correlation between the allotments of these shares to Ebbers and WorldCom's allocation of investment banking work to SSB. Grubman was under pressure to provide favorable reports on certain companies in order for SSB to obtain more investment banking business from them. This was not an isolated problem. Arthur Levitt (2002) reported: "In April 2002, the Justice Department, Securities and Exchange Commission, and state regulators opened investigations of possible wrongdoing by research analysts at major Wall Street firms" (p. 65). These investigations were prompted by subpoenaed e-mails that seemed to confirm many rumors:

> Wall Street analysts often recommended to investors shares of companies that have an investment banking relationship with their firm; yet privately, analysts deride these same companies…. [A Merrill Lynch analyst] in one e-mail referred to a company that he had bullishly recommended as "a piece of junk." (Levitt, 2002, p. 65)

In the rush to jump on the bandwagons of IPOs, hot dot-coms, and other get-rich-quick schemes, many investment bankers and analysts lost their independence, their impartiality, and their ability to provide their clients with sound and objective investment advice. Analysts' reports on the results of their research into companies became one more gatekeeping function that could not be relied upon. The promise of lucrative investment banking work may have been the driving force behind an upgrade of a company's stock, and signals that the financial statements might be fraudulently prepared may have been ignored … for a fee.

Internal Controls

However, even if every one of the gatekeepers previously discussed failed in their duties, were there no other checks and balances in the form of internal control systems and internal audit departments to guard against the production and publication of fraudulent financial statements? Once again, Enron and WorldCom were symptomatic of the recurrent problems of inadequate and flawed systems of internal controls, as well as indicative of understaffed internal audit departments that came under the authority of the very managers they were meant to audit. The responsibility of management to institute controls ensuring the integrity of the accounting information captured was not clearly defined. The duties of the external auditors regarding the system of internal control were not well specified. Although members of WorldCom's internal audit department were finally instrumental in uncovering the financial reporting frauds and reporting them to the board of directors, WorldCom's Bankruptcy Examiner faulted both the company's system of internal controls and the understaffing of its internal audit department. It was also problematic that the internal audit department ultimately reported to the CFO, Scott Sullivan, who was the major originator of the tall tales underlying WorldCom's accounting fraud.

Such was the financial reporting environment at the turn of the 21st century as the management of so many companies, blinded by the lure of stock option riches, recklessly pushed and pressurized everyone in the system to go along with the fabricated financial statements. What happened to WorldCom and Enron was the result of a seriously flawed financial reporting environment that permitted all of their gatekeepers to fail them in the same ways that hundreds of other companies' custodians failed their stakeholders. The frauds were not limited to any particular industry or sector of the economy, nor were they limited to just a couple of varieties of sham reporting. The suspect companies ranged from medical corporations to theatrical companies, from manufacturers of kitchen electrics to conglomerates that sold electricity. In the five-year period ending July 30, 2002, the SEC filed 515 enforcement actions against "164 entities and 705 individuals" (SOX Report, 2002, p. 1).

In an attempt to deal with the morass of corporate problems and the huge public outcry, in July 2002, Congress passed the Public Company Accounting Reform and Investor Protection Act of 2002, also known as the Sarbanes-Oxley Act or the SOX Act.

THE SARBANES-OXLEY ACT OF 2002

The major goals of the SOX Act are "to enhance corporate responsibility, enhance financial disclosures and combat corporate and accounting fraud, and [create] the 'Public Company Accounting Oversight Board,' also known as the PCAOB, to oversee the activities of the auditing profession" ("The Laws …," 2012). The PCAOB "ended more than 100 years of self-regulation by the public company audit profession" ("The Sarbanes-Oxley Act at 10," 2012).

This act—sponsored by Senator Paul Sarbanes (D-Md.) and Congressman Michael Oxley (R-Ohio)—was intended to restore what Senator Sarbanes called the "fundamental integrity" of U.S. markets. Initially, some ardent supporters of the legislation regarded it as a type of magic potion, a cure-all for the problems plaguing the corporate world. Although it was drawn up and passed quite rapidly, it took several years, countless squabbles, and many millions of dollars for the various facets of the SOX Act to be implemented.

The expensive, complex, and often vague internal control requirements of the contentious and much-maligned Section 404 of SOX caused critics to argue that the hefty compliance costs actually impeded corporations. The question of corporate compensation—only partially addressed by the SOX Act—remains another difficult issue with no easy answers in a free market economy. A 2013 report published by the Institute for Policy Studies points out: "The pay gap between CEOs and average American workers has grown from 195-to-1 in 1993 to 354-to-1 in 2012" (Anderson, Klinger, & Pizzigati, 2013).

The SOX Act also had its quirky side with some unexpected consequences. For example, Section 301 of SOX mandated the establishment of hotlines for anonymous whistleblowers. This caused problems for some U.S. companies with European subsidiaries because very few countries in Europe have laws that protect whistleblowers.

In spite of the glitches encountered implementing SOX, the reform was a rational response to problems that endangered the fundamental stability of our capital markets. In addition to the SEC's efforts to fulfill the requirements of the SOX Act, a number of other organizations set to work to clean up the corporate environment and create greater financial statement transparency.[6] For example:

- The Financial Accounting Standards Board (FASB) issued or updated several accounting standards.
- The PCAOB developed an extensive inspection program.
- The New York Stock Exchange (NYSE) and the National Association of Securities Dealers Automated Quotations (NASDAQ) added new requirements for their member companies.
- The Department of Justice made corporate fraud a priority, with increased penalties for corporate fraud and other corporate crimes.
- Business schools from coast to coast established courses in business ethics and corporate governance issues.
- An ongoing project was launched to integrate U.S. generally accepted accounting principles (GAAP) with international financial reporting standards (IFRS).

Some of the main areas of corporate governance reform as a result of the SOX Act of 2002 included the following:

- Internal control requirements (SOX Section 404)
- Responsibilities of corporate management (SOX Section 302)
- Loans to executives
- Independence and oversight of external auditors
- Audit committees
- Independence of boards of directors
- Independence of analysts
- Corporate crime enforcement

---

[6] Information in this section is mainly from Glassman (2005).

Internal Control Requirements (Section 404 of SOX)

While internal control is certainly not new, SOX emphasized it to such an extent that one of the most hotly contested parts of the SOX legislation was Section 404 on the grounds that compliance was extremely expensive and time-consuming. Section 404(a) "requires management to report on the effectiveness of the company's internal controls over financial reporting, and Section 404(b) requires the auditor's attestation regarding their effectiveness" ("The Sarbanes-Oxley Act at 10," 2012). In response to some of the criticisms, changes have been made to Section 404(b). The Dodd-Frank Act of 2010 eliminated certain Section 404(b) requirements for public companies "with less than $75 million in market capitalization," and the Jumpstart Our Business Startups Act (JOBS Act) of 2012 granted a five-year postponement to "certain emerging growth companies" after an initial public offering (Amato, 2012). Former Senator Sarbanes referred to the JOBS Act exemptions as "a scandal waiting to happen" (qtd. in Amato, 2012).

In a 2012 statement, the American Institute of CPAs came out in firm support of Section 404(b): "The AICPA has consistently urged implementation of Section 404(b) for all publicly held companies. It has led to improved financial reporting and greater transparency, and the AICPA believes all investors in public companies should have equal benefit of the same protections" (Melancon, 2012).

Responsibilities of Corporate Management (Section 302 of SOX)

Section 302 requires that the chief executive officers (CEOs) and the chief financial officers (CFOs) of public companies assume responsibility for certifying specific areas of "each annual or quarterly report filed or submitted" to the SEC. The *Executive Summary of the Sarbanes-Oxley Act* presents guidelines for CEOs and CFOs who are required to certify the following:

- The report does not contain untrue statements or material omissions.
- The financial statements fairly present, in all material respects, the financial conditions and results of operations.
- Such officers are responsible for internal controls designed to ensure that they receive material information regarding the issuer and consolidated subsidiaries.
- The internal controls have been reviewed for their effectiveness within 90 days prior to the report.

Other SOX Regulations

In addition to Sections 404 and 302, SOX established legislation covering a variety of other issues. Some of these include the following:

- *Loans to Executives*: Some of the most outrageous corporate looting prior to SOX occurred via a two-step loan process. First, boards of directors authorized huge loans to company officers. Second, the board sometimes conveniently authorized "forgiveness" of the loans. This process of granting outrageous company loans was particularly rampant in the case of WorldCom; for example, in 2001, the WorldCom Compensation Committee authorized loans or loan guarantees to Ebbers for $150 million. SOX now prohibits company loans to company officers and directors.

- *Independence and Oversight of External Auditors*: The SOX Act of 2002 established the PCAOB for the oversight of the audit of public companies. The act requires public accounting firms to register with the PCAOB, and it requires the board to establish or modify, as required, standards for auditing, reporting, ethics, and quality control. It equips the PCAOB with disciplinary powers and requires the PCAOB to inspect and investigate registered accounting firms and to enforce compliance with the established standards.

   The NYSE and the NASDAQ have also strengthened corporate governance and filing requirements.

   The SOX Act also prohibits public accounting firms from performing specified non-audit services for the firms that they audit. If a senior executive of a company was previously employed by the company's auditor and worked on the company's audit, the audit firm is prohibited from auditing that company for a period of one year. (It is worth noting that Enron was notorious for hiring ex-Arthur Anderson employees who had worked on Enron audits.) SOX mandates auditor rotation by prohibiting an audit partner from being the lead or reviewing auditor of the same company for more than five consecutive years.

   In an attempt to decrease the likelihood of auditors being pressured by management into adopting manipulative accounting treatments, SOX requires reporting of the following to the board's audit committee for its review:
   - Critical accounting policies and practices used by the organization, including methods, assumptions, and judgments.
   - Alternative accounting treatments that were discussed with management, as well as their possible effects. (This provision could prevent the situation that arose at Enron, where Arthur Andersen's technical oversight partner, Carl Bass, objected to some of Enron's accounting treatments and was removed from involvement with the audit at Enron's request.)
- *Audit Committees*: Audit committees consisting of a minimum of three independent directors are required. In addition, the SEC requires disclosure as to whether at least one financial expert is serving on the audit committee or the reason why there is no financial expert on that committee.
- *Independence of Boards of Directors*: SOX instituted a number of requirements for boards of directors to improve their gatekeeping duties and to ensure the independence of the majority of directors on company boards.
- *Independence of Analysts*: Several of the accounting scandals discussed in this book involved investment banking analysts who publicly gave certain company stocks "buy" ratings but left e-mail trails revealing that they believed those stocks were actually poor investments. To deal with this issue, SOX added provisions mandating independence of analysts from their investment banking employers.
- *Corporate Crime Enforcement*: More generally, SOX legislation also increased penalties for other corporate crimes beyond the certification of false financial statements.

It has been well over a decade since the implementation of SOX. While there have been sweeping changes to the financial reporting environment (and many agree that SOX has instigated some positive changes), others maintain that SOX may have gone too far in its attempts to clean up the U.S. business landscape. Yet accounting fraud still continues to rear its ugly head. In their September 2012 article discussing the collapse of Peregrine Financial, Drawbaugh and Aubin commented: "When Peregrine Financial collapsed earlier this month, a nagging question resurfaced. As in the implosion of Lehman Brothers, the fall of Bernard Madoff and other cases in recent years, many asked: Where were the accountants?"

While there are those who say that the SOX reforms have not done enough to transform the financial-reporting environment, others believe that SOX "has strengthened auditing, made the accounting industry a better steward of financial standards, and fended off Enron-sized book-cooking disasters" (Drawbaugh & Aubin, 2012).

The fact remains that in 2002, after the SOX Act was signed into law, the corporate community heaved a collective sigh of relief and went back to business on Main Street. Little did anyone suspect what was brewing on Wall Street.

ACCOUNTING FRAUD AND THE FINANCIAL CRISIS OF 2008

Ironically, in 1999, about two-and-a-half years before the SOX Act was signed into law, the Glass-Steagall Act was repealed and the Financial Services Modernization Act was passed to deregulate the banking sector in the United States. This deregulation marked what many believe to be the origin of the financial crisis of 2008.

Past SEC Chairman Mary L. Schapiro (2010) describes the summer of 2008 as follows:

> That July, against the backdrop of the growing subprime crisis, the federal government seized control of what was then the second-largest bank to fail in United States history. Unemployment was only 5.5 percent, but oil prices were surging towards a new high of $147 a barrel and the Dow was plunging, down 20 percent year-over-year and headed much lower.
>
> Everyone knew the situation was precarious, but very few seemed to understand the seismic shift that was already underway. Merrill Lynch was still independent, AIG was still solvent, and Lehman Brothers was still trading.
>
> We were only seeing the tip of the iceberg, however. In the coming months, the Reserve Primary Money Market Fund would break the buck. Wachovia and WaMu's banking operations would be sold off. The SEC would issue a series of emergency orders prohibiting short-selling of securities of financial institutions. And the financial sector would deliver the biggest bankruptcies and bailouts in American history.

As the housing market took a nosedive and housing prices plunged, countless homeowners who had toxic mortgages (mortgages that were likely to go into default) began to lose their homes, and the problem caused a domino effect. By the end of 2008, millions of Americans were unemployed, billions of dollars in mortgages and mortgage-related securities had been lost, Lehman Brothers had collapsed, and the American International Group (AIG) had to be bailed out by the federal government. The SEC would later file charges "against nearly 100 individuals and entities—actions against Goldman Sachs, Citigroup, J.P. Morgan and top executives at Countrywide, Fannie Mae and Freddie Mac" (Schapiro, 2012).

The *Financial Crisis Inquiry Report* (2011), published by the National Commission on the Causes of the Financial and Economic Crisis in the United States, came to the following conclusions:

- We conclude this financial crisis was avoidable.
- We conclude widespread failures in financial regulation and supervision proved devastating to the stability of the nation's financial markets.
- We conclude dramatic failures of corporate governance and risk management at many systemically important financial institutions were a key cause of this crisis.
- We conclude a combination of excessive borrowing, risky investments, and lack of transparency put the financial system on a collision course with crisis.
- We conclude the government was ill prepared for the crisis, and its inconsistent response added to the uncertainty and panic in the financial markets.
- We conclude there was a systemic breakdown in accountability and ethics.
- We conclude collapsing mortgage-lending standards and the mortgage securitization pipeline lit and spread the flame of contagion and crisis.
- We conclude over-the-counter derivatives contributed significantly to this crisis.
- We conclude the failures of credit rating agencies were essential cogs in the wheel of financial destruction. (pp. xvii–xxv)

There are many familiar themes in the above findings, as many of the characteristics found in the corporate failures at the turn of the 21st century were also features of the financial crisis of 2008, such as the following:

- Failure of existing regulations and supervisory bodies.
- Failure of corporate governance and risk management.
- Lack of transparency.
- Inconsistent government response.
- A breakdown in responsibility and ethical standards.

The lack of transparency—particularly in relation to the financial statements of prominent lending institutions—certainly fueled the fire that was in the process of destroying the economy. *The Financial Crisis Inquiry Report* (2011) explained:

> The Panic fanned by a lack of transparency of the balance sheets of major financial institutions, coupled with a tangle of interconnections among institutions perceived to be "too big to fail," caused the credit markets to seize up. Trading ground to a halt. The stock market plummeted. The economy plunged into a deep recession. (p. xvi)

This widespread concern over the lack of transparency in financial statements was certainly not unfounded. There were colossal understatements of allowances for mortgage loan losses, whether by fraudulent intention or by an innocent but naïve belief that house prices could continue to increase forever. This underestimation of loan losses corresponded with overstatements of investments in loans and mortgage-backed securities and understatements of liabilities for repurchase of loans and for insuring investors against defaults by mortgage borrowers. To fight the rampant fraud revealed by the 2008 crisis, President Obama established the Financial Fraud Enforcement Task

Force in November 2009. (This task force replaced the Corporate Fraud Task Force that was created in 2002 in response to SOX.)

Just as the response to the earlier crisis had been additional regulation (in the form of SOX), the 2008 crisis resulted in more regulation in the form of the Dodd-Frank Wall Street Reform and Consumer Protection Act of 2010.

THE DODD-FRANK ACT OF 2010

The major objectives of Dodd-Frank are to "reshape the U.S. regulatory system in a number of areas including but not limited to consumer protection, trading restrictions, credit ratings, regulation of financial products, corporate governance and disclosure, and transparency" ("The Laws …," 2012).

Dodd-Frank established the Financial Stability Oversight Council (FSOC) as well as the Consumer Financial Protection Bureau (CFPB). The FSOC is tasked with the detection of those institutions that have the power to potentially bring about another financial crisis, whereas the main task of the CFPB is to safeguard consumers. Dodd-Frank also revised and increased the responsibilities and power of the SEC.

Past SEC Chairman Schapiro (2012) summarized the highlights of the SEC's response to Dodd-Frank, as follows:

- In the area of corporate governance, we have finalized rules concerning share-holder approval of executive compensation and "golden parachute" arrangements.
- Led by the Division of Investment Management, we have adopted new rules that have already resulted in approximately 1,200 hedge fund and other private fund advisers registering with the SEC. It's a process by which they agree to abide by SEC rules and provide critical systemic risk information that can give regulators better insight into their practices.
- And we have established a whistleblower program that is already providing the agency with hundreds of higher-quality tips, helping us to avoid investigatory dead-ends and—at the same time—prodding companies to enhance their internal compliance programs.

In another area, response to the meltdown of the mortgage-backed securities market, the SEC has proposed rules that will protect investors by:

- Increasing dramatically investors' visibility into the assets underlying all types of asset backed securities.
- Requiring securitizers—in conjunction with our banking colleagues—to keep skin in the game, giving them an incentive to double-check originators' underwriting practices.
- Changing the practices of the rating agencies whose gross mis-ratings of billions of dollars of mortgage-backed securities were kerosene on kindling.

Of all the changes brought about by Dodd-Frank, its whistleblower program has garnered a great deal of attention from the media because the whistleblowers not only are offered more protection than under SOX but also can now receive monetary awards from the SEC, which is pursuing whistleblower tips very seriously.

The Dodd-Frank Act made several changes to the whistleblower provisions in the SOX Act in order to "clarify and improve OSHA's[7] procedures for handling SOX whistleblower claims" ("Procedures for the Handling ...," 2011). These changes seem to be effective. In October 2013, the SEC awarded over $14 million to a whistleblower:

> The whistleblower, who does not wish to be identified, provided original information and assistance that allowed the SEC to investigate an enforcement matter more quickly than otherwise would have been possible. Less than six months after receiving the whistleblower's tip, the SEC was able to bring an enforcement action against the perpetrators and secure investor funds. ("SEC Awards ..." 2013).

Furthermore, in response to Title VII of Dodd-Frank, the SEC is working with the Commodity Futures Trading Commission (CFTC) to develop regulations that will stabilize and fortify our financial system in the following ways:

- Increasing centralized clearing of swaps and ensuring that capital and margin requirements reflect the true risks of these products.
- Improving transparency to regulators and to the public by shedding light on opaque exposures and assisting in developing more robust price discovery mechanisms.
- Increasing investor protection by enhancing security-based swap transaction disclosure, mitigating conflicts of interest, and improving our ability to police these markets. (Schapiro, 2012)

Some of the important financial reporting consequences of Dodd-Frank are as follows[8]:

- Smaller public companies will be exempt from Section 404(b) of the SOX Act of 2002.
- Auditors of non-public broker-dealers will be subject to oversight by the PCAOB.
- Changes to asset-backed securitization practices.
- Stricter regulations for credit rating agencies.
- Changes to executive compensation and corporate governance practices.
- The reduction of risky investments on the balance sheets of large financial firms, as well as other requirements. This has come to be known as the "Volcker Rule" (Sarno, Mueller, & Burns, 2010).

The debate surrounding Dodd-Frank continues, with some alleging that it does not do enough to stop future crises and others maintaining that it goes too far. Although regulation has its place in the business world, rules and laws without a sense of why they matter will always be problematic because there will always be those who look for loopholes in order to abide by the letter of the law, rather than the spirit of the law. As noted in *The Financial Crisis Inquiry Report* (2011):

> Unfortunately ... we witnessed an erosion of standards of responsibility and ethics that exacerbated the financial crisis. This was not universal, but these breaches stretched from the ground level to the corporate suites. They resulted not only in significant financial consequences but also in damage to the trust of investors, businesses, and the public.... (p. xxii)

---

[7] OSHA is the Occupational Safety and Health Administration Division in the United States Department of Labor.

[8] For more details, refer to Sarno, Mueller, and Burns (2010) who present a well-written overview.

To fight accounting fraud effectively, it is essential that those who prepare and use financial statements understand the ethical underpinnings necessary for a healthy and functional business environment and why it is imperative that investors have access to and trust in "high quality" financial information. Chapter 2 of this book, "Ethics at Work," examines the major ethical frameworks and how they apply to the business world.

It is also critical that users of financial statements learn to identify the major methods that companies use to manipulate financial statements, as well as the key signals that indicate a company's financial statements may have been falsified.

THE TOP-TWENTY METHODS OF FICTITIOUS FINANCIAL REPORTING

The first systematic study of the incidence of financial reporting enforcement actions was the *Report Pursuant to Section 704 of the Sarbanes-Oxley Act of 2002* (or SOX Report of 2002). In this Report, the SEC examined enforcement actions over the period of July 31, 1997, through July 30, 2002. The Report found 227 enforcement investigations in that five-year period, which led to the filing of "515 enforcement actions for financial reporting and disclosure violations" (p. 1). This Report classified the fictitious methods in terms of their effect on income (i.e., overstatement of revenue and understatement of expense). This categorization of the methods of fictitious financial reporting provides a particularly useful pedagogical progression for studying the methods that companies may use to manipulate their financial statements. The organization of Table 1.1, which follows, is based on the categories provided by the SOX Report (2002) and provides a list of the most prevalent methods of fictitious financial reporting leading to SEC enforcement actions. Table 1.1 adapts the terminology of the SOX Report for each method of fictitious overstatement of income to note the corresponding overstatement of assets or understatement of debt.

There are as many methods of categorizing financial reporting violations as there are studies of financial reporting enforcement actions. Some studies categorize the fictitious reporting methods in terms of how the method manipulates income (revenue or expense), whereas other studies categorize the fictitious methods according to the corresponding effect on misstating assets or liabilities. Either way, if one considers the overstatement of assets in terms of the corresponding overstatement of revenue or understatement of expense, the most frequently used methods of fictitious financial reporting as described in Table 1.1 continue to occur.

Since the financial crisis of 2008, however, there has been an increase in SEC enforcement actions in respect of the disclosure of mortgage loans and in the understatement of reserves for loan losses and the corresponding overstatement of investments in loans and investments in mortgage-backed securities. This method of manipulating financial statements has been added as a separate category in Table 1.1.

Chapters 3–9 of this book tell the story of real-world companies that illustrate the top 20 methods of fictitious financial reporting and also identify the signals left in financial statements that alert readers to the possibility that reported income, as well as assets and liabilities, may have been influenced by these methods.

Finally, the Appendix at the end of this book presents an overview of the top 25 signals indicating possible fictitious reporting in financial statements.

TABLE 1.1   The Top 20 Methods of Fictitious Financial Reporting*

Fictitious Reporting Method	Illustrating Company**
The following schemes involve ***improper revenue recognition*** and overstatement of receivables:	
1. Bill and Hold Sales, Consignment Sales, and other Contingency Sales for the purpose of improper timing of revenue recognition	SUNBEAM
2. Holding Books Open after the Close of a Reporting Period for the purpose of improper timing of revenue recognition	SENSORMATIC
3. Multiple Element Contracts or Bundled Contracts when used for the purpose of improper timing of revenue recognition	XEROX
4. Fictitious Revenue	CUC/CENDANT
5. Improper Valuation of Revenue	INSIGNIA
The following schemes involve ***improper expense recognition*** and a corresponding overstatement of assets or understatement of liabilities or reserves:	
6. Improper Capitalization of Expenses or Losses as Assets	WORLDCOM
7. Improper Deferral of Expenses or Losses and Overstatement of Assets	LIVENT
8. Failure to Record Expenses or Losses and Understatement of Liabilities	LIVENT
9. Overstatement of Ending Inventory Values in order to understate the cost of goods sold	RITE AID
10. Understatement of Reserves for Bad Debts and Overstatement of Accounts Receivable	ALLEGHENY
11. Incomplete Disclosure of Loans or Underestimation of Allowance for Loan or Mortgage Losses and Overstatement of Loans Held for Investment and/or Investments in Mortgage-Backed Securities	COUNTRYWIDE
12. Failure to Record Asset Impairments	LOCKHEED
13. Improper Use of Restructuring and Other Liability Reserves. The overstated reserves are released in future periods to fictitiously understate future periods' expenses.	SUNBEAM
The following schemes involve ***improper accounting in connection with business combinations:***	
14. Improper Use of Acquisition and Merger Reserves. Overstated reserves are created in order to use their later release to overstate future periods' earnings.	WORLDCOM
15. Improper Valuation of Assets	WORLDCOM

(continued)

* Table 1.1 was updated in 2013. The Table was originally adapted from SEC's *Report Pursuant to Section 704 of the Sarbanes-Oxley Act of 2002* and published in *Business Fairy Tales* by Cecil W. Jackson: Thomson/Cengage, 2006.

**All of the illustrating companies except Lockheed were the subject of SEC enforcement actions.

Fictitious Reporting Method	Illustrating Company**
Miscellaneous schemes:	
16. Improper Use of Off-Balance Sheet Arrangements. Special Purpose Entities (SPEs) are used to overstate earnings and understate debt via contrived transactions.	ENRON
17. Inadequate Disclosures in Management Discussion and Analysis (MD&A) and Improper Disclosure of Non-GAAP Financial Measures	EDISON ADELPHIA
18. Failure to Disclose Related-Party Transactions	ADELPHIA
19. Improper Accounting for Foreign Payments in Violation of the Foreign Corrupt Practices Act (FCPA)	BELLSOUTH
20. Inappropriate Accounting for Roundtrip Transactions	KRISPY KREME

Assignments

TRUE/FALSE QUESTIONS

Answer the following questions with T for true or F for false for more practice with key terms and concepts from this chapter.

1. In civil fraud, the burden of proof is higher than in criminal fraud.

   T   F

2. By 2001, very little of top management compensation was in the form of stock options.

   T   F

3. To deal with the turmoil caused by the various accounting scandals, the SOX Act was passed in 1999.

   T   F

4. The PCAOB ended the self-regulation of the external auditing profession.

   T   F

5. The financial frauds at the turn of the millennium were limited to just a couple of varieties of sham reporting.

   T   F

6. The *National Crisis Inquiry Report* (2011) concluded that the financial crisis was unavoidable.

   T   F

7. According to the *Financial Crisis Inquiry Report*, the lack of transparency in the balance sheets of major financial institutions was one of the causes of the financial crisis of 2008.

   T   F

8. The Glass-Stegall Act revised and increased the power of the SEC.

   T   F

9. When companies settle a charge of civil fraud, they usually accept the SEC's findings.

   T   F

10. Most countries in Europe do not have stringent laws to protect whistleblowers.

    T   F

FILL-IN-THE-BLANK QUESTIONS

Fill in the blanks with information and concepts from this chapter.

11. One of the most contentious parts of the SOX legislation was Section _____, which addressed internal controls.

12. It was problematic for WorldCom that its internal _____ department reported to the CFO, Scott Sullivan, who was the major originator of the company's accounting fraud.

13. In 1999, the Glass-Steagall Act was repealed and the Financial Services Modernization Act was passed to deregulate the _____ sector in the United States.
14. According to Lawrence and Wells, the three elements necessary to prove fraud are "a material false statement made with intent to deceive, a victim's reliance on the statement and _____."
15. In the year _____, the Dodd-Frank Act established the Financial Stability Oversight Council (FSOC) as well as the Consumer Financial Protection Bureau (CFPB) in response to the financial crisis of 2008.
16. For the last few years, the FBI has had special _____ working in place at the SEC.
17. CEO compensation in 2012 was _____ than CEO compensation in 2002.
18. One of the reforms of the Dodd-Frank Act is the requirement that has become known as the _____ Rule, which calls for a reduction of risky investments on the balance sheets of large financial firms.
19. In this text, the company used to illustrate the failure to disclose related-party transactions is _____.
20. In 2008, countless investors held mortgage-backed securities that were backed by _____ mortgage loans.

MULTIPLE-CHOICE QUESTIONS

21. Which of the following gatekeepers or gatekeeping functions was *not* identified by WorldCom's Bankruptcy Examiner as having failed WorldCom in some way?
    (a) The structure of its internal audit department.
    (b) Its external auditors.
    (c) The SEC.
    (d) Its board of directors.
22. According to SEC enforcement releases, which of the following was a major reason company executives orchestrated accounting frauds at the turn of the millennium?
    (a) Receiving government-based subsidies.
    (b) Meeting Wall Street analysts' earnings expectations.
    (c) Meeting international bankers' expectations.
    (d) Meeting employees' expectations.

23. Which of the following statements about the PCAOB is *not* true?
    (a) It was established to oversee the activities of the auditing profession.
    (b) It was created by the Dodd-Frank Act.
    (c) It ended 100 years of self-regulation by the auditing profession.
    (d) It replaced the Public Oversight Board (POB).
24. Which of the following situations would *not* limit a director's autonomy, according to Levitt?
    (a) "Inside" directors who are company employees.
    (b) "Outside" directors who are either friends or relatives of the company's CEO.
    (c) "Outside" directors who are associated with competing businesses or had been involved in business transactions with the corporation and earned lucrative fees.
    (d) "Outside" directors who do not have a stake in the company.
25. Which of the following is *not* a goal of the Dodd-Frank Act?
    (a) To increase the number of audit firms.
    (b) To regulate financial products.
    (c) To increase transparency.
    (d) To protect consumers.
26. Which of the following is an important financial reporting consequence of Dodd-Frank?
    (a) Smaller public companies will be exempt from Section 404(b) of the SOX Act of 2002.
    (b) Auditors of nonpublic broker-dealers will be subject to oversight by the PCAOB.
    (c) Changes to asset-backed securitization practices.
    (d) All of the above.
27. Judy, an internal auditor at Fermented Fruits, has found evidence of accounting fraud at the company. She is worried about the repercussions of reporting her firm to the SEC. You remind her that under Dodd-Frank, a whistleblower:
    (a) Is eligible to receive money from a $453 billion SEC fund.
    (b) Is not eligible to receive a monetary award.
    (c) Will likely be ignored by the SEC.
    (d) Will likely be vilified by the SEC.

28. Which of the following might undermine the independence of a member of the board of directors at Fermented Fruits?
    (a) One of the outside directors works for another dried fruit company, Raining Raisins.
    (b) One of the outside directors is a high school teacher.
    (c) One of the outside directors is a former CEO of a law firm.
    (d) One of the outside directors is an actor.

29. Ethical Auditors is the external auditor for Fermented Fruits. Which of the following might undermine the ability of Ethical Auditors to impartially audit Fermented Fruits?
    (a) Some auditors don't like dried fruit.
    (b) Judy does not like the personality of the CEO of Fermented Fruits.
    (c) Fermented Fruits has added nuts to its inventory.
    (d) Ethical Auditors has been auditing Fermented Fruit since it went public ten years ago, and Judy has always been the managing partner on the job.

30. The SOX Act of 2002 introduced reforms in which of the following areas?
    (a) Internal control reporting requirements.
    (b) The registration of hedge funds with the SEC.
    (c) Changes in the practices of ratings agencies.
    (d) All of the above.

CHAPTER 2

Ethics at Work

Learning Objectives

After studying this chapter, you should be able to:

- Identify and describe the three major normative ethical theories or schools of thought: consequentialism, deontology, and virtue ethics.
- Explain the utilitarian approach to making ethical decisions.
- Explain the *rights-and-duties* approach to ethical decision making.
- Explain the *justice* approach to analyzing ethical dilemmas.
- Apply the American Accounting Association Ethical Decision-Making Model to dilemmas in the business world.

CHAPTER OUTLINE

- Theories of Ethics
- Applied Ethics: Ethical Decision-Making Models in the Business World
- An Ethical Decision-Making Model for Accountants
- Key Terms

- Assignments
- Case Study: Peter Madoff, Former Chief Compliance Officer and Senior Managing Director of Bernard L. Madoff Investment Securities, LLC

Everything that can be counted does not necessarily count; everything that counts cannot necessarily be counted.

—ALBERT EINSTEIN

According to a recent article in the *Boston Business Journal*, "CPAs are sexy" (Pratt, 2013). And so are forensic accountants (Blake, 2012). One of the reasons for the newfound appeal of accountants is the increased demand following the ratification of the Sarbanes-Oxley Act of 2002 and the Dodd-Frank Wall Street Reform and Consumer Protection Act of 2010. One of the main goals of Dodd-Frank is to "promote the financial stability of the United States by improving accountability and transparency in the financial system" (Dodd-Frank, 2010). The word *ethics* is used 20 times in Dodd-Frank, emphasizing "the reason for the Act's creation—a compelling lack of business ethics as evidenced by a growing number of cases involving insider-trading, financial misdeeds and bad corporate governance in the financial services industry" (Peluso, 2012). However, a focus on external rules, regulations, and laws, without any authentic understanding of the essential nature of ethics and morality, could prove to be ineffective.

A combined study by the American Institute of CPAs (in the United States) and the Chartered Institute of Management Accountants (in the United Kingdom) reports the following: "Four out of five businesses worldwide have committed to ethical performance, but rhetoric does not always match reality…. The report found a weakened 'tone from the top' and more pressure on financial professionals—especially in emerging economies—to act unethically" ("CGMA Report," 2012). Flanagan and Clarke point out, "Rather than relying essentially on an imposed set of external regulations, guidelines and exemplars, the professional accountant's decisions, while reflecting community expectations, will of necessity be derived from each practitioner's individual internalized decision-making processes" (2007, p. 496). In order to develop meaningful and principled decision-making practices, it is necessary for accountants to understand the fundamental approaches to the philosophy of ethics. A grasp of ethics is also important for the establishment of what is known as an "ethical work climate" (Buchan, 2009).

THEORIES OF ETHICS

There are three major branches of ethics: *metaethics*, *normative ethics*, and *applied ethics*. **Metaethics** addresses foundational issues and presuppositions of ethical frameworks. It ponders perennial questions such as what makes the good *good* and the bad *bad*? While important, this branch of ethics is beyond the scope of our discussion.

Because *rightness* and *wrongness* are in a different category from *goodness* and *badness*, a separate branch of ethics, **normative ethics**, addresses issues of right and wrong actions. A normative theory makes claims or offers guidelines or norms about how to discern the right action. This chapter is concerned with identifying the most common types of normative ethics.

Applied ethics investigates how a normative system plays out in a practical situation and/or within a specific field. *Business ethics* is a type of applied ethics, and the necessity, limits, and boundaries of business ethics—specifically in relation to the accounting profession—are addressed throughout this text.

The Three Major Normative Ethical Theories

We can identify three major normative ethical theories, or schools of thought, according to what is most important in the pursuit of morality—namely, **consequentialism**, **deontological theory**, and **virtue ethics**.

To the consequentialist, the most important issue in morality is to choose the right action, and this choice is determined by examining the consequences of that action. On the other hand, to the deontologist, the most important issue in morality is to do the right thing because it is right or, as often stated by the deontologist: "Do your duty for duty's sake." Under this view, if it is right to be honest, then avoiding lying and telling the absolute truth is always right, irrespective of the consequences. There is a moral imperative to be honest no matter what the situation. Coming from a third perspective, the virtue ethicist holds that the most important aspect of morality is having the right character or set of traits, or "dispositions," as they are often called. In a nutshell, according to the virtue ethicist, possessing the right set of virtues is central to morality because what makes an action right is that it is the action that a virtuous person would take. In other words, the integrity of an action flows from the virtuous character performing such an action, and that character embodies the virtuous traits.

A potential whistleblower who is deciding whether or not to reveal unethical or unlawful practices may use one of the three approaches. If she is a consequentialist, she will determine right action by the consequences and effect on the stakeholders, such as the impact it will have on her future employment, as well as the impact on employees, shareholders, the board of directors, managers, and consumers. If she is a deontologist, she will act according to the duty she thinks is most important. If she thinks truth-telling is a duty, she will reveal the fraud because it is her duty to be forthcoming. Finally, if she follows virtue ethics, she will use her character and virtues to guide her. She may think that the virtue of courage requires her to tell the truth even in an adverse situation and that the virtue of wisdom requires that she tell the truth in an astute and effective way.

Let us now examine these three theories more closely and then discuss how they apply to business ethics.

CONSEQUENTIALISM While the term *consequentialism* refers to all approaches to the study of morality that evaluate conduct or actions in terms of the consequences that they produce, it is possible to distinguish between different forms of consequentialism. Some schools of thought focus on actions in terms of the proportion of benefits to costs, whereas others evaluate actions in terms of their benefits to the nation (nationalism) or benefits to oneself only (egoism).

The leading and best-known form of consequentialism is identified as *utilitarianism.* Conceived by Jeremy Bentham (1748–1832), utilitarianism holds that the right action ethically is the action that maximizes *the good.* Bentham thought that there was only one *good* (namely, pleasure) and one *evil* (namely, pain). Bentham's protégé, John Stuart Mill (1806–1873), defined happiness as the presence of pleasure and the absence of pain and believed that actions have *utility* when they maximize happiness. According to Mill, actions are *right* in proportion to the happiness they tend to promote and the morally best action of those open to us is the action that maximizes happiness—or (in his sense) has utility. Mill, who became the leading utilitarian scholar, specified that the net pleasure to be maximized when performing the right action referred to the pleasure of all who would be affected by the action, and not just one's own pleasure.

This type of utilitarianism is known as *hedonism*, encapsulated by the phrase "The greatest happiness for the greatest number" (Sinnott-Armstrong, 2012). Hedonism uses pleasure (and/or pain) to judge the consequences of an action. Right action corresponds with the act that produces the greatest amount of pleasure.

As consequentialist philosophy has developed over the years, different philosophers have specified different definitions of *the good*, or what ought to be maximized, but the unifying thread is that all consequentialists judge actions according to the sum of the net good that they cause among all those affected by the actions. To the strict utilitarian, it is the total of the pleasure for all parties in the aggregate that determines whether the action is right, irrespective of how that pleasure or utility or *good* is allocated among the parties involved.

The term *consequentialism* often refers to all the utilitarian approaches, whether they refer to Mill's strict definition of *the good* to be maximized or to more flexible definitions. Philosopher Stephen Cohen (2004) succinctly described the essence of modern consequentialism: "It is the effects, or consequences, that are morally significant, not intentions or rules or commitments." Of all forms of moral analysis, *utilitarianism* is probably the most widespread, and many argue that it is the most intuitive approach to judging what action is right and what action is wrong. Philosopher Peter Singer is a prominent proponent of utilitarianism. Singer explains that his form of utilitarianism "furthers the interests of those affected, rather than merely what increases pleasure and reduces pain" (1993, p.14).

However, consequentialists are vulnerable to the argument that one cannot predict all the consequences that will follow in perpetuity from one's actions. Further, even if we could predict all the consequences, consequentialists are criticized on the basis that the different *goods* are not homogeneous and there is no common denominator by which to measure and aggregate the benefits or harmful effects of actions to determine which actions to follow or which to avoid. As such, utilitarianism is capable of being either overly permissive or overly stringent. For instance, a utilitarian framework could theoretically permit violence toward a marginal group in the name of protecting the majority. Or on the other hand, the same framework could also be critical of someone spending $4 on gourmet coffee in the United States when the $4 could save lives if given to provide electrolytes to children in impoverished countries. As it pertains to hedonism, the Victorian-era philosopher Henry Sidgwick famously pointed out that when one's objective is pleasure, pleasure becomes elusive. This is known as the *hedonist's paradox*, and it is an ongoing obstacle for those who try to obtain pleasure or argue for it as a moral goal.

DEONTOLOGY   The word *deontology* is derived from the Greek *deon*, which means "duty." The *deontologist* does not look to the future or to the effect of actions in order to judge an action as right or wrong. The deontologist chooses moral action not because of its consequences, but because it is the right thing to do. Right actions correspond to the moral law, and according to Kant, these actions are universally discernible and universally applicable by our ability to reason.

Essentially, deontologists assert that one must do the right thing because it is one's duty to do so. The leading deontologist was Immanuel Kant (1724–1804). According to Kant, if you perform an action—for example, if you tell the truth mainly because of the positive consequences of telling the truth—the act does not have the same moral value as telling the truth out of your duty to always tell the truth. An action is moral if it is performed because it is right, not if it is performed because of its consequences.

Kant went even further by saying that if you perceive telling the truth as a duty, you must *always* tell the truth for that reason in itself. Moreover, you must tell the truth even if telling the truth will cause a negative consequence. A common hypothetical example of this proposition is a situation where you may know the location of a person who is hiding from an ax murderer. According to Kant's deontological view of ethics, if that murderer asks you if you know the whereabouts of the person in hiding, you are duty bound not to lie. Kant's view holds that if you perceive telling the truth as a duty, then it is an unassailable duty, and telling a lie is *always* wrong, irrespective of the consequences.

Kant's standard test was that one ought to act as though a personal maxim were a universal moral law and that law could be stipulated for everyone without it leading to contradiction. Kant's concept of the **categorical imperative** encompasses a binding moral obligation that must be universal, rational, and impartial. John Finnis presents Kant's three formulations of the *categorical imperative*:

1. Act only according to that maxim by which you can at the same time will that it should become a universal law.
2. Act so that you treat humanity, whether in your own person or in that of another, always as an end and never as a means only.
3. Act according to a maxim which harmonizes with a possible realm (i.e., a systematic union of different rational beings through common laws).... (qtd. in Finnis, 1983, p. 121)

For Kant, the moral law admitted no exception. If we have a duty, there are no exceptions. Further, for Kant, in order for our actions to have moral worth, we must have the right motive, which is to fulfill our duty simply because it is our duty. Although no list of duties has ever been specified as prescriptive, some of the more common duties that Kant and his followers have suggested include the duty to develop one's talents, the duty to avoid dishonest promises, and the duty to respect the freedom of others.

Deontology is often critiqued on two grounds. First, the universal impetus of Kantian-deontology renders it incapable of adjusting for particular situations or different world views, which has become an increasing concern of modern ethics. Furthermore, duty-based ethics may seem somewhat lacking to those who regard motivation as a crucial factor in ethical decision making. For example, some may question spousal fidelity that is rooted in a general sense of duty, rather than in an authentic love that leads a person to stay faithful to his or her spouse.

VIRTUE ETHICS   As we have already noted, the three major ethical theories can be distinguished by their answer to the question, "What is the most important aspect of morality?" According to Stephen Cohen, both utilitarians and deontologists look outside the individual (i.e., outside the decision maker) to determine the answer to that question. The utilitarian or consequentialist focuses on the consequences of the action to establish the morality of the action, whereas the deontologist insists that morality is determined by doing one's duty at all times. An examination of the outer world ascertains what that duty is.

According to the virtue theory of ethical behavior, the most important aspect of morality is found within the individual. According to this philosophy of *virtue ethics*, having the right character is the most important aspect of morality. Here, as distinct from utilitarian or deontological theory, the most important issue in morality is having the right set of dispositions or *virtues*. In other words, having a moral character is the basis for choosing the right actions because a person of fundamental integrity can be trusted to do the right thing. Cohen (2004) describes this approach as follows:

> A virtue ethics view may see the process more "inside out." Moral behavior should be the result of, and flow from, a person's character. This is not to say that moral behavior is only automatic or spontaneous. It can indeed involve difficult and perplexing thinking and deliberation.... Cultivation of an ethical person, then, is very largely a matter of developing the right character. (pp. 49, 50)

Aristotle is the most famous proponent of virtue ethics. He saw the virtues as those dispositions or traits that were in accord with the *golden mean* or the middle course. To him, extremes in behavior or tastes were vices, whereas moderation—the golden mean—was the primary virtue. For example, in conversation, either constant chattering or complete silence would be vices, but a reasonable amount of discussion would be a virtue. To Aristotle, the ultimate objective of the golden mean was the *good* or well-being of both the individual and the society, and he offered a non-exhaustive list of virtues or character traits that included honesty, courage, temperance, friendship, and the intellectual virtues. The intellectual virtue of practical wisdom is, according to Aristotle, a prerequisite for all the other virtues.

Other virtue ethicists have suggested some different traits as conditions of being virtuous. Phillipa Foot emphasized the "four cardinal virtues: courage, temperance, wisdom, and justice" (qtd. in Kellenberger, 1995, p. 200). Further, Foot pointed out that what is virtue in one context may not be virtue in another context. For example, courage in carrying out a random act of violence would not be considered a virtue. For virtue ethics, the driving question is "What kind of person ought I be?" The answers are inextricably related to one's notion of the human *telos* (or ultimate purpose) and what defines human flourishing.

To identify the nature of virtue, Alasdair MacIntyre sought a common thread in five different views of the nature of virtue over the ages. First, he noted that during the time of Homer, bodily strength and physical courage were considered major virtues on the grounds that they enabled one to fulfill one's social role. Second, according to Aristotle, "the *telos* of man as a species ... determines what human qualities are virtues." Traits such as temperance and practical wisdom are considered to be virtues. Third, MacIntyre noted the *New Testament* virtues of faith, hope, love, and humility that also focus on the good of humanity, but here the *good* includes a spiritual or mystical good. Fourth, MacIntyre identified a "Jane Austen" view of the virtues, which included elements of the three approaches discussed previously and included a "real affection for people" as a virtue. Finally, MacIntyre described Benjamin Franklin's utilitarian and functional view of virtue, where hard work and early rising are seen as virtues. (Quotes from Kellenberger, 1995, p. 196)

MacIntyre (2007) found coherency within these different (and sometimes seemingly contradictory) views of virtue in the fact that whenever a practice is being performed, such as playing chess (or auditing!), we can perform the practice for either external (extrinsic) benefits or internal (intrinsic) benefits. For MacIntyre, performing a practice in such a way as to benefit inherently from that practice is a virtue because one achieves an intrinsic benefit that can be obtained only from performing the practice properly. To illustrate this, he used the example of playing chess. Assume that you enjoy the game of chess. Now assume further that you want to play chess, but there are no chess players on hand, and the only person available is a child who does not know the game. If you ask the child to learn chess, he or she will probably refuse. If you offer the youngster candy as an incentive to learn the game, he or she may then agree to be taught. If you then offer the child extra candy to play and some additional candy as a prize for winning, he or she may be more inclined to put extra effort and concentration into the game. Now, if the child were to leave the room during a game, you—who enjoy the game so much— would not be inclined to cheat and move a chess piece. However, if you leave the room, the youngster playing for candy would almost certainly be tempted to cheat in order to win and obtain the prize. MacIntyre pointed out that the child would be playing for the extrinsic benefit of the prize, but you would be playing for the intrinsic benefit attached to the practice of playing the game as skillfully as possible. To MacIntyre, virtue can be found in performing an action or a practice for its intrinsic benefits.

While virtue ethics is able to address the utilitarian and deontological shortcomings of not attending to ethical agents, it is liable to be critiqued for its vague prescriptions. Critics ponder how one determines the virtues. Modern philosophy is skeptical of Aristotle's understanding of the human *telos* that grounds his virtues, and others worry that deriving virtues for a certain group may lead to **moral relativism**. This is the view that morality possesses no universal appeal and is not tethered to any truth claims; right action and the good are wholly dependent on, and relative to, the situation, actors, culture, group, or time period. Furthermore, how does one proceed when the virtues are at odds in a certain situation?

In dealing with the problem of how to teach and cultivate the virtues, virtue ethics often uses narratives to illustrate how a virtuous person acts.

In spite of some difficulties in the virtue-ethics model, the significance of applying virtue ethics to the business world, and to accounting in particular, is quite far-reaching. Philosopher Joel Schickel (2009) explains that "because good accounting practice antecedently requires the formation of good moral character, professional ethics in accounting presupposes that practitioners come to the profession already having been formed in certain moral virtues."

APPLIED ETHICS: ETHICAL DECISION-MAKING MODELS IN THE BUSINESS WORLD

Having considered the approach of the three major normative ethical theories, we must now examine how these ethical theories apply to decision making and ask, "How do we decide what the right action is?" In answering this question, John E. Fleming suggests an eight-step decision-making model developed by Bowie and Velasquez:

1. What are the facts?
2. What are the ethical issues?
3. What are the alternatives?
4. Who are the stakeholders?
5. What is the ethical evaluation of the alternatives?
6. What are the constraints?

   • Ignorance or uncertainty?
   • Ability?

7. What decision should be made?
8. How should the decision be implemented? (qtd. in Pincus, 2002, p. 28)

Under this decision-making model, Fleming describes four approaches to Step 5 (i.e., the ethical evaluation of the alternatives):

- The consequentialist/utilitarian model
- The rights approach
- The duties approach
- The justice approach

The rights approach is often combined with the duties approach, so we will examine three distinct approaches to the ethical evaluation of alternative actions.

The Consequentialist/Utilitarian Approach to the Decision-Making Model

The consequentialist theory of ethics and morality, as previously discussed, is a particularly practical ethical decision-making approach because it stresses that the most important aspect of morality is to do the right act, and it specifies that the right act is the one that produces the best consequences considering all the parties affected. Therefore, under this approach to the decision-making model, when you are faced with an ethical dilemma in a business environment, it is vital to identify all of the stakeholders in the decision; that is, you should consider everyone who might be affected by the decision. Further, modern consequentialists agree that it is essential to consider the sum or aggregate of all the benefits and disadvantages to all of the stakeholders.

USING THE CONSEQUENTIALIST/UTILITARIAN APPROACH IN THE BUSINESS WORLD Let us consider, for example, the case of an auditor who contemplates bowing to pressure from a client to give an unqualified audit opinion on a knowingly incorrect set of financial statements because the client wants to boost the company's stock price. Using this approach, the auditor should first consider all the people who could be affected by the decision:

- **Investors** could suffer losses if they trade stock at prices based on the incorrect information in fraudulent financial statements.
- All the **employees** of the company being audited are stakeholders. Many internal operating decisions of the firm are made on the basis of accounting data that is used for the financial statements. If that information is wrong, it is very likely that suboptimal operating decisions will be made with damaging consequences for the company, such as lower profits and bonuses, or even bankruptcy of the company, causing employees to lose their jobs.
- Employees may choose to contribute to retirement plans that invest in a company's stock, but they may decide on different plans if they were presented with correct financial statements.
- **Potential employees** may accept jobs at firms that they may not have joined had they been in possession of correct financial statements.
- **Banks** and other lenders could make erroneous decisions based on the false information, which could have serious consequences.
- The **auditor** could be sued or face other legal action for fraudulently issuing an audit opinion.

- The **auditor's family** could suffer public humiliation if the auditor were criminally prosecuted.
- The **auditor's business partners** and employees are also stakeholders, and their reputations could suffer, as could the entire audit firm as a result of public scrutiny that could follow a failed audit. The firm itself could be sued for monetary damages.
- Our **stock markets** require valid information in order to operate efficiently. When fraudulent financial statements are allowed to be presented after corrupt audits, this decreases confidence in the capital markets, which, in turn, makes it harder for American firms to raise capital either locally or internationally.

Now let us consider the stakeholders who potentially could suffer negative utility or hardship if the auditor *refuses* to issue a fraudulent audit opinion:

- The **auditor** could be fired and lose compensation and status; he or she may suffer workplace hostility from colleagues who wanted the auditor to "be more of a team player" and go along with the client and the rest of the team; or the auditor may keep his or her job but lose the client and the fees and possibly lose status or promotion in the firm.
- The **family members** of the auditor are potential stakeholders because they could suffer due to the auditor losing his or her job; for example, they may have to move to a different house or change schools.
- The **audit firm** could lose an important client, which could cause other employees at the audit firm to lose their jobs.

According to the consequentialist ethical decision-making model, after identifying all the stakeholders and estimating the potential consequences to them, the decision maker (in this case, the auditor) must choose the action that he or she believes will lead to the *maximum utility* or *benefit in the aggregate,* taking all the stakeholders into account. Moreover, the mere process of identifying the possible consequences to all the stakeholders would likely increase the decision maker's awareness of the *wrongness* of the unethical act, the risks associated with the *wrong* action, and the importance of doing the *right* or ethical thing. If some of the executives who were found guilty in recent financial frauds had considered their own families as potential stakeholders in their decisions to go along with criminal activity—on the grounds of their families' future suffering or public humiliation—it is possible that some of them may have paused long enough to remember the reasons society made laws against issuing fraudulent financial statements in particular and against fraud in general. If some of these company officers had paused to imagine their mortification as television cameras filmed their "perp" walks when they were arrested for possible indictments on criminal charges, perhaps they may have had second thoughts before embarking upon unethical paths of action.

The Rights-and-Duties Approach to the Decision-Making Model

Under this approach, when faced with an ethical decision, the decision maker would again attempt to identify all the facts and all of the stakeholders affected by a particular decision. However, here, when considering the effects of the decision on others, the most important issue to consider is that of the *rights* of those concerned; thus, following the rights-and-duties approach, the correct decision is the one that would appear to best serve or uphold these rights.

It is important to remember that ethical dilemmas frequently involve the possibility of actions that violate or fail to recognize the rights of others. Seen from a slightly different angle, the rights of those concerned usually involve a corresponding duty on the part of others to honor those rights. Therefore, this approach requires the decision maker to fulfill his or her obligation to *recognize and respect the rights of others.* These rights may be either legal rights or moral rights that are not necessarily protected by law. For instance, a company that adheres to the rights-and-duties approach may believe that workers have a right to a fair wage even if this standard is higher than the legal minimum wage.

In addition to the focus on natural human rights, issues such as animal rights and potential cruelty to animals could also be a concern. For example, while factory farms are not illegal, certain beef-producing companies may believe that they have a moral right to provide more natural living conditions for their animals.

Philosophers classify rights in many different ways. James Sterba has identified four kinds of rights:

1. There are "action" rights, or the rights to do things, such as to express your opinion.
2. There are "recipient rights," which are the "rights to receive something" (e.g., the right to be paid for services rendered).
3. There are what Sterba has called "*in persona*" rights, which hold against some "specific, nameable person or persons." An example of an *in persona* right is the right to have a loan repaid or the right to have a promise kept.
4. Sterba has also identified "*in rem*" rights, which hold against the world. An example of such a right is the right to liberty. (Quotes from Kellenberger, 1995, pp. 212, 213)

USING THE RIGHTS-AND-DUTIES APPROACH IN THE BUSINESS WORLD   Using this approach to the ethical evaluation of alternatives in a decision-making model, a manager under pressure to publish fraudulent financial statements in order to keep his or her job should consider all the people whose rights may be affected by this decision. Note that the list of those affected is virtually identical to the list in the utilitarian model, but the emphasis here is not so much on the negative impact of the decision, but rather on upholding the *rights* of the people involved.

- Users of financial statements, such as stockholders, potential investors, and people making loans or extending credit to the company, have the right to truthful financial statements.
- Society at large relies on the capital markets, which rely on accurate information, and so society has a right to expect that public companies publish honest financial statements.
- Employees of the company have a right to truthful information about the company.

It is therefore important that the auditor who is under pressure to give an unqualified audit opinion on fraudulent financial statements has a clear awareness of the rights of all the stakeholders. On the other hand, what about the rights of the family of the manager or the auditor who may be fired for resisting fraudulent financial statements? What about children's rights to be supported by their parents? How does one balance these rights against the rights of the employees or other users of the financial statements? Conversely, do the relatives of the manager or auditor have the right to expect not to be embarrassed by family members who are criminally charged for presenting fraudulent financial statements? For situations when rights clash, ethicist James Kellenberger (2004) makes the following two suggestions:

- We should examine the consequences of a decision or course of action—an extension of the utilitarian approach.
- We should also examine the situation of conflicting rights in the context of relationship morality—an extension of the rights and duties model. Relationship morality requires that we treat all human beings with human dignity. It may be helpful for us to consider the special rights and duties that our particular relationships with specific persons demand.

Examining this approach in the auditing context, it is important to remember that the purpose of the external auditor's assignment is to express an independent opinion of the financial statements of a company for users of that company's financial statements. Auditors cannot allow their relationship with the people who appoint them to interfere with the special relationship they have with users of financial statements. Focusing on the resulting *rights* of financial statement users to receive a fair, independent opinion and on the *relationship* between the auditors and all those who may use the financial statements, should lead auditors to better understand their duties and to better understand why they must not accept limits on the scope of their audits without qualifying their reports. The same goes for the duty of management to produce honest financial statements in the first place.

The Justice Approach to the Decision-Making Model

The third approach presented by Fleming for analyzing ethical dilemmas in the decision-making model in order to identify the *right* or the moral action is the *justice* approach. Once again, as in the other models, all the facts and all the stakeholders impacted by the decision must be identified. Under this model, the matter of paramount importance is the fairness of treatment of all the individuals involved. Also important is the access to goods such as clean water and services such as health care and education. Justice, in the ethical sense, is focused more on *distributive* justice than on *retributive* justice—which is more the focus of legal justice. Kellenberger (1995) points out, "Distributive justice is concerned with fairness in the comparative treatment of persons" (p. 167). The *good* being distributed in this context is very broad and applies to benefits generally or, conversely, to the general avoidance of burdens or hardships.

Philosophers differ as to the principles of distributive justice. In particular, one school of thought (*universalism*) argues in favor of universal principles of justice, whereas the *communitarianism* school recognizes a plurality of communities in which the diversity of the communities must be taken into account. In this case, justice will be determined with reference to community values. At the core, both schools have the concept of *equality* in common: "Distributive justice, both universalism and communitarianism agree, is treating persons equally" (Kellenberger, 1995). According to Joel Feinberg (1993), the principles of distributive justice are equality, need, merit, contribution, and effort.

Certainly, basic human rights must be equally accorded to all people. In some situations, need would be paramount in driving fair distribution, and in other situations, one may see merit, contribution, or effort as paramount. For example, when it comes to the distribution of material goods, we can all see the necessity of providing disaster relief to those in need after a natural catastrophe, such as those affected by tornadoes in Oklahoma or earthquakes in Mexico. In the case of employment compensation, many would argue in favor of extra distribution of benefits on the basis of merit, contribution, or effort. However, there is little consensus among philosophers on just how far equality in distribution extends and where merit, contribution, or effort overrides equal distribution in the allocation of material goods. Nevertheless, certain aspects of distributive justice are clear enough to be useful.

Both law and morality require that factors such as race, religion, gender, sexual orientation, or national origin should not affect the distribution of benefits or burdens to citizens. Further, the justice approach clearly requires us to ensure that no partiality is used so as to ensure that all persons falling into the same category are treated equally. For example, in absence of special needs, all the students taking a particular class must fulfill the same requirements. Some students cannot be required to write more essays than other students or take more tests or attend more class sessions. Yet all students taking one course can be required to write five essays in a semester, whereas all students taking a different course could be required to write seven essays in the same semester, and so on.

USING THE JUSTICE DECISION-MAKING APPROACH IN THE BUSINESS WORLD In applying the justice approach to an ethical dilemma in the business arena, the decision maker should:

- Identify all the stakeholders impacted by the decision,
- Identify the different categories of stakeholders, and
- Consider whether all persons in the same category are being treated in the same manner—that is, that all are being treated equally and fairly.

Let us consider the example of year-end bonuses being distributed in a company. In a decision about the size of the bonuses, the justice approach requires that all employees of the same category (or rank) must be equally eligible for the bonus and all employees achieving the same target of performance must receive the same size of bonus. Examining this approach in the accounting context, let us consider the case of a manager who knows that the earnings in the financial statements of Company X are overstated and this manager sells his or her shares to a member of the public who does not know that the earnings are inflated. The justice approach requires that both parties deserve equal information in order to make a rational decision. An auditor who knowingly fails to qualify incorrect financial statements fails to justly distribute the correct information. Under the justice approach, we also can better understand why insider trading is unethical: The parties involved do not have equal information. The overriding concern in the justice approach is the absence of partiality and prejudice in the treatment of all persons.

AN ETHICAL DECISION-MAKING MODEL FOR ACCOUNTANTS

All of the previous applied approaches to the ethical evaluation of alternatives in a decision-making model address the ethical problems quite clearly and offer paradigms to help identify the following:

- The facts and the alternatives
- The stakeholders
- The dominant ethical issues involved (such as benefits and consequences, rights and duties, or justice and equality)
- The way in which the decision making may affect the stakeholders

   To choose the right action, each system requires the consideration of the alternatives and the application of principles in an analytical attempt to make ethical decisions and to select appropriate actions.

   A number of professional organizations, as well as individuals, have submitted models that combine and/or adapt the major philosophical frameworks for the evaluation of ethical issues in the business world. One model that is particularly useful for the accounting profession is the American Accounting Association Decision-Making Model.

The American Accounting Association Ethical Decision-Making Model

The American Accounting Association Model (see Table 2.1) is a frequently cited model that has strong elements of consequentialism and the rights-and-duties approach while specifying some virtues—such as integrity—together with a call to the decision maker's own "primary principles or values" (qtd. in Cohen, 2004, p. 134).

TABLE 2.1   The American Accounting Association Ethical Decision-Making Model[*]

1. Determine the facts—what, who, where, when and how?
    What do we know or need to know, if possible, that will help define the problems?

2. Define the ethical issue.
    a) List the significant stakeholders
    b) Define the ethical issues
       Make sure precisely what the ethical issue is—for example, conflicts involving rights, questions over limits of an obligation, etc.

3. Identify major principles, rules, or values.
    For example, integrity, quality, respect for persons, and profit.

4. Specify the alternatives.
    List the major alternative courses of action, including those that represent some form of compromise or point between simply doing or not doing something.

5. Compare values and alternatives. See if a clear decision is evident.
    Determine if there is one principle or value, or combination, which is so compelling that the proper alternative is clear—for example, correcting a defect that is almost certain to cause loss of life.

6. Assess the consequences.
    Identify short and long, and positive and negative consequences for the major alternatives. The common short-run focus on gain or loss needs to be measured against long-run considerations. This step will often reveal an unanticipated result of major importance.

7. Make your decision.
    Balance the consequences against your primary principles or values and select the alternative that best fits.

---

[*]Quoted in Stephen Cohen, 2004. *The Nature of Moral Reasoning: The Framework and Activities of Ethical Deliberation, Argument, and Decision-Making*. New York: Oxford University Press. pp. 133–134. Model adapted by William W. May for the American Accounting Association from a model suggested by H.Q. Langenderfer and J.W. Rockness. Published with permission.

All ethical dilemmas should initially be examined against the background of the three major ethical theories of morality: consequentialism, deontology, and virtue ethics. Such analysis and contemplation is highly likely to increase the decision maker's awareness of all the nuances and issues at stake. Like the child who does not appreciate the intricacies of chess and plays the game for an extra piece of candy, the business manager or accountant who does not understand the essence of ethics or morality will be tempted to cheat at the game when no one is looking.

Joseph L. Badaracco, Jr., Professor of Business Ethics at Harvard Business School, offers the following succinct description of those who have the ability to make prudent and ethical decisions in the business world:

> They are able to dig below the busy surface of their daily lives and refocus on their core values and principles. Once uncovered, those values and principles renew their sense of purpose at work and act as a springboard for shrewd, pragmatic, politically astute action. By repeating this process again and again throughout their work lives, these executives are able to craft an authentic and strong identity based on their own, rather than on someone else's, understanding of what is right. (2006)

As we proceed from the major ethical theories of morality toward a decision-making model and test the different approaches for their applicability or usefulness in relation to an ethical evaluation of all the options in a specific business dilemma, the likelihood increases that we will better discern what the right action is and why it is important to do what is right.

Key Terms

Applied ethics *24*
Categorical imperative *27*
Consequentialism *25*
Deontological theory *25*

Hedonism *26*
Metaethics *24*
Moral relativism *29*
Normative ethics *24*

Utilitarianism *25*
Virtue ethics *25*

Assignments[1]

TRUE/FALSE QUESTIONS

Answer the following questions with T for true or F for false for more practice with key terms and concepts from this chapter.

1. Virtue ethics offers strict prescriptions for how to act.

   T   F

2. Consequentialism is agent-centered.

   T   F

3. Business ethics is a type of metaethics.

   T   F

4. A consequentialist framework always is able to predict every foreseeable outcome of any given action.

   T   F

5. Utilitarianism is a form of deontology.

   T   F

6. Deontology judges right action based on one's duties.

   T   F

7. Developing good character is crucial to consequentialism.

   T   F

8. The purpose of an audit is to make the company feel positive about its business plan.

   T   F

9. The rights approach to the analysis of ethical dilemmas is usually combined with the justice approach.

   T   F

10. An example of an *in persona* right is the right to have a loan repaid.

    T   F

FILL-IN-THE-BLANK QUESTIONS

Fill in the blanks with information and concepts from this chapter.

11. _____ formulated the categorical imperative.

12. Bentham's protégé, John Stuart Mill (1806–1873), defined happiness as the presence of pleasure and the absence of pain and believed that actions have *utility* when they _____ happiness.

13. Distributive justice is concerned with how goods are _____.

14. Equality, _____, merit, contribution, and effort are the principles of distributive justice, according to philosopher Joel Feinberg.

15. To the virtue ethicist, the most important aspect of morality is having the right _____.

16. The most famous proponent of virtue ethics was _____.

---

[1] Assignments in this chapter were developed in collaboration with Kate Jackson, Ph.D. student in Theological Ethics, Boston College.

17. The leading form of consequentialism is _____.

18. "The greatest happiness for the greatest number" is the main tenet of _____.

19. Investors are considered to be _____ when the utilitarian model is used by an auditor making a decision about whether to qualify an audit report.

20. According to virtue ethics, the _____ is one's ultimate purpose and the virtues are derived from this end.

MULTIPLE-CHOICE QUESTIONS

21. "The most important issue in morality is to choose the right actions, and this choice is determined by examining the consequences of the action." This statement is best aligned with:
    (a) Utilitarianism.
    (b) Deontology.
    (c) Virtue ethics.
    (d) All of the above.

22. Which of the following statements is not consistent with Kant's concept of the categorical imperative?
    (a) Act only according to that maxim by which you can at the same time will that it should become a universal law.
    (b) In some circumstances, the end justifies the means.
    (c) Always treat persons as an end and never as a means.
    (d) Act according to a maxim that harmonizes with a possible realm (i.e., a systematic union of different rational beings through common laws).

23. "The cultivation of ethical behavior is very largely a matter of developing the right character." This statement is best aligned with:
    (a) Deontology.
    (b) Utilitarianism.
    (c) Virtue ethics.
    (d) All of the above.

24. Which one of the following does *not* describe Aristotle's virtue approach to ethics?
    (a) Behavior related to human flourishing.
    (b) An unwavering commitment to duty.

(c) The mean between extremes.
(d) Developed by good character.

Questions 25–28 are about a fictitious shoe manufacturing company, Stylish Shoes, and the audit performed by the fictitious audit firm Ethical Auditors, Inc.

Ethical Auditors is on a tight deadline to finish the audit of Stylish Shoes soon after its financial year end. Despite the deadline, Lucas Cypher, CPA, leaves work surreptitiously to take his daughter to dance class. He tells his coworker, Eva Numeral, CPA, that he will be back in an hour. The managing partner asks Eva where Lucas is. Eva reflects carefully before she answers the managing partner.

25. Based on some stern e-mails sent by the managing partner in the past, Eva believes that if she tells him Lucas left, he will fire Lucas. Unemployment will be detrimental to Lucas and his daughters, who rely on Lucas's salary for all their needs. Eva also believes that Lucas will be back soon and that he will make up the missed work. Based on this analysis, she decides that the best course of action with the best results for everyone is to lie. "Lucas is in the bathroom," Eva tells the managing partner. What ethical system is she predominantly using to make her decision?
    (a) Consequentialism.
    (b) Deontology.
    (c) Virtue ethics.
    (d) Justice.

26. Eva decides she has a duty to tell the truth at all times. What ethical system will Eva be using to make her decision?
    (a) Consequentialism.
    (b) Deontology.
    (c) Virtue ethics.
    (d) Hedonism.

27. Based on their audit, Lucas and Eva determine that someone is embezzling money from Stylish Shoes. After further research, the CEO learns that the embezzler is most likely one of three employees. In light of the consequences of continuing embezzlement (loss of profit to shareholders and employees, no bonuses for employees, and low morale), the CEO decides it is reasonable to interrogate each of the three suspects until he knows for

sure who did the crime. The CEO believes that it is ethical to mistreat a few people for the greater good of many. This incident illustrates the possibility for overly permissive ethics from which one of the following theories?
(a) Consequentialism.
(b) Deontology.
(c) Virtue ethics.
(d) Hedonism.

28. Ethical Auditors determines that Stylish Shoes has an unexpected surplus of $200,000. The CEO and CFO debate how best to spend the money. Knowing the financial difficulties of a number of company employees, the CEO thinks that the greatest good for the greatest number will be best served if the excess is split among the employees. On the other hand, the CFO thinks the greatest good for the greatest number will be best served if the money is sent to starving children in a poor country. This conflict of how to assess the repercussions of an action is a shortcoming of which ethical theory?
(a) Consequentialism.
(b) Deontology.
(c) Virtue ethics.
(d) Nihilism.

29. Which of the following is *not* one of the cardinal virtues?
(a) Courage.
(b) Autonomy.
(c) Temperance.
(d) Justice.

30. Which of the following is *not* one of the categories of rights articulated by James Sterba?
(a) Action rights.
(b) *In persona* rights.
(c) Self-defense rights.
(d) *In rem* rights.

FOR DISCUSSION

31. List and describe the virtues that you think comprise a "virtuous" accountant. Discuss how these virtues may be cultivated.

32. Do you think that to be virtuous in business, it is also necessary to be virtuous in other areas of your life, such as in your marriage or in your friendships? Or do you think you can possess some virtues without the others? Support your answer.

33. In your opinion, what role does intention play in moral decision making? For instance, is it permissible to do the right action for the wrong reasons (e.g., to gain fame or acclaim) or to do the wrong thing for good reasons (e.g., to embezzle money from a Fortune 500 company and give it to the poor)? Which ethical theory discussed in this chapter is most likely to take intention into account?

34. Aristotle believed we are happiest when we act ethically. For Aristotle, the human *telos* is to comprehend the good, and so we will be happiest when we are achieving our *telos*. Because our ultimate end is to comprehend the good, Aristotle thought we are happiest when we perform right action. Kant did not think that right action was necessarily rewarded on Earth or that right action was accompanied by happiness in this life. In fact, Kant postulated that there is a heaven because following the moral law does not always seem to benefit us on Earth. Think about your own life in light of these two positions. Do you think you are happiest when you are acting ethically, or do you think morality is sometimes at odds with your well-being? Explain your answer.

35. Your manager at Ethical Auditors is an avid Kantian. Over the course of the last two years, you have had many personality conflicts with her, as well as major arguments over what are the best accounting practices. Despite these conflicts, you always completed your tasks accurately and on time. At your two-year review, she recommends you for promotion. You know the recommendation is rooted in her sense of duty and not her kind feelings for you.
(a) Do you think her duty-based approach to ethics supports or undermines your promotion? Why?
(b) Do you think your manager's duty-based approach to ethics supports or undermines her status as an ethical person? Why?

36. Justice is named as one of the cardinal virtues; it is also sometimes thought of as a duty, and the justice approach is one of the decision-making models offered by Fleming for business ethics. Considering justice in terms of equal treatment of the sexes, do you think that the business environment is sometimes unfair to women? Why or why not? If possible, use examples from your work or internship experience to support your view.

CASE STUDY

Peter Madoff, Former Chief Compliance Officer and Senior Managing Director of Bernard L. Madoff Investment Securities, LLC

- **Read** the June 29, 2012, press release on Peter Madoff, younger brother of Bernard Madoff.
- **Respond** to the following Case Study Questions.

Required

a. **Utilitarianism requires the identification of stakeholders who could suffer consequences due to the choice of a particular action.**

   i. Identify each of the stakeholders that the U.S. Attorney's office recognized as parties that suffered consequences of Peter Madoff's actions. Describe the kinds of consequences they may have suffered.

   ii. Based on this utilitarian analysis, determine what Peter Madoff should have done.

   iii. One form of consequentialism is egoism. Describe the concept of egoism. Identify how the U.S. Attorney's office addresses egoism in the case of Peter Madoff.

b. **Deontology requires the identification of rationally derived duties.**

   i. Describe Peter Madoff's duties as a company officer and the ways he fell short of fulfilling his obligations.

   ii. According to Kant, we are bound by the moral law because we can rationally discern right action. Do you think "pure, practical reason" offers a compelling incentive to choose the right course of action, or do you think external forces are necessary to keep people honest? Why or why not? Be sure to use the situation of Peter Madoff in your answer.

c. **At times, we must choose between competing ethical systems.**

   i. Compare and contrast the ethical analysis of Peter Madoff's actions by a consequentialist with the analysis of a deontologist.

   ii. In your view, which theory better identifies the salient moral issues at stake? Why?

   iii. Do you think one system is more applicable to business ethics, or do you think it varies depending on the situation? Explain your answer.

d. **The American Accounting Association Ethical Decision-Making Model.** Use the American Accounting Association's Model to analyze this case from the point of view of a chief compliance officer who wants to act ethically in this situation.

Press Release on Peter Madoff

Peter Madoff, Former Chief Compliance Officer and Senior Managing Director at Bernard L. Madoff Investment Securities LLC, Pleads Guilty to Securities Fraud and Tax Fraud Conspiracy in Manhattan Federal Court[1]

Madoff Also Pleads Guilty to Falsifying Books and Records and Making False Statements to Investors

U.S. Attorney's   Southern District of New York
Office June 29, 2012

Preet Bharara, the United States Attorney for the Southern District of New York; Janice K. Fedarcyk, the Assistant Director in Charge of the New York Field Office of the Federal Bureau of Investigation (FBI); Toni Weirauch, the Acting Special Agent in Charge of the New York Field Office of the Internal Revenue Service, Criminal Investigation (IRS-CI); Robert L. Panella, Special Agent in Charge for the New York Regional Office of the U.S. Department of Labor's Office of the Inspector General, Office of Labor Racketeering and Fraud Investigations (DOL-OIG); and Jonathan Kay, the Director for the New York Regional Office of the U.S. Department of Labor, Employee Benefits Security Administration (DOL-EBSA), announced that Peter Madoff, the former chief compliance officer and senior managing director of Bernard L. Madoff Investment Securities LLC (BLMIS), pled guilty today to a two-count superseding information charging him with, among other things, conspiracy to commit securities fraud, tax fraud, mail fraud, ERISA[2] fraud, and falsifying records of an investment advisor. The overt acts in the conspiracy count also include, among other things, making false statements to investors about BLMIS's compliance program and the nature and scope of its Investment Advisory business. Madoff pled guilty in Manhattan federal court before United States District Judge Laura Taylor Swain.

Manhattan U.S. Attorney Preet Bharara said, "Peter Madoff enabled the largest fraud in human history. He will now be jailed well into old age, and he will forfeit virtually every penny he has. We are not yet finished calling to account everyone responsible for the epic fraud of Bernard Madoff and the epic pain of his many victims."

FBI Assistant Director in Charge Janice K. Fedarcyk said, "The Madoff investment empire, built on a foundation of deceit, was a house of cards that grew to skyscraper proportions. As Peter Madoff has admitted today, he was one of the chief architects. For years he certified that periodic reviews established the firm's compliance with internal and regulatory rules. In fact, Peter Madoff conducted no reviews. He certified that his examination of the firm's trading process established its integrity. He did not—indeed, he could not—conduct any such examination: despite the façade, the investment advisory business did not actually trade any stocks. Peter Madoff played an essential enabling role in the largest investment fraud in U.S. history. He made a pretense of compliance; he was really about complicity."

IRS-CI Acting Special Agent in Charge Toni Weirauch said, "This scheme relied on sophisticated teamwork to prevent its discovery by investors and law enforcement. One

---

[1] Obtained from the website of the Federal Bureau of Investigation. *www.fbi.gov*.
[2] ERISA refers to the Employee Retirement Income Security Act of 1974, a federal law set up to protect employee retirement plans.

of the consequences of the concealment is that the IRS was hindered from performing its lawful duty, thus harming our nation's law abiding taxpayers, along with the defrauded victims. IRS-Criminal Investigation is proud to bring our financial investigative skills to this complex joint investigation and be part of the team that is helping to untangle the web of lies and sort out the culpabilities of the individuals involved. Today's plea represents an important step forward."

DOL-OIG Special Agent in Charge Robert L. Panella said, "During today's plea, Peter Madoff admitted to his role in a fraud scheme that harmed the savings of thousands of investors. The investigation that led to today's guilty plea by Madoff serves as a stern warning to those who would knowingly undermine the financial well-being of workers. In addition, by conspiring to make false statements and to falsify documents required by the Employee Retirement Income Security Act, he failed to protect the integrity of employee benefit plan assets and personally benefited from proceeds gained as a result of these false statements. The OIG will continue to work tirelessly with the U.S. Attorney and our law enforcement partners to investigate such crimes." DOL-EBSA New York Regional Director Jonathan Kay said, "Today's plea is a testament to the good work and strong collaboration among multiple federal agencies. This agency remains committed to protecting worker benefit plans from those who would defraud them for personal gain."

According to the superseding information to which Madoff pled and other court filings:

Madoff was employed at BLMIS from 1965 through at least December 11, 2008. Beginning in 1969, he became the chief compliance officer (CCO) and senior managing director of BLMIS. In his role as CCO, Madoff created false and misleading BLMIS compliance documents, as well as false reports that were filed with the U.S. Securities and Exchange Commission (SEC) that materially misstated the nature and scope of BLMIS's Investment Advisory (IA) business.

Specifically, in his capacity as CCO, Madoff created numerous false compliance documents in which he stated that he had performed compliance reviews of the trading in the BLMIS IA business on a regular basis, when, in reality, the reviews were never performed. The false statements were designed to mislead regulators, auditors, and IA clients.

Further, in August 2006, BLMIS registered as an investment adviser with the SEC. As a registered investment adviser, on at least an annual basis, BLMIS was required to file forms with the SEC that are used to guide the examination programs of investment advisors. Madoff was integrally involved with both the SEC registration process and in the creation of the forms, known as "Forms ADV," which were materially false and misleading. The numerous false statements in the Forms ADV created the false appearance that BLMIS's IA business had a small number of highly sophisticated clients and far fewer assets under management than was actually the case. For example, the Forms ADV stated that there were only 23 IA accounts under management at BLMIS when, in fact, there were more than 4,000 at the time of the firm's collapse in 2008 and that its IA services were available "only to institutional and high net worth clients." The forms also stated that, in 2008, BLMIS had $17.1 billion in assets under management when, on paper, it had more than $65 billion at that time. Madoff also misrepresented that he, as CCO, ensured that reviews of the IA trading were being performed.

In addition, from 1998 through 2008, Madoff engaged in a tax fraud scheme involving the transfer of wealth within the Madoff family in ways that allowed him to avoid paying millions of dollars in required taxes to the IRS. Most, if not all of the "wealth," came directly or indirectly from IA client funds held at BLMIS. The schemes in which he engaged also allowed Bernie Madoff to evade his tax obligations. The methods by which Madoff engaged in tax fraud included the following:

- Madoff received approximately $15,700,000 from Bernard L. Madoff and his wife and executed sham promissory notes to make it appear that the transfers were loans, in order to avoid paying taxes;
- Madoff gave approximately $9,900,000 to family members, and in order to avoid paying taxes, executed sham promissory notes to make it appear that the transfers of these funds were loans;
- Madoff did not pay taxes on approximately $7,750,000 that he received from BLMIS;
- Madoff received approximately $16,800,000 from Bernard L. Madoff from two sham trades, and disguised the proceeds of the trades as long-term stock transactions in order to take advantage of the lower tax rate for long-term capital gains;
- Madoff charged approximately $175,000 in personal expenses to a corporate American Express card and did not report those expenses as income. Madoff also arranged for his wife to have a "no-show" job at BLMIS from which she received between approximately $100,000 and $160,000 per year in salary, a 401(k), and other benefits to which she was not entitled.

In December 2008, when the collapse of BLMIS was virtually certain, Madoff agreed with others to send the $300 million that remained in the IA accounts to preferred employees, family members, and friends. BLMIS collapsed before the funds were ever disbursed. On December 10, 2008, one day prior to BLMIS's collapse, Madoff also withdrew $200,000 from BLMIS for his personal use.

Madoff, 66, of Old Westbury, New York, faces a statutory maximum sentence of 10 years in prison. The statutory maximum sentences for each of the charged offenses are set forth in the attached chart. Pursuant to his plea agreement with the government, Madoff agrees not to seek a sentence of other than 10 years in prison. Madoff is also subject to mandatory restitution and criminal forfeiture and faces criminal fines up to twice the gross gain or loss derived from the offense. He has agreed to forfeiture of more than $143.1 billion, including all of his real and personal property. This amount represents all of the investor funds paid into BLMIS from 1996—the start of Madoff's involvement in the conspiracy—through December 2008.

As part of the defendant's forfeiture, the government has entered into a settlement with Madoff's family that requires the forfeiture of all of his wife Marion's and daughter Shana's assets and assets belonging to other family members. The surrendered assets include, among other things, several homes, a Ferrari, and more than $10 million in cash and securities. Marion Madoff is being left with approximately $771,733 to live on for the rest of her life. The forfeited assets, including the net proceeds from the sale of the forfeited properties, will be used to compensate victims of the fraud, consistent with applicable Department of Justice regulations.

Judge Swain set a sentencing date for Madoff of October 4, 2012 at 3:30 p.m.[3]

Mr. Bharara praised the investigative work of the Federal Bureau of Investigation. He also thanked the U.S. Securities and Exchange Commission, the Internal Revenue Service, and the U.S. Department of Labor for their assistance.

These cases were brought in coordination with President Barack Obama's Financial Fraud Enforcement Task Force, on which Mr. Bharara serves as a Co-Chair of the Securities and Commodities Fraud Working Group. President Obama established the interagency Financial Fraud Enforcement Task Force to wage an aggressive, coordinated, and proactive effort to investigate and prosecute financial crimes. The task force includes representatives from a broad range of federal agencies, regulatory authorities, inspectors general, and state and local law enforcement who, working together, bring to bear a powerful array of criminal and civil enforcement resources. The task force is working to improve efforts across the federal executive branch and, with state and local partners, to investigate and prosecute significant financial crimes, ensure just and effective punishment for those who perpetrate financial crimes, combat discrimination in the lending and financial markets, and recover proceeds for victims of financial crimes.

The case is being handled by the Office's Securities and Commodities Fraud Task Force. Assistant United States Attorneys Lisa A. Baroni, Julian J. Moore, Matthew L. Schwartz, Arlo Devlin-Brown, and Barbara A. Ward are in charge of the prosecution.

United States v. Peter Madoff, S7 10 Cr. 228 (LTS)

---

[3] Peter Madoff was ultimately sentenced on December 19, 2012, to ten years in prison. He also consented to forfeit all his assets (Van Voris & Glovin, 2012). In June 2009, Bernard Madoff was sentenced to 150 years in prison (Henriques, 2009).

CHAPTER 3

The Sizzling Saga of Sunbeam[1]

Learning Objectives

After studying this chapter, you should be able to:

- Recognize how a record of problematic executive leadership and a flashy leadership style may signal potential problems within a company.
- Explain the meaning of the term *improper revenue recognition*.
- List the methods that Sunbeam used to recognize future periods' sales in current periods.
- Identify the conditions under which "bill and hold sales" can legitimately be recognized in accordance with Generally Accepted Accounting Principles (GAAP).
- Identify the signals in financial statements that could alert one to the possibility that future periods' revenue has been recognized in current periods.
- Explain how restructuring reserves can be used to overstate earnings in future periods.
- Identify the signals in financial statements that could alert one to the possibility that a company may be misusing restructuring reserves in order to overstate earnings.
- Explain why downsizing by closing segments that report an accounting loss often leads to a decrease in profits, rather than an increase.

Sunbeam is presented in this chapter mainly as an example of:

- Improper Timing of Revenue Recognition via bill and hold sales, consignment sales, and other contingency sales
- Improper Expense Recognition via the use of restructuring and other liability reserves (refer to Table 1.1.)

---

[1] Background information in this chapter is mainly from Byrne (2003), Byron (2004), Laing (1997; 1998a; 1998b), Scherer (1996), and Schifrin (1998).

CHAPTER OUTLINE

THE HISTORY OF SUNBEAM

The Sunbeam story is ultimately the tale of a company that was gutted by management in a scorching turnaround attempt made at the same time that Sunbeam's executives falsely overstated profits in the vain effort to find a buyer for the charred company and cut themselves loose from the havoc they had wreaked. However, it is also the story of the collision and collusion of the forces that came together when fund managers who acquired Sunbeam hired a slash-and-burn chief executive officer. This is the saga of the analysts and journalists who watched and applauded while the auditors over-looked the false profits reported by a company that had the guts ripped out of it after the appointment of Albert J. "Chainsaw Al" Dunlap as CEO in 1996.

Why did Sunbeam hire a CEO with a reputation for slashing, burning, and "dumb-sizing" companies? Why was Al Dunlap so enthusiastic about cutting plants and jobs so ruthlessly? Why did Wall Street not question how production, sales, and profits could possibly increase as a result of having fewer plants, fewer product lines, and fewer workers? Why did virtually no one take heed of demoralized and scared employ-ees looking for safer jobs, while key executives resigned in droves? What accounting mechanisms were used to overstate sales and earnings? Why did none of the executives inform the board of directors of the unfolding chaos? What went wrong, and why did it go wrong so rapidly and so relentlessly?

To answer these questions, we must look at how Sunbeam was performing in the 1990s as compared with the stock market in general and the company's irrational expec-tations. We must examine the background and personality of Al Dunlap, as well as Wall Street's reactions to Dunlap's previous "turnaround" **downsizings**—reductions in the size of a company by reducing the number of product lines, factories, offices, and/or personnel in a business—and "cost-cutting-at-any cost" efforts in general.

Sunbeam began its life in 1897 as the Chicago Flexible Shaft Company, a manu-facturer of agricultural implements. With the innovation of electricity, it began pro-ducing toasters and irons and changed its name to Sunbeam Corp. In the 1960s, it acquired Oster Co. and added blenders and electric blankets to the array of its then "high-tech" product range. However, competition for household electrical goods grew quickly, and in 1981, under increasing pressure, Sunbeam believed that its best option was to be acquired by Allegheny International, Inc. This turned out to be a poor choice because Allegheny's CEO, Robert Buckley, was a man somewhat ahead of his time in that he was a forerunner of the high-living CEOs we are all too familiar with today.

He regarded the company he ran as his own. Traveling the world in his corporate jets and staying in lavish corporate apartments and condominiums, he felt entitled to large company loans at very low interest rates and to a salary of over $1 million a year. It was not surprising that his business focus became a little distracted. Between spectacular losses and extravagant expenditures, corporate profits soon evaporated and the unfortunate Buckley was fired in 1986.

The new management team began what would be a recurring theme for Sunbeam—team members instituted an aggressive downsizing program whereby they cut one-third of the company's jobs and sold off a number of the product lines. Not surprisingly, sales went down—not up. In early 1988, the company filed for bankruptcy.

Sunbeam emerged from bankruptcy under the control of Michael Price of the Mutual Series Investment Fund and Michael Steinhardt of the Steinhardt Partners Fund. Each had contributed around $60 million, at the urging of two dealmakers—Paul Kazarian and Michael Lederman—who were then appointed to manage the company, with Kazarian as CEO. They renamed the business Sunbeam-Oster. Kazarian performed a true turnaround of the company, producing genuine profits and taking the company public very successfully.

Although Kazarian cut the extravagant waste of the Buckley era and stopped the wild downsizing of his predecessor's turnaround attempt, he appeared to be a workaholic and was too intense for some. He was fired and replaced with Roger Schipke, who was as laid-back and gentlemanly as Kazarian had been intense. He may have overdone the gentility, however, for Sunbeam at this stage had many strong personalities pulling in opposite directions. Without a powerful leader, profits fell quickly and steadily.

As a result of basically buying Sunbeam out of bankruptcy, Price and Steinhardt, the fund managers, had an enormous amount of stock and an enormous amount of control over Sunbeam, even after it went public. It was now 1996, and these were giddy times for Wall Street. Price prided himself on being an exceptional stock selector. He knew how to find bargain stocks and he felt sure that Sunbeam could be made very profitable again and that its stock price could soar. He believed that he just needed to appoint the right kind of CEO—a leader who could do another turnaround of Sunbeam. He needed a leader who had slashed costs in companies, who had cut production plants and products, and who had reported a profit so quickly after a period of losses that it was almost too good to be true. In fact, he knew of such a man—Al Dunlap—who had done all this for Scott Paper Co. What is more, Dunlap had then sold Scott Paper to Kimberly-Clark at a huge profit.

Perhaps Price had not followed what had happened to Scott Paper after its reported quick turnaround profits and its rapid sale to Kimberly-Clark. Perhaps he had followed but didn't care. Perhaps he believed that the problems had not been caused by the downsizing. The trouble was that after Kimberly-Clark acquired Scott Paper, management found it to be a mess. Scott Paper had had the guts ripped out of it. However, Michael Price needed a man who could slash costs and perform a company turnaround in no time at all, and he thought that Dunlap was just the man he needed to be the new CEO of Sunbeam.

The History of Al Dunlap

Al Dunlap's history—both his personal background and his business history of down-sizing businesses that later suffered—was the first warning sign that alerted analysts, such as Andrew Shore of the PaineWebber, Inc. brokerage house, to be on the lookout for unsustainable profits at Sunbeam.

Dunlap was 59 years old when he was appointed CEO of Sunbeam in 1996. Although he claims that he was born poor and grew up even poorer, his sister said that his childhood was "very comfortable." Until he was 11 years old, he lived in a "three-story redbrick row house on Garden Street in Hoboken" in New Jersey. When he turned 11, "his family moved to Hasbrouck Heights, New Jersey, a middle-class com-munity of peaceful, tree-lined streets and modest homes." Both Dunlap's sister and his high school football coach reported that he had always had a temper, "an aggressive one," according to his coach. His sister said that he "would just spin on you in a sec-ond." (Quotes from Byrne, 2003, pp. 97–98)

Dunlap's childhood behavior sounds mild compared to his legendary temper tan-trums at Sunbeam, where he would go into screaming rants that Christopher Byron described as "extreme fighting in the boardroom," in *Testosterone Inc. Tales of CEOs Gone Wild* (2004, p. 254).

Dunlap worked hard at high school and got into the United States Military Academy at West Point. He completed his three-year military obligation, during which time he married Gwyn Donnelly when he was 24 and she was 19. Gwyn soon began to see another side of Al Dunlap. A few years later, in Gwyn's divorce complaint, she alleged that once, while cleaning his gun collection, Dunlap had remarked, "You better watch out and toe the line." He would become enraged if she had not cleaned the apart-ment to his satisfaction. The complaint also stated that he had once threatened to bash her over the head with a telephone if she did not give the telephone to him. Dunlap emphatically denied the divorce complaint. Ultimately, however, the judge found that Dunlap had engaged in "extreme cruelty" and awarded Gwyn sole custody of their son. (Quotes from Byrne, 2003, pp. 101–104)

Dunlap remarried in 1968 and his new wife, Judy, was always supportive of Chainsaw Al. She appeared to admire his aggression. It has been reported that she once proudly told a party of people that Dunlap did not get heart attacks himself, but he gave them to others. Al Dunlap and Judy appeared to be very well matched. They did not have children, but both were dog enthusiasts and their German shepherds were their pride and joy. However, Dunlap's rage continued unabated toward the rest of the world. He "'was the most unpleasant, personally repulsive businessman I ever met in my life' said a New York image consultant who Dunlap had wanted to hire" (qtd. in Byron, 2004, pp. 18–19).

Dunlap's business career echoed the same rocky pattern as his personal life. After graduating from West Point and completing his three-year military obligation, Dunlap got a job at Kimberly-Clark's New Milford plant in Connecticut. In 1965, he was trans-ferred to Kimberly-Clark's plant in Wisconsin. The plant's superintendent was a can-tankerous man who liked to chastise his employees. Not surprisingly, Dunlap got on well with him and perhaps even imitated him. Dunlap was recommended for the job as plant manager at Sterling Pulp and Paper, also in Wisconsin. Between his military train-ing and his angry management style, he was soon giving unpopular orders for layoffs.

In Dunlap's own autobiography, he relates that soon after assuming this new position, he began receiving death threats. Nevertheless, he kept that job for about six years, leaving only when the owner died.

Dunlap's next job was at Max Phillips and Sons, where he was allegedly fired after less than two months for his ill manners and insolence toward his boss. Undeterred, he got a job as chief operating officer at Nitec Paper Corp. in Niagara Falls, New York. Dunlap was hired to do a turnaround at Nitec, which was in a bit of a slump. However, Dunlap's sojourn there lasted only about two years and ended badly as well. Nitec's chairman, George Petty, fired him, declaring that "Dunlap had so completely alienated those around him that Nitec faced the mass resignation of all the company's vice presidents if he weren't let go." At that time, it appeared that profits had turned around positively, and so Dunlap negotiated a $1.2 million severance package. However, just after Dunlap left the company, "Nitec's auditors at the accounting firm of Arthur Young & Co. reported that the anticipated profits that Dunlap had been promising were apparently the result of massive falsifications and fraudulent accounting entries on the company's books." Even though there is no evidence that Dunlap had anything to do with the falsification, there had been no real turnaround. As a result, Nitec reneged on its promise of the severance pay, and Dunlap sued and settled for $50,000. (Quotes from Byron, 2004, p. 77)

From Nitec, Dunlap eventually found a middle-management job at American Can, where he rose to become head of the plastics division. From there, he moved on to Manville Corp., which, as a result of asbestos lawsuits, filed for bankruptcy within a year after his arrival.

Serendipitously, Dunlap's next position truly seemed to be a perfect match with his genetic makeup. He was recruited by Lily-Tulip, Inc., to cut costs and perform a turnaround of the company that was operating at a loss and had too much debt. The specific mandate of slashing costs was almost too good to be true for Dunlap and he tackled the task with gusto. He even began to cultivate an image in the press of an executive who did not shy away from cutting jobs or offending colleagues. The press ran several articles on Dunlap in 1984, indicating that he was instilling fear into his workforce. This was the beginning of what would become the long saga of an angry man who cultivated and was even proud of a tough, ruthless public image that fed his apparently already ruthless streak. He interpreted "mean" as "strong," and he titled his memoir *Mean Business: How I Save Bad Companies and Make Good Companies Great.* Dunlap took his cue from the media: Nothing captured the business press's attention more than a slash-and-burn downsizing. And the more jobs he cut, the tougher and smarter the press made him look. By the end of his time at Lily-Tulip, Dunlap had cemented his public image as a ruthless downsizing and turnaround specialist—and he was proud of it.

After Lily-Tulip, Dunlap went on to work in Britain and then in Australia for Kerry Packer's Consolidated Press Holdings. He left Consolidated Press embroiled in conflict with a number of colleagues, as described in an article titled "Al Dunlap's Disgrace" (Williams, 2001). However, the controversy in Australia did not seem to count against him at all when he went after the job of CEO of Scott Paper, which was also badly in need of a turnaround.

By the last quarter of 1993, Scott Paper was sustaining large losses and its CEO, Philip Lippincott, wanted out. There were not many seasoned executives who wanted his job. Lippincott had already publicized a downsizing plan that would require laying off more than 8,000 employees over a number of years. For Chainsaw Al, it looked like a magnificent opportunity. Al Dunlap arrived to take the helm of Scott Paper in April 1994 and he slashed more than 11,000 jobs in less than one year. He sold off large publishing and printing businesses as well as the company's domestic timberlands and a number of overseas paper mills. It is difficult to second-guess which of these should have stayed and which should have gone, if any. However, when research and development expenditure is deeply cut and maintenance on property, plant, and equipment is deferred, it is usually a fairly good guess that management is focused on short-term earnings instead of long-term growth and profit. It is easy to get profits up in the current year by cutting R&D, but that will kill future growth and profits.

In an interview with an executive from Scott Paper, John Byrne was told that "by the end of 1994, it just became a volume-driven plan to pretty up the place for sale.... We're talking about a whole new definition of short-term." In addition, "Dunlap slashed the company's research and development budget in half, to about $35 million, and eliminated 60% of the staffers in R&D." Dunlap also cut back on memberships in industry organizations and "eliminated all corporate gifts to charities." (Quotes from Byrne, 2003, p. 27)

In a precursor to what would happen at Sunbeam, big sales discounts were given to accelerate sales, and "in the final months before the company was sold, the discounts were doubled." The stock price went up dramatically based on reported profits. Dunlap managed to sell Scott Paper to Kimberly-Clark in July 1995 and he left Scott Paper $100 million the richer. Not surprisingly, Kimberly-Clark soon realized that Scott Paper, in fact, had had the guts ripped out of it. Predictably, with the highly discounted sales before Scott was sold, its sales were slow in the next period. With plants closed, businesses cut, and workers retrenched, combined with little R&D and sparse maintenance, growth did not increase; inevitably, it fell. Kimberly-Clark took a $1.4 billion restructuring charge in respect of its integration of Scott Paper. Al Dunlap did not seem to care; he was out of Scott's as a very rich man—and a lucky one. Kimberly-Clark was left with the mess. Chainsaw Al, however, was not ready to retire. He was looking for a new company to "turn around." (Quotes from Byrne, 2003, pp. 28–32)

How Wall Street Embraced Sunbeam's Downsizing Plans

When Dunlap went looking for a new job after selling off Scott Paper, the general attitude toward downsizing at the time was that it was effective and that Dunlap had the world's leading reputation for downsizing. In 1996, Sunbeam was sustaining losses. The board was looking for a replacement for its CEO, Roger Schipke, who was considered too placid to provide the assertive leadership that the troubled company needed. Dunlap was the man for the job. On July 18, 1996, Albert J. Dunlap was appointed CEO of Sunbeam, Inc.

Although it was becoming obvious that Dunlap's cost-cutting turnarounds were not turning out to be such positive transformations after all, the business press generally ignored the short-lived nature of the profits that followed his ruthless downsizings. In the 1990s, Wall Street was happy to read optimistic news into almost any confidently announced plan. The more dramatically a plan predicted a spectacularly profitable vision of the future, the more the press and the analysts loved it. This was a time when companies were going public with no records of profits—sometimes not even of sales—and a time when a simple click on a website was enough to be counted as a customer.

So when Dunlap announced not only a vision of a profitable future for Sunbeam but also a plan to achieve it, the press embraced his vision with gusto. After all, he was a brilliant businessman with a simple strategy—he was going to slash costs. And how was he going to slash costs? He was going to close production plants, drop product lines, and slash workers' jobs. That was Dunlap's vision for Sunbeam. If the CEO of a company that was sustaining losses suddenly and miraculously reported a profit in the financial statements without dramatically announcing a **restructuring plan**— a major plan to reorganize the company in the form of downsizing or changing the company's capital structure or reorganizing the company's debt agreements—this would be a little suspicious. One might wonder whether the financial statements had been fraudulently reported, or at least one might question whether they had been erroneously reported. Similarly, if management announced that it was going to increase sales by cutting products and increase production by closing plants and firing employees, that would sound counterintuitive; the logic might be questioned, and the predictions of increased earnings might not sound credible. However, if the CEO announced that he or she was going to perform a turnaround in a brief period by embarking on an aggressive downsizing and cost-cutting plan, Wall Street would embrace the plan and celebrate the vision of a quick turnaround with high profits and even higher stock prices.

The fact of the matter is that profits are maximized when total revenues exceed total costs by the greatest amount, which is not achieved by just cutting production facilities and employees or cutting R&D and marketing costs. Cutting is likely to reduce revenues more than it reduces costs and that will lead to less profit. If the object is just to cut costs, you can cut costs all the way to zero by liquidating the company. That will not maximize profits; it will produce a profit of zero. So cost-cutting is not an end in itself. It must be done scientifically, taking care to cut only costs that do not support greater revenues. Analysis, discernment, and precision are vital. The unintended consequences of cutting costs to increase short-term profits can easily cause long-term losses.

"Downsizing or Dumbsizing?"

An article in *BYU Magazine* titled "Downsizing or Dumbsizing?" succinctly captured the perils of these unintended consequences. It told the story of how, in 1994, Professors Lee Tom Perry and Eric L. Denna presented a cost-cutting plan to the executive committee of Scott Paper Co. The plan was well received, but before any implementation, Perry and Denna's consultancy was ended when Al Dunlap took over as CEO of Scott Paper. Professor Perry later remarked, "Obviously, something needed to be done. But what bothers me about Al Dunlap is his lack of precision. He has a very simplistic view: smaller is better" (qtd. in Jenkins, 1997).

Sunbeam apparently did not realize that there is a crucial difference between a downsizing and a dumbsizing. Clearly, companies must respond to changes and initiate changes. The economist, Val Lambson, observed:

> The way capitalism works is that it sends signals through prices telling people what they ought to be doing based on what's valued by consumers. The advantage of a free-market system is that it allocates the resources in a productive and efficient way. The results are beneficial for the whole. (Qtd. in Jenkins, 1997)

The organizational behavior specialist in downsizing, Kim S. Cameron, explained that downsizing must be an improvement process, not a target: "If they merely cut positions and headcount, but do not address the fundamental problems causing inefficiency and lack of competitiveness, the problems are still going to be there even after downsizing." Cameron acknowledged that while downsizing is sometimes necessary, when it is done badly, it is a most unproductive and futile method of trying to improve a company. Cameron likened it to a "grenade strategy," explaining that when you fling "a grenade into a company … it explodes, eliminating the positions of a certain number of people. The problem is you have no way of telling precisely who is going to be affected." (Qtd. in Jenkins, 1997)

Cameron pointed out:

> In the end, a corporation almost always loses company memory and company energy. The first is caused when informal networks are destroyed, information sharing is restricted, and experienced employees depart. The second is caused by declining morale, loss of loyalty and commitment, and the departure of the most talented employees, who know that they are marketable. (Qtd. in Jenkins, 1997)

Of course, cutting R&D and maintenance expenditures is going to hurt you in the future. At the same time, as Lambson pointed out, "When there's a technological change, or a change in consumer tastes, the changes are reflected in the prices. That's a signal to industry producers—the black-and-white television industry, for example—to retrain, retool, and move into other areas, which may cause some downsizing." As Perry explained: "Increased resource utilization is good for both business and society. That doesn't mean downsizing is out of the picture, but the Al Dunlaps would be." (Qtd. in Jenkins, 1997)

Cost-accounting analysis shows that when a company closes down a segment, although it does lose that segment's revenues, it does not lose all of the costs that are allocated to it in typical income statements. Some of those costs—the **common or allocated fixed costs** that support more than one segment of the business and will not decrease if any one segment is eliminated—will remain and will simply have to be carried by the remaining divisions. Only the costs that are truly caused by the division continuing—the **traceable fixed costs and the variable costs**—will be saved if the division is closed. Frequently, segments are closed without this analysis being done, and the result is often that the company is surprised to find that it has less profit, not more, after the segment is closed.

Dunlap's Carrot-and-Stick Approach

Dunlap structured control over his management team at Sunbeam with one of the most severe *carrot-and-stick* combinations ever implemented in U.S. business. The *carrot* was that executives and managers were allocated large numbers of stock options that would make them multimillionaires if the Sunbeam stock price went up dramatically. This was a large carrot that caused many executives, even those who despised Dunlap from past experience, to join him again for the Sunbeam turnaround. It also encouraged a number of managers who were working for Dunlap for the first time at Sunbeam to stay put because another key part of the carrot-and-stick deal was that the options Dunlap doled out vested after only three years. Many executives spent their entire tenure under

Dunlap caught in a dilemma: They desperately wanted to leave, but they would be walking away from potentially millions of dollars of stock-option gains, as long as the price of Sunbeam shares stayed up or went higher. The *stick* ingredient in Dunlap's carrot-and-stick approach was the raw fear he instilled in everybody who worked for him. All reports are that this really did apply to *everyone*.

The installation of fear began on Al Dunlap's very first day on the job at Sunbeam. All the top executives assembled for a meeting in the boardroom of the Fort Lauderdale, Florida office. Dunlap walked into the meeting and began a "monologue on himself and the company." He then turned to the gathering of company officers and began ranting and raving, admonishing them for the "demise of Sunbeam!" He kept repeating that the "old Sunbeam is over today. It's over." In his description of the scene, Byrne wrote: "Glaring fiercely, Dunlap kept repeating the phrase, again and again, saliva spitting from his lips. His chest was puffed out and his face flushed bright red. The men stared in silence, incredulous at this outrageous performance." (Quotes from Byrne, 2003, pp. 2–3)

Dunlap then confronted the CFO, Paul O'Hara, and blamed him for Sunbeam's failure to meet the previous year's financial performance estimates. Next, Dunlap began asking the executives to present their summaries of the state of their units or departments. He started with the unfortunate James Clegg, the chief operating officer, who had expected to get Dunlap's job. Dunlap "cut him off and accused him of not knowing the details of his businesses." Dunlap snapped at anybody who hesitated. Richard Boynton, Sunbeam's national sales manager, later said, "He [Dunlap] just yelled, ranted and raved." Dunlap kept this up for the entire first day. On the second day, Dunlap called Clegg out of the meeting and told him to leave the company and immediately sign the release form that honored his contract, including his salary for a year and his vested options. "Less than fifteen minutes after leaving the boardroom [Clegg] returned to pick up his briefcase. 'I'm out,' he said to his shocked colleagues." (Quotes from Byrne, 2003, pp. 5–8)

Over the next few days, Dunlap fired five more executives. The fear factor was firmly in place. The big stick was looming over every senior executive and manager. The carrot in the form of extremely generous options beckoned to the remaining executives with the promise of great riches.

To grasp the unpleasant yet enticing position that the Sunbeam management team found itself in, one must remember that the year was 1996. Stock prices were rising boisterously; restructuring and downsizings were in vogue among Wall Street analysts and journalists; and the king of downsizing and restructuring, Al Dunlap himself, was promising to turn Sunbeam around in twelve months, maybe even less. On July 19, the day after the announcement of Dunlap's appointment as CEO, Wall Street analysts gave *buy* ratings to the stock and its market price jumped from $12.50 to $18.63.

By early November, the stock was trading around $25 per share. Considering how fast the stock market as a whole was climbing in 1996, Sunbeam's stock had moved upward relatively modestly after the initial jump on the announcement of Dunlap's appointment. To propel the stock price much higher, he wanted to produce a spectacular slash-and-burn downsizing plan for Wall Street. To get a truly dramatic, aggressive cost-cutting plan together, Dunlap turned to a long-trusted consultant at Coopers & Lybrand to head the project.

Dunlap announced his stunning cost-cutting plan on a conference call with analysts on November 12, 1996. The next day, the *Wall Street Journal* ran an article dramatically titled, "Dunlap's Ax Falls—6,000 times—at Sunbeam." In the article, Frank and Lublin (1996) gave details of the plan announced by Dunlap:

- Immediately get rid of half of Sunbeam's 12,000 employees.
- Shut down about 40 of its 61 warehouses.
- Cut loose almost 90 percent of its product line.
- Get rid of more than half of its 26 factories.
- Eliminate the majority of its offices.

The article went on to say that "Albert Dunlap all but gutted Sunbeam Corp. and demonstrated once again the genesis of his nickname: 'Chain-Saw Al.'" Dunlap's plan estimated "a one-time pretax charge of $300 million, of which $75 million will be paid as severance costs associated with plant closings." Furthermore, the reduction of 6,000 people "appears to represent one of the single biggest percentage cutbacks ever announced by a major US corporation." The downsizing expert and author, Alan Downs, commented, "You don't cut that dramatically without creating chaos inside the company." (Qtd. in Frank & Lublin, 1996)

Surprisingly, for the first time Wall Street was not impressed with a Dunlap slash-and-burn announcement. The stock price did not rise. Perhaps the plan was so stunning that it gave cause for concern that Sunbeam was in worse shape than anyone had realized. Perhaps Kimberly-Clark's troubles with Scott Paper, after Dunlap's alleged turnaround, had left Wall Street a little wary of Dunlap's cost-cutting strategies. Maybe word had leaked that some managers were in shock about what they considered to be economic suicide: the closing of plants that they regarded as efficient low-cost/high-profit facilities. Whatever the reason, Wall Street did not respond to this ruthless announcement. In fact, Sunbeam's stock price actually dropped 50 cents on the day of the announcement.

No wonder the stock market was a little skeptical. How could closing so many factories lead to increased production and sales? How could fewer people produce and sell more? However, whether by design or by coincidence, the dramatic announcements of cost cutting had laid the foundation for lending credibility to the suddenly increasing false profits that would be reported in the near future. If Sunbeam had begun falsely reporting overstated sales and profits in 1997, without any dramatic plan at all, the numbers in the financial statements probably would have been questioned much sooner. All Sunbeam had to do after this dramatic slash-and-burn action was report sales and profit growth and all would be believed. Accompanied by *reported* increases in profits, the plant and warehouse closings didn't have to be logical—they just had to be dramatic—and they were.

Two plant closings stood out as particularly ill conceived. Byrne reported conversations with employees and managers at the McMinnville, Tennessee plant indicating that this was one of the most profitable plants at Sunbeam. It produced 15,000 hair clippers and trimmers a day and its sales were growing. Further, the quality of its products was very high and its profit margins were much higher than Sunbeam's margins on its blenders or blankets. Sunbeam also had a very low lease cost at McMinnville, only "pennies per foot in rent, some $29,000 a year" (Byrne, 2003, p. 131). However, there were plans to move the plant to Mexico to save on labor costs, even though transport costs would be higher and moving the factory would cost millions of dollars. The plant manager and Donald Uzzi, senior vice president for sales (who had replaced Newt White), as well as general manager William Kirkpatrick, fought to keep the McMinnville plant open and managed to save some of the jobs. Nevertheless, a line of clippers was moved out of McMinnville and large numbers of sales were lost because of unanticipated production shortages caused by the restructuring plan.

In the small town of Bay Springs, Mississippi, Dunlap's decision to close the plant that made the high-quality wire for Sunbeam's electric blankets was possibly his most economically unfeasible. The city had given Sunbeam the rent-free use of the building for the plant. To keep jobs in the town, the mayor went on a public campaign to point out the economic stupidity of moving the plant. It was going to cost millions of dollars to relocate the plant in an absurd attempt to save a few hundred thousand dollars of transportation costs a year. As much as the mayor made sense, Dunlap resented the opposition and the plant was closed.

The numerous problems of trying to run Sunbeam after it was gutted by the restructuring plan were documented in a *Wall Street Journal* article by Lublin and Suris (1997). There were bar-coding problems with shipping to its biggest customer, Wal-Mart, as well as a failed delivery of 150,000 irons, among other items. There were also problems with the invoicing system and the computer system. In fact, Wal-Mart considered ending its relationship with Sunbeam due to these glitches. Other large customers claimed that shipments were late and that the staff turnover made continuity difficult.

Having pushed ahead with cutting jobs and closing plants, Dunlap began to apply his trademark brand of motivation—the fear and the dreams of stock option riches—to put the pressure on management. With gutted production facilities and a demoralized workforce, Dunlap began to pressure his management team to agree to incredibly high target estimates for sales and production.

The pressure to meet the sales figures fell first to the head of the sales department, who had to pass it down the line, and the same applied to the head of the production department. Managers simply couldn't achieve the unrealistic numbers, but they felt there would be repercussions if they didn't agree to them. And they didn't want to lose their stock options, which had increased in value, but for the most part had not yet vested. They were in a bind. A number of employees left. Those who remained and accepted their unfeasible target numbers had to find ways to meet them.

One of the things that had swayed some of the mangers in their decision to work for Dunlap in spite of their aversion to him was that he had told them that his plan for Sunbeam was to make a very quick turnaround and then to find an outright buyer for the company, as he had done with Scott Paper. If that could be done in a year, many of the managers thought it would be worthwhile to stick around and wait for their stock options to turn into huge financial windfalls. With such an incentive, they believed they could stomach anything for a year. However, the combination of what amounted to the gutting of the company with the restructuring plan, together with Wall Street's lukewarm reaction to it, caused some of the management to become skeptical. This was certainly the case with Newt White, executive vice president for consumer products. A few days after Sunbeam's downsizing announcement and Wall Street's cool response, White realized that this was not going to be a quick turnaround and there was not going to be a company gullible enough to acquire Sunbeam and rescue the current management team from Sunbeam's mess. So less than a week after Dunlap announced his plan, White left Sunbeam.

Many believe that Sunbeam never recovered from the blow of losing White. When Sunbeam lost White, it lost an extremely talented and capable manager and a crucial amount of "company energy" (qtd. in Jenkins, 1997). His departure represented the loss of "informal networks" and "information sharing," of which Cameron spoke (qtd. in Jenkins, 1997). White's leaving represented one of the unintentional consequences of indiscriminate downsizing: Due to "declining morale," the most talented employees leave. According to White's friends, he "despised Dunlap" (Byrne, 2003, p. 68). White could not tolerate the thought of a long stay in the environment that Dunlap was creating.

AN OVERVIEW OF SUNBEAM'S FICTITIOUS FINANCIAL REPORTING SCHEMES

Sunbeam engaged in two major schemes to make its financial statements appear much healthier than they really were: **improper timing of revenue recognition** (the process of formally recording a revenue item in the financial statements in an earlier or later period than the period in which the item should have been recorded) and **improper use of restructuring reserves**.

Let's examine Sunbeam's ploys.

Scheme #1: Improper Timing of Revenue Recognition via Bill and Hold Sales, Consignment Sales, and other Contingent Sales

Under intense pressure to make the sales and profit targets, Sunbeam recorded future periods' sales in current periods. The U.S. Securities and Exchange Commission (SEC) findings explained how, for almost two years, Sunbeam's senior management deliberately embarked on a series of deceptive activities to increase the perceived value of the company (AAER 1393).[2]

The following is a summary of the alleged tactics that Sunbeam used, beginning with the first quarter of 1997 until the second quarter of 1998, to accelerate future quarters' sales in order to boost current periods' profits and give a misleading impression of sales growth:

1. Beginning in the first quarter of 1997, Sunbeam offered deep discounts and extended payment terms to get customers to place the next period's orders early. This acceleration of future quarters' sales into the present quarter "provided a misleading impression of the Company's results of operations for the present period." A worse consequence, of course, was that it "also resulted in the erosion of the company's profit margins and impoverished sales in later periods." In a nutshell, this began a death spiral because the ploy would have to be repeated in the future in order for the company to announce success in meeting target sales. Further, the SEC reported that Sunbeam "failed to disclose this practice in its quarterly filing on Form 10-Q, as required under Regulation S-IC, Items 101 and 103." (Quotes from AAER 1393, 2001)

2. Beginning in the first quarter of 1997, Sunbeam recorded contingent sales or guaranteed sales as normal current-period sales. These were sales to customers where

---

[2] Sunbeam consented to the entry of the order without admitting or denying the findings or conclusions of law as set out in AAER 1393, May 15, 2001.

the sales agreements allowed the customers to return the goods to Sunbeam if they did not sell the goods and some of these agreements even provided that, if returned, Sunbeam would pay for shipping and storage costs. Some of these customers did return the goods to Sunbeam in later quarters. Such non-GAAP sales increased Sunbeam's reported earnings; however, "GAAP does not permit the recognition of revenue in transactions lacking economic substance" (Cullinan & Wright, 2003, p. 192). **Revenue recognition** refers to the process of recording a transaction in the financial statements, indicating that the conditions have been met for the earning of revenue. Generally, revenues refer to sales, the rendering of services, or other operating activities that result in an increase in assets or a decrease in liabilities.

According to the Financial Accounting Standards Board (FASB) Statement of Financial Accounting Concepts No. 5, two conditions must be satisfied before entities can recognize revenue:

i. The revenue must be realized or realizable.

ii. The revenue must be earned.

Current GAAP has many industry-specific and transaction-specific rules for revenue recognition. The FASB is working closely with the International Accounting Standards Board (IASB) to issue a new principles-based converged revenue recognition statement. The FASB tentatively requires that the new standard will be effective "for annual reporting periods beginning after December 15, 2016," for public companies (*Revenue Recognition Project*, 2013, p. 15).

3. Beginning the second quarter of 1997, Sunbeam became more aggressive and desperate and began using **bill and hold sales**, in which the customer is billed and a sale is recorded when the order is placed but the goods are held for delivery until a later date to entice customers to place future periods' sales orders early. Sunbeam again offered discounts and extended payment terms and sometimes even provided the right to return the goods to Sunbeam if they could not be sold. However, because the orders were so far in the future, the customers did not want to hold the goods in their inventory ahead of time; so Sunbeam agreed to hold the goods that it had "sold" in the current period until the customers really needed them in the next period. There are a number of criteria that must be met before bill and hold sales are allowed to be recorded in a current period's sales and earnings:

   a. The buyer, not the seller, must request that the transaction be on a bill and hold basis.

   b. The buyer must have a substantial business purpose for ordering the goods on a bill and hold basis.

   c. The risks of ownership must have passed to the buyer. To ascertain when the risks of ownership are passed to the buyer, one should refer to the terms of the deal to see whether the sales contract specifies **FOB shipping**, where ownership passes to the customer when the goods are handed over to the shipper, or **FOB destination**, where ownership passes when the goods arrive at their final destination.

Other relevant factors include "whether [the seller] has modified its normal billing and credit terms for this buyer" and "the seller's past experiences with and pattern of bill and hold transactions" (AAER 1393, 2001).

Sunbeam, nevertheless, recorded these sales as current-period sales even though they did not meet the criteria.

4. To coax even more sales orders, Sunbeam increasingly gave customers the right to return goods, yet did not increase the reserve for returns in its accounting records. This overstated reported income. In addition, the SEC's findings alleged that in January 1998, the CFO, Russell Kersh, "ordered the deletion of all return authorizations from the company's computer system … [and] deleting the authorization file delayed acceptance of some quantity of pending returns long enough so that they did not count against net sales for the first quarter" (AAER 1393, 2001). Further, while sales with rights of return were growing, at year end 1997, Sunbeam actually reduced its reserve for returns from $6.5 million to $2.5 million.

5. In the first quarter of 1997, Sunbeam sold products that it planned to discontinue as part of its restructuring plan. Sunbeam knew that sales of these items would not be continued because the product lines had been dropped. Also, they were sold at huge discounts to dispose of the products fully. These sales should have been reported separately from continuing sales as an infrequent event, but they were recorded as regular ongoing sales. (This gave a misleading impression of Sunbeam's sales "growth" and its future profitability.) The SEC findings showed that such sales totaled $19.6 million in the first quarter of 1997 (AAER 1393, 2001).

6. Also, pursuant to product lines that were to be closed as part of the restructuring in 1996, Sunbeam overstated the amount by which the inventory had to be written down for all the segments that were going to be closed. This was part of its creation of **cookie-jar reserves**—reserves created by overstating a future liability in one period in order to release it in a future period, thereby implying that the company has less expense in the future period. Then beginning in the first quarter of 1997, profits were overstated as these inventories were sold at amounts above the amount recorded in 1996. In the first quarter of 1997, quarterly income was inflated "by approximately $2.1 million" (AAER 1393, 2001).

7. In the fourth quarter of 1997, Sunbeam entered into a thoroughly inconclusive "sales" agreement with a fulfillment house to sell an indeterminate amount of spare parts to the customer. The contract stated that it "would terminate in January 1998, absent agreement between the parties on the value of the inventory." Sunbeam even guaranteed a profit of 5 percent to the "customer" on any future resale of this inventory. Despite the conditional and indeterminate nature of this agreement, Sunbeam recorded $11 million sales and $5 million profit on the "sale" in 1997, even though, as the SEC stated, "The sale price had no practical relationship to any payment Sunbeam might obtain." Upon the auditor's unwillingness to classify such an agreement as a sale, Sunbeam agreed to create a reserve of $3 million against the profit it had raised, but left the balance of the income in the 1997 financial statements. (Quotes from AAER 1393, 2001)

8. Sunbeam recorded rebates on future purchases as deductions from the current period's cost of goods sold expense. In 1997, the company aggressively negotiated with suppliers to secure rebates that applied to purchase contracts covering future periods' purchases. One rebate contract included an up-front payment in respect of future purchases. Naturally, according to GAAP, rebates should decrease the cost of goods sold expense in the period that the goods are sold. Instead of prorating them, Sunbeam applied these rebates to decrease cost of goods sold in the period that it signed the rebate contracts. The Commission found that "the suppliers' rebates obtained by Sunbeam beginning in the second quarter of 1997

were made in contemplation of future purchases, and therefore should have been recognized as the related sales were made" (AAER 1393, 2001).

9. Sunbeam captured extra revenue by extending its quarter-end date by two days. In the first quarter of 1998, in order to include the results of its newly acquired company, Coleman. Sunbeam changed its quarter end from March 29 to March 31. This is legal. However, in its press release on April 3, Sunbeam made no mention of the fact that the shortfall in sales for the quarter was after *adding* two days' sales to the quarter. Sunbeam did, however, disclose the change in its 8-K filing on April 13, 1998, and in the 10-Q that it filed on May 15, 1998.

10. Sunbeam was also accused of issuing misleading press releases, as well as conducting ambiguous and deceptive press conferences and conference calls with analysts. Sunbeam categorically denied its "**channel stuffing**"—persuading customers to place a later period's orders in the current period. Essentially, the seller "stuffs" more inventory into the customer's warehouse than the customer currently needs. For example, using big discounts and extended payment terms, the seller entices the customer to order goods ahead of time. Sunbeam also blatantly overstated its sales and earnings estimates and deliberately failed to disclose any of the previously mentioned nine manipulations that it had used to present a misleading impression of its sales and profit growth. In the press release announcing its results for the first quarter of 1997, Sunbeam's sales showed growth of 10 percent compared to the first quarter of 1996. However, in publicizing its results, Sunbeam did not disclose that much of that growth came from the sales of discontinued products and from the guaranteed sales, as explained earlier in point 2. Furthermore, the SEC declared, "As members of Sunbeam's management knew or were reckless in not knowing, these misstatements and omissions rendered Sunbeam's press release materially false and misleading." The SEC also found that although Sunbeam had ostensibly met its earnings targets for the third quarter of 1997 by relying on accelerating future periods' sales, "management publicly denied the contention of certain analysts that Sunbeam relied on channel stuffing to achieve its revenue targets." (Quotes from AAER 1393, 2001)

When it came to the fourth quarter of 1997, all the tricks (as previously described—and more) were still not enough to meet Sunbeam's unlikely targets. Dunlap then blamed the warm weather for its effect on sales of electric blankets. However, "What investors didn't know would have caused Sunbeam stock to suffer a total collapse" (Byrne, 2003, pp. 169–170). Although just short of Sunbeam's own unrealistic targets, the *reported* results after all the ploys to accelerate future sales were supposedly record results. In its press release on January 28, 1998, Sunbeam maintained that the increase in its sales was a "clear indication that [Sunbeam's] strategy is working." The SEC subsequently concluded that "this press release and the associated conference call between Sunbeam and its analysts communicated substantially overstated results of operations" (AAER 1393, 2001).

With reluctance, Dunlap issued another (rather sudden) press release on March 19, 1998. The impetus for this was the "due diligence" examination that Morgan Stanley had done in respect of the $500 million bond offering that it was underwriting for Sunbeam. This "due diligence" study had picked up on the fact that major Sunbeam customers were overstocked with Sunbeam inventories and that Sunbeam's sales were going very slowly in the first quarter of 1998. Morgan Stanley's attorneys and Sunbeam's internal and external counsels insisted on a press release disclosing that the company's sales in the first quarter of 1998 might not meet analysts' expectations. Sunbeam issued a statement saying that net sales for the first quarter of 1998 "may be lower than the range of Wall Street analysts' estimates for $285 million to $295 million, but net sales are expected to exceed 1997 first quarter net sales of $253.4 million." It also stated that the shortfall "if any, would be due to changes in inventory management and order patterns at certain of the company's major retail customers." (Quotes from AAER 1393, 2001)

The SEC maintained that the "release inaccurately implied that Sunbeam's lower sales to retailers stemmed from a generalized effort among retailers to reduce inventory levels, rather than from Sunbeam's 1997 accelerated sales. In addition, information available to Sunbeam management did not provide any basis for projecting net sales in excess of those achieved in the first quarter of 1997" (AAER 1393, 2001).

Indeed, Sunbeam, in an April 3 press release just after its debt offering, announced that it expected to show a loss for the first quarter of 1998. The SEC release noted the following:

> In the release and related conference call, Sunbeam management did not disclose:
>
> • the inadequacy of Sunbeam's reserves for returns,
> • bill and hold sales that pulled $35 million in net sales into the quarter, and
> • the extension of the quarter by two days, which added $20 million in net sales to the quarter. (AAER 1393, 2001)

On May 11, 1998, Sunbeam issued its first-quarter 1998 earnings release. It did not disclose how accelerated sales in 1997 had drained its current quarter's sales as it disclosed its loss of 52 cents per share. It also failed to disclose the "positive effect of the first quarter bill and hold sales and the failure to adequately reserve for returned product." Furthermore, Sunbeam made predictions for the year that were "contrary to internal analyses." (Quotes from AAER 1393, 2001)

Scheme #2: Improper Use of Restructuring Reserves

According to SEC allegations, the other major category of misreporting by Sunbeam was that it created big reserves for the write-down of assets and for future losses or liabilities in order to boost future profits. It later "discovered" that these reserves were not needed, and it then released those cookie-jar reserves back into earnings. Sunbeam created these overstated restructuring reserves upon the implementation of its downsizing and restructuring ploy and upon its acquisitions of Coleman, First Alert, and Signature Brands.

A legitimate reserve is usually created in recognition of a future liability or loss. The expense is recognized in the current period. When the future payment or loss occurs, the amount is offset against the reserve, and it is not reported as an expense in that later period. Sometimes companies abuse this procedure, and the SOX Report (*SEC Report Pursuant to the Sarbanes-Oxley Act, 2002*) described the abuse or improper use as follows:

> Reserves may be improperly used to manage earnings. These companies typically create reserves (by initially over-accruing a liability) in one accounting period and then reduce the excess reserves in later accounting periods. The reversal of the reserve creates net income that can be used to meet earnings shortfalls. (p. 17)

What deceptive companies especially like to do is recognize the future expense in the current period as a special charge. The special charge is likely to be regarded as something that will not recur; therefore, it often does not impact the stock price negatively when recognized. It is best if the one-time charge has a positive-sounding name, such as a "restructuring reserve." In the future, when the expense actually occurs and is offset against the reserve instead of being recognized as an expense, the earnings are inflated because the expense was moved to an earlier period. It then appears as though the "restructuring" worked and higher profits will recur, and the stock price often increases in response. Meanwhile, all that happened after the restructuring was that the company did not have to account for the expenses that were offset by the overstated cookie-jar reserves that had been created earlier.

Sunbeam was not shy when it came to creating reserves on its spectacular downsizing restructuring plan. In the last quarter of 1996, it took a very significant restructuring charge. The SEC found that at least $35 million of this was overstated (AAER 1393, 2001).

In addition, the SEC found that upon its restructuring, Sunbeam had decreased the carrying value not only of inventory that it was dropping but also of inventory that it would continue to carry normally. As a result, inventory at the end of 1996 was understated by $2.1 million. Earnings in 1997 would be overstated by this amount when inventory was sold.

Sunbeam also created a $12 million litigation reserve in the last quarter of 1996 in respect of a possible environmental action. However, the Commission found that at least $6 million of this reserve was overstated. Also in the last quarter of 1996, Sunbeam created a cooperative advertising reserve of $21.8 million, which the commission found was created "without any test of the reasonableness" of the amount (AAER 1393, 2001).

Throughout 1997, Sunbeam overstated earnings by releasing parts of these overstated reserves in each quarter. For instance, in the second quarter of 1997, the company overstated its earnings by releasing $8.2 million of the non-GAAP overstated restructuring reserve, and another $5.8 million overstatement of earnings came from the release of the cooperative advertising reserve. By way of further example, Sunbeam's fourth-quarter earnings were overstated by the release of $1.5 million of the restructuring reserves and by $9 million when the company settled an environmental litigation case for $3 million and could release back into profit the remaining $9 million of the $12 million litigation reserve that it had created (AAER 1393, 2001).

It was in the area of accelerating the recording of future sales that Sunbeam presents itself as the ultimate case study in pulling every trick in the book to boost sales and profits. Sunbeam created a whole new approach to playing fast and loose as it milked the widespread practice of channel stuffing for every last dollar.

THE SUNBEAM INFERNO

On July 19, 1996, the day that Al Dunlap was appointed CEO of Sunbeam, the stock price jumped 56 percent, from $12.50 to $18.63. Wall Street was enthralled at the thought that this slash-and-burn downsizing specialist would quickly boost Sunbeam's stock price as he had boosted previous companies' share prices—irrespective of what had happened to those companies after the quick boost. The stock continued to rise after Dunlap said, in July, that he had begun a study for a downsizing plan that would produce a turnaround. By November 12, 1996, the stock price was up in the high $20s. That was the day that Sunbeam announced the actual details of the massive downsizing.

This time, the stunning magnitude of the planned cuts in jobs, plant facilities, and products shocked Wall Street. The stock price dropped a little that day but remained in the high $20 range right into March 1997.

It was during this first quarter of 1997 that Sunbeam began producing financial reports that made it look as though the slashing of facilities, products, jobs, and research and development could, in fact, grow sales and earnings. Early in 1997, Sunbeam began to release back into earnings the false reserves that it had created upon its restructuring in 1996. It also began to accelerate future periods' sales into current periods via the wide array of tricks discussed earlier. Sunbeam did this for every quarter in 1997, with its earnings management reaching its greatest level in the fourth quarter of that year (AAER 1393, 2001).

As previously mentioned, Sunbeam accompanied these misleading sales and earnings reports with unrealistic estimates of future growth and without any reference to the acceleration of future periods' sales. Based on these illusory reports of earnings and sales growth, as well as unrealistic estimates of future performance, the stock price broke out of the high $20 range in March 1997 and began a steady, steep rocketlike climb until it peaked at about $52 in March 1998. This occurred a few days after the announcement of Sunbeam's acquisition of three companies in one day: Coleman, First Alert, and Signature Brands. Sunbeam's stock price had risen 400 percent since Dunlap's appointment in July 1996.

However, Sunbeam was on the verge of a blazing disintegration. By November 1998, the stock price had tumbled to about $7 (AAER 1393, 2001). The more Sunbeam accelerated future periods' sales into current periods, the harder it became to achieve the future periods' sales estimates. The company was caught in an ever-intensifying vicious circle. The customers weren't paying ahead of time for sales that were recorded ahead of time, and worse still, their inventories of Sunbeam products were building up steadily. Further, Sunbeam itself was storing massive amounts of these "sold" inventories.

While so many accepted the downsizing program as an explanation for that all-too-quick turnaround, for others, the downsizing made a quick growth in sales seem implausible. Some skeptics kept a careful watch for signs of overstated sales and earnings. As early as mid-June 1997, an article in *Barron's* questioned the validity of the sales growth in light of the increase in both accounts receivable and inventories (Laing, 1997). However, this went unheeded by the market, which was blinded by the dazzling stock prices. William H. Steele, an analyst for Buckingham Research Group in San Francisco, downgraded Sunbeam to a neutral rating in July 1997 based on the increase in inventories and on him noticing that "changes in cash from working capital were negative" (Byrne, 2003, p. 152). On March 2, 1998, when Dunlap's new employment contract was announced during a conference call, a Bear Stearn's analyst, Constance Maneaty, questioned Dunlap on whether his generous new options package would be a drag on earnings in the future.

During this period, a real threat to the Sunbeam trajectory had been approaching in the form of Morgan Stanley's "due diligence" test for the debt offering that it was underwriting to raise the cash for Sunbeam's acquisitions of Coleman, First Alert, and Signature Brands. While Dunlap was talking up Sunbeam as part of the road show to drum up support for the debt offering, Morgan Stanley's "due diligence" team had been speaking to Sunbeam managers as well as to Arthur Andersen, the external auditors, and to Sunbeam's biggest customers. Everything they heard indicated that Sunbeam's sales estimates for the first quarter of 1998 were not going to be met. Morgan Stanley then approached Sunbeam's internal counsel, David Fannin, and its external counsel, Blaine Fogg, who investigated further. On March 18, it was agreed that a press release had to be issued the next day announcing that Sunbeam might not makes its sales estimates. When released, however, the statement did not capture the severity of the problem. The company acknowledged that sales may be lower than the range of Wall Street analysts' estimates, but it "expected sales to exceed those of the first quarter of 1997." It also blamed the shortfall on "changes in inventory management and order patterns." Sunbeam's customers had so much inventory from 1997's accelerated sales that it was catching up with them in 1998. (Quotes from AAER 1393, 2001).

The announcement represented the first crack in the armor of Sunbeam's façade as a company whose sales and earnings were growing rapidly. Sunbeam stock fell to $45.375 on the day of the announcement. In spite of this, the company still raised $750 million on the debt offering. Later, this would be to the chagrin of those debtholders. However, the questions as to the validity of Sunbeam's real sales growth and its estimates were now exposed, and with inventory piled up in Sunbeam's warehouses and in its customers' warehouses, the answers to those questions would continue to impede management's efforts to maintain the Sunbeam illusion.

One day after the Sunbeam press release, on March 20, 1998, the *New York Post* carried an article entitled "Sunbeam's Cloudy Outlook: Chairman Al Warns on Profits." The article questioned whether Dunlap would be able to deliver on Sunbeam's estimates of sales growth. More ominously, analyst Andrew Shore was reconsidering his earlier upgrade of Sunbeam's stock. Never a fan of Al Dunlap, Shore was again hot on the trail of stories of inventory piling up. He had also heard stories of turmoil within Sunbeam.

In early April, Shore received a tip-off that Sunbeam's head of domestic sales, Donald Uzzi, had been fired. The company was desperate to keep this quiet because Uzzi had been carrying an enormous load in trying to keep Sunbeam's sales from falling apart altogether. With the rumors of Uzzi's departure, as well as the resignation of Richard Goudis, head of corporate planning, Shore thought he had to take the risk of downgrading Sunbeam's stock on a "conference call that linked analysts in New York with more than 5,000 stockbrokers around the world. It had an electrifying effect. Sunbeam's stock began to plunge, falling $4 within minutes" (Byrne, 2003, pp. 241, 242). If he was wrong, Shore's reputation would be in shreds. A few hours later, Shore was relieved to get confirmation that his call was correct when Sunbeam's internal counsel insisted on the release of a press statement explaining the following:

- Sunbeam now expected to make a loss in the first quarter of 1998.
- Sales would not meet the amount predicted in Sunbeam's March release a few weeks earlier.
- Sales would be less than in the comparative first quarter of 1997 (AAER 1393, 2001).

That same day, Sunbeam's stock fell almost 25 percent, to $34.38. Andrew Shore was vindicated and congratulated. Sunbeam's internal auditor, Deidra DenDanto, who had been sidelined by management with her concerns about the bill and hold sales, resigned the same day. Russell Kersh, the chief financial officer of Sunbeam who had the ultimate responsibility for the accounting misstatements, could now just watch as the fireworks of falsely stated profits exploded before his eyes. As for Dunlap, he continued to "gloss over the first quarter repercussions of [Sunbeam's] 1997 earnings management as a surprising slowdown" (AAER 1393, 2001).

Wall Street analysts began to downgrade Sunbeam's stock and investigative journalists began to search for the telltale signs of fraud: growing accounts receivable and mounting inventory. The problem with a fictitiously recorded sale is that it remains as accounts receivable. It does not turn into cash like an honest sale. Also, the inventory of a bill and hold sale must build up somewhere—either at the seller's or the buyer's warehouses. Furthermore, **cash flow from operations (CFFO)** lags the falsely reported profits and it becomes difficult to make sales in the following periods. CFFO refers to the amount of cash generated from the company's main operating activities. It generally refers to the increase or decrease in the actual amount of cash in a period as a result of sales or services rendered or the performance of some other operating activities and the related expenses. It is more formally referred to as *cash flows from operating activities*. Wall Street was finally catching on to Dunlap's "turnarounds," and so was the media. According to an article in *Forbes* magazine, "Seven months ago Al Dunlap declared victory in turning around … Sunbeam…. But since the middle of March its stock has fallen nearly 50% from $52 to a recent $28…. This turnaround hasn't turned and it isn't likely to." The article went on to point out how, in December 1997, Sunbeam had "sold $60 million in accounts receivable to raise cash." Unfortunately, however, analysts had not questioned Sunbeam's numbers. "If they had, they might have seen that Sunbeam was coming apart." (Quotes from Schifrin, 1998)

During a meeting with financial analysts on May 11, Sunbeam announced another downsizing plan. In respect of its acquisition of Coleman, Signature Brands, and First Alert, Sunbeam planned to eliminate 6,400 jobs and close 8 of 24 plants. The *New York Times*, on May 12, noted that in the analysts' meeting, "Mr. Dunlap attributed the 'early buy' debacle to everything from a marketing executive who approved 'stupid deals' with retailers to El Nino…. Whatever the reason, the dismal performance was worse than investors had anticipated" (Canedy, 1998c). Worse was coming.

The final blast of the explosion for Dunlap and CFO Russell Kersh came a few weeks later in the form of an article by Jonathan Laing in *Barron's* magazine. Laing believed that "the earnings from Sunbeam's supposed breakthrough year appear to be largely manufactured." The article speculated that much of the supposed earnings had come from releasing back into earnings the overstated reserves that had been created upon Sunbeam's restructuring charge in 1996. Furthermore, the exposé assumed that, at the time, Sunbeam had also written down property, plant, and equipment values to reduce future depreciation expenses and observed that earnings were boosted by a drop in Sunbeam's allowance for doubtful debts and discounts. It was also suspicious that "Sunbeam's inventories exploded by some 40% or $93 million, during 1997." In addition, there were "indications that Sunbeam jammed as many sales as it could into 1997 to pump both the top and bottom lines." The article in *Barron's* provided the final spark that exploded the Sunbeam façade. (Quotes from Laing, 1998b, pp. 18–19)

The following Monday, Sunbeam put out a press release saying that there was no factual support for the accusation in the *Barron's* article that Sunbeam had largely invented its profits. The release was rather problematic, however, because it was very general and did not answer the specific questions raised. The next day, Sunbeam held a directors' meeting to consider the accusations against the company. The gathering included internal and external counsel, as well as Russell Kersh (CFO), Robert Gluck (controller), and Phillip Harlow (external auditor from Arthur Anderson). At the meeting, the directors found no comfort from the answers they received about the accounting numbers or about the strength of the current quarter. Further, Dunlap and Kersh indicated that if they didn't get more support from the board of directors, they might tender their resignations. After the meeting broke up, the external directors discussed the situation and concluded that it looked like the end of the line for Dunlap—and possibly for Sunbeam as well. In the next few days, Fannin, the general counsel, met with the external counsel. They carried out further internal investigations. In his book, *Chainsaw*, John Byrne (2003) explained how, on Saturday, June 13, Fannin and the outside directors met secretly. They decided that they should get rid of Dunlap and Kersh by accepting their offers to resign as tendered at the previous board meeting. Another board meeting was convened, and telephone calls were made to Dunlap and Kersh. With the jobs of the two men on the line, Peter Langerman, one of the directors, read to them from a prepared statement:

Here is what we propose:

1. You be removed from all positions with the company and its subsidiaries immediately. You may continue to serve as a director of Sunbeam unless you choose to resign from that position.
2. The board names a new Chairman of the Board and we expand our ongoing search to encompass a search for your successor.... (Qtd. in Byrne, 2003, p. 324)

After firing Dunlap and Kersh, Langerman continued to investigate the depth of Sunbeam's problems. He learned that Sunbeam might contravene its debt covenants by the end of the month and that huge loans could become repayable. The board of directors realized that bankruptcy was a possibility and they decided to ask Ron Perelman (of Revlon Cosmetics) if he would arrange for Jerry Levin (who had been the CEO of Coleman) to run Sunbeam for a while. (Perelman had acquired a significant amount of Sunbeam stock on the sale of his company, Coleman, to Sunbeam.) Levin agreed to the request and began by rehiring executives who had quit under Dunlap. Then he initiated a thorough analysis of the financial statements. The SEC also began an investigation of Sunbeam in June. Arthur Andersen, the external auditors, began a review of Sunbeam's previous financial statements. It was immediately apparent to Levin, Arthur Andersen, and the SEC that Sunbeam's financial statements would have to be restated. An ongoing investigation would have to determine the amount of the restatements.

In November 1998, as a result of the investigations, Sunbeam "issued substantially restated financial statements for the six quarters from the fourth quarter of 1996 through the first quarter of 1998. As a result of the restatement for 1997, Sunbeam reported $93 million in income, approximately one half of the amount it had previously reported" (AAER 1393, 2001). Sunbeam had inflated its 1997 income alone by close to 100 percent. Sunbeam's amazing resurrection had been nothing more than a "manufactured illusion" (Byrne, 2003, p. 345).

Within weeks of the firing of Dunlap, the stock price had fallen to below $10 per share. After the October announcements of the required restatements, Sunbeam was trading in the $7 range, a spectacular plunge from its peak of about $52 per share a mere eight months earlier (AAER 1393, 2001).

Although Jerry Levin did a valiant job in attempting to reverse the destruction of Sunbeam, the company filed for Chapter 11 bankruptcy protection in 2001, after suffering heavy losses in the previous year. Under the reorganization plan, most of the bank debt would be converted to equity and shareholders would receive nothing ("Bankruptcy Judge," 2002).

SIGNALS OF SUNBEAM'S SCHEMES

There were several indications that Sunbeam may have engaged in fictitious financial reporting. Here is an examination of some of these signals.

Signals of Sunbeam's Fictitious Reporting Scheme #1—Improper Timing of Revenue Recognition via Bill and Hold Sales, Consignment Sales, and Other Contingency Sales

Numerous signals could have alerted investors to the fictitious reporting schemes associated with improper timing of revenue recognition.

SIGNAL #1: QUALITY OF LEADERSHIP The quality of a company's leadership is an important signal with regard to whether its financial statements are likely to be fraudulently reported. The ethics, ability, management style, and track record of the leadership of the company should be the first piece of evidence an analyst or investor looks at in conjunction with examining financial reports for credibility. The track record of the companies that Dunlap had managed before joining Sunbeam, most notably Scott Paper, made Andrew Shore a skeptic of Sunbeam's reported "turnaround" right from the start. Because of his long-term doubts about Dunlap, on the morning of April 3, 1998, just before Sunbeam's press release that it was not going to make its estimates for the first quarter of 1998, Shore was the first analyst to put in a downgrade on Sunbeam stock.

This general signal of the quality and track record of company leaders should be combined with an analysis of whether the business plan outlined by management is likely to produce the reported results as published in the financial statements. Sunbeam's vicious cost-cutting plan of closing production plants and cutting products, jobs, and R&D expenditure was not likely to lead to fast sales growth as reported in record numbers in 1997. The implausibility of the reported financial results in relation to Sunbeam's major downsizing plan was a major signal of fictitious financial reporting.

SIGNAL #2: INCREASE IN ACCOUNTS RECEIVABLE AS A PERCENTAGE OF SALES The leading sign of an overstatement of sales is when accounts receivable increase as a percentage of sales, which is often measured as days sales outstanding (DSO). If the next period's sales have been accelerated into the current period or if the sales are completely fictitious, the company will debit accounts receivable and credit sales, as for legitimate sales. However, whereas legitimate sales will be paid relatively soon by the customers and will turn into cash, the next period's sales will probably be paid only in the next period and will remain on the balance sheet in the current period as accounts receivable instead of turning into cash.

This signal of an overstatement of sales (and the accompanying profit) is easy to spot. We simply look at the income statement, extract the sales figures, look at the balance sheet and extract the accounts receivable amounts, and then calculate accounts receivable as a percentage of sales. To illustrate the validity of this technique, let us examine an extract from Sunbeam's income statements in Table 3.1 and an extract from its balance sheet in Table 3.2. If we divide accounts receivable at the end of any quarter by the addition of the sales for the four quarters ending on that date (i.e. the trailing twelve months' sales), we see the trend of accounts receivable growing as a percentage of sales, as shown in Table 3.3, from 29 percent of sales in the first quarter of 1997 to almost 49 percent of sales in the first quarter of 1998.

SIGNAL #3: SUDDEN CHANGE IN GROSS MARGIN PERCENTAGE   The third sign to look for as an indicator of illegitimately reported sales is a sudden change in the **gross margin percentage**—sales less the cost of goods sold expressed as a percentage of sales. It is difficult for a manufacturer suddenly to increase the company's gross margin percentage; it is also suspicious if the gross margin fluctuates downward suddenly. It is easy to find this signal. A simple perusal of the income statements over a number of quarters will alert the investor to suspicious changes in the gross margin percentage. Look at extracts from Sunbeam's quarterly income statements in Table 3.1. Calculating gross margin as a percentage of sales, as shown in Table 3.4, reveals sudden changes in the gross margin over the quarters, from 19 percent in the second quarter of 1996 to negative 15 percent in the fourth quarter of 1996. This was followed by a suspicious improvement in 1997 (after the so-called "turnaround") to 27 percent in the first quarter of 1997 to 31 percent in the third quarter of 1997, then falling to 13 percent in the first quarter of 1998 and to negative 9 percent in the second quarter of 1998.

These sudden changes in gross margins were probably due, in part, to practices such as selling inventory in 1997 at higher prices than the restructuring purported to anticipate because some inventory had been valued at incorrectly low amounts. Also, Sunbeam's schemes—for example, understating the reserve for returns and taking the benefits of rebates for future purchases into the current period—would have falsely boosted the gross margins in 1997 and in the first quarter of 1998.

SIGNAL #4: CFFO FALLING BEHIND OPERATING INCOME   The fourth signal of inappropriately recorded sales is when CFFO lags behind operating income or when CFFO falls relative to operating income. For this information, once again we simply look at the financial statements filed with the SEC. For the first three quarters of 1997, we see that Sunbeam reported operating income of $132 million in its income statement. However, looking at the statement of cash flows, we see that Sunbeam's CFFO for the same period was *negative*. This signal is a huge red flag. If Sunbeam was operating at such a great profit, why would it be burning through operating cash?

The statement of cash flows is separated into three segments: the cash flows from operating activities, the cash flows from investing activities, and the cash flows from financing the business. So the "cash flow from operations" (CFFO) should *not* show an amount of cash generated that is significantly less than the profit from operations—listed as "operating income" or "operating earnings" in the income statement—without a very specific explanation.

Certainly, from the first four signals alone, anybody reading Sunbeam's financial statements at the end of 1997 should have been alerted to the fact that its reported sales and operating profits were unreliable. The sales were simply not turning into

TABLE 3.1 Extracts from Sunbeam's Income Statements[3]

Extracts from Quarterly Income Statement (in Thousands)

| | 1996 | | | 1997 | | | | 1998 | |
	Q2	Q3	Q4	Q1	Q2	Q3	Q4	Q1	Q2
Net Sales	253,896	231,770	268,863	253,450	287,609	289,033	338,090	244,296	578,488
(Cost of Goods Sold)	206,685	202,998	309,282	185,669	213,080	200,242	238,692	211,459	630,965
Gross Profit	47,211	28,772	(40,419)	67,781	74,529	88,792	99,398	32,837	(52,477)

TABLE 3.2 Extracts from Sunbeam's Balance Sheets

Extracts from Quarterly Balance Sheets (in Thousands) PRIOR TO RESTATEMENT

| | 1996 | | | 1997 | | | | 1998 | |
	Q2	Q3	Q4	Q1	Q2	Q3	Q4	Q1	Q2
Balance Sheet Accounts									
Cash and cash equivalents	35,794	24,638	11,526	30,415	57,970	22,811	52,378	193,543	43,151
Receivables, net	228,749	194,559	213,438	296,716	252,045	309,095	295,550	562,294	523,065
Inventories	327,093	330,213	161,252	14,811	208,374	290,875	256,180	575,109	646,626
Total current assets	621,411	586,012	624,163	609,654	634,848	692,552	658,005	1,438,638	1,278,465
Total assets	1,230,310	1,196,333	1,072,709	1,053,155	1,089,345	1,145,071	1,120,284	3,443,422	3,519,121
Total current liabilities	187,535	253,331	2,771,583	260,154	258,149	245,997	198,099	443,719	1,861,243
Retained earnings			35,118				141,134		(310,233)

[3] Tables 3.1 and 3.2 are derived from Sunbeam's filings at the U.S. Securities and Exchange Commission. *www.sec.gov.*

TABLE 3.3	Increase in Receivables as a Percentage of Sales

Receivables-to-Sales Ratio

	1997				1998	
	Q1	Q2	Q3	Q4	Q1	Q2
Receivables-to-Sales Ratio	29.43%	24.20%	28.13%	25.30%	48.51%	36.08%

TABLE 3.4	Changes in Gross Margin Percentages

Quarterly Gross Margin Percentages

	1996			1997				1998	
	Q2	Q3	Q4	Q1	Q2	Q3	Q4	Q1	Q2
Gross Profit Margin %	19%	12%	−15%	27%	27%	31%	29%	13%	−9%

cash received at the rate they should have been if they were legitimate sales, and the gross margin percentages were fluctuating wildly, without a clear explanation for the volatility.

SIGNAL #5: ADOPTING A MORE AGGRESSIVE REVENUE RECOGNITION POLICY   The fifth signal that a company is overstating its sales is when it begins a policy of more aggressively recognizing revenue. The leading example of such an aggressive policy is the practice of recognizing sales revenue before the goods are shipped to the customer. The two major accounting strategies for doing this are "bill and hold sales" and "percentage of completion" accounting for contracts in progress. For Sunbeam, the relevant method in this category of overstatement of sales and profit was its bill and hold sales to get customers to place later periods' orders long before they would pay for the goods and long before Sunbeam delivered the goods to the customers. Of $35 million of bill and hold sales that Sunbeam recognized in the fourth quarter of 1997, $29 million was later reversed and restated as future periods' sales.

In the case of Sunbeam, this signal was easy to spot. One of the notes to the financial statements in the company's 1997 Annual Report mentioned this policy.

The lesson here is to read the notes and footnotes to quarterly and annual financial statements and search for any new, aggressive policies indicating that the company records sales before the goods are delivered.

SIGNAL #6: LARGE DISCOUNTS AND EXTENDED PAYMENT TERMS   When a company offers large discounts and extended payment terms to entice its customers to order early, it is a signal that the reported sales for the current period are overstated and that future sales will be impoverished by the early placement of the orders. The notes to the financial statements in Sunbeam's quarterly reports (Form 10-Q) should have disclosed this under Regulation S-K, items 101 and 103. However, Sunbeam failed to divulge this information (AAER 1393, 2001). To get information on this kind of channel stuffing, analysts and investors should scan the 10-Q and 10-K reports and conduct article searches via search engines such as Google and databases such as LexisNexis or ProQuest. They should search for data indicating that the company is offering unusually generous payment terms or discounts. If necessary, one could even interview the company's staff and customers, as was done in the due diligence tests by the underwriters of Sunbeam's debt offering in 1998.

In addition, any news reports of large warehouses being built to house the company's inventory (as was the case with Sunbeam) or of a company's major customers building warehouses or "reclamation centers" to store unsold or returnable inventory should be taken as huge red flags that companies may have accelerated current sales at the expense of future sales.

SIGNAL #7: GUARANTEED SALES   The recording of sales when the customer has a right to return the product is a signal of the overstatement of sales. Such sales are often known as "guaranteed sales," where the customers can return goods if they are unable to resell them or they can get a reimbursement if they cannot achieve a certain resale selling price or a guaranteed markup. In Sunbeam's case, the SEC found that "in total, $24.7 million in fourth quarter [1997] sales to distributors were subject to rights of return" (AAER 1393, 2001). A reserve for such returns should be accounted for in the financial statements according to the Financial Accounting Standards Board's SFAS 48[4]. However, the SEC reported that because such sales were a significant change in approach for Sunbeam and the likely return amounts were not known, it should not have reported these sales.

An investor or analyst should search the financial statements for any disclosure of recording such sales (although in some cases, like that of Sunbeam, a change in approach may not be properly disclosed). One should also look for media reports about significant changes in company policy or about either the company or its customers building reclamation centers or warehouses. Again, these are all telltale signs of returns waiting to happen.

SIGNAL #8: PRESS RELEASES STATING INABILITY TO MEET SALES ESTIMATES   Press releases indicating that previous sales growth estimates will not be met are clear warning signals. It is a strong indication of a desperate overstatement of sales and sales estimates when a company issues a second press release, downwardly revising the numbers of an earlier press release that was, itself, a downward revision of sales estimates. This was the case with Sunbeam's March and April press releases discussed earlier. Perform Internet or database searches for press releases or for articles referring to press releases that revise earlier public statements in quick succession.

Signals of Sunbeam's Fictitious Reporting Scheme #2—Overstating Earnings via Improper Use of Restructuring Reserves

There were also signals that should have uncovered the overstatement of earnings through the improper use of restructuring reserves.

---

[4] Statement of Financial Accounting Standards No. 48. *www.fasb.org*.

SIGNAL #1: LARGE ONE-TIME CHARGES   Large one-time charges in the income statement, such as restructuring charges and the creation of reserves on the balance sheet, should alert the reader to the possibility that future periods' earnings may be inflated as the reserves are released back into profits or as the written-down assets are sold at normal prices. Sunbeam's income statement showed a massive restructuring charge of $154.9 million in the last quarter of 1996 that included the over-accruals for items such as the advertising reserve and the litigation reserve.

SIGNAL #2: RESTRUCTURING RESERVES   If restructuring reserves or reserves resulting from other one-time charges appear in the financial statements upon the arrival of a new CEO, it is an even stronger alert that future expenses are possibly being recognized early with the creation of improper reserves. Al Dunlap was appointed CEO of Sunbeam on July 18, 1996, and the massive restructuring reserves were created in the last quarter of 1996.

SIGNAL #3: RAPID DECREASE IN RESERVES   When reserves decrease rapidly, it is an indication that earnings in the period may have been inflated by avoiding expenses through the reversal of the reserves. One has to consider how the company will be able to continue showing profits in the future when it can no longer release reserves to bolster profits. Sunbeam's restructuring accrual decreased from $63.8 million in the last quarter of 1996 to $45.3 million in the first quarter of 1997, and then it was released steadily until it reached zero at the end of the first quarter of 1998.

SIGNAL #4: CFFO SIGNIFICANTLY LESS THAN OPERATING INCOME   The release of cookie-jar reserves boosts operating income but does not produce cash flow. Therefore, once again, CFFO lagging or falling behind operating income is a signal of this method of fictitious reporting. In Sunbeam's financial statements, the effect of releasing cookie-jar reserves together with accelerating sales (as discussed in Scheme 1), combined to provide a very strong signal of its extremely aggressive earnings management.

To discover this manipulation, search the financial statements for large one-time charges in the income statement or for reserves decreasing in later periods on the balance sheet. When Sunbeam simultaneously reported large operating profits in 1997 but negative CFFO, it was a signal to bail out of the company and its stock as quickly as possible.

ARE THEY LIVING HAPPILY EVER AFTER?[5]

- **Al Dunlap,** Sunbeam's former CEO and chairman, settled a $15 million class-action lawsuit with Sunbeam shareholders in 2002. In a civil settlement with the SEC that same year, and without admitting or denying the allegations, Dunlap agreed to a civil penalty of $500,000 and was prevented from ever again acting as an officer or a director of a public company (LR 17710, 2002).

  Dunlap and his wife Judy are reportedly living on a horse farm in Ocala, Florida, and have a summer home in Hilton Head, South Carolina. In 2006, the Dunlaps gave a substantial gift to Florida State University (Murphy & Ray, 2006).

---

[5] The "Are They Living Happily Ever After?" sections in this book present selected information about certain people and companies and are not meant to be definitive or exhaustive lists.

In September 2007, Dunlap received an honorary doctorate from Florida State University, one year after his $5 million donation to the university. He was soon dubbed "Dr. Chainsaw" (Porter & Dizik, 2007).

In 2009, Dunlap was named the sixth worst CEO of all time ("Portfolio's Worst American CEOs of All Time").

Now in his late 70s, Dunlap insists that he is not the ferocious person the media reported him to be while he was at Sunbeam. He is described as a life-long German shepherd lover and apparently despises his infamous nickname of Chainsaw Al (Florian & Adamo, 2010).

- **Russell Kersh,** Sunbeam's former chief financial officer, agreed to a civil penalty of $200,000 without admitting or denying the allegations. He was barred from ever again acting as an officer or director of a public company (LR 17710, 2002).
- **Morgan Stanley** was found liable for fraud by a jury in May 2005. The investment firm was ordered to pay a total of over $1.4 billion in "compensatory and punitive damages" in respect of the sale of Ron Perelman's Coleman Company to Sunbeam in 1998. Perelman had lost close to $1 billion when Sunbeam collapsed. Morgan Stanley appealed the verdict, claiming that it too was "a victim of the Sunbeam fraud" ("Morgan Stanley ...," 2005).

  In 2007, an appeals court in Florida reversed the jury verdict against Morgan Stanley (Thomas, Jr., 2007).
- **Sunbeam** emerged from bankruptcy in 2002 as American Household, Inc., which was then acquired by Jarden Corporation in January 2005 ("Jarden," 2005).

Key Terms

Bill and hold sales *13*	Cookie-jar reserves *14*	Improper timing of
Cash flow from operations (CFFO) *20*	Downsizing *2*	revenue recognition *12*
	FOB destination *13*	Restructuring plan *7*
Channel stuffing *15*	FOB shipping *13*	Revenue recognition *13*
Common or allocated fixed costs *8*	Gross margin percentage *23*	Traceable fixed costs *8*

ETHICS AT WORK

Questions:

a. Approaching ethics from a *utilitarian* framework, discuss whether or not the management of Sunbeam was unethical in issuing financial statements that improperly timed Sunbeam's revenue recognition. Identify the *major* stakeholders in this case. (Refer to Chapter 2, "Ethics at Work," for a description of the utilitarian framework.)

b. Do you believe that trading a company's stock with the knowledge that the company's earnings are overstated is unethical? Explain why or why not within the context of the *justice* approach to ethical decision making. (Refer to Chapter 2 for a description of the justice approach.)

Assignments

TRUE/FALSE QUESTIONS

Answer the following questions with T for true or F for false for more practice with key terms and concepts from this chapter.

1. Bill and hold sales that are reported in an income statement in the period before the goods are shipped to a customer are always a contravention of GAAP.

    T   F

2. When a company solicits bill and hold orders from its customers and recognizes the sales in its income before delivery of the goods, this represents improper timing of revenue recognition.

    T   F

3. The closing of unprofitable segments sometimes causes companies to lose more revenue than they save in cost reductions.

    T   F

4. According to the SEC's AAER, Sunbeam recorded contingent sales or guaranteed sales as normal, current sales.

    T   F

5. Sunbeam overstated its income by failing to maintain large enough provisions for doubtful debts.

    T   F

6. Sunbeam overstated goodwill on the acquisition of companies in order to create cookie-jar reserves.

    T   F

7. After its downsizing, Sunbeam released overstated reserves into profit.

    T   F

8. According to the SEC, Sunbeam gave customers the right to return goods, yet Sunbeam did not increase the reserves for returns.

    T   F

9. When a previously overstated reserve is reversed in a later period, this increases operating income but not net income in the later period.

    T   F

10. For a some quarters during the time of Sunbeam's bill and hold sales and heavily discounted sales, it reported positive operating income but negative CFFO.

    T   F

FILL-IN-THE-BLANK QUESTIONS

Fill in the blanks with information and concepts from this chapter.

11. When a company closes a segment, the common or _____ fixed costs will remain.

12. When a company closes a segment, the continuing costs that were allocated to it will have to be carried by the _____ divisions.

13. During downsizings, informal networks are often destroyed and experienced employees depart, resulting in the loss of company _____ and energy.

14. When Sunbeam offered deep discounts and extended payment terms to get customers to place orders early, this resulted in _____ future quarters' sales into the current period.

15. To coax even more orders for sales, Sunbeam increasingly gave customers the right to return goods, yet Sunbeam did not increase the _____ for _____ in the its accounting records.

16. Sunbeam entered into a(n) _____ sales agreement to sell an indeterminate amount of spare parts to a customer.

17. Sunbeam recorded rebates on future purchases as _____ from the current period's cost of goods sold expense.

18. Sunbeam captured extra sales revenue by extending its _____–_____ date by two days.

19. With an improper use of reserves, companies usually over-accrue a liability in one period and then reduce the _____ reserves in later periods.

20. When creating a false reserve, companies often recognize the future expense in the current period as a(n) _____ charge.

MULTIPLE-CHOICE QUESTIONS

21. Ace Company is a manufacturer of electrical appliances. The following transaction occurred near Ace Company's December 31 fiscal year-end date:

A packing case containing products costing $10,000 was found in Ace's branch office warehouse when the physical inventory count was taken on December 31. The case was labeled: "Hold for shipping to customer on January 5." The shipping documents show that the sale to Ace's customer is "FOB Shipping."

For the preparation of Ace's December 31 financial statements, which of the following is correct?

(a) The packing case should not be included in Ace's December 31 inventory balance. Ace should recognize a sale in respect of the inventory's selling price.

(b) The packing case should be included in Ace's December 31 inventory. Ace should recognize a sale in respect of the inventory's selling price.

(c) The packing case should be included in Ace's December 31 inventory. Ace should not recognize a sale in respect of the inventory's selling price.

(d) The packing case should not be included in Ace's December 31 inventory. Ace should not recognize a sale in respect of the inventory's selling price.

22. Bolt Company is a clothing manufacturer. The following items relate to transactions that occurred close to Bolt's December 31 fiscal year-end date.

Item I: Merchandise costing $5,000 was shipped to a retail customer on December 27. The merchandise is part of a consignment agreement with the retailers. The goods were received by the retail customer on December 30 and were on the customer's shelves and available for sale on January 2.

Item II: Merchandise costing $3,000 was shipped by Bolt to a retail customer on December 26, using FOB shipping. The merchandise was received by the retailer on January 3.

For the preparation of Bolt's December 31 financial statements, which of the following is correct?

(a) Item I's and Item II's inventory should both be included in Bolt's December 31 inventory.

(b) Item I's inventory should be included in Bolt's December 31 inventory, and Item II's inventory should be excluded from Bolt's December 31 inventory.

(c) Bolt should recognize sales in its income statement for both Item I and Item II.

(d) Bolt should not recognize a sale for either Item I or Item II.

23. Push Company is a lawn mower manufacturer. Push was falling short of meeting its sales estimates for its December 31 fiscal year end. The company expected to receive a large order for $40,000 of lawn mowers from Pull Company, a major customer, in April the next year, for goods to be delivered to Pull in May. In December, Push approached Pull with the suggestion that Pull place its upcoming April order immediately. Push offered Pull a significant discount for placing the order early and said that it would hold the inventory for several months before shipping it to Pull in May the next year. Pull agreed and placed the order with Push on December 29. Push set the goods aside in its warehouse in December and recognized a bill and hold sale for the goods on December 30. The goods were shipped to Pull in May the next year.

The bill and hold sale should not have been recognized as a sale in Push Company's December 31 financial statements because:

(a) Push Company, not Pull Company, requested the early order for the bill and hold transaction.

(b) Nothing in the preceding description of the transaction indicates that Pull Company had a substantial business purpose for ordering the goods on a bill and hold basis.

(c) With a bill and hold sale, the seller recognizes revenue in its income statement but does not recognize cost of goods sold.

(d) Both a and b are correct.

24. On December 20, Zee Company, an office-supply company, placed an order for goods from Papyrus Company, a paper manufacturer. Zee wanted the goods to be shipped only in March the next year (FOB destination), and a clause to that effect was included in the sales contract. Zee placed the order early to ensure that it would receive the goods in March in the event that Papyrus Company received orders for more inventory than it could fulfill the next quarter.

Papyrus Company should not have recognized the sale to Zee Company as a bill and hold sale in its December 31 financial statements because:

(a) The buyer must have a substantial business purpose for ordering the goods on a bill and hold basis.

(b) Bill and hold sales recognize the revenue from a sale, but fail to recognize the cost of goods sold.

(c) The risks of ownership must have passed to the buyer.

(d) Zee Company had not paid for the goods by December 31.

Use the following data for Questions 25 and 26:

XYZ Company has finalized its financial statements for its fiscal year ended December 31. At this stage, all of its transactions have been recorded properly in terms of GAAP. On January 10, XYZ Company is considering securing a back-dated order for a bill and hold sale from one of its customers. The back-dated order would be for goods with a selling price of $10,000 and a cost of $4,000. The goods would be delivered on February 28, two months after the year end. The order would be back-dated as though it were placed on December 28.

25. If XYZ goes ahead and secures the back-dated order and recognizes it as a bill and hold sale in its December 31 financial statements, which of the following is correct?

(a) Operating income would be overstated by $6,000, and sales would be overstated by $10,000.

(b) Cash flow from operations (CFFO) would be overstated by $10,000.

(c) CFFO would be overstated by $4,000.

(d) Net income would be overstated by $10,000.

26. If XYZ goes ahead and secures the back-dated order and recognizes it as a bill

and hold sale, which of the following is correct?

(a) This would cause operating income to exceed CFFO by $10,000.

(b) This would cause CFFO to be $6,000 smaller than operating income.

(c) This would have the same effect on both operating income and CFFO.

(d) This would have no effect on operating income but would increase CFFO by $6,000.

Use the following information for Questions 27 and 28:

Mac Company's correctly prepared financial statements for its December 31 year end show an accounts receivable balance of $50,000, operating income of $25,000, and CFFO of $24,000.

Mac has an inconclusive sales transaction to supply Donald & Co. with merchandise costing $10,000 and a likely selling price of $15,000. A sales contract was not fully agreed upon by December 31. If the transaction is completed, the merchandise will be delivered on January 20 and paid for on January 30. Mac has the goods on hand on December 31.

27. If Mac goes ahead and recognizes a sale of $15,000 in its December 31 financial statements for this inconclusive agreement, which of the following is correct?

(a) CFFO will increase by $15,000.

(b) CFFO will increase by $10,000.

(c) Operating income will increase by $15,000.

(d) Operating income will increase by $5,000.

28. If Mac goes ahead and recognizes a sale of $15,000 in its December 31 financial statements, which of the following is correct?

(a) The accounts receivable balance will be stated as $65,000.

(b) Operating income will be stated as $40,000.

(c) CFFO will be stated as $39,000.

(d) Operating income will be stated as $25,000.

29. With reference to Sunbeam's financial statements, in the period that Sunbeam overstated its restructuring expense and restructuring reserves, what was the effect?

(a) Increased net income.

(b) Decreased total liabilities and reserves.

(c) Increased operating income.

(d) Decreased net income.

30. Which of the following was *not* a method used by Sunbeam to recognize future periods' sales in current periods?

(a) Inventing fictitious customers.

(b) Recording contingent sales as current-period sales.

(c) Offering deep discounts and extended payment terms.

(d) Using bill and hold sales.

FOR DISCUSSION

31. Perpetrators of improper revenue recognition schemes often attempt to offer the defense that recognizing future periods' revenue in the current period is *only* a "timing" error. Discuss whether the fact that the overstated revenue will likely be earned in later periods reduces the impact of the overstatement or reduces the responsibility of the perpetrator to report revenue accurately in the current period.

32. What is the incentive for managers to overstate a restructuring reserve in the current period in order to reverse it in future periods, since overstating the restructuring reserve decreases net income in the current period?

SHORT-ANSWER QUESTIONS

33. Explain how a company's overstatement of its restructuring reserve may not cause it to understate its operating income in the period that it overstates the reserve.

34. Explain why a bill and hold sale causes cash flow from operations (CFFO) to lag behind operating income.

35. Explain why downsizing a company by closing segments or product lines that report an accounting loss often leads to a decrease in profits rather than an increase.

36. Why is an "increase in accounts receivable as a percentage of sales" a signal of improper revenue recognition?

37. Why do overstatements of restructuring reserves sometimes cause gross margin percentages to change suddenly?

EXERCISES

38. Examine these extracts from Moonshine Company's income statement and balance sheet for the previous three years:

Income Statement	Year 1 $	Year 2 $	Year 3 $
Sales	2,000	3,000	4,000
Operating Income	500	700	800

Income Statement	Year 1 $	Year 2 $	Year 3 $
Balance Sheet			
Accounts receivable	300	600	1,500

Now calculate the ratio of accounts receivable as a percentage of sales for Years 1, 2, and 3.

39. Saturn Company's income statement for the current year shows $100,000 as its net income. Its depreciation expense is $5,000. The only changes to its working capital balances over the last year were that accounts receivable increased by $40,000, inventory decreased by $10,000, and accounts payable increased by $5,000. What is Saturn's cash flow from operations (CFFO) for the year?

40. Before finalizing its financial statements for the year, Jupiter Company decides to create a restructuring reserve of $20,000 in preparation for a downsizing to be implemented the following year. Jupiter's income statement for the year before it created the restructuring reserve was as follows:

Sales	$160,000
Cost of goods sold	60,000
Gross margin	100,000
Selling and administrative expenses	40,000
Operating income	60,000
Taxation	12,000
Net income	$ 48,000

The company does not want to reduce operating income as a result of creating the reserve this period.

Required

a. What is the journal entry this year with regard to the creation of the restructuring reserve?

b. Restate the company's income statement for the year, taking the creation of the restructuring reserve into account and assuming that it does not change the company's income tax expense.

CASE STUDY

Beazer Homes USA. Inc.

- **Read** the Accounting and Auditing Enforcement Release (AAER 2884) for Beazer Homes,[6] given below.
- **Examine** the summarized Financial Statements of Beazer Homes for 2004–2007, given below.
- **Respond** to the following Case Study questions.

Required

a. **Overstatement of Revenue Scheme:** (Note: This question refers to the Sale-Leaseback Transactions.) According to AAER 2884, Beazer Homes overstated its 2006 revenues by $117 million and understated its cumulative revenue for the first two quarters of 2007 by 2.6 million. Refer to The Top Twenty Methods of Fictitious Financial Reporting in Table 1.1 (p. 19). Then answer the following questions regarding the SEC's action, AAER 2884, against Beazer Homes.

    1. How would you characterize Beazer Homes' method of overstating its revenue? Do you see it primarily as a method of "improper timing of revenue," or as "fictitious revenue," or as "improper valuation of revenue"? Explain.

    2. Describe Beazer Homes' method of overstating its revenue.

3. Refer to Beazer's financial statements for the following fiscal years: 2004–2007. What signals can you identify to indicate that Beazer Homes overstated its revenues? (Note: Do not use restated amounts; use amounts as originally stated because analysts did not have restated figures until 2007.)

b. **Overstatement of Accruals and Reserves Scheme:** According to AAER 2884, Beazer Homes also overstated its earnings by first overstating accruals and reserves and then releasing the reserves into earnings.

    1. Regarding the use of certain of its land inventory accounts, describe and explain how Beazer Homes created a cookie-jar reserve that it later reversed into earnings.

    2. Consider how Beazer Homes used its land inventory accounts as a cookie-jar reserve and explain how this scheme is similar to Sunbeam's scheme of "Improper Use of Restructuring and Other Liability Reserves."

    3. Explain the major way in which Beazer's land inventory accounts scheme differs from Sunbeam's use of improper reserves.

---

[6] Beazer consented to the entry of the Order without admitting or denying the findings.

Accounting and Auditing Enforcement Release (AAER 2884) for Beazer Homes[7]

UNITED STATES OF AMERICA
Before the
SECURITIES AND EXCHANGE COMMISSION

SECURITIES ACT OF 1933
Release No. 8960 / September 24, 2008

SECURITIES EXCHANGE ACT OF 1934
Release No. 58633 / September 24, 2008

ACCOUNTING AND AUDITING ENFORCEMENT
Release No. 2884 / September 24, 2008

ADMINISTRATIVE PROCEEDING
File No. 3-13234

In the Matter of BEAZER HOMES USA, INC., Respondent.	ORDER INSTITUTING CEASE-AND-DESIST PROCEEDINGS PURSUANT TO SECTION 8A OF THE SECURITIES ACT OF 1933 AND SECTION 21C OF THE SECURITIES EXCHANGE ACT OF 1934, MAKING FINDINGS, AND IMPOSING A CEASE-AND-DESIST ORDER

I.

The Securities and Exchange Commission ("Commission") deems it appropriate that cease-and-desist proceedings be, and hereby are, instituted pursuant to Section 8A of the Securities Act of 1933 ("Securities Act") and Section 21C of the Securities Exchange Act of 1934 ("Exchange Act") against Beazer Homes USA, Inc. ("Beazer" or "Respondent").

II.

In anticipation of the institution of these proceedings, Respondent has submitted an Offer of Settlement (the "Offer") which the Commission has determined to accept. Solely for the purpose of these proceedings and any other proceedings brought by or on behalf of the Commission, or to which the Commission is a party, and without admitting or denying the findings herein, except as to the Commission's jurisdiction over it and the subject matter of these proceedings, which are admitted, Respondent consents to the entry of this Order Instituting Cease-and-Desist Proceedings Pursuant to Section 8A of the Securities Act of 1933 and Section 21C of the Securities Exchange

---

[7] Obtained from U.S. Securities and Exchange Commission. *www.sec.gov*. Beazer consented to the entry of this Order without admitting or denying the findings.

Act of 1934, Making Findings, and Imposing a Cease-and-Desist Order ("Order"), as set forth below.

III.

On the basis of this Order and Respondent's Offer, the Commission finds[1] that:

Summary

1. In certain periods between 2000 and 2007, Beazer, acting through certain of its officers and employees, fraudulently misstated its net income for the purpose of improperly managing its quarterly and annual earnings. In May 2008, as a result of its earnings management and other errors, Beazer restated its financial statements to reflect adjustments for the fiscal years 1998 through 2006, as well as the first and second quarters of fiscal year 2007. Beazer restated its fiscal year 2006 net income from $389 million to $369 million (a reduction of $20 million or 5%). Beazer also restated its fiscal 2005 net income from $263 million to $276 million (an increase of $13 million or 5%) and increased its beginning retained earnings for the fiscal year 2005 by $34 million (from $742 million to $776 million or 5%) to reflect the cumulative effect of adjustments for the fiscal years 1998 through 2004. Finally, Beazer also restated its net loss for the first quarter of fiscal year 2007 from $59 million to $80 million (an increased loss of $21 million or 36%), and its net loss for the second quarter of fiscal year 2007 from $43 million to $57 million (an increased loss of $14 million or 33%).

Respondent

2. Beazer, a Delaware corporation headquartered in Atlanta, Georgia, is a homebuilder with operations in at least twenty-one states. Since March 1994, Beazer's common stock has been registered with the Commission pursuant to Section 12(b) of the Exchange Act and listed on the New York Stock Exchange under the symbol BZH. On June 6, 2006, Beazer issued and sold a $275 million aggregate amount of its 8.125% Senior Notes due 2016 in a private placement to qualified institutional buyers pursuant to Rule 144A and in offshore transactions pursuant to Regulation S. On August 15, 2006, Beazer filed an S-4 registration statement offering to exchange $275 million in new notes for the notes issued on June 6, 2006. The prospectus filed with the registration statement incorporates by reference Respondent's annual and quarterly reports. In a June 2006 private placement, Beazer also issued $103 million of junior subordinated notes. Additionally, in November 2005, Beazer announced an increase to 10 million shares of its prior repurchase plan which resulted in 3.65 million of its shares being repurchased during fiscal 2006 for an aggregate purchase price of $205.4 million.

Beazer's Earnings Management

3. Between approximately 2000 and 2007, Beazer, acting through certain of its officers and employees, fraudulently misstated certain of its quarterly and annual

---

[1]The findings herein are made pursuant to Respondent's Offer of Settlement and are not binding on any other person or entity in this or any other proceeding.

net income by intentionally managing its earnings. From approximately 2000 to 2005, a period of strong growth and financial performance for Beazer, Beazer decreased its reported net income by improperly increasing certain reported operating expenses. This created improper accruals, or "reserves," in Beazer's books and records. In certain quarters, the existence of these reserves had the effect of smoothing Beazer's earnings, *i.e.*, allowing Beazer to report earnings that still met or exceeded analysts' expectations for its quarterly net income and earnings per share ("EPS") while permitting it to improperly defer a portion of its income to future periods.

4. Beginning in the first quarter of fiscal year 2006, Beazer's financial performance began to decline. In order to continue to meet or exceed analysts' expectations for its quarterly net income and EPS, Beazer began reversing many of its previously created, improper reserves. In certain instances, Beazer also began purposefully not recognizing certain current period expenses. These actions had the effect of reducing Beazer's operating expenses and thereby improperly increasing its net income.

5. Additionally during fiscal 2006 and the first two quarters of fiscal 2007, Beazer, again acting through certain of its officers and employees, improperly recognized income from the sale of approximately 360 model homes to three separate investor pools compiled and sponsored by a third party entity (the "Investor Pools").

The Improper Accruals and Reversals

6. Between approximately 2000 and 2007, Beazer created, and later reversed, improper accruals and reserves by, among other ways, manipulating the amounts recorded in two series of accounts in order to manage earnings. These accounts were the land inventory accounts and the house cost to complete accounts.

7. The Land Inventory Accounts. As part of its homebuilding and sales operations, Beazer regularly acquired large parcels of land upon which it constructed houses. Beazer recorded this purchased land as an asset on its balance sheet in accounts denoted as "land inventory accounts." Also recorded in these accounts were capitalized costs for the common development of the parcel, such as costs for sewer systems and streets. Each Beazer subdivision under construction had at least one land inventory account associated with it in Beazer's general ledger.

8. As subdivisions were built, Beazer allocated the land acquisition cost, as well as past and future common development costs, to individual home lots which were then offered for sale. When a home sale was recorded in Beazer's general ledger, all associated homebuilding costs, including the costs of the land recorded in the land inventory account, were expensed to cost of sales. As part of these journal entries, the land inventory account was reduced and a cost of sales expense account increased to reflect the value of the land and improvements that Beazer sold with the house. Because Beazer sold houses within a subdivision as the development of that subdivision progressed, the land expense recorded for any particular house sale was necessarily an estimate. As individual houses in a development were sold, the land inventory accounts were decreased by an amount representing the amounts of the land and development costs allocated to each individual house. Shortly after the final

house in a development had been sold, the balance in the land inventory account would be at or near zero.

9. In certain quarters between 2000 through 2007, however, Beazer, acting through certain officers and employees, manipulated the amounts recorded in the land inventory accounts in order to manage earnings. Specifically, in various quarters during fiscal years 2000 through 2005, Beazer over-allocated land inventory expense to individual properties sold. This over-allocation caused Beazer to report more expense and less profit on each sold house in certain subdivisions. When all or most of the houses in a development were eventually sold, these over-allocations resulted in the affected land inventory accounts having negative (or credit) balances. The credit balances that resulted from the intentional over-allocation were then improperly held open in Beazer's general ledger—acting, in effect, as improper reserves. By these actions, Beazer understated its net income by a total of $42 million for fiscal years 2000 through 2005.

10. Beginning at least by the second quarter of 2006, Beazer, acting through certain officers and employees, began to reverse the excess reserves existing in the land inventory accounts, which increased then-current period earnings. The credit balances in land inventory accounts were debited, *i.e.*, zeroed out, and a cost of sales expense credited, *i.e.*, reduced. This improperly reduced expenses and increased Beazer's earnings. During 2006, Beazer overstated its cumulative reported net income of $389 million by $16 million by "zeroing out" credit balances in its land inventory accounts. For the first two quarters of fiscal 2007, Beazer understated its cumulative reported net loss of $102 million by $1 million due to the reversal of improper land inventory reserves.

11. The House Cost to Complete Accounts. Under its accounting policies, Beazer recorded revenue and profit on the sale of a house after the close of the sale of that house to a third party. In the journal entries to record the sale, Beazer typically reserved a portion of its profit earned on the house. This reserve, called a "house cost to complete" reserve, was established to cover any known and unknown expenses that Beazer might incur on the sold house after the close, such as outstanding invoices, unbudgeted cost overruns, minor repairs or final cosmetic touchups. Although the amount of this reserve varied by region, it was typically $2,000 to $4,000 per house, above known outstanding invoices. Beazer's policy was to reverse any unused portion of the house cost to complete reserve within four to nine months after the house's close, taking any unused portion into income at that time. Although creation of such a house cost to complete reserve is proper, in some instances, Beazer, acting through certain officers and employees, utilized these reserves to manage improperly its earnings. In various quarters between 2000 and 2005, Beazer over-reserved house cost to complete expenses in order to defer profit to future periods. In later periods, Beazer eliminated these cost to complete reserves, resulting in inflated profits for those periods. In certain instances, Beazer also purposefully did not recognize certain current period house cost to complete expenses, again resulting in inflated profits for those periods.

12. Between fiscal years 2000 and 2005, Beazer understated its net income by $6 million due to excess house cost to complete accruals. During fiscal year 2006, when Beazer began to reverse some of the excess accruals, Respondent overstated its net

income by over $1.2 million. Beazer also understated its cumulative net loss for the first two quarters of fiscal 2007 by $1 million.

The Sale-Leaseback Transactions

13. As part of its marketing activities, Beazer typically builds and furnishes between one and five model homes for each of its housing developments. Prior to 2006, Beazer typically retained ownership of the large majority (upwards of 70–80%) of its model homes, and entered into sale-leaseback arrangements with third parties for the remaining ones. Beginning in fiscal 2006, Beazer significantly increased the number of model homes it leased. At the end of fiscal 2006, Beazer had leased 557 of its 793 model homes or 70%. Beazer improperly accounted for more than half of these leased model homes as sale-leasebacks in order to improve Beazer's financial results.

14. Specifically, beginning near the end of fiscal 2005, Beazer, acting through certain of its officers and employees, engaged in negotiations with the third party entity representing the Investor Pools concerning possible sale-leaseback transactions for Beazer's model homes. Pursuant to the transaction terms under discussion, the Investor Pools would purchase certain Beazer model homes at 92% of the homes' appraised value. Beazer would then lease the model homes, at monthly lease payments equal to the Investor Pools' purchase price multiplied by the current 30 day LIBOR rate plus 450 basis points (prorated on a monthly basis). Beazer would also retain a right to receive a percentage of the appreciation of the model home upon its sale at the end of the lease term (the "Appreciation Rights").

15. However, Beazer's outside auditor informed certain Beazer officers and employees that any Appreciation Rights represented a "continuing interest" that, pursuant to Generally Accepted Accounting Principles ("GAAP"), required Beazer to record the transactions as financing, not as sale-leasebacks. This proper accounting treatment would not have permitted Beazer to record the model home sales revenue and profit at the beginning of the lease term.

16. In order to circumvent GAAP, and deceive its outside auditor, Beazer, acting through certain officers and employees, caused the model home sale-leaseback written agreements with the Investor Pools to omit any reference to Appreciation Rights and recorded the model home transactions as sale-leasebacks, recognizing home sales revenue in fiscal 2006. Based upon the terms of the written agreements, the outside auditor agreed that the transactions qualified for sale-leaseback accounting. However, unbeknownst to the outside auditor, Beazer, acting through certain officers and employees, and the Investor Pools had also entered into oral side agreements which contained the Appreciation Rights, and allowed Beazer to receive a percentage of the model homes' price appreciation upon their sale at the end of the lease term.

17. As a result of Beazer's improper recording of these transactions as sale-leasebacks, Beazer overstated its fiscal year 2006 revenues by $117 million and net income by $14 million. For the first two quarters of fiscal 2007, Beazer understated its cumulative revenue by $2.6 million and overstated its cumulative net loss by $3.9 million due to the improper sale-leasebacks accounting.

Beazer's Anti-fraud Violations: Section 17(a) of the Securities Act and Section 10(b) of the Exchange Act and Rule 10b-5 Thereunder

18. As a result of the conduct described above, Beazer violated Section 17(a) of the Securities Act, which prohibits materially false or misleading statements, or material omissions in the offer or sale of any security. Specifically, Beazer knowingly departed from GAAP and misstated its net income for certain periods in its registration statements and other filings with the Commission and other investor disclosures by using certain reserves and other accrued liabilities to recognize profits in 2006 and 2007 that were earned from 2000 through 2005. Beazer also intentionally and improperly recognized sales revenue from certain model home lease transactions, due to Respondent's use of sale-leaseback accounting treatment for these transactions despite knowing that such treatment was not in accordance with GAAP.

19. Additionally, Beazer violated Section 10(b) of the Exchange Act and Rule 10b-5 thereunder, which prohibit fraudulent conduct in connection with the purchase or sale of securities. As set forth above, Beazer made untrue statements of material facts in registration statements, periodic reports filed with the Commission and other investor disclosures or omitted to state therein any fact necessary in order to prevent the statements made therein, in the light of the circumstances under which they were made, from being materially misleading. Specifically, Beazer falsely stated its net income in certain periods in various Commission filings and other investor disclosures.

Beazer's Reporting Violations: Section 13(a) of the Exchange Act and Rules 12b-20, 13a-1, 13a-11 and 13a-13 Thereunder

20. Also as a result of the conduct described above, Beazer violated Section 13(a) of the Exchange Act and Rules 12b-20, 13a-1, 13a-11 and 13a-13 promulgated under the Exchange Act, which require that every issuer of a security registered pursuant to Section 12 of the Exchange Act files with the Commission information, documents, and annual and quarterly reports as the Commission may require, and mandate that periodic reports contain further material information as may be necessary to make the required statements not misleading.

Beazer's Record Keeping and Internal Control Violations: Sections 13(b)(2)(A) and 13(b)(2)(B) of the Exchange Act

21. As a result of the conduct described above, Beazer violated Section 13(b)(2)(A) of the Exchange Act, which requires reporting companies to make and keep books, records, and accounts, which, in reasonable detail, accurately and fairly reflect the transactions and dispositions of the assets of the issuer.

22. As a result of the conduct described above, Beazer violated Section 13(b)(2)(B) of the Exchange Act, which requires all reporting companies to devise and maintain a system of internal accounting controls sufficient to provide reasonable assurances that transactions are recorded as necessary to permit preparation of financial statements in accordance with GAAP. Beazer's insufficient internal controls failed to prevent the recording of the fraudulent accounting entries in its general ledger and

caused Respondent to file with the Commission financial statements that failed to conform with GAAP.

Beazer's Remedial Efforts

23. In determining to accept the Offer, the Commission considered remedial acts promptly undertaken by Respondent and cooperation afforded the Commission staff.

Undertakings

24. Respondent shall cooperate fully with the Commission in any and all investigations, litigations or other proceedings relating to or arising from the matters described in this Order. In connection with such cooperation, Respondent has undertaken:

To produce, without service of a notice or subpoena, any and all documents and other information requested by the Commission's staff;

To use its best efforts to cause its employees to be interviewed by the Commission's staff at such times as the staff reasonably may direct;

To use its best efforts to cause its employees to appear and testify truthfully and completely without service of a notice or subpoena in such investigations, depositions, hearings or trials as may be requested by the Commission's staff; and

That in connection with any testimony of Respondent to be conducted at deposition, hearing or trial pursuant to a notice or subpoena, Respondent:

i Agrees that any such notice or subpoena for Respondent's appearance and testimony may be served by regular mail on its attorney, David G. Januszewski, Esq., at Cahill Gordon & Reindel LLP, Eighty Pine Street, New York, New York 10005-1702; and

ii Agrees that any such notice or subpoena for Respondent's appearance and testimony in an action pending in a United States District Court may be served, and may require testimony, beyond the territorial limits imposed by the Federal Rules of Civil Procedure.

25. In determining whether to accept the Offer, the Commission has considered these undertakings.

IV.

In view of the foregoing, the Commission deems it appropriate to impose the sanction agreed to in Respondent Beazer's Offer.

Accordingly, it is hereby ORDERED that:

Pursuant to Section 8A of the Securities Act and Section 21C of the Exchange Act, Respondent Beazer cease and desist from committing or causing any violations and any future violations of Section 17(a) of the Securities Act and Sections 10(b), 13(a), 13(b)(2)(A) and 13(b)(2)(B) of the Exchange Act and Rules 10b-5, 12b-20, 13a-1, 13a-11 and 13a-13 promulgated under the Exchange Act.

By the Commission.

Florence E. Harmon Acting Secretary

FINANCIAL STATEMENTS

UNITED STATES
SECURITIES AND EXCHANGE COMMISSION
Washington, D.C. 20549

Extracts from FORM 10-K[8]

Annual report pursuant to Section 13 or 15(d) of the Securities Exchange Act of 1934

For the fiscal year ended September 30, 2007

BEAZER HOMES USA, INC.

Consolidated Statements of Operations
(in thousands, except per share amounts)

	Year Ended September 30		
	2007	**2006**	**2005**
		As Restated	
Total revenue	**$ 3,490,819**	$ 5,356,504	$ 4,992,973
Home construction and land sales expenses	**2,944,385**	4,061,118	3,766,517
Inventory impairments and option contract abandonments	**611,864**	44,175	5,511
Gross (loss) profit	**(65,430)**	1,251,211	1,220,945
Selling, general and administrative expenses	**454,122**	629,322	548,161
Depreciation and amortization	**33,594**	42,425	36,068
Goodwill impairment	**52,755**	—	130,235
Operating (loss) income	**(605,901)**	579,464	506,481
Equity in (loss) income of unconsolidated joint ventures	**(35,154)**	1,343	5,021
Other income, net	**7,775**	2,450	1,712
(Loss) income before income taxes	**(633,280)**	583,257	513,214
(Benefit from) provision for income taxes	**(222,207)**	214,421	237,315
Net (loss) income	**$ (411,073)**	$ 368,836	$ 275,899

---

[8] Extracted from 10-K filings for Beazer Homes, USA, Inc. 2005–2007. Obtained from U.S. Securities and Exchange Commission. *www.sec.gov*.

Beazer Homes USA, Inc.
Consolidated Balance Sheets
(in thousands, except share and per share amounts)

	September 30	
	2007	**2006**
		As Restated
ASSETS		
Cash and cash equivalents	$ 454,337	$ 167,570
Restricted cash	5,171	4,873
Accounts receivable	45,501	338,033
Income tax receivable	63,981	—
Inventory		
Owned inventory	2,537,791	3,137,021
Consolidated inventory not owned	237,382	471,441
Total Inventory	2,775,173	3,608,462
Residential mortgage loans available-for-sale	781	92,157
Investments in unconsolidated joint ventures	109,143	124,799
Deferred tax assets	232,949	71,344
Property, plant and equipment, net	71,682	76,454
Goodwill	68,613	121,368
Other assets	102,690	109,611
Total Assets	$ 3,930,021	$ 4,714,671
LIABILITIES AND STOCKHOLDERS' EQUITY		
Trade accounts payable	$ 118,030	$ 140,008
Other liabilities	453,089	557,754
Obligations related to consolidated inventory not owned	177,931	330,703
Senior Notes (net of discounts of $3,033 and $3,578, respectively)	1,521,967	1,551,422
Junior subordinated notes	103,093	103,093
Warehouse Line	—	94,881
Other secured notes payable	118,073	89,264
Model home financing obligations	114,116	117,079
Total Liabilities	2,606,299	2,984,204
Stockholders' Equity:		
Preferred stock (par value $0.01 per share, 5,000,000 shares authorized, no shares issued)	—	—
Common stock (par value $0.001, 80,000,000 shares authorized, 42,597,229 and 42,318,098 issued, 39,261,721 and 38,889,554 outstanding)	43	42
Paid in capital	543,705	529,326
Retained earnings	963,869	1,390,552
Treasury stock, at cost (3,335,508 and 3,428,544 shares)	(183,895)	(189,453)
Total Stockholders' Equity	1,323,722	1,730,467
Total Liabilities and Stockholders' Equity	$ 3,930,021	$ 4,714,671

Beazer Homes USA, Inc.
Consolidated Statements of Cash Flows
(in thousands)

	Year Ended September 30		
	2007	**2006**	**2005**
Cash flows from operating activities:		**As Restated**	
Net (loss) income	**$ (411,073)**	$ 368,836	$ 275,899
Adjustments to reconcile net (loss) income to net cash provided by (used in) operating activities:			
Depreciation and amortization	**33,594**	42,425	36,068
Stock-based compensation expense	**11,149**	15,753	11,945
Inventory impairments and option contract abandonments	**611,864**	44,175	5,511
Goodwill impairment charge	**52,755**	—	130,235
Deferred income tax (benefit) provision	**(161,605)**	25,963	(51,186)
Tax benefit from stock transactions	**(2,635)**	(8,205)	11,551
Equity in loss (income) of unconsolidated joint ventures	**35,154**	(1,343)	(5,021)
Cash distributions of income from unconsolidated joint ventures	**5,285**	352	5,844
Changes in operating assets and liabilities:			
Decrease (increase) in accounts receivable	**292,532**	(181,639)	(84,637)
Increase in income tax receivable	**(63,981)**	—	—
Decrease (increase) in inventory	**134,953**	(486,727)	(593,521)
Decrease (increase) in residential mortgage loans available-for-sale	**91,376**	(92,157)	—
Decrease (increase) in other assets	**9,180**	(20,736)	(16,780)
(Decrease) increase in trade accounts payable	**(21,978)**	(1,641)	18,336
(Decrease) increase in other liabilities	**(108,809)**	(83,044)	208,794
Other changes	**1,610**	(8)	806
Net cash provided by (used in) operating activities	**509,371**	(377,996)	(46,156)
Cash flows from investing activities:			
Capital expenditures	**(29,474)**	(55,088)	(48,437)
Investments in unconsolidated joint ventures	**(24,505)**	(49,458)	(42,619)
Changes in restricted cash	**(298)**	(4,873)	—
Distributions from and proceeds from sale of unconsolidated joint ventures	**2,229**	4,655	5,597
Net cash (used in) investing activities	**(52,048)**	(104,764)	(85,459)
Cash flows from financing activities:			
Repayment of term loan	**—**	—	(200,000)
Borrowings under credit facilities and warehouse line	**169,888**	1,937,528	439,700
Repayment of credit facilities and warehouse line	**(264,769)**	(1,842,647)	(439,700)
Repayment of other secured notes payable	**(31,139)**	(20,934)	(16,776)
Borrowings under senior notes	**—**	275,000	346,786
Borrowings under junior subordinated notes	**—**	103,093	—
Repurchase of senior notes	**(30,413)**	—	—
Borrowings under model home financing obligations	**5,919**	117,365	—
Repayment of model home financing obligations	**(8,882)**	(286)	(1,118)

(continued)

	Year Ended September 30		
	2007	**2006**	**2005**
		As Restated	
Debt issuance costs	**(2,259)**	(7,206)	(4,958)
Proceeds from stock option exercises	**4,422**	7,298	5,875
Common stock redeemed	**(348)**	(2,624)	—
Treasury stock purchases	—	(205,416)	(8,092)
Tax benefit from stock transactions	**2,635**	8,205	—
Dividends paid	**(15,610)**	(16,144)	(13,884)
Net cash (used in) provided by financing activities	**(170,556)**	353,232	107,833
Increase (decrease) in cash and cash equivalents	**286,767**	(129,528)	(23,782)
Cash and cash equivalents at beginning of year	**167,570**	297,098	320,880
Cash and cash equivalents at end of year	**$ 454,337**	$ 167,570	$ 297,098

Extracts from FORM 10-K[9]

For the fiscal year ended September 30, 2006

BEAZER HOMES USA, INC.

Consolidated Statements of Income

(in thousands, except per share amounts)

	Year Ended September 30		
	2006	**2005**	**2004**
Total revenue	**$ 5,462,003**	$ 4,995,353	$ 3,907,109
Home construction and land sales expenses	**4,201,318**	3,823,300	3,099,732
Gross profit	**1,260,685**	1,172,053	807,377
Selling, general and administrative expenses	**649,010**	554,900	429,442
Goodwill impairment	—	130,235	—
Operating income	**611,675**	486,918	377,935
Equity in (loss) income of unconsolidated joint ventures	**(772)**	5,021	1,561
Other income, net	**2,311**	7,395	7,079
Income before income taxes	**613,214**	499,334	386,575
Provision for income taxes	**224,453**	236,810	150,764
Net income	**$ 388,761**	$ 262,524	$ 235,811
Weighted average number of shares:			
Basic	**39,812**	40,468	39,879
Diluted	**44,345**	45,634	42,485
Earnings per share:			
Basic	**$ 9.76**	$ 6.49	$ 5.91
Diluted	**$ 8.89**	$ 5.87	$ 5.59
Cash dividends per share	**$ 0.40**	$ 0.33	$ 0.13

---

[9] Extracted from 10-K filings for Beazer Homes, USA, Inc. Obtained from U.S. Securities and Exchange Commission. *www.sec.gov*.

Beazer Homes USA, Inc.
Consolidated Balance Sheets
(in thousands, except share and per share amounts)

	September 30	
	2006	2005
ASSETS		
Cash and cash equivalents	$ 162,570	$ 297,098
Restricted cash	9,873	—
Accounts receivable	333,571	161,880
Inventory		
Owned inventory	3,048,891	2,671,082
Consolidated inventory not owned	471,441	230,083
Total Inventory	3,520,332	2,901,165
Residential mortgage loans available-for-sale	92,157	—
Investments in unconsolidated joint ventures	122,799	78,571
Deferred tax assets	59,842	101,329
Property, plant and equipment, net	29,465	28,367
Goodwill	121,368	121,368
Other assets	107,454	80,738
Total Assets	$ 4,559,431	$ 3,770,516
LIABILITIES AND STOCKHOLDERS' EQUITY		
Trade accounts payable	$ 141,131	$ 141,623
Other liabilities	547,014	636,106
Obligations related to consolidated inventory not owned	330,703	166,163
Senior Notes (net of discounts of $3,578 and $4,118, respectively)	1,551,422	1,275,882
Junior subordinated notes	103,093	—
Warehouse Line	94,881	—
Other notes payable	89,264	46,054
Total Liabilities	2,857,508	2,265,828
Stockholders' Equity:		
Preferred stock (par value $0.01 per share, 5,000,000 shares authorized, no shares issued)	—	—
Common stock (par value $0.001, 80,000,000 shares authorized, 42,318,098 and 41,844,414 issued, 38,889,554 and 41,701,955 outstanding)	42	42
Paid in capital	528,376	534,523
Retained earnings	1,362,958	990,341
Treasury stock, at cost (3,428,544 and 142,459 shares)	(189,453)	(8,092)
Unearned compensation	—	(12,126)
Total Stockholders' Equity	1,701,923	1,504,688
Total Liabilities and Stockholders' Equity	$ 4,559,431	$ 3,770,516

Beazer Homes USA, Inc.
Consolidated Statements of Cash Flows
(in thousands)

	Year Ended September 30		
	2006	2005	2004
Cash flows from operating activities:			
Net income	$ 388,761	$ 262,524	$ 235,811
Adjustments to reconcile net income to net cash used in operating activities:			
Depreciation and amortization	10,304	9,229	8,374
Stock-based compensation expense	15,753	11,945	7,381
Goodwill impairment charge	—	130,235	—
Impairment and write-off of inventory-related assets	43,477	5,511	3,180
Deferred income tax provision (benefit)	41,487	(54,631)	(22,740)
Tax benefit from stock transactions	—	11,551	8,127
Equity in loss (earnings) of unconsolidated joint ventures	772	(5,021)	(1,561)
Cash distributions of income from unconsolidated joint ventures	352	5,844	—
Changes in operating assets and liabilities:			
Increase in accounts receivable	(171,251)	(91,306)	(4,571)
Increase in inventory	(430,345)	(572,114)	(413,705)
Increase in residential mortgage loans available-for-sale	(92,157)	—	—
Increase in other assets	(19,462)	(16,775)	(16,828)
(Decrease)/increase in trade accounts payable	(492)	18,336	(2,234)
(Decrease)/increase in other liabilities	(92,342)	199 76	123,210
Other changes	680	1,333	1,837
Net cash used in operating activities	(304,463)	(84,263)	(73,719)
Cash flows from investing activities:			
Capital expenditures	(11,542)	(13,448)	(10,271)
Investments in unconsolidated joint ventures	(49,458)	(40,619)	(25,844)
Changes in restricted cash	(9,873)	—	—
Distributions from and proceeds from sale of unconsolidated joint ventures	4,655	5,597	5,639
Net cash used in investing activities	(66,218)	(48,470)	(30,476)
Cash flows from financing activities:			
Proceeds from term loan	—	—	200,000
Repayment of term loan	—	(200,000)	(200,000)
Borrowings under credit facilities	1,937,528	439,700	—
Repayment of credit facilities	(1,842,647)	(439,700)	—
Repayment of other notes payable	(20,934)	(16,776)	—
Borrowings under senior and junior notes payable	378,093	346,786	380,000
Debt issuance costs	(7,206)	(4,958)	(10,654)
Proceeds from stock option exercises	7,298	5,875	5,362
Common stock redeemed	(2,624)	(8,092)	—
Treasury stock purchases	(205,416)	—	(17,546)
Tax benefit from stock transactions	8,205	—	—
Dividends paid	(16,144)	(13,884)	(5,459)
Net cash provided by financing activities	236,153	108,951	351,703

(continued)

	Year Ended September 30		
	2006	**2005**	**2004**
(Decrease)/increase in cash and cash equivalents	**(134,528)**	(23,782)	247,508
Cash and cash equivalents at beginning of year	**297,098**	320,880	73,372
Cash and cash equivalents at end of year	**$ 162,570**	$ 297,098	$ 320,880
Supplemental cash flow information:			
Interest paid	**$ 111,501**	$ 79,088	$ 65,237
Income taxes paid	**$ 228,181**	$ 233,965	$ 170,475
Supplemental disclosure of non-cash activity:			
Increase in consolidated inventory not owned	**$ 164,540**	$ —	$ 188,585
Land acquired through issuance of notes payable	**$ 64,144**	$ 40,608	$ 21,502

Extracts from FORM 10-K[10]

For the fiscal year ended September 30, 2005

BEAZER HOMES USA, INC.

Consolidated Balance Sheets
(in thousands, except per share amounts)

	September 30	
	2005	**2004**
ASSETS		
Cash and cash equivalents	$ 297,098	$ 320,880
Accounts receivable	161,880	70,574
Inventory		
Owned inventory	2,671,082	2,089,330
Consolidated inventory not owned	230,083	254,765
Total Inventory	2,901,165	2,344,095
Investments in and advances to unconsolidated joint ventures	78,571	44,748
Deferred tax assets	101,329	47,052
Property, plant and equipment, net	28,367	24,671
Goodwill	121,368	251,603
Other assets	80,738	59,407
Total Assets	$ 3,770,516	$ 3,163,030
LIABILITIES AND STOCKHOLDERS' EQUITY		
Trade accounts payable	$ 141,623	$ 123,287
Other liabilities	636,106	437,608
Obligations related to consolidated inventory not owned	166,163	219,042
Term Loan	—	200,000
Senior Notes (net of discounts of $4,118 and $1,095, respectively)	1,275,882	928,905
Other notes payable	46,054	22,067
Total Liabilities	2,265,828	1,930,909
		(continued)

---

[10] Extracted from 10-K filings for Beazer Homes, USA, Inc.. Obtained from U.S. Securities and Exchange Commission. *www.sec.gov*.

	September 30	
	2005	2004
ASSETS		
Stockholders' Equity:		
Preferred stock (par value $0.01 per share, 5,000,000 shares authorized, no shares issued)	—	—
Common stock (par value $0.001 and $.01 per share, 80,000,000 and 30,000,000 (pre-split) shares authorized, 41,844,414 and 53,605,047 issued, 41,701,955 and 41,191,419 outstanding)	42	54
Paid in capital	534,523	593,874
Retained earnings	990,341	741,701
Treasury stock, at cost (142,459 and 12,413,628 shares)	(8,092)	(88,150)
Unearned compensation	(12,126)	(14,748)
Accumulated other comprehensive loss	—	(610)
Total Stockholders' Equity	1,504,688	1,232,121
Total Liabilities and Stockholders' Equity	$ 3,770,516	$ 3,163,030

Hocus Pocus

After studying this chapter, you should be able to:

- Explain the various methods that Sensormatic and Xerox used to recognize future periods' sales in current periods.
- Describe CUC's method of reporting fictitious revenue.
- Describe Insignia's method of improper valuation of revenue.
- Identify the signals in financial statements that could alert you to the possibility that a company may be overstating its revenues.
- Adjust for sales of accounts receivable in order to ensure that such sales do not dilute the signals that could alert you to an overstatement of sales.

- Sensormatic, Xerox, CUC, and Insignia are presented in this chapter as examples of various forms of Improper Revenue Recognition (see Table 1.1 on p. 19–20)

CHAPTER OUTLINE

- Sensormatic: Madness at Midnight
- Xerox: Do Not Duplicate
- CUC: Phony Funds
- Insignia: Return to Sender
- Key Terms
- Ethics at Work
- Assignments
- Case Study: Peregrine Systems, Inc.

In a speech given several years ago, past SEC chairman Arthur Levitt (1998) spoke about the numerous companies that "operate in the gray area between legitimacy and outright fraud." He observed, "Integrity may be losing out to illusion." In order to achieve these illusory earnings and fabricated balance sheets, many companies resort to what Levitt described as "hocus pocus."

This chapter presents a brief overview of, at worst, some of the lesser-known, intentional revenue-recognition accounting frauds or, at best, misguided attempts to "improve" a company's financial statements with aggressive accounting. In all cases, however, the main objective was either to boost the appearance of corporate profits or to enhance the seeming strength of the balance sheets. In most cases, company personnel achieved this using their own versions of hocus pocus.

Why are so many company executives prepared to resort to such desperate measures to misrepresent or falsify accounting records? Some of the reasons are quite obvious: better balance sheets or greater earnings mean more investors, increased stock prices, more valuable stock options, bigger bonuses, improved financing terms, and so on. Essentially, all these reasons boil down to one basic and obvious motivating force—greed. However, there are other reasons that are not quite so apparent. As with Enron and WorldCom, many of the companies discussed in this chapter were managed predominately by men who at times seemed charismatic and plausible, men with strong personalities and even stronger egos. Some were desperate to avoid the embarrassment of failure at any cost. Others started to believe that they were immune to mundane rules and regulations.

SENSORMATIC: MADNESS AT MIDNIGHT

> **Sensormatic is presented mainly as an example of Improper Timing of Revenue Recognition via holding books open after the close of a reporting period.**

Sensormatic Electronics Corporation was a publicly traded company, registered in Delaware, with its head office located in Boca Raton, Florida. The company is still in existence but is no longer a public company. Sensormatic manufactures electronic security systems and is probably best known for its anti-shoplifting security devices. It was known on Wall Street for meeting its budgeted figures for revenues and earnings. Moreover, these estimates were quite aggressive. For example, Sensormatic budgeted for revenue growth of over 20 percent per year over the period of 1988–1995. The company began facing enormous difficulty in meeting these phenomenal growth projections from at least the first quarter of its 1994 fiscal year. Surprisingly, despite this difficulty, Sensormatic's quarterly financial reports continued to meet analysts' earnings forecasts almost to the cent. Sensormatic's management was fully committed to meeting these forecasts and apparently became quite creative in this regard.

In its proceedings against Sensormatic, the SEC examined the roles of a number of former senior executives of the company, including Ronald Assaf (former CEO), Michael Pardue (former COO and CFO), and Lawrence Simmons (former vice president of finance).

Sensormatic is presented mainly as an example of improper timing of revenue recognition via holding books open after the close of a reporting period. Sensormatic's stock was used to finance acquisitions, and the stock price was sensitive to the company's revenue growth and to analysts' revenue and earnings estimates. Therefore, senior management was highly motivated to communicate positive information on Sensormatic's financial position and prospects to stock analysts. Management was also aware of Sensormatic's high price-to-earnings ratio as well as the effect that faltering growth would have on the stock price. Senior executives became too eager in their quest to deliver earnings and revenue figures that met analysts' high growth expectations in every single quarter. Sales were lower in the third quarter of each year due to seasonal variables, and this quarter generally provided the biggest challenge. By the 1994 fiscal year, all quarters received significant assistance from nifty accounting that recognized the next quarter's sales a little early.

AN OVERVIEW OF SENSORMATIC'S FICTITIOUS FINANCIAL REPORTING SCHEMES

The SEC found that Sensormatic misstated its quarterly revenue and earnings from at least the first quarter of fiscal year 1994 until the third quarter of fiscal year 1995.[1] Further, the SEC claimed that Sensormatic's senior management, including Pardue and Simmons, were "aware of the methods used to effectuate the scheme, [and] also condoned and directed them. Others at various levels and in various departments also participated in these practices" (AAER 1017, 1998).

According to the SEC, memoranda were prepared close to the end of each quarter, specifying sales goals that needed to be met before the close of the quarter, in order to comply with the aggressive sales budgets that had been published and distributed to senior management and to the various departments. When it became clear that the company could not reach the budget targets, "Sensormatic engaged in a variety of **improper revenue recognition** practices . . . that were not in conformity with Generally Accepted Accounting Principles ('GAAP') . . ." (AAER 1017, 1998). Improper revenue recognition refers to incorrectly recording a transaction in the financial statements, indicating that the conditions have been met for the earning of revenue.

Scheme #1: Holding Books Open after the Close of a Reporting Period

The SOX Report, which examined all the SEC Enforcement Actions for July 31, 1997, through July 30, 2003, found 25 enforcement actions in this period "involving the failure of issuers to close their books properly at the close of a reporting period" (2002, p. 8). Simply put, **holding books open** enables a company to report the next quarter's sales in the current period by simply keeping the current period's books and records open for a few extra days after the close of a reporting period to record additional sales. This strategy was one of a "variety of improper revenue recognition practices" that Sensormatic allegedly used. The Commission contended that Sensormatic devised a

---

[1] Sensormatic consented to the issuance of the order without admitting or denying the findings contained in the order. As set out in AAER 1017, March 25, 1998.

complicated and expensive procedure whereby the computer records of goods or equipment shipped were actually backdated:

> Shortly before midnight on the last day of the quarter, the computer system that recorded and dated shipments was "brought down" so that the computer clock date would reflect the last day of the prior quarter. The company system then falsely recorded shipments as having occurred on the last day of the prior quarter (AAER 1017, 1998).

Scheme #2: False Recognition of Early Shipments

The next improper revenue recognition practice Sensormatic used to meet its quarterly sales budgets was the ploy of shipping goods that customers had ordered for the next period to Sensormatic's own warehouses at the end of the current period. Then in the financial records, the company would recognize this revenue *at the time of* the shipment to its own warehouse. This scheme was so elaborate that the company needed to create a set of what were known as "off-books" records in order to keep track of the prematurely shipped goods to ensure that they were later shipped from the warehouses to the customers at the appropriate time, as originally requested by the customer. Sometimes the goods remained in the warehouses for several months before they were shipped to the customers.

Scheme #3: Slow Shipping Requests

Another tactic Sensormatic allegedly used to accelerate its revenue recognition was what is called "**slow shipping**," or requesting the shipping company to delay the shipment of goods. When a customer ordered items for the next quarter, Sensormatic sometimes shipped the goods early in order to record the sale in the current quarter. However, according to the SEC, to avoid having the goods arrive at the customer before the requested date, Sensormatic would instruct the carrier to delay the delivery for anything from a few days to a few weeks. Using this slow shipping strategy, the company could record a few extra days' sales in a particular quarter.

Scheme #4: Recognizing "FOB Destination" Sales at the Time of Shipment

When a sales order stipulates "**FOB destination**," it means that there is a sales agreement specifying that ownership passes to the customer only when the purchased goods arrive at their destination. According to GAAP, the sale can be recognized only when the customer takes ownership. However, the SEC alleged that in the last week of some quarters, Sensormatic recognized some of its FOB destination sales at the time of shipping instead of the time the goods reached their destination. This was yet another of the "variety of improper revenue recognition practices" that the Commission alleged Sensormatic used in its attempt to meet analysts' quarterly revenue and earnings expectations.

Table 4.1 summarizes Sensormatic's misstatements over a two-year period.

Scheme #5: Misleading the Auditors

The SEC also stated that Sensormatic carefully concealed its deceptive practices. Besides the computer clock being stopped to backdate sales after the end of a period, documents were also provided indicating that shipments to the company's own warehouses were

TABLE 4.1	Summary of Sensormatic's Quarterly Misstatements[2]			
	1994–1995			
	Amount of Improperly Recognized Revenue	**Net Income as Reported by Sensormatic**	**Over/[Under] Statement of Net Income**	**% Over/[Under] Statement of Net Income**
1994 Q1	$8.5 M*	$14.8 M	[$0.8 M]	[5.3%]
1994 Q2	$4.6 M	$18.8 M	[$1.9 M]	[9.1%]
1994 Q3	$15.8 M	$16.4 M	$3.6 M	28.1%
1994 Q4	$15.5 M	$22.0 M	[$0.9 M]	[3.8%]
1995 Q1	$12.8 M	$20.1 M	[$0.5 M]	[2.2%]
1995 Q2	$13.8 M	$25.3 M	$0.3 M	1.2%
1995 Q3	$30.2 M	$24.1 M	$6.7 M	38.3%
1995 Q4	$29.3 M	$18–$21 M**	$5.2 M	40.5%

*M = millions.
**Sensormatic's reported estimate in press release.

sales to customers. According to the Commission, Sensormatic instructed employees to withhold certain bills of lading from the auditors because they would have indicated a practice of **premature revenue recognition**, in which revenue was recorded in the financial statements in an earlier period than it should have been recorded. Through a concerted and deliberate effort to conceal information from the auditors, company executives "caused accounting records to be falsified, made false statements to the independent auditors, and intentionally circumvented the company's internal accounting controls" (AAER 1020, 1998). The SEC findings also alleged that during the 1994 audit, an employee was instructed to withhold documents from the auditors that would have "disclosed the improper recognition of revenue on out-of-period shipments." Furthermore, the employee was apparently told to "follow orders or quit" (AAER 1027, 1998).

SIGNALS OF SENSORMATIC'S FICTITIOUS REPORTING SCHEMES #1–#4

Although Sensormatic used different methods compared to those of Sunbeam, all of Sensormatic's reporting frauds accelerated and overstated sales, which ultimately had the same effect as Sunbeam's accelerated sales. The two signals listed below may apply to any method of overstating sales.

SIGNAL #1: INCREASE IN ACCOUNTS RECEIVABLE AS A PERCENTAGE OF SALES The leading sign of an overstatement of sales is when accounts receivable increase as a percentage of sales, which is often measured as days sales outstanding (DSO). If the next period's sales have been accelerated into the current period or if the sales are completely fictitious, the company will debit accounts receivable and credit sales, as for legitimate sales. However, while legitimate sales will be paid relatively soon by the

---

[2] Obtained from AAER 1017, 1998. *www.sec.gov*.

customers and will turn into cash, the next period's sales will probably be paid only in the next period and will remain on the balance sheet in the current period as accounts receivable instead of turning into cash.

SIGNAL #2: CASH FLOW FROM OPERATIONS FALLING BEHIND OPERATING INCOME   The second signal of inappropriately recorded sales is when cash flow from operations (CFFO) lags or falls behind operating income or net income. This is a prime signal; if a company is operating at a profit, why would it not be generating CFFO at a similar pace?

ARE THEY LIVING HAPPILY EVER AFTER?

- **Assaf, Pardue, and Simmons** consented to the SEC's final judgment "without admitting or denying the allegations." Assaf, Pardue, and Simmons were ordered to pay "civil money penalties of $50,000, $40,000, and $50,000, respectively" (AAER 1020, 1998).
- **Sensormatic** was acquired by Tyco Inc. in November 2001 and was removed from the New York Stock Exchange because "fewer than 600,000 shares remain[ed] publicly held" (NYSE, 2001).
- **Ronald Assaf** resigned after Sensormatic was acquired by Tyco. Mr. and Mrs. Assaf are reportedly living in Boca Raton, Florida, where they are very active in the community. In January 2012, Mr. and Mrs. Assaf were awarded Nova Southeastern University's highest honor, the President's Community Award, for their "leadership and philanthropic gifts" ("NSU to Honor Ron and Kathy Assaf . . . ," 2012).

XEROX: DO NOT DUPLICATE

> **Xerox is presented mainly as an example of Improper Timing of Revenue Recognition via the misuse of multiple-element contracts or bundled contracts.**

The Xerox Corporation is a multibillion-dollar Connecticut-based company that specializes in the production, sale, and lease of duplicating machines and services. The company is known worldwide, and its name has become synonymous with "photocopying." In the period from 1997 to 2000, Xerox paid its auditors (KPMG) the sum of "$55.8 million for auditing [its] financial statements" (AAER 2234, 2005).

AN OVERVIEW OF XEROX'S FICTITIOUS FINANCIAL REPORTING SCHEMES

The SEC found that Xerox accelerated recognition of its equipment revenue by more than $3 billion over the period 1997 through 2000 and "increased pre-tax earnings by $1.5 billion."[3] The SEC findings also alleged that "KPMG's failure to comply with

---

[3] "Pursuant to a consent to settlement by Xerox, the company also was assessed a civil penalty of $10 million. In consenting to settlement, Xerox neither admitted nor denied the allegations of the Commission's Complaint." As set out in AAER 2234, April 19, 2005.

generally accepted auditing standards (GAAS) caused and willfully aided and abetted Xerox's violations."[4] (Quotes from AAER 2234, 2005)

Xerox provides a dramatic illustration of fictitious reporting by improper timing of revenue recognition through the misuse of multiple-element contracts or bundled contracts.

Scheme #1: Improper Use of Multiple-Element Contracts or Bundled Contracts

The major offending accounting actions in the SEC complaint were concerned with Xerox's treatment of its lease contracts. Typically, Xerox customer leases generate revenue from three streams:

1. The equipment revenue known at Xerox as the "box" revenue. This revenue is earned by making the physical asset (the copy machine itself) available to the customer, and it is legitimately recognized at the beginning of the lease in sales-type leases.
2. Revenue for servicing the equipment. GAAP requires this revenue to be recognized over the life of the lease.
3. The financing of revenue on the effective loans to the lessees. GAAP also requires this revenue to be recognized over the life of the lease.

The SEC found that Xerox shifted revenue in the following ways:

- Xerox shifted revenue from its servicing revenue stream to the box revenue stream, making it appear as revenue received for physically transferring the equipment to the customer. This was done in order to recognize future service revenue at the beginning of the lease. Xerox's internal name for the accounting method whereby it shifted this revenue was its "return on equity" method.
- Xerox also shifted certain portions of its financing revenue to the box or equipment revenue stream so as to recognize that revenue at the beginning of the lease. Xerox's name for the accounting method under which it made this shift was the "margin normalization" system.

According to the SEC, "These two methodologies, which did not comply with GAAP, increased Xerox's equipment revenues by $2.8 billion and its pre-tax earnings by $660 million from 1997 to 2000." The SEC complaint alleged that Xerox failed to disclose its use of these methods, "which were changes in accounting methods and changes in accounting estimates." (Quotes from AAER 1542, 2002)

Scheme #2: Estimates of Discount Rates and Residual Values

Further, an article in *The Accountant* described an SEC complaint against the Xerox auditors, KPMG, as follows: "Between 1995 and 2000, Xerox always assumed a 15 percent return . . . despite significant volatility in the returns actually earned by leasing companies" ("SEC Complaint . . .," 2003). Leasing companies discount future cash flows when they recognize the amounts in current income. (**Discounted future cash flows** refer to the present value of the future cash that a company expects to receive or pay.) By choosing a particular discount rate, a leasing company can manipulate its reported

---

[4] KPMG consented to the entry of this order without admitting or denying the finding therein, except as to the Commission's jurisdiction over it and the subject matter of these proceedings. As set out in AAER 2234, April 19, 2005.

income. The SEC also alleged that Xerox increased its reported earnings by changing estimates of the residual values of its leased assets. (Note: KPMG strongly defended its audit work at Xerox.)

Scheme #3: Improper Disclosure of Sales of Leases

Xerox also sold approximately $400 million of its existing leases. This occurred after Xerox Brazil changed its emphasis from sales-type leases to operating leases. This revenue from the operating leases would have been received over a number of years over the durations of the leases. However, the sale of the receivables to a lender caused the revenue to be recognized immediately and the cash to be received immediately. The nondisclosure of these sales had the dual effects of making the operating income in the period of the sale look better than it was, as well as making the cash-flow situation look stronger: "This added $182 million in pre-tax profits to Xerox's 1999 results" (AAER 1542, 2002).

OTHER MISSTATEMENTS   The SEC also alleged that Xerox boosted its earnings by creating cookie-jar reserves[5] and then reversing those unneeded reserves back into profits in later periods. In addition, the company improperly disclosed the gain on a one-time event with the result of boosting the appearance of extra profits from ordinary, recurring operations.

SIGNALS OF XEROX'S FICTITIOUS REPORTING SCHEMES

The first two signals listed next apply to all methods of overstating revenue. The next two signals apply to Xerox's specific methods of overstating revenue.

SIGNAL #1: INCREASE IN ACCOUNTS RECEIVABLE AS A PERCENTAGE OF SALES   Examine the accounts receivable-to-sales ratio as measured, for example, by DSO or by days' revenues outstanding (DRO). When a company shifts revenue from a stream that should be recognized in a later period in order to have it recognized in a current period, its revenues, operating income, and net income increase, but its cash received does not. Instead, the company's accounts receivable increase.

SIGNAL #2: CFFO FALLING BEHIND OPERATING INCOME OR NET INCOME   When CFFO decreases relative to operating income or net income, this is the prime signal of a company recognizing any form of profit ahead of time. CFFO refers to the amount of cash generated after expenses from the company's main operating activities, such as sales, services rendered, or other operating activities. At Xerox, CFFO went from 26% of net income for 1996, to 33% for 1997. Then for 1998, the company actually generated a *negative* CFFO of $1,165 million compared to positive reported net income of $395 million. This dramatic lagging of CFFO behind net income should have been a major red flag, signaling that something was seriously amiss regarding Xerox's reported

---

[5] Recall that "cookie-jar" reserves refer to reserves created by overstating a future liability in one period to release it in a future period, thereby fictitiously implying that the company has less expense in the future period.

profit. Suddenly, in 1999, CFFO turned around dramatically, to positive $1,224 million, compared to net income of $1,424 million—a ratio of 86 percent.

It was later revealed that in 1999 Xerox had sold approximately $400 million of its accounts receivable. When a company sells its accounts receivable, this increases its reported CFFO. To test whether CFFO is lagging behind operating income or net income, one must deduct the amount of sold accounts receivable from CFFO before comparing CFFO to operating income or net income. After making this adjustment, anyone looking at the signal of CFFO lagging reported net income should have been suspicious that Xerox was dramatically accelerating its reported income. (For this signal and Signal #1, securitized or sold receivables should be added back to accounts receivable and deducted from CFFO.)

SIGNAL #3: CHANGES IN PROPORTIONS OF REVENUE STREAMS If the revenue streams are reported separately and the stream in which revenue is immediately recognized increases in proportion to the stream(s) where revenue recognition is delayed (over the life of the contract), it is a signal that the company could be shifting revenue to accelerate its recognition. If this is accompanied by Signal #1 (an increase in the accounts receivable-to-sales ratio), the alert becomes stronger.

SIGNAL #4: SALES OF ACCOUNTS RECEIVABLE Any disclosure in the financial statements (or in the press) that a company has "factored" or sold its accounts receivable—or any future revenue stream—should alert the reader to test for all signals of accelerating revenue recognition. Xerox sold accounts receivable without disclosing it immediately. In such a case, as soon as information is released that a company has factored its accounts receivable, one should realize that this, in itself, could be a signal that the company has accelerated its sales. In addition, one should be aware that this factoring of accounts receivable would have concealed Signal #1 because the factoring would have reduced the buildup in accounts receivable.

ARE THEY LIVING HAPPILY EVER AFTER?

- **Six former Xerox company officials** agreed to pay over $22 million in penalties, without admitting or denying the SEC's allegations (SEC Press Release, 2003).
- A criminal investigation into **Xerox's** accounting practices was concluded in October 2004, and U.S prosecutors did not file charges ("Xerox Cleared . . . ," 2004).
- **KPMG** "agreed to settle the SEC's charges against it in connection with the audits of Xerox Corp. from 1997 through 2000" (LR 19191, 2005). As a result of this civil litigation, KPMG agreed to pay a total of $22.475 million in penalties. KPMG was also ordered to develop reform plans to ensure that SEC violations do not recur (LR 19191, 2005).
- "KPMG consented to the entry of the Order without admitting or denying the SEC's findings" (LR 19191, 2005).
- In March 2008, **Xerox** agreed to pay $670 million and **KPMG LLP** agreed to pay $80 million to settle a "lawsuit filed on behalf of Xerox investors who claimed Xerox committed accounting fraud to meet Wall Street earnings expectations" (Taub, 2008). The case was settled without any admissions of wrongdoing.

CUC: PHONY FUNDS[6]

> **CUC is presented mainly as an example of Improper Revenue Recognition via reporting fictitious revenue.**

CUC International, Inc., was a company (registered in Delaware) that sold club memberships to its customers for automobile, dining, shopping, and travel services. Another Delaware company, HFS Incorporated, controlled franchise brand names in the hotel, real estate brokerage, and car rental industries. These two companies merged in December 1997, taking the name of Cendant Corporation, which carried on the combined activities of the two formerly separate companies.

The SEC maintained that the fraud began with the original CUC as far back as 1985 and was allegedly directed by CUC's chairman and CEO, Walter Forbes, from the very beginning. The SEC's complaint also alleged that CUC's president and COO, E. Kirk Shelton, joined Forbes in directing the scheme from at least 1991 onward (AAER 1372, 2001; LR 16919, 2001). The Commission also contended that Cosmo Corigliano, who served as controller of CUC from 1983 to 1995 and as CFO from 1995 to 1997, "assisted senior CUC officers who initiated the long-running financial reporting fraud and later, as CUC's Chief Financial Officer, proceeded to orchestrate and refine the fraud" (AAER 2014, 2004; LR 18711, 2004).[7] Referring to the CUC case, Richard Walker, SEC Director of Enforcement, noted that "large, complex, and long-running financial frauds often originate at the highest levels of a company" (AAER 1372, 2001; LR 16919, 2001).

According to SEC records, another pivotal individual involved in the execution of the schemes was Mary Sattler Polverari, a CPA who was hired by CUC in December 1995 and became manager of financial reporting in 1997. The SEC maintained that Polverari carried out instructions that "included adjustments increasing revenue . . . and decreasing particular expense line items" (AAER 1275, 2000).[8]

AN OVERVIEW OF CUC'S FICTITIOUS FINANCIAL REPORTING SCHEMES

According to the Securities and Exchange Commission, beginning in at least 1985, "certain members of CUC's senior management implemented a scheme designed to ensure that CUC always met the financial results anticipated by Wall Street analysts. The CUC managers utilized a variety of means to achieve their goals" (AAER 1275, 2000).

The SOX Report (2002) found 80 enforcement matters in which companies reported fictitious revenue, and the report described several ways in which improper revenue recognition involving fictitious revenue occurred: "The manipulation of revenue was accomplished through, among other means, the falsification of sales documents, side agreements with customers that were not recorded, and top-side adjustments by senior management" (p. 11).

---

[6] The fraud occurred at CUC before the company merged with Cendant.

[7] Cosmo Corigliano and others "consented to the entry of the Final Judgment without admitting or denying the allegations of the complaint." As set out in LR 18711, 2004.

[8] Mary Sattler Polverari consented to the entry of the order without admitting or denying the findings. As set out in AAER 1275, 2000.

One of CUC's primary methods of fictitious revenue reporting was through the use of top-side adjustments. In addition to the **top-side entries**, entries recorded in the financial statements but not in the general ledger or other formal accounting records, CUC also transferred some amounts for deferred club membership revenues to current periods' revenues. Further, the company created huge overstated merger reserves, which it used as cookie-jar reserves to be released into profits in later periods. After the merger of CUC with HFS, Inc., the newly established Cendant discovered the CUC fraud. In 1998, this represented the biggest accounting fraud ever revealed in the United States. However, in the first decade of the 21st century, the CUC fraud was surpassed by several much larger accounting frauds. CUC is presented in this chapter as an example of overstating revenue by the use of *fictitious revenue*. (Note that WorldCom is examined in this text as an illustration of the fraudulent use of merger acquisition reserves.)

The CUC Scheme of Reporting Fictitious Revenue via Top-Side Adjustments

For the hands-on part of the scheme that required actually making the top-side adjustment (adjustments made in the financial statements and not in the general ledger), the alleged role of Polverari was important. She received the financial reports from all the business units and compiled a monthly report showing the results of each unit. Each quarter she submitted the quarterly consolidated report to her supervisors. This was when the scheme started. Polverari's supervisors would devise instructions describing adjustments for her to make: "Typically the instructions included adjustments increasing revenue by a certain amount and decreasing particular expense line items by certain amounts" (AAER 1275, 2000). Most of the alterations were concentrated on the Comp-U-Card division. The adjustments always increased earnings, and they never had supporting documentation. The SEC commented:

> The adjustments were entirely top-side adjustments. That is, the adjustments were simply entered into Polverari's spreadsheet at Stamford—no journal entries were created, no entries were made to CUC's general ledger, and the adjustments were not carried down to the books and records of Comp-U-Card or any of the company's other divisions. (AAER 1275, 2000)

Clearly, the revenue recognized in this manner was entirely fictitious, with no accounting explanation provided for the entries. However, the explanation given to Polverari for the entries was amazingly frank. She was apparently informed that "CUC's chief financial officer had generated the adjustments to inflate CUC's quarterly results so that the results would meet earnings expectations of Wall Street analysts." Polverari was even told that some of the adjustments were made to achieve percentage targets for some expenses and that some of the adjustments were "to ensure that items such as receivables and cash were at levels he [the CFO] thought desirable." (Quotes from AAER 1275, 2000)

The Commission found that for the fiscal years ended January 31, 1996; January 31, 1997; and December 31, 1997, the top-side alterations aggregated $31 million, $87 million, and $176 million, respectively. Because the top-side entries were not entered in the company's general ledger, something had to be done to align retained earnings with the annual financial statements. The SEC maintained that in April 1998, after the filing of Cendant's annual financial statements, "Polverari directed the subsidiaries to give the entries March 1998 effective dates and stated that the entries that 'would normally be charged to the P&L can be charged directly to Retained Earnings to avoid opening last year's books'" (AAER 1275, 2000). The Commission also found that in January 1998, managers ordered approximately $115 million in unsupported post-closing journal entries, reversing the company's merger reserves. This dramatically inflated reported profits. (Refer to the WorldCom chapter of this text, Chapter 5, "WorldCom Wizardry: From WorldCom to WorldCon," for a detailed analysis of improper use of merger reserves.)

SIGNALS OF CUC'S SCHEME OF REPORTING FICTITIOUS REVENUE

The major signals for overstatement of revenues are the same as those discussed in the analysis of Sunbeam's accelerated revenue reporting. In addition, CUC manipulated membership subscriptions and suspiciously met analysts' earnings targets on a regular basis.

SIGNAL #1: INCREASE IN ACCOUNTS RECEIVABLE AS A PERCENTAGE OF SALES Once again, accounts receivable as a percentage of sales as captured in such measures as DSO is a leading signal of this fraud. (Refer to Sunbeam's signals in Chapter 3, "The Sizzling Saga of Sunbeam.")

SIGNAL #2: CFFO FALLS BEHIND OPERATING INCOME Also, CFFO lagging reported operating income or net income is a strong signal of a possible overstatement of revenue in the income statement. When examining financial statements, one must be concerned when the reported income is not being earned in cash.

SIGNAL #3: DEFERRED REVENUE DECREASES AS A PERCENTAGE OF TOTAL REVENUES In a company that sells membership subscriptions, deferred revenue decreasing as a percentage of total revenue is an indication that the company may be aggressively recognizing subscription revenues that will actually be earned only in future periods. This falsely boosts current revenues and earnings at the expense of future periods.

SIGNAL #4: PRECISELY MEETING ANALYSTS' TARGETS Yet again, when a company precisely meets analysts' earnings and revenue expectations quarter after quarter, it is often a sign that things may be too good to be true. SEC enforcement actions frequently comment on how companies in violation of reporting standards consistently met their own earnings targets.

SIGNAL #5: FIXED COSTS REMAINING A CONSTANT PERCENTAGE OF SALES When major expense items remain identical quarter after quarter as a percentage of revenues, it is frequently a signal that the reported expenses and revenues are being manipulated. This is an especially strong alert when an expense contains a significant fixed-cost element. One would expect a fixed-expense component to increase as a percentage of revenues when revenues decrease. Likewise, it would be expected that the fixed-cost component of an expense would decrease as a percentage of revenues when revenues increase.

ARE THEY LIVING HAPPILY EVER AFTER?

- **E. Kirk Shelton,** former CUC president and COO was convicted in January 2005 by a federal jury "of all 12 counts of an indictment: including conspiring to fraudulently inflate reported earnings at Cendant and at a predecessor company, CUC International" ("E. Kirk Shelton Is Guilty," 2005). On August 3, 2005, he was sentenced to ten years in prison and ordered to pay $3.27 billion to Cendant (Haigh, 2005). He appealed the sentence but lost the appeal and was ordered to serve his original ten-year sentence (Farrell, 2006). In addition, in June 2010, the SEC barred Shelton from ever serving as an officer or a director of a public company (LR 21548, 2010).
- **Cosmo Corigliano, Anne Pember, and Casper Sabatino,** three of Shelton's co-conspirators, each pleaded guilty in federal courts under plea agreements in which "the three defendants admitted participating in the conspiracy and acting under the instruction of their superiors" ("E. Kirk Shelton Is Guilty," 2005). In January 2007, Pember and Sabatino were sentenced to two years of probation and 200 hours of community service (Taub, 2007, Jan. 29). Corigliano was sentenced to three years of probation. In addition, his sentencing included six months of home confinement, electronic monitoring, and a total of 300 hours of community service. Corigliano apologized and took full responsibility for his actions. "I realize it was very wrong," Corigliano reportedly told the judge. "My one wish is I had clarity of mind" (Taub, 2007, Jan. 30).
- **Walter Forbes,** former CUC chairman and CEO, stood trial with Shelton. Forbes's case ended in a mistrial. A retrial began in October 2005 in Hartford, Connecticut (Mills & Voreacos, 2005). The retrial ended in February 2006, with the jury unable to reach a verdict and the judge declaring another mistrial ("Another Cendant Hung Jury," 2006). In early 2007, Mr. Forbes was finally sentenced to 12 years and 7 months in federal prison. He was also ordered to pay Cendant and its investors over $3 billion in restitution ("Ex-Cendant Chairman . . . ," 2007). While in jail, Mr. Forbes sold his Canaan, Connecticut mansion in the fall of 2010 for a reported $7 million (Kershaw, 2010).
- **Mary Polverari** settled with the SEC without admission or denial of illegal behavior. Polverari agreed to pay a civil penalty of $25,000 (Norris & Henriques, 2000).

INSIGNIA: RETURN TO SENDER

Insignia is presented here mainly as an example of Improper Valuation of Revenue.

Insignia Solutions was a publicly traded British company that did business in the United States through its subsidiary company, Insignia Solutions, Inc. It developed and supported cross-platform compatibility software, which it generally sold to resellers, to whom it granted certain rights of return. Insignia specialized in software that allowed "operators of mobile devices [to] update and repair them remotely . . ." (Graebner, 2006).

THE INSIGNIA SCHEME OF FAILING TO VALUE REVENUE CORRECTLY

The SOX Report (2002) listed Insignia Solutions PLC as an example of the failure to value revenue properly via providing **inadequate allowances for returns**. This means that the amount the company had set aside in the income statement to allow for customer returns was insufficient. The SEC found that Insignia Solutions allegedly "overstated its Revenue and Net Income . . . [and] . . . understated its allowance for returns" for the first and second quarters of 1996.[9] Insignia had a standard practice of recording an allowance for returns—in respect of inventory at resellers—that exceeded an estimated 45 days of sales: "In effect, Insignia subtracted this allowance from its gross revenue to arrive at revenue." Therefore, if Insignia understated the amount of inventory held by its resellers, this would cause it to understate its allowance for returns and overstate its revenue. This was the method the company used for the improper valuation of its revenue. The Commission's findings quoted Insignia's own revenue recognition policy as stating that revenue is "recognized upon shipment if no significant vendor obligations remain and if collection of the resulting receivables is deemed probable." (Quotes from AAER 1133, 1999)

In December 1995, the sales manager effected a shipment of $1.2 million to a reseller. A side letter was signed, giving the reseller generous rights of return. According to the SEC release of May 1999, "After the shipment, the supervisors instructed a subordinate to 'drop the zero' or report only 10% of the inventory held by the reseller. . . . This had the effect of decreasing Insignia's allowance for product returns, thereby increasing reported revenue" (AAER 1133, 1999).

No restatement was needed for this in 1995 because there was a large enough allowance for returns at that point. However, at the end of the first quarter of 1996, when most of the goods were still unsold, the Commission found this resulted in the revenue being overstated by $1.1 million. Also, because the later return of the goods due to obsolescence was concealed from the finance department, a replacement order was recorded as a new sale. Further, in June 1996, a sale of $750,000 with a 60-day right of return was recognized without an allowance for returns.

Insignia restated its financial statements for the first and second quarters of 1996. It reported restated revenue of $13.1 million in the first quarter, compared to $14.7 million previously reported. For the second quarter, the company reported restated revenue of $14.9 million, compared to $15.7 million previously reported.

On February 27, 1997, Insignia announced that it was restating its financial statements for the first two quarters of 1996. Following this announcement, the company's shares fell 35 percent, from $3.88 to $2.53, in one day.

SIGNALS OF INSIGNIA'S FICTITIOUS REPORTING SCHEME OF FAILING TO VALUE REVENUE PROPERLY

Since overstatement of revenue via failing to provide adequate allowances for returns leads to accounts receivable that do not get realized in the form of cash, the first two signals that follow are the same as the major signals for the overstatements of revenue

---

[9]Insignia consented to the order without admitting or denying the findings. As set out in AAER 1133, 1999.

discussed in the Sunbeam case in Chapter 3, "The Sizzling Saga of Sunbeam." The second two signals listed are related specifically to manipulation of the allowance for returns.

SIGNAL #1: INCREASE IN ACCOUNTS RECEIVABLE AS A PERCENTAGE OF SALES The leading sign of an overstatement of sales is when accounts receivable increase as a percentage of sales, which is often measured as DSO. If the next period's sales have been accelerated into the current period or if the sales are completely fictitious, the company will debit accounts receivable and credit sales, as for legitimate sales. However, whereas legitimate sales will be paid relatively soon by the customers and will turn into cash, the next period's sales will probably only be paid next period and will remain on the balance sheet in the current period as accounts receivable instead of turning into cash.

SIGNAL #2: CFFO FALLING BEHIND OPERATING INCOME The second signal of inappropriately recorded sales is when CFFO lags, or falls behind, operating income or net income. This is a prime signal. If a company is operating at a profit, why would it not be generating CFFO at a similar pace?

SIGNAL #3: DECREASE IN ALLOWANCE FOR RETURNS If the company separately reports the amount of its allowance for returns, a significant decrease in allowances for returns as a percentage of sales is a signal that the allowance for returns may be understated.

SIGNAL #4: CHANGE IN ACCOUNTING POLICY Any reference in the financial statements' notes to a change in policy regarding the method of recognizing the allowance for returns or any changes in estimates for returns that lead to decreasing the allowance should be taken as signals that the company may be understating its returns.

ARE THEY LIVING HAPPILY EVER AFTER?

- **Insignia** was briefly in danger of losing its listing on the Nasdaq due to falling out of compliance with Nasdaq capitalization requirements. However, the company obtained additional funding, and in January 2006, Nasdaq agreed that Insignia could "continue to be listed on the exchange" (Graebner, 2006).
- In December 2009, Insignia was taken over by America's Suppliers, Inc. "Insignia is now a wholly owned subsidiary of ASI" ("Insignia Solutions," 2009).

Key Terms

Discounted future cash flows *99*

FOB destination *96*

Holding books open *95*

Improper revenue recognition *95*

Inadequate allowances for returns *106*

Premature revenue recognition *97*

Slow shipping *96*

Top-side entries *103*

ETHICS AT WORK

Questions:

a. Approaching ethics from a *deontological* framework, discuss whether or not Xerox's management was unethical in issuing financial statements that accelerated Xerox's revenue recognition. (Refer to Chapter 2, "Ethics at Work," for a description of the ethical frameworks.)

b. Past SEC Chairman Arthur Levitt (1998) stated that numerous companies "operate in the gray area between legitimacy and outright fraud." He also noted, "Integrity may be losing out to illusion." Keeping Levitt's comments in mind, consider a situation in which a company's financial statements comply with GAAP but nevertheless present a misleading picture of the company's operating performance and its financial position. Is it unethical for management to issue such financial statements? Should companies abide by the letter of the law or the spirit of the law? Explain.

Assignments

TRUE/FALSE QUESTIONS

Answer the following questions with T for true or F for false for more practice with key terms and concepts from this chapter.

1. Sensormatic is presented in the text as an example of overstating revenue via recording fictitious revenue.

   T   F

2. Sensormatic also overstated its revenues by shipping goods before the customer needed them and instructing the carrier to delay delivery.

   T   F

3. Sensormatic overstated its earnings by creating false reserves in one period and reversing those reserves into earnings in future periods.

   T   F

4. It was fully legitimate for Xerox to record the present value of the future period's payments for servicing equipment in the period in which the leases were concluded.

   T   F

5. When a company factors or sells its accounts receivable, it is required to disclose this information in its annual report.

   T   F

6. Xerox's sale of its account receivable increased its reported CFFO.

   T   F

7. When a company sells its accounts receivable, the signal of its accounts receivable increasing as a percentage of sales is diluted.

   T   F

8. When a company sells its accounts receivable, it is important to deduct the amount received on the sale from CFFO before comparing CFFO to operating income when looking for signals of overstatement of revenues.

   T   F

9. When a company overstates its earnings via the use of top-side adjustments, the general ledger balances do not reflect the amounts shown in the financial statements.

   T   F

10. Insignia's understatement of its allowance for returns is an example of improper valuation of revenue.

    T   F

FILL-IN-THE-BLANK QUESTIONS

Fill in the blanks with information and concepts from this chapter.

11. According to AAER 1017, at Sensormatic shortly before midnight on the last day of the quarter, the computer system that _____ and _____ shipments was manipulated to change the date and time on the computer clock.

12. Sensormatic shipped goods that customers had ordered for the next period to Sensormatic's own _____ at the end of the current period.

13. Xerox presents an example of the misuse of multiple-element contracts or _____ contracts.

14. For sales-type leases, GAAP requires the financing revenue to be recognized over the _____ of the _____.

15. When accounts receivable are factored or sold, this _____ the signal of CFFO lagging behind operating income.

16. When a company sells its accounts receivable, it is important to _____ the amount received to accounts receivable *before* comparing accounts receivable to sales.

17. CUC transferred some amounts from _____ club membership revenues to current periods' revenues.

18. Regarding CUC's _____- _____ adjustments, no entries were made to CUC's general ledger.

19. In a company that sells membership subscriptions, deferred revenue _____ as a percentage of total revenue is an indication that the company may be overstating revenues.

20. Insignia subtracted its allowance for _____ from its gross revenue to arrive at net revenue.

MULTIPLE-CHOICE QUESTIONS

21. Sensormatic's overstatement of earnings via holding its books open after the close of a reporting period is an example of:
    (a) Recording fictitious revenue.
    (b) Improper timing of revenue.
    (c) Improper valuation of revenue.
    (d) None of the above.

22. Xerox's bundled sales were improperly recorded in its financial statements because:
    (a) All of the revenue streams for its leases should have been recorded over the life of the leases.
    (b) Some of the revenue relating to the finance charges included in monthly lease payments over the life of the leases was recognized upon the signing of the lease agreements and delivery of the goods.

    (c) The revenue (known as box revenue) related to making the equipment available to the customer—and paid over the life of the lease—was recorded in Xerox's financial statements in the period in which the lease agreements were signed and the equipment was delivered.
    (d) Future lease payments should not be discounted when revenue is recorded.

23. According to the SEC's AAER, which of the following fictitious practices was/were used by Xerox in preparing it financial statements?
    (a) Improper estimates of discount rates in recognizing its income.
    (b) Holding its books open at the close of a reporting period.
    (c) Improper estimates of residual values of leased items.
    (d) Both (a) and (c).

24. Jay Company sells $100,000 of its accounts receivable. To test whether any of the signals of overstatement of sales are present, it will be necessary to:
    (a) Add $100,000 back to its accounts receivable amount before calculating its accounts receivable as a percentage of sales.
    (b) Add $100,000 to both its accounts receivable and its sales amounts before calculating its accounts receivable as a percentage of sales.
    (c) Add $100,000 to its CFFO before comparing CFFO to operating income.
    (d) Deduct $100,000 from both its CFFO and its operating income before comparing them to each other.

25. CUC's use of top-side adjustments to overstate its earnings is an example of:
    (a) Improper timing of revenue recognition.
    (b) Recording of fictitious revenue.
    (c) Improper valuation of revenue.
    (d) None of the above.

26. When CUC transferred some amounts for deferred club membership revenues to current period revenues, it had the following effect on CUC's financial statements.
    (a) Increasing the deferred revenue amount on the balance sheet.

(b) Decreasing the prepaid asset amount on the balance sheet.

(c) Decreasing the deferred revenue amount on the balance sheet.

(d) Decreasing expenses on the income statement.

27. According to the SEC's AAER, which of the following was a method used by CUC to overstate its earnings?
(a) Falsification of sales documents.
(b) Side agreements with customers that were not recorded.
(c) Creation of cookie-jar merger reserves.
(d) All of the above.

28. Insignia's understatement of its allowance for returns is an example of overstating revenue via:
(a) Improper valuation of revenue recognition.
(b) Improper timing of revenue recognition.
(c) Recording of fictitious revenue.
(d) None of the above.

29. Which of the following manipulations by the lessor would have the effect of overstating revenues for sales-type leases?
(a) Selling or factoring legitimate sales-type leases.
(b) Using a higher discount rate when discounting future lease payments.
(c) Overstating the estimated residual values of its leased assets.
(d) None of the above.

30. When Xerox factored or sold its accounts receivable to avoid reclassifying them as operating leases instead of sales-type leases, this had the effect of:
(a) Decreasing the amount of revenue it reported.
(b) Increasing the amount of revenue it reported.
(c) Decreasing its reported CFFO.
(d) None of the above.

FOR DISCUSSION

31. Issuers of financial statements that fail to disclose that accounts receivable have been sold or factored sometimes attempt to offer the defense that this is *only* a disclosure issue that does not affect earnings. If the nondisclosure of the sale of accounts receivable does not affect earnings, does this reduce the responsibility of management to properly disclose the sale of accounts receivable? Give reasons for your answer.

32. Xerox sold $400 million of its South American lease agreements. Explain Xerox's possible incentive for selling those accounts receivable.

SHORT-ANSWER QUESTIONS

33. If a company sells or factors a material portion of its accounts receivable, what adjustments must you make to accounts receivable before doing your test to see whether the financial statements contain any signals indicating an overstatement of sales? Explain why.

34. Explain why overstating sales by holding books open after the close of a period would cause CFFO to lag behind operating income.

35. If a company sells a significant portion of its accounts receivable, what adjustments must you make to CFFO before testing whether the financial statements contain signals of overstatement of earnings? Explain why these adjustments should be made.

36. Why are multiple-element lease contracts a fertile ground for overstating revenue?

37. Explain how deferred revenue can be misused to overstate earnings.

EXERCISES

38. XYZ Co. is an equipment leasing company. The following is an extract from its income statement for the previous three years.

	Year 1 $	Year 2 $	Year 3 $
Revenues	4,000	6,000	8,000

The following is an extract from XYZ's notes to its financial statements:

Note: Revenues

All revenues reported are in respect of sales type leases. Included in the majority of lessees' monthly payments are amounts for financing and for servicing of equipment. The servicing fees for years 1, 2, and 3 were $400, $300, and $200 respectively. The financing revenue for years 1, 2, and 3 were $400, $600, and $800, respectively.

Calculate servicing revenue and financing revenue as a percentage of total revenue for years 1–3 and then comment on your findings.

39. Examine the following extracts from Blake Co.'s income statement and balance sheet for the previous three years.

Income Statement	Year 1	Year 2	Year 3
	$	$	$
Sales	6,000	9,000	12,000
Operating Income	1,500	2,100	2,400

Balance Sheet	Year 1	Year 2	Year 3
	$	$	$
Accounts receivable	1,200	1,800	2,400

You also read in the financial press that Blake Co. sold $2,000 of its accounts receivable in year 3.

Required

a. Calculate the ratio of accounts receivable as a percentage of sales for years 1, 2, and 3 without taking into account what you read about the sale of Blake's accounts receivable.

b. Calculate the ratio of accounts receivable as a percentage of sales for years 1, 2, and 3 after adjusting for the sale of Blake's accounts receivable.

40. Examine these extracts from Collin Company's income statements and statements of cash flow for the previous three years.

Income Statement	Year 1	Year 2	Year 3
	$	$	$
Operating income	1,000	1,000	1,000

Statement of Cash Flows	Year 1	Year 2	Year 3
	$	$	$
Cash flow from operating activities	1,000	1,000	1,000

You also read in the notes to the financial statements that Collin Company sold $1,000 of its accounts receivable in year 3. Adjust for the sale of accounts receivable in year 3 and calculate CFFO as a percentage of operating income for years 1–3.

CASE STUDY

PEREGRINE SYSTEMS. INC.

- **Read** Litigation Release No. 18205A for Peregrine Systems, Inc., given below.
- **Examine** the financial statements of Peregrine Systems for the following year-ends: March 31, 1999; March 21, 2000; and March 21, 2001, given below.
- **Respond** to the Case Study questions.

Required

a. **Overstatement of Revenue Scheme:** Litigation Release (LR) No. 18205A describes the ways in which Peregrine overstated its revenue in its financial statements.

1. Identify and briefly describe Peregrine's main methods of overstating its revenue.

2. Examine Peregrine's financial statements for the following yearends: March 31, 1999; March 31, 2000; and March 31, 2001. Consider "accounts receivable as a percentage of sales" as a possible signal indicating that Peregrine overstated its revenue. Perform your calculations for this signal without any knowledge of sales of accounts receivables and without any knowledge of misclassification of the write-off of accounts receivable as "acquisition costs." Comment on your findings.

b. **Improper "Sales" of Accounts Receivable and Improper Disclosure of "Sales" of Accounts Receivable:** Describe Peregrine's scheme of improperly "selling" its accounts receivable and improperly disclosing its "sales" of accounts receivable.

c. **Improper Classification of Write-Off of Accounts Receivable as "Acquisition Costs":** According to the SEC, "[A]s part of the cover up, Peregrine personnel wrote off millions of dollars in uncollectible—primarily sham—receivables, to acquisition-related accounts" (LR 18205A).

1. Explain how this would affect the signal of CFFO lagging, or falling behind, operating income that would normally indicate an overstatement of revenue.

2. Explain how the improper write-off of accounts receivable as "acquisition costs" would affect the signal of accounts receivable increasing as a percentage of sales.

d. **Calculation of Accounts Receivable as a Percentage of the Trailing 12 Months' Sales:** Now examine Exhibit 4.1 below and use the sales and receivable amounts from Peregrine's quarterly financial statements to calculate accounts receivable as a percentage of the trailing 12 months' sales for fiscal 2000-Q3, 2000-Q4, and 2001-Q1. Comment on your calculations as a signal of overstatement of revenue.

e. **Recalculation of Accounts Receivable for Comparison with Sales:** Consider the following information: The SEC complaint* alleged that there was a plan for Peregrine to write off $26.65 million of channel receivables as "Acquisition Costs and Other" (par. 28) in fiscal 2001.

Assume that this amount was written off accounts receivable. Now add the amount back to accounts receivable and recalculate accounts receivable as a percentage of sales that you calculated in Case Study question a2 above. Comment on the new calculation as a signal of overstatement of sales.

EXHIBIT 4.1   Extracts from Peregrine's Quarterly Financial Statements (in Thousands) 1999–2001[10]

	Mar. 31-1999	June 30-1999	Sept. 30-1999	Dec. 31-1999	Mar. 31-2000	June 30-2000
Sales	46,110	51,605	57,807	67,544	76,344	94,324
Accounts Receivable	38,947	43,737	51,058	59,629	69,940	127,845

*Case No. 03 CV. United States District Court for the Southern District of California. June 2003. *www.sec.gov*.

[10] Obtained from U.S. Securities and Exchange Commission. *www.sec.gov*

Litigation Release for Peregrine Systems, Inc.

U.S. Securities and Exchange Commission

Litigation Release No. 18205A/June 30, 2003*

Accounting and Auditing Enforcement Release No. 1808/June 30, 2003

Securities and Exchange Commission v. Peregrine Systems, Inc., Civil Action No. 03 CV 1276 K (LAB) (S.D. Cal.) (June 30, 2003)

SEC Charges Peregrine Systems, Inc. With Financial Fraud And Agrees To Partial Settlement

The Securities and Exchange Commission today sued San Diego-based software company Peregrine Systems, Inc., in the United States District Court for the Southern District of California, for a massive financial fraud at the company that spanned 11 fiscal quarters. Simultaneously with the filing of the complaint, the Commission submitted to the Court, for its approval, a partial settlement with Peregrine.

According to the Commission's complaint, the purpose of the fraudulent scheme was to inflate the company's revenue and stock price. To achieve that end, Peregrine filed materially incorrect financial statements with the Commission concerning the quarter ended June 30, 1999, through the quarter ended December 31, 2001. In 2003 Peregrine restated its financial results for those quarters. In its restatement, Peregrine reduced previously reported revenue of $1.34 billion by $509 million, of which at least $259 million was reversed because the underlying transactions lacked substance.

The complaint alleges that Peregrine improperly booked millions of dollars of revenue for purported software license sales to resellers. These transactions were non-binding sales of Peregrine software with the understanding—reflected in secret side agreements—that the resellers were not obligated to pay Peregrine. Those involved in the scheme called this "parking" the transaction. Peregrine personnel parked transactions when Peregrine was unable to complete direct sales it was negotiating (or hoping to negotiate) with end-users, but needed revenue to achieve its forecasts. Peregrine engaged in other deceptive practices to inflate the company's revenue, including entering into reciprocal transactions in which Peregrine essentially paid for its customers' purchases of Peregrine software. Peregrine routinely kept its books open after fiscal quarters ended, and improperly recorded as revenue, for the prior quarter, software transactions that were not consummated until after quarter end. Certain Peregrine officers characterized these transactions as having been completed on "the 37th of December." Peregrine senior officers, and sales and finance personnel knew, or were reckless in not knowing, that the applicable accounting rules prohibited revenue recognition on these and other transactions for which Peregrine booked revenue.

The complaint alleges that, by various means, certain Peregrine officers and employees fraudulently concealed the revenue inflation scheme. When Peregrine booked revenue for the non-binding reseller contracts, and the customers predictably did not pay, receivables—some of them bogus—ballooned on Peregrine's balance sheet.

---

*Obtained from U.S. Securities and Exchange Commission. *www.sec.gov*. Peregrine agreed to a partial settlement without admitting or denying the findings.

Large aged accounts receivable were not being paid, an indication that Peregrine's financial health was deteriorating. To make it appear to investors that Peregrine was collecting its receivables more quickly than it was, a senior officer entered into financing arrangements with banks to exchange receivables for cash. Peregrine improperly accounted for these financing arrangements as sales of the receivables and removed them from the company's balance sheet. There were several problems with this. First, because Peregrine had given the banks recourse, and frequently paid or repurchased unpaid receivables from them, Peregrine should have accounted for the financing arrangements as loans and left the receivables on its balance sheet. Second, some of the "sold" receivables were not valid because the customers were not obligated to pay Peregrine. Third, several of the "sold" invoices were fake. For example, in June 2001, Peregrine's senior treasury manager, with senior management's approval and encouragement, created a false $19.59 million invoice and sold it to a bank. As a result, Peregrine's financial statements and books and records overstated Peregrine's cash flow from operations, and understated its accounts receivable.

The complaint also alleges that, as part of the cover up, Peregrine personnel wrote off millions of dollars in uncollectible—primarily sham—receivables, to acquisition-related accounts in Peregrine's financial statements and books and records. These write-offs were improper because they had nothing to do with acquisitions, and because the Peregrine personnel who directed the write-offs knew, or were reckless in not knowing, that certain written-off receivables should not have been recorded as revenue in the first place. Peregrine misled investors by not including the write-offs in its pro forma operating results, and by making the write-offs appear on Peregrine's income statement as one-time charges rather than expenses from operations. Through its officers and employees, Peregrine knew that (a) a substantial portion of these receivables should not have been recorded as revenue in the first place, (b) the receivables were not impaired by acquisitions, and (c) it was inappropriate to make it appear to the investing public that the write-offs related to non-recurring events.

The Commission's complaint seeks to permanently enjoin Peregrine from violating certain antifraud provisions of the federal securities laws (Section 17(a) of the Securities Act of 1933, Section 10(b) of the Securities Exchange Act of 1934 (Exchange Act) and Exchange Act Rule 10b-5), and from violating certain reporting, books and records, and internal controls provisions (Exchange Act Sections 13(a), 13(b)(2)(A) and 13(b)(2)(B), and Exchange Act Rules 12b-20, 13a-1, and 13a-13). The complaint also seeks disgorgement of ill-gotten gains, prejudgment interest, and civil monetary penalties.

Peregrine, without admitting or denying the allegations of the Commission's complaint, has agreed (1) to be enjoined from violating the antifraud, reporting, books and records, and internal controls provisions of the federal securities laws, (2) to disclose the current condition of its internal controls and financial reporting procedure, when a reorganization plan under Chapter 11 of the Bankruptcy Code becomes effective, (3) to comply, on an accelerated basis, with the rules regarding management's report on internal controls, implementing Section 303 of the Sarbanes-Oxley Act of 2002, (4) to retain an Internal Auditor to ensure that Peregrine's financial results are accurately reported in Peregrine's public financial statements, (5) to appoint a Corporate Compliance Officer to perform an ongoing review of Peregrine's corporate governance policies and practices, and (6) to commence a training and education program for its officers and employees, to prevent violations of the federal securities laws. The partial settlement provides that the amount of disgorgement and/or civil penalty to be paid by Peregrine, if any, shall be determined at a later date. In determining to accept Peregrine's offer of partial settlement, the Commission considered remedial acts promptly undertaken by Peregrine and cooperation afforded the Commission staff.

This is the fourth civil fraud action the Commission has filed in this investigation. In November 2002, the Commission filed a civil injunctive action against Ilse Cappel, the former senior treasury manager at Peregrine (Litigation Release No. 17859A). In April 2003, the Commission filed a civil injunctive action against Matthew C. Gless, Peregrine's former chief financial officer (Litigation Release No. 18093). In June 2003, the Commission filed a civil injunctive action against Steven S. Spitzer, a former vice president of sales at Peregrine (Litigation Release No. 18191).

The Commission's investigation of participants in the financial fraud at Peregrine is continuing.

The Commission thanks the U.S. Attorney's Office for the Southern District of California and the Federal Bureau of Investigation for their cooperation in this matter.

FINANCIAL STATEMENTS

UNITED STATES
SECURITIES AND EXCHANGE COMMISSION
Washington, D.C. 20549

Extracts from FORM 10-K[11]
Annual report pursuant to Section 13 or 15(d) of the Securities Exchange Act of 1934

For the fiscal year ended March 31, 2001

PEREGRINE SYSTEMS, INC.

CONSOLIDATED BALANCE SHEETS
(IN THOUSANDS, EXCEPT PER SHARE AMOUNTS)

	MARCH 31, 2001	MARCH 31, 2000
ASSETS		
Current Assets:		
Cash and cash equivalents	$ 286,658	$ 33,511
Accounts receivable, net of allowance for doubtful accounts of $11,511 and $2,179, respectively	180,372	69,940
Other current assets	62,811	22,826
Total current assets	529,841	126,277
		(continued)

[11] Extracted from 10-K filings for Peregrine Systems, Inc. 1998-2002. Obtained from U.S. Securities and Exchange Commission. *www.sec.gov.*

	MARCH 31, 2001	MARCH 31, 2000
Property and equipment, net	82,717	29,537
Goodwill, net of accumulated amortization of $334,178 and $54,406, respectively.	1,192,855	233,504
Other intangible assets, investments and other, net of accumulated amortization of $24,015 and $1,398, respectively.	198,353	134,112
	$2,003,766	$523,430
LIABILITIES AND STOCKHOLDERS' EQUITY		
Current Liabilities:		
Accounts payble	$ 36,024	$ 19,850
Accrued expenses	200,886	49,064
Current portion of deferred revenue	86,653	36,779
Current portion of long-term debt	1,731	74
Total current liabilities	325,294	105,767
Deferred revenue, net of current portion	8,299	4,556
Other long-term liabilities	17,197	—
Long-term debt, net of current portion.	884	1,257
Convertible subordinated notes	262,327	—
Total liabilities	614,001	111,580
Stockholders' Equity:		
Preferred stock, $0.001 par value, 5,000 shares authorized, no shares issued or outstanding	—	—
Common stock, $0.001 par value, 500,000 shares authorized, 160,359 and 109,501 shares issued and outstanding, respectively.	160	110
Additional paid-in capital.	2,342,235	480,957
Accumulated deficit	(917,104)	(64,863)
Unearned portion of deferred compensation.	(22,151)	(678)
Cumulative translation adjustment	(3,950)	(666)
Treasury stock, at cost	(9,425)	(3,010)
Total stockholders' equity	1,389,765	411,850
	$2,003,766	$523,430

(continued)

Extracts from FORM 10-K[12]

For the fiscal year ended March 31, 1999

PEREGRINE SYSTEMS, INC.

CONSOLIDATED BALANCE SHEETS

(IN THOUSANDS, EXCEPT SHARE AMOUNTS)

	MARCH 31,	
	1998	1999
ASSETS		
Current Assets:		
Cash and cash equivalents	$ 14,950	$ 21,545
Short-term investments	7,027	2,000
Accounts receivable, net of allowance for doubtful accounts of $485 and $1,248, respectively	16,761	38,947
Deferred tax assets	7,297	5,798
Other current assets	2,905	10,370
Total current assets	48,940	78,660
Property and equipment, net	5,455	15,895
Intangible assets, net and other	29,173	113,158
	$ 83,568	$207,713

Extracts from FORM 10-K[13]

For the fiscal year ended March 31, 2001

PEREGRINE SYSTEMS, INC.

CONSOLIDATED STATEMENTS OF OPERATIONS

(IN THOUSANDS, EXCEPT PER SHARE AMOUNTS)

	YEAR ENDED MARCH 31,		
	2001	2000	1999
Revenues:			
Licenses	$ 354,610	$168,467	$ 87,362
Services	210,073	84,833	50,701
Total revenues	564,683	253,300	138,063
Costs and Expenses:			
Cost of licenses	2,582	1,426	1,020
Cost of services	111,165	51,441	31,561
Amortization of purchased technology	11,844	1,338	50

(continued)

---

[12] Extracted from 10-K filings for Peregrine Systems, Inc. Obtained from U.S. Securities and Exchange Commission. *www.sec.gov.*

[13] Extracted from 10-K filings for Peregrine Systems, Inc. Obtained from U.S. Securities and Exchange Commission. *www.sec.gov.*

	YEAR ENDED MARCH 31,		
	2001	**2000**	**1999**
Sales and marketing	223,966	101,443	50,803
Research and development	61,957	28,517	13,919
General and administrative	48,420	19,871	10,482
Acquisition costs and other	918,156	57,920	43,967
Total costs and expenses	1,378,090	261,956	151,802
Loss from operations before interest			
(net) and income tax expense	(813,407)	(8,656)	(13,739)
Interest income (expense), net	(538)	38	664
Loss from operations before income tax			
expense	(813,945)	(8,618)	(13,075)
Income tax expense	38,296	16,452	10,295
Net loss	$ (852,241)	$ (25,070)	$ (23,370)
Net loss per share basic and diluted:			
Net loss per share	$ (6.16)	$ (0.24)	$ (0.27)
Shares used in computation	138,447	102,332	87,166

Peregrine Systems, Inc.

CONSOLIDATED STATEMENTS OF CASH FLOWS

(IN THOUSANDS)

	YEAR ENDED MARCH 31,		
	2001	**2000**	**1999**
Cash flows from operating activities:			
Net loss	$ (852,241)	$(25,070)	$(23,370)
Adjustments to reconcile net loss to net cash (used in) provided by operating activities:			
Depreciation, amortization, acquisition costs and other	954,231	68,293	47,781
Increase (decrease) in cash resulting from changes in:			
Accounts receivable	(100,474)	(24,364)	(18,984)
Other current assets	(25,955)	1,485	(5,678)
Other assets	7,648	2,717	(245)
Accounts payable and other liabilities	18,563	4,755	2,939
Accrued expenses	(32,794)	17,328	12,486
Deferred revenue	20,851	12,467	4,874
Net cash (used in) provided by operating activities	(10,171)	57,611	19,803
Cash flows from investing activities:			
Acquisitions and investments, net of cash acquired	17,974	(41,249)	(11,128)
Purchases of short-term investments	—	—	(49,000)
Maturities of short-term investments	—	2,000	54,027
Purchases of property and equipment	(49,031)	(20,713)	(12,426)
Net cash used in investing activities	(31,057)	(59,962)	(18,527)

(continued)

	YEAR ENDED MARCH 31,		
	2001	**2000**	**1999**
Cash flows from financing activities:			
Issuance (repayments) of long-term debt	1,284	(7,832)	(1,174)
Issuance of common stock	42,501	23,427	7,921
Issuance of notes receivable	(1,611)	—	—
Treasury stock purchased	(6,415)	(1,285)	(1,463)
Issuance of convertible subordinated notes	261,900	—	—
Net cash provided by financing activities	297,659	14,310	5,284
Effect of exchange rate changes on cash	(3,284)	7 35	
Net increase in cash and cash equivalents	253,147	11,966	6,595
Cash and cash equivalents, beginning of period	33,511	21,545	14,950
Cash and cash equivalents, end of period	$ 286,658	$ 33,511	$ 21,545
Cash paid during the period for:			
Interest	$ 1,069	$ 451	$ 26
Income taxes	$ 1,587	$ 3,015	$ 155
Supplemental Disclosure of Noncash Investing Activities:			
Stock issued and other noncash consideration for acquisitions and investments	$1,762,952	$253,209	$105,499

WorldCom Wizardry: From WorldCom to WorldCon[1]

Learning Objectives

After studying this chapter, you should be able to:

- Identify WorldCom's improper accounting in connection with business combinations (via improper use of acquisition or merger reserves and improper asset valuation).
- Recognize WorldCom's improper capitalization of expenses.
- Identify and explain the signals in the financial statements that could alert you to the possibility that a company may be overstating its earnings by improper use of acquisition or merger reserves.
- Identify and explain the signals in the financial statements that could alert you to the possibility that a company may be understating its expenses via improper capitalization of expenses.
- Describe each of the major categories of gatekeepers that the WorldCom Bankruptcy Examiner identified as being responsible for the overall control of a company.

WorldCom is presented mainly as an example of:

- Improper accounting in connection with business combinations via improper use of acquisition or merger reserves and improper asset valuation
- Improper capitalization of expenses

---

[1] Background information in this chapter is mainly from Jeter (2002), Krim (2002), Malik (2003), *First Interim Report of Dick Thornburgh* (2002), *Second Interim Report of Dick Thornburgh* (2003), and *Third and Final Report of Dick Thornburgh* (2004).

CHAPTER OUTLINE

- The Wizards of WorldCom
- The Acquisitions Spree
- Problems at WorldCom
- An Overview of WorldCom's Fictitious Financial Reporting Schemes
- The Collapse of Wizard World

- The Gatekeepers Who Failed WorldCom
- Signals of the WorldCom Fraud
- Key Terms
- Ethics at Work
- Assignments
- Case Study: Tyco International, Ltd.

THE WIZARDS OF WORLDCOM

During a CNBC television interview hosted by David Faber in September 2003, Robert Hudspeth, a former WorldCom vice president, described how there appeared to have been a discrepancy between WorldCom's internal numbers and the numbers touted on Wall Street. Hudspeth added that it had been hard to explain to members of his 4,000-person sales force why investors were told that WorldCom's revenue was increasing while the sales force knew that revenue was declining (Faber, 2003). A few years after that television interview, several WorldCom officers were found guilty of fraud.

The Chief Wizard: Bernard Ebbers

At 6 feet 4 inches, Bernard J. Ebbers was a starter on the varsity basketball team at Victoria Composite High School in downtown Edmonton, Canada. He already had the ambiguous traits of coming across either as painfully shy or as powerfully driven and charismatic. His basketball team won the city championship in his senior year. For Bernie Ebbers and Brent Foster, best friends on the team, it looked as though that championship was going to be the peak of their careers. For a few years after high school, both spun their wheels doing odd jobs such as delivering milk. Then their former high school coach took Brent Foster on a trip to Seattle. While Foster waited for the coach in a bank, he picked up a brochure lying on a desk in the lobby—a seemingly trivial, distracted act that changed the course of so many lives. The brochure was, oddly, an advertisement for Mississippi College in the town of Clinton. The charming pictures of the campus and town looked enticing, and Foster decided that this was the fresh start that he needed.

The very traditional Mississippi College is the oldest Baptist college in America, and the town of Clinton is lined with tall, old oak trees interspersed with striking magnolias. On a subsequent visit to Mississippi College, the deeply religious and conservative young Foster had a good feeling about the college and the town, with its many grand Victorian-era homes. The fact that Clinton's city hall had been the site of General Sherman's headquarters during the siege of Jackson struck a chord with the competitive young Foster, who enrolled in the school. When Foster returned home to Edmonton for the summer, it was clear to his old high school pal, Bernard Ebbers, that Foster was back to his peak.

By the end of that summer, Bernard Ebbers joined Foster and his new wife on their honeymoon road trip back to Mississippi College. Even more devoutly Baptist than Foster, Ebbers liked the school and the town of Clinton immensely and took to southern small-town life, finding the green openness a refreshing change from downtown Edmonton. Ebbers joined the college basketball team and soon was awarded a basketball scholarship. Before long, he too was back to his peak and growing in confidence every day, his earlier shyness now counteracted by a kind of arrogant swagger.

Ebbers's basketball scholarship, however, ended after one year, when his Achilles tendon was torn by a broken bottle during a fight with some local thugs. To get by financially, he helped coach the junior varsity team. This led to a high school coaching job at nearby Hazelhurst after he graduated with a degree in physical education.

A year later Ebbers went to work for a clothing manufacturer, where he remained for five years, before buying a cheap, run-down hotel and restaurant in Columbia, Mississippi. By this time, he was married to Linda Pigott, and they had three children: Treasure, Joy, and Faith. In 1977, he combined with a few friends and began an expansion that led to nine hotels by 1983. This was the year that a court order instigated the breakup of AT&T into AT&T and seven local phone companies to allow more competition in the long-distance telephone industry. "The divestiture forced AT&T to lease long-distance phone lines at deeply discounted rates to small, regional companies who could then resell the lines' data-carrying capacity, or bandwidth, to small businesses" (Jeter, 2003, pp. 17, 18). That was the impetus for WorldCom. The actual inception of WorldCom occurred when Murray Waldron, a businessman from Tennessee, decided to get into the business of reselling long-distance phone service in country towns.

Ebbers—now living in Brookhaven, Mississippi, and running nine hotels—was introduced to this business venture by David Singleton, a friend from Ebbers's prayer group at the First Baptist Church in Brookhaven. Singleton invited Ebbers to a meeting about starting a company to resell long-distance phone service. Ebbers was aware of the court-ordered breakup of AT&T and had heard of small companies that were taking advantage of the leases that AT&T was forced to option out. He was ready to listen when he got the call from Singleton.

Waldron, Singleton, and Ebbers met with Waldron's friend, Bill Fields, in a coffee shop in Hattiesburg, Mississippi. It was September 1983. They had chosen Hattiesburg because it looked like a rural area's hub town on the map and it didn't have a long-distance phone company. Legend has two competing stories about how the company's initial name was concocted. Either way, what both stories have in common is that the first meeting about starting a company to resell long-distance phone service was in a coffee shop in Hattiesburg and that Waldron was present. One story is that the men at the meeting asked their waitress to suggest a name for their new company. On a napkin, the waitress wrote the letters *LDDC*, for "Long Distance Discount Company." The group at the meeting made one small change to "Long Distance Discount Services." At this point, LDDS, the company that was destined to evolve—with over 70 acquisitions—into the infamous WorldCom, was born. (An **acquisition** occurs when one business entity issues stock or pays cash or other assets for the voting stock of another business entity. The acquired business continues operating as a separate entity.)

Cynics of corporate folklore say that the story of the napkin and the waitress is not completely accurate and that the meeting occurred without all four founders. However, it sounded better for company mythology if the arrogant, self-conscious, yet charismatic Bernie Ebbers and the other three founders were present at the site of this slice of Americana being lived out on a cold night in an unpretentious but warm Hattiesburg coffee shop. These men were about to embark on a wild roller-coaster ride with their new company. Almost 20 years later, on July 21, 2002, that same company would declare one of the most spectacular bankruptcies in corporate history.

WorldCom, in the end, was betrayed by virtually every single entity or division entrusted with any fiduciary duty intended to guarantee the honest reporting of its financial affairs—from the preparation of the financial reports to the gatekeeping intended to provide the checks and balances to ensure the proper accounting behind the preparation of those reports. Even the board of directors abrogated its responsibility and ignored the outrageously unfocused growth of WorldCom with more than 70 uncoordinated acquisitions of other companies. The failed checks and balances listed by Richard Thornburgh, WorldCom's Bankruptcy Examiner, in his *First Interim Report* (2002), included failures by the following:

- The internal control system
- The audit committee
- The compensation and stock-option committee
- Arthur Andersen, WorldCom's external auditors
- WorldCom's Internal Audit Department
- The board of directors
- The management
- The investment banking company of Salomon Smith Barney (SSB)
- The chief investment banker and analyst Jack Grubman
- Members of WorldCom's senior accounting staff

For many years, thousands of employees, customers, corporate investors, and private individuals were hoodwinked by accounting manipulations of massive proportions. How did WorldCom spin so out of control? Why did all the checks and balances fail? How did Arthur Andersen neglect to detect the massive and poorly hidden frauds? Why did SSB's analyst recommend the deteriorating company so highly? Why did the directors allow the chaotic list of acquisitions and the colossal loans to Bernie Ebbers?

After the September meeting in the Hattiesburg coffee shop, Ebbers, Singleton, Fields, and Waldron contacted friends and acquaintances. Together with an additional five investors, the nine of them incorporated LDDS with about $600,000 capital. They divided its 1,000 shares among themselves. On January 14, 1984, the first long-distance telephone call was made on LDDS's system. At this stage, LDDS basically leased bandwidth and resold it for long-distance telephone calls. The company's switching equipment, which it had purchased for $450,000, was located in a small building opposite the University of Southern Mississippi. The first customer was a realty company, Floyd Franks & Associates, which was owned by Ole Miss's former wide receiver, Floyd Franks. With Franks's recommendation, LDDS had 200 customers soon after opening. Still, it had capacity for many more customers, and with fixed costs so high, it needed to expand its customer base. (**Fixed cost** refers to a category of a business entity's expenses that one would expect to remain constant for a range of volume of units produced or services rendered.)

Also, without a technical expert to optimize the configuration of the circuits, its line costs were very high. After the AT&T breakup, LDDS wasn't the only company to get the idea of long-distance discounting. There were a number of start-ups, most of them running at a loss, just like LDDS, which was losing about $20,000 a month in 1984. By the end of that year, LDDS had gone into debt to the tune of over $1.5 million.

Ebbers took over the running of the company in 1985, and besides a ferocious focus on cutting costs, he immediately set his sights on acquiring some of the small, long-distance resellers. Between the market competition and the requirements of the Public Utility Commission, the charges to customers were more or less set. However, the cost of bandwidth depended on the volume. Larger volume led to lower costs per minute. Ebbers decided that he had to get more customers and bandwidth—and sell the bandwidth cheaper than the other small-town competitors. Most importantly, he had to do this while the big boys such as MCI were focused elsewhere. Ebbers craftily decided that the best way to increase customers and bandwidth—without getting the attention of the big players—was to buy the smaller companies. His first acquisition was The Phone Company in Jackson, Tennessee, where Waldron had once worked briefly to get experience in the telephone business. After this, Ebbers and his associates bought ReTel Communications, also in Tennessee. Next, in order to acquire a small telephone reseller in Arkansas, Ebbers convinced his colleagues to do something they would do over and over and over again until WorldCom's final bankruptcy—they issued shares in their company (LDDS) to get the cash to pay for the acquisitions.

Many folks around Brookhaven, Mississippi, became multimillionaires from the stocks they bought in LDDS in those early years. With these acquisitions, the company's sales grew and the volume of reswitching equipment grew as well. With each acquisition, the new company's revenue, assets, and profits were included with those of the original LDDS. Around that time, LDDS's first two CPAs quit the company—ostensibly because of "personality clashes." Looking back, one has to wonder if there were other reasons.

By now, Ebbers was a keen acquirer of companies and was growing into a fanatical one. He became convinced that it was time for LDDS to go public. He realized that if LDDS was listed on the stock exchange, it would be able to raise cash readily by issuing stock. Furthermore, instead of paying cash for additional acquisitions, LDDS could pay for new companies simply by issuing LDDS shares to the shareholders of those companies. As long as the publicly traded stock price of LDDS increased, there would be no end to the number of acquisitions it could make. As long as LDDS publicly *reported* increasing profits and increasing sales in its financial statements, it could carry on acquiring companies, and there would be no limit to the growth of its stock price. To Ebbers, there was no doubt—LDDS had to go public.

There were two ways that LDDS could become a public company. It could make a public offering, or it could acquire a publicly traded company, and in the process, LDDS would then become publicly listed and traded. It chose the latter approach. In 1989, LDDS purchased the publicly listed Advantage Companies, Inc., of Atlanta. With that purchase, LDDS became a public company.

The Assistant Wizard: Jack Grubman

Ebbers now had to interface with investors as well as public institutions. As a result, he had his first fateful meeting with Jack Grubman, the SSB stock analyst. Ebbers and Grubman had an instant rapport. Both had colossal ambition-to-knowledge ratios—always a dangerous set of attributes—and both were newly rich, having come from working-class roots. Both possessed the need to impress. Grubman, for example, had lied about having "attended the Massachusetts Institute of Technology" (Jeter, 2003, p. 62). Interestingly, both men also shared the need to be generous with money gained dubiously. Both were driven and troubled, yet charismatic. They formed a bond and sometimes drank beer and shot pool together.

Ebbers and Grubman would later go on to overestimate the demand for Internet traffic capacity at that time. Neither of them had much of a clue about the technicalities of either the Internet or Internet traffic or the workings of the telecom industry as a whole (Jeter, 2003).

The Accounting Wizard: Scott Sullivan

Shortly after going public, LDDS swapped some of its new publicly traded stock for stock in Advanced Telecommunications Corp. (ATC). With this transaction, Ebbers and Grubman acquired another associate who seemed very different from them. Scott Sullivan was a brilliant, quiet, reserved, and conservative young CPA who had previously audited for one of the Big Eight audit firms. Sullivan had moved to south Florida to become CFO of a telecommunications company. When Ebbers acquired ATC, he also got Sullivan, who became vice president and assistant treasurer of LDDS. Sullivan commuted from his home in Florida to a condo in Mississippi, where he seemed to be almost obsessive about his job and often worked into the early hours of the morning. He was just what Ebbers needed: a serious and seriously smart sidekick—the brains to Bernie's brawn. In spite of their differences (or perhaps because of them), Sullivan and Ebbers got along extremely well, and Sullivan became "the real force" behind Ebbers's deals (Malik, 2003, p. 7).

Sullivan apparently liked the idea of acquisitions as much as Grubman and Ebbers did—but for a different reason. Sullivan understood the potential of acquisitions to provide opportunities to manipulate the profits, or earnings, that a company reports in its financial statements. Of course, reported earnings drive share price, and a high share price can, in turn, be used to finance more acquisitions to begin the whole cycle again. Thornburgh, the WorldCom Bankruptcy Examiner would eventually explain, "WorldCom grew in large part because the value of its stock rose dramatically. Its stock was the fuel that kept WorldCom's acquisition engine running at a very high speed. WorldCom needed to keep its stock price at high levels to continue its phenomenal growth" (*First Interim Report*, 2002, p. 6).

Sullivan seemed to believe that a company didn't need actual earnings to *report* profits of a given amount. The Bankruptcy Examiner went on to observe, "WorldCom put extraordinary pressure on itself to meet the expectations of securities analysts. This pressure created an environment in which reporting numbers that met these expectations, no matter how these numbers were derived, apparently became more important than accurate financial reporting" (*First Interim Report*, 2002, p. 7).

THE ACQUISITIONS SPREE

The three men who influenced WorldCom used the company for their own convoluted reasons. Ebbers wanted the company to grow as big as possible and as fast as possible, Grubman seemed to want a leadership role in the telecom-analyst sector, and Sullivan worked on producing high reported earnings and high stock prices.

The acquisition of ATC in 1992 seemed like a good move. The lease cost of lines was high, and with ATC, Ebbers got a large supply of his own fiber-optic lines. With these lines, LDDS could use the Internet to transmit not only data but also voice and video.

At the end of 1994, on the quest for more acquisitions, LDDS acquired IDB Communications, Inc., a global satellite business that included IDB WorldCom—a company with a large international division. Possession of IDB WorldCom gave the company an international platform in Eastern Europe and eventually gave LDDS its new name, WorldCom.

Still high from that deal, Ebbers and Sullivan went on to acquire a company that had undergone a very interesting change to its core business. WilTel, previously Williams Oil and Gas, had experienced a severe drop in demand for its gas and wondered what to do about the idle capacity in its gas pipelines. When the demand for fiber-optic lines grew, it figured that it could save a great deal of money by simply threading fiber-optic lines through its existing but idle natural gas pipelines. LDDS acquired WilTel in 1995 for $2.5 billion cash, gaining a cable network with over 11,000 miles of fiber-optic cable. After that gratifying deal, Sullivan was promoted to CFO, the name of LDDS was formally changed to WorldCom, and the three cohorts were gearing up to rock the financial world.

By now, with all the acquisitions, too many companies had been added to the collection without being properly integrated into a synergetic whole. There was little liaison between the companies, and much of the work was duplicated. Employees had already started to mock WorldCom. They ridiculed the famous Michael Jordan/ WorldCom "teamwork" commercial because the various WorldCom companies actually eschewed teamwork and despised each other.

In 1996, the Telecommunications Act was passed, allowing for more competition in the local telephone market. This gave WorldCom another boost, and the company grew exponentially that year.

Ebbers's ego also continued to grow. The folksy part of his personality became more pronounced; he dressed and swaggered more and more like John Wayne. People who saw him only from afar—and he was very visible around Mississippi— couldn't get over what a down-to-earth billionaire he was, always in blue jeans and boots. He was also a big donor to a variety of civic causes and colleges all over Mississippi. In addition, WorldCom was a boon to the state, providing employment to so many Mississippi College graduates that the college even structured courses specifically for WorldCom's needs. While folks from a distance saw Ebbers as a hero, some of those closer to him were beginning to see him get meaner as he got bigger. Although he was down-to-earth around town, with his down-home clothes and his unpretentious truck, he was always on the prowl for companies. He also bought huge ranches and other properties, as well as a 60-foot yacht that he appropriately called *ACQUASITION*.

The misspelled *Acquasition* fittingly described his ego as well as his only real business strategy of collecting an increasingly out-of-focus conglomeration of companies. Ebbers was a walking mass of contradictions: devoutly religious and a generous donor, yet bad-tempered and penny-pinching. He was controlling on minute details, yet had no macro plan or focus for all the acquisitions that he was pushing through management and the board of directors at an unprecedented, frenzied pace.

The Bankruptcy Examiner would eventually assert, "WorldCom did not achieve its growth by following a predefined strategic plan, but rather by opportunistic and rapid acquisitions of other companies. The unrelenting pace of these acquisitions caused the company to constantly redefine itself and its focus" (*First Interim Report*, 2002, p. 6).

WorldCom continued to grow too fast and in too many directions. In 1996, the company set its sights on becoming a major Internet provider and turned its attention to UUNet, which was the leading Internet provider in the world at that time. UUNet had been one of the first companies to offer e-mail and Internet access to individual users. As the company began to attract a vast amount of investment money, John Sidgmore, from General Electric, was appointed CEO. UUNet then began providing large businesses the means to transmit data via the Internet. Next, the company provided hardware for Microsoft's online service, MSN. UUNet had gone public in 1995, and its stock price had soared until competition from AT&T and MCI began to knock down the price in 1996. As a result, Sidgmore led UUNet to accept a buyout offer from MFS Communications on August 12, 1996. About two weeks later, on August 26, 1996, WorldCom acquired MFS Communications, swapping WorldCom stock for MFS stock. This was a $12 billion deal whereby WorldCom acquired UUNet at the same time. By this time, UUNet had over 4 million dial-up ports for users to log on to the Internet.

With this acquisition, WorldCom had broadband and networks all over the world and had become a major provider of Internet access and data transmission. WorldCom's stock price soared on the grounds of its reported profits combined with its vast Internet capacity and the world's belief in the projected astronomical growth in Internet traffic.

The Myth of Internet Growth

Everyone accepted the enthusiastic claim that Internet traffic was "doubling every 100 days." The only problem was that this expectation of Internet growth was not accurate. Om Malik (2003) clarified the misconception in his book *Broadbandits* by saying, "Think of 'Internet traffic doubles every 100 days' as an urban legend" (p. 13). Compared to demand at that time, there had been a massive overinvestment in fiber-optic lines and Internet backbone hardware; in fact, the investment anticipated at least ten times the actual demand. Not only was the demand grossly overestimated, but all the large companies, including WorldCom, Global Crossing, Qwest, AT&T, Enron, and Sprint, were building and acquiring capacity to meet that fictitious demand. Each company was seemingly unconcerned about the fact that what each of them was doing was being done ten times over by their competitors.

Broadbandits points out that Andrew Odlyzko and Kerry Coffman, two AT&T scientists, couldn't believe that Internet traffic was doubling every 100 days, so they undertook a research study to analyze its growth. In their paper "The Size and Growth of the Internet," Odlyzko and Coffman "proved that the whole notion of Internet traffic was doubling every 100 days was hogwash." The actual growth rate of the Internet at that time was about 70–150 percent per year. The researchers found that every reference to Internet traffic doubling every 100 days led back to Sidgmore and Ebbers at WorldCom. In August 1997, Sidgmore had stated in an interview with *Telecommunications Magazine*, "We're seeing growth at an unprecedented level. Our backbone doubles every 3.7 months. . . . So three years from now, we expect our network to be 1,000 times the size it is today. There's never been a technology model with such an extraordinary rate of growth like this before." (Quotes from Malik, 2003, pp. 13–15)

Besides the demand for the Internet growing more slowly, at least 30 percent of Internet access was still ordinary, old-fashioned dial-up access, and the broadband capacity for demand at that time was being vastly overbuilt. However, to justify the acquisitions in Internet capacity, WorldCom had to insist that the demand for it was growing at an incredible speed. Grubman joined in spreading the hysteria about Internet traffic and broadband growth. With Sidgmore, Grubman, and Ebbers screaming about capacity being the only limitation, nobody in the industry wanted to believe the Odlyzko and Coffman study about the truth of Internet traffic growth. The rest of the industry ignored the proverbial iceberg and chanted their mantra, "Internet traffic is doubling every 100 days," as they swarmed across the nation and under the oceans, installing ten times more fiber-optic lines than was necessary at the time.

Ebbers and Sullivan continued their acquisition frenzy. They were perhaps driven by a quest for power as well as intense greed. They did not want to lose the value of all the shares they held in WorldCom, and the pursuit of acquisitions was their method of hiding the fact that the motley group of companies that WorldCom had put together was not nearly as profitable as they were reporting in their financial statements. Sullivan and Ebbers had to have more acquisitions in order to maintain the mirage of soaring earnings and stock value. They did it with smoke and mirrors—and accounting magic.

Making Accounting Magic with Acquisitions

Acquisitions provide an easy vehicle for companies to employ accounting tricks to overstate earnings after the acquisition. (Acquisitions can also make a corporate group's revenue appear to be growing when, in fact, the parent company and the acquired company may be stagnating.) The falsely overstated earnings, in turn, drive the group's stock price higher, and then the company can use its stock as currency for the next acquisition, which can again be used to overstate profits after the acquisition period. The entire cycle can then be repeated again and again. In the *First Interim Report* (2002), the Bankruptcy Examiner described WorldCom's efforts to overstate its profits:

> We have found that as early as at least 1999, responding to the pressures on WorldCom's earnings, management undertook a succession of measures designed to shore up the Company's income statement. These measures deteriorated into a concerted program of manipulation that gave rise to a smorgasbord of fraudulent journal entries and adjustments. (p. 105)

When a company acquires another company, the parent company can use a number of time periods to manipulate profits. For example, sometimes the parent company recognizes a big one-time expense or restructuring charge with respect to the acquired company *in the period immediately after the acquisition.* This expense ostensibly is to anticipate some event in the future and to provide for it in the current period—that is, to set aside current-period profit and create a reserve now for when the expense, or liability, materializes in the future. Examples of situations for which reserves could be set up include the following:

- The parent or acquiring company anticipates that the realizable value of the acquired company's assets is less than the assets' value as stated on the balance sheet—in other words, the asset will have to be sold at a loss in the future. For example, the company's inventory may have to be sold below its currently stated cost. Hence, a reserve is created for this probable, expected future loss.

- It is "probable" that the company will have liabilities in the future for a situation for which the liability has not yet been recorded in the acquired company's books—for example, a liability for taxes or litigation or employee severance payments.

Of course, all the previously mentioned reserves should only be created if it is probable that the unfavorable future condition actually will come to pass. Falsely creating such reserves for the future—when the unfavorable condition is not really probable—has two advantages for the acquiring company. First, because the charge is described as a "one-time charge" in the period immediately after the acquisition, analysts may not see the expense as recurring, meaning that they do not see it as indicative of the future—and the value of any financial instrument, such as a share certificate, is the present value of its future income stream. So the current charge (expense) in the income statement is often "discounted" by analysts and investors. In other words, it may be largely ignored by the market because it was related to the previous management, and the current thinking tends to be that the new owners are going to turn things around.

The second advantage of false reserves is the big payoff. As the future periods approach, when the earnings fail to meet the hyped expectations, the company has a "cookie jar" in the form of the reserves that it does not really need. It can then conveniently discover that the reserve wasn't required and release this surplus reserve back into the earnings in the income statement for the new period. So when a reserve that was created is reversed because it isn't needed, it erroneously appears to be an increase in the earnings in the period into which it is released. Conversely, at the origin of the reserve, it overstates expenses and understates profits in an apparently nonrecurring manner in the period in which it was first created. As the Bankruptcy Report pointed out, "It is the inappropriate release of these reserves that results in one form of earnings management" (*First Interim Report*, 2002, p. 107). WorldCom got to the point that it needed acquisition after acquisition in order to release false reserve after false reserve to prop up its earnings period after period.

There is another similar accounting trick that a company can employ to use acquisitions to present false earnings and a false balance sheet. In this ploy, the parent company, *at the time of the acquisition,* creates a purchase acquisition accounting reserve. An unscrupulous company can overstate this reserve and manipulate future profits by releasing the reserve in the future. To the extent that a company overstates the reserves, it overstates goodwill by a corresponding amount. (**Goodwill** refers to the excess of the cost of an acquired company over the fair value of its net assets.)

This would be done at the exact time of recording the purchase of the acquired company (as opposed to the period immediately following the acquisition). No expense needs to be recorded.

Also at the time of the acquisition, the company can understate the fair value of the assets it is acquiring by making it look as though it has paid a greater part of the purchase price for goodwill—and less for the acquired assets. To economists, **economic goodwill** is an ability to earn future supernormal profits on its net assets. (Accountants, on the other hand, while having the same concept in mind, have some cursory rules about how to calculate and allocate a portion of the purchase price of an entity to goodwill.) At the time of the acquisition, the parent company ascribes a fair value to the acquired company's assets, and its liabilities. If the parent pays more than the net value for the company, the excess of the purchase price over the fair value of the net assets is all allocated to goodwill. The advantage of ascribing part of the purchase price to goodwill instead of, say, to plant and machinery is that plant and machinery would have to be amortized reasonably quickly over the estimated useful life of the asset. However, until 2001, goodwill had to be amortized over only 40 years, resulting in much smaller amortization expenses during each period in the company's income statement, and therefore higher reported earnings. Since 2001, goodwill need not be amortized at all unless it becomes impaired. Also, overstating the amount of the purchase price attributed to goodwill means a company can understate its assets and create false reserves to release back into earnings as previously described.

A further, especially egregious version of this accounting sleight of hand is when, in *the period after an acquisition*, a company decides that the value of the assets acquired is less than originally calculated and then creates a reserve for this decrease in anticipated, realizable value. However, instead of recognizing a charge (as discussed in the first version of this trick), in this version, in the financial statements of the period immediately following the acquisition, the other side of the entry is a false reevaluation of the portion of the purchase price that is allocated to *goodwill*. This indicates that the parent company has now decided that the net assets acquired were of less value than was originally estimated. Hence, this creates the *need* for a reserve for the purported potential for the anticipated loss to be realized on those assets, and a corresponding increase is made to the allocation of the amount of the purchase price that was paid for *goodwill*.

WorldCom focused on the use of acquisitions to overstate reserves at the point of acquisition or in the period soon after acquisition. This was achieved by either a one-time charge (expense) in the income statement or an allocation of a portion of the purchase price to goodwill on acquisition. WorldCom would then reverse these cookie-jar reserves in later periods by releasing them back into earnings (profits), when it conveniently "discovered" that they were no longer needed because the projected negative events were not materializing. As the Bankruptcy Examiner stated, "It is inappropriate to record reserves unless a risk is probable and estimable. . . . WorldCom appears to have violated this principle" (*First Interim Report* 2002, p. 106). Furthermore, the SEC findings in its enforcement action against Sullivan alleged that "the false adjustments and entries, among other things, improperly reduced expenses by drawing down certain reserves" (AAER 1966, 2004).

WorldCom needed to continue recording unnecessary reserves. Ebbers and Sullivan went after bigger and better acquisitions to create larger and larger false reserves, which would then be released into profits in future periods in order to prop up inadequate earnings. This helped to boost the stock price, which was then used for more acquisitions—and so the Ponzi scheme's engine kept running.

By 1997, WorldCom's acquisition frenzy became quite manic. Ebbers and Sullivan became a duo on the path to mayhem. They went on from the MFS/UUNet acquisition to acquire BLT Technologies, which supplied prepaid phone cards. Back in the office, Ebbers installed Sullivan onto the board of directors, after unceremoniously giving another member the boot. The turmoil was not confined to Ebbers's boardroom. Unconfirmed rumors had swirled for a while that Ebbers, the pious Sunday school teacher, had been having an affair. Whether true or not, this devout deacon divorced his wife, Linda, and soon remarried. Through it all, he managed to find time and energy to acquire ANS Communications from America Online.

One would think 1997 had been a busy enough year, but seemingly without taking a breath, Ebbers and Sullivan set their sights on acquiring a company three times bigger than their own—they decided to go after MCI.

MCI Falls under the WorldCom Spell

MCI got its start in 1963, when ex-General Electric employee John (Jack) Goeken formed a group to pursue an investment idea. Goeken had sold two-way radios for truckers to stay in touch with dispatchers and, of course, to "rap" with each other. Goeken figured out that they should put some microwave towers between St. Louis and Chicago, on the famous Route 66, to support two-way radio communications and then sell the radios—hence the name "Microwave Communications, Inc." (MCI). This was such an innovative idea that MCI immediately had to raise money to fight the legal battles launched by AT&T and General Electric to shut it down. MCI recruited William (Bill) McGowan, a Harvard law alumnus, to help raise money and fight for the fledgling company. McGowan took over from Goeken as CEO in 1974. After AT&T's breakup in 1984, MCI expanded astronomically under McGowan's leadership, developing a huge fiber-optic network that supported the long-distance phone service that we all know. After McGowan's gradual retreat from the company's affairs following heart surgery in 1987 and his retirement in 1991, the company lost some of its focus and discipline. MCI's overhead grew disproportionately to its revenue as it made spectacular losses on its experiments with Internet business and its "Music-Now" service.

In 1996, British Telecom (BT) made an offer of $24 billion for MCI, and GTE also put in an offer. The British press generally convinced BT that it was paying too much for MCI, so BT withdrew its first offer and later offered $19 billion. Jack Grubman, the telecom analyst, added to the hype, arguing that MCI was worth the inflated price. Lynne W. Jeter's book *Disconnected: Deceit and Betrayal at WorldCom* (2003)maintained that BT needed MCI for the American market, GTE needed MCI for the overseas market, and the Baby Bells needed MCI for both the long-distance and overseas markets.

If WorldCom could snag MCI, it would thwart all these competitive efforts, and WorldCom would then be the only telecom company with a huge local service, while at the same time being the second-largest long-distance service in the United States. WorldCom already controlled half of all the domestic Internet traffic through UUNet and commanded a stunning investment in bandwidth through the IDB, WilTel, and MFS acquisitions. If WorldCom could pull MCI out of the hat, it would have revenues estimated at between $28 billion and $30 billion.

In the heated competition between WorldCom, GTE, and BT for MCI, WorldCom began with a bid of $30 billion and eventually purchased MCI for approximately $42 billion. Most of this was paid for with WorldCom stock. Because BT already owned 20 percent of MCI, it had to be paid $7 billion in cash. WorldCom made this payment by taking on billions of dollars of more debt. (Jeter, 2003)

Virtually every U.S. business magazine, newspaper, and journal was impressed with Ebbers and gushed that he was a brilliant entrepreneur. He was regarded as an ingenious visionary and a farsighted genius. Everyone repeated the chant "Internet traffic is doubling every 100 days." Ebbers had become the Midas of the business world, as everything he touched seemed to turn to gold.

Jack Grubman, of Salomon Brothers, did his part in spreading the WorldCom myth. In 1997, he told *Red Herring*, "WorldCom is at the intersection of everything we like—no carrier in the world can offer the integrated set of facilities that it does. The company has nothing to lose and everything to gain" (qtd. in Malik, 2003, p. 21). This was, however, the opposite of what the European press was saying after WorldCom outbid BT. An editorial in *Information Society Trends* blamed the U.S. stock markets for "enabling a second-rank company such as WorldCom to become a global giant in a matter of a few years" (qtd. in Jeter, 2003, p. 81).

Meanwhile, the U.S. telecom industry was in denial. Because everyone had swallowed the fabrication that Internet traffic was doubling every 100 days, WorldCom's competitors were building up massively expensive bandwidth and data networks. Ebbers and his enchanted circle believed they had a vast capacity of a commodity that was in short supply, whereas they actually had a commodity that was in oversupply. Although they claimed that WorldCom had amazing synergy with MCI and that the integration of the companies was going well, in reality, the infighting festered and the unnecessary duplications were nothing short of ludicrous. While WorldCom reported skyrocketing earnings, behind the scenes, company management was raiding the cookie-jar reserves created on acquisitions in order to meet earnings' expectations.

WorldCom's internal turmoil was so well hidden that in 1998, Sullivan made the cover of *CFO Magazine* when he was selected for an "Excellence Award" (McCafferty, 1998). Ebbers (the CEO), Scott Sullivan (the CFO), and David Myers (the controller), as well as other members of WorldCom's senior personnel, were the toast of the town; they had almost everyone fooled.

PROBLEMS AT WORLDCOM

After the MCI **merger** (in which WorldCom acquired all of MCI's stock), things started to spin out of control. However, WorldCom was undeterred. After acquiring a company more than three times its size, WorldCom went on, in 1998, to acquire Brooks Fiber for $2.9 billion and then CompuServe for $1.2 billion of WorldCom stock. Wall Street applauded, but back home the workforce was restless. For a start, the UUNet Internet employees believed that they were the "technocrats" and far superior to the "low-tech" MCI telephone operation proletariats. The MCI staff had already lost a great deal of morale during the decline after McGowan's departure. The lack of enthusiasm was exacerbated by the superior attitudes of the Internet division. To add insult to injury, WorldCom decided to do something about the cash flow problems it faced as a result of all the debt it had incurred to pay for mergers, combined with the debt it had inherited from the merged companies. It decided to reduce MCI's hefty overhead costs with a dramatic cost-cutting program, including cutbacks such as no longer flying first class and staying in expensive hotels on business trips.

Whenever a customary company perk is withdrawn, it typically causes a negative reaction. If this is combined with a merger after a hostile bid, together with one company feeling superior to another, feelings are hurt and morale usually plunges. In fairness, Ebbers tried to get the entire WorldCom hodgepodge onto a shoestring budget—except, of course, his own hundreds of millions of dollars of compensation, existing loans, guaranteed loans, and forgiven loans. Rumors of problems in the company began seeping into the media. It was starting to become clear that there was no communication between the different departments at WorldCom, resulting in wasteful duplication of resources. The problem became worse in 1998 when WorldCom acquired MCI and increased the number of departments selling the same products (Krim, 2002).

In addition, as a result of acquiring MCI, WorldCom had two billing systems. Some employees would even switch existing customers to the other system and get an extra commission for a "new" account. The famous whistleblower and internal auditor Cynthia Cooper reported in June 2001 that such switches of existing accounts purporting to be new ones had led to commissions being overpaid by close to $1,000,000. WorldCom, however, reported publicly that the practice had been limited to a small number of cases (Krim, 2002).

There was such confusion between the various merged companies that inefficiency set in and disorganization spilled over to every level. There was a great deal of double billing as well as billing of customers for work that was not done. Also, outside contractors were billed for work that had not been done, and sometimes friends of employees were hired to do simple data entry work at exorbitant fees. Furthermore, because the divisions were under pressure to meet sales growth targets and the sales staff wanted commissions, sales often were made at below cost. A 2002 article in the *Washington Post* reported that sales staff sometimes signed such outrageous contracts with clients that the company actually lost money. After all the acquisitions, most employees did not know what inventory WorldCom carried. Sometimes items that WorldCom already had in inventory would be sold to WorldCom by an outside supplier for a higher cost than WorldCom had originally paid. By 2000, WorldCom had become an incompetent, unwieldy conglomeration of over 60 telecom companies. (Krim, 2002)

Ignoring all of the turmoil, Ebbers turned his attention to insignificant and petty issues. In a subsequent CNBC interview, Robert Hudspeth, the former WorldCom vice president, explained how—as WorldCom crumbled—Ebbers became obsessed with small and trivial details such as travel expenses, meals for employees, or smoking breaks (Faber, 2003).

While WorldCom reported immense earnings for 1999 and still greater growth in both revenues and profits for the first quarter of 2000, the bitter truth was that the company was already in dire trouble. Not only had operations become chaotic and confused with all the uncoordinated and incongruent companies, but the telecom industry itself was feeling the effects of having built capacity for an overestimated future growth projection (Krim, 2002).

With growing losses, slowing revenue, and debt spiraling out of control, Sullivan knew the true peril the company was in, and he knew that one way WorldCom could prolong its façade of profits—and prolong its existence—was to make yet another colossal acquisition. This would give WorldCom an additional source of false reserves to reverse back into earnings. There were only two telecommunication companies left of such magnitude: Sprint and AT&T. So WorldCom went after Sprint.

In fairness, the acquisition of Sprint would have added an important wireless presence to WorldCom's long-distance and Internet traffic capacity to complete its all-round telecommunications clout. On October 5, 1999, a $129 billion deal was made between WorldCom and Sprint for the purchase of Sprint. Most of the price was to be paid by the issue of WorldCom shares that were trading at $43.53 on that date.

Shareholders approved the deal at their April 28, 2000 meeting. However, the deal still needed approval from regulators at the FCC in the United States, and European regulators worried that the merged companies would control too much of the long-distance and Internet traffic markets. On June 27, 2000, the U.S. Department of Justice filed a suit to put a stop to the merger of the two telecom giants.

What the world didn't know was that WorldCom's merger with Sprint was its last hope for continuing its Ponzi-type scheme. By now, WorldCom was an inefficient mess. It was a colossal, unmanageable charade, with $30 billion of debt, stalling revenues, and spiraling costs. The end of the Sprint merger was, in effect, the end of WorldCom. The stock price began to fall and Sullivan reached desperation point in his attempts to portray the company as profitable in the financial statements. According to the later Indictment against Sullivan and Buford Yates, WorldCom's director of general accounting, members of WorldCom's accounting staff were instructed "to reduce WorldCom's reported lines costs and thereby increase WorldCom's reported earnings." The staff was told "to make journal entries crediting line cost expense accounts." In order for these entries to balance on the general ledger, the staff was further instructed "to debit, in amounts corresponding to the line cost credits, various reserve accounts on WorldCom's balance sheet, such as accrued line costs, deferred tax liability, and other long-term liabilities." After certain entries were booked in WorldCom's general ledger, it had the "net effect of reducing line costs by approximately $828 million, and thereby increasing WorldCom's publicly reported earnings for the third quarter of 2000 by the same amount." (Quotes from United States of America v. Scott D. Sullivan, 2002)

Then in the first quarter of 2001, in his desperation, Sullivan began a further ploy. He directed the first of the now infamous and spectacular fraudulent transfers of line-cost expenses to asset accounts. (Of course, money spent on expenses goes into the income statement and reduces profit. However, money spent on assets is recorded in the balance sheet and does not reduce profits. Capital expenditure changes one asset, cash, into another asset.) But if Sullivan did not want to own up to the scheme that the cycle of acquisitions had been paid for with overpriced WorldCom stock based on overstated earnings, what else could he do? He could embark on a series of magical accounting manipulations.

The Bankruptcy Examiner, Thornburgh, summed up the major accounting hoaxes that Sullivan directed to falsify the financial statements:

> It appears that once income could no longer be sufficiently enhanced by the release of reserves, Mr. Sullivan and certain other WorldCom personnel directed a series of adjustments to its line costs in successive reporting periods beginning with the first quarter of 2001. (*First Interim Report*, 2002, pp. 105, 106)

AN OVERVIEW OF WORLDCOM'S FICTITIOUS FINANCIAL REPORTING SCHEMES

At this stage, it is important to examine the two major schemes that WorldCom used to overstate its earnings:

1. WorldCom artificially created unnecessary cookie-jar reserves, usually on the acquisition of companies or in the period following an acquisition, in order to reverse those reserves back into earnings in later periods. This was done to boost

those later earnings and to present a false picture of financial health and growth, which inflated the price of WorldCom shares on the stock market.

2. WorldCom reclassified $3.8 billion of line-cost expenses as capital assets, thereby presenting those costs as assets on the balance sheet instead of as expenses in the income statement, in order to falsely overstate the earnings that it reported.

These two schemes were perpetrated in an unscrupulous and brazen manner with a total disregard for veracity and accurate reporting.

Scheme #1: Improper Use of Merger Reserves

WorldCom's favored method of creating false reserves was on the acquisition of companies. All Sullivan and his cohorts had to do was acquire numerous companies and pretend they were paying for large amounts of goodwill as they overstated the reserves and undervalued the assets. In future periods, they would just reverse those reserves into profits as it was "discovered" that the reserves weren't really needed. This gave the impression of a financially healthy company.

The WorldCom Bankruptcy Examiner (Thornburgh) subsequently stated, "The manipulation of reserve accounts comprises a prominent part of the story of the irregularities in the WorldCom financial statements" (*First Interim Report*, 2002, p. 106). He reviewed the appropriateness of the following seven reserves (*First Interim Report*, 2002, p. 107):

- Revenue reserves
- Bad debt reserves
- Tax reserves
- Depreciation
- Purchase acquisition account reserves
- Legal reserves
- Line-cost reserves

Apparently, Sullivan and his buddies had gone wild in understating the net value of assets of the companies they were acquiring and overstating liabilities while allocating large portions of the purchase price to "goodwill." Their audacity can be seen in an extract of the Examiner's schedule of the amounts allocated to goodwill, with respect to WorldCom's major acquisitions. The size of the number is hard to believe; however, what follows is not a typographical error. By December 31, 2001, WorldCom showed an asset named "Goodwill" on its balance sheet in the amount of *$50.5 billion*. Of this, $49.8 billion of goodwill was comprised of payments for acquired companies in excess of the net value of the assets of those companies, after the cookie-jar reserves were created by writing down the value of the acquired assets or by anticipating liabilities. The Bankruptcy Report provided the goodwill allocation schedule outlined in Table 5.1.

In its interim investigation in 2002, Ernst and Young estimated an impairment write-down of $15 billion to $20 billion of this goodwill. WorldCom later announced a write-off of approximately $50 billion of goodwill in its bankruptcy filing in 2002. The *Third and Final Report* (2004) on the WorldCom bankruptcy analyzed the inappropriate release of reserves to overstate earnings in two categories: (1) the manipulation of line cost accruals to boost profits by reducing reported line costs and (2) the improper release of revenue and other reserves into profits to "close the gap" between earnings targets predicted by Wall Street and actual earnings.

TABLE 5.1	As of December 31, 2001, Goodwill Related to the Following Acquisitions (in billions)*	
Legacy WorldCom		$ 1.9
MCI		28.2
WNS		2.2
Technologies, Telecom, MESI, MFSCC		8.3
Intermedia, PA		4.7
Other**		4.5
		$49.8 billion

*Obtained from *First Interim Report of Dick Thornburgh, Bankruptcy Court Examiner*. 2002, p. 113.
**Includes more than 12 acquisitions.

TABLE 5.2	WorldCom's Adjustments*	
Fourth Quarter	1999	$239 million
First Quarter	2000	$369.9 million
Third Quarter	2000	$828 million

*Derived from *Third and Final Report*. 2004, p. 273.

Concerning the manipulation of line costs, it must be noted that by 1999, both local and international line costs had mushroomed out of control. To diminish the amount of the line costs, Sullivan and his crew simply released the line-cost reserves that they had created earlier and allocated the reversal to line-cost expenses. In accounting terminology, they debited the reserve on the balance sheet and made a corresponding credit or reduction to line-cost expense in the income statement. Because the dollar size of the debit was equal to the credit, everything still balanced and expenses went down while profits went up. Never mind that the expenses were now understated and the earnings were overstated. Arthur Andersen never did press WorldCom for an explanation of these entries. The auditors either passed or missed the adjustments listed in Table 5.2.

Thornburgh stated that for the $239 million entry, "The sole support for the entry consisted of a post-it note bearing the notation '$239,000,000.'" At certain times, the reserves were released even though personnel had determined "that such reserves were needed to ensure that the company had accrued the appropriate level of reserves in relation to its liabilities." At other times, the releases were cookie-jar reserves that had been kept for when costs needed to be reduced. About $3.3 billion of reserves was released to reduce line costs inappropriately. At the close of each quarter, Sullivan's office tapped any reserve necessary to boost reported profits to "close the gap" between Wall Street expectations and actual earnings. Overall, the release of reserves accounted for the overstatement of profit before tax of approximately $3.3 billion through the understatement of line costs. In addition, the Examiner's *First Interim Report* identified at least another $633 million in the release of reserves to satisfy Wall Street's expectations. (Quotes from *Third and Final Report*, 2004, p. 274)

Scheme #2: Improper Capitalization of Expenses

Once they had run out of reserves to falsely reverse into earnings, the WorldCom gang turned to a much simpler, more old-fashioned ruse to inflate earnings. They merely pulled the oldest financial fraud in the world: **improper capitalization of expenses**. They recorded money spent on expenses as though it had been spent on acquiring assets—as though the money was spent on acquiring capital goods that held their value into the following periods.

The Bankruptcy Examiner described the scam:

> The Examiner understands that, beginning in the first quarter of 2001, Mr. Sullivan directed that hundreds of millions of line-cost expenses be capitalized, subtracting them from what otherwise would have been expenses against the company's earnings for the successive quarter, and disguising most of those reductions by transferring them as additions to the company's fixed assets. (*Third and Final Report*, 2004, p. 278)

The entries, which were passed after the close of each quarter, amounted to $3.8 billion, mainly reducing line costs and overstating property, plant, and equipment (PPE) over the period January 2001 to March 2002. Further, "The journal entries lacked any supporting documents or explanations" (*Third and Final Report*, 2004, p. 278). In addition, the findings of the SEC alleged that over 2001 and 2002, WorldCom falsely portrayed its profitability:

> WorldCom did so by capitalizing (and deferring) rather than expensing (and immediately recognizing) approximately $3.8 billion of its costs: the company transferred these costs to capital accounts in violation of established generally accepted accounting principles ("GAAP"). These actions were intended to mislead investors and manipulate WorldCom's earnings to keep them in line with estimates by Wall Street analysts. (AAER 1585, 2002)

The obvious question in the face of such a brazen and crude fraud is, where were the auditors? According to the Examiner, the auditors—Arthur Andersen—did not demand total and simultaneous access to all of WorldCom's general ledger and journal entries. In addition, WorldCom gave Arthur Andersen misleading special "MonRevs"; namely, monthly revenue schedules that concealed the top-side journal-entry adjustments. These adjustments were used for "closing any gaps between targeted and projected actual earnings." They also spread the irregular amount over a number of months and over a number of asset accounts so that no one amount would stand out dramatically. WorldCom also transferred the false assets out of certain accounts into other accounts according to when Arthur Andersen planned to review the financial records. "By engaging in this shell game, those responsible for the improper entries stayed several steps ahead of Arthur Andersen in shielding these entries from the auditors." (Quotes from *Third and Final Report*, 2004, pp. 276, 283)

The combination of Arthur Andersen's restricted access to the accounting records together with the machinations by WorldCom to deceive the auditors led to Arthur Andersen's being oblivious of these top-side transfers from expenses to assets. As to whether the auditors actually knew of the accounting exploits, the Bankruptcy Examiner stated the following:

> The evidence is not in dispute: Arthur Andersen had no knowledge of the improper capitalization of line costs or the Company's improper manipulation of its line cost, revenue and other reserves to inflate its earnings. (*Third and Final Report*, 2004, p. 279)

However, whether Arthur Andersen should have conducted its audit in a more conscientious manner that would have revealed irregular entries is another matter. It can be argued that WorldCom's external auditors should not have accepted so many limitations on their access to the complete general ledger at a given time.

Auditors need to demand necessary access, and if that demand is not met, they are obliged to give a disclaimer audit opinion or a qualified opinion on the financial statements. There is not much point in auditing documents if the auditors are not going to reconcile the audited documents with the financial statements that they must approve. The whole point in auditing schedules is to test their support of the financial statements. If adjustments are made to the company's documentation or accounts or to schedules after they have been audited via massive journal entries for the preparation of the financial statements, it is futile to audit the underlying information in the first place.

In its discussion of the auditors, the *Third and Final Bankruptcy Report* (2004) alleged that "the company has claims against Arthur Andersen due to its responsibility for the failure to detect any aspect of the company's accounting fraud" (p. 261).

THE COLLAPSE OF WIZARD WORLD

Like most financial frauds, WorldCom's problems began with relatively small steps down the slippery slope. Those steps, however, soon escalated into a major avalanche.

Ebbers Loses Control

In addition to fraudulently misreporting its earnings and net assets, WorldCom personnel also enabled Ebbers to raid the company of huge sums of money by granting or guaranteeing him loans that totaled over $400 million. Some of these loans were unethical in that they were made at very low interest rates. In addition, there was little chance that Ebbers could repay them. Further, Ebbers did not disclose his problematic financial position to the compensation committee until 2002, and even then his disclosures were misleading.

When WorldCom was doing well in the 1990s, Ebbers began applying for bank loans on his own behalf or for his other business interests. The crucial point is that he dragged WorldCom interests into his private activities by pledging his WorldCom stock to secure his personal bank loans. Caught between a genuine desire to engage in philanthropy and a strong need to assuage an insatiable ego desperate for recognition, Ebbers also pledged his WorldCom stock for loans on behalf of Mississippi College. As these loans grew—and grow they did—significant amounts of Ebbers's WorldCom stock were held as security—so much so, in fact, that Ebbers could argue that if he were forced to sell his WorldCom stock to pay the loans, such a large volume of selling would put considerable downward pressure on the WorldCom stock price. Astoundingly, Ebbers had pledged or guaranteed hundreds of millions of dollars of WorldCom stock.

The kicker for WorldCom was that clauses in many of these loans required Ebbers to make repayments if WorldCom stock fell below specified levels, and that is exactly what the stock did. It fell from a high of $64.50 per share in June 1999 to $46.07 in mid-July 2000, after the Sprint merger was called off. To pay his enormous debts, Ebbers began borrowing large amounts from WorldCom. The Bankruptcy Examiner observed that WorldCom's compensation committee alleged it was Ebbers's idea that WorldCom lend him money to avoid the sale of his WorldCom stock to repay his outside loans. Ebbers, on the other hand, disputed this, claiming that the compensation committee had asked him to borrow money from WorldCom rather than sell his stock, which would put further downward pressure on the stock price. Ebbers's version makes it appear that accepting massive loans from WorldCom was a magnanimous favor he did for the company; it was a gesture of all heart. The point, of course, is that if Ebbers had not pledged vast quantities of company stock for personal loans and guarantees, neither he nor the WorldCom shares would have had to be rescued. It seemed to be lost on Ebbers that his argument of helping WorldCom by taking the loans was merely tautological. In fact, he appeared to favor this kind of circular logic to rationalize his actions.

The first loan of $50 million was made to Ebbers by the WorldCom compensation committee on September 6, 2000. In October, the committee authorized another $25 million guarantee with respect to Ebbers's personal bank loans. In January 2001, the guarantee was increased to $100 million and then to the even more staggering amount of $150 million. (Ebbers eventually signed a note in September 2001 agreeing to repay the amounts extended under the guarantees.)

The Global Crossing bankruptcy filing in January 2001 hit WorldCom's stock hard, putting another nail in Ebbers's coffin. That month the stock price fell below $10 per share. Ebbers continued his desperate acquisition strategy and went after Intermedia to get control of Digex, an Internet company. The handling of this acquisition later caused special criticism by the Bankruptcy Examiner. Ebbers was accused of withholding information from WorldCom's board of directors as well as misleading them. The board of directors was criticized for not performing due diligence before its approval of the acquisition. Ebbers's acquisition price of over $6 billion for Intermedia in July 2001 was generally considered an overpayment. To make matters worse, WorldCom became embroiled in an expensive lawsuit with Digex shareholders. The stock price of WorldCom continued to fall, and blame was increasingly aimed at the formerly untouchable Bernie Ebbers. In spite of his increasing debacles, in January 2002, the compensation committee authorized another $65 million loan to Ebbers. What were they thinking?

The *Third and Final Report* shows that by April 2, 2002, the loans and guarantees to Ebbers exceeded $379 million. On that date, in an agreement letter, WorldCom formally protected its interest in Ebbers's WorldCom stock as security for his loans. A couple of weeks later, on April 18, Ebbers pledged his other personal and business interests as security. On April 29, all Ebbers's loans and guarantees were consolidated into one promissory note of $408.2 million—a staggering sum by any measure. The Report shows that of this amount, $198.7 million was to satisfy loans to Ebbers for other companies controlled by him, $36.5 million was for a letter of credit used to support Mississippi College, $165 million was a personal loan to Ebbers, and $7.6 million was for interest on these loans. This, in a nutshell, is the story of an ego gone wild, of an insane spending spree, and of a compensation committee that acquiesced to the CEO's wishes.

Thornburgh, the Bankruptcy Examiner, faults primarily Ebbers as well as two members of the compensation committee for the loan fiasco. However, because the remaining members of the board of directors "ratified compensation committee actions with virtually no data and without inquiring about or questioning the low interest rates," the Examiner believed that claims could be pursued against all of WorldCom's former directors (*Third and Final Report*, 2004, p. 18).

On March 7, 2002, the SEC finally and inevitably questioned WorldCom formally on a wide range of items, including the loans to Ebbers, as well as the accounting for acquisitions. On April 3, 2002, WorldCom laid off 3,700 people. The stock price continued to fall, and the pressure on Ebbers burst through his wall of resolve to stay in charge. On April 9, 2002, Ebbers resigned as CEO of WorldCom and John Sidgmore was appointed in his place. The compensation committee, again, did the unbelievable for their (rather tarnished) golden-boy Ebbers. They presented him with a generous severance package that included $1.5 million per year for life and use of the WorldCom jet for 30 hours per year.

The End of the Sullivan Era

By this time, a storm was brewing that would uncover the massive accounting fraud of Scott Sullivan and his cohorts. Business was declining; WorldCom had run out of acquisitions to falsify profits; the stock price was falling; Ebbers's loans were eating cash; and a number of suspicious events had caught the attention of WorldCom's now famous internal auditor, Cynthia Cooper.

In March 2002, John Stupka—of WorldCom's wireless division—complained to Cooper that Sullivan was taking a reserve for doubtful debts from Stupka's division to use elsewhere. Cooper noted this as suspicious, but not clearly illegal. She raised the issue with the Andersen auditors, who brushed her off. An Andersen spokesperson said that Stupka's division did not need the reserve of $400 million. Pulliam and Solomon (2002) later reported in the *Wall Street Journal* that Norton's response galvanized Cooper's determination to find out what was going on, and she assembled a team consisting of herself, Gene Morse, and Glyn Smith of the Internal Audit Department.

Cooper, having decided not to accept Andersen's answer, reported it to Max Bobbit, head of the audit committee, on March 6, 2002. Sullivan backed down on the issue of the reserve, but did not forget. Pulliam and Solomon reported that the next day Sullivan tracked down Cooper at her hair salon and warned her not to interfere with Stupka's business again. One day later the SEC delivered a "Request for Information" concerning its investigation into WorldCom. That gave Cooper a little more leeway to go beyond the Internal Audit Department's narrow operational audit and into the realm of a financial audit. In May, Sidgmore, the new CEO, appointed Cooper to head a complete investigation into WorldCom's books.

On May 21, Glyn Smith, of the internal audit team, received an e-mail from Mark Abide, who was in charge of the PPE records in Texas. Abide attached an article from the *Fort Worth Weekly Online* of May 16, 2002, about Kim Emigh, a WorldCom employee in Texas who had been fired for questioning the accounting for PPE. This caught the attention of the investigative team. The entire sham that was WorldCom may have been set in play by Ebbers following his high school basketball teammate to Mississippi College, but it was about to be unraveled by a different kind of team altogether—a team of trustworthy internal auditors. Cooper, Morse, and Smith began to triple-team Sullivan. The team had already come across an item of $1.4 billion in capital equipment that was suspicious. By that stage, the investigators were already suspicious about almost $2 billion of unauthorized capital expenditure. (Pulliam & Solomon, 2002)

The team kept investigating, and on May 21, it found $500 million of unsupported computer expenses that were improperly classified as capital expenditure. Cooper became convinced that operating expenses were being fraudulently booked as capital assets when Myers tried to stop the inquiry. Undeterred but without full access to the accounting computer system, the internal audit team became creative and surreptitious in their search for the information they needed. Gene Morse contrived to be testing a new software program in order to retrieve the journal entry source of items in the general ledger. Initially, Morse downloaded so much data that he almost shut down the entire system. To avoid detection, he started working in the windowless audit library each day. He even started copying accounting information on CD-ROMs in case others tried to remove the evidence by destroying the financial records. Sullivan became suspicious and tried to find out what Morse was working on, but Morse deflected the questions. (Pulliam & Solomon, 2002)

On June 11, Sullivan called the internal audit team into his office to ask what they were working on. Among other items, Gene Smith casually mentioned the capital expenditure audit, at which point Sullivan asked them to delay it a few months. They refused and left. Cooper and Smith then informed Bobbit, the head of the audit committee, of the $3.8 billion misallocation of operating expenses as assets. Bobbit advised them to inform WorldCom's new auditors, KPMG, who had replaced Arthur Andersen after the Enron debacle. (Interestingly, Bobbit did not mention the issue at a board of directors meeting the next day.) When KPMG asked Cooper to recheck her facts, she questioned Betty Vinson (the director of management reporting) and Buford Yates about the capital expenditure entries. Vinson said that she had been instructed to make the entries but had not been given any explanations. Yates claimed that he did not know anything about them. Cooper and Smith then questioned David Myers, the controller, who acknowledged that he had known about the incorrect accounting. According to the Grand Jury Indictment:

> SULLIVAN, David F. Myers, and BUFORD YATES, JR. . . . agreed that it was no longer possible to disguise WorldCom's rising ratio of expenses to revenue by reducing various reserves on WorldCom's general ledger. Therefore, the conspirators discussed a scheme to hide WorldCom's increasing expenses by causing substantial portions of WorldCom's line costs to be transferred from current expense accounts into capital expenditure accounts. This transfer would allow WorldCom to defer recognizing a substantial portion of its current operating expenses, thereby allowing WorldCom to report higher earnings. (United States of America v. Scott D. Sullivan, 2002, par. 23)

On June 20, Cooper and Smith, along with KPMG, told the audit committee that the line-cost transfers did not conform to GAAP. Sullivan prepared a white paper to try to provide theoretical support for the transfers, but nobody bought his arguments.

On June 24, WorldCom stock fell to below $1 on the stock exchange. The next day WorldCom announced to the world that it had uncovered a massive fraud that had overstated profits by $3.8 billion over the last few years. That same day the CFO, Scott Sullivan, and the controller, David Myers, were asked to resign. When WorldCom filed for bankruptcy a month later, on July 21, 2002, it attained the record for the largest bankruptcy in the United States at that time. (Today it stands as the third-largest bankruptcy in the United States, having been overtaken by Lehman Brothers—which holds the top spot—and Washington Mutual.)

THE GATEKEEPERS WHO FAILED WORLDCOM

Over the years, the capitalization of expenses and manipulation of reserves had overstated WorldCom's profits by more than $9 billion:

> The Commission's Amended Complaint alleges that WorldCom misled investors from at least as early as 1999 through the first quarter of 2002, and further states that the company has acknowledged that during that period, as a result of undisclosed and improper accounting, WorldCom materially overstated the income it reported on its financial statements by approximately $9 billion. (AAER 1678, 2002)

This estimate of $9 billion would increase, after further investigation, to close to $11 billion.

Two of the main perpetrators, Sullivan and Myers, were arrested on August 1, 2002, and charged with securities fraud, conspiracy to commit securities fraud, and filing false statements with the SEC. On August 28, a further seven-count indictment was filed against Sullivan, charging him with conspiracy to boost earnings by hiding operating expenses. Sullivan pleaded guilty to three fraud-related counts. Myers pleaded guilty and agreed to assist prosecutors with the case. The next month Buford Yates, Betty Vinson, and Troy Normand pleaded guilty to charges of fraud, conspiracy, and securities fraud. Ebbers was later arrested and subsequently convicted "on all nine counts that he helped mastermind an $11 billion accounting fraud at WorldCom" (Crawford, 2005).

The responsibility for the repugnant financial reporting failure does not rest solely with the WorldCom management and staff who perpetrated the frauds or with Arthur Andersen, whose audits failed to detect the irregularities. As mentioned earlier, the Bankruptcy Examiner showed how every single gatekeeping entity failed to perform its function effectively.

Concerning Arthur Andersen, the Examiner's *Third and Final Report* went further than earlier reports and concluded that Arthur Andersen allegedly failed "to carry out the kinds of substantive tests that were warranted by the risks." Even though it was "significantly deceived," Andersen lacked due "professional skepticism" (p. 20).

Turning his attention to the board of directors, Thornburgh scrutinized the impact of the "scant involvement" of the board in the massive acquisitions. As poor as this aspect of corporate governance was, Thornburgh conceded, "In the

end, however, only one acquisition . . . Intermedia . . . seemed truly questionable."
This huge acquisition had been approved without apparent due diligence. The first
Intermedia agreement, on September 1, 2000, was presented to the board of directors
for its approval without "meaningful or advance data," and the directors "passively"
approved the transaction. In the opinion of the Examiner, the board would probably
have approved this purchase even with better information. However, the price of
Intermedia increased, and by the time of the amended merger contract in February
2001, "a vigilant and properly informed Board would have rejected the merger."
Sullivan and Ebbers, without authorization, finalized the revised merger agreement,
and the Examiner concluded that the directors breached their "fiduciary duty of care
in not learning all the circumstances concerning the merger amendment." This Report
also apportioned blame (in varying degrees) to the former board of directors for the
fiasco of over $400 million of loans and guarantees made by WorldCom on behalf of
Ebbers and to Ebbers, who "breached his duties of loyalty and good faith." (Quotes
from *Third and Final Report*, 2004, pp. 17–21)

Certainly, WorldCom's Internal Audit Department failed to properly carry out
the function that an internal audit division should fulfill and was rebuked for this by
the Bankruptcy Examiner. However, the department was set up with a flawed focus
and was not truly independent. It did not have sufficient resources and was geared to
perform operational audits only—not financial audits. Taking this into consideration,
the Examiner pointed out, "Given this focus on operational issues, it was a credit to the
personnel of the Internal Audit Department that they investigated the line cost capitalization issue in 2002" (*First Interim Report*, 2002, p. 7). The *Third and Final Report* of 2004
did not recommend that claims be pursued against the Internal Audit Department
staff. Similarly, although the audit committee of the board of directors was ineffective
and the Examiner referred to "the mistaken deference" that this committee showed
to senior financial management, Thornburgh did not recommend claims against the
audit committee.

WorldCom's major investment bank, SSB, represented yet another major gatekeeping failure. The Examiner claimed that Ebbers breached his fiduciary duties and
"that SSB aided . . . and abetted those breaches" (*Third and Final Report*, 2004, p. 17).
The Report maintained that in exchange for WorldCom's investment banking business
from Ebbers, SSB gave Ebbers preferential treatment in two significant ways. First, the
investment bank allocated huge amounts of initial public offering (IPO) shares to him
when it took other companies public; second, Salomon favored Ebbers by providing
him with unusual financial assistance.

While the practice of investment bankers allocating some IPO shares to their best
retail customers is a long established one, certain aspects of the distribution of these
shares to Ebbers was strikingly unusual. First, when Salomon initially allotted IPO
shares to Ebbers, besides not being one of its good customers, he was not a customer at
all. Second, the size of the allocation to Ebbers was staggering—bigger than was given
to any other individual customer and even bigger than the amounts offered to most
institutional investors. Third, and most incriminating of all, soon after the first allocation of valuable IPO shares to Ebbers by Salomon, Ebbers used Salomon as WorldCom's
investment banker for the first time.

The first IPO stock allotted to Ebbers was for Salomon's IPO of McLeod, Inc.,
before Ebbers was even a customer of the banking firm. Ebbers paid $4 million for

200,000 shares and sold them four months later for $6.1 million. By a startling fluke, two months after the sale of his McLeod shares, Ebbers saw to it that WorldCom employed SSB as its investment bank when it merged with MFS Communications Company. Coincidence? The Examiner did not think so: "The evidence supports the conclusion that Mr. Ebbers received his huge McLeod allocation, at least in part, because the large allocation made it more likely that Mr. Ebbers would award Salomon investment banking work" (*Third and Final Report*, 2004, pp. 14, 15). Salomon earned a fee of $7.5 million from its work on the WorldCom/MFS merger.

Over the span of all WorldCom's subsequent mergers, Salomon earned over $100 million in fees and Ebbers made over $12 million in gross profits on various IPO shares. The investment bankers attempted to justify the IPO shares, claiming that Ebbers had been one of their best customers. The Examiner, however, rejected the argument on the grounds that Ebbers had not traded at all on his SSB account, except for his IPO shares.

Apart from favoring Ebbers with IPO shares, SSB also gave him another brand of preferential financial assistance when he could not buy any more shares because of the margin calls with respect to his personal bank loans. The bankers requested their affiliate, Citibank, not to sell any of Ebbers's stock that Citibank held as security for its $40 million loan to him. SSB also guaranteed Ebbers's loan to Citibank. One week after Ebbers resigned as CEO of WorldCom and had no more business to extend to the banks, SSB sold—at a loss—the stock that had been held as security for his loan.

The following chart shows the interrelationship between Ebbers's IPO allocations and SSB's investment-banking work for WorldCom.

Summary of Salomon's IPO Allocations to Mr. Ebbers and Investment Banking Activity for WorldCom in 1996 and 1997*

- *June 10, 1996.* Salomon first allocates IPO shares to Mr. Ebbers—200,000 shares in the McLeod IPO. He realizes profits of $2,155,000.
- *August 14, 1996.* Salomon is engaged for the first time by WorldCom on the Company's acquisition of MFS, receiving fees of $7,500,000.
- *November 15, 1996.* Salomon allocates 89,286 shares to Mr. Ebbers in the McLeod Secondary Offering. He realizes profits of $390,172.
- *March 18, 1997.* Salomon is engaged by WorldCom on its issuance and sale of $2 billion in senior notes, receiving fees of $8,330,600.
- *May 15,1997.* Salomon is engaged by WorldCom on its exchange offering for MFS Bonds, receiving fees of approximately $1,500,000.
- *June 23, 1997.* Salomon allocates 205,000 shares to Mr. Ebbers in the Qwest IPO. He realizes profits of $1,957,475.
- *September 26, 1997.* Salomon allocates 200,000 shares to Mr. Ebbers on the Nextlink IPO. He realizes profits of $1,829,869.
- *September 29, 1997.* Salomon is engaged by WorldCom on the MCI transaction, receiving fees of more than $48 million, including fees from a related investment-grade debt offering.
- *October 26, 1997.* Salomon allocates 100,000 shares to Mr. Ebbers in the MFN IPO. He realizes profits of $4,558,71.

*Obtained *Third and Final Report of Dick Thornburgh, Bankruptcy Court Examiner*. January 26, 2004, p. 176.

All of this happened while Jack Grubman, SSB's "independent" star telecom analyst, wined and dined and shot pool with Ebbers. Grubman also touted WorldCom stock, attended some WorldCom board meetings, and echoed the absurd "demand for broadband is doubling every 100 days" line. SSB earned $100 million in investment banking fees as WorldCom's stock skyrocketed (before it plunged). Grubman steadfastly refused to give the stock a "sell" rating. In his analysis of Ebbers's relationship with SSB, the Bankruptcy Examiner stated:

> The Examiner believes that Mr. Ebbers breached his fiduciary duties of loyalty and good faith by putting his personal interest ahead of those of the Company. The Examiner also believes that SSB aided and abetted those breaches. . . . Indeed, SSB is jointly and severally liable along with Mr. Ebbers for these breaches. The recoveries could include . . . disgorgement for the fees WorldCom paid to SSB. (*Third and Final Bankruptcy Report*, 2004, p. 17)

So it was that all of the institutional gatekeepers failed in their corporate gatekeeping duties.

SIGNALS OF THE WORLDCOM FRAUD

WorldCom overstated its earnings in two major ways. The first was its improper use of acquisition or merger reserves, and the second was the capitalizing of its line-cost expense.

Signals of WorldCom's Fictitious Reporting Scheme #1—Improper Use of Acquisition or Merger Reserves

Using business combinations to overstate earnings leaves a number of signals in financial statements. Let us examine a few of these signals.

SIGNAL #1: PARENT COMPANY ALLOCATES LARGE AMOUNTS TO GOODWILL WHEN ACQUIRING OTHER COMPANIES

The prospective investor should be on the lookout for large amounts allocated to goodwill on the acquisition of other companies. This is an indication that false cookie-jar reserves may have been created and released back into earnings to falsely boost post-acquisition profits.

As reported earlier in this chapter, WorldCom had $49.8 billion of goodwill recorded as amounts paid in excess of **net asset values** on acquisitions. (The net asset value of a business refers to the net amount of the fair value of a business entity's assets less the value of its liabilities and reserves.) Of this colossal amount, $28.2 billion was related to its acquisition of MCI. In subsequent restatements of WorldCom's financial statements, and in its bankruptcy accounts, virtually all of the $49.8 billion was written off as valueless. Whenever goodwill, as a factor of earnings, increases dramatically over time with consecutive acquisitions, it is a sign to be very skeptical about a company's financial statements. Also, when goodwill increases over time with consecutive acquisitions as a percentage of total assets, one should be on the alert.

SIGNAL #2: GOODWILL RELATED TO ACQUISITION OF COMPANIES WITHOUT SUPERNORMAL RETURN ON ASSETS   When the goodwill on an acquisition relates to a company that does not have or is not very likely to have a supernormal return on assets, it is a signal that the goodwill may be false because, in economic terms, goodwill is an ability to earn supernormal profits. If the parent company is not paying for supernormal profits, what is it paying for when it pays more for a company than the value of its net assets? One should keep a skeptical watch to see whether these profits materialize.

SIGNAL #3: PARENT COMPANY CREATES SIGNIFICANT RESERVES WHEN ACQUIRING OTHER COMPANIES   When a company that makes a number of acquisitions also creates significant reserves, it is a signal that the company may be creating false reserves to boost later periods' earnings. WorldCom created a number of reserves that later became the subject of the Bankruptcy Examiner's inquiry.

SIGNAL #4: LARGE ONE-TIME CHARGES IN INCOME STATEMENT   Investors should be wary of large one-time charges in the income statement, especially around the time of an acquisition period, because these often signal that the company is creating false reserves to boost later earnings.

SIGNAL #5: PARENT COMPANY MAKES LATER ADJUSTMENTS TO INCREASE GOODWILL AFTER AN ACQUISITION   Adjustments that increase goodwill in a later period with respect to an acquisition are further signs that a company may be creating false reserves. Sometimes companies want additional false reserves, in excess of the reserves created at the time of the acquisition. The parent company may even want to avoid taking a large one-time charge in its income statement to acquire the cookie-jar reserves. In such a case, the company may reopen the value placed on goodwill at acquisition by creating false reserves in a later period and increasing the goodwill paid for an acquisition by a complementary amount. These later adjustments increasing goodwill are a huge red flag that false reserves are being created to boost later profits.

Signals of WorldCom's Fictitious Reporting Scheme #2—Understating Expenses via Improper Capitalization of Expenses

This fraud overstates earnings reported on the income statement and inflates assets on the balance sheet. In addition, this fraud overstates the cash flow from operations (CFFO) and inflates the amount reported as "cash used in investing activities" in the statement of cash flows.

WorldCom, of course, fraudulently reallocated billions of dollars out of its line-cost expense into the asset designated as PPE.

SIGNAL #1: DECREASE IN RATIO OF SALES TO ASSETS   The first signal of this kind of fraud is often a decrease in the **ratio of sales to assets** (i.e., the asset-turnover ratio), which is the ratio of a business entity's total sales to the total amount that it has invested in all of its assets).

Ultimately, the reason that a company invests in assets is to generate revenue with those assets. Obviously, a fictitious asset cannot produce revenue. Because PPE is one of the most common assets chosen for fraudulent companies to misclassify expenses, a frequently used way to identify this fraud is to check the ratio of sales to PPE.

TABLE 5.3	WorldCom: A Selection of Ratios*							

Third Quarter 2000–First Quarter 2002

	2000	2000	2000	2001	2001	2001	2001	2002
	06/30	09/30	12/31	03/31	06/30	09/30	12/31	03/31
Line-Costs/ Revenues	40.73%	38.49%	42.53%	42.26%	41.86%	41.77%	42.09%	42.84%
Sales/Total Assets	10.47%	10.06%	9.71%	9.76%	8.74%	8.55%	8.16%	7.82%
Sales/PPE	59.2%	55.1%	47.4%	45.5%	44.1%	40.7%	35.6%	32.2%

*Derived from WorldCom's 10-K filings submitted to U.S. Securities and Exchange Commission. www.sec.gov.

In Table 5.3, note that over the period during which WorldCom manipulated its financial statements by understating its line costs in its income statements—and allocating the amounts spent to PPE instead—its revenue as a percentage of PPE assets grew smaller and smaller. In the second quarter of 2000, revenue was 59.2 percent of PPE, and it fell steadily to 44.1 percent by the second quarter of 2001. Then as WorldCom increased its fraudulent transfers from line costs to PPE, revenue as a percentage of PPE dropped precipitously to only 35.6 percent in the fourth quarter of 2001 and to just 32.2 percent in the first quarter of 2002.

SIGNAL #2: INCREASE IN PPE WITH DECREASE IN REVENUE When the PPE amount on the balance sheet increases while revenue actually decreases, this is a double red flag that something is likely to be seriously wrong with the company. The **sales-to-PPE ratio** is the ratio of a business entity's sales to the amount it has invested in PPE. This signal is, of course, based on the same logic and dynamics as Signal #1, but it is a more pronounced signal and very easy to spot. Without even calculating a percentage, the prospective investor reading the financial statements can simply check to see that revenue does not decrease over time while the amount reportedly invested in PPE increases.

From an examination of Table 5.4, we see that for WorldCom, the amount of dollars reportedly invested in PPE grew steadily from $17.2 billion in the second quarter of 2000 to $20.2 billion in the second quarter of 2001 and jumped to $25.2 billion in the first quarter of 2002, at the height of the fraud. Over that same time, revenues dropped from $10.2 billion to $8.9 billion to $8.1 billion.

The logic behind this signal, of course, is that companies invest their cash in PPE to *increase* their capacity to produce goods and services and earn revenue with these goods and services. A company cannot continue for an extended period of time by increasing its cash spent on production capacity while reducing the revenue it gets from that capacity. If such a trend *continues over time*, at least one of two things has happened—and they are both bad. Either the company is falsely reporting some of its cash spent on operating expenses as cash invested in PPE or it is reporting honestly and its business model has serious problems. In the latter case, the investment in PPE assets is not producing the revenue for which the investment was made in the first place. In the absence of clearly understandable explanations in the Management Discussion and Analysis (MD&A) section of the company's annual report or in coherent press releases,

TABLE 5.4	WorldCom: Extracts from Quarterly Statements and Balance Sheets[*]

(In Millions) Third Quarter 2000–First Quarter 2002

	2000	2000	2000	2001	2001	2001	2001	2002
	06/30	09/30	12/31	03/31	06/30	09/30	12/31	03/31
Revenues	10,193	10,047	9,607	9,720	8,910	8,966	8,478	8,120
Line Costs Originally Reported	4,152	3,867	4,086	4,108	3,730	3,745	3,568	3,479
Improperly Capitalized Line Costs	292	292	292	1,063	902	1,035	1,223	1,089
Less Tax Shield	119	117	197	419	352	403	474	390
Total Assets	97,373	99,893	98,903	99,580	101,944	104,902	103,914	103,803
Goodwill	46,670	46,594	46,594	46,113	50,820	50,820	50,531	50,607
PPE	17,226	18,243	20,288	21,381	20,191	22,053	23,814	25,219
Accumulated Depreciation	6,104	6,707	7,204	7,770	8,241	9,061	9,852	10,807

*Obtained from U.S. Securities and Exchange Commission. www.sec.gov.

either of these signals in the financial statements is a strong alert for an investor to consider a downgrade of the stock.

In the case of WorldCom, these two signals could have easily been revealed by going to the EDGAR Database on the U.S. Securities and Exchange Commission's website (www.sec.gov/edgar.shtml) and perusing WorldCom's income statement and balance sheet in the 10-Q and 10-K filings, then comparing the amounts reported as revenues to the amounts reported as total assets and as PPE over time. It would have been evident that something was very wrong.

Over a period of time, WorldCom's comparison of sales to PPE produced a strong signal of overstatement of PPE because so much of the misallocation of the line-cost expense went specifically into PPE. The misallocation of expenses could also go to other assets. Thus, it is also useful to test each of the following ratios, looking for the same trend of a decline in sales as a percentage of these particular assets:

- Ratio of sales to each fixed-asset category on the balance sheet
- Ratio of sales to total fixed assets
- Ratio of sales to total assets

SIGNAL #3: DECREASE IN REVENUE WHILE FIXED-COST EXPENSE REMAINS CONSTANT AS PERCENTAGE OF SALES REVENUE When an expense that has a fixed-cost component remains a constant percentage of sales revenue as revenue decreases, it is a signal that the expense is being understated. When revenues decrease over time, one should test all expenses that have a fixed-cost element against sales revenue, checking for such expenses that have not increased as a percentage of sales.

When revenues decrease over time, variable costs can usually be cut back proportionately. However, fixed costs, by definition, do not respond to changes in scale of operation; hence, the fixed cost becomes a greater percentage of the shrinking sales revenue amount. (For example, if a company produces and sells less, the landlord charges the same amount of factory rent; so the rent expense becomes a greater percentage of the sales revenue amount.)

In the case of WorldCom, the line cost was a very significant expense that had a fixed-cost element as well as a variable-cost element. Looking at Table 5.4, you can see that revenue declined from $10.2 billion in the second quarter of 2000, to $8.9 billion in the second quarter of 2001, and to $8.1 billion in the first quarter of 2002. However, in Table 5.3, we see that the "line-cost" expense remained amazingly close to 41 percent throughout the period. It would have looked very suspicious if so much had been reallocated out of line costs that the expense actually declined as a percentage of sales. Nobody checked to see why this expense with a fixed-cost element had remained a suspiciously constant percentage as sales revenue declined. We now know that WorldCom was calculating how much it needed to reduce expenses to hit profit targets. If necessary, the company would understate line costs down to the constant amount of close to 41 percent of sales revenue each quarter.

In fact, whenever any expense fluctuates too wildly as a percentage of sales or stays at a constant percentage of sales quarter after quarter, it is cause for suspicion. When the expense that stays constant to within a percentage of sales has a fixed-cost component, it becomes more likely that part of the expense is being recorded as an asset. When, in addition, the assets are growing at a faster rate than sales, some expenses probably are being reported as assets. The signals combine to create a siren when, simultaneously, assets (such as PPE at WorldCom) grow while sales actually decline and expenses (such as line costs at WorldCom) hold constant or decline as a percentage of sales. At WorldCom, these signals indicated that the line-cost expense was being misallocated as the asset PPE.

SIGNAL #4: NOTES TO FINANCIAL STATEMENTS REVEAL CAPITALIZING OF COSTS THAT ARE USUALLY EXPENSED   A fourth signal of misclassifying expenses as assets occurs when the notes to the financial statements indicate that the company is capitalizing costs that other companies—in the same industry—expense. One can browse through a company's accounting policy note to look for such evidence. Although WorldCom's note did not reveal much, often the note will indicate that the company is capitalizing questionable costs. In general (although not in the case of WorldCom), these kinds of aggressive capitalizations of expenses occur in the areas of:

- direct response advertising costs.
- customer acquisition costs and subscriber acquisition costs.
- software development costs.
- capitalized interest costs (which occur when interest is incurred on amounts invested in assets under construction). The interest must relate to the period beginning with construction costs and ending when the asset is complete and ready for service.

SIGNAL #5: CHANGE IN ACCOUNTING POLICY TO BEGIN CAPITALIZING A COST   If a company changes its accounting policy to begin capitalizing a cost as an asset that was previously classified as an expense, it should alert the reader to the possibility of an aggressive capitalization policy. Investors should be warned to use all the signals in this chapter to test whether an expense has been misclassified as an asset.

SIGNAL #6: WRITING OFF PREVIOUSLY CAPITALIZED COSTS   If in the past the company had a special charge in the income statement for writing off a previously capitalized cost, this is a signal that the company could be aggressive in its approach to the classification of items as assets rather than expenses. (In 1989, Cendant Corporation had written off previously capitalized membership acquisition costs long before the company's spectacular problems in 1997. In 1999, American Software had to write off previously capitalized software costs.)

It is important to note that for this particular fraud of misallocating expenses as fixed assets, CFFO lagging operating income is usually not as helpful as it is in uncovering other frauds. The reason is that in the statement of cash flows, the fraud simultaneously overstates CFFO and the amount of cash used in investing activities. Therefore, this fraud makes it look as though the company did generate cash in its operating activities, but that it spent that cash on investing in fixed assets such as PPE. Thus, we must rely more on the previously mentioned signals for this scam.

ARE THEY LIVING HAPPILY EVER AFTER?

- **Bernard Ebbers**, former WorldCom CEO, was convicted of securities fraud, conspiracy to commit securities fraud, and false filings on March 17, 2005. He was sentenced to 25 years in prison. After a failed appeal, he entered the Oakdale Federal Correctional Institution in Louisiana in 2006. His wife, Kristie, filed for divorce in 2008. Ebbers is scheduled to be released from prison in July 2028 ("Ebbers' wife files . . . ," 2008).
- **Jack Grubman**, analyst and crony of Bernie Ebbers," accepted a lifetime ban from the securities industry and paid a $15 million fine" (Guyon, 2005). Grubman was never charged with any criminal misconduct relating to WorldCom.
- **David Myers**, former WorldCom controller, pleaded guilty to one count of conspiracy to commit securities fraud. In August 2005, he was sentenced to one year plus one day in prison (*Bureau of Prisons*, 2005; "WorldCom Ex-Controller . . . ," 2005).
- **Scott Sullivan**, former WorldCom CFO, pleaded guilty to three fraud-related counts on March 2, 2004. He was the chief witness for the prosecution in the trial of Bernard Ebbers. Sullivan reportedly admitted "that he repeatedly lied to the board about the company's financial plight and its fraudulent accounting maneuvers" ("WorldCom's Finance Chief . . . ," 2005). Sullivan was sentenced to five years in prison, with his sentence commencing in November 2005 ("Sullivan Gets Five Years . . . ," 2005). In 2009, after receiving one year off his sentence for good behavior, Sullivan was released from prison and moved back to Boca Raton, Florida. He did not move into "the $15 million dream house he was building in the exclusive Le Lac enclave west of the city. Instead, he's back at the modest Woodbury neighborhood home he bought for $170,000 in 1990" (Clough, 2009).
- **Betty Vinson**, accounting executive, pleaded guilty to one count of conspiracy to commit securities fraud and one count of securities fraud. She was sentenced to five months in prison and five months home detention ("Ex-WorldCom Executive Sentenced . . . ," 2005).

- **Buford Yates, Jr.**, director of general accounting, pleaded guilty to one count of conspiracy to commit securities fraud. He was sentenced to one year plus one day in prison, with his sentence commencing in October 2005. He also received a fine of $5,000 ("Ex-WorldCom Exec Gets a Year . . . ," 2005).
- **WorldCom** emerged from bankruptcy in April 2004, doing business as MCI. On January 6, 2006, Verizon Communications, Inc., completed its merger with MCI. The new business unit is named Verizon Business ("Verizon Business"). The WorldCom bankruptcy is the third-largest bankruptcy in the history of the United States, superseded in recent years by Washington Mutual and Lehman Brothers, the second-largest and largest, respectively (Tkaczyk, 2009).

Key Terms

Acquisition *122*
Economic goodwill *129*
Fixed cost *123*
Goodwill *129*

Improper capitalization of
   expenses *137*
Merger *132*
Net asset value *145*

Sales-to-PPE ratio *147*
Turnover ratio or sales-
   to-total assets ratio *146*

ETHICS AT WORK

Questions:

a. Describe the role of Cynthia Cooper and the rest of WorldCom's internal audit team in revealing the accounting frauds at WorldCom.

b. Consider whistleblowing in the context of virtue ethics. What "virtuous" character traits are required of the whistleblowing?

c. Describe the most important characteristics or qualities of an effective internal audit department and explain whether or not these qualities were missing in WorldCom's Internal Audit Department.

Assignments

TRUE/FALSE QUESTIONS

Answer the following questions with T for true or F for false for more practice with key terms and concepts from this chapter.

1. When goodwill on the acquisition of a company relates to a company that does not have or is unlikely to have a supernormal return on assets, it is a signal that the stated goodwill may be fictitious.

   T   F

2. WorldCom overstated its sales by holding its books open at the close of a reporting period.

   T   F

3. WorldCom overstated its earnings by capitalizing rather than expensing approximately $3.8 billion of its costs.

   T   F

4. WorldCom overstated its earnings by improper accounting for multiple element contracts.

   T   F

5. If a company overstates merger reserves at the time of acquiring another company, it can release the surplus reserves into earnings in a later period without decreasing net income at the time of the creation of the reserve.

   T   F

6. When a company that makes a number of acquisitions also creates significant reserves, it is a signal that the company may be creating false reserves.

     T   F

7. When the PPE amount on the balance sheet increases while revenue decreases, it is a signal that expenses may be improperly capitalized.

     T   F

8. If the notes to the financial statements indicate that a company is capitalizing costs that other companies in the same industry recognize as expenses, it is a signal that the company is capitalizing questionable costs.

     T   F

9. Special charges in the income statement that write off previously capitalized costs are always a sign that a company has become conservative in recognizing earnings and that the quality of its earnings is increasing.

     T   F

10. If a parent company discovers that the assets of an acquired company are worth less than it believed at the time of the acquisition, it is appropriate to increase goodwill because this means that the excess of the purchase price over the net asset value of the acquired company was greater than what the parent company originally believed.

     T   F

FILL-IN-THE-BLANK QUESTIONS

Fill in the blanks with information and concepts from this chapter.

11. The opportunity for the creation of WorldCom was the court-ordered breakup of _____, which was then forced to lease long-distance phone lines.

12. WorldCom's Bankruptcy Examiner alleged that WorldCom's _____ was the fuel that kept its acquisition engine running.

13. When a company inappropriately overstates purchase acquisition reserves, it also overstates _____ by a corresponding amount.

14. When a company overstates reserves at the time of acquisition, in later periods, it can release the _____ reserves back into earnings.

15. Adjustments that increase _____ in a later period, with respect to an earlier acquisition, are further signs that a company may be creating false reserves.

16. Investors should be wary of large _____ - _____ charges in the income statement around the acquisition period because these are often signals that the company could be creating false reserves.

17. The misallocation of expenses as assets is known as the improper _____ of expenses.

18. A signal of the fictitious reporting of expenses as assets is a decrease in the ratio of _____ to assets.

19. When a(n) _____ cost remains constant as a percentage of sales while sales decrease, it is a signal that the cost is being understated.

20. If a company changes its accounting policy to begin capitalizing a cost that it previously recorded as an expense, it is a signal that the _____ of the company's earnings may be deteriorating.

MULTIPLE-CHOICE QUESTIONS

21. WorldCom is presented in this textbook as an illustration of overstating earnings by:
    (a) Holding books open after the close of a reporting period.
    (b) Misuse of multiple element contracts.
    (c) Improper use of merger reserves and improper capitalization of expenses.
    (d) Understatement of reserves for bad debts.

22. Which of the following is *not* a signal of overstatement of earnings by improper use of merger reserves?
    (a) When goodwill on acquisition relates to a company that does not have or is unlikely to have a supernormal return on assets.
    (b) When the sales-to-PPE ratio decreases after an acquisition.

(c) When a company that makes a number of acquisitions also creates significant reserves.

(d) Adjustments that increase goodwill in a later period, with respect to an earlier acquisition.

23. When revenue decreases, one would expect fixed costs to:
(a) Remain constant as a percentage of sales.
(b) Increase as a percentage of sales.
(c) Decrease as a percentage of sales.
(d) None of the above.

24. Which of the following costs can be capitalized without contravening GAAP?
(a) Customer acquisition costs.
(b) Software development costs.
(c) Interest costs related to amounts invested in assets under construction.
(d) All of the above.

25. Which of the following reserve accounts was not examined by WorldCom's Bankruptcy Examiner?
(a) Bad debt reserves.
(b) Tax reserves.
(c) Legal reserves.
(d) Cooperative advertising reserves.

26. If a company overstates the reserves of a company that it acquires and increases goodwill by a corresponding amount in the period of the acquisition in order to release the reserves in a later period, which of the following will occur?
(a) A decrease in the amount of the group's operating income in its consolidated income statement in the period of the acquisition.
(b) No decrease in operating income, but a decrease in net income in the group's consolidated income statement in the period of the acquisition.
(c) No decrease in operating income and no decrease net income in the period of the acquisition.
(d) An increase net income in the period of the acquisition.

27. If a company misclassifies an expense as an asset, this will likely cause which of the following signals?
(a) Accounts receivable increase as a percentage of sales.

(b) Fixed expenses increase as percentage of sales.
(c) Asset turnover ratio increases.
(d) Asset turnover ratio decreases.

28. WorldCom improperly accounted for its line cost expense by:
(a) Allocating line-cost expense to PPE in its first recording of the line-cost transactions.
(b) Initially properly debiting the line-cost expense to an expense account and later transferring the expense to PPE.
(c) Misclassifying part of its line-cost expense as goodwill.
(d) Adding its line-cost expense to inventory to reduce cost of goods sold.

29. An overstatement of goodwill on the acquisition of a company can be accomplished by:
(a) An understatement of the value of the assets of the acquired company.
(b) An understatement of the liabilities of the acquired company.
(c) An understatement of reserves required for the restructuring of an acquired company.
(d) A bargain purchase price of the acquired company that is below its net asset value.

30. With which of the following gatekeepers did WorldCom's Bankruptcy Examiner find fault?
(a) The board of directors.
(b) The investment banking company.
(c) Both (a) and (b).
(d) None of the above.

FOR DISCUSSION

31. Signal #1 for the scheme of improper use of acquisition or merger reserves is a parent company allocating large amounts to goodwill when acquiring other companies. Explain why this could be a signal of "improper use of acquisition or merger reserves."

32. Signal #4 for the scheme of improper use of merger reserves is the occurrence of large, one-time charges in the income statement around the time of the acquisition period. Compare the use of one-time charges in the income statement to the use of large amounts of goodwill for the improper use of merger reserves.

SHORT-ANSWER QUESTIONS

33. When Company A acquires Company B, does the fact that Company A paid more for Company B than its net asset value mean that "goodwill" has been acquired? Explain.
34. Why is a decreasing sales-to-PPE ratio a signal of possible overstatement of assets?
35. Explain why the overstatement of a reserve for accumulated depreciation of an acquired company at the time of acquisition would cause an overstatement of goodwill.
36. How was WorldCom able to continue to acquire so many companies and overstate goodwill by so much?

EXERCISES

37. Action Co. has agreed to pay $45,000 to acquire 100 percent of the shares of Sub Co. Action Co. believes that the fair value of Sub Co.'s assets, liabilities, and reserves at the date of acquisition are as follows:

Assets	$ 100,000.00
Liabilities and reserves	$ 60,000.00

Action Co. believes that based on Sub Co.'s future earnings potential, it is prepared to pay $5,000 more for Sub Co. than its net asset value. Action Co. decides to overstate reserves related to Sub Co. by $10,000 at the time of acquisition and to overstate goodwill by a corresponding amount.

How much goodwill will be recorded in respect of the acquisition of Sub Co.?

38. At the time of Big Company's acquisition of Small Company, Big Company believed that Small Company's reserve for doubtful debts was correctly stated at $30,000. Big Company purposely overstated the reserves at the time of acquisition by $20,000 by specifically stating that it believed that this reserve was understated by this amount.

At the end of the next accounting period following the acquisition, the reserve for doubtful debts balance was $50,000 before considering any entries for that period.

Based on aging of the accounts receivable, it appeared that the reserve for doubtful debts balance needed to be stated at $55,000.

Required

a. As a result of the overstatement of the doubtful debts reserve in the acquisition period, what is the bad debt expense in the period following the acquisition?
b. If the reserve for doubtful debts had not been overstated at the time of the acquisition, what would the bad debt expense have been in the period following the acquisition?

39. Extracts for Zeddy Company's quarterly income statements and balance sheets for quarters 1–4 are as follows:

	Q1	Q2	Q3	Q4
	$	$	$	$
Sales	200,000	150,000	100,000	75,000
Selling & admin expenses	50,000	37,000	25,000	19,000

Calculate selling and administrative expenses as a percentage of sales for quarters 1–4 and comment on the results.

40. Extracts from Zee's quarterly income statements and balance sheets for the four quarters of year 1 are as follows:

	Q1	Q2	Q3	Q4
	$	$	$	$
	Millions	Millions	Millions	Millions
Sales	1,000	1,020	1,030	1,040
PPE	1,000	1,000	1,500	1,500
Total assets	5,000	5,100	5,600	5,700

Required

a. Calculate the sales/PPE ratio for quarters 1–4.
b. Calculate the sales/total assets ratio for quarters 1–4.
c. Comment on the above ratios.

CASE STUDY

Tyco International, Ltd.

- **Read** Litigation Release No. 19657 for Tyco International Systems, Ltd., given below.
- **Read** extracts from the April 2006 SEC Complaint against Tyco, given below.
- **Examine** the financial statements of Tyco International for the fiscal years ended 1998–2002, given below.
- **Respond** to the following Case Study Questions.

Required

a. **Chapter 5 of this text lists a number of signals of the misuse of acquisition or merger reserves.** Identify some of these signals in Tyco's financial statements (given below) and explain how your findings could have indicated to users of Tyco's financial statements that the company may have been misusing reserves–that could have been created at the time of the acquisitions–to increase post-acquisition income.

b. **Tyco's Ratio of Sales to Total Assets:** Calculate the trend in Tyco's ratio of Sales to Total Assets over the period 1998–2002 and then discuss whether investors should have been troubled by the trend in this ratio.

c. **Understating assets or overstating liabilities and reserves when acquiring a new company:** When a new company is acquired, how does understating assets or overstating liabilities and reserves increase the reported post-acquisition income of the parent company?

Litigation Release (LR 19657) for Tyco International

U.S. Securities and Exchange Commission

Litigation Release No. 19657/April 17, 2006*

Accounting and Auditing Enforcement Release No. 2414/April 17, 2006

SEC v. Tyco International Ltd., 06 CV 2942 (S.D.N.Y. filed April 17, 2006)

SEC Brings Settled Charges Against Tyco International Ltd. Alleging Billion Dollar Accounting Fraud

The U.S. Securities and Exchange Commission today filed a settled civil injunctive action in the United States District Court for the Southern District of New York against Tyco International Ltd. The Commission's complaint in that action alleges that, from 1996 through 2002, Tyco violated the federal securities laws by, among other things, utilizing various improper accounting practices and a scheme involving transactions with no economic substance to overstate its reported financial results by at least one billion dollars.

---

* Obtained from U.S. Securities and Exchange Commission. *www.sec.gov*. Tyco consented to the entry of a final judgement without admitting or denying the allegations.

The Commission's complaint alleges that Tyco inflated its operating income by at least $500 million as a result of improper accounting practices related to some of the many acquisitions that Tyco engaged in during that time. Tyco's improper acquisition accounting included undervaluing acquired assets, overvaluing acquired liabilities, and misusing accounting rules concerning the establishment and utilization of purchase accounting reserves. The complaint further alleges that, apart from its acquisition activities, Tyco improperly established and used various kinds of reserves to make adjustments at the end of reporting periods to enhance and smooth its publicly reported results and to meet earnings forecasts.

The complaint alleges that Tyco inflated its operating income by $567 million from its fiscal year 1998 through its fiscal quarter ended December 31, 2002, by means of connection fees that Tyco's ADT Security Services, Inc. subsidiary charged to dealers from whom it purchased security monitoring contracts. Because the connection fee was fully offset by a simultaneous increase in the purchase price ADT allocated to the dealers' security monitoring contracts, the connection fee transaction lacked economic substance and should not have been recorded in Tyco's income statement. In 2003, Tyco restated its operating income and cash flow relating to the connection fees.

The complaint further alleges that, from September 1996 through early 2002, Tyco failed to disclose in its proxy statements and annual reports certain executive compensation, executive indebtedness, and related party transactions of its former senior management. Tyco also incorrectly accounted for certain executive bonuses it paid in its fiscal years 2000 and 2001, thereby excluding from its operating expenses the costs associated with those bonuses. Finally, the complaint alleges that Tyco violated the anti-bribery provisions of the Foreign Corrupt Practices Act when employees or agents of its Earth Tech Brasil Ltda. subsidiary made payments to Brazilian officials for the purpose of obtaining or retaining business for Tyco.

Between 1996 and 2002, as a result of these various practices, Tyco made false and misleading statements or omissions in its filings with the Commission and its public statements to investors and analysts.

Without admitting or denying the allegations in the Commission's complaint, Tyco has consented to the entry of a final judgment permanently enjoining it from violating Section 17(a) of the Securities Act of 1933, Sections 10(b), 13(a), 13(b)(2)(A), 13(b)(2)(B), 14(a), and 30A(a) of the Securities Exchange Act of 1934, and Exchange Act Rules 10b-5, 12b-20, 13a-1, 13a-13, 13b2-1, and 14a-9. The proposed final judgment also orders Tyco to pay $1 in disgorgement and a $50 million civil penalty.

The Commission's investigation is continuing with respect to individuals. The Commission acknowledges the assistance and cooperation of the Manhattan District Attorney and the New York City Police Department.

Extract from Complaint against Tyco International
Case 06-CV-2942 Filed April 13, 2006*
UNITED STATES DISTRICT COURT
SOUTHERN DISTRICT OF NEW YORK

16. Understating acquired assets benefited Tyco's earnings by decreasing depreciation expense in future periods for long-lived assets and, for current assets, by allowing Tyco to record larger profits as the assets were utilized. Overstating acquired liabilities allowed Tyco to maintain on its books and records inflated reserves, which Tyco used in future periods to improve its earnings.

17. In certain acquisitions made in 1996, Tyco officials convinced the companies that were being acquired to make entries to their books and records that understated the assets and overstated the liabilities that Tyco would acquire. For example, at the urging of Tyco officials, Thorn-EMI, whose fire protection operations Tyco acquired, made adjustments that reduced its assets and increased its liabilities by $76.5 million, resulting in Tyco's operating income in future financial periods being overstated by approximately $29 million. At Zettler AG, a security monitoring company Tyco acquired, adjustments were made to Zettler's books that overstated its liabilities and resulted in Tyco's operating income in subsequent reporting periods being increased by approximately $6.6 million. And at Carlisle Plastics, Carlisle management made entries to its books and records, at Tyco's request, that reduced its assets and increased its liabilities by $36.4 million, resulting in an overstatement of Tyco's post-acquisition earnings.

---

* Obtained from U. S. Securities and Exchange Commission. *www.sec.gov.*

FINANCIAL STATEMENTS

UNITED STATES
SECURITIES AND EXCHANGE COMMISSION
Washington, D.C. 20549

Extracts from FORM 10-K[2]

Annual report pursuant to Section 13 or 15(d) of the Securities Exchange Act of 1934

For the fiscal years 1998-2002

TYCO INTERNATIONAL LTD.

Consolidated Balance Sheet 1999

(in millions, except share data)

	SEPTEMBER 30,	
	1999	**1998**
CURRENT ASSETS:		
Cash and cash equivalents	$ 1,762.0	$ 1,072.9
Receivables, less allowance for doubtful accounts of $329.8 in 1999 and $317.6 in 1998.	4,582.3	3,478.4
Contracts in process	536.6	565.3
Inventories	2,849.1	2,610.0
Deferred income taxes	711.6	797.6
Prepaid expenses and other current assets	721.2	430.7
Total current assets	11,162.8	8,954.9
PROPERTY, PLANT AND EQUIPMENT, NET	7,322.4	6,104.3
GOODWILL AND OTHER INTANGIBLE ASSETS, NET	12,158.9	7,105.5
LONG-TERM INVESTMENTS	269.7	228.4
DEFERRED INCOME TAXES	668.8	320.9
OTHER ASSETS	779.0	726.7
TOTAL ASSETS	$32,361.6	$23,440.7
CURRENT LIABILITIES:		
Loans payable and current maturities of long-term debt	$ 1,012.8	$ 815.0
Accounts payable	2,530.8	1,733.4
Accrued expenses and other current liabilities	3,599.7	3,069.3
Contracts in process—billings in excess of costs	977.9	332.9
Deferred revenue	258.8	266.5
Income taxes	798.0	773.9
Deferred income taxes	1.0	15.2
Total current liabilities	9,179.0	7,006.2
LONG-TERM DEBT	9,109.4	5,424.7
OTHER LONG-TERM LIABILITIES	1,236.4	976.8
DEFERRED INCOME TAXES	504.2	131.2
TOTAL LIABILITIES	20,029.0	13,538.9

(continued)

---

[2] Extracted from 10-K filings for Tyco International LTD. 1999-2002. Obtained from U.S. Securities and Exchange Commission. *www.sec.gov.*

	SEPTEMBER 30,	
	1999	**1998**
COMMITMENTS AND CONTINGENCIES (NOTE 17)		
SHAREHOLDERS' EQUITY:		
Preference shares, $1 par value, 125,000,000 authorized, none issued	—	—
Common shares, $0.20 par value, 2,500,000,000 shares authorized; 1,690,175,338 shares outstanding in 1999 and 1,620,463,428 shares outstanding in 1998, net of 11,432,678 shares owned by subsidiaries in 1999 and 6,742,006 shares owned by subsidiaries in 1998	338.0	324.1
Capital in excess:		
Share premium	4,881.5	4,035.0
Contributed surplus, net of deferred compensation of $30.7 in 1999 and $67.3 in 1998	3,607.6	2,584.0
Accumulated earnings	3,955.6	3,162.6
Accumulated other comprehensive loss	(450.1)	(203.9)
TOTAL SHAREHOLDERS' EQUITY	12,332.6	9,901.8
TOTAL LIABILITIES AND SHAREHOLDERS' EQUITY	$32,361.6	$23,440.7

Tyco International

Consolidated Statements of Operations 1998–1999[3]

(in millions, except share data)

	YEAR ENDED SEPTEMBER 30, 1999	YEAR ENDED SEPTEMBER 30, 1998
NET SALES	$22,496.5	$19,061.7
Cost of sales	14,433.1	12,694.8
Selling, general and administrative expenses	4,436.3	4,161.9
Merger, restructuring and other non-recurring charges	928.8	256.9
Charge for the impairment of long-lived assets	507.5	—
Write-off of purchased in-process research and development	—	—
OPERATING INCOME	2,190.8	1,948.1
Interest income	61.5	62.6
Interest expense	(547.1)	(307.9)
Income (loss) before income taxes, extraordinary items and cumulative effect of accounting changes	1,705.2	1,702.8
Income taxes	(637.5)	(534.2)
Income (loss) before extraordinary items and cumulative effect of accounting changes	1,067.7	1,168.6
Extraordinary items, net of taxes	(45.7)	(2.4)
Cumulative effect of accounting changes, net of taxes	—	—
NET INCOME	1,022.0	1,166.2

---

[3] Extracted from 10-K filings for Tyco International LTD. 1998-2002. Obtained from U.S. Securities and Exchange Commission. *www.sec.gov*

Tyco International

Consolidated Statements of Cash Flows 1998–1999[4]

	YEAR ENDED SEPTEMBER 30, 1999	YEAR ENDED SEPTEMBER 30, 1998
CASH FLOWS FROM OPERATING ACTIVITIES:		
Net income (loss)	$ 985.3	$ 1,166.2
Adjustments to reconcile net income (loss) to net cash provided by operating activities:		
Merger, restructuring and other non-recurring charges.....	517.1	253.7
Charge for the impairment of long-lived assets	335.0	—
Write-off of purchased in-process research and development	—	—
Extraordinary items	45.4	2.4
Effect of accounting changes	—	—
Depreciation	979.6	895.1
Goodwill and other intangibles amortization	331.6	242.6
Debt and refinancing cost amortization	10.4	11.3
Interest on ITS vendor note	(12.1)	(11.5)
Deferred income taxes	334.3	(8.2)
Provisions for losses on accounts receivable and inventory	211.5	192.9
Other non-cash items	(6.7)	2.5
Changes in assets and liabilities, net of the effects of acquisitions and divestitures:		
Receivables	(796.0)	(88.9)
Proceeds from accounts receivable sale	50.0	—
Contracts in process	642.2	(91.4)
Inventories	(124.4)	(226.2)
Prepaid expenses and other current assets	(154.1)	(57.7)
Accounts payable, accrued expenses and other current liabilities	361.1	(96.4)
Income taxes payable	(10.2)	66.3
Deferred revenue	(54.1)	(6.5)
Other, net	(96.1)	35.6
Net cash provided by operating activities	3,549.8	2,281.8
CASH FLOWS FROM INVESTING ACTIVITIES:		
Purchase of property, plant and equipment	(1,632.5)	(1,317.5)
Purchase of leased property (Note 2)	(234.0)	—
Acquisition of businesses, net of cash acquired	(4,901.2)	(4,251.8)
Disposal of businesses	926.8	—
Decrease (increase) in investments	10.5	6.4
Other	(13.7)	(83.1)
Net cash utilized by investing activities	(5,844.1)	(5,646.0)
CASH FLOWS FROM FINANCING ACTIVITIES:		
Net receipts of short-term debt	162.3	287.1
Net proceeds from issuance of public debt	1,173.7	2,744.5
Repayment of long-term debt, including debt tenders	(2,057.8)	(1,074.6)
Proceeds from long-term debt	3,665.6	802.0
Proceeds from sale of common shares	—	1,245.0

(continued)

---

[4] Extracted from 10-K filings for Tyco International LTD. 1998-2002. Obtained from U.S. Securities and Exchange Commission. *www.sec.gov*

	YEAR ENDED SEPTEMBER 30, 1999	YEAR ENDED SEPTEMBER 30, 1998
Proceeds from exercise of options and warrants	872.4	348.7
Dividends paid	(187.9)	(303.0)
Purchase of treasury shares	(637.8)	(283.9)
Other	(7.1)	(36.5)
Net cash provided by financing activities	2,983.4	3,729.3
Net increase in cash and cash equivalents	689.1	365.1
CASH AND CASH EQUIVALENTS AT BEGINNING OF YEAR, AS RESTATED	1,072.9	707.8
CASH AND CASH EQUIVALENTS AT END OF YEAR	$ 1,762.0	$ 1,072.9
SUPPLEMENTARY CASH FLOW DISCLOSURE:		
Interest paid	$ 509.1	$ 250.7
Income taxes paid (net of refunds)	$ 209.7	$ 345.9

Extracts from FORM 10-K[5]

TYCO INTERNATIONAL LTD.
2000–2002

Consolidated Statements of Operations 2000–2002[5]
(in millions, except share data)

	YEAR ENDED SEPTEMBER 30,		
	2002	2001	2000
Revenue from product sales	$ 28,794.8	$ 28,987.4	$ 24,958.4
Service revenue	6,848.9	5,049.2	3,973.5
NET REVENUES	35,643.7	34,036.6	28,931.9
Cost of product sales	19,510.8	18,334.4	15,959.8
Cost of services	3,570.2	2,615.9	1,971.4
Selling, general and administrative expenses	8,086.8	6,361.5	5,252.0
Restructuring and other unusual charges, net	1,203.9	233.6	175.3
Charges for the impairment of long-lived assets	3,489.5	120.1	99.0
Goodwill impairment	1,343.7	—	—
Write-off of purchased in-process research and development	17.8	184.3	—
OPERATING (LOSS) INCOME	(1,579.0)	6,186.8	5,474.4
Interest income	117.3	128.3	75.2
Interest expense	(1,077.0)	(904.8)	(844.8)
Other (expense) income, net	(233.0)	250.3	(0.3)
Net gain on sale of common shares of a subsidiary	(39.6)	64.1	1,760.0
(Loss) income from continuing operations before income taxes and minority interest	(2,811.3)	5,724.7	6,464.5
Income taxes	(257.7)	(1,275.7)	(1,925.9)
Minority interest	(1.4)	(47.5)	(18.7)
(LOSS) INCOME FROM CONTINUING OPERATIONS	(3,070.4)	4,401.5	4,519.9

(continued)

---

[5] Extracted from 10-K filings for Tyco International LTD. 1998-2002. Obtained from U.S. Securities and Exchange Commission. *www.sec.gov.*

	YEAR ENDED SEPTEMBER 30,		
	2002	2001	2000
(Loss) income from discontinued operations of Tyco Capital (net of tax expense of $316.1 million and $195.0 million for the year ended September 30, 2002 and 2001, respectively)	(6,282.5)	252.5	—
Loss on sale of Tyco Capital, net of $0 tax	(58.8)	—	—
(Loss) income before cumulative effect of accounting changes	(9,411.7)	4,654.0	4,519.9
Cumulative effect of accounting changes, net of tax	—	(683.4)	—
NET (LOSS) INCOME	$ (9,411.7)	$ 3,970.6	$ 4,519.9

Tyco International
Consolidated Balance Sheets 2001–2002[6]
(in millions, except share data)

	SEPTEMBER 30,	
	2002	2001
ASSETS		
Current Assets:		
Cash and cash equivalents	$ 6,186.8	$ 1,779.2
Restricted cash	196.2	—
Accounts receivables, less allowance for doubtful accounts ($629.1 at September 30, 2002 and $550.4 at September 30, 2001	5,848.6	6,453.2
Inventories	4,716.0	5,101.3
Deferred income taxes	1,338.1	980.2
Other current assets	1,478.9	1,532.3
Total current assets	19,764.6	15,846.2
Net Assets of Discontinued Operations	—	10,598.0
Tyco Global Network	581.6	2,342.4
Property, Plant and Equipment, Net	9,969.5	9,970.3
Goodwill, Net	26,093.2	23,264.0
Intangible Assets, Net	6,562.6	5,476.9
Other Assets	3,442.9	3,524.8
TOTAL ASSETS	$66,414.4	$71,022.6
LIABILITIES AND SHAREHOLDERS' EQUITY		
Current Liabilities:		
Loans payable and current maturities of long-term debt....	$ 7,719.0	$ 2,023.0
Accounts payable	3,170.0	3,692.6
Accrued expenses and other current liabilities	5,270.8	5,181.8
Contracts in process—billings in excess of cost	522.1	935.0
Deferred revenue	731.3	973.5
Income taxes payable	2,218.9	1,845.0
Total current liabilities	19,632.1	14,650.9
Long-Term Debt	16,486.8	19,596.0
Other Long-Term Liabilities	5,462.1	4,736.9
TOTAL LIABILITIES	41,581.0	38,983.8

(continued)

[6] Extracted from 10-K filings for Tyco International LTD. 1998-2002. Obtained from U.S. Securities and Exchange Commission. *www.sec.gov.*

	SEPTEMBER 30,	
	2002	**2001**
Commitments and Contingencies (Note 20) Minority Interest	42.8	301.4
Shareholders' Equity:		
Preference shares, $1 par value, 125,000,000 shares authorized, one share outstanding at September 30, 2002 and 2001	—	—
Common shares, $0.20 par value, 2,500,000,000 shares authorized; 1,995,699,758 and 1,935,464,840 shares outstanding, net of 22,522,250 and 17,026,256 shares owned by subsidiaries at September 30, 2002 and 2001, respectively	399.1	387.1
Capital in excess:		
Share premium	8,146.9	7,962.8
Contributed surplus, net of deferred compensation of $51.2 at September 30, 2002 and $85.3 at September 30, 2001	15,042.7	12,561.3
Accumulated earnings	2,794.1	12,305.7
Accumulated other comprehensive loss	(1,592.2)	(1,479.5)
TOTAL SHAREHOLDERS' EQUITY	24,790.6	31,737.4
TOTAL LIABILITIES AND SHAREHOLDERS' EQUITY	$66,414.4	$71,022.6

Tyco International

Consolidated Statements of Cash Flows 2000–2002

(in millions, except share data)

	YEARS ENDED SEPTEMBER 30,		
	2002	**2001**	**2000**
CASH FLOWS FROM OPERATING ACTIVITIES:			
(Loss) income from continuing operations	$ (3,070.4)	$ 4,401.5	$ 4,519.9
Adjustments to reconcile net (loss) income from continuing operations to net cash provided by operating activities:			
Non-cash restructuring and other unusual charges (credits), net	851.5	145.2	(84.2)
Write-off of purchased in-process research and development	17.8	184.3	—
Charges for the impairment of long-lived assets	3,489.5	120.1	99.0
Goodwill impairment	1,343.7	—	—
Minority interest in net income of consolidated subsidiaries	1.4	47.5	18.7
Net loss (gain) on sale of businesses	(7.2)	(410.4)	—
Loss on investments	270.8	133.8	—
Net loss (gain) on sale of common shares of subsidiary	39.6	(64.1)	(1,760.0)
Depreciation	1,465.5	1,243.1	1,095.0
Goodwill and intangible assets amortization	567.4	897.5	549.4
Deferred income taxes	(535.6)	219.0	507.8
Provision for losses on accounts receivable and inventory	493.9	593.5	354.3
Debt and refinancing cost amortization	194.0	108.4	6.8
Charges related to prior years (see Note 1	222.0	—	—

(continued)

	YEARS ENDED SEPTEMBER 30,		
	2002	**2001**	**2000**
Other non-cash items	(26.0)	81.8	60.0
Changes in assets and liabilities, net of the effects of acquisitions and divestitures:			
Accounts receivable	1,014.5	(434.1)	(992.4)
(Decrease in) proceeds under sale of accounts receivable program	(56.4)	490.6	100.0
Contracts in progress	(336.5)	(192.5)	28.9
Inventories	(47.2)	(678.8)	(850.0)
Other current assets	(51.9)	313.7	100.2
Accounts payable	(833.7)	(249.1)	443.9
Accrued expenses and other current liabilities	272.2	(606.1)	53.1
Income taxes	335.1	370.7	896.4
Deferred revenue	(35.5)	304.1	(0.2)
Other	117.0	(94.2)	128.4
Net cash provided by operating activities from continuing operations	5,695.5	6,925.5	5,275.0
Net cash provided by (used in) operating activities from discontinued operations	1,462.9	(260.2)	—
Net cash provided by operating activities	7,158.4	6,665.3	5,275.0
CASH FLOWS FROM INVESTING ACTIVITIES:			
Purchase of property, plant and equipment, net	(1,708.7)	(1,797.5)	(1,703.8)
Construction in progress—Tyco Global Network	(1,146.0)	(2,247.7)	(111.1)
Acquisition of businesses, net of cash acquired	(3,084.8)	(10,956.6)	(4,246.5)
Cash paid for purchase accounting and holdback/earn-out liabilities	(624.1)	(894.4)	(544.2)
Net proceeds from the sale of CIT	4,395.4	—	—
Disposal of other businesses, net of cash sold	138.7	904.4	74.4
Net purchases of investments	(16.8)	(142.8)	(353.4)
Restricted cash	(196.2)	—	—
Other	(83.2)	(177.2)	(52.9)
Net cash used in investing activities from continuing operations	(2,325.7)	(15,311.8)	(6,937.5)
CIT cash balance acquired	—	2,156.4	—
Net cash provided by investing activities from discontinued operations	2,684.3	1,516.8	—
Net cash provided by (used in) investing activities	358.6	(11,638.6)	(6,937.5)
CASH FLOWS FROM FINANCING ACTIVITIES:			
Net proceeds from debt	1,951.3	8,535.6	680.4
Proceeds from sale of common shares	—	2,196.6	—
Proceeds from exercise of options	185.7	545.0	355.3
Net proceeds from sale of common shares by subsidiary	—	—	2,130.7
Dividends paid	(100.3)	(90.0)	(86.2)
Repurchase of Tyco common shares	(789.2)	(1,326.1)	(1,885.1)

(continued)

	YEARS ENDED SEPTEMBER 30,		
	2002	**2001**	**2000**
Repurchase of minority interest shares of subsidiary	—	(270.0)	—
Capital contributions to Tyco Capital	(200.0)	(675.0)	—
Other	(9.7)	(15.4)	(29.8)
Net cash provided by financing activities from continuing operations	1,037.8	8,900.7	1,165.3
Net cash used in financing activities from discontinued operations	(2,874.6)	(2,605.0)	—
Net cash (used in) provided by financing activities	(1,836.8)	6,295.7	1,165.3
NET INCREASE (DECREASE) IN CASH AND CASH EQUIVALENTS	5,680.2	1,322.4	(497.2)
TYCO CAPITAL'S CASH AND CASH EQUIVALENTS TRANSFERRED TO DISCONTINUED OPERATIONS	(1,272.6)	(808.0)	—
CASH AND CASH EQUIVALENTS AT BEGINNING OF PERIOD	1,779.2	1,264.8	1,762.0
CASH AND CASH EQUIVALENTS AT END OF PERIOD	$ 6,186.8	$ 1,779.2	$ 1,264.8
SUPPLEMENTARY CASH FLOW DISCLOSURE:			
Interest paid	$ 943.8	$ 896.5	$ 814.2
Income taxes paid	$ 668.3	$ 798.9	$ 491.1

Tyco International

Consolidated Balance Sheet 2000[7]
(in millions, except share data)

	SEPTEMBER 30
	2000
CURRENT ASSETS:	
Cash and cash equivalents	$ 1,264.8
Receivables, less allowance for doubtful accounts of $442.1 in 2000 and $329.8 in 1999	5,630.4
Contracts in process	357.3
Inventories	3,845.1
Deferred income taxes	683.3
Prepaid expenses and other current assets	1,034.8
Total current assets	12,815.7
CONSTRUCTION IN PROGRESS—TYCOM GLOBAL NETWORK	111.1
PROPERTY, PLANT AND EQUIPMENT, NET	8,218.4
GOODWILL AND OTHER INTANGIBLE ASSETS, NET	16,332.6
LONG-TERM INVESTMENTS	1,653.7
DEFERRED INCOME TAXES	532.5
OTHER ASSETS	740.3
TOTAL ASSETS	$40,404.3
CURRENT LIABILITIES:	
Loans payable and current maturities of long-term debt	$ 1,537.2
Accounts payable	3,291.9

(continued)

---

[7] Extracted from 10-K filings for Tyco International LTD. 1998-2002. Obtained from U.S. Securities and Exchange Commission. *www.sec.gov*

	SEPTEMBER 30
	2000
Accrued expenses and other current liabilities	4,038.2
Contracts in process—billings in excess of costs	835.0
Deferred revenue	265.7
Income taxes	1,650.3
Deferred income taxes	60.6
Total current liabilities	11,678.9
LONG-TERM DEBT	9,461.8
OTHER LONG-TERM LIABILITIES	1,095.3
DEFERRED INCOME TAXES	791.6
TOTAL LIABILITIES	23,027.6
COMMITMENTS AND CONTINGENCIES (NOTE 17)	
MINORITY INTEREST	343.5
SHAREHOLDERS' EQUITY:	
Preference shares, $1 par value, 125,000,000 shares authorized, none issued	—
Common shares, $0.20 par value, 2,500,000,000 shares authorized; 1,684,511,070 shares outstanding in 2000 and 1,690,175,338 shares outstanding in 1999, net of 31,551,310 shares owned by subsidiaries in 2000 and 11,432,678 shares owned by subsidiaries in 1999........	336.9
Capital in excess:	
Share premium	5,233.3
Contributed surplus, net of deferred compensation of $59.4 in 2000 and $30.7 in 1999	2,786.3
Accumulated earnings	8,427.6
Accumulated other comprehensive income (loss)	249.1
TOTAL SHAREHOLDERS' EQUITY	17,033.2
TOTAL LIABILITIES AND SHAREHOLDERS' EQUITY	$40,404.3

Abracadabra

After studying this chapter, you should be able to:

- Describe Livent's methods of failing to record expenses and improperly deferring expenses.
- Explain Rite Aid's method of understating cost of goods sold.
- Identify Allegheny's understatement of bad debt expense.
- Describe Lockheed's failure to record its asset impairment.
- Identify and explain the signals in financial statements that could raise concern that a company might be understating its expenses.

- Livent, Rite Aid, Allegheny (AHERF), and Lockheed are presented as examples of understatements of expenses (see Table 1.1 on p. 19)

CHAPTER OUTLINE

- Livent: Phantom of the Finances
- Rite Aid: "The Keys to the Kingdom"
- Allegheny (AHERF): Trick or Treatment?
- Lockheed: Sky High
- Key Terms

- Ethics at Work
- Assignments
- Case Study: Navistar International Corporation

LIVENT: PHANTOM OF THE FINANCES

Livent is presented mainly as an example of improper expense recognition via failure to record expenses and via improper deferral of expenses.

Livent, Inc, was a Canadian theater company that originated in Toronto toward the end of the 1980s. It expanded quickly, trading its stock on NASDAQ in the United States after only a few years. Two of the main performers in the dramatic saga of Livent were its founders, Garth Drabinsky and Myron Gottlieb, who staged many large and lavish shows such as *Ragtime*, *Showboat*, and *Phantom of the Opera*. Not satisfied with creating grand fantasies on stage, it seems they may have, according to the SEC, also performed some creative artifice on the company's financial statements.

In 1998, Livent was purchased by a U.S. consortium headed by Michael Ovitz, the well-known Hollywood icon. However, it did not take long before "the new owners said that they had uncovered accounting irregularities" (Simon, 2002). Toward the end of 1998, Livent declared bankruptcy in both the United States and Canada. In January 1999, Drabinsky and Gottlieb were indicted in the United States on 16 counts of fraud and conspiracy, but they refused to face these charges and remained in Canada.

In October 2002, the Royal Canadian Mounted Police filed 19 charges of fraud against Drabinsky and Gotlieb.

Livent's irregular reporting schemes are particularly interesting because they were implemented not only to present a better-looking overall income statement and balance sheet, which inflated the stock price, but also to make particular shows appear to be more successful than they really were. For instance, if *Ragtime*'s ticket sales fell below $500,000, the Schubert Theater (in Los Angeles) could evict the company. Further, if *Ragtime* had been evicted, according to the SEC, this would have undermined its planned opening on Broadway (AAER 1095, 1999). Therefore, it became important for Livent to report high ticket sales even if the seats were not filled.

The Livent case is presented here because it contains some clear examples that alert the reader to the frequently committed, old-fashioned fraud of omitting expenses and the corresponding liabilities by simply failing to record invoices in the ledger during the correct period. Such improper expense recognition understates both expenses and liabilities and overstates earnings. (**Improper expense recognition** refers to the omission of expenses or movement of expenses from the financial statements in the period in which they should be recorded to an earlier or later period.) Livent is also presented as a good example of the scheme of improperly deferring expenses via transferring costs from their correct accounts to other accounts to delay amortization. (**Improper deferral of expenses** refers to any technique that avoids the recording of an expense in the current period by shifting the recognition of the expense to a later period's financial statements.)

The Sarbanes-Oxley (SOX) Report's study of SEC enforcement actions found that the most common method of misstating financial reports was improper expense recognition via a "lack of accrual" of expenses and their corresponding liabilities. This is a subset of the SEC category described as "Failure to Record Expenses or Losses via

Improper Capitalization/Deferral or Lack of Accrual" (SOX Report, 2002), which can actually be broken down into the following three components:

- Failure to Record Expenses or Losses
- Improper Deferral of Expenses or Losses
- Improper Capitalization of Expenses or Losses

Whereas WorldCom represents the leading and largest case of the Improper Capitalization part of this category, the Livent case is presented to complete the category with an interesting and illustrative example of the first and second components listed above. Livent's financial statements also contained some examples of improper capitalization.

As is usually the case, the SEC findings also alleged other overlapping irregularities in Livent's financial reporting. The company understated some expenses by capitalizing them as assets (and moved expenses to different periods by transferring the expenses to different assets or theatrical shows) to amortize them more slowly and defer recognition of the expense. The SEC also found that Livent employees recorded revenues before they should have by recognizing revenues that were subject to side agreements. In addition, they recorded fictitious ticket sales. Furthermore, the SEC found that Livent's management was involved in a "kickback scheme designed to misappropriate funds for their own use" (AAER 1095, 1999).

AN OVERVIEW OF LIVENT'S FICTITIOUS FINANCIAL REPORTING SCHEMES

Allegedly, Livent's manipulations were carefully orchestrated by senior management. After two controllers produced the general ledger each quarter, they gave the information to Gordon Eckstein, the former vice president of finance and administration, who summarized the information. The SEC alleged that Eckstein then met with Livent's top executives. At these meetings, they "agreed on the approximate nature and quantity of adjustments to be made . . . in order to achieve a predetermined false financial picture"[1] (AAER 1095, 1999). After the adjustments were completed, Eckstein met with top management again, with an adjusted general ledger, and further specific adjustments were directed.

The SEC states that senior management provided "approximate dollar adjustments that they [i.e. staff] were required to make to various accounts in the balance sheet and income statement, including expense categories, specific shows and fixed-asset accounts." In addition, the SEC found that Drabinsky, Livent's former CEO, and Gottlieb, the company's former president, ". . . from at least 1994 through the first quarter of 1998 . . . engaged in a deliberate manipulation of Livent's books and records." As a result of these manipulations, which were orchestrated together with other officers and employees of the company, expenses were understated for the purpose of inflating profits. There were many adjustments that they could not enter, however, because such adjustments "would have left a trail of 'red flags' for the auditors." Therefore, senior

---

[1] Livent submitted an offer of settlement and consented to the entry of the order without admitting or denying the findings as set out in AAER 1095 (1999).

company officials had a special computer program designed that would enable accounting personnel to "override the accounting system without a paper or transaction trail." The Commission also maintained, "This process had the effect of falsifying the books, records and accounts of the company so completely that the adjustments appeared as original transactions, and no trace of the actual original entries remained in the company's general ledger." (Quotes from AAER 1095, 1999)

By means of the previously mentioned schemes, Livent's financial statements understated expenses in three ways:

- They erased expense invoices from the accounting system.
- They deferred expenses by transferring costs from a current theatrical show to other shows to defer amortizing the assets.
- They transferred production costs to fixed assets.

Scheme #1: Understatement of Expenses via Removing Invoices from the Records

Of particular interest for the financial reporting ploy of failure to record expenses was Livent's erasure of expense invoices. The SEC findings described the company's actions as follows:

> . . .at the end of each quarter, Livent simply removed certain expenses and the related liabilities from the general ledger, literally erasing them from the company's books. In the succeeding quarter, the expenses and related liabilities would be re-entered in the books as original entries. This blatant accounting manipulation violated the basic tenets of GAAP. The amount of expenses moved from current periods to future periods was tracked at Livent as the "Expense Roll." This manipulation permitted significant redirection in show expenses while also increasing profits. For example, the total expenses rolled from the first to the second quarter of 1997 was [sic] approximately $10 million. (AAER 1095, 1999)

Specific invoices were periodically identified as part of the effort to adjust reported profits. Then, on an invoice-by-invoice basis, they were deleted from the accounting system. This understatement of expenses and liabilities of $10 million for the first quarter of 1997 was a significant part of the financial misstatements. The Commission found that for 1997, Livent reported a pretax loss of $62.1 million, when its actual loss was a minimum of $83.6 million.

Scheme #2: Improper Deferral of Expenses

Livent also represents an example of the failure to record expenses or losses by means of improper deferral. In this instance, as is often the case, Livent achieved the deferral of expenses by moving the cost from one asset account to another, where the amortization could be delayed. This is a prevalent method of moving expenses from current periods to future periods. According to the SEC:

> Livent transferred costs from one show currently running to another show that had not yet opened or that had a longer amortization period. This accounting manipulation increased profits in a particular quarter by reducing the charge for

amortization of preproduction costs, since amortization is only appropriate once a production has begun. For example, in 1996 and 1997, approximately $12 million relating to seven different shows and twenty-seven different locations was transferred to the accounts of approximately thirty-one different future locations and ten other shows then in process. (AAER 1095, 1999)

Livent internally tracked the amortization moved in this manner from current periods to future periods under the clandestine label of the "Amortization Roll."

Variations on this scheme of deferring current expenses to later periods include extending the time period over which assets are amortized and making changes in accounting policies regarding the capitalization of costs. Two possible manipulations to look out for are changes regarding policies for the capitalization of software costs and the capitalization of pre-opening costs.

Scheme #3: Improper Capitalization of Expenses

As an example of improper capitalization of expenses, Livent also transferred preproduction costs for shows to fixed asset accounts, such as those for construction of theaters. Livent's preproduction costs should have been expensed through amortization over the life of the shows (up to a period of not more than five years) once the shows began. However, fixed assets were amortized over periods up to 40 years. In 1997, Livent transferred preproduction costs and operating expenses "totaling $15 million from six different shows in thirty locations to three different fixed asset accounts" (AAER 1095, 1999).

Additional Miscellaneous Schemes

In addition to finding that Livent understated expenses in the previously noted matters, the SEC also found that Livent misstated revenues. During 1996 and 1997, Livent recognized $34 million of revenue on transactions that utilized side agreements that required Livent to repay the revenues that it received. This is an example of either improperly timed revenue (if a later transaction with full economic substance materializes) or fictitious revenue (if there is no intention of finalizing a proper transaction later on).

Further, in an effort to make the Los Angeles production of *Ragtime* look more successful, senior management of Livent arranged for outside associates to purchase approximately $381,000 of tickets on personal credit cards and to make future ticket purchases using personal checks. The amounts were reimbursed to these individuals' companies and recorded as Livent's payments for fixed assets. This is a clear example of both reporting fictitious revenue and overstating assets. Also, even before Livent was a listed company in the United States, the SEC alleged that Drabinsky and Gottlieb engineered a kickback scheme in which the two got outside individuals to inflate invoice amounts to Livent, which Livent paid and for which approximately $7 million was kicked back to Drabinsky and Gottlieb between 1990 and 1994 (AAER 1095, 1999).

All in all, as a result of an independent investigation by KPMG Peat Marwick, Livent restated its financial statements for the years 1996 through the first quarter of 1998. These restatements resulted "in a cumulative adverse effect on net income in excess of $98 million (Cdn.)" (AAER 1095, 1999). Trading of Livent stock was suspended, and when trading briefly recommenced after the restatement, Livent's stock "plummeted over ninety-five percent from $6.75 (US) per share to approximately $0.28 cents per share and lost over $100 million (US) in market capitalization" (AAER 1095,1999). The SEC further claimed that for each of Livent's years as a U.S. public company, Livent either reported inflated pretax earnings or understated its pretax losses:

> For fiscal 1995, Livent reported pretax earnings of $18.2 million. In fact, the company's true earnings were approximately $15 million. For fiscal 1996, Livent reported pretax earnings of $14.2 million. In fact the company incurred a loss of more than $20 million in that year. For fiscal 1997, Livent reported a pretax loss of $62.1 million. In fact, the company's true loss in fiscal 1997 was at least $83.6 million. (AAER 1095, 1999)

SIGNALS OF UNDERSTATEMENT OF EXPENSES

Here is an examination of some of the signals indicating that a company may have engaged in improper expense recognition.

Signals of Fictitious Reporting Scheme #1—Understating Expenses and the Corresponding Liabilities via Lack of Accrual

Numerous signals can alert investors to the fictitious reporting scheme of simply omitting the recording of expenses in the current period.

SIGNAL #1: DECREASE IN EXPENSE AS A PERCENTAGE OF SALES   As with any understatement of expenses, you should test each category of expense as a percentage of sales to see whether it represents a decreasing percentage compared to previous quarters or periods or whether the expense is a smaller percentage of sales than the average for the industry. Also, if a category of expense has a significant fixed-cost element and the expense remains the same percentage of sales as sales decrease, it is an indication that some of the fixed expenses may not be recorded. Fixed costs increase as a percentage of sales when sales volume declines.

SIGNAL #2: DECREASE IN CURRENT LIABILITIES AS A PERCENTAGE OF CURRENT ASSETS OR OF SALES   When the company first omits recording expenses and current liabilities, this omission decreases the company's current liabilities as a percentage of current assets and as a percentage of sales. Such a change could, of course, be the result of an improvement in efficiency or of legitimately paying off current liabilities earlier—for example, by obtaining a long-term loan. However, if the decrease in current liabilities does not seem to be explained by efficiency or by a form of longer-term financing on the balance sheet and Signal #1 is also in force—that is, expenses show a decrease as a percentage of sales—the warning signs get stronger. If the Notes to the Financial Statements show the makeup of current liabilities, check to see whether accruals for individual current liabilities decrease as a percentage of sales compared to previous periods.

The existence of both signals could be a strong alert that there has been a failure to record expenses and the corresponding liabilities. With these frauds, attempts should be made to locate these signals early on. Although the initial omissions of the expenses decrease reported expenses and liabilities, remember that the expense is rolled forward to later periods, with the result that later periods' expenses will not appear small, relative to sales, to the extent that they include the previous period's omitted expenses.

SIGNAL #3: REGULAR VENDOR NOT ON ACCOUNTS PAYABLE LIST   If you have access to the company's internal records, you can test lack of accrual by selecting vendors that the firm does business with, checking that they are on the list of accounts payable, and then reconciling the amount accrued with the vendors' statement of amounts owing. To test for an unrecorded liability, it is pointless to start with the list of current liabilities recorded by the firm and simply check those amounts. It is vital to remember that since this test is for understatement, it must begin at the origin. Choose a known vendor and trace that vendor to the list of accounts payable that supports the amount listed on the final record, the balance sheet.

If you do not have access to the company's internal records, you must rely on alerts, such as the signals mentioned earlier, from the published financial statements. However, when a firm omits recording its expenses and liabilities, it often also understates expenses by capitalizing them as fixed assets and deferring them to later periods. Therefore, being alert to the signals of those misstatements will strengthen the overall alert for this method of understatement of expenses.

Signals of Fictitious Reporting Scheme #2—Understating Expenses via Deferral of the Expenses

Here is an examination of some of the signals indicating that a company may have engaged in improper deferral of expenses.

SIGNAL #1: INCREASE IN DEFERRED COSTS OR PREPAID EXPENSES AS A PERCENTAGE OF TOTAL ASSETS   If deferred costs or prepaid expenses increase significantly as a percentage of total assets, it could be a sign that operating expenses are being capitalized.

SIGNAL #2: DECREASE OF EXPENSES AS A PERCENTAGE OF SALES   As with Scheme #1 (omitting expenses), if a category of expense decreases as a percentage of sales compared to the industry or compared to previous periods, it is an alert that part of the expense may be deferred to future periods.

SIGNAL #3: UNUSUALLY LONG PERIOD FOR DEPRECIATION OF ASSETS   If an accounting policy note to the financial statements indicates that an asset is being depreciated or amortized over a longer period than in the past or over longer periods than the average for the industry, it is a red flag that the company may be aggressive in deferring the current cost to future periods.

SIGNAL #4: INCREASE IN RATIO OF DEFERRED ASSETS TO SALES   When there is concern that a company may have engaged in aggressive deferral of expenses by means of recording them as assets (for example, recording preproduction costs as assets), test the ratio of the deferred assets to sales in comparison to companies in a comparable situation. Be sure to take into account the stage in the life cycle of the companies and the logic of the deferment as described in the accounting policy notes.

Signals of Fictitious Reporting Scheme #3—Understating Expenses via Capitalization of the Expenses[2]

Here is an examination of some of the signals indicating that a company may have engaged in improper capitalization of expenses.

SIGNAL #1: LOWER ASSET-TURNOVER RATIO   Compare the asset-turnover ratio and the fixed-asset turnover ratio of the company to that of the industry and to that of the company itself in previous periods. If the ratio is lower than the industry average or if it is decreasing, it is an indication that some expenses may be recorded as assets or that the investment in assets is not efficient in that it is not producing sufficient revenue.

SIGNAL #2: CHANGE IN POLICY FOR CAPITALIZATION OF COSTS   Be on the alert for notes to the financial statements that indicate that there has been a change in policy regarding the capitalization of costs. Although this signal was not present in the case of Livent, because the SEC found that Livent contradicted its own accounting policy description when it miscapitalized costs, a note regarding a change in capitalization policy is often a blatant signal of an aggressive accounting policy to intentionally decrease recorded expenses.

SIGNAL #3: WRITE-OFF OF COSTS PREVIOUSLY CAPITALIZED   One must be on the alert for aggressive capitalization of costs when a company writes off costs that were formerly capitalized. According to Mulford and Comiskey (2002), a good example of possible aggressive accounting with regard to capitalization policies is American Software, which capitalized the majority of its software costs in 1997, wrote down a large amount of capitalized software costs in 1999, and then increased the percentage amount capitalized again in 2000. A write-off of previously capitalized costs shows that the company has been wrong in the past about the ability of a current cost to hold value in future periods.

SIGNAL #4: UNUSUAL CAPITALIZATION POLICY   Read the notes to the financial statements to compare the company's capitalization policy to the capitalization policy of other companies in the same industry. If a company capitalizes costs that other companies in the industry do not, it could be an alert that the company may be aggressive in capitalizing expenses.

ARE THEY LIVING HAPPILY EVER AFTER?

- **Garth Drabinsky and Myron Gottlieb** were convicted of fraud and forgery by the Ontario Superior Court of Justice in Canada in 2009. Drabinsky was sentenced to seven years in prison and Gottlieb to six years. In 2011, their convictions were upheld by the Ontario Court of Appeal, but their sentences were reduced by two years each (Dobby, 2011). Drabinsky "served 18 months of a five-year sentence before being released from jail on day parole last October [i.e., 2012]. Mr. Gottlieb, who was also convicted and was sentenced to four years in jail, had already been released" (Shecter, 2013).

---

[2] For a thorough discussion of the signals for this fraud, see the discussion in Chapter 5, "WorldCom Wizardry: From WorldCom to WorldCon." WorldCom is the leading example of this kind of fraud.

RITE AID: "THE KEYS TO THE KINGDOM"

> Rite Aid is presented mainly as an example of overstating ending inventory values to reduce the cost of goods sold.

Founded by Alex Grass in 1962 in the town of Scranton, Pennsylvania, Rite Aid grew from a single drugstore to one of the biggest pharmacy conglomerates in the United States, operating over 3,500 stores across the country. In February 1995, Alex Grass handed what he reportedly called "the keys to the kingdom" to his eldest son, Martin Grass, who became CEO of Rite Aid. Several years earlier Martin's younger brother, Roger, had resigned from his position as a senior vice president at Rite Aid because "he recognized that the top job would go to a brother he considered incompetent." (Quotes from Berner & Maremont, 1999)

Less than five years after taking charge of Rite Aid, Martin Grass was fired. That same week an article in the *Wall Street Journal* remarked that the impact of Martin Grass's tenure at Rite Aid had been "disastrous" (Quote from Berner & Maremont, 1999).

According to the grand jury, Rite Aid was riddled with "massive accounting fraud, the deliberate falsification of financial statements, and intentionally false SEC filings" (qtd. in "8-Year Sentence," 2002). Documents from the SEC alleged that for over two years—from the fiscal year 1998 through the first quarter of 2000—Rite Aid overstated its net income and that former senior management failed to disclose material information, including related-party transactions in 1999 (AAER 1579, 2002). The SEC maintained that Rite Aid's resulting restatements in July and October 2000—in which the company restated reported cumulative pretax income by a total of $2.3 billion and restated cumulative net income by $1.6 billion—represented what the SEC called "the largest financial restatement of income by a public company" at the date of that report (AAER 1579, 2002).

Although Rite Aid did understate various expenses, most of its understatement of expense was its understatement of **cost of goods sold**, which refers to the cost of inventory sold during the period. Rite Aid represents a leading example of overstating earnings via understating cost of goods sold. It manipulated cost of goods sold through a number of mechanisms.

RITE AID'S FICTITIOUS FINANCIAL REPORTING SCHEMES

Rite Aid engaged in a number of schemes to reduce the cost of goods sold.

Scheme #1: Overstating Ending Inventory Values to Reduce Cost of Goods Sold

One of the three most significant methods that Rite Aid used to understate its cost of goods sold amount was that it overstated its ending inventory by failing to write down its inventory amount for the full amount of the shrinkage that it suffered. (**Shrinkage** refers to the loss of inventory between the point of production or purchase from the vendor and the point of sale.) This failure did not account for the largest portion of the understatement of cost of goods sold, but it is presented first because understating cost of goods sold by overstating ending inventory values is a very common financial reporting fraud. The SOX Report (2002) found that this method of improper expense recognition accounted for 25 SEC enforcement matters in the study period.

Rite Aid conducted periodic physical inventory counts at many of its stores. To the extent that the physical count revealed less inventory on hand than was reflected in its records, Rite Aid's official policy, of course, was to write down its inventory amount in its records via a "shrink" expense on the assumption that the difference was due to theft or loss. The SEC's findings alleged, "In FY [fiscal year] 1999, Rite Aid failed to record $8.8 million in shrink"[3] (AAER 1579, 2002). For those stores in which Rite Aid did not conduct a physical inventory count, Rite Aid's policy was to estimate a shrink amount and accrue that amount. The SEC further alleged,"In FY 1999, Rite Aid improperly reduced the accrued shrink expense for 2,000 stores resulting in an aggregate increase to income of $5 million" (AAER 1579, 2002). Thus, in total, pretax income for 1999 was allegedly overstated by $13.8 million due to overstating ending inventory by not recognizing the full amount of shrinkage.

Scheme #2: Adjusting Gross Profit Entries to Reduce Cost of Goods Sold

Of all its manipulations of cost of goods sold and net income, Rite Aid's manipulation of cost of goods sold via adjusting gross profit journal entries represented the largest dollar amount of its distortions, by far. It was also its most brazen scheme. Rite Aid simply put through journal entries decreasing cost of goods sold and decreasing accounts payable by a corresponding amount. These entries were known internally as "gross profit entries."According to the SEC, they were "determined by one person without input or review by anyone and were completely unsubstantiated." The size of these adjustments was staggering. The most egregious entries were in the second quarter of FY 1999. The SEC found that Rite Aid allegedly "improperly reduced cost of goods sold and accounts payable by approximately $100 million." It is interesting to note that in each of the years that Rite Aid adjusted its cost of goods sold in this way, it did so for the first three quarters of the year and then reversed the entries in the fourth quarter of each year. The reversal led Rite Aid to find new adjustments in the fourth quarter to offset the reversal. One of these adjustments was the misstatement of the inventory shrink, discussed previously. Another adjustment was Rite Aid's treatment of vendor rebates. (Quotes from AAER 1579, 2002)

Scheme #3: Improper Recognition of Vendor Rebates to Reduce Cost of Goods Sold

Rite Aid was entitled to receive rebates on amounts owing to certain vendors, contingent upon Rite Aid's sales of the vendors' products. In its income statement, Rite Aid should have applied the rebate only to purchases relating to goods that it had already sold. The SEC stated that regarding $77 million of such refunds that Rite Aid recognized for FY 1999, the sales had not yet occurred. In addition, the purchasing agreements had not yet been legally finalized. Nevertheless, on the last day of FY 1999, Rite Aid reduced cost of goods sold and accounts payable by $42 million and, in the same way, reopened its books to recognize the other $33 million of those rebates after the close of FY 1999. The SEC noted quite pertinently that at that particular stage, it "was readily apparent that

---

[3] Rite Aid consented to the issuance of the order without admitting or denying the findings as set out in AAER 1579 (2002).

the Company's results would fall short of Wall Street analysts' projections. These entries violated GAAP because the credits were unearned as of FY 1999" (AAER 1579, 2002).

Other Rite Aid Manipulations

According to the SEC, Rite Aid also employed a number of other methods to overstate its reported income. One ploy was that it failed to write off capitalized costs, such as legal services and title searches in respect of possible new stores, when it decided not to construct such stores. Another alleged Rite Aid ruse, according to the Commission, involved the company's "will-call" accounts payable. A number of prescription medications had been ordered but not collected by Rite Aid customers. Rite Aid, however, had been paid for these medications by the customers' insurance carriers. Instead of returning the payments to the insurance companies, Rite Aid reversed the accounts payable into profit "without sufficient justification or basis in violation of GAAP. Ultimately, the accrual was re-established and the $6.6 million attributable to the will-call payable was repaid to the insurance carriers" (AAER 1579, 2002).

The SEC also found that Rite Aid allegedly failed to properly accrue an expense each quarter with respect to the stock appreciation rights (SARS) that the company granted to certain field managers. (**Stock appreciation rights** refer to compensation in which employees receive the opportunity to participate in any increase in value of the company's stock without having to incur the cost of actually purchasing shares.) Each quarter, Rite Aid should have accrued an expense based on the market price of its stock at the end of the quarter. The Commission found that in FY 1998 and 1999, Rite Aid allegedly "should have recorded an accrued expense of approximately $22 and $33 million respectively" (AAER 1579, 2002).

The SEC's summary of Rite Aid's overstatement of pretax income is presented in Table 6.1.

SIGNALS OF THE FICTITIOUS REPORTING SCHEMES OF REDUCING COST OF GOODS SOLD

The three methods of understating cost of goods sold all produce similar signals. Overstating inventory to reduce cost of goods sold, as well as other methods of understating cost of goods sold, affect similar key ratios. For instance, inventory as a percentage of cost of goods sold increases when cost of goods sold is understated. This occurs whether the reduction of cost of goods sold is achieved by the overstatement of inventory or by another means. The ratio is distorted by an even greater amount if ending inventory is overstated. Therefore, the signals for the various methods of understating cost of goods are considered together.

SIGNAL #1: INCREASE IN INVENTORY AS A PERCENTAGE OF COST OF GOODS SOLD When inventory increases as a percentage of cost of goods sold (COGS), it is an indication that inventory could be overstated and that COGS could be understated. This measure is calculated or presented in a number of ways. The **inventory turnover ratio** is a common measure of how many times an entity's inventory has been sold or replaced during a period. The ratio is calculated as follows:

$$\text{Inventory turnover ratio} = \text{COGS} \div \text{Average inventory}$$

TABLE 6.1 Summary of Rite Aid's FY 1998, FY 1999, and 1st Quarter FY 2000 Overstatements of Pre-tax Income*

The quantifiable effect of Rite Aid's practices in the above-described areas on Rite Aid's reported pre-tax income are summarized below. [in millions]

	1st Q FY 1998	2nd Q FY 1998	3rd Q FY 1998	FY 1998	1st Q FY 1999	2nd Q FY 1999	3rd Q FY 1999	FY 1999	1st Q FY 2000
Reported Pre-tax Income	114.3	101.5	113.7	530.0	151.3	135.2	144.7	199.6	141.1
Adjustments									
Corporate Entries									17.5
Retail Entries	0.0	9.0	(4.0)		1.0	12.2	1.7		8.0
Gross Profit Entries	25.3	26.2	5.9		47.1	100.4	39.6		23.8
Undisclosed Up-Charge	2.6	1.7	1.5	7.6	5.9	6.5	7.0	27.8	
Undisclosed Markdowns								29.7	
Vendor Rebates								75.6	
Litigation Settlement								17.0	
Dead Deals								10.6	
SARS	3.4	3.6	12.6	22.1	9.0	13.7	21.9	33.2	
Will-Call Payables								6.6	
Inventory Shrink								13.8	
Depreciation				14.6					
Total Adjustments	31.3	40.5	16.0	44.3	63.0	132.8	70.2	214.3	49.3
Corrected Pre-tax Income/ (Loss)	83.0	61.0	97.7	485.7	88.3	2.4	74.5	(14.7)	91.8
Overstatement Percentage	38	66%	16%	9%	71%	5533%	94%	N/A	54%

*Obtained from AAER 1579, 2002. www.sec.gov

Notes:
1) Reported Pre-tax Income for the 2nd quarter of FY 99 is before a pre-tax charge for store closings of $289.7 million
2) This table does not purport to show a complete listing of the adjustments recorded in Rite Aid's restatements.

Another frequently used measure is the number of **days' sales in inventory**, which refers to the length of time it takes a company to turn its inventory into sales. This is calculated as follows:

Days sales in inventory = Number of days in period ÷ Inventory turnover ratio

Therefore:

Days' sales in inventory = 365^4 ÷ Inventory turnover ratio (if period is one year)

If the inventory turnover ratio decreases or if days' sales in inventory increases, it is an indication of possible overstatement of inventory and understatement of COGS. If the days' sales in inventory increase significantly, even if the cause is not the actual overstatement of inventory, it is an alert to the fact that sales are not keeping up with production.

SIGNAL #2: UNEXPECTED AND UNUSUALLY LARGE INCREASES IN GROSS MARGIN AS A PERCENTAGE OF SALES   Sudden, significant increases in gross margin as a percentage of sales are indications of possible overstatement of inventory and understatement of COGS. Sudden changes (either increases or decreases) should be accompanied by simple, logical explanations, such as, for example, a new manufacturing technique or a change in the selling price. The Management Discussion and Analysis (MD&A) section of the company's annual report ought to explain significant changes in the gross margin percentage measure. Without clear explanations, suspicion and skepticism should be aroused.

SIGNAL #3: REDUCTION IN INVENTORY RESERVE AS A PERCENTAGE OF INVENTORY   When the reserve for the obsolescence or shrinkage of inventory decreases as a percentage of inventory, it is a signal that the company may be overstating its inventory by understating its reserve for obsolescence or shrinkage.

SIGNAL #4: CASH FLOW FROM OPERATIONS DROPPING BELOW OPERATING INCOME   As is so often the case, cash flow from operations (CFFO) falling significantly below operating income and net income is a useful signal that profit may be misreported. In fact, Rite Aid's net income for the thirteen weeks ended May 30, 1998, was $90.8 million, whereas CFFO for that same period was negative $9.0 million. This signal, in itself, should have broadcast a warning to anyone examining that set of Rite Aid's financial statements.

ARE THEY LIVING HAPPILY EVER AFTER?

- **Martin Grass**, former CEO of Rite Aid, pleaded guilty to a conspiracy charge, and in May 2004, Judge Sylvia Rambo sentenced him to eight years of imprisonment ("8-Year Sentence," 2004), but later reduced his term to seven years. He served his sentence in federal prisons in Florida. According to reports, Grass was a model prisoner (Scolforo, 2005). Grass was released after seven years and placed on three years' probation. He is now in his late fifties and reportedly resides in Florida, where he "is a principal in a real estate firm and in a company that makes hair-care products" (Miller, 2011).

---

[4] By convention, 90 days is usually used as the approximate number of days in a period of one quarter (or three months).

- **Franklin C. Brown**, former vice chair and chief counsel, was found guilty of playing a major role in the Rite Aid case. He was sentenced to ten years of imprisonment (Scolforo, 2005). Citing Brown's advanced age, 76 at that time, his attorneys described the sentencing as "a *de facto* death sentence" (Scolforo, 2004). However, after several appeals and almost six years in prison, Brown was released on probation (Miller, 2011).
- **Karen Brown**, Franklin Brown's wife, brought a lawsuit against Grass for almost $5 million in 2011 (Miller, 2011). Karen Brown lost the case (Reisinger, 2012).
- **Timothy J. Noonan**, former COO and interim CEO, left Rite Aid before the fraud was discovered. Although not actively involved in the schemes, he was nevertheless accused of neglecting to report the Rite Aid fraud. He eventually cooperated with investigators and pleaded guilty to a "misprision" charge for not reporting the fraud. He received two years of probation and a small fine (Federwisch, 2007).

ALLEGHENY (AHERF): TRICK OR TREATMENT?

> Allegheny (AHERF) is presented mainly as an example of understating reserves for bad debts.

The Allegheny Health Education & Research Foundation (aka AHERF) was described by the SEC Enforcement Files as a collection of nonprofit, acute-care hospitals, with a medical university, physicians groups, and other affiliated entities. AHERF grew very rapidly from its inception in Pittsburgh in 1983 to the largest nonprofit healthcare provider in Pennsylvania before its sudden decline and bankruptcy in July 1998. The SEC subsequently found that AHERF and some of its subsidiaries, collectively known as Delaware Valley, allegedly "issued annual financial statements and municipal disclosure reports that materially misrepresented, among other things, AHERF's and Delaware Valley's net income" (AAER 1283, 2000).

AHERF's swift growth came at the expense of large debt, and along with the debt came the pressure to appear financially stable. When a company appears to be in a financially stressful situation, this situation can instigate a vicious cycle by making it difficult for a company to obtain future financing as well as driving up its interest rates. This, in turn, can increase the likelihood of debt repayments being demanded, which can eventually lead to bankruptcy. Due to such an environment of high debt, the SEC concluded that "AHERF, through certain of its senior officers, and in violation of applicable accounting principles, misstated its financial statements and schedules" (AAER 1283, 2000).

As a holding company, AHERF did not assume liability for the preexisting debt of its acquired entities. The obligation to repay debt was placed on Delaware Valley, the nonprofit's "obligated groups." AHERF's obligated groups were responsible for over $900 million of debt by the time of the bankruptcy in 1998. The misstated reports, in this case, went beyond annual financial statements and included municipal securities disclosure reports known as Nationally Recognized Municipal Securities Information Repositories. In a speech to the AICPA National Healthcare Industry Conference in August 2000, SEC attorney Stephen Weinstein pointed out that "the Disclosure Reports were made available to the public through the Repositories and were the most easily accessible source of information for investors and potential investors in AHERF bonds."

AHERF'S FICTITIOUS FINANCIAL REPORTING SCHEMES

AHERF's Fictitious Financial Reporting Scheme of Understating Bad Debts

According to the SEC, during 1996, AHERF's senior management became aware that there were significant problems with the collection of Delaware Valley's patient accounts receivable. They were also aware of the considerable growth in the amount of these accounts receivable and attempted to solve the problem with changes in management. However, the SEC found that as early as October 1996, "AHERF decided to write off approximately $81 million in Delaware Valley patient accounts receivable."[5] To do this, the company needed to increase the bad debt reserve on the June 30, 1996 financial statements, in which the reserve was short of this amount by approximately $40 million. AHERF should have increased that reserve by $40 million and recognized the expense of $40 million in the income statement. However, the conglomerate did not adjust its 1996 financial statements. Instead, it decided to write off the uncollectible accounts receivable in quarterly installments. The SEC found that in the audited financial statements as well as in the Disclosure Report distributed by AHERF to the public, properly adjusting the bad debt reserve of Delaware Valley would have "reduced its reported net income of $27 million before extraordinary item and change in accounting principle by approximately $40 million and similarly reduced its reported net accounts receivable figure of $253 million by approximately $40 million." Furthermore, the MD&A section of the AHERF Disclosure Report "implied that the $72.2 million increase in Delaware Valley accounts receivable during fiscal year 1996 was a temporary phenomenon that would resolve itself." (Quotes from AAER 1283, 2000)

AHERF's Other Fabrications

The SEC also found that AHERF inappropriately transferred $99.6 million of reserves from the various hospitals to Delaware Valley in 1997 to avoid recognizing the expense in its income statement when it had to write off accounts receivable and did not have a sufficient bad debt reserve. Also in 1997, AHERF overstated its reported consolidated net income by incorrectly recognizing over $54 million of irrevocable trusts' income as its own income.

SIGNALS OF THE FICTITIOUS REPORTING SCHEME OF UNDERSTATING BAD DEBTS

Here is an examination of some of the signals indicating that a company may have understated its reserve for bad debts.

SIGNAL #1: UNUSUALLY LARGE NET ACCOUNTS RECEIVABLE   When a company fails to recognize its bad debts by failing to increase the reserve for bad debts, the net accounts receivable is larger than it should be. This is likely to show up in ratios that measure accounts receivable as a percentage of sales (for example, an increase in DSO).

---

[5] AHERF consented to the entry of the findings and the issuance of the order without admitting or denying the findings as set out in AAER 1283, 2000.

SIGNAL #2: DECREASE IN RESERVE FOR BAD DEBTS AS A PERCENTAGE OF ACCOUNTS RECEIVABLE   When the reserve for bad debts decreases as a percentage of accounts receivable, it is an indication that the company may be understating its bad debt reserve. If the reserve or allowance for doubtful debts decreases while the gross amount for receivables increases, consider that a red alert.

SIGNAL #3: INCREASE IN ACCOUNTS RECEIVABLE AS A PERCENTAGE OF TOTAL CURRENT ASSETS   When net accounts receivable increase as a percentage of total current assets, it could be a signal that the company is not writing off bad debts or is not appropriately estimating its reserve for doubtful debts.

SIGNAL #4: CASH FLOW FROM OPERATIONS LAGGING BEHIND OPERATING INCOME   When a company does not appropriately recognize an expense, CFFO will lag behind operating income. Bad debts that are not written off represent operating profit that is recognized in the income statement but that should be expensed because the profit will not be liquidated. In other words, the accounts receivable asset will not be paid and will not turn into a cash asset. Therefore, the bad debts not written off will show up in the form of CFFO being less than operating profit if it is not disguised by some further misstatement in the statement of cash flows.

ARE THEY LIVING HAPPILY EVER AFTER?

- **Sherif Abdelhak**, former CEO of AHERF, pleaded no contest to charges of raiding the company's charitable endowments in order to bolster AHERF's deteriorating healthcare system. In August 2002, he received up to 23 months in prison (Becker, 2002). After serving three months of his sentence, Abdelhak was released on parole (Becker, 2003). According to a November 2007 newspaper article, "For Mr. Abdelhak, the period after the demise of AHERF has included jail time, a divorce, an aborted oil-buying venture, a personal bankruptcy filing and a recent U.S. Tax Court order that he pay more than $500,000 in back taxes" (Fitzpatrick, 2007).
- **David McConnell**, former CFO of AHERF, agreed to participate in an "accelerated rehabilitative disposition program" and was fined $25,000 by the SEC (Bowling, 2013).

LOCKHEED: SKY HIGH[6]

> Lockheed is presented mainly as an example of failing to record impairments of assets.

As jet travel boomed in the 1960s, there was such a demand by the airlines for larger wide-bodied jets to carry more passengers that two large airline manufacturing companies, McDonnell Douglas and Lockheed, pursued plans to design similar aircraft with similar ranges and load capacities. While McDonnell Douglas launched its DC-10 project, Lockheed began its design and production of the TriStar. Although pilots and aviation enthusiasts still rank the TriStar's performance and safety record highly, the ambitious and costly TriStar program was dogged with financial problems almost from its outset.

---

[6]Background information in this section is mainly from "Lockheed L-1011 TriStar," "Lockheed L-1011 TriStar History" (2003), and Mondout and Schilit (2002).

As gas prices soared in the 1970s and demand for air travel fell, it became clear that there was only enough traffic for one of the new plane designs. By this time, however, too many sunk costs had already been invested in the production of the aircraft. (A **sunk cost** refers to a cost that has already been incurred and the expenditure cannot be reversed by any future decision or action.) As Patrick Mondout explained, "Even if the L-1011 [TriStar] was 'technically superior' to the DC-10, it cost more to purchase and more per passenger mile than its competitor." Furthermore, Lockheed's initial estimates were that the break-even point on the TriStar would be sales of 300 aircraft. However, with cost overruns, the break-even point actually required sales of 500 aircraft.

Lockheed's problems with the TriStar originally began with its choice of the British Rolls-Royce RB-211 engine for its new plane. Interestingly, David Huddie, head of Rolls-Royce's Aero Engine Department at that time, later received a knighthood from the Queen of England for securing the contract to supply the engine for the TriStar. However, the Rolls-Royce engine was still in the design stage and the costs for this engine skyrocketed long before it was ready to propel an aircraft. Lockheed, therefore, had to carry a share of the climbing Rolls-Royce costs while its own development costs were growing well over budget.

In December 1970, the TriStar took off from Palmdale, California, on its first flight. That same year Rolls-Royce was driven into quasi-bankruptcy which, according to some sources, was a result of the TriStar project. The entire venture was now in jeopardy, and for the program to continue, it took the combined efforts of the British government taking over Rolls-Royce and the U.S. government providing a federal guarantee for Lockheed to receive a $250 million line of credit.

Ultimately, Lockheed's accounting tale is the story of misstating earnings by failing to write off an impaired asset, which was the development cost of its TriStar L-1011 wide-body jet. (An **impaired asset** refers to an asset whose carrying value is less than the fair or recoverable value.) This evidently inadvertent accounting failure certainly drew the attention of the shareholders when the company suddenly wrote off over $400 million of the TriStar's development costs in 1981, after the program had been losing a fortune for over a decade.

LOCKHEED'S FICTITIOUS FINANCIAL REPORTING SCHEME OF FAILING TO ACCOUNT FOR ASSET IMPAIRMENTS

Lockheed had an accounting policy in which it capitalized the TriStar's development costs with the intention of writing them off as the planes were sold. The company estimated the total development costs as well as the total number of TriStar aircraft that it would sell and then calculated an average development cost per airplane. As each aircraft was sold, this average development cost was expensed and a corresponding amount was written off the development-cost asset.

By late 1975, Lockheed had capitalized $500 million in TriStar development costs (Schilit, 2002). The TriStar program was continuing to suffer losses. It became clear that future sales were not going to be made at a profit and that this "asset" was impaired and needed to be written off. However, instead of writing off the entire $500 million, Lockheed wrote off that amount in annual installments of $50 million. The TriStar program lost over $900 million up to 1981, when Lockheed finally wrote off the remaining amount of this impaired asset in one lump sum of $400 million (Mondout, "Lockheed L-1011"). By the end of 1983, when Lockheed ceased production of the TriStar, only

250 planes had been built, far short of the break-even point of approximately 500 aircraft ("Lockheed L-1011 TriStar").

Lockheed's delay in writing off the impaired asset caused both assets and earnings to be overstated for the duration of the delay.

SIGNALS OF THE FAILURE TO RECORD ASSET IMPAIRMENTS

Here is an examination of some of the signals indicating that a company may have failed to record an impairment of an asset.

SIGNAL #1: SIGNIFICANT INTANGIBLE ASSETS ACCOMPANIED BY OPERATING OR PRODUCTION PROBLEMS   When the development of a product or program is accompanied by the recording of a significant intangible asset such as development costs or start-up costs and the product or program hits scheduling problems and runs at a loss, it is a strong indication that the associated asset is impaired and should be written off. The indication that a product or program associated with the intangible asset is incurring problems or setbacks can often be found in press articles, notes to the financial statements, the segmented income statement, or the MD&A section of the annual report. In Lockheed's case, press articles pointing toward the losses of the TriStar program were abundant, and the capitalization of significant development costs for the program were clearly indicated on the balance sheet and in notes to the financial statements. This signal ought to have alerted users of the financial statements to the possibility that, eventually, Lockheed would have to recognize a huge expense to write off this asset.

SIGNAL #2: A COMPANY WITH LARGE INTANGIBLE ASSETS INCURRING A LOSS   When there are significant intangible assets and a company is incurring a loss overall, it is an indication that the intangible assets are impaired. Although this signal is not always clear as to which assets are impaired, it is logical to assume that the purpose of assets overall is to produce future profits, and if they are not producing profits currently, it is an indication that they might not produce them in the future. It may even be argued that if a company is not likely to produce a supernormal return on its tangible assets, the net value of all its intangible assets is zero. Certainly, a company cannot continue to incur losses indefinitely, and if it goes into bankruptcy or scraps a segment, certain intangible assets—such as development costs, start-up costs, and goodwill—will not be saleable.

SIGNAL #3: DECREASE IN A COMPANY'S ASSET-TURNOVER RATIO   When a company's asset-turnover ratio declines, either for a category of assets or for total assets, it is an indication that the assets may be impaired. When the sales-to-total-assets ratio declines or the ratio of sales to a specific asset declines, the user of financial statements should be alert to the possibility that either some assets are failing to achieve their objectives (and the assets may be impaired) or the assets should not have been capitalized in the first place.

SIGNAL #4: ACCOUNTING POLICY INDICATING SLOW ASSET WRITE-OFF   Accounting policy notes to the financial statements indicating that the company has a policy that is slower than other companies in the industry to write off assets—such as development costs or start-up costs—should alert the reader to the possibility that the company is aggressive in its efforts to overstate the value of assets. Such aggressive policies often include the failure to record the impairment of assets.

SIGNAL #5: UNUSUAL RESTRUCTURING CHARGES   Restructuring charges in a current period can indicate that the company failed to recognize impairments of assets in previous periods. Always carefully scrutinize the notes explaining restructuring charges. If there is an indication that the company failed to write off assets that were impaired previously, it may be an indication that the company is in the habit of being aggressive in overstating its earnings by failing to recognize the impairment of its assets.

ARE THEY LIVING HAPPILY EVER AFTER?

- There was no SEC enforcement action or allegation of intentional wrong doing at **Lockheed**.
- **Lockheed** merged with Martin Marietta Corp. in 1995 to form one of the largest aerospace companies in the world.
- **Lockheed Martin** was ranked 59th on the 2013 list of Fortune 500 companies ("Fortune 500," 2013). Its revenue for the financial year ending March 2013 was $47.2 billion (Madhusudanan, 2013).

Key Terms

Cost of goods sold *175*
Days' sales in inventory *179*
Impaired asset *183*
Improper deferral of expenses *168*

Improper expense recognition *168*
Inventory turnover ratio *177*
Shrinkage *175*

Stock appreciation rights *177*
Sunk cost *183*

ETHICS AT WORK

Read the article below, "Exploring Ethical Lapses During the Rite Aid Crisis" by Anne Federwisch.

Questions:

a. What does Timothy Noonan, former COO and former interim CEO of Rite Aid, see as his mistakes or failures in Rite Aid's legal and ethical crisis?
b. Besides the vendor fraud, what other signs of ethical disintegration does Noonan now believe were present at Rite Aid?

Exploring Ethical Lapses During the Rite Aid Crisis[7]

By Anne Federwisch

Timothy J. Noonan, former COO, interim CEO and member of the board of directors at Rite Aid Corp., spoke to a recent meeting of the Business and Organizational Ethics Partnership about his experiences during a legal and ethical crisis at the company from 1999–2000. Though he offered insights on his behavior, he did not offer excuses or shift blame. Rather, he presented a frank account of an ethical lapse that he wished he had avoided.

---

[7]Originally published in 2007 by the Markkula Center for Applied Ethics, at Santa Clara University, California: *www.scu.edu/ethics*. Published with permission.

As Jim Balassone, executive-in-residence at the Markkula Center for Applied Ethics, noted in his introduction, "Tim and I are the same age, with similar backgrounds and education. Perhaps the only difference is that I went to work for a company where it was easy to be ethical and Tim went to work for Rite Aid. I'd like to think that I would have acted differently or escaped some of the traps Tim will talk about—I would like to think that, but I'm far from sure that would be true."

Noonan outlined his purpose by saying, "I'm here today to spend a little bit of time with you to talk about the crisis at Rite Aid. It could have been your company, your associations. It could be anyone's. It was a real crisis. And I hope it's the kind of crisis that none of you ever get yourself caught up in," he said. "I made some bad decisions, but ultimately, you've got to make some right decisions. I'm no different than you. I want you to understand that this could happen to you, it could happen to anybody."

History of the Rite Aid Crisis

Alex Grass founded Rite Aid, a mom-and-pop health and beauty aids store, in Scranton, Pa., in 1962. The company went public in 1968, and by 1995, Grass's son forced him out as CEO. Amid rapid expansion, numerous acquisitions, and costly innovations, Rite Aid got involved in a financial crisis resulting in a $1.6 billion restatement, shareholder lawsuits, and ultimately, indictments and convictions of officers of the company. Noonan himself eventually pled guilty to misprision, defined as the failure by someone who is not an accessory to prevent or notify the authorities of a felony.

Noonan began at his career at a pharmacy that was eventually acquired by Rite Aid, moving from stock boy, to pharmacist, to COO and eventually to interim CEO of Rite Aid. The company had state-of-the-art warehouses and an innovative robotic pharmaceutical system industry leading technology, unique store design, and was very active in acquisitions. "The company was a great company. The employees were great employees. The jobs I had were the greatest jobs you'd ever want to have," he said.

Not that there weren't ethical questions even early in his career. He confronted management about a possibly illegal 50-cent surcharge on Medicare prescriptions and refused to make questionable payments.

Should he have left the company then, he asked. "These things were few and far between, but they did happen. And they did raise eyebrows." Taken as a whole, they did not reflect well on the company's ethical culture but were minor transgressions, Noonan concluded.

The Whole Truth

But there was a definite crisis when Noonan left the company; there was a cash flow crisis, a major drop in the stock price, and rumors of manipulation of the company's financials. He got called in to speak to a law firm brought in to investigate the situation.

"There is no question that when I went to those interviews, I wasn't fully truthful. No question about it," he admitted. "I was perfectly honest with them, upfront, the vast majority of the time. But there were some items I wasn't truthful about that became part of this case."

For example, although he admitted to investigators that he had gotten a severance package, he neglected to tell them about the secret, backdated package (which he never exercised) that the former chief legal counsel and former vice chairman handed him. It was signed by the ousted CEO after he left the company, backdated almost a year, and worth millions of dollars more than his official deal. And although he told them some of what he knew about pharmacy rebates, "I didn't fully tell them all I knew."

After Noonan's third meeting with investigators, he said, rumors ran rampant, innuendoes abounded, and he decided to speak directly with government officials. "I wanted to clean up any of the interviews I had in the past," he said.

Lying to the investigators was a big mistake, he said. "Ultimately, you have to correct it. You have to face reality," he said. "What I would share today is whenever you get yourself into these situations, you're better off right up front facing the issues. Kind of difficult, I'll tell you that."

Eventually, Noonan told the government what he knew. He wore a wire when talking to other principals in the case. He did not get immunity, and as a result of his guilty plea to the felony misprision charge, he got two years' probation, and a $2,600 fine. He eventually paid significant dollars to resolve the shareholder lawsuit, lost his severance, and was left with huge legal bills. "No question, your reputation gets damaged," he said.

"You might ask why I wasn't candid to the internal investigators when I went to them," he mused. "First and foremost, I'll tell you it was my fault. No question about it. My fault. But those long-term friendships—30-plus years of relationships—they do get in the way. They do have an impact on how things go."

Compounding the problem, he said, were "years of legal coaching—how to take a deposition, what to say, what not to say, say it this way, don't say it that way, change the subject on this question. All that stuff comes into play. It's not right, but it comes into play."

Retrospective Red Flags

Did Rite Aid have ethical lapses before the crisis? "Looking at it in retrospect, yes," he admitted. The company did not communicate or discuss ethical values. The code of conduct and ethics hotline were more form than substance. Positive leadership role models were lacking. The company stressed the short-term result rather than the long-term. Gatekeepers were ineffective.

Using Marianne Jennings' seven signs of ethical collapse as a guide, he noted that he could probably give a concrete example of each one. Pressure to achieve numbers. Pervasive fear and silence. Larger-than-life CEO. Weak board. Conflicts of interest. Innovation like no other. Goodness "there" atones for wrong-doing "here."

"They were all there. Were they something that you could have looked at and seen? Probably not," he said. "I don't want to paint the picture that you could see this on the wall. There were a lot of other things going on."

But were there warning signs that he probably should have paid attention to? "Sure," he admitted. He knew the company was operating in gray areas. "I knew about vendor fraud because I was at an executive meeting where the former CEO brought it up and said, 'I want the marketing and financial people to do it this way.' And it was done that way, way into the '90s."

But, as he asked rhetorically throughout his talk, where do you go when an ethical problem arises? What do you do?

With 20/20 hindsight, he can look back and see the red flags clearly. He can look at his behavior and identify better alternatives. He said he wasn't the one directing the fraud, "but maybe I should've been doing something about it and said, 'We are not going to do it.'"

There is no doubt, he said, that he made some bad decisions. So he talks about his experiences as a lesson to others not to let themselves get caught up in a cascade of events with such a high personal and professional cost.

He summed up his advice by saying, "Sooner or later, you have to make the right choice. Sooner is better than later."

Assignments

TRUE/FALSE QUESTIONS

Answer the following questions with T for true or F for false for more practice with key terms and concepts from this chapter.

1. The improper deferral of an expense moves the recognition of the expense from the current period's financial statement to a later period.

   T   F

2. Vendor rebates on inventory purchases must be prorated over the periods in which the related inventory is sold.

   T   F

3. An improper capitalization of an expense would cause the current period's earnings to be overstated and would not cause any increase or decrease in later periods' earnings.

   T   F

4. One of the methods that Rite Aid used to reduce its cost of goods sold was to pass journal entries that decreased cost of goods sold and decreased accounts payable by a corresponding amount.

   T   F

5. When inventory decreases as a percentage of cost of goods sold, it is a signal that cost of goods sold could be understated.

   T   F

6. A decrease in the reserve for obsolescence of inventory could be a signal that cost of goods sold is understated.

   T   F

7. AHERF's failure to increase its reserve for bad debts caused it to understate its expenses and overstate its income.

   T   F

8. When accounts receivable decreases as a percentage of sales, it could be a signal that a company is understating its reserve for bad debts.

   T   F

9. When company discovers that an intangible asset is impaired, it can write the asset down over the remaining expected life of the asset.

   T   F

10. An accounting policy note indicating that a company is writing off a category of assets over a longer period of time than other companies in the industry is a signal that the company may be improperly deferring the recording of its expenses.

    T   F

FILL-IN-THE-BLANK QUESTIONS

Fill in the blanks with information and concepts from this chapter.

11. The SEC's enforcement action against Livent alleged that senior company officials had a special computer program designed that would enable accounting personnel to _____ the accounting system without leaving a paper or transaction trail.

12. At the end of each quarter, Livent simply _____ certain expenses and the related liabilities from the general ledger.

13. In order to defer expenses, Livent moved expenses from one asset account to another where the _____ could be delayed.

14. According to the SEC, one of the methods that Rite Aid used to understate its cost of goods sold was to recognize vendor _____ on sales that had not yet occurred.

15. Rite Aid failed to write down its inventory amount for the full amount of the _____ that it suffered.

16. When inventory _____ as a percentage of cost of goods sold, it is an indication that inventory could be overstated and that cost of goods sold could be understated.

17. In the case of AHERF, the misstated reports went beyond annual financial statements and included municipal securities disclosure reports known as Nationally Recognized Municipal _____ Information Repositories.

18. Instead of writing off its uncollectible amounts immediately, AHERF decided to write off its uncollectible accounts receivable in _____ installments.

19. Lockheed had an accounting policy in which it capitalized TriStar's development costs with the intention of writing them off as the planes were _____.

20. Restructuring charges in a current period can indicate that the company failed to recognize _____ of assets in previous periods.

MULTIPLE-CHOICE QUESTIONS

21. Which of the following methods of overstating earnings was not identified in the SEC's Enforcement Action against Livent?
    (a) Understating expenses via the release of cookie-jar reserves.
    (b) Understatement of expenses by removing invoices from accounting records.
    (c) Improper deferral of expenses.
    (d) Improper capitalization of expenses.

22. If a company amortizes or depreciates a category of its fixed assets over a longer period than in the past or over a longer period than the average for the industry, it is a signal that the company may be:
    (a) Understating expenses via improper capitalization of expenses.
    (b) Understating expenses by removing invoices from the accounting records.
    (c) Understating expenses via improper deferral of expenses.
    (d) Understating expenses by overstating inventory to decrease the amount reported for cost of goods sold.

23. Which of the following methods of fictitious accounting were used by Rite Aid to understate its cost of goods sold?
    (a) Overstatement of ending inventory values.
    (b) Adjusting gross profit entries to reduce cost of goods sold.
    (c) Improper recognition of vendor rebates.
    (d) All of the above.

24. Which of the following is *not* a signal of possible understatement of cost of goods sold?
    (a) A significant increase in inventory as a percentage of cost of goods sold.
    (b) A sudden increase in the gross margin percentage.
    (c) An increase in accounts payable as a percentage of sales.
    (d) A significant decrease in the reserve for obsolescence of inventory.

25. Which of the following methods of fictitious accounting was not identified by the SEC in its Enforcement Action against Rite Aid?
    (a) Understatement of bad debt expense.
    (b) Failure to write off capitalization costs such as costs of title searches.
    (c) Reversal of accounts payable amounts for "will-call" prescriptions.
    (d) Improper accrual of expense in respect of stock appreciation rights.

26. Allegheny (AHERF) is presented in this chapter mainly as an example of understating expenses via:
    (a) Improper capitalization of expenses.

(b) Understatement of cost of goods sold.

(c) Understatement of reserves for bad debts.

(d) Understatement of expenses by improper use of restructuring reserves.

27. Which of the following would not be a signal that a company may have understated its reserve for doubtful debts?

(a) Accounts receivable increases as a percentage of sales.

(b) The reserve for bad debts decreases as a percentage of accounts receivable.

(c) The net amount for accounts receivable decreases as a percentage of total current assets.

(d) All of the above.

28. Lockheed is presented in this chapter mainly as an example of:

(a) Failure to record asset impairments.

(b) Overstatement of sales.

(c) Understatement of reserve for bad debts.

(d) Improper use of cookie-jar reserves.

29. In the first quarter of the fiscal year, Brace Company discovers that an asset is impaired and the asset will need to be written down by $4 million. Which of the following statements is correct?

(a) Brace Company can write down the asset by $4 million when it prepares its annual financial statements.

(b) Brace must write off the $4 million by writing off $1 million in each quarter's financial statements in the year that it discovered that the asset was impaired by $4 million.

(c) Brace must write down the asset by $4 million in the first quarter's quarterly financial statements.

(d) Brace can write down the asset by $4 million evenly over three years, beginning in the year that it discovered that the asset was impaired.

30. If the value of a company's beginning inventory is overstated but its ending inventory is correctly stated, then:

(a) Its cost of goods sold expense will be understated.

(b) Its gross margin will be understated.

(c) Its gross margin will be overstated.

(d) None of the above.

FOR DISCUSSION

31. Describe and compare Lockheed's capitalized development costs and Livent's capitalized preproduction costs.

32. How did the development costs at Lockheed and the preproduction costs at Livent differ from preproduction costs related to long-term supply arrangements?

SHORT-ANSWER QUESTIONS

33. Explain how Livent's improper deferral of expenses and Rite Aid's improper recognition of vendor rebates shifted the recognition of expenses from one period to a later period.

34. Explain why Rite Aid's failure to write down its ending inventory amount—to agree with values determined by physical inventory counts—caused it to overstate its income.

35. Explain why sudden unexplained increases in gross margin as a percentage of sales could be an indication that a company is understating its cost of goods sold.

36. What balance sheet item did AHERF misstate, and what effect did this have on its reported income?

37. Explain how Lockheed's treatment of its development costs overstated its reported income.

EXERCISES

38. LivePlay Company has incurred $300,000 in scenery production costs for the play *Cat Trap*. It estimates that *Cat Trap* will run for three years, beginning January 1, 2012. However, to the company's surprise, it becomes clear in October 2012 that *Cat Trap* will run for only one year and close on December 31, 2012. By the end of Q3 of 2012, LivePlay had amortized an accumulated amount of $75,000 of the scenery production costs of $300,000.

Required

a. How much amortization expense or impairment costs should LivePlay Company recognize in respect of the scenery production costs in its income statement in Q4 of 2012?

b. LivePlay has a second play running at another theater. It estimates that the second play, *Dogs*, will run until December 31, 2014. On October 1, 2012, in its books and records, LivePlay transfers the scenery assets of $225,000 from the *Cat Trap* to the *Dogs* production in order to avoid fully writing off the asset in its 2012 financial statements. By how much would LivePlay understate its amortization expense (or its impairment loss) in Q4 of 2012 by falsely transferring the scenery assets from *CatTrap* to *Dogs*?

39. Brite Company's ending inventory values and its cost of goods sold (COGS) amounts for Q1–Q4 are listed below.

| | **Mar 31** | **June 30** | **Sept 30** | **Dec 31** |
	Q1	**Q2**	**Q3**	**Q4**
Inventory	$20,000	$30,000	$40,000	$50,000
COGS	$60,000	$62,000	$60,000	$60,000

Required

a. Calculate Brite's inventory turnover ratio for Q2, Q3, and Q4.

b. Calculate Brite's days' sales in inventory for Q2, Q3, and Q4.

40. Aerial, Inc., an airplane manufacturing company, incurred $1 million in development costs during the design and manufacture of a new airplane. Aerial estimates no further development costs, and it estimates that it will need to sell 100 airplanes to break even on this line of aircraft. It believes it will easily sell this number of planes and adopts the policy of writing off the development costs over the sale of the 100 planes that it estimates it will be required to sell in order to break even. Its policy is to add this development cost to the cost of goods sold as each airplane is sold.

If the company sells ten airplanes in the following year and the cost of goods sold is $2 million per airplane excluding development costs, how much must the company recognize as its total cost of goods sold for the year?

CASE STUDY

NAVISTAR INTERNATIONAL CORPORATION

- **Read** the extracts from AAER 3165, August 5, 2010.
- **Examine** the Statements of Income and Statements of the Statement of Financial Condition (i.e., Balance Sheets) for Navistar's fiscal years ended October 31, 2002 and 2003.
- **Read** extracts 1–4 from the Notes to Navistar's Financial Statements (10-K) for 2002 and 2003.
- **Respond** to the following Case Study Questions.

Required

a. Warrantee Reserve. Calculate Navistar's "Product Warranty Accrual" as a percentage of sales of manufactured products for fiscal years ended 2002 and 2003; then comment on your results. [*Hint 1:* Remember that Signal #2 for Livent's Scheme 1 (understating expenses and the corresponding liabilities) is a decrease in current liabilities as a percentage of sales. Furthermore, if the makeup of current liabilities is given in a note, it is important to check whether the accruals for the individual current liabilities decrease as a percentage of sales compared to previous periods.]

[*Hint 2:* You must isolate the Product Warranty section of the Product Liability and Warranty Accrual.]

b. **Deferred Start-Up Costs.** Review Signals #1–#4 in the discussion of Livent's scheme 3 (understating expenses via capitalization of expenses); then respond to the following.

   1. Indicate which of these signals is present in Navistar's 10-K notes.
   2. Explain why the signal identified in the previous question (b.1) should alert the reader to the possibility of aggressive recognition of reported income.

c. **Vendor Rebates.** After reading the extracts from AAER 3165, answer the following:

1. Explain how Navistar's improper treatment of its rebates was similar to Rite Aid's improper accounting for its rebates, as described in this chapter.
2. Explain how Navistar's accounting for its improper use of rebates differs from Rite Aid's improper accounting for its rebates.
3. If you were to write journal entries to describe how Rite Aid and Navistar improperly accounted for the rebates, which accounts would be debited and credited in the books or ledger of each company?

Extracts from Accounting and Auditing Enforcement Release (AAER 3165) for Navistar International Corporation*

UNITED STATES OF AMERICA
Before the
SECURITIES AND EXCHANGE COMMISSION

SECURITIES ACT OF 1933
Release No. 9132 / August 5, 2010

SECURITIES EXCHANGE ACT OF 1934
Release No. 62653 / August 5, 2010

ACCOUNTING AND AUDITING ENFORCEMENT
Release No. 3165 / August 5, 2010

ADMINISTRATIVE PROCEEDING File No. 3-13994

In the Matter of
NAVISTAR INTERNATIONAL CORPORATION,

---

*Obtained from U.S. Securities and Exchange Commission. *www.sec.gov*. Navistar consented to the entry of this Order without admitting or denying the findings.

SUMMARY FROM AAER 3165

1. This is a financial fraud, reporting, and internal controls case against Navistar, a Fortune 200 manufacturer of commercial trucks and engines, and certain current and former employees. At times from 2001 through 2005, Navistar overstated its pre-tax income by a total of approximately $137 million as the result of various instances of misconduct. Fraud at a Wisconsin foundry and in connection with certain vendor rebates and vendor tooling transactions accounted for approximately $58 million of that total. The remaining approximately $79 million resulted from improper accounting for certain warranty reserves and deferred expenses. These findings do not reflect a coordinated scheme by senior management to manipulate the Company's reported results or conduct committed with the intent of personal gain. Instead, these findings reflect misconduct that resulted in large part from a deficient system of internal controls, evidenced in part by insufficient numbers of employees with accounting training, a lack of written accounting policies and procedures, and flaws in the Company's organizational structure. The internal control deficiencies, in turn, resulted from senior management's failure to dedicate sufficient resources and attention to the adequacy of Navistar's accounting and reporting functions. The deficient internal controls failed to provide adequate checks on certain employees' efforts to meet the Company's financial targets.

PARAGRAPHS 17–22 FROM AAER 3165:

Vendor Rebates

17. During the 2001 to 2004 time period, Navistar ramped up its engine production beyond initial expectations and correspondingly increased its purchases of engine parts from suppliers. Navistar sought to share in those suppliers' unanticipated profits by asking them to pay a portion back to the Company in the form of rebates. Under GAAP, a company could recognize rebates only when they were actually earned, i.e., when the entity had substantially accomplished what was necessary to be entitled to such rebates. Accordingly, Navistar could record the full rebate as income in the then-current period only if no contingencies existed on its right to receive the rebate. Conversely, the Company was prohibited from booking rebates as income in the then-current period if they were based on future business.

18. During this period, Navistar booked 35 rebates and related receivables from its suppliers. Of those rebates and receivables, as many as 30 were improperly booked. While these rebates and receivables took different forms—including volume-based rebates and so-called "signing bonuses" for Navistar's award of new business—all were improperly booked as income in their entirety upfront, even though, in whole or in part, they were earned in future periods. The Company's eventual restatement of these rebates and receivables totaled $9.7 million of pre-tax income in 2004 and $8.5 million in 2003, which represented 27.7 percent and 2.7 percent, respectively, of the restated loss before income taxes for those years.

19. The vast majority of these receivables were volume-based rebates that Navistar obtained from its suppliers at the end (or even after the end) of the fiscal

---

* The findings herein are made pursuant to Respondents' Offers of Settlement and are not binding on any other person or entity in this or any other proceeding.

year. As contingent consideration for paying these rebates, however, many suppliers required the Company either to agree to new business or to repay the amount of the rebate in the form of waived price concessions on already-agreed upon future business. The Engine Division booked these rebates, often using the same form letter (which in certain instances was back-dated) that falsely stated that the rebate was based on past purchases and had no contingencies. In some instances, certain Engine Division employees also generated side-letter arrangements with vendors that detailed that the rebates were contingent on future purchases and/or the vendor could recoup the rebate through inflated future prices by which the Company would forego agreed-upon price reductions. Additionally, these side-letters stated that Navistar would refund the rebate accordingly if the Company failed to make sufficient future purchases. These side-letters made clear that these rebates had not actually been earned at the time the amounts were recognized.

20. In one instance, "Vendor Rebate 1," a supplier executed a form rebate letter drafted by Navistar, and dated October 19, 2004, that said the supplier was providing the Company a $2.1 million rebate based on "2004 volume and piece price productivity improvements." However, the very next day, October 20, 2004, the parties executed a side-letter arrangement that specifically stated that half of the rebate was based on pulling forward productivity improvements expected to be achieved in 2005. Navistar also agreed to refund any shortfall to the supplier should these 6 improvements not be achieved. Thus, the side-letter made clear that the supplier's rebate was contingent on future business with the Company. Nevertheless, Navistar approved the rebate and booked the entire dollar amount in fiscal year 2004.

21. Another form of these improperly-booked rebates were so-called "signing bonuses" that Navistar demanded and received from certain suppliers in exchange for awarding new business. Despite the fact that the suppliers' payments were contingent on receiving that new business from Navistar, the Company booked the rebates in their entirety during the then-current period in which they were received, instead of when earned over the period of the future business.

22. In one such instance, "Vendor Rebate 2,"McIntosh contacted Stanaway four days after the 2003 fiscal year-end to discuss the need to fill an earnings shortfall. Stanaway, in turn, discussed the shortfall with Akers, who in exchange for promising to provide future business to a particular supplier in 2004, convinced the supplier to agree to pay a $6.2 million signing bonus to the Company and to provide Navistar with a letter that would allow the Company to book the full amount in 2003. The vendor had never before done business with Navistar. Akers had engaged in previous discussions with the vendor about possible future business and the payment of a signing bonus, but the terms of the signing bonus were not finalized until after the 2003 fiscal year-end. Stanaway, who had no direct role in acquiring the rebate, then approved an entry recording the $6.2 million as income in 2003.

PARAGRAPHS 33–43 FROM AAER 3165

Warranty Reserve

33. Beginning in fiscal year 1999, the Engine Division assumed responsibility for accounting for its warranty reserve, which reflected the Company's estimated future warranty costs on engines installed in the majority of Navistar

manufactured trucks. The warranty accrual estimate process began with the Engine Division's Reliability & Quality ("R&Q") group, which generated an estimated warranty cost per unit, or CPU, for each engine sold. This calculation incorporated certain "above-the-line" items, including well-established or known steps (e.g., implemented engineering fixes) that were viewed, based on historical trends or data, to have effectively reduced warranty costs. The CPU was the primary basis for the warranty reserve amount; the higher the CPU, the higher the reserve.

34. The warranty reserve-setting process should have been governed by accounting rules related to contingent liabilities. Pursuant to Statement of Financial Accounting Standards ("SFAS") No. 5, *Accounting for Contingencies - Appendix A; With Respect to Obligations Related to Product Warranties and Product Defects*, warranty reserves must be established when it is probable that a liability has been incurred and the amount of the loss can be reasonably estimated.

35. When R&Q's CPU calculation was presented to Stanaway, and then ultimately to McIntosh, both typically stated that the initial estimated reserve number was too high for the Engine Division's business plan. Without sufficient consideration for the relevant accounting rules, Stanaway and McIntosh typically then directed R&Q to add certain "below-the-line" items to the warranty reserve calculation process because they thought these items would reflect potential reductions that the Company hoped to achieve in future warranty costs. These "below-the-line" items included anticipated vendor reimbursements and engineering fixes* that lacked historical trend or other data evidencing their likely effectiveness. For example, Stanaway and McIntosh directed R&Q to include anticipated vendor reimbursements in the warranty reserve calculation despite the lack of any specific language in the vendor contracts providing for such recoveries. Instead, the Company relied on the existence of standard provisions in supply agreements or the Illinois Commercial Code to support the contemplated vendor reimbursements. During the relevant period, approximately 50 percent of the vendor recoveries deducted below the line from warranty reserve calculations were based on something other than specific contractual language. Moreover, the Company often did not receive reimbursements from vendors for engine warranty claims. Stanaway and McIntosh also directed the inclusion in the warranty accrual calculation of anticipated engineering fixes that lacked historical and empirical data evidencing their likely effectiveness. Certain anticipated fixes were incorporated into the CPU calculation before they had even been implemented. At McIntosh and Stanaway's insistence, R&Q included these "below-the-line" items in its warranty reserve calculation, and these components consistently reduced the warranty reserve.

36. The inclusion of these anticipated vendor reimbursements and engineering fixes was not in compliance with GAAP. Stanaway and McIntosh knew or should have known that the warranty reserve-setting process was governed by accounting rules relevant to contingent liabilities, yet failed to consider or apply such rules in establishing Navistar's

---

* Vendor reimbursements concerned payments that Navistar sought to receive from manufacturers of the failed engine parts that were the source of warranty claims against the Company. Engineering fixes included engine design changes (e.g., modifications to engines not yet built) and service kits (e.g., modifications implemented after sale to address engine problems that arose in the field).

warranty reserve. Stanaway and McIntosh also knew or should have known that includ-ing anticipated vendor reimbursements and engineering fixes without data evidencing their effectiveness was not in compliance with GAAP.

37. The below-the-line items inappropriately included in the reserve calculation caused the warranty expense to be understated by $17 million in fiscal year 2002 and by $18.5 million in fiscal year 2003. The $18.5 million total represented 5.9 percent of the restated loss before income tax for that year.

Reporting Failures Regarding Certain Deferred Start-up Costs

38. In 2000, the Company entered into a long-term supply contract (the "Agreement") with an automobile manufacturer (the "Automaker") to develop and manufacture V-6 diesel engines commencing with model year 2002 and extending through 2012. From the fourth quarter of 2001 through the fourth quarter of 2002, the Company incurred substantial start-up costs relating to the Agreement, including expenses developing the engine, constructing a plant in Huntsville, Alabama, and leasing engine assembly assets. The Company began deferring some of these start-up costs in the fourth quarter of fiscal 2001 and as of the fourth quarter of 2002 had accumulated $57 million of deferred pre-production costs. Production of these engines was continually delayed by the Automaker until October 2002, when it cancelled the Agreement and discontinued its V-6 engine program with Navistar.

39. Relevant accounting rules provided that such start-up costs could be deferred only if there existed an objectively verified and measured contractual guarantee of reimbursement. *See* FASB Emerging Issues Task Force Issue No. 99-5, *Accounting for Pre-Production Costs Related to Long-Term Supply Arrangements* ("EITF 99-5").

40. The terms of the Agreement standing alone did not provide for reimbursement in a manner sufficient to satisfy the requirements for start-up cost deferral pursuant to EITF 99-5. The start-up costs could be appropriately deferred only if the Company had received from the Automaker a written guarantee of specific reimbursement. Without such a written guarantee, the Company was not entitled to defer these costs.

41. The Company never received from the Automaker a sufficiently specific written guarantee of reimbursement. Beginning in September 2001 and continuing until October 2002, when the Automaker cancelled the Agreement, Company management repeatedly sought such a guarantee in the form of a letter. These efforts were continually rebuffed by the Automaker.

42. Nevertheless, the Company, through its senior accounting staff, deferred these start-up costs from the fourth quarter of 2001 through the fourth quarter of 2002. Specifically, the Company deferred $4.3 million in the fourth quarter of fiscal year 2001, $12.8 million in the first quarter of fiscal year 2002, and $13.3 million in each of the second and third quarters of fiscal year 2002.*

43. These deferred start-up costs were not in compliance with GAAP. While senior management did receive oral assurances from Navistar senior managers that the

---

* The Company did not file an adjusted consolidated statement of operations for fiscal year 2002 or for the 2002 quarterly periods. *See supra* n. 2. Nevertheless, the dollar amounts that were deferred instead of being expensed are considered material for each of the first three quarters of fiscal year 2002. The $12.8 million and the $13.3 million totals represent 12.5 percent, 65.5 percent, and 25.4 percent, respectively, of the Company's previously reported loss before income tax if adjusted to reverse these deferrals for each of the first three quarters of fiscal year 2002.

Automaker had in fact committed to reimburse the Company for these start-up costs and Navistar's outside auditor was aware of and accepted the continuing deferral, the Company should not have allowed the deferral because it had not received the aforementioned written guarantee of reimbursement. Navistar, like all issuers registered with the Commission, is ultimately responsible for the accuracy of its books, records, and accounts.

FINANCIAL STATEMENTS

UNITED STATES
SECURITIES AND EXCHANGE COMMISSION
Washington, D.C. 20549

Extracts from FORM 10-K[8]

Annual report pursuant to Section 13 or 15(d) of the Securities Exchange Act of 1934

For the fiscal years 2002-2003

NAVISTAR INTERNATIONAL CORPORATION

Statement of Income 2003

	Navistar International Corporation and Consolidated Subsidiaries	
For the Years Ended October 31 Millions of dollars, except share data	2003	2002
Sales and revenues		
Sales of manufactured products	**$ 7,033**	$ 6,493
Finance revenue	**287**	271
Other income	**20**	20
Total sales and revenues	**7,340**	6,784
Costs and expenses		
Cost of products and services sold	**6,229**	5,817
Cost of products sold related to restructuring	**9**	23
Total cost of products and services sold	**6,238**	5,840
Restructuring and other non-recurring charges	**(41)**	521
Postretirement benefits expense	**297**	228
Engineering and research expense	**242**	260
Selling, general and administrative expense	**487**	521
Interest expense	**136**	154
Other expense	**26**	29
Total costs and expenses	**7,385**	7,553

(continued)

---

[8] Extracted from 10-K filings for Navistar International Corporation 2002-2003. Obtained from U.S. Securities and Exchange Commission. *www.sec.gov.*

For the Years Ended October 31	Navistar International Corporation and Consolidated Subsidiaries	
Millions of dollars, except share data	2003	2002
Income (loss) from continuing operations before income taxes	(45)	(769)
Income tax expense (benefit)	(31)	(293)
Income (loss) from continuing operations	(14)	(476)
Discontinued operations:		
Loss from discontinued operations (less applicable Income taxes of $0, $2 and $0, respectively)	—	(14)
Loss on disposal	(4)	(46)
Loss from discontinued operations	(4)	(60)
Net income (loss)	$ (18)	$ (536)

Navistar International Corporation

Statement of Financial Condition 2003

As of October 31	Navistar International Corporation and Consolidated Subsidiaries	
Millions of dollars	2003	2002
ASSETS		
Current assets		
Cash and cash equivalents	$ 447	$ 620
Marketable securities	78	—
Receivables, net	869	1,043
Inventories	494	595
Deferred tax asset, net	176	242
Other assets	146	107
Total current assets	2,210	2,607
Marketable securities	517	116
Finance and other receivables, net	955	1,239
Property and equipment, net	1,350	1,479
Investments and other assets	339	167
Prepaid and intangible pension assets	66	63
Deferred tax asset, net	1,463	1,286
Total assets	$ 6,900	$ 6,957
LIABILITIES AND SHAREOWNERS' EQUITY		
Liabilities		
Current liabilities		
Notes payable and current maturities of long-term debt	$ 214	$ 358
Accounts payable, principally trade	1,079	1,020
Other liabilities	911	1,029
Total current liabilities	2,204	2,407

(continued)

As of October 31 Millions of dollars	Navistar International Corporation and Consolidated Subsidiaries	
	2003	**2002**
Debt: Manufacturing operations	**863**	747
Financial services operations	**1,533**	1,651
Postretirement benefits liability	**1,435**	1,354
Other liabilities	**555**	547
Total liabilities	**6,590**	6,706
Commitments and contingencies		
Shareowners' equity		
Series D convertible junior preference stock	**4**	4
Common stock and additional paid in capital (75.3 million shares issued)	**2,118**	2,146
Retained earnings (deficit)	**(824)**	(721)
Accumulated other comprehensive loss	**(786)**	(705)
Common stock held in treasury, at cost (6.5 million and 14.8 million shares held)	**(202)**	(473)
Total shareowners' equity	**310**	251
Total liabilities and shareowners' equity	**$ 6,900**	$ 6,957

From NAVISTAR's 10-K 2002 NOTES, Page 53[9]

Other Liabilities

Major classifications of other liabilities at October 31 are as follows:

Millions of dollars	2002	2001
Product liability and warranty	$ 273	$ 241
Employee incentive programs	26	34
Payroll, commissions and employee-related benefits....	79	88
Postretirement benefits liability	282	257
Dealer reserves	21	22
Taxes	206	211
Sales and marketing	41	37
Long-term disability and workers' compensation	48	48
Environmental	10	11
Interest	34	36
Restructuring and other non-recurring charges	296	90
Other	246	155
Total other liabilities	1,562	1,230
Less current portion	(1,021)	(758)
Other long-term liabilities	$ 541	$ 472

---

[9] Extracted from 10-K filings for Navistar International Corporation. Obtained from U.S. Securities and Exchange Commission. *www.sec.gov*.

From NAVISTAR's 10-K 2002 NOTES, Page 55

From NAVISTAR's 10-K 2002 NOTES, Page 55

Restructuring and Other Non-Recurring Charges

In addition to the 2002 Plan of Restructuring charges, the company has recorded non-recurring charges of $170 million primarily related to the company's V-6 diesel engine program with Ford. In 2000, the company and Ford finalized a contract for the supply of V-6 diesel engines commencing with model year 2002 and extending through 2012. The contract provided that the company is Ford's exclusive source for these diesel engines and the company would sell these engines only to Ford for certain specified vehicles. To support this program, the company developed a V-6 diesel engine, constructed an engine assembly plant in Huntsville, Alabama, entered into non-cancelable lease agreements for V-6 diesel engine assembly assets and incurred certain pre-production costs. During 2002, the company deferred certain pre-production expenses related to the launch of the Ford V-6 diesel engine program in accordance with Emerging Issues Task Force Issue No. 99-5, "Accounting for Pre-Production Costs Related to Long-Term Supply Arrangements." As of October 31, 2002, $57 million of such costs and expenses had been deferred. In October 2002, Ford advised the company that their current business case for a V-6 diesel engine in the specified vehicles is not viable and it has discontinued its program for the use of these engines. Ford is seeking to cancel the V-6 supply contract. As a result, the company has determined that the timing of the commencement of the V-6 diesel engine program is neither reasonably predictable nor probable. Accordingly, the company has recorded a non-recurring pre-tax charge of $167 million to write-off the deferred pre-production costs, write-down to fair value certain V-6 diesel engine-related fixed assets that will be abandoned, accrue future lease obligations under non-cancelable operating leases for certain V-6 diesel engine assembly assets that will not be used by the company, accrue for amounts contractually owed to suppliers related to the V-6 diesel engine program and write-down to fair value certain other assets.

From NAVISTAR'S 10-K 2003 NOTES, Page 58

Other Liabilities

Major classifications of other liabilities at October 31 are as follows:

Millions of dollars	2003	2002
Product liability and warranty	$ 253	$ 273
Employee incentive programs	26	26
Payroll, commissions and employee-related benefits	63	79
Postretirement benefits liability	294	282
Dealer reserves	22	21
Taxes	235	206
Sales and marketing	56	41
Long-term disability and workers' compensation	52	48
Environmental	8	10
Interest	30	34
Restructuring and other non-recurring charges	157	296

(continued)

Millions of dollars	2003	2002
Other	270	260
Total other liabilities	1,466	1,576*
Less current portion	(911)	(1,029)
Other long-term liabilities	$ 555	$ 547

*Author's Note:** In the 2003 notes, there was a small change to the 2002 *Total other liabilities* amount, as compared to the amount for *Total other liabilities* stated in the 2002 note.

From NAVISTAR'S 10-K 2003 NOTES, Page 68

Product Warranty

Provisions for estimated expenses related to product warranty are made at the time products are sold. These estimates are established using historical information about the nature, frequency and average cost of warranty claims. Management actively studies trends of warranty claims and takes action to improve vehicle quality and minimize warranty claims. Management believes that the warranty reserve is appropriate; however, actual claims incurred could differ from the original estimates, requiring adjustments to the reserve.

Changes in the product warranty accrual for the year ended October 31, 2003, were as follows:

Millions of dollars	
Balance, beginning of period	$185
Change in liability for warranties issued during the period	166
Change in liability for preexisting warranties	11
Payments made	(189)
Balance, end of period	$173

Enron and the Tale of the Golden Goose[1]

After studying this chapter, you should be able to:

- Explain Enron's abuse of mark-to-market accounting.
- Identify the various ways in which Enron used off-balance sheet entities to understate debt and overstate earnings.
- Describe how Enron misclassified "prepays" as sales.
- Identify and explain the signals in financial statements that could have alerted one to Enron's use of special purpose entities (SPEs) to overstate earnings and understate debt.
- Identify and explain the general signals of Enron's overstatement of earnings, overstatement of cash flow from operations (CFFO), and problematically high debt levels.

Enron is presented here mainly as an example of:

1. The abuse of mark-to-market accounting

2. The improper use of special purpose entities (or unconsolidated off-balance sheet entities), which it used to:

   - Understate debt

   - Overstate earnings via:

     - Related-party sales

     - Loans disguised as sales

---

[1] General background information in this chapter is from Bankruptcy *Report #1* (2002), *Bankruptcy Report #2* (2003), *Bankruptcy Report #3* (2003), Bryce (2002), Eichenwald (2005), Enron Timeline (2005), Gruley and Smith (2002), McLean and Elkind (2004), Powers Report (2002), and Swartz and Watkins (2003).

- Related-party management fees

- Contrived put options purporting to lock in profits on investments in shares

- Mark-to-market revaluations of assets via references to contrived sales to these contrived entities

- Recognition of profits on its own stock that was issued to off-balance-sheet entities

3. Misclassification of "prepays" as sales (see Table 1.1 on p. 19)

CHAPTER OUTLINE

- The Start of Enron
- Enron Capital and Trade (ECT)
- How Enron Lost a Fortune
- The Electricity Fiasco in California
- Enron's Fictitious Financial Reporting Schemes

- Signals of the Enron Frauds
- Key Terms
- Ethics at Work
- Assignments
- Case Study: Basin Water, Inc.

THE START OF ENRON

The company that once represented the pinnacle of corporate success—and the company that became the golden goose for so many—is now a symbol of all that can go horribly wrong in the corporate world. In August 2000, Enron's stock was at an all-time high, trading at $90 a share. By November 2001, an Enron share was worth less than $1. What happened? Why was it allowed to happen? How did the golden goose become the cooked goose?

The real story of Enron goes back to May 1985, when InterNorth—the company that owned the biggest and best gas-pipeline network in the United States—merged with Houston Natural Gas (HNG), whose ancestry went back to the Houston Oil Company that had been formed in 1901. Twenty-four years later, in 1925, Houston Oil entered the gas business and formed two companies: the Houston Pipeline Company (to pipe natural gas) and Houston Natural Gas (to distribute the gas). By the early 1980s, Houston Natural Gas owned hundreds of gas wells and had annual revenue of $3 billion. Around this time, the HNG board of directors started searching for a dynamic chief executive officer (CEO), and they believed that they had found such a man in Kenneth Lay, who was appointed CEO in 1984. Both HNG and InterNorth were first-rate companies with impeccable credentials, and both were targets for hostile takeovers. In an attempt to avoid such takeovers, the two companies merged in 1985, and Lay became CEO of the new conglomerate, which took the name of *Enron*.

So perhaps the real story of Enron starts with the story of Kenneth Lay.

Kenneth Lay

Born in Missouri in 1942, Kenneth Lay was the son of respectable, down-to-earth parents who constantly struggled to make ends meet. At one stage in Lay's early childhood, after his parents' feed store had gone bankrupt, Lay and his family "bounced around Missouri and Mississippi. Thanksgiving dinner that year was lunch meat with bread" (Gruley & Smith, 2002). The family was then taken in by in-laws who lived on a small, meager farm. After that, the Lays never really regained their financial footing. There are several accounts of Kenneth Lay sitting on a tractor as a child and gazing at the downtown buildings he saw in the distance, daydreaming about inhabiting that remote world that seemed so elusive.

As so many before him, Kenneth Lay's route out of poverty was higher education. After high school, he attended the University of Missouri, where he studied economics and apparently became "captivated by theories of how markets and companies work." He went on to complete a master's degree in economics in 1965 and later earned a doctorate from the University of Houston. Lay married his college sweetheart, Judith, in 1966, and within a few years, they were the proud parents of a son and daughter. A couple of years after his marriage, Lay enrolled in the U.S. Navy. In the early 1970s, Lay's undergraduate economics professor, Pinkney Walker, was appointed to the Federal Power Commission, and Walker selected Lay as his chief aide. During this time, Lay wrote speeches for Walker that "shook up Washington with their fervor for deregulation." Washington was impressed, and Lay was appointed interim deputy undersecretary for energy. (Quotes from Gruley & Smith, 2002)

As steep as his ascent had been from underprivileged farm boy to deputy undersecretary, nobody observing the likeable, unfailingly courteous Lay would have guessed at the ambition that grew as he surveyed the country's energy sector. His attention was particularly riveted on the natural gas segment of the energy sector. Lay saw a highly regulated business in which the price of gas was mandated. Pipeline companies paid regulated amounts to the gas producers and, in turn, received regulated prices from industrial customers and gas utilities for piping the gas to them. Lay believed in free markets. He was certain that deregulation would eventually come to the gas industry and that it would unleash vast opportunities for making a fortune from natural gas. Adhering to this belief, he left the public sector, and with the help of another letter of recommendation from Walker, he landed a job in the corporate planning office of Florida Gas in 1974. By 1979, he was president of the company, and by anybody's standards, the once poor farm boy was rich.

In 1981, Lay was appointed president of the Houston-based Transco Energy. Lay moved to Houston with his secretary, Linda Phillips, whom he then married after divorcing his first wife. When HNG came looking for a new CEO in 1984, Lay jumped at the opportunity to become CEO and chairman of this old and highly respected Houston gas production company. Lay was 42 years old, and he had arrived.

Lay soon began fretting that HNG did not have a large enough network of pipelines. Quite coincidentally, he received an unexpected call from Sam Segnar, the CEO of InterNorth, asking if Lay was interested in a plan for InterNorth to acquire HNG. Segnar was keen to shut out the chance of a hostile takeover by a corporate raider and believed that all the debt InterNorth would incur by buying HNG would make it immune to a future takeover. In May 1985, InterNorth acquired HNG for $2.3 billion.

Although InterNorth was three times the size of HNG, the deal was done on terms that were unusually favorable to HNG. The agreement included paying HNG $70 per share for shares that were trading at $48 at the time of the amalgamation of the two companies. Also, according to the contract, after 18 months, Lay would replace Segnar as CEO of InterNorth. The InterNorth board soon regretted the merger and blamed Segnar for persuading them to agree to it. As a result of the inexplicably poor terms and other difficulties with the merger, the board of the merged companies decided to replace Segnar sooner rather than later. In November 1985, it appointed Kenneth Lay as the CEO of the new conglomerate.

Lay was now CEO of a huge company that, with over 37,000 miles of pipeline, controlled "the largest gas-distribution system in the country, running from border to border, coast to coast" (McLean & Elkind, 2004, p. 10). It also had natural gas exploration plants, productions plants, hundreds of gas wells, and other energy businesses. Lay himself had a lot to offer the new company—he was good at cajoling politicians, and he was on friendly terms with the future governor of Texas, Ann Richards. Lay's support was also courted by then Governor George W. Bush. Yet in spite of Lay's talents and the power and reach of this awesome combination of companies, the merger had a strange and difficult start.

After InterNorth's bout of merger remorse, the next blunder—minor, yet indicative of a troubled future—involved the naming of the new company. The board of InterNorth/HNG had decided to change the name of the combined companies to *Enteron*. However, "Within days of the announcement, the soon-to-be Enteron was a laughing stock." Apparently, the dictionary definition of *enteron* is "digestive tube." The name was rather "unfortunate, given that Lay's company produced natural gas." So the board decided to adjust the name to *Enron*. (Quotes from Eichenwald, 2005, pp. 33–34)

More ominous than the embarrassing name, Enron had another problem right from its inception—a problem that was concealed for years until it mushroomed into a monster. The predicament was simply this: Enron began its life with too much debt. InterNorth's borrowing of hundreds of millions of dollars to acquire HNG for $2.4 billion, combined with other debt, meant that the newly formed Enron began its life *with over $4 billion of debt.*

While such debt would—for good reason—discourage future hostile takeovers, such large debt also presented significant problems for the company itself. High debt means high interest expenses, which eat into profits. Also, the higher the debt relative to profits and to equity, the higher the risk that the debtor will default on payments. For this reason, lenders charge higher interest rates for future borrowing, exacerbating the problem of the high cost of capital. More troubling still, a company's high debt can cause analysts to lower their "buy" ratings on the company's stock. Perhaps most disturbing of all is that the debt must be repaid eventually, and if it cannot be repaid, the company will face bankruptcy. (Ironically, about 20 years later, at Lay's criminal trial in early 2006, his attorney would lament the fact that the banks had wanted their loans to be repaid and argued that if the banks had not made this inconvenient request, Enron would still be in business.)

It is unlikely that Kenneth Lay, or "Kenny boy" (as then Texas Governor George W. Bush had named him) worried too much about the existence of debt—it was the appearance of debt that he did not like. Although Lay was master of all the pipelines and gas wells that Enron possessed, he did not become master of its debt. While Enron's management certainly manipulated the *reporting* of its debt, they never controlled the debt itself; indeed, eventually it mastered all of them.

Enron had yet another crisis early on. At the time of the merger, a large part of InterNorth had moved to Houston, but its small oil-trading division, which became known as Enron Oil, remained in New York and was largely allowed free rein by the Houston office. Louis Borget, who ran Enron Oil, liked it that way. However, a bank that was doing business with Borget became suspicious and contacted Enron. Kenneth Lay and a few other Enron employees paid a visit to Enron Oil and soon discovered that "the traders were keeping two sets of books, one for legitimate purposes … and another in which to record their ill-gotten gains" (Swartz & Watkins, 2003, p. 31). It emerged that Borget had been incurring losses and concealing them by selling his losing oil futures at a "profit" to sham companies that he had set up in order to report false profits to inflate his bonus.

Everyone assumed that Borget would be fired, and everyone was surprised when Lay overlooked the fraud and kept Borget on. According to rumor, Lay explained his decision by saying that Borget would be kept in line. An accountant from Arthur Andersen, Enron's auditors, apparently commented later, "No one pounded the table and said these guys are crooks. They thought they had the golden goose, and the golden goose just stole a little money out of their petty cash" (qtd. in McLean & Elkind, 2004, p. 19). Lay's decision would come back to haunt him.

Borget was unrepentant and actually accelerated his oil futures trading. In October 1987, Lay was in Europe and received an emergency call from Enron president John M. "Mick" Seidl, who set up an urgent meeting with Lay in Newfoundland. At the meeting, Seidl told Lay that Enron was on the brink of collapse. Borget had committed the company to delivering a staggering $1.5 billion of oil—oil that it did not have. If word got out that Enron was short this amount, other dealers would buy up the spot oil, driving up the price, and Enron would be bankrupted.

Lay put one of his traders, Mike Muckleroy, in charge of the salvage effort. Muckleroy fooled the markets by buying 8 million barrels of spot oil and then offering each of the major dealers 1 million barrels of oil, saying that Enron had a surplus. This trick worked, and Enron was able to buy up spot oil and offload enough of Borget's contracts in the next 60 days for the company to survive. Eventually, word got out of Enron's near miss, and Lay did what he would do again in 2002 on Enron's final collapse—he denied that he had ever known of the magnitude of the trading operation or its risks. Borget was later convicted of fraud, jailed for a year, and fined $6 million. Lay did not realize it then, but he was peering into a crystal ball and gazing at Enron's future.

Initially, no problems were obvious to outsiders. The golden goose appeared to be sleek and plump. Over the next few years, Enron was to offer dizzying numbers of stock options to its executives. In fact, Lay would eventually unload over $100 million of his Enron stock before it became worthless.

Although Lay had moved from the public energy sector in the 1970s in anticipation of deregulation and the opportunity for the profits he was sure this would bring, he had not yet figured out a way for Enron to capitalize on deregulation, which had started but had not unfolded as neatly as he had hoped. In fact, while the previously regulated gas business had been steady and predictable, the process of semi-deregulation had produced some unintended consequences. With fixed purchase prices and fixed selling prices, the pipeline companies had entered into long-term contracts to purchase gas for years to come. When the purchase prices were deregulated, prices fell and companies were stuck with these take-or-pay contracts to purchase gas at prearranged fixed prices that were above-market. In addition, because of earlier price caps, a number of gas producers had closed down, and many industrial gas plants and utilities had experienced shortages of gas.

After deregulation, selling prices shot up during times of higher demand but plunged at other times, making it difficult for users to predict future purchase prices and estimate whether or not an industrial gas plant or a gas utility would be profitable. Therefore, new utility companies and industrial plants increasingly used alternative energy sources—such as oil and coal—and avoided gas. Soon there was an oversupply of gas on the market and Enron, like the other pipeline businesses, had a huge problem. Kenneth Lay—indeed the whole gas industry—needed someone who could figure out a way to make the deregulated gas industry profitable.

Jeffrey Skilling

The man that Kenneth Lay turned to was a Harvard MBA—and intermittent risk taker—named Jeffrey Skilling, who worked at the prominent consulting firm of McKinsey & Company. Born in Pittsburgh in 1953, Skilling was the son of an engineer-turned-traveling salesman who lost his job, forcing the family to move to Chicago, where Skilling, with very little effort, did exceptionally well in high school. Interestingly, Skilling turned down Princeton University and selected Southern Methodist University, in Dallas, for his undergraduate degree. After getting married and working briefly in a bank, Skilling was accepted at Harvard Business School, where he graduated in the top 5 percent of his MBA class and then joined McKinsey.

As a consultant to InterNorth, which subsequently became part of Enron, Skilling began to realize that without stable, long-term gas prices, energy users—including industrial plants, utilities, and private customers—would not want to be dependent on gas. In addition, power producers were hesitant to explore and produce gas, and even willing potential producers could not raise financing because the banks required more reliable estimates of future prices in order to assess whether the producers would be profitable enough to repay their bank loans. The daily fluctuating spot prices of natural gas were just too volatile. Natural gas as a significant energy source would only make sense if one could get the wild instability out of the prices.

The industry was in desperate need of a business model that would provide the producers and users with the mechanism to reliably predict the prices as well as the demand and supply of gas. As a consultant to Enron, Skilling provided the answer—what he called the *Gas Bank* (Swartz & Watkins, 2003, p. 45).

SKILLING'S GAS BANK The plan was for Enron itself to be the Gas Bank. Gas producers could contract to make deposits of gas with Enron for future years at previously agreed-upon prices. In addition, gas users could contract in advance to make withdrawals (purchases) of gas from Enron at specified prices for future years. Enron would make a percentage on the spread, much the same way a bank borrows from lenders at a certain interest rate and lends to borrowers at a higher interest rate. Gas producers, industrial gas users, and utilities would be able to estimate future prices and cash flows more reliably. Potential producers could obtain bank loans more easily for the exploration and production of new gas.

In 1987, on the advice of Skilling, Enron launched its Gas Bank. Industrial users and utilities quickly signed long-term contracts to buy gas at fixed prices. However, the plan faltered when gas producers were not as keen to lock themselves into long-term selling prices. Skilling became convinced that if *he* ran Enron's Gas Bank, he would be able to solve the problems and make it work. In 1990, Skilling left McKinsey & Company to join Enron as chairman and CEO of a new division known as *Enron Finance*.

Skilling expanded his Gas Bank concept by announcing that Enron would get gas producers on board by paying them up front for their contracts to deliver gas in future periods; Enron was now financing gas production companies. The producers would later have to deliver an assured supply of gas at fixed prices, and Skilling knew what price to set for the supplies of gas in order to make a profit on the spread because Enron already had contracts to sell the gas at fixed prices in the future. The Gas Bank was a brilliant concept.

Skilling had still bigger plans, intending to transform the gas industry even further. He decided to chop up Enron's long-term supply contracts, as well as its long-term purchase contracts, into smaller ones and offer all of them sale. In other words, Skilling transformed the contracts into financial instruments to be sold on the free market. He set up traders to buy and sell these financial instruments. The public could now buy the right to purchase gas or to supply gas at fixed prices in the future. Skilling had invented a futures market in natural gas! (A **futures market** is an exchange where parties can trade futures contracts—financial instruments in which parties agree to buy or sell quantities of a commodity at a specified price on a specified future date.) Soon, companies on Wall Street followed Skilling's lead, and in 1990, the New York Mercantile Exchange began trading gas futures. Enron dominated the market and "was the dominant company when it came to setting prices as well" (Swartz & Watkins, 2003, p. 47).

SKILLING AND MARK-TO-MARKET ACCOUNTING Once Skilling had established a trading floor and staffed it with traders selling financial instruments, he started to declare that his division—Enron Finance—was the real business of Enron. Financial service firms usually have a ready market price to refer to in order to establish the value of the financial instruments that they own and can readily sell. According to generally accepted accounting principles (GAAP), financial service firms should normally carry the value of their financial instruments on their balance sheets at market price. If an instrument's market value increases while a *financial services* company owns it, the company revalues the asset on the balance sheet (that is—marks it up to market value) and correspondingly records the increased amount as profit on its income statement, a practice known as mark-to-market accounting. (**Mark-to-market accounting** refers to the revaluation of an asset or a liability on an entity's balance sheet to its market or fair value and the corresponding recording of the increased or decreased amount as income on the income statement or as other comprehensive income.) Although Enron was not primarily a financial services company, Skilling believed that he had an argument for his division to use mark-to-market accounting on the grounds that his division traded financial instruments (gas futures).

Unfortunately, there is a strong potential for abuse of mark-to-market accounting. It is one thing to have a market value for a futures contract to sell an asset in the not-too-distant future and to recognize or record the increase in value of that contract. In fact, it is even possible to sell that contract today on the futures market and receive the market price in cash. It is quite another matter if you have a contract to sell gas for the next 23 years and there are no market prices to indicate what you will have to pay for the gas you intend to sell in 23 years' time. The longer the contract extends into the future, the less likely it is to estimate prices accurately. Because of this risk, the futures market does not usually enter into such long-term contracts.

Recognizing such future profit now—that is, revaluing the asset and booking the revaluation amount to current profit—involves unreliable estimates and is highly susceptible to abuse. Further, if the transaction involves actual work that must be done in the future to realize a future profit, the profit can only be recognized once the work has been done. Mark-to-market accounting cannot be used in such situations. Bethany McLean and Peter Elkind, in their book *The Smartest Guys in the Room: The Amazing Rise and Scandalous Fall of Enron* (2004), pointed out, "This line of thinking suggests that General Motors should book all the future profits of a new model automobile at the moment the car is designed, long before a single vehicle rolls off the assembly line" (pp. 39–40).

Since his arrival at Enron in 1990, Skilling had been intrigued with the idea of being able to currently record future profits using mark-to-market accounting. Then in late 1990, Enron signed a 23-year contract—valued at over a billion dollars—with the New York Power Authority (NYPA) (Bryce, 2002, p. 65). According to accepted accounting practice, Enron could report only 1/23 of this revenue each year for the next 23 years. Using mark-to-market accounting, however, Enron would be able to report the entire 23 years of profit in the current quarter.

According to Bryce (2002), the potential for reporting profits on such a long-term contract convinced Skilling to adopt mark-to-market accounting. In May 1991, Skilling persuaded Enron's audit committee to adopt mark-to-market accounting. With the help of lobbying from Arthur Andersen, the Securities and Exchange Commission (SEC) granted its permission to Enron to use mark-to-market accounting in its Gas Services division. It was unusual for a company that was *not* a financial institution to receive permission from the SEC to use mark-to-market accounting. Enron wrote back to the SEC and said that it planned to go ahead and use mark-to-market accounting *a year earlier* than the date approved by the SEC. To this day, it remains a mystery as to why the SEC did not object to that subsequent letter from Enron. On the day that the letter arrived from the SEC giving Skilling permission to use this new accounting policy, he bought champagne to celebrate with his division's staff (Bryce, 2002, p.68).

From this point on, Enron began to focus more on recording accounting profit than on making cash—so a huge problem was born. Enron began to use mark-to-market accounting wherever it could. The magnitude of that loss of focus *cannot* be underestimated. Enron began to lose colossal amounts of cash on ill-advised projects while it reported "estimated" future profits as current-period profits and hid the mounting debt it incurred to cover the huge amounts of cash it squandered. In May 1991, when Skilling cracked open the champagne to celebrate his right to use mark-to-market accounting, he was focused on the ability to report massive amounts of expected future earnings as current-period profits and the boost this would give to Enron's stock price as well as to his compensation.

Around this time, Enron Finance, Skilling's Enron division, merged with Enron Gas Marketing, and the segment was renamed *Enron Capital and Trade (ECT) Resources*. Skilling became the CEO of this new division. As head of ECT, Skilling was an Enron star on the rise. He had remade himself as the coolest guy at Enron, and Enron was the coolest company in all of Texas.

Skilling appointed Lou Pai, a brilliant trader with little respect for the hard-asset pipeline business, as head of the floor and trading operations. From then on, Skilling allegedly wanted Enron to focus on its trading business as opposed to the hard-asset business of actually piping gas. Over the next few years, Enron's trading operations grew in many different directions until, eventually, the trading division opened Enron Online, which bought and sold *over 800* different commodities. For the rest of Enron's business life, there would always be a tension within the company between those who wanted Enron to expand its "asset-lite" trading arm and those who wanted to consolidate its hard-asset pipeline business.

Andrew Fastow

To fulfill his ultimate vision of Enron as a trading company, Skilling realized he had to find a financial expert who knew his way around the system and who could wheel and deal for Enron. Just a few months after moving to Enron, Skilling contacted a company of headhunters to locate such a person. They came up with Andrew Fastow. At the time, Fastow was a young banker—with a degree from Tufts University and an MBA from Northwestern University—living in Chicago with his wealthy wife, Lea Weingarten, who was originally from Houston. Fastow was working at Continental Bank, where he had become an expert in "securitization deals, or as they were known more commonly, structured finance." (**Securitization** refers to the pooling of loans and the trading of portions of these loans on securities markets in the form of collateralized debt obligations.) By the time he interviewed at Enron, Fastow was already adept at using SPEs, which enabled a company to "monetize," or "literally turn its assets into money and generate revenue." (Quotes from Swartz & Watkins, 2003, pp. 154–155)

Fastow was doing well, but he wanted to do better. He had never heard of Enron, however, and was rather skeptical when he traveled to Houston to meet Skilling. After all, he dwelled in the elevated world of finance, not "in pipelines—expensive, dirty pipelines" (Eichenwald, 2005, p. 51). Skilling, however, with his unbridled enthusiasm and vision of Enron as a trading company, soon won over the younger man. Fastow was exactly the sort of Enron executive that Skilling had in mind: "Fastow's motto—'never say no to a deal'—came to mean pushing for any transaction, no matter how complex or how irrational" (Swartz & Watkins, 2003, p. 156). As Enron grew larger and louder, so did Andrew Fastow.

Lay, Skilling, and Fastow

The three men who would steer Enron to eventual ruin were all in place by the beginning of 1990. Armed with the power to report virtually any fictitious profit it wished and to hide almost immeasurable amounts of debt, Enron burned through billions of dollars on foolhardy projects on several continents. Enron would use the infamous system of prepays to facilitate overstatement of earnings and cash flow by essentially borrowing against future receipts for future deliveries of commodities and related-party transactions. (**Prepays** refer to transactions in terms of contracts in which one party enters into a contract with another party to deliver a commodity in the future at a specified price.) The party required to deliver the commodity in the future sells the contract to a third party for the amount of the future cash selling price, less a discount. The net result is cash received up front but an obligation to deliver the commodity in the future. Enron would construct SPEs such as Chewco, LJM, and the Raptors that would use mark-to-market accounting and related-party transactions to overstate earnings and hide the debt related to all the cash that had been recklessly lost.

For several years, three things kept Enron going—and growing—throughout its reckless and convoluted projects:

1. Enron constantly overstated its earnings and understated its debt with fictitious accounting via mark-to-market accounting and contrived transactions with SPEs.
2. Enron employed misleading transactions, using the infamous prepays, which essentially took out loans on the strength of future contracts and recorded those loans as revenues.
3. Enron's energy trading—especially its gas trading and its trading on the manipulated California electricity market—generated profit and cash that staved off the inevitable crash from its huge losses and fictitiously reported profits.

Once the energy prices stabilized and energy trading profits waned, not even falsely reported profits and hidden debt could save Enron. Eventually, the debt had to be repaid. The game was up for Enron once the banks refused to continue extending credit to the company either directly or indirectly through its SPEs.

To understand what went wrong with this behemoth company and why it went so wrong, it is necessary to take a closer look at the following phases in the rise and fall of Enron:

- Enron's energy-trading business (ECT).
- Enron's bizarre projects and how the company managed to burn through billions of dollars.
- Enron's exploitation of California's electricity problems.
- Enron's outrageous accounting manipulations to hide its vast losses.
- The signals of the alleged frauds that were scattered throughout Enron's financial statements, while the business community did not bother to look too closely at the golden goose.

ENRON CAPITAL AND TRADE (ECT)

Jeffrey Skilling's bright idea to develop a futures market in natural gas in 1990 was the beginning of Enron's venture into the trading business. In the 1990s, ECT developed quickly from a small trading department into a large and highly profitable division.

Given that Enron was involved in all aspects of the gas business, Enron's traders had extremely useful information to trade on. Enron had gas production supply contracts as well as pipelines and orders for gas from big gas consumers such as utilities and industrial power plants. Enron's traders knew better than anyone how much gas was going to be needed, what supplies were available, and how much was going to be supplied. If Enron discovered that a gas producer was having production problems or that a big consumer needed more gas, the traders knew that they should invest in options contracts that gave them the right to buy gas in the future at today's price; in other words, they "went long on gas."

Bolstered by their success in trading gas, the traders became more inventive in writing derivative financial instruments and started regarding themselves as the Enron elite. To the eventual peril of the company, the trading arm expanded trading to a variety of businesses and commodities in areas that Enron knew absolutely nothing about. One particularly imaginative type of derivative that Enron began trading was its "weather derivative." The idea for this grew out of Enron's attention to fundamental weather information for its gas trading. Enron traders knew that if a cold front was advancing, it would cause gas prices to increase; so the company employed meteorologists to help them predict the weather and, in turn, to predict future gas prices. In fact, all the electric and gas utilities faced risks due to changing prices as a result of fluctuating weather conditions. Enron saw this as an opportunity and began trading weather derivatives with the utility companies. Essentially, Enron would insure its customers against unusual weather conditions (Bryce, 2002, p. 243).

Electricity trading worked well for Enron because several of the fundamentals behind the successful trading of gas futures also worked for trading electricity futures. In 1997, Enron moved into yet another branch of energy and began trading coal. Again, Enron's knowledge of gas and electricity trading provided the basics it needed for success in coal trading. At this point, however, because of the company's increasing conviction that the future of Enron lay in *trading* rather than *energy* per se, Enron began to drift outside the energy business that it understood and into areas where it had little expertise. This would cause a great deal of friction within the company.

HOW ENRON LOST A FORTUNE

Some of the imprudent projects that caused Enron to lose billions of dollars included the infamous Dabhol Power Plant in India, the Azurix water debacle in England, the massive Enron Online venture that went spinning out of control, and the hugely incompetent Enron Broadband Services (EBS), among others.

The Projects of Rebecca Mark

Rebecca Mark was a glamorous Harvard MBA graduate who had worked with John Wing from the division that later became Enron Development. This division began huge power projects overseas, including the massive Teesside project in England. When Wing left Enron in 1991, Mark was made CEO of Enron Development and caught Lay's attention—so much so that she became real competition to Skilling in his quest to be appointed the next CEO of Enron.

Mark apparently recognized that Enron had lost focus on making money and was more focused on recording profit in its income statement. Mark also appeared to have realized that Enron had access to massive amounts of borrowed cash, which it often lost on ill-advised projects while continuing to report earnings up front. As the new CEO of Enron Development, Mark set out to win power projects all over the world and to extend Enron's international reach. In sharp contrast to Skilling's trading operation (which was "asset-lite"), Mark's mandate was to build hard-asset projects such as pipelines, production fields, and other energy sources to supply power plants overseas. She developed these international projects with gusto. For example, by 1992, Enron had part ownership in a pipeline in Argentina, and by "early 1994 Mark also had power plants in the Philippines, Guatemala and Guam." Next, Enron Development was "busy laying a pipeline in Columbia … [and] constructing a plant in China." Soon Enron was working on a pipeline that was intended to go all the way from Bolivia to Brazil. (Quotes from McLean & Elkind, 2004, p. 74)

However, there were a number of problems associated with this frenetic rate of growth. The first problem was that Mark got an up-front bonus on the signing of many of these huge deals. Clearly, this policy encouraged large projects that might not be prudent. Second, "Enron often ended up guaranteeing some or all of the debt." Third, hugely optimistic assumptions were made at the beginning of the projects, assuming that little or nothing would go wrong. Not surprisingly, problems and roadblocks usually did emerge. For example, a power project in the Dominican Republic caused soot to be blown onto a neighboring hotel, resulting in an extremely expensive lawsuit: "For Enron, the deal was a complete bust; through mid-2000 the company had collected a pathetic $3.5 million from its $95 million investment." Possibly the most infamous hard-asset losses for Enron—and the deals that Mark pushed hardest to accomplish—were the Dabhol Power Project in India and the Azurix water project in England. (Quotes from McLean & Elkind, 2004, pp. 77–78)

MARK IN INDIA: THE DABHOL POWER PROJECT In 1992, Mark tried to convince India's Maharashtra State Energy Board (MSEB) to authorize a 20-year power contract with Enron for the province of Maharashtra. This would require Enron to build a massive energy plant estimated to cost just under $4 billion. During its first phase, the plant planned to use a fuel known as "naphta," and in the second phase, it would use liquefied natural gas (LNG), a rather expensive form of energy. The project was never really viable on at least two counts. First, coal was probably a better option than gas for India's electricity production. Second, the payment arrangements as set out in the contract were outrageously favorable to Enron but were not really feasible considering that in India, the government often had to forgive many unpaid electricity bills.

The project seemed doomed when the World Bank refused to finance it and the MSEB wanted to end negotiations. However, Mark pushed ahead and managed to get partial financing from banks and additional financing from the U.S. federal government via the Overseas Private Investment Corporation (OPIC). Mark also lobbied over the head of the local MSEB in India, and in December 1993, the Indian government signed a contract for the first phase of the 20-year project. In fact, if the terms of the contract were fully realized, Enron would receive over $25 billion from India (Bryce, 2002, p. 103). However, just after Enron began construction, India's Congress Party in Maharashtra lost power, and the new party stopped all work on the project, claiming that Enron was guilty of gross overcharging.

Mark worked hard to renegotiate the contract and get the venture back on track, lowering the costs for the first phase and giving the MSEB a 15 percent share in the project. In spite of these amendments, the size of the financial obligation to MSEB was still outrageous and would probably have bankrupted the province. The first phase began producing power in May 1999, two years behind schedule. Around this time, charges of bribery and corruption at the Dabhol plant began to circulate, exacerbated by an anonymous letter sent to Enron's head office. The letter also claimed that MSEB could not pay its bills. The company denied the bribery charges, which were never proven, but the nameless writer certainly proved to be correct in one respect: MSEB refused to pay for the power from Dabhol, saying it could not afford it. In spite of all their attempts, there was nothing Enron executives could do to resuscitate the project. The plant remained empty and useless for five years, a stark symbol of incompetence and greed. In 2006, "Dabhol reopened as Ratnagiri Gas and Power ... under the tutelage of two Indian government-owned firms" (Bajaj, 2010). It has, however, continued to be plagued with problems (Jore, 2013).

MARK IN ENGLAND: THE AZURIX ACCOUNT Mark's status began to diminish with the failure of many of her international power projects. Her decline from glory was aided by her nemesis, Jeffrey Skilling, who led the charge to have her removed from her position as CEO of Enron International (as the development division of Enron had been renamed). Mark's Enron career was finally undone by her plan to start a water utilities company—a sector in which she and Enron had absolutely no experience.

Toward the end of the 1990s, some countries had begun the slow process of privatizing their water utilities and wastewater facilities. Mark believed that this privatization would lead to deregulation, as had happened with the gas industry, and there would be a great deal of money to be made in water. Two French companies, Vivendi and Suez Lyonnaise, were already operating water utilities for local governments around the world, and they were doing very well. So in 1998, Mark began the start-up water company called Azurix, which she financed with money from Enron via an Enron off-balance-sheet entity named *Marlin*. It was extremely difficult to get a foothold in this industry, and Azurix was plagued with problems from beginning to end even though Mark was a hard worker and was always ready to fly around the world to drum up business.

The first Azurix project involved Wessex Water, a successful water utility company in England. In July 1998, Azurix purchased Wessex Water for $2.88 billion. However, by the end of the following year, seven weeks after Azurix had gone public, the company was shocked when Britain's water regulation agency announced that water companies would have to drop prices. Wessex would have to cut its customer rates by 12 percent. To make matters worse, the Wessex facilities had to be upgraded, and the cost for this was astronomical. By some accounts, Azurix lost more than a billion dollars in its first year of operation (Bryce, 2002, pp. 178, 187).

The next problem Mark had to face involved development costs. She had expected Wessex Water to be the silver bullet that would facilitate Azurix's entrance into the water world, after which it could easily buy out privatized utilities or win contracts to manage utilities for municipalities. However, this did not happen in spite of Mark's optimism and her large development teams. In June 1999, even though Azurix was in a state of disarray and not developing enough new business, its initial public offering (IPO) raised $695 million (Smith & Lucchetti, 2000).

Azurix was still desperate for new business, and it seemed as though the answer lay in Argentina. Buenos Aires was taking bids from private companies for a 30-year contract to essentially rent and manage the Buenos Aires water utility and wastewater plants. While preparing to go public, Azurix had submitted an incredibly high bid of $439 million for the contract. The next highest bid was less than $200 million. In its haste to put the deal together, Azurix had ignored some significant information. For example, it had not realized that the actual office buildings were not included in the bid and that the plant had not been well maintained. In fact, it soon became obvious that Azurix had made a mistake. The fatal blow to the Buenos Aires project occurred when an algae outbreak contaminated the drinking water in early 2000 and Azurix had to purchase containers of water and deliver them to its customers at a huge additional expense.

Not everyone believed that the failure of Azurix was entirely Mark's fault. From the outset, her company was saddled with debt when Enron financed it via the off-balance-sheet entity known as Marlin. In fact, "some of the $900 million of the money Fastow had raised [for Azurix] was paid right back to Enron." Even though Azurix burned through cash with its own ill-fated projects and mismanaged development costs, some claimed that Enron was not particularly supportive of Azurix and that—in the battle to gain control of Enron—the "entire expensive episode had all been a grand conspiracy" to depose Rebecca Mark. (Quotes from McLean & Elkind, 2004, pp. 249–250).

Whether or not the plot existed, Jeffrey Skilling retained his position as future king of Enron, and at the end of 2000, Rebecca Mark was cut loose. In spite of her desperate plans to shore up the drowning company, the Enron board had lost confidence in her. Even Kenneth Lay agreed that Azurix had been a tremendous waste of money and that Mark had to resign.

The Enron board ended the Azurix hemorrhage when it paid over $300 million to buy back the shares—held by the public—at just over $8 a share, when the shares were trading at around $3.50 per share. In early 2001, Enron's entire international division was sold. However, because Azurix had initially been funded by the off-balance-sheet entity, Marlin, Enron was still on the hook for Marlin's loans that had been used mainly on Azurix.

Before she left Enron, Mark made a fortune by selling Enron shares. Although it did not seem so at the time, "Rebecca Mark was one of the lucky ones—she got out at the top" (McLean & Elkind, 2004, p. 263). Indeed, Mark managed to hold on to the golden goose just long enough to snatch a golden egg.

Enron Energy Services

Meanwhile, buoyed by its rapid and spectacular success in gas trading, Enron purchased the Portland General Electric utility company in 1997 to establish itself in the electricity industry. As it transpired, Enron's experience and information base in the gas-trading business transferred quite well to the wholesale component of electricity trading. However, Enron also decided to launch into the retail electricity market and, that same year, formed Enron Energy Services (EES) to manage and provide electricity and gas directly to business organizations and households. Enron's expertise did not transfer well to the retail division of supplying and managing electricity services, and this venture became rather problematic.

In attempting to sell its electricity, Enron had to aggressively seek business by promising various other companies and state organizations that it could provide their power supplies at rates that were cheaper than the rates they were currently paying. Unfortunately, Enron did not plan ahead as to how they would fulfill such promises of cheap power. In addition to selling power at bargain-basement prices, Enron had to start managing and maintaining electrical power plants—and it knew almost nothing about this aspect of the electricity industry.

While most of Enron's wholesale traders expected that the cost of electric power would increase, Lou Pai, one of Skilling's chief traders, decided to take a huge gamble that prices would decrease. As it transpired, the price of electricity increased dramatically toward the end of 2000 and EES lost a fortune. (Behind the scenes, of course, many of the wholesale traders made big profits on California's manipulated electricity prices, but this will be covered in a later section.)

It was not too long before some of the problems at EES were noticed by other Enron employees. In February 2001, an accountant named Wanda Curry reported to Enron's chief accounting officer that she was investigating several discrepancies at EES. Some of these problems included the following:

- Many of the contracts were overvalued. Enron Energy "hadn't done much more than guess at energy loads its customers would require" (McLean & Elkind, 2004, p. 300).
- EES had used "faulty price curves with their excessively optimistic assumptions" (McLean & Elkind, 2004, p. 300). It is important to note that with mark-to-market accounting, these contracts were valued using these estimates for the balance sheet and that the expected future profit was recognized in current-period income statements.
- The contracts were not fully hedged, so that if price changes deviated from expectations, Enron would not have other contracts that would increase in value by compensating amounts.
- EES faced huge losses if the California energy crisis forced Enron's customers into bankruptcy, as had occurred, for example, in the case of Pacific Gas.
- There were various speculative trading losses because EES had been trading on the bet that electricity prices would fall when, in fact, prices rose astronomically.

Overall, based on Curry's investigation, EES needed to recognize "a loss that would likely total more than $500 million" (McLean & Elkind, 2004, p. 303). But mysteriously, a disclosure of these losses was nowhere to be found in Enron's financial statements.

Enron Online

Moving into new trading markets usually meant that Enron had no comparative advantages, and there were often huge disadvantages to having absolutely no knowledge of the new industry. It also involved spending and losing vast sums of money to get started. For example, Enron purchased a couple of paper mills to begin a market for trading pulp and paper.

Next, Enron attempted trading in metals and bought the British metals company, MG Plc. Greg Whalley, a talented trader in charge of Enron's wholesale trading operation, supervised the acquisition of MG Plc. Enron was in such a rush to complete the purchase that most of the deal was accomplished in four days and "most of it done with heavy drinking in London bars" (McLean & Elkind, 2004, p. 225). A Wall Street commodity trader is reported to have said that the metals company was worth only a fraction of what Enron had paid for it. Nobody seemed to care, however, because the executives at Enron were imbued with a form of hysteria.

Around this time, an Enron team led by a British trader named Louise Kitchen had developed the technology to launch Enron's trading business on the Internet—and so Enron Online was born and went live in November 1999. From a purely technological point of view, the system was a marvel.

Now the trading arm of Enron really surged, and Enron became predominantly a trading company. Through Enron Online, the Enron traders saw the prices that buyers and sellers were offering, and with that advantage, they made a great deal of money on the products they really understood. However, unlike eBay, which offers a marketplace for other buyers and sellers, Enron Online actually purchased everything that it resold. This caused a huge cash flow problem for Enron and the company borrowed well over $3 billion in order to keep Enron Online afloat (Bryce, 2002, pp. 220–221).

While Enron made profits on many of the commodities, the company was losing money due to its interest expense and the trading of commodities that the brokers did not understand. In addition, the trading volumes were so large that even in gas trading—where they had all the advantages—when the traders bet the wrong way, the losses were astounding. For example, when a cold arctic air front was moving toward Texas in early December 2000, many gas traders went "long" on gas, expecting the price to increase. However, the cold weather never arrived and gas prices fell, with the result that on December 12, "The traders lost $550 million according to one report and $630 million according to another report" (McLean & Elkind, 2004, p. 219).

The traders were young, egotistical, belligerent, and partial to obscene language. They were rich beyond their wildest dreams—and totally unmanageable. But ultimately, they were gamblers, and they "bet—on anything" (Swartz & Watkins, 2003, p. 79). Eventually, the gambling—like the rest of Enron—spun totally out of control.

Enron Broadband Services

In 1997, when Enron acquired the Portland General utility company to get into the utility business, an unintended consequence was that it also acquired FirstPoint, a small telecommunications Internet start-up company that was a tiny division of Portland General. As luck would have it, the stock prices of Internet companies and telecommunication companies began to rise dramatically. These companies had price-earnings ratios far higher than Enron's. In fact, in the late 1990s, these companies enjoyed soaring stock prices even when they had negative earnings! This was a situation ripe for exploitation.

Never one to miss an opportunity, Jeffrey Skilling turned to his newfound tele-communications division and came up with four big, bad ideas:

1. Skilling decided that Enron would join the broadband investment boom by expanding FirstPoint's investment in broadband capacity. At this time, Global Crossing, AT&T, and all the other big telecommunication companies were overin-vesting in broadband capacity and chanting the erroneous mantra "Internet traffic is doubling every 100 days" (Malik, 2003, p. 13). So Enron joined the rush to lay fiber-optic lines and to acquire small telecommunications companies with broad-band capacity. Like everyone else, Enron would be caught with a huge overin-vestment in broadband capacity that was in oversupply.

2. Skilling decided that Enron would trade broadband capacity, figuring that it would be much like trading gas futures—but he was sorely mistaken. Enron could move gas in its own pipelines with its own connections all the way from the power plant to the utility company. However, although Enron owned a great deal of fiber-optic lines, it did not have the connection facilities or the lines to transmit data all the way to its customers. This meant that it could not guarantee the security of the transmitted information and that it would have to invest in connection facilities to move the data to its customers. Skilling, therefore, planned to build "two dozen pooling points across the globe. These pooling points would use sophisticated equipment [and] ... would act as hubs. Enron would buy and sell capacity on the Internet so that corporations and other carriers could get reliable network connec-tions." However, there was a huge problem in that the technology necessary for Skilling's plan to work did not yet exist: "No one had built equipment that could provide instant bandwidth on demand." Furthermore, while Enron was spend-ing a fortune on these highly dubious plans, it had yet to find any customers. The potential buyers of broadband capacity were the big telephone companies that did not like Enron very much and believed that Enron's entry into their busi-ness was going to become a comedy of errors; they had no incentive to trade with Enron. (Quotes from Malik, 2003, p. 104)

3. FirstPoint was renamed Enron Broadband Services (EBS), and Skilling appointed his trusted friend, Ken Rice, as co-CEO. (The other CEO was Joe Hirko of the original FirstPoint.) Rice had been an exceptional salesman, landing enormous gas power plant deals, but he had little experience in telecommunications and actually wanted to retire. To his credit, he first rejected the job, but Skilling talked him into accepting the position. As co-CEO with Hirko—and as Skilling's friend—Rice could do as he wished and had the final say, albeit with no knowl-edge of the industry. Predictably, the co-CEO arrangement did not work and Joe Hirko left the company in July 2000. Kevin Hannon, a trader who had risen to the top of Enron's trading operations, was appointed Ken Rice's deputy. With Rice and Hannon at the helm of EBS, Skilling believed that Enron would trans-form the telecom world. On the contrary, however, now neither the CEO nor his deputy had any deep broadband knowledge or experience, and the result was disastrous.

4. Enron was going to stream movies directly into television sets in all homes. Once again, this grandiose plan was not backed by the necessary technology and never even approached fruition.

All four of these ideas failed—some sooner, others later. But before the failures came the hype, and some of the people at Enron—as well as many of the Wall Street financial analysts—actually believed some of the misinformation.

In January 2000, at a meeting of financial analysts in Houston, Enron and Sun Microsystems announced that they were going into partnership to focus on Internet development. Bryce (2002) explained how the analysts went wild and Enron's stock jumped.

The stock increase was based on fiction. The technology for most of the plans had not been perfected (or even developed), there were not nearly enough customers to support the ostentatious plans, and the price of bandwidth would soon plunge. By the second quarter of 2000, Enron Broadband's revenues were way behind predictions. However, the accounting and financial problems were "solved" with the help of Andrew Fastow's SPE named LJM2. In his later article in *Forbes Magazine*, Daniel Fisher (2002) explained to readers how Enron had "sold" a portion of its unused fiber to LJM2 at an inflated price, adding $100 million to Enron's revenue and about $67 million to its profit.

Clearly, EBS would not let a little obstacle like the falling price of fiber capacity mess up its rosy picture of growth. Soon there would be a way to make real money with broadband. In fact, the Web weavers were already spinning another yarn. In April 2000, a few months after the formation of Enron Online, EBS had signed a 20-year contract with Blockbuster. Under this agreement, Blockbuster would persuade the movie studios to give it partnership licensing rights to stream movies directly into private residences, using Enron's broadband network. The trouble was that Enron had not yet worked out the technical details to solve the "last mile problem—getting the content from Enron's network into people's homes" (McLean & Elkind, 2004, p. 292). In addition, Blockbuster was having enormous difficulty convincing the studios to cooperate because there was not much incentive in it for them. All these roadblocks did not stop Kenneth Lay from announcing in July 2000 that Enron was about to enter the entertainment business.

Without the technology in place, the Blockbuster project was a disaster and never went beyond a feeble pilot program. The cities in the pilot program were especially chosen because they were located in areas where Enron had found small providers to solve the problem of moving the movie material from Enron into private homes. Ultimately, however, even the trial run was a dismal failure. "Broadband executives sat in meetings poring over reports of the pilots' comically pathetic results: *the Care Bears Movie*: Seven purchases—$8.40" (McLean & Elkind, 2004, p. 293).

To deal with the losses from the Blockbuster debacle, Enron decided to spin a web of SPEs. A variety of these SPEs were used to confuse the situation in order to book a profit via a project known as *Braveheart*. Essentially, Enron persuaded the Canadian Imperial Bank of Commerce (CIBC) to finance a deal that appeared to be a sale of Enron's share in the 20-year Blockbuster contracts. The contracts were first "sold" to a joint venture called nCube and to an SPE called Thunderbird—which, in turn, was owned by the Enron entity called Whitewing. The joint venture then "sold" the rights to another SPE called Hawaii 125-0 at a price that had wildly off-target estimates of profits for Enron in the contracts. A few months after recording millions of dollars in profits on the Braveheart project, Enron cancelled its deal with Blockbuster.

Finally, in mid-2001, the charade came to an end when EBS was gutted. On July 12, it was officially announced that EBS would be merged into Enron's wholesale division. The EBS farce had caused Enron to lose more than $1 billion.

In July 2005, several EBS executives were tried on various charges of fraud, insider trading, and money laundering. The jury deadlocked on some charges and found the defendants not guilty on the other charges. The judge "declared a mistrial on the dozens of counts on which the jury could not agree" (Flood, 2005, July 21). Ben Campbell, the prosecutor at this trial, pointed out that "EBS' highly touted core software packages never worked properly and failed to generate much income" ("Enron Defendants Not Guilty for Charges," 2005). This point is actually not in dispute. What is in dispute, however, is whether or not the senior managers of EBS believed their own stories. At this particular trial, the defense argued that the EBS executives assumed that their network was viable; evidently, the jury was unable to ascertain otherwise.

Linda Chatman Thomsen, the SEC's deputy director of the Enforcement Division, commented that the Enron executives "played important roles in perpetuating the fairy tale that Enron was capable of spinning straw—or more appropriately, fiber—into gold" (qtd. in "SEC Files Amended Complaint," 2003).

THE ELECTRICITY FIASCO IN CALIFORNIA

To comprehend the intricacies of the electricity saga in California, a little background information is necessary. In the late 1990s, the California Public Utilities Commission (CPUC) was in charge of revamping the rules for what was then referred to as California's electricity *deregulation*. This, however, was a misnomer, as California was really engaged in what amounted to a *semi*-deregulation of the prices that customers paid the utility companies for electricity and the prices that the utilities paid the power companies. The CPUC initiated a 10 percent price cut for the end users and capped the amount paid by the utilities to the power companies at $750 per megawatt hour, but *did not cap the amount paid for power purchased from outside California*.

California's much-vaunted *deregulation* contained several other interesting rules:[2]

- The utilities were required to sell their power plants and buy their power on a daily (or even hourly) basis from on-the-spot markets, yet sell the power at the fixed reduced rate.
- The utilities were required to fulfill their purchasing obligations on existing long-term contracts while selling at reduced fixed rates to customers.
- No new long-term contracts were allowed.
- The state created two new agencies that were subject to additional rules:
  1. The California Power Exchange (CAL PX): Power had to be bought and sold through CAL PX, which established hourly prices.
  2. The Independent System Operator (ISO): When there were emergency energy shortages, power had to be purchased and sold though ISO auctions, subject to

---

[2] Information on these rules is from Swartz and Watkins (2003, p. 238), Eichenwald (2005, p. 342), and McLean and Elkind (2004, pp. 256, 266).

the $750 per megawatt cap on purchases of power from within California. ISO also administered California's electricity transmission lines.

- If at any time a transmission line's electricity flow exceeded its capacity, the ISO would pay a premium fee for removal of the congestion.

California's energy system was a formula for disaster—even without the pervasive abuse that engulfed it on so many fronts. There were just too many potential problems. What if the market price the utilities had to pay for the power went above the fixed price at which they were forced to sell the power? Obviously, if that situation continued too long, the utilities would go bankrupt. If future power prices rose above the $750 cap for power purchased from California, would this be a disincentive for the construction of power plants in California?

Conversely, the cap on customer rates would decrease customers' incentives to use less power at times when the utilities were paying more for power.

In addition to all this, some traders and power companies were eager to "game the system" and take advantage of the unintended consequences of this dysfunctional set of regulations. For Enron, "[t]he easy money was just too tempting to pass up" (Eichenwald, 2005, p. 342).

Ironically, California's bizarre regulations came into effect on April Fools' Day—April 1, 1998. While the system worked well at first, the power companies and traders soon began to see the potential loopholes. In fact, about a year after the new regulations came into effect, Timothy Belden, former head of Enron's Western energy trading desk, did an experiment to test weaknesses in California's power system. On May 24, 1999, Belden negotiated a deal to sell 2,900 megawatts of power to CAL PX, and "he identified a transmission route called Silverpeak as the means for getting the electricity to the state" (McLean & Elkind, 2004, p. 268). Silverpeak was deliberately chosen because its lines could transmit only a small amount of electricity, with the result that suddenly, California was facing an energy shortage and had to buy a large quantity of power at the last minute when prices increased dramatically. When the California authorities called Belden to find out whether the choice of Silverpeak had been an error, he was blatant that it had been done deliberately.

By May 2000, all the adverse forces had combined and California's power nightmare began in earnest. A long, dry season reduced the supply of hydroelectricity, and the start of a long, hot summer increased the demand for electric power. The utility companies were caught in a bind: They were receiving income from the same regulated rates from customers, but they were paying astronomical prices for power on the CAL PX auctions and the ISO emergency auctions because the utilities had been forced to sell their own power plants and had not been allowed to sign any long-term purchase contracts. In addition, there was some suspicion about just how much downtime the power plants really needed for maintenance.

Before May 2000, prices had hovered in the range of $25 – $40 per megawatt hour. On May 22, 2000, the ISO had to declare an emergency as prices "quickly hit the price cap of $750 per megawatt hour" (McLean & Elkind, 2004, p. 272). Rolling blackouts began in June 2000, with schools, companies, and homes experiencing power cuts for two hours at a time during the day. By the time summer ended, California was experiencing an energy crisis. In August, the California utilities requested that the Federal Energy Regulatory Commission (FERC) conduct an investigation into trading abuses.

However, this Commission was largely ineffective; it lacked subpoena power, and its weak efforts did not uncover the scams.

California's problems continued unabated through the winter, and in January 2001, California's Governor Gray Davis began calling for price caps over the whole western region to prevent California's power from being sent out of state to areas where there were no price caps. Enron, of course, argued vehemently against price caps on the grounds that it favored market prices—a most disingenuous argument because these electricity prices were certainly not purely market driven. There was no fully deregulated market to produce market prices. Instead, the prices were artificially inflated due to manipulations by unscrupulous individuals and a set of dysfunctional regulations.

The artificially high prices in this semi-deregulated market were making much more profit for Enron than market prices ever could. In fact, an October 2002 article in the *Wall Street Journal* reported that Enron's "overall electricity-trading profit soared to $1.8 billion during 2000 and 2001" (Smith & Wilke, 2002). Back in California, the price of electricity was out of control.

The jokers at Enron were laughing all the way to the bank. At a conference in Las Vegas in mid-2001, Skilling quipped at California's expense: "What's the difference between California and the *Titanic*? At least when the *Titanic* went down ... the lights were on" (Swartz & Watkins, 2003, p. 267). Skilling chuckled over California's plight while schools and companies closed down during rolling blackouts and Pacific Gas and Electric filed for bankruptcy.

Throughout this time, emboldened by the Silverpeak experiment, many of the other power companies and their traders used numerous ploys to manipulate power prices and congestion fees. Those fees enabled the traders to earn more money by intentionally sending electricity on congested routes. Furthermore, the sellers could file inflated demand schedules to make an electricity line appear to be congested when it was not, and the ISO had no way of checking this information. The various bilking schemes became so pervasive that they had their own names. For example, making a line appear congested became known as "Load Shift" or "Death Star." An article in the *San Francisco Chronicle* described the scheme in this way: "To pull off Load Shift, Enron submitted false schedules to the state's power grid that appeared to cause transmission line congestion, and forced grid officials to pay Enron to relieve the congestion." The same article described how Jeffrey Richter, an Enron trader, who later pleaded guilty to conspiracy to commit wire fraud and making false statements, also assisted in the development of Enron's "Get Shorty" scheme, which "involved Enron's selling power to the state at high prices in the day-ahead market and then buying it back the next day at much lower prices. In company memos, Enron officials admitted the company often did not have the power it was selling and then buying back." (Quotes from Berthelson & Martin, 2003)

Another loophole pounced upon by unscrupulous suppliers and traders was based on the regulation cap that existed for the price of Californian power—but *not* for power from outside California. The traders simply directed the electricity supplies out of California and then redirected it back into the state. Presto! With a wave of a magic wand, the power was no longer from California. This dazzling scheme, which became known as "Ricochet," allowed traders to charge higher prices for out-of-state electricity (Eichenwald & Richtel, 2002).

After leading the charge to exploit the weaknesses in California's energy grid, Timothy Belden played the system for several years, but eventually, he became too clever for his own good. In October 2002, the *Wall Street Journal* reported:

> Timothy Norris Belden, 35 years old, pleaded guilty to a single count of fraud. He told U.S. District Judge Martin Jenkins in San Francisco that he helped devise "schemes" to manipulate the California wholesale electricity market from when it was first deregulated in 1998 until Enron's collapse in 2001, "because I was trying to maximize profit for Enron." (Smith & Wilke, 2002)

That same month, another article (in the *New York Times*) described how Belden admitted to "transmitting energy into a fictional world, complete with bogus transmission schedules, imaginary congestion in power lines and fraudulent sales of 'out of state' energy that, in fact, came from California itself." As a reward for creating this fine work of fiction, Enron paid Belden large bonuses, "totaling about $5 million ... the seventh-highest amount of bonuses paid to any executive at the company that year." (Quotes from Eichenwald & Richtel, 2002)

Erik Saltmarsh, then the executive director of California's Electricity Oversight Board, was emphatic that Enron did not merely participate in California's energy upheaval, but Enron "was the cause of them" (Peterson, 2005).

Although California's electricity situation emerged from crisis mode in June 2001, concerns about the adequacy of its power supply persist, and the specter of Enron lives on. In July 2012, an article in the *Los Angeles Times* discussed a recent Enron-type scheme in California's energy market:

> To the extent it was designed to exploit loopholes in energy trading rules, ... the scheme allegedly perpetrated by JPMorgan Venture Energy Corp. is cut from the same cloth as Enron's infamous "fat boy" swindle, which cost the state's ratepayers an estimated $1.4 billion in 2002. (Hiltzik, 2012)

The enormous profit that Enron made on wholesale electricity futures, as well as its lucrative trading in natural gas, merely delayed its inevitable downfall from the huge losses it was incurring in the retail electricity business and on projects such as Dabhol, Cuiába, Azurix, and EBS.

ENRON'S FICTITIOUS FINANCIAL REPORTING SCHEMES

As its plans and projects imploded one after the other, Enron fought to remain afloat the only way it knew: by receiving cash up front in the infamous prepays, reporting false earnings, and keeping its huge debts off the balance sheet—in short, by fabricating its financial statements.

Scheme #1: The Abuse of Mark-to-Market Accounting via Mariner Energy

When the SEC originally opened the door to mark-to-market accounting in 1991, Enron searched for every possible loophole to exploit this opportunity to overstate its earnings. Essentially, mark-to-market accounting allowed Enron to look at an asset—be it a merchant asset or a contract or publicly traded stocks—and revalue it to its "fair" value. This process involved increasing the asset's value on the balance sheet and increasing the profit on the income statement.

One of Enron's most spectacular abuses of mark-to-market accounting involved its investment in a private oil and gas exploration company named Mariner Energy, Inc., that Enron acquired in 1996. If Mariner had been a publicly traded company where shares could be sold at a moment's notice, there would have been valid, objective guidelines to use when revaluing Enron's shares in Mariner. Also, because publicly traded shares can be sold easily (if there is no sale restriction), it would have been fair to revalue Enron's shares in Mariner according to the objective market price and to recognize the corresponding profit (or loss) in the income statement. However, because Mariner Energy was a private company, it had no verifiable market price. Mariner specialized in highly speculative deepwater exploration, which made the value of its shares even more volatile. Nevertheless, the clairvoyants at Enron knew exactly what the shares of this private company were worth. Not surprisingly, the Enron executives deemed the shares to be exceptionally valuable and they became the shares that kept on sharing. In fact, one Enron vice president reportedly said that when Enron's earnings were tight, "People were asked to look and see if there's anything more we can squeeze out of Mariner" (qtd. in McLean & Elkind, 2004, p. 129).

The SEC, in a subsequent discussion of Enron's approach to the non-publicly traded businesses in its portfolio, alleged:

> Enron valued the businesses according to its own internal "models." Enron then manipulated these models in order to produce results necessary to meet internal budget targets. For example, under the direction of Causey [Enron's chief accounting officer] and others, company personnel fraudulently increased the value of one of the largest of Enron's merchant assets, Mariner Energy, Inc., by $100 million in the fourth quarter of 2000. (LR 18851)

Enron had acquired Mariner Energy for $185 million and by "the second quarter of 2001, Enron had Mariner on its books for $367.4 million" (McLean & Elkind, 2004, p. 129).

Scheme #2: The Abuse of SPEs

The Powers Report (2002) of the U.S. Congressional Special Investigative Committee on Enron stated that many of Enron's transactions involved "an accounting structure known as a 'special purpose entity'" (p. 5). (A **special purpose entity (SPE)** is a business entity such as a partnership, trust, or joint venture created as legally separate from a company in order to conduct "special" or specific kinds of business transactions that are not part of the company's normal operating activities.) In accounting terms, if certain conditions are met, the SPE's debt need not be "consolidated" with the company's debt and its assets are also not added into the company's consolidated balance sheet. Because such entities operate for a specific purpose, in pre-Enron accounting, the SPEs were allowed to be excluded from consolidation with the sponsor's group financial statements if the equity interest of a third-party owner was a minimum of 3 percent of the SPEs' total equity capital and an independent party owned the majority of the voting equity rights of the SPE and controlled the SPE. Post Enron, accounting for SPEs was updated by the Financial Accounting Standards Board Interpretation FIN 46 (R) as amended by FASB No. 167 (2009). The latest guidance for consolidation is the ASC 810 proposed update issued in 2011. The Board estimates a final update will be issued in the second half of 2014.

The beauty for the unscrupulous sponsoring company is that via **equity accounting**, the company's share of the SPE's earnings is accounted for in the company's income statement and the company can still record profits on its transactions with the SPE. Under the equity method of accounting, the investor includes its share of the investee's net income in its income statement and the original cost of the investment is increased or decreased by a corresponding amount on the balance sheet. However, there needs to be an arm's-length distance between the control of the SPE and the company. The Powers Report (2002) summarized these *pre-Enron* requirements[3] as follows:

A company that does business with an SPE may treat that SPE as if it were an independent outside entity for accounting purposes if two conditions are met:

1. An owner independent of the company must make a substantive equity investment of at least 3 percent of the SPE's assets, and that 3 percent must remain at risk throughout the transaction; and
2. The independent owner must exercise control of the SPE.

In those circumstances the company may record gains and losses on transactions with the SPE and the assets and liabilities of the SPE are not included in the company's balance sheet even though the company and the SPE are closely related. (2002, p. 5)

The problem with Enron's SPEs arose because often the person who managed the SPE was not independent of Enron and often the minimum of 3 percent of equity capital that was purportedly provided by the independent outsider was, in fact, indirectly provided or guaranteed by Enron. Further, Enron often guaranteed the SPEs' debts. When these facts were revealed, it became clear that the SPEs' debts should have been consolidated with Enron's other debts and this ultimately resulted in Enron being forced to restate its financial statements.

As mentioned earlier, although SPEs often take the form of partnerships, they can also be structured as corporations, trusts, or joint ventures. The charter of an SPE limits its activities, while its assets and debts are its own and "off balance sheet" (that is—off the sponsor's balance sheet as long as the sponsor is not at risk for more than its invested capital). Enron used a multiplicity of these kinds of off-balance-sheet entities to generate false profits with contrived sales and to keep debt off its balance sheet.

Although Enron began its SPE activity as a means to keep a joint venture's debt off its balance sheet, the SPE activity grew to include transactions with the SPEs that both hid debt and overstated Enron's profits. Eventually, Enron used vast interlocking sets of SPEs to borrow huge amounts of money and to transfer the money to itself.

---

[3]For more information, see page 242 of this chapter.

These transfers were carried out via related-party sales of poorly performing Enron assets to the SPEs at inflated prices, thereby overstating Enron's earnings. Enron also used the SPEs to overstate earnings via mark-to-market accounting and to recognize profits on the increase in value of Enron's own shares.

Of course, financial institutions did not lend these huge sums of money to Enron without receiving guarantees, and eventually, when Enron was called on to repay the debts of the SPEs, the company was bankrupted. By the time Enron collapsed, it had a confusing jumble of over 3,000 interrelated SPEs.

An examination of six of Enron's major SPE clusters reveals how Enron deviously used these SPEs.

SPECIAL PURPOSE ENTITY #1: JEDI In 1993, Enron entered into an off-balance-sheet joint venture with the California Public Employees Retirement System (CALPERS). The joint venture was named JEDI, an acronym for Joint Energy Development Investments, and a tongue-in-cheek reference to Andrew Fastow's admiration of the *Star Wars* film. Enron's $250 million was contributed in the form of issuing its own shares to JEDI, whereas CALPERS contributed its $250 million in cash. The purpose of JEDI was to invest in energy projects. As a legal entity, JEDI could, of course, borrow cash—and the resulting debt incurred would be JEDI's debt, not Enron's. At the same time, Enron could account for 50 percent of JEDI's profits in its income statement. This particular accounting operation was completely legal; the debt really was JEDI's and not Enron's. There was no need to consolidate JEDI's assets and debts into Enron's balance sheet. It was equally true that 50 percent of JEDI's profits did belong to Enron and ultimately would be distributed to it or reinvested in JEDI for eventual distribution to Enron. By the same token, CALPERS had contributed its 50 percent share of JEDI's equity.

At this stage, Enron was not doing any related-party transactions with JEDI, which was doing its own successful transactions with outsiders. These investments did fairly well for Enron and CALPERS. By 1997, the CALPERS half of JEDI was valued at $383 million—an increase of $133 million in about four years. At that point, Enron wanted CALPERS to enter into a second, even larger joint venture. CALPERS was willing to do this as long as it was bought out of its share of JEDI. Herein lay a problem: If Enron purchased CALPERS' share, it would own 100 percent of JEDI and would have to consolidate JEDI's assets and debts into its group balance sheet, because Fastow could not find another party willing to buy CALPERS' half of JEDI.

While it is difficult to pinpoint exactly when Enron crossed the line from legal to fraudulent financial accounting, Fastow's next step must have been one of the first in that direction: Fastow constructed an SPE to buy CALPERS' half of JEDI. He named it Chewco, apparently after the *Star Wars* character, Chewbacca.

SPECIAL PURPOSE ENTITY #2: CHEWCO There were two major problems facing Fastow in financing Chewco as an SPE that could keep its assets and liabilities off Enron's balance sheet. First, it had to be controlled by someone independent of Enron. Second, it had to have a minimum of 3 percent of its equity capital contributed independently of Enron. Fastow selected Michael Kopper, an employee at Enron, to be the person who would "independently" run Chewco and purportedly contribute the required 3 percent of the equity capital—amounting to $11.4 million—to Chewco. The only problem was that Kopper, together with his partner, could come up with only $125,000. Undeterred, Fastow simply got Barclays Bank to provide the $11.4 million via ostensible "equity loans" (ownership capital that is at risk). Barclays stipulated that $6.6 million cash collateral had to be provided for repayment of the loan; Enron obligingly provided this cash collateral.[4]

The Powers Report (2002) later concluded:

> The existence of this cash collateral for the Barclays funding was fatal to Chewco's compliance with the 3% equity requirement.... As a result, Chewco should have been consolidated into Enron's consolidated financial statements from the outset, and because JEDI's non-consolidation depended upon Chewco's non-consolidation status, JEDI also should have been consolidated beginning in November 1997. (p. 52)

In addition to the feeble attempt to provide outside equity of $11.4 million to satisfy the 3 percent rule, the remainder of Chewco's financing came from another $240 million loan (which Enron guaranteed) from Barclays Bank, as well as a $132 million advance from JEDI itself. From this financing, CALPERS was paid $383 million for its 50 percent share of JEDI.

Michael Kopper was now in control of Chewco—a phantom entity. Although Kopper was not a senior officer at Enron, the fact that he was an Enron employee meant it was likely that Chewco would fail the off-balance-sheet SPE test on the grounds that Chewco was not controlled independently of Enron. This test would have been hypothetical because Chewco definitely failed the 3 percent outside-equity test anyway. The situation was further complicated by the fact that Kopper later transferred his controlling interest to his partner but continued to run Chewco. In fact, Kopper received $1.6 million for managing Chewco.

According to the SEC's ensuing investigation, "Fastow secretly controlled Chewco and Kopper, and by virtue of that control, received a share of Chewco's profits as kickbacks from Kopper" (LR 17762, 2002). The fact that an Enron employee ran Chewco was not revealed to the board of directors and was a contravention of Enron's own policies and procedures guidelines. Moreover, Chewco's debt was guaranteed by Enron, and as soon as it became likely that any debt guaranteed by Enron would have to be paid by Enron, such debt should have been accounted for on Enron's balance sheets.

Chewco and JEDI were significant in two major ways. First, as Bryce (2002) explained, JEDI had to be kept out of Enron's financial statements. Second, Enron used Chewco and JEDI to overstate its earnings with related-party transactions—it boosted its profits by essentially doing transactions with itself—since JEDI and Chewco were really part of Enron. The Powers Report identified three sources of false earning streams:

1. A guarantee fee;
2. Management fees;
3. Revenue recognized on Enron's own stock.

---

[4] To complicate matters further, these loans were made via a contrived set of transactions with two other entities: Big River and Little River. Big River was designated as Chewco's limited partner, and Little River was selected to be Chewco's sole member.

To guarantee the repayment of the $240 million Barclays Bank loan to Chewco, JEDI "paid" Enron $17.4 million as a guarantee fee. Because neither JEDI nor Chewco were independent entities, this amount was a related-party transaction that, in effect, amounted to Enron paying itself. Further, Enron recognized the up-front amount of $10 million paid in 1997 as revenue for that period instead of spreading the fee for the guarantee over the life of the guarantee. In addition, JEDI was required by Enron and Chewco to pay Chewco a management fee from 1998 to 2003. In 1998, using mark-to-market accounting, Enron recognized the present value of the entire five-year period's management fees of $25.7 million in its income statement. The phony fees earned by Enron via the management and financing of the bogus entities really amounted to Enron managing and financing itself. To bring this wily illusion full circle, we must not forget that Enron invested its original $250 million in JEDI in the form of Enron stock.

The Powers Report (2002) stated that in the first quarter of 2000, "Enron recorded $126 million in Enron stock appreciation during that quarter" (2002, p. 59). In effect, Enron was actually recording the appreciation of its own stock on its income statement. To add to the cunning subterfuge, when the value of Enron stock owned by JEDI fell by approximately $94 million in 2001, "Enron did not record its share of this loss" (2002, p. 59). Exhibit 7.1 provides a diagram from the Powers Report showing how Chewco and JEDI were financed.

Kopper and Dodson, who had originally come up with the paltry $125,000 portion of the $383 million financing for Chewco, also received strangely favorable treatment by Fastow during Enron's final repurchase of Chewco. The Powers Report (2002) stated: "As a result of the buyout, Kopper and Dodson received an enormous return on their $125,000 investment in Chewco. In total, they received approximately $7.5 million (net) cash during the term of the investment, plus an additional $3 million cash payment at closing" (2002, p. 64). In addition, Kopper had also received $1.5 million in management fees for running Chewco for a few years. The SEC's Litigation Release No. 17692 (2002) alleged that Kopper "shared the $1.5 million management fee with Enron's CFO"—none other than Andrew Fastow. Furthermore, the same SEC Release claimed that Fastow also "received a share of Chewco's profits as kickbacks from Kopper."

SPECIAL PURPOSE ENTITY #3: LJM1   Emboldened by the ease with which he had manipulated JEDI and Chewco to enhance Enron's balance sheet, Fastow concocted another SPE that he dubbed LJM, a name based on the initials of the first names of his wife, Lea, and children, Jeffrey and Matthew. This SPE was registered in the Cayman Islands in June 1999 as a Limited Partnership officially named LJM Cayman L.P., but was subsequently referred to as LJM1.

The Powers Report (2002) described how Fastow concealed and disguised the ownership of LJM1 with a series of interlocking partnerships: "Fastow became the sole and managing member of LJM Partners, LLC, which was the general partner of LJM Partners, L.P. This, in turn, was the general partner of LJM1" (p. 69). Exhibit 7.2 provides a diagram of the LJM1 structure.

By this time, Fastow had realized that he had complete control of the cash borrowed by an SPE, and the golden goose was his for the plucking. He persuaded Lay and Skilling to convince the board of directors to appoint *him* as general partner of LJM1. Fastow offered to invest $1 million of his own cash into LJM1, with a further

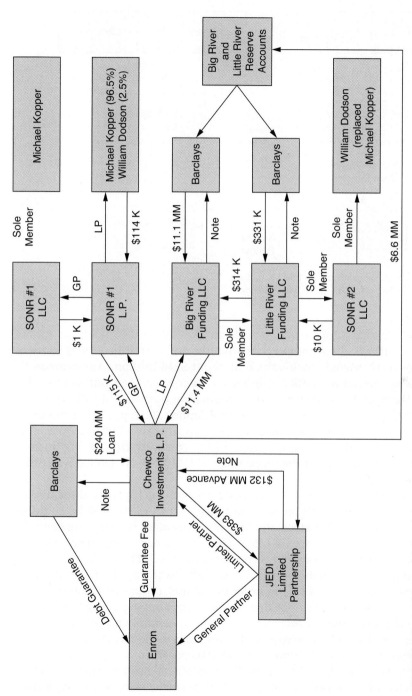

EXHIBIT 7.1   A Diagram of the Chewco Transaction. *www.sec.gov.*
From Powers Report, 2002, p. 51.

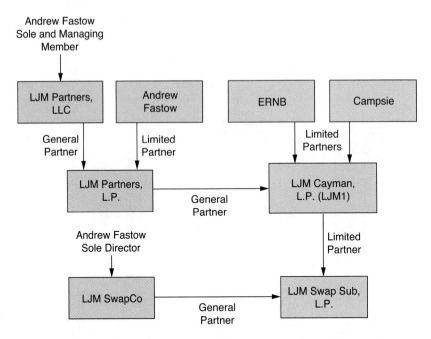

EXHIBIT 7.2 A Diagram of the LJM1 Structure.
From Powers Report, 2002, p. 70. *www.sec.gov.*

$15 million to be controlled by limited partnerships, and Enron itself was to invest 3.4 million shares of restricted stock valued at about $246 million. Any worries the board may have had about a conflict of interests must have been put to rest when Fastow assured them that his participation as managing partner of LJM1 would not "adversely affect the interests of Enron" (Powers Report, 2002, p. 69). At the Enron board meeting on June 28, 1999, the directors agreed to waive Enron's own ethics rule—which was supposed to prevent officers of the company from doing business with the company—and approved the formation of LJM1 to be controlled by Enron's own CFO, Andrew Fastow.

The Enron board's approval of an arrangement with such potential for disaster was astonishing. Fastow now had an ownership interest in LJM1, and he could get financing for the SPE via Enron's stock and Enron's guarantees of loans. Furthermore, he could buy and sell Enron's assets via LJM1. Did it not occur to any members of the board that the profits that Enron would record on sales to LJM1 would be absolutely meaningless? Did it not occur to them that Fastow had a large interest in getting Enron to guarantee numerous loans for LJM1 in order to acquire substantial amounts of cash that could be used for his own gain? Or that he could start buying and selling Enron's assets at prices more favorable to LJM1 than to Enron? It certainly must have occurred to Fastow. This was perhaps why he ensured that the trails to the ownership and financing of his SPEs were as complicated and convoluted as possible.

Essentially, via contrived sales with an SPE, Enron gave itself revenue that would simply be eliminated upon consolidation of the SPE's financial statements with Enron's financial statements. The trick, however, was that Enron had no intention of consolidating the SPE. Did Fastow know that an SPE had to be consolidated with the parent company if it was controlled by a senior officer of that company? He appeared to have forged ahead blatantly, without consolidating LJM1 into Enron's financial statements, in direct contravention of conventional accounting practice.

The hidden problem at the heart of this accounting fantasy was that Enron secretly had to guarantee the SPE's debt in order for the SPE to get the loans. Eventually, Enron would have to recognize these secret debts when it was forced to pay them. This, however, did not seem to bother Fastow whose creation of illusory earnings via LJM1 far exceeded his comparatively modest manipulations with Chewco. His dress rehearsal with Chewco had given him practice in the exploitation of SPEs. It had shown him how easy it was to create artificial revenue in Enron's books—simply by charging an amount (for example, for a management fee or a contrived sale) to an SPE that he ultimately controlled. The SPE would then borrow money to pay Enron. With a deft sleight of hand, the ensuing debt was *the SPE's* debt—and not Enron's!

LJM1 and Rhythms NetConnections   Enron first used LJM1 to create a false put option "hedge" for its investment in Rhythms NetConnections. (A **put option** is a financial instrument that gives the owner the right to sell an ownership interest, usually an equity interest in another company, at a specified price on a specified future date.) The owner of the interest has the option, or choice, to sell the interest at that price on the future date. The Rhythms transaction was actually the motivation for the formation of LJM1. Rhythms was an Internet service provider and Enron had purchased 5.4 million shares of Rhythms NetConnections stock in March 1998 at $1.85 per share. In April 1999, the company went public and the stock jumped to $21 per share, and by May 1999, Enron's investment was worth almost $300 million. However, Enron was not allowed to trade its Rhythms stock before the end of 1999, and with the wild fluctuations of Internet companies, it was impossible to estimate what the stock would be worth by then. Precisely because of that uncertainty, GAAP rules do not allow a company to record the profit on such stock until it is marketable. Fastow, however, wanted to recognize the profit in Enron's books immediately—in May. He had to find a way around the GAAP rules.

At that point, Fastow decided that LJM1 would agree to "purchase" the Rhythms shares at a specific, profitable price on a future date. Accordingly, the actual amount of profit Enron would make on its Rhythms stock in the future would be "known" in May 1999. Because it was now guaranteed that Enron would make that minimum profit from selling the stocks to LJM1, Enron could use mark-to-market accounting to revalue the Rhythms stock and it could book at least that amount of profit. Fastow ordered Enron to buy a put option from LJM1 in May 1999, which would give Enron the right to sell its Rhythms stock to LJM1 in June 2004 at $56 per share. This way, if the stock price fell by the end of 1999, Fastow reasoned that he did not have to devalue this investment because he had the right to sell it at $56 per share in *June 2004*. Enron then went ahead in 1999 and "recognized after-tax income of $95 million from the Rhythms transaction" (Powers Report, 2002, p. 14).

The next piece of the puzzle was for Fastow to determine what LJM1 would use for cash to buy the Rhythms stock from Enron. Furthermore, he had to work out how LJM1 would handle the loss if the Rhythms shares fell in price. Because LJM1 had received 3.4 million shares of Enron stock as part of its formation capital, the logic behind this hedge was that LJM1 would just sell its Enron stock to buy the Rhythms shares from Enron at $56 per share, irrespective of the market value of the shares. Did Fastow ever stop to consider what would happen if the Enron shares held by LJM1 fell so much in value that the sale of these shares was not enough to purchase the Rhythms shares at the option price? Fastow probably thought things would never get that bad.

Jeffrey Skilling—an ardent supporter of mark-to-market accounting—apparently supported Fastow's misguided thinking. On the other hand, Vince Kaminski, Enron's chief research analyst (who had an MBA and a PhD in mathematical economics) was shocked to discover this hedge maneuver. Allegedly, because Kaminski objected to the formation of LJM so vehemently, Skilling transferred Kaminski and his group of analysts to other projects. Several years later, at the criminal trial of Lay and Skilling in 2006, Kaminski explained that using LJM had been like placing bets in a casino that was bankrupt. "'If you lose you lose, and if you win you lose because the house can't pay your winnings" (qtd. in Mulligan, 2006). The put option hedge would fail if the value of both Rhythms' and Enron's shares fell at the same time. When the stock bubble burst, that is, exactly what happened because the "hedge guarantee" that Enron would sell its Rhythms stock at $56 a share to LJM1 was not a guarantee at all. The so-called "profit" on the Rhythms stock had not really been earned in May 1999, and Enron could not legitimately recognize the profit in its income statement in 1999.

While Fastow liked to obscure the structure of his SPEs, he liked to complicate their transactions even more. He did not merely arrange for LJM1 to sell Enron the put option for Rhythms stock, he also created LJM Swap Sub L.P. and LJM SwapCo for the transaction. He then used LJM1 to transfer $1.6 million of Enron shares and about $3.75 million in cash into LJM Swap Sub. The SPE known as LJM SwapCo was made general partner of LJM Swap Sub. It was actually LJM Swap Sub that issued the put option to Enron, giving Enron the right to sell 5.4 million of Rhythms shares to Swap Sub at $56 per share in June 2004. Originally, Enron had issued 3.4 million restricted shares to LJM1. In exchange, Enron received the put option (from Swap Sub) valued at approximately $104 million, in addition to a note for $64 million.

Commenting on the convoluted, contrived set of SPEs involved in the exchange, the Powers Report (2002) concluded, "We do not know why Swap Sub was used, although a reasonable inference is that it was used to shield LJM1 from legal liability in any derivative transactions with Enron" (2002, p. 81). The complicated structure of the Rhythms transactions can be seen in Exhibit 7.3.

With these absurd procedures injected into Fastow's interlocking SPEs, it is no wonder that later, in attempting to unravel it all, Enron's post-bankruptcy CEO, Stephen Cooper, declared, "It looks like some deranged artist went to work one night" (qtd. in McLean & Elkind, 2004, p. 155). Further, regarding Swap Sub, the CEO of Arthur Andersen, which was Enron's external audit firm, stated in Congressional testimony on December 12, 2001, "When we reviewed this transaction again in October 2001, we determined that our team's initial judgment that the 3 percent test was met was in error. We promptly told Enron to correct it" (Powers Report, 2002, p. 84).

The Powers Report (2002) went on to explain:

> On November 8, 2001, Enron announced that Swap Sub was not properly capitalized with outside equity and should have been consolidated. As a result, Enron

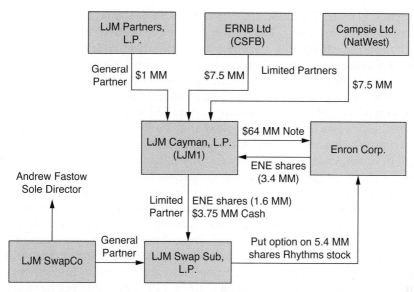

EXHIBIT 7.3 A Diagram of the Rhythms Transaction
From Powers Report, 2002, p. 81. *www.sec.gov.*

said it would restate prior period financial statements to reflect the consolidation retroactive to 1999, which would have the effect of decreasing Enron's net income by $95 million in 1999 and $8 million in 2000. (p. 84)

In the first quarter of 2000, Enron decided to sell its Rhythms shares and unwind the Rhythms put option. The period during which the Rhythms stock could not be sold by Enron had passed, the stock had fallen in value, and its price continued to be volatile. According to the Powers Report (2002), Enron analysts had reviewed the financial viability of the structure of SPEs created for the Rhythms put option and "determined there was a 68% probability that the structure would default and would not be able to meet its obligations on the Rhythms put" (p. 87)

LJM1 and the Cuiába Power Plant   Fastow amused himself with SPEs for several years before his maneuvers caught up with him. One of his favorite fabrications had its origin in South America, where Enron owned 65 percent of a Brazilian company called Empressa Productura de Enerain Ltd. This company, also known as EPE, was building the Cuiába Power Plant in Brazil, and Cuiába was meant to connect to a natural gas pipeline that Enron was constructing through tropical forests from Bolivia to Brazil.

By mid-1999, the project had experienced several setbacks. It was far behind schedule and was experiencing opposition from environmentalists who were concerned that the project would harm the tropical forests and delicate ecosystem. Enron wanted to decrease its ownership of this problematic investment. Not surprisingly, no buyer was foolish enough to buy into this messy situation. So what did Fastow do? He conjured up a buyer—his own LJM1—and sold a 13 percent stake in Cuiába/EPE to LJM1 for the sum of $11.3 million. (Essentially, Enron sold part of its own share of the Brazilian company back to itself, like a dog chasing its tail.) Fastow then concluded that with its reduced ownership in Cuiába/EPE, Enron no longer needed to consolidate Cuiába/EPE into its financial statements. Further, Fastow decided that Enron now had a market price for the Cuiába project based on the price of "selling" Cuiába/EPE back to Enron itself. In the third quarter of 1997—with circular logic—Enron figured if this 13 percent share that it had sold was worth $11.3 million, then using mark-to-market accounting, the remainder of its share must be worth an extra $34 million in the income statement. In the fourth quarter of 1999, Enron booked another $31 million using mark-to-market accounting on a further revaluation of this same plant.

Back in Brazil, Cuiába's problems worsened for the next few years, but in Texas, everything was just swell. Then Enron repurchased LJM1's stake of Cuiába in August 2001 for $14 million. Why on earth would anyone have wanted to buy the ailing project back when he or she had already "sold" it due to its difficulties? Obviously, the entire exercise had been for the purpose of generating some mark-to-market revaluation profits based on the ludicrous "market value" claim determined by the "outside" sale of 13 percent of Cuiába/EPE to LJM1. The Powers Report (2002) stated that if Enron had agreed to make LJM1 whole (i.e., compensate it for any loss on its investment), "Enron would have been required to consolidate Cuiába/EPE, and could not have recognized the mark-to-market gains" (2002, p. 138). McLean and Elkind (2004) pointed out:

> … a June 1999 email from an Enron accountant named Kent Castleman described LJM as a "short-term warehouse" for the Cuiába stake. Kopper later disclosed that the buy-back provision had even been included in drafts of the original Cuiába sale documents. One thing was certain: the deal provided yet another windfall for LJM's investors. (p. 203)

After the Cuiába deal, Enron began a series of transactions using LJM1 (and later LJM2) to purportedly sell poorly performing assets or a share thereof to various SPEs, thereby recording profits or avoiding losses on the sales. With these schemes, it was no wonder that Enron insider jokes began to circulate referring to Enron's mark-to-market accounting as "HFV" or "Hypothetical Future Value" accounting (McLean & Elkind, 2004). Fastow also utilized mark-to-market accounting from time to time to revalue the remaining unsold part of the poorly performing assets based on the contrived sales and booked more profits on the revaluation of the assets. The strategy was essentially for Enron to use interlocking SPEs as a front to borrow cash from a financial institution; then some of the money would be passed on to Enron via the contrived sale of Enron's poorly performing assets to that SPE. (In addition, Enron would generously guarantee the loan; so the banks thought that their money was secure!) Cash would actually have been loaned to Enron disguised as a sale, thus overstating Enron's profits and understating its debt.

There would be clandestine side agreements to guarantee that the "sold" assets would be repurchased by Enron and that the cash received from the financial institutions would be repaid. Assets were parked in an SPE with the entire financing arrangement masquerading as a sale when, in fact, it was a loan. The false categorization of the loan as a sale overstated both earnings and cash flow in Enron's financial statements and understated its debt.

Riding high on his make-believe business acumen, Fastow also used LJM1 to make a brief investment in Osprey, which was part of the infamous Whitewing entity, one of Enron's wildest and most ambitious off-balance-sheet entities. Osprey will be discussed in more detail later in this chapter, as part of the analysis of Whitewing.

The Liquidation of LJM1   To add insult to injury, Fastow hoodwinked a whole group of individuals in the final winding up of LJM1 and Swap Sub. The two limited partners that put up a joint amount of $15 million in the financing of LJM1 were Credit Suisse First Boston Bank and National Westminster Bank. Certain employees from the banks allegedly misled their own banks as to the amounts Enron would pay for the dismantling of the SPEs. Astoundingly, Fastow constructed yet another SPE, named Southampton, which he controlled and used—together with other Enron employees and the banks' employees—to buy out the interests of Credit Suisse and NatWest in the LJM1 set of partnerships. The SEC explained:

> In approximately February 2000, Fastow and others caused Enron to buy out the partnership interests of LJM1's limited partners, Credit Suisse First Boston and National Westminster Bank (NatWest). In connection with this transaction, Fastow and others told Enron that NatWest wanted $20 million for its interest in the partnership assets, but paid NatWest only $1 million of that sum and pocketed the rest. A purported charitable foundation in the name of Fastow's family received $4.5 million in proceeds of this fraud. (LR 17762, 2002)

Fastow's audacity was unbelievable, and it did not end there. A few months later, in July 2000, Fastow received another $18 million from LJM1. In addition, his "management fees" from this SPE came to $2.6 million. According to McLean and Elkind (2004), "The Fastows' total secret take, just from this one partnership, ultimately reached a staggering $25.1 million" (p. 197).

With LJM1, Enron had overstated its earnings via its related-party transactions, had overstated the cash flow reported in its financial statements, and had falsely driven up its stock price. Furthermore, with LJM1, Fastow caught even Skilling and Lay off guard with the extent to which he profited from the SPE.

SPECIAL PURPOSE ENTITY #4: LJM2 AND THE RAPTORS   The false profits generated by LJM1 for Enron, by artificially hedging the Rhythms stock gain, was preparation for Fastow's far more ambitious manipulations of earnings with his next SPE creation—LJM2. With LJM2, Fastow would not only dramatically expand his overstatement of Enron's earnings, but he would also fatten his own bank balance in various conflict-of-interest dealings between Enron and LJM2. Via a series of dizzyingly contrived and interlocking partnerships, LJM2 basically borrowed money—and used Enron's own stock—to purchase poorly performing assets from Enron in order to inflate Enron's earnings, hide its debt, and provide cash to keep Enron going.

Perhaps the most infamous of the LJM2 deals concerned the formation of four SPEs called the Raptors (numbered Raptor I through Raptor IV). The Raptors were devised by Fastow and approved by Enron's board of directors in May 2000. (These SPEs were named for the Raptor Golf Course where the scheme was devised, but ironically, *raptor* is also the name of a type of dinosaur believed to have been egg thieves and predators. Like the dinosaur, Enron was destined for extinction.) Ultimately, "Enron used the extremely complex Raptor structured finance vehicles to avoid reflecting losses in the value of some merchant investments in its income statement" (Powers Report, 2002, p. 97).

By way of example, let us consider the convoluted transactions of Raptor I, which was started with the formation of an SPE officially called Talon LLC. (A *talon* is a vicious claw—another telling choice of name.) According to the Powers Report (2002), LJM2 invested $30 million in cash in Talon, and Enron invested "stock and stock contracts with a fair market value of $537 million," as well as a $50 million promissory note but only $1,000 cash in Talon (p. 100). The $30 million investment by LJM2 was meant to cover the 3 percent rule requiring an SPE to have at least 3 percent of its at-risk capital contributed by an *independent* entity in order for Enron to avoid consolidating the SPE into its own financial statements.

Not surprisingly, there were numerous problems with this devious plan. First, LJM2's $30 million investment in Talon was not at risk, as the SEC later pointed out:

> Fastow allegedly entered into an undisclosed side deal in which Enron agreed that, prior to conducting any hedging activity with Raptor I, Enron would return LJM2's investment ($30 million) plus a guaranteed return ($11 million). As a result, Raptor I should have been consolidated into Enron's financial statements. (LR 18543, 2004)

Generally, Talon entered into hedges known as "total return swaps" on interests in Enron's merchant assets. The Powers Report (2002) described these return swaps as "derivatives under which Talon would receive the amount of any future gains on the value of those investments, but would also have to pay Enron the amount of any future losses" (p. 108).

The main problem was that Talon was really another division of Enron and Enron was just shifting its losing assets to another part of itself; after all, what sort of a business would purchase only investments that were on the verge of collapse? Another problem was that Talon's main asset was its Enron stock, and its fate was inexorably tied up with Enron's fate.

Soon, Enron began parking poorly performing assets in other Raptor structures to avoid recognizing losses on those poor investments. Then, of course, the inevitable happened. The assets that had been transferred to the Raptors fell in value, and Enron's stock plunged at the same time. This led to the possibility that Enron would have to devalue the Raptors by $500 million at the end of the first quarter of 2000 and recognize this enormous loss in its financial statements because the Raptors could not meet their obligations. Still unwilling to face the reality of extinction, Enron contrived yet another structure to help the Raptors extend their artificial lives a little longer. However, the floundering investments moved to the Raptors continued to fall and Enron's stock price continued to decline.

In the midst of all the tricks, Stuart Zisman, an attorney in Enron's legal department, sent an e-mail to his superiors in September 2001, expressing concern about the accuracy of Enron's financial statements.

Zisman's suspicions were later confirmed. The Powers Report (2002) presented a diagrammatic representation of the complicated set of interlocking structures that were

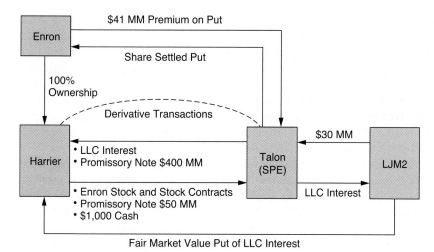

EXHIBIT 7.4 A Very Simplified Diagram of Raptor 1
From Powers Report, 2002, p. 101. *www.sec.gov.*

used for the process through which Enron basically transacted with itself in an endless hall of mirrors. Refer to Exhibit 7.4 for a copy of this diagram.

The Powers Report examined the extent to which Enron used the Raptors to manipulate its reported earnings during the period from the third quarter of 2000 through the third quarter of 2001: "Transactions with the Raptors during that period allowed Enron to avoid reflecting on its income statements almost $1 *billion* in losses on its merchant investments." Without these manipulations, Enron's pretax earnings for that period would have been "$429 million, a decline of 72%." Now the writing was on the wall for all to see (Powers Report, 2002, p. 99).

In the third quarter of 2001, "Enron finally terminated the vehicles. In doing so, it incurred the after-tax charge of $544 million ($710 million pre-tax) that Enron disclosed on October 16, 2001, in its initial third quarter release" (Powers Report, 2002, p. 98). Of course, all the debt incurred by the SPEs—debt for which Enron was ultimately responsible—was kept off Enron's balance sheet until it became absolutely clear that the SPEs could not repay their debts. Enron was finally trapped and had no method or means of borrowing more money to keep hiding the situation.

As news of the chaos spread and Enron rapidly fell apart, the world was shocked to learn that the Raptors' connivances were just one part of the SPE labyrinth.

SPECIAL PURPOSE ENTITIES #5 AND #6: WHITEWING AND OSPREY Whitewing, yet another illusion devised by Fastow, was initially concocted with the apparent purpose of purchasing Enron assets. However, behind this fantasy, Whitewing was borrowing money to transfer to Enron in such a manner as to disguise the loan as the sale of Enron assets. These loans were made to a group of Enron's off-balance-sheet entities known as the Whitewing structure and filtered through this structure to Enron. The loans, which were disguised as sales, overstated Enron's sales, earnings, and CFFO. They also under-stated Enron's contingent liabilities in the notes to Enron's financial statements. Further, as it became clear that Enron's contingent liability for Whitewing's debt would become an actual liability due to Whitewing's inability to repay its own debt, Enron's failure to record its liability for this debt understated Enron's own debt.

In addition, in the event that Whitewing lost money on the resale of the assets it had purchased from Enron (at inflated prices), Enron had guaranteed that it would compensate the Whitewing structure with the issue of Enron stock to make up the shortfall. This meant that the more Enron's share price fell, the more shares it would have to issue if Whitewing made losses on the assets it had purchased from Enron. Predictably, that is what ultimately happened.

As always, Fastow and his helpers made the actual flow of money rather difficult to follow through a dazzling maze of off-balance-sheet entities. To assist Whitewing, an off-balance-sheet share trust entity called Osprey Trust was created and it immediately borrowed over $3 billion. Amazingly, no one seemed inclined to ask why in the world any financial institution would lend money to a newly formed trust with no track record. Surely, the answer would have been obvious: because Enron ultimately guaranteed the repayment of the debt. However, Enron's gatekeepers who reviewed the Whitewing structure and Enron's financial statements apparently did not ask that question.

After borrowing this money, Osprey invested $1.5 billion in the specially created partnership of Whitewing Associates. Enron also invested 250,000 shares of its preferred convertible stock in Whitewing, as well as $135.2 million of Enron notes. Whitewing then paid "$1.6 billion to purchase assets from Enron." Continuing with its tricks, "Enron recorded the proceeds of its sales of assets to the Whitewing Investment Entities as cash flow from operating activities." (Quotes from *Bankruptcy Report #2*, 2003, p. 75)

The Bankruptcy Examiner concluded that the Whitewing Associates should have been consolidated by Enron, and if this had been the case, the CFFO on the sale of Enron's assets to Whitewing would have been eliminated. In the case of Osprey Trust, the Examiner acknowledged that it was debatable whether or not Osprey should have been consolidated. However, even without consolidation, the portion of Osprey's debt that was guaranteed by Enron should have been disclosed in the notes to Enron's financial statements as a contingent liability.

Adding to its impending financial implosion, Enron agreed to issue shares to cover losses made by Whitewing's resale of any assets that it had "bought" from Enron. In another dangerous maneuver, Enron tried to pacify investors by proposing what was, in effect, **death-spiral financing**—an arrangement in which a borrower agrees to repay a loan amount in the form of the issue of the borrowing company's own stock. The number of shares issued depends on the market value of the stock on the repayment date. If loans must be repaid by the issue of shares, the more the stock price falls, the more shares have to be issued, which, in turn, drives the stock price down. This is similar to slicing a pizza into smaller and smaller slices; yes, there are more slices, but they are being reduced to mere slivers.

Originally, Enron had set up Whitewing and another major share trust entity, Marlin, in order to create "in the aggregate, $3.8 billion dollars in off-balance-sheet financing using support provided by Enron's preferred stock, related contractual obligations of Enron, and Enron notes." The Examiner concluded that "the Whitewing transaction functioned more like revolving financing with the aggregate amount of advances made by Whitewing entities to Enron over a two-year period exceeding $2.7 billion." (Quotes from *Bankruptcy Report #2*, 2003, p. 67)

As Enron's share price began its inevitable downward spiral, the Whitewing structure—like an albatross—circled back to accelerate Enron's demise. The Bankruptcy Examiner calculated that the remaining assets in the Whitewing structure had "an estimated aggregate value between $700 million and $1 billion" (*Bankruptcy Report #2*, 2003, p. 67). By the end, Whitewing owed $2.43 billion in respect of the Osprey notes.

Scheme #3: The Prepay Transactions

Even with all the disguised financing from sales to the SPEs, Enron was still desperately short of cash. Much of the reported earnings was in the form of mark-to-market accounting, while many of the losing assets were hidden elsewhere but not actually sold. Furthermore, the income from operations reported on Enron's income statement would be way above the CFFO reported in its statement of cash flows unless something drastic was done to manipulate the CFFO.

Enron, with its usual innovative flair, came up with an answer—or rather, it came up with a temporary and rather short-sighted solution known as "prepays." In essence, with prepays, Enron would enter into a contract with a party to deliver a commodity, such as gas, in the future at a specified price. That in itself would not have produced any cash in a current period, nor should it have produced any profit until the gas was delivered. However, Enron would *sell* the contract to a financial institution for the amount of the total future cash selling price, less a discount, and Enron would get the cash up front. Presto! The cash problem was "solved," or at least it appeared to be. However, Enron would have to agree to guarantee the repayment of all the cash received, plus interest, at some point in the future.

The beauty of the scheme for the current period was that Enron was able to report this loan transaction as a sale in its financial statements. It then raised similar amounts of current assets and current liabilities on the balance sheet under the headings "Assets from Price Risk Management Activities" and "Liabilities from Price Risk Management Activities" with respect to these contracts. To confuse the deals even more, Enron would have a conduit entity agree to deliver the commodities in the future and to receive the prepaid cash. The cash would then be paid by the conduit entity to an Enron affiliate, usually Enron North America (ENA), which would agree to make the future repayments plus interest. For a diagram of a typical prepay transaction, refer to Exhibit 7.5. For a short while, this strategy produced cash and inflated the CFFO reported on Enron's statement of cash flows. It also overstated sales and income and kept the long-term debt—which was the true source of the temporary cash inflow—off Enron's balance sheet.

To illustrate how the prepays worked, Bryce (2002) described one prepay with JP Morgan Chase in which Enron entered into a contract to deliver $394 million of natural gas to a customer over the period 2001–2005. Enron sold the contract to the conduit, Mahonia—owned by JP Morgan Chase—for $330 million. Enron then agreed to buy the full $394 million of gas from another conduit, Stoneville Aegean, and pay for it in installments. Enron had just received $330 million cash and had to repay $394 million. In a 1998 e-mail, a Chase banker wrote, "Enron loves these deals ... as they are able to hide funded debt from their equity analysts" (qtd. in McLean & Elkind, 2004, p. 160).

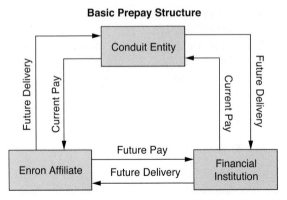

EXHIBIT 7.5 Typical Prepay Transaction Structure
From Powers Report, 2002, p. 63. *www.sec.gov.*

Within a few years, Enron was, predictably, immersed in legal problems. In January 2003, the Bankruptcy Examiner reached the following conclusions on the pre-pay transactions:

> Collectively, the Prepay Transaction may have been Enron's single largest source of cash during the four-year period prior to the petition date, providing Enron with $5 billion of cash. Yet, Enron's accounting, cash-flow reporting and disclosure of transactions were inappropriate. (*Bankruptcy Report #2*, 2003, p. 66)

Furthermore, the Bankruptcy Examiner concluded:

> Enron should have accounted for the Prepay Transactions as debt rather than as price risk management activities, and ... Enron should have reported the cash received as cash flows from financing activities instead of from operating activities. As a result, the Examiner has concluded that, pursuant to the Prepay Transaction, Enron:
>
> - Understated its debt by approximately $5 billion in its June 30, 2001 balance sheet; and
> - Incorrectly reported the cash obtained through the Prepay Transactions as cash flows from operating activities. (*Bankruptcy Report #2*, 2003, p. 59)

According to the Examiner's findings, Enron's cash flow from prepays in 1999 was $1.2 billion, which was greater than Enron's reported total CFFO. The Examiner showed that the Prepays, if properly reported in 2000, would have increased Enron's debt from $10.2 billion to $14.24 billion. He pointed out, "The prepay technique was a powerful tool employed by Enron to maintain its investment credit grade rating." In fact, the Examiner cited William Brown, who managed Enron's corporate finance group, as saying that "he understood the amount of any given prepay transaction was determined by the targeted cash flow Enron wanted to show the Rating Agencies." (Quotes from *Bankruptcy Report #2*, 2003, p. 62)

SIGNALS OF THE ENRON FRAUDS

A number of red flags in Enron's financial statements indicated that Enron had been using off-balance-sheet entities or SPEs to understate debt and overstate earnings.

Signals of Enron's Fictitious Reporting Schemes of Using SPEs (or Unconsolidated Affiliates) to Understate Debt and Overstate Earnings

Because SPEs are usually equity investments—investments in which the investor acquires an ownership interest in the investee—the information about SPEs is often included but hidden among the other equity investments on the investor's balance sheet.

Generally, equity investments in companies fall into one of three categories:

1. Holdings of less than 20 percent, where the investor has a passive interest in the investee. The investee's assets and liabilities are not consolidated into the investor's group balance sheet. Income is recognized when dividends are declared.

2. Holdings of between 20 percent and 50 percent, where the investor is deemed to have significant influence, but not control, unless information to the contrary exists. These investments are often classified as "investments in unconsolidated affiliates" on the balance sheet. The assets and liabilities of the affiliate are not consolidated into the investor's group balance sheet. The investor accounts for its share of the investee's income using the equity method.

3. Holdings of more than 50 percent of the equity of the investee, where the investee is deemed to have a controlling interest. The investee's financial statements are consolidated into the investor's group financial statements.

The three categories become blurred, however, when investors or sponsors create SPEs. SPEs are usually "created by a party (the transferor or the sponsor) by transferring assets to another party (the SPE) to carry out a specific purpose, activity or series of transactions. Such entities have no purpose other than the transactions for which they were created" (Soroosh & Ciesielski, 2004). They are often partnerships, joint ventures, or trusts, and sometimes they are corporations.

In pre-Enron accounting, because such entities operate for a specific purpose, the Emerging Issue Task Force (EITF 90-15) allowed SPEs to be excluded from consolidation with the sponsor's group financial statements "as long as the equity interest of a third-party owner was at least 3% of the SPE's total capitalization; at the same time, the majority of equity voting rights cannot reside with the beneficiary" (Soroosh & Ciesielski, 2004).

Many companies began to bend the rules and create entities over which they had control, in which they had invested most of the equity capital (except for 3 percent), and for which they had further obligations for the entities' debt. They used the non-consolidation rule to avoid including such SPEs' debt in their balance sheets and to avoid eliminating profit on related-party transactions with these entities. These investments in off-balance-sheet entities were often lost or hidden in the investor's balance sheets as though they were typical investments in unconsolidated affiliates where the investor holds between 20 percent and 50 percent of the investee.

As previously mentioned, post Enron, accounting for SPEs was updated by the Financial Accounting Standards Board Interpretation FIN 46 (R) as amended by FASB No. 167 (2009). The latest guidance for consolidation is the ASC 810 proposed update issued in 2011. The Board estimates a final update will be issued in the second half of

2014. In essence, under FIN 46(R), if a sponsoring company has an investment in an entity that is not self-supportive and there is a possibility that the investor may need to provide further financial support, the investee must be defined as a variable interest entity (VIE).

VIEs must be consolidated into a company's group financial statements if the company is a primary beneficiary of the VIE. The FASB Summary of Statement No. 167 (2009) identifies the primary beneficiary as:

[T]he enterprise that has both the following characteristics:

1. The power to direct the activities of a variable interest entity that most significantly impact the entity's economic performance.
2. The obligation to absorb losses of the entity that could potentially be significant to the variable interest entity or the right to receive benefits from the entity that could potentially be significant to the variable interest entity.

In addition, disclosure is also required in the MD&A section regarding certain details of off-balance-sheet arrangements. The proposed accounting standards update, ASC 810, "provides criteria for a reporting entity to evaluate whether a decision maker is using its power as a principal or an agent. These criteria would affect the evaluation whether an entity is a variable interest entity and, if so, whether the reporting entity should consolidate the entity being evaluated" (FASB News Release, Nov. 2011). It is important to note that pre-Enron accounting rules also required many of Enron's unconsolidated SPEs to be consolidated into Enron's financial statements, but Enron failed to consolidate many of its now infamous SPEs. If some companies broke the old rules requiring certain off-balance-sheet entities to be consolidated, some will likely be tempted to break the new rules as well. Therefore, hints in financial statements and notes are instructive for telltale signs of problematic SPEs.

Enron's SPEs were hidden mainly among its investments in unconsolidated affiliates and other investments. Hints were left in references in the notes to the financial statements regarding unconsolidated affiliates and also in the notes regarding related-party transactions, guarantees, and "sales" where some ownership rights in the "sold assets" were retained by the seller. There were also vague references, in notes to the financial statements, to investments in partnerships and trusts and the financing of such entities with Enron's own stock.

SIGNAL #1: ASSETS AND LIABILITIES OF UNCONSOLIDATED AFFILIATES OR SPEs INCREASING SIGNIFICANTLY When the amount of the assets and liabilities of unconsolidated affiliates or SPEs grows significantly, it is an indication that the company could be using off-balance-sheet entities to hide its debt or overstate its earnings.

In Enron's "Notes to the Consolidated Financial Statements" in its Annual Report, the note titled "Unconsolidated Equity Affiliates" showed that the magnitude of the assets and liabilities of the unconsolidated affiliates was alarming—the total liabilities grew from $8.3 billion in 1997 to $20.6 billion in 2000. Given that off-balance-sheet entities are often used to hide debt by removing it from a company's balance sheet, large amounts of debt held by unconsolidated affiliates must raise concern that the company may be liable for the debts of the affiliated entities. There should have been suspicion as to why Enron was investing so much in unconsolidated entities.

SIGNAL #2: VAGUE REFERENCES TO UNCONSOLIDATED AFFILIATES IN NOTES TO THE FINANCIAL STATEMENTS   Vague references in the notes to the financial statements or in the management discussion and analysis (MD&A), particularly regarding investments in unconsolidated affiliates or off-balance-sheet entities, should be regarded as warning signals. Be very cautious when notes are unclear as to one or more of the following:

- The nature of the transactions with the entity;
- The reason for using the special entity;
- The name of the entity;
- The nature of the entity—whether it is a partnership, a trust, a joint venture, or an established corporation.

When investments in unconsolidated affiliates or related-party transactions occur with specially constructed entities such as partnerships, trusts, or joint ventures—as opposed to independently established companies—one should be on the alert that the company could be using SPEs to understate debt and boost earnings. The company also may be blending the disclosure of these SPEs with regular investments in independently established companies. Therefore, users of financial statements must be on high alert for unconsolidated affiliates that are described in vague terms.

Unless a company operates in an industry where the use of SPEs is widespread, the financial statements and the MD&A should make very clear the nature of the SPE, as well as the reason for its use.

In an examination of the notes to Enron's financial statements, the following selection of alerts was revealed:

- In 1998, Enron's consolidated balance sheet already showed a $4.433 billion investment in unconsolidated affiliates. In the related notes, the relationships between Enron and some of these affiliates were described briefly, whereas others were not named or described at all. In fact, $1.199 billion of the $4.433 billion was simply described as "other." The notes also stated, "From time to time, Enron has entered into various administrative service, management, construction, supply and operating agreements with its unconsolidated affiliates."
- In the 1998 Annual Report, the note titled "Merchant Assets" stated, "The investments made by Enron included public and private equity, debt, production payments and interests in *limited partnerships*." (Emphasis added.)
- In the 1999 annual financial statements, several of the LJM SPEs are mentioned in the notes under "Related Party Transactions" without using the term *special purpose entities*. It becomes clear that Enron's own stock was invested in these partnerships from the statement: "LJM received $6.8 million shares of Enron common stock."
- Also in the 1999 notes to the financial statements, an alarming number of new affiliates were added to the list of "Unconsolidated Equity Affiliates," including the now infamous Whitewing structure that hid enormous debt and losses from Enron's financial statements. Vague descriptions were given of the Whitewing structure without a clear rationale for its existence in the first place. (The LJM structure of unconsolidated entities was not even listed in the unconsolidated affiliates' note, although it was mentioned under "Related-Party Transactions.")

- In 2000, the "Unconsolidated Affiliates" note provided an incomplete list of entities, and although some significant SPEs were omitted, the note did mention the sale of Enron's merchant assets to Whitewing. This piece of information sheds some light on why the entity was created in the first place and why it was shrouded in vagueness in the financial reports. Enron was selling its own assets to this affiliated entity. Why would it do that? No rationale was given. (In the previous year, sales of merchant assets to Whitewing had not been mentioned in Enron's unconsolidated affiliates' note concerning Whitewing.)

By the time Enron's 2000 Annual Report was issued, investors should have been aware of Enron's investments in the partnerships and joint venture entities of Whitewing, LJM, and JEDI, and they should have realized that it was unclear as to why and how these entities were being used. This level of vagueness about off-balance-sheet entities should have been a strong alert that Enron may have been concealing something.

SIGNAL #3: UNCONSOLIDATED AFFILIATES USED TO GENERATE SIGNIFICANT PROFITS When unconsolidated affiliates—especially constructed entities such as partnerships—are used to generate a significant portion of a company's profit, it is a signal that the company may be using SPEs to manipulate its financial statements.

A company could be using the SPEs to move poorly-performing assets off its financial statements to avoid dilution of reported earnings or to generate gains. It is therefore important to search the notes to the financial statements for "gains" or profits earned outside of regular operations, especially where such gains appear to have been made in connection with unconsolidated affiliates of the company.

In Enron's case, an examination of the "Merchant Investments" notes and "Merchant Activities" notes in its annual reports revealed important information regarding the sales of Enron's merchant assets. Refer to Table 7.1 for Enron's pretax gains on sales of merchant assets from 1997 to 2000.

Table 7.2 presents the calculation of Enron's "Pretax Gains on Sales of Merchant Assets" as a *percentage of "Operating Income."*

It is mind boggling to discover that in 1997, without these gains on sales of merchant assets, Enron's consolidated operating income of $15 million would have been an operating loss of $121 million. It is even more alarming because the "Merchant Investment" note in 1998 shows that the majority of the merchant investments, totaling $1.859 billion, were held through unconsolidated affiliates, including partnerships.

TABLE 7.1	Enron's Pretax Gains on Sales of Merchant Assets*	
Year	**Amount**	
1997	$136 M**	
1998	$628 M	
1999	$756 M	
2000	$104 M	

* Derived from Enron's Notes to the Consolidated Financial Statements.
** M = million.

TABLE 7.2	Enron's Pretax Gains on Sales of Merchant Assets and Investments as a Percentage of Operating Income*

Year	Percentage
1997	906%
1998	46%
1999	94%
2000	5%

* Derived from Enron's Notes to the Financial Statements.

Therefore, without these transactions with unconsolidated entities, a significant portion of Enron's "profits" would not have existed.

Certainly, examining the income statement on the basis of normal, regular operating profit, one had to consider whether Enron stock had a value anywhere near the price at which it was trading. Ultimately, of course, it turned out that Enron was virtually worthless.

SIGNAL #4: RELATED PARTY TRANSACTIONS NOTE TO THE FINANCIAL STATEMENTS REFERRING TO TRANSACTIONS WITH UNCONSOLIDATED SPEs When the note to the financial statements on "Related Party Transactions" refers to transactions with unconsolidated affiliates, especially specifically constructed entities, such as partnerships or trusts, it is a signal that the company may be using the SPEs to hide debt or generate fictitious profits.

Enron's "Related-Party Transactions" note to the financial statements in its 1999 Annual Report stated, "A senior officer of Enron is the managing member of LJM's general partner." Furthermore, it explained that "LJM2, which has the same general partner as LJM, acquired, directly or indirectly approximately $360 million of merchant assets from Enron, in which Enron recognized pretax gains of approximately $16 million." Although the term *special purpose entity* was not used in this note, the warning signs were unmistakable:

- An Enron officer was doing business with Enron for an Enron-constructed entity in a potential conflict of interest with Enron.
- Enron was selling its assets to itself.

The same note to the 1999 Annual Report also revealed that "Whitewing acquired $192 million of merchant assets from Enron. Enron recognized no gains or losses in connection with these transactions." Whitewing was another unconsolidated Enron entity, and here again, Enron was doing transactions with itself and moving assets to this structure. In such a case, one had to wonder whether the reason for this was to avoid recording large losses.

In the 2000 Annual Report, the "Related-Party Transactions" note referred to a "Related Party" that "acquired approximately $371 million of merchant assets and investments and other assets from Enron" in 2000. That same Annual Report revealed that Enron had expanded its investment in SPEs to an outrageous degree: "Enron ...

contributed to newly-formed entities (the Entities) assets valued at approximately $1.2 billion, including $150 million in Enron notes payable, [and] 3.7 million restricted shares of outstanding Enron stock."

Although Enron was not forthcoming about the fact that it was moving losing assets to these SPEs at values that hid the losses, the mere disclosure of the magnitude of the transactions—together with the involvement of Enron officials in the SPEs' transactions with Enron—should have alerted interested parties to the following:

- There was the opportunity for hiding losses in these transactions.
- There was no reliable market price for the sale of the assets.
- There was no objective way of calculating Enron's real profit.

Interested parties had to blindly trust Enron and Enron's external auditor, Arthur Andersen, concerning the validity of the prices used for the related-party transactions.

SIGNAL #5: SECURITIZATION OF CURRENT ASSETS   Securitizations by nonfinancial institutions of current assets—whether accounts receivable or financial instrument assets—indicate that a company may be experiencing cash-flow problems and that it needs to accelerate the realization (or liquidation) of an asset into cash faster than the asset would be liquidated in the ordinary course of business.

To test for an indication of a fictitious receivable, one should add the amount of the securitization—the cash received by selling a receivable that would normally be paid to the company later—back to the receivables (accounts receivable or, in Enron's case, "assets from price risk management activities") before calculating the ratio of the receivables-to-sales.

By the same logic, to test for an indication of overstated income that is not being realized in the form of CFFO, one should deduct the amount of the securitization from CFFO before calculating the ratio of operating income or net income to CFFO.

In Enron's annual financial statements for 2000, the note titled "Price Risk Management Activities and Financial Instruments" contained a subsection identified as "Securitizations," which stated, "During 2000, gains from sales representing securitizations were $381 million and proceeds were $2,379 million ($545 million of the proceeds related to sales to Whitewing Associates L.P.)." This meant that close to half of Enron's CFFO came from securitizations of its current assets. Further, part of the securitization included a related-party transaction with an off-balance-sheet partnership entity (Whitewing).

It is time to sit up and become suspicious when a review of financial statement notes reveals the following:

- A company invests significant amounts in unconsolidated SPEs.
- That company engages in significant related-party transactions with these entities.
- The transactions include significant securitizations or sales of current assets to accelerate cash collections.

These are clear indications that a company may be sprucing up its reported financial statements—and that one cannot rely on the financial statements for analyzing the profit, the cash-flow generation, or the debt of the company.

(As a case in point, the securitizations signal for Xerox, as discussed in Chapter 4, "Hocus Pocus," indicated the importance of adjusting ratios to test the validity of accounts receivable and CFFO. This is done by adding back the securitized amount to accounts receivable and deducting the securitized amount from CFFO. With Xerox, the CFFO as adjusted for the "sold receivables" revealed that the amount by which CFFO lagged operating income was quite alarming.)

In Enron's case, the securitizations occurred together with references to related-party transactions, specially constructed entities, and sales where some ownership interests in the "sold" assets were retained by Enron. That combination of factors was more than a signal; it was a siren. It is important to search the 10-Ks and 10-Qs, and to pay attention to the notes to the financial statements, and to look for the words *securitization* and *factoring* and for the phrase *sales of accounts receivable* to pick up this acceleration of cash flow.

SIGNAL #6: RETAINING PARTIAL OWNERSHIP IN ASSETS SOLD When a company has sales in which it retains any of the ownership interests in the asset sold, it is a signal that the company may actually be obtaining a loan and classifying it as a sale.

When such transactions involve off-balance-sheet entities, it is especially troubling. In Enron's 1998 Annual Report, the note titled "Merchant Activities" stated, "Some of these sales are completed in securitizations in which Enron retains certain interests through swaps associated with the underlying assets." We now know that many of these sales were, in fact, disguised loans in which the "certain interests" that Enron retained were the ownership interests, meaning that the "sales" were actually loans. Further, the profit or gains on these so-called sales were included in operating income.

SIGNAL #7: A COMPANY GUARANTEEING THE DEBT OF ITS SPEs When a company guarantees the debt of its unconsolidated (off-balance-sheet) entities, it is a signal that these entities are being used to raise debt and hide the debt by keeping it off the company's own balance sheet and the group's consolidated balance sheet.[5]

In Enron's 1998 Annual Report, there is a note to the financial statements titled "Commitments." According to this note:

> Enron also guarantees the performance of certain of its unconsolidated affiliates in connection with letters of credit issued on behalf of those unconsolidated affiliates. At December 31, 1998, a total of $209 million of such guarantees were outstanding.... In addition, Enron is a guarantor on certain liabilities of unconsolidated affiliates and other companies totaling approximately $755 million.

The growth of Enron's guaranteed liabilities over the three-year period from 1998 to 2000 was quite staggering, as can been seen from Table 7.3.

---

[5] In post-Enron accounting, we are less likely to find a disclosure of such a guarantee of an unconsolidated entity because such a guarantee would probably lead to the entity being classified as a VIE and to its consolidation by the entity's primary beneficiary in terms of FIN 46(R).

| TABLE 7.3 | Guaranteed Liabilities Extracted from Notes to Enron's Annual Reports: 1998–2000 |

	December 1998	December 1999	December 2000
Guaranteed Liabilities for Letters of Credit on behalf of unconsolidated affiliates	$209 M*	$ 303 M	$ 264 M
Guaranteed Liabilities on behalf of certain liabilities of unconsolidated affiliates and other companies	$755 M	$1,501 M	$1,863 M

* M = million.

Although Enron did not fully disclose all the guarantees or the fact that it was likely the entities would default and that Enron itself would be liable for the guaranteed amounts, these notes were unmistakable red flags due to the magnitude of Enron's unconsolidated affiliates and its related-party transactions with them.

The combination of these signals indicated that the off-balance-sheet activity was sufficiently significant as to render the published balance sheet wholly inadequate for analysis of the company. Indeed, we now know that the guarantees relating to special purpose unconsolidated entities actually bankrupted Enron within one year of the issue of its 2000 Annual Report.

General Signals of Enron's Assorted Financial Problems

Enron's financial statements revealed warning signs of a variety of financial problems, including overstatement of earnings, overstatement of CFFO, and problematic debt levels.

SIGNAL #1: ACCOUNTS RECEIVABLE INCREASING AS A PERCENTAGE OF REVENUE When the accounts receivable amount increases as a percentage of revenue, it is a signal that the revenue recognized may be accelerated or fictitious.

This signal becomes an even greater alert if there is evidence (as disclosed in notes to the financial statements) that the company has created SPEs and that the company is also involved in related-party transactions. In Enron's case, unrealized revenues were split between accounts receivable and assets from price risk management activities (PRMA). The associated revenue from PRMA was specified in the note and included in the category "Other Revenues" in the income statement. Over time, Enron's accounts receivable and its PRMA grew as a percentage of revenues and "other revenues," respectively. From 1997 to 2000, Enron's trade receivables as a percentage of revenues (excluding Other Revenues) grew from 7.23 percent to 11.12 percent. Refer to Table 7.4.

SIGNAL #2: CASH FLOW FROM OPERATIONS LAGGING OPERATING INCOME When CFFO significantly lags behind operating income, it is a signal that the profit generated may be fictitious or that its recognition has been accelerated.

In Enron's case, the prepays and securitizations overstated the CFFO dramatically, so this signal was blurred. Nevertheless, if one had deducted securitizations from the CFFO before comparing it to operating income, the ratio would not have presented

TABLE 7.4	Growth of Enron's Accounts Receivable as a Percentage of Revenue: 1997–2000			
	1997	**1998**	**1999**	**2000**
Trade Receivables	$ 1.37 B*	$ 2.06 B	$ 3.03 B	$10.40 B
Revenues (Excluding Other Revenues)	$18.96 B	$27.84 B	$34.77 B	$93.56 B
Percentage of Revenues	7.23%	7.40%	8.71%	11.12%

* B = billion.

quite so rosy a picture. One dramatic example of this can be found in 1997, when CFFO was stated as $211 million, but after adjusting for possible securitizations, it was reduced to *negative* $128 million. For 1999, the effect of the adjustment is even more dramatic. For an analysis of these numbers over the four-year period from 1997 to 2000, refer to Table 7.5.

With these adjustments, the CFFO lagged operating income in each year of the period from 1997 to 1999, and the CFFO as adjusted was, in fact, negative for two of those years. Of course, we now know that Enron was burning through cash at an amazing rate while it was pretending to have a healthy CFFO. By 2000, the prepays were disguising the cash-flow problem so heavily that the reported CFFO was positive—and greater than operating income—even after this adjustment. For example, in December 2000, the Mahonia project produced $330 million of illusory CFFO on one contract alone.

All the mechanisms discussed earlier regarding Enron's use of mark-to-market accounting, in conjunction with its false sales via SPEs, led to a gap not only between reported earnings and generated cash but also to a lack of a strategic business focus on projects that generated real profits and real cash. A former Enron trader remarked, "No one ever talked to me about cash. It [cash] wasn't on our annual review or included

TABLE 7.5	Enron's Adjusted Cash Flow from Operations Compared to Its Operating Income: 1997–2000			
	1997	**1998**	**1999**	**2000**
CFFO	$211 M	$1,640 M	$1,228 M	$4,779 M
Possible Securitizations**	($339 M)	($1,434 M)	($2,217 M)	($2,379 M)***
CFFO, Excluding Possible Securitizations	($128 M)	$ 206 M	($ 989 M)	$2,400 M
Operating Income	$ 15 M	$1,378 M	$ 802 M	$1,953 M

* M = million.

** For 1997 to 1999, this is the amount referred to in the Enron notes as "sales of merchant assets and investments," and according to Enron's 1998 Annual Report, "Some of these sales are completed in securitizations." Not all of these sales were completed as securitizations, and there could have been other securitizations. Because the financial statements in those years did not specify the amount of the securitizations portion, it is safest to regard them all as securitizations because these sales were also the sales in which "Enron retains certain interests" (*Enron Annual Report*, 1998). As such, these were sales that may, in fact, have been loans masquerading as sales.

*** In 2000, the securitizations amount was specified as $2,379 million, which was greater than the amount of the sales of merchant assets and investments.

in our targets. It had nothing to do with how we were measured for our bonus. It was nothing we were paid for, so who cares?" (qtd. in McLean & Elkind, 2004, p. 228).

SIGNAL #3: LATE PUBLICATION OF FINANCIAL STATEMENTS When a company is late in publishing its balance sheet and statement of cash flows, it is a signal that the company may be taking time to manipulate these statements because it has something to hide.

Enron generally issued only its income statement at the time of its earnings release conference call and made the balance sheet and statement of cash flows available much later, when it filed its financial statements with the SEC. The analyst and short-seller Richard Grubman picked up this delay as a signal of problems at Enron. When Skilling held a conference call on March 22, 2001, in an attempt to allay investors' fears about the $5.06 drop in Enron's stock price the previous day, Grubman questioned Skilling about the delay. The exchange was heated, with Skilling losing his temper and swearing at Grubman:

[Grubman] pointed out: "You're the only financial institution that cannot produce a balance sheet or cash-flow statement with their earnings."

Skilling very eloquently responded, "Well, you're—you—well, uh thank you very much. We appreciate it."

Grubman replied, "Appreciate it?"

Whereupon Skilling snapped, "Asshole."

(Qtd. in McLean and & Elkind, 2004, p. 326)

Skilling clearly appeared tense about the cash-flow situation, and Grubman had obviously exposed a real problem. Furthermore, Skilling's angry response to Grubman alerted everyone on that conference call to the fact that something sinister lay behind the late financial statements. From then on, analysts and business journalists adopted an increasingly skeptical attitude toward Enron's financial statements.

SIGNAL #4: HIGH INTEREST EXPENSE IN RELATION TO INCOME When the interest expense of a company is so large that it uses a significant portion of its income—or when interest increases significantly as a percentage of income—it is an indication that the company may not be able to continue to pay its interest and, ultimately, may not be able to repay its debt.

In Table 7.6, an examination of Enron's **times-interest-earned ratio** over the period 1998 to 2000 clearly reveals that Enron had too much debt. This ratio is used as a measure of an entity's ability to meet its interest obligations from the income that it generates. It is calculated by adding back interest and taxation expense to net income and dividing that amount by the entity's interest expense. Each period this huge debt led to large interest expenses relative to Enron's income. This became a vicious circle because the company did not produce enough profit to repay its debt—and the debt kept growing.

In spite of that fact that Enron was hiding massive amounts of debt and interest via SPEs, the times-interest-earned ratio extracted from Enron's reported income statement was, nevertheless, a signal that the company may not have been able to sustain its debt with its operating plan. The ratio did not deteriorate over the period, but the

TABLE 7.6 Times-Interest-Earned Ratio:* 1998–2000			
	1998	**1999**	**2000**
NI**	$ 703 M***	$ 893 M*	$ 979 M
Interest Expense****	$ 550 M	$ 656 M	$ 838 M
Income Tax	$ 175 M	$ 104 M	$ 434 M
NI before Interest and Tax	$1,428 M	$1,653 M	$2,251 M
NI before I&T***** / Interest	2.596	2.520	2.686

* Times interest earned is most often calculated as net income before interest and taxation expenses, divided by the interest expense.

** NI = net income.

*** M = million.

**** This is interest expense only. Interest income has not been offset.

***** I & T = interest and tax.

interest remained too high as a percentage of income for the debt to be maintained and repaid. The times-interest-earned ratio remained between 2.5 and 2.6 over the period.

Apart from Enron's trading income, which was extremely volatile, nothing in Enron's financial statements indicated any recurring true operating income to handle this large debt. Enron's continued existence depended on its ability to borrow more and more money to repay earlier loans and finance its upcoming operations.

SIGNAL #5: SUBSTANTIAL GROWTH OF DEBT   When the portion of a company's finance that is provided by lenders or outsiders (as opposed to being provided by owners) increases significantly, it is an indication that the company may be taking on too much debt.

It is therefore important to examine the company's debt-equity ratio. Of course, if a company takes on a large debt and uses that capital to earn profit at a rate of return that is much higher than the interest rate, it will be a very profitable company. However, when debt grows substantially and the times-interest-earned ratio does not improve, there is cause for concern that the company will be unable to maintain or repay its debt.

At Enron, the times-interest-earned ratio remained low while the debt-to-equity ratio increased even though Enron understated its debt on its balance sheets. In the period from 1998 to 2000, there was a dramatic increase in the amount of Enron's capital that was financed by debt as opposed to equity, as can be seen in Table 7.7. Over that period, the debt-to-equity ratio increased from 2.86 to 4.50. Even with its debt understated, this—together with the low times-interest-earned ratio—was a signal that Enron had a severe debt problem.

SIGNAL #6: THE USE OF "DEATH-SPIRAL" FINANCING   When a company uses death-spiral financing, it is a signal that the company's future earnings per share could be diluted by the need to issue shares.

TABLE 7.7 Debt-to-Equity Ratio: 1998–2000

	1998	1999	2000
Total Debt	$20,159 M*	$21,381 M	$51,619 M
Total Equity	$ 7,048 M	$ 9,570	$11,470 M
Debt: Equity Ratio	2,860	2.234	4.500

*M = million.

Death-spiral financing refers to an arrangement with another party that if certain circumstances occur, the company must compensate the other party for a required amount in the form of the issue of the company's own stock. The number of shares issued depends on the market value of the stock at the date of the share issue. The most common form of death-spiral financing is a loan in which the terms specify that the amount must be repaid at a specified date by the issue of the borrower's shares. The problem, of course, is that the lower the stock price falls, the greater the number of shares that must be issued which, in turn, dilutes the earnings per share and reduces the stock price even further, requiring more shares to be issued—and so the spiral continues.

In Enron's case, as discussed earlier in the sections on Whitewing, LJM, and the Raptors, Enron used its SPEs to purchase its poorly performing assets. These SPEs were partially funded by the issue of Enron's shares. In some cases, Enron had guaranteed to compensate the SPEs for any losses they may incur on the resale of Enron's assets by issuing additional Enron stock to the entities. In other cases, because the entities depended on their Enron stock as a major asset, Enron had guaranteed that if the Enron stock price fell below certain specified amounts, Enron would issue more shares or cash to the entities to compensate them. Obviously, this resulted in a further decline in the Enron stock price.

Such death-spiral financing indicates the risk inherent in the potential dilution of the value of the shares, and the adoption of the high-risk strategy itself also signals that the company is probably in a desperate position. This should warn the reader that the company may be tempted to hide debt, just as Enron used SPEs to keep what was effectively its own debt off its balance sheet.

SIGNAL #7: STRAYING FROM CORE BUSINESS When a company misrepresents the nature of its core business or when a large portion of its profit is dependent on a type of business that is not its core business, it should be regarded as a signal that the company's ability to maintain its earnings is more risky than it wants to disclose.

Profits that are made via trading depend on the volatility of prices and on betting successfully on the direction of the price changes. Because of the increased risks involved, investors usually demand a higher earnings-yield percentage for a trading company than for a hard-asset operating company. Price-earnings ratios are therefore usually lower for trading companies than for operating companies.

Enron, while holding itself out as an operating or logistics company, became increasingly dependent on profits from trading, especially in its energy trading sector, whose massive profits had, for a time, concealed Enron's fundamental problems.

However, trading profits are extremely erratic, and Jim Chanos, a broker and short-seller, called Enron a "hedge fund sitting on a pipeline." Chanos also noted that "Enron was a speculative trading shop, which meant that, at an absolute minimum, its outsize price-to-earnings multiple made no sense." (Qtd. in McLean & Elkind, 2004, p. 321)

Skilling, of course, insisted that Enron was not a trading business. In fact, Enron's 2000 Annual Report stated, "We have metamorphosed from an asset-based pipeline and power generating company to a marketing and logistics company" (p. 5). The problem was that when one excluded the gains from sales of its merchant assets and its trading profits, there was not enough traditional recurring income for its "logistic" operations to sustain its stock price.

The company that had once been regarded as a golden goose was, in fact, a cooked goose!

ARE THEY LIVING HAPPILY EVER AFTER?

- **Timothy Belden** (a former head of Enron's energy trading) pleaded guilty "to engaging in a conspiracy that illegally manipulated the California power market." Belden "agreed to forfeit $2.1 million he maintained in two brokerage accounts at Charles Schwab" (Eichenwald & Richtel, 2002). In February 2006, Belden appeared as a prosecution witness in the Lay and Skilling trial in Houston, Texas. Belden was sentenced (with Jeff Richter) in February 2007 to "two years of court-supervised release," and avoided prison ("Two Enron Traders Avoid Prison," 2007). In 2009, Belden and Richter established an energy consulting company in Portland ("The Defendants of the Enron Era," 2011).
- **Richard Causey** (former Enron chief accountant) entered into a last-minute plea bargain agreement toward the end of December 2005, just a few weeks before the start of the trial of Lay and Skilling. Causey "pleaded guilty to securities fraud and agreed to cooperate with prosecutors. He was the 16th ex-Enron executive to plead guilty" (Hays, 2006). Causey began his prison sentence in January 2007 at a minimum-security prison near Austin, Texas (Stinebaker, 2007). He was released in October 2011 (Inmate Locator). He now works as an "independent accounting professional" ("The Defendants of the Enron Era," 2011).
- **Andrew Fastow**, former CFO of Enron, "pleaded guilty in January 2004 to two counts of conspiracy, admitting to orchestrate schemes to hide the company's debt and inflate profits while pocketing millions of dollars" ("Status of High-Profiles Corporate Scandals," 2005). Fastow cooperated with prosecutors and was sentenced to six years in prison (Partington, 2012). Fastow served the last months of his sentence in a halfway house and was released in December 2011 (Inmate Locator). Fastow forfeited $24 million. He is now reportedly a "document review clerk" at the Houston law firm that worked his civil cases (Partington, 2012).
- **Lea Fastow**, Andrew's wife, completed a one-year sentence "on a misdemeanor tax charge for failing to report her husband's kickbacks" ("Status of High-Profile Corporate Scandals," 2005). She now reportedly runs an art consulting firm ("The Defendants of the Enron Era," 2011).

- **Kenneth Lay,** 64, went on trial (with Jeffrey Skilling) in Houston, Texas, in early 2006. The jury found Lay guilty of three counts of securities fraud, one count of conspiracy, and two counts of wire fraud. Further, on the same day, "after a separate three-day nonjury trial, US District Judge Sim Lake found Lay guilty of one count of bank fraud and three counts of making false statements to banks" (Mulligan, 2006). In an interview after the trial, jurors revealed that "Lay's credibility was severely damaged by evidence that he quietly sold $70 million in Enron stock ... in 2001, while telling employees that the company was in fine shape and that the stock was a great buy" (Mulligan, 2006). While awaiting sentencing, Lay died from heart disease during a vacation in Aspen, Colorado, in July 2006, at age 64 (Pasha, 2006). After Lay's death, his conviction was expunged (Partington, 2012).
- **Rebecca Mark** left Enron before its collapse and was not prosecuted. However, in early 2005, Mark "was one of 10 former Enron officers and directors who settled a lawsuit by shareholders—she contributed $5.2 million of the $13 million settlement" (Lavelle, 2005). She is reportedly the president of an oil and gas consultancy firm (Partington, 2012).
- **Jeffrey Skilling**, 52, went on trial (with Kenneth Lay) in Houston, Texas in early 2006. In May 2006, the jury "convicted Skilling of one count of conspiracy, 12 counts of [securities] fraud, five counts of making false statements and one count of insider trading. He was acquitted of nine other insider-trading counts" (Mullligan, 2006). Skilling was sentenced to 24 years in prison. After hearing an appeal in March 2011, the Supreme Court sent Skilling's case to the 5th U.S. Circuit Court of Appeals in New Orleans to determine whether a new trial was necessary. The 5th U.S. Circuit ruled against the need for a new trial. In April 2012, the Supreme Court rejected another appeal by Skilling (Lattman, 2012). In June 2013, a deal was made in which Skilling's sentence was reduced by ten years: "Under the deal, more than $40 million of Skilling's fortune, which has been frozen since his conviction in 2006, will be distributed to victims of Enron's collapse" (Hays & Driver, 2013). Skilling currently resides in a Federal Detention Center in Houston, Texas (Inmate Locator).
- **Sherron Watkins**, Enron's now-famous whistle-blower, is a successful writer, speaker, and consultant (Partington, 2012).
- **Enron**, once the biggest energy trading company in the world, was worth over $68 billion before it went bankrupt in December 2001. "Enron-related litigation has so far resulted in settlements of over $21.7 billion" ("Payments to Date," 2011). It is now the sixth-largest bankruptcy in U.S. history (Ovide, 2011).

Key Terms

Death-spiral financing 238	Mark-to-market accounting 208	Securitization 210
Equity accounting 225	Prepays 211	Special purpose entity 224
Futures market 208	Put option 231	Times-interest-earned ratio 250

ETHICS AT WORK

Questions:

a. After reading the Enron chapter and the article below: "Andrew Fastow, Former Enron CFO, Talks Ethics with Students," discuss what you think Fastow's has learned about maintaining ethical business practices.

b. Do you believe that principles-based accounting standards would be more effective than rules-based accounting standards for financial reporting? Give reasons for your response.

Andrew Fastow, Former Enron CFO, Talks Ethics With Students*

By Kirk Kardashian

Fastow is proof that the road to ignominy is most often not well marked. His talk was part of the Choices & Challenges series organized by the Center for Business and Society.

There was a time, about 13 years ago, when Andrew Fastow had achieved the pinnacle of success and fame that could be expected of a chief financial officer. At the tender age of 36, he had been appointed the CFO of Enron, the hundred-billion dollar energy company. Just two years later, CFO Magazine gave Fastow an award for capital structure management.

But as the world learned in 2001, the laws of physics don't apply to fame. When Enron imploded, causing $40 billion in market value to disappear along with the pensions of thousands of people, Fastow fell much further than he had ever risen, becoming the most hated person in America. Even his eight-year old son knew the right term for him now. "Dad, you're not famous," he said, "you're infamous."

Fastow, who served more than five years in federal prison for securities fraud, recounted the arc of this journey with candor and conciliation to Tuck students on October 8, during an event moderated by Richard Shreve, adjunct professor of business ethics at Tuck. The talk was part of the Choices & Challenges series on business ethics organized by the Center for Business and Society.

Fastow's story is a perfect case study for business school students on the blurry line between genius problem solving and fraud. The same much-lauded "off-balance-sheet" strategies that Fastow innovated to make Enron seem financially healthy were the ones that, upon closer review, landed him in jail. His main mistake, he said, was ignoring the principles behind the rules he creatively circumvented. "I used loopholes in the rules to get around the principles of the rules," he explained. "But it's not always easy to know when you're doing that."

Indeed, it was not as if Fastow acted alone. According to Fastow, every sketchy deal he made was approved by accountants, attorneys, and the Enron board—the usual gatekeepers who guard against illegal action. The salient lesson was that these gatekeepers can also act as enablers. All it takes is a change in attitude. Lawyers, instead of warning about fraudulent statements, can delight in crafting disclosures that are "technically legal but completely incomprehensible," Fastow said. Auditors and consultants, instead of raising red flags, can help shape the numbers to comply with generally accepted accounting principles.

Another important lesson was that a series of minor indiscretions can slowly accrete into a major crime. Fastow went astray not with one shocking act of fraud, but by degrees. Time after time, he chose from a menu of justifications: he was helping shareholders, "it was just a timing problem," everyone was doing it. "We had a lot of immaterial stuff that added up to being material," he said. In retrospect, these justifications were just a manifestation of his lack of character, he admitted. Greed, ego, and hubris all played an underlying role. "I wanted to be a hero by solving the problem," he said.

When the talk became more of a dialogue between Fastow, Shreve, and students, the most daunting question was how to prevent another Enron-scale disaster, in a business environment where firms still employ legions of people to dream up ways to get around laws. The best hope for reform, Shreve

---

*Originally published on Oct. 10, 2012, by the Tuck School of Business at Dartmouth. *http://www.tuck. dartmouth.ed.* Published with permission.

said, is to educate the next generation of business leaders, something that Tuck does with its Ethics and Social Responsibility requirement in the core program. All students are required to take at least one mini-course that explores the complex ethical and social challenges of business.

"You're going to find yourself in a position where you're incented to do things really close to the line," Shreve told students. "That's why there's an ethics program at Tuck."

Fastow, by most accounts a brilliant man, is proof that the road to ignominy is most often not well marked. "No one's going to say, 'Hey, I've got a Ponzi scheme I want you to sign on to,'" he remarked. "It's going to be much more insidious."

"Mark-to-market accounting is like crack," Fastow replied. "Don't do it."

Assignments

TRUE/FALSE QUESTIONS

Answer the following questions with T for true or F for false for more practice with key terms and concepts from this chapter.

1. Enron used off-balance-sheet entities to overstate earnings via related-party sales and loans disguised as sales.

   T   F

2. Enron used contrived put options from an off-balance-sheet entity to justify the revaluation of an investment in a company's shares that it was not allowed to sell until a later date.

   T   F

3. An SPE's assets and liabilities did not have to be consolidated into the sponsoring company's consolidated balance sheet as long as the required percentage of equity capital was owned by an outside party even if the sponsor guaranteed the financing of the outsider's equity capital.

   T   F

4. According to GAAP, a company is allowed to recognize a profit in its financial statements in respect of the increase in the price of its own shares.

   T   F

5. Enron's SPE Whitewing was used to borrow money that was paid to Enron for Whitewing's purchase of Enron assets, and Enron recorded the cash received as cash flow from operating activities.

   T   F

6. Enron's Bankruptcy Examiner concluded that the "Prepay Transactions" may have been Enron's single largest source of cash during the four-year period prior to Enron's filing for bankruptcy.

   T   F

7. Enron's note to its financial statements on related-party transactions for the fiscal year ended 2000 fully disclosed the extent to which it was using SPEs to generate its reported income.

   T   F

8. Information in Enron's note to its financial statements on related-party transactions for the fiscal year ended 2000 was a signal that Enron was generating a significant portion of its income from related-party transactions with SPEs.

   T   F

9. Enron did *not* disclose in its financial statements that it engaged in sales transactions in which it retained certain ownership interests in the items sold.

   T   F

10. When a company guarantees the debt of its unconsolidated affiliates, it is a signal that these entities may be used to raise debt without recording it on the sponsoring company's balance sheet.

    T   F

FILL-IN-THE-BLANK QUESTIONS

Fill in the blanks with information and concepts from this chapter.

11. In order to finance Chewco as an SPE that did not have to become consolidated into

Enron's consolidated financial statements, it had to have a minimum of 3 percent of its equity _____ contributed independently of Enron.

12. In respect of Enron's SPEs Chewco and Jedi, the Powers Report identified three sources of fictitious income streams: a _____ fee, management fees, and revenue recognized on Enron's own stock.

13. Enron used LJM1 to create a false _____ option hedge for its investment in Rhythms NetConnections.

14. According to McLean and Elkind, a "June 1999 email from an Enron accountant named Ken Castleman described LJM as a 'short term _____' for the Cuiaba stake."

15. The Powers Report concluded that transactions with Enron's Raptors SPEs allowed Enron to avoid reflecting almost $1 billion in _____ on its income statement on its merchant investments.

16. In a contrived sale to its SPE LJMI, Enron used what it referred to as the _____ price to justify a mark-to-market revaluation of its ownership in the Cuiaba Power Plant.

17. When Enron accounted for its share of JEDI's income, it actually recorded the _____ of its own stock in its income statement because JEDI owned Enron stock.

18. References in notes to the financial statements regarding investments in specially constructed unconsolidated affiliates that are _____ as to the reason for the special entity or the nature of the transactions with the entity should be regarded as a signal that the SPEs could be used to overstate the sponsor's earnings or to understate its debt.

19. Enron's note to the financial statements on related-party transactions that revealed transactions with its SPEs indicated that Enron was, in effect, selling its assets to _____.

20. It was a signal that Enron's debt was understated when its notes to the financial statements titled "Commitments" stated that Enron also _____ the performance of certain of its unconsolidated affiliates in connection with letters of credit issued on behalf of those unconsolidated affiliates.

MULTIPLE-CHOICE QUESTIONS

21. In which of the following ways did Enron not use off-balance-sheet entities to overstate its earnings?
    (a) Related-party sales.
    (b) Creation of cookie-jar reserves.
    (c) Recognition of profits on its own stock.
    (d) All of the above.

22. Enron arranged for Barclays Bank to provide $11.4 million for an Enron employee to acquire 3 percent of the equity capital of the SPE named Chewco, and Enron provided a $6.6 million collateral for its repayment. The Powers Report later concluded that Chewco "should have been consolidated into Enron's consolidated financial statements" because:
    (a) The existence of the cash collateral was fatal to Chewco's compliance with the 3 percent equity requirement.
    (b) The SPE had to be controlled by someone independent of Enron to avoid consolidation.
    (c) Chewco's activity was not part of Enron's main operating activity.
    (d) Both (a) and (b).

23. According to Enron's Bankruptcy Examiner, the effect of Enron's "prepay transactions" on its financial statements was:
    (a) Understatement of its debt.
    (b) Overstatement of its cash flow from operating activities.
    (c) Understatement of its cash flow from financing activities.
    (d) All of the above.

24. In respect of its investment in stock in Rhythms NetConnections, Enron used SPE LJM1 to:
    (a) Create a false put option hedge.
    (b) Overstate its sales revenue.
    (c) Understate its cost of goods sold.
    (d) All of the above.

25. Which of the following is a signal that a company may be using SPEs to overstate its earnings or understate its debt?
    (a) When references in the notes to the financial statements regarding unconsolidated affiliates are vague as to the reason for using the SPE, the name of the SPE, or the nature of the transactions with the SPE.
    (b) When unconsolidated affiliates—especially constructed entities such as

partnerships—are used to generate a significant portion of the company's profit.

(c) When a note to the financial statements on "Related Party Transactions" refers to transactions with unconsolidated, specially constructed entities such as partnerships or trusts.

(d) All of the above.

26. With its Prepay Transactions, Enron would enter into a contract to deliver a commodity in the future at a specified price. It would then sell the contract at a discount and receive cash up front. It then would take on an obligation to buy the commodity required for delivery and to pay for it in installments. How did Enron describe the resulting rights and obligations on its balance sheet?

(a) As accounts receivable and accounts payable.

(b) As loans payable and loans receivable.

(c) As "assets from price risk management activities" and "liabilities from price risk management activities."

(d) Enron completely omitted the resulting rights and obligations from its balance sheet.

27. Which of the following is *not* true regarding disclosure by Enron *in its financial statements*?

(a) Enron disclosed that it guaranteed the performance of certain of its unconsolidated affiliates in connection with letters of credit.

(b) Enron disclosed that a significant portion of its CFFO came from securitizations of its current assets.

(c) Enron disclosed all the names of all of its unconsolidated affiliates as well as the total assets and total debt of each one.

(d) Enron disclosed that it engaged in related-party transactions with unconsolidated, specially constructed entities.

28. For which of the following purposes did Enron *not* use its investment in Empressa Productura de Enerain (EPE) and the off-balance-sheet entity LJM1?

(a) To enter into a contrived sale of a percentage of Enron's ownership in the Cuiaba Power Plant to LJM1.

(b) To cause EPE to obtain a loan from a bank and divert the funds to Enron.

(c) To use mark-to-market accounting to revalue its investment in the Cuiaba Power Plant by reference to a contrived sale of a percentage of Enron's ownership in the Cuiaba Power Plant to LJM1.

(d) To buy back Enron's stake in the Cuiaba Power Plant from LJM1 after having recorded profits on the earlier sales of parts of its stake in the power plant to LJM1.

29. Which of the following was *not* a signal in Enron's financial statements of its financial problems?

(a) Receivables increased as a percentage of sales.

(b) Its debt-to-equity ratio decreased over time.

(c) It used death-spiral financing in which it guaranteed that if Enron's stock fell below certain specific amounts, it would issue more shares or pay cash to SPEs.

(d) All of the above were signals.

30. Which of the following was *not* a false revenue stream that was generated by Enron's use of off-balance-sheet entities Chewco and Jedi, as identified by the Powers Report?

(a) A guarantee fee.

(b) Management fees.

(c) Gain on revaluation of an asset.

(d) Revenue recognized on Enron's own stock.

FOR DISCUSSION

31. Two ways in which Enron used SPEs to overstate earnings were the abuse of mark-to-market accounting and contrived related-party sales. Choose one asset that Enron used to employ both of these methods and describe how the asset was used to overstate earnings via contrived sales and to overstate earnings via mark-to-market accounting.

32. Another way in which Enron used off-balance-sheet entities to overstate earnings was via the recognition of profit on its own stock. With reference to an off-balance-sheet entity discussed in the text, explain how Enron recognized profit on the appreciation of its own stock.

SHORT-ANSWER QUESTIONS

33. Explain why Enron had so much debt from the time of its inception onward and explain why it was under pressure to hide this debt.

34. Explain how Enron used the "Prepay Transactions" to overstate CFFO.

35. Describe how SPE LJM1 was used to assist Enron to fictitiously recognize income on its investment in Rhythms NetConnections (RHYTHMS).

36. Explain why vague references to off-balance-sheet entities or unconsolidated affiliates in notes to a company's financial statements or in its MD&A may be a signal that a company could be engaging in fictitious financial reporting.

EXERCISES

37. Bronto Company invested in 10,000 shares in Saurus Company, which it purchased in June 2012 for $1 per share, before Saurus went public. On December 1, 2012, Saurus Company went public, and by December 31, 2012, its shares were trading at $5 per share. However, Bronto was not allowed to sell its shares in Saurus until March 31, 2013.

On December 31, 2012, Bronto Company formed an SPE in the form of a partnership that it named SPOCK1. The CFO of Bronto Company became the managing partner of SPOCK1, and SPOCK1 wrote a put option, which it sold to Bronto Company for $1,000 in terms of which SPOCK1 gave Bronto the option to sell all 10,000 shares that Bronto owned in Saurus to SPOCK1 on June 30, 2013, for $50,000. On December 31, 2012, Bronto paid SPOCK1 the $1,000 for the put option. Bronto then used mark-to-market accounting to revalue its shares in Saurus through its income statement to the market price on the grounds that the put-option "hedge" gave it the certainty that the value of the shares would not fall below $50,000.

Required

a. Prepare the journal entry in Bronto Company's books, accounting for the purchase of the put option and specifying whether each account in the entry is a balance sheet item or an income statement item.

b. Prepare the journal entry accounting for the revaluation of the investment

in Saurus Company in the manner that Bronto Company accounted for it.

c. Do you believe that the treatment illustrated in part b is in contravention of GAAP? Why or why not?

38. Power Company acquires 80 percent of the shares (80 shares) in Emperor Company for $20 million on January 1, 2012. On December 31, 2012, Power Company forms an unconsolidated partnership named P2 and issues 1,000 Power Company shares to P2 for a 90 percent share in P2. The CFO of Power Company buys the remaining equity interest in P2 with cash loaned to him by Power. On December 31, 2012, Power Company sells 10 percent of its stake in Emperor to P2 for $4 million.

Using this sale as evidence of the market value of its investment in Emperor, Power Company revalues the remainder of its holdings in Emperor, recognizing the alleged appreciation in value as current income. Power does not consolidate P2 into its consolidated financial statements.

Required

a. Calculate the amount of pretax income that Power Company recognizes in its income statement for the year ended December 31, 2012, if it accounts for the revaluation on the basis described above.

b. How much pretax income would Power recognize on the sale of 10 percent of its stake in Emperor to P2?

39. Sabre Company's summarized income statements for the last three years are presented below.

	Year 1	Year 2	Year 3
Net sales	$100,000	$90,000	$80,000
Cost of sales	60,000	58,000	56,000
Gross margin	40,000	32,000	24,000
Selling, general, and administrative expenses	20,000	19,000	18,000
Operating income	20,000	13,000	6,000
Interest expense	3,000	4,000	5,000
Interest before tax	17,000	9,000	1,000
Tax	5,100	2,700	300
Net Income	$ 11,900	$ 6,300	$ 700

Required

a. Calculate the times-interest-earned ratio for years 1–3.

b. Comment on Sabre Company's times-interest-earned ratio over the three-year period as a signal of its ability to continue to meet its interest payments.

40. On January 1, Khaan Company obtained a $30,000 loan from Raptorex Company. The loan terms specify that the loan amount must be repaid on three specific repayment dates by the issue of shares in Khaan. The number of the shares to be issued depends on the market value of the Khaan shares on each repayment date.

Loan Repayment Dates	March 31	June 30	Sept. 30
Loan repayment amounts	$10,000	$10,000	$10,000
Khaan Company's share price	$ 10	$ 5	$ 2

Required

a. Calculate the number of Khaan shares that must be issued on each repayment date.

b. Comment on the risk inherent in this form of financing.

CASE STUDY

BASIN WATER. INC*.

- **Examine** extracts from the selected financial statements from Basin Water, Inc., for the fiscal years ended 2005, 2006, and 2007.
- **Examine** Note 9 and Note 15 to Basin Water's Consolidated Financial Statements for 2007.
- **Respond** to the following Case Study questions.

Required

a. **Improper Use of SPEs:** The SEC's Complaint (2011) against Basin Water, Inc. alleged: "The Defendants Materially Overstate Basin's Q2 2007 And Year-To-Date Revenues By Engaging In A Sham $3.8 Million Sale To A Special Purpose Entity They Directly Or Indirectly Cause To Be Created" (section F). After reviewing the signals for Enron's schemes of using SPEs to understate debt and to overstate earnings, identify the signals of the improper use of unconsolidated

affiliates, or SPEs, that were present in the Enron case and can allegedly be found in Basin Water's notes to its financial statements. Explain why those signals could have been indications that Basin Water may have allegedly overstated its sales and understated its loss.

b. **Improper Recognition of Sales:** The SEC Complaint (2011) alleged that Basin also overstated revenues via contingent sales. Further, according to the SEC Complaint, "Several sales did not occur in the quarter for which revenue was recognized" (par. 3). These alleged methods described by the SEC are similar to some of Sunbeam's methods of overstating sales.

Review Sunbeam's signals of overstatement of sales (see Chapter 3) and identify which of those signals could have been found in an analysis of Basin Water's financial statements. Provide supporting calculations.

*In early November, 2013, the bench trial for the Basin Water case was concluded, pending decision by the court. According to Litigation Release 22014, "In February 2009, Basin Water restated its financial results. In July 2009, the Rancho Cucamonga, Calif.-based company declared Chapter 11 bankruptcy and is now defunct.

FINANCIAL STATEMENTS[6]

UNITED STATES
SECURITIES AND EXCHANGE COMMISSION
Washington, D.C. 20549

Extracts from FORM 10-K

Annual report pursuant to Section 13 or 15(d) of the Securities Exchange Act of 1934

For the fiscal year ended September 31, 2006

BASIN WATER, INC.

Balance Sheets
(in thousands except share and per share data)

	December 31, 2006	December 31, 2005
ASSETS		
Current assets		
Cash and cash equivalents	$ 54,567	$ 2,724
Accounts receivable, net of $67 and $0 allowance for doubtful accounts	2,416	3,927
Unbilled receivables, net of $433 and $0 allowance for doubtful accounts	9,123	3,123
Inventory	714	347
Prepaid expenses and other	634	189
Notes receivable	—	100
Total current assets	67,454	10,410
Property and equipment		
Property and equipment	13,621	10,445
Less: accumulated depreciation	1,394	962
Property and equipment, net	12,227	9,483
Other assets		
Long-term unbilled receivables	7,466	2,744
Patent costs, net	383	286
Loan costs, net	37	428
Other assets, net	2,485	447
Total other assets	10,371	3,905
Total assets	$ 90,052	$ 23,798
LIABILITIES AND STOCKHOLDERS' EQUITY		
Current liabilities		
Accounts payable	$ 1,562	$ 2,150
Current portion of notes payable	2,007	674
Current portion of capital lease obligations	17	15
Current portion of deferred revenue and advances	292	741
Current portion of contract loss reserve	1,321	—
Accrued expenses and other	2,291	273
Total current liabilities	7,490	3,853

(continued)

---

[6] Extracted from 10-K filings for Basin Water, Inc. 2005–2007. Obtained from U.S. Securities and Exchange Commission. *www.sec.gov*

	December 31, 2006	December 31, 2005
Notes payable, net of current portion and unamortized discount	10	6,878
Capital lease obligations, net of current portion	24	40
Deferred revenue, net of current portion	387	439
Contract loss reserve, net of current portion	2,404	—
Redeemable convertible Series A preferred stock, no par value—6,000,000 shares authorized, 0 and 627,500 shares issued and outstanding	—	2,250
Redeemable convertible Series B preferred stock, no par value—5,000,000 shares authorized, 0 and 1,734,125 shares issued and outstanding	—	6,529
Total liabilities	10,315	19,989
Commitments and contingencies		
Stockholders' equity		
Common stock, no par value—40,000,000 shares authorized, 10,303,047 shares issued and outstanding	—	7,927
Common stock, $0.001 par value—100,000,000 shares authorized, 19,887,672 shares issued and outstanding	20	—
Additional paid-in capital	95,002	—
Accumulated deficiency	(15,285)	(4,118)
Total stockholders' equity	79,737	3,809
Total liabilities and stockholders' equity	$ 90,052	$ 23,798

Extracts from FORM 10-K[7]

For the fiscal year ended December 31, 2007

BASIN WATER, INC.

Consolidated Balance Sheets

(In thousands, except share and per share data)

	December 31, 2007	December 31, 2006
ASSETS		
Current assets		
Cash and cash equivalents	$ 35,456	$ 54,567
Accounts receivable, net of $72 and $67 allowance for doubtful accounts	3,167	2,416
Unbilled receivables, net of $524 and $433 allowance for doubtful accounts	11,443	9,123
Inventory	1,055	714
Current portion of notes receivable	338	—
Prepaid expenses and other	1,233	634
Total current assets	52,692	67,454
Property and equipment		
Property and equipment	15,945	13,621
Less: accumulated depreciation	1,645	1,394
Property and equipment, net	14,300	12,227

(continued)

---

[7] Extracted from 10-K filings for Basin Water, Inc. Obtained from U.S. Securities and Exchange Commission. *www.sec.gov*

	December 31, 2007	December 31, 2006
Other assets		
Goodwill	8,682	—
Unbilled receivables, net of current portion	7,664	7,466
Notes receivable, net of current portion	3,015	—
Intangible assets, net	3,416	1,641
Patent costs, net	2,274	383
Investment in affiliate	4,502	—
Other assets	1,667	881
Total other assets	31,220	10,371
Total assets	$ 98,212	$ 90,052
LIABILITIES AND STOCKHOLDERS' EQUITY		
Current liabilities		
Accounts payable	$ 3,553	$ 1,562
Current portion of notes payable	—	2,007
Current portion of capital lease obligations	11	17
Current portion of deferred revenue and advances	266	292
Current portion of contract loss reserve	1,964	1,321
Accrued expenses and other	3,140	2,291
Total current liabilities	8,934	7,490
Notes payable, net of current portion	—	10
Capital lease obligations, net of current portion	15	24
Deferred revenue, net of current portion	296	387
Deferred revenue—affiliate	1,920	—
Contract loss reserve, net of current portion	5,311	2,404
Deferred income tax liability	2,268	—
Other long-term liabilities	179	—
Total liabilities	18,923	10,315
Commitments and contingencies		
Stockholders' equity		
Common stock, $0.001 par value—100,000,000 shares authorized, 21,948,704 and 19,887,672 shares issued and outstanding	22	20
Additional paid-in capital	110,354	95,002
Treasury stock	(552)	—
Accumulated deficiency	(30,535)	(15,285)
Total stockholders' equity	79,289	79,737
Total liabilities and stockholders' equity	$ 98,212	$ 90,052

The accompanying notes are an integral part of these consolidated financial statements.

Basin Water, Inc.
Consolidated Balance Sheets
(In thousands, except per share data)

	Years Ended December 31,		
	2007	**2006**	**2005**
Revenues			
System sales	$ 13,477	$ 13,861	$ 10,016
Contract revenues	5,307	3,253	2,215
Total revenues	18,784	17,114	12,231
Cost of revenues			
Cost of system sales	13,790	12,161	4,467
Cost of contract revenues	10,698	7,522	2,323
Depreciation expense	443	423	340
Total cost of revenues	24,931	20,106	7,130
Gross profit (loss)	(6,147)	(2,992)	5,101
Research and development expense	564	634	651
Selling, general and administrative expense	13,685	6,827	3,334
Income (loss) from operations	(20,396)	(10,453)	1,116
Other income (expense)			
Interest expense	(98)	(2,781)	(621)
Interest income	2,736	2,061	52
Gain on sale to affiliate	2,500	—	—
Other income	8	6	16
Total other income (expense)	5,146	(714)	(553)
Income (loss) before taxes	(15,250)	(11,167)	563
Income tax benefit	—	—	—
Net income (loss)	$ (15,250)	$ (11,167)	$ 563
Net income (loss) per share:			
Basic	$ (0.76)	$ (0.70)	$ 0.06
Diluted	$ (0.76)	$ (0.70)	$ 0.04
Weighted average common shares outstanding:			
Basic	20,185	16,048	9,924
Diluted	20,185	16,048	12,849

Basin Water, Inc.
Consolidated Statements of Cash Flows
(In thousands)

	Years Ended December 31,		
	2007	**2006**	**2005**
Cash flows from operating activities			
Net income (loss)	$ (15,250)	$ (11,167)	$ 563
Adjustments to reconcile net loss to net cash provided by operating activities:			
Depreciation and amortization	995	1,024	506
Stock-based compensation expense	1,706	744	31
Gain on sale to affiliate	(2,500)	—	—
Issuance of warrants for services	—	34	417
Write off of loan acquisition costs	—	401	—

(continued)

	Years Ended December 31,		
	2007	2006	2005
Changes in operating assets and liabilities:			
Accounts receivable including unbilled	(1,817)	(4,489)	(6,279)
Inventory	103	(367)	(268)
Prepaid expenses and other	(542)	(445)	(80)
Accounts payable	1,600	(588)	1,468
Deferred revenues	(117)	(501)	(354)
Accrued expenses and other	(1,515)	2,018	397
Contract loss reserve	3,550	3,725	—
Net book value of systems sold	4,091	636	—
Issuance of notes receivable	(3,353)	—	—
Other assets and other liabilities	(207)	(3,386)	(2,810)
Net cash used in operating activities	(13,256)	(12,361)	(6,409)
Cash flows from investing activities			
Purchase of property, plant and equipment	(5,347)	(3,942)	(1,913)
Acquisition of business, net of cash acquired	(6,214)	—	—
Collection of notes receivable	—	100	325
Patent costs	(31)	(99)	(107)
Net cash used in investing activities	(11,592)	(3,941)	(1,695)
Cash flows from financing activities			
Issuance of common stock	—	75,178	3,584
Repurchase of common stock	(552)	—	—
Proceeds from employee stock option exercises	527	162	—
Proceeds from warrant exercises	8,060	—	—
Issuance of redeemable preferred stock	—	—	596
Proceeds from notes payable	—	2,000	5,156
Loan origination fees	—	(100)	(100)
Repayments of notes payable and capital lease obligations	(2,298)	(9,095)	(112)
Net cash provided by financing activities	5,737	68,145	9,124
Net increase (decrease) in cash and cash equivalents	(19,111)	51,843	1,020
Cash and cash equivalents, beginning of period	54,567	2,724	1,704
Cash and cash equivalents, end of period	$ 35,456	$ 54,567	$ 2,724

From Basin's 10-K 2007 NOTES, Pages F20-F22[8]

Note 9: OTHER ASSETS

Goodwill

The table below summarizes the changes in the carrying amount of goodwill for the year ended December 31, 2007:

Balance at December 31, 2006	$ —
Acquisition of business during the period	8,682
Balance at December 31, 2007	$ 8,682

Long-term Accounts Receivable and Notes Receivable The Company has four customer system sales agreements which provide for payment terms ranging from two to five years, unless certain conditions are met, in which case the payment terms are

---

[8] Source: U.S. Securities and Exchange Commission. *www.sec.gov*

accelerated. At December 31, 2007 and 2006, the amount of long-term accounts receivable was $7,664 and $7,466, respectively, which represents the balance due from these four customers under the extended payment terms.

In 2004, in connection with the sale of a system, the Company received a $300 unsecured note that provides for interest at a rate of 3% per annum. The Company received a payment of $200 in connection with this note in 2005. The final principal payment of $100 became due in 2006, and as such, the note has been classified as current. The Company has reserved $67 of this note as of December 31, 2007 and 2006. Both the note and the related allowance for doubtful accounts have been classified as current assets and are included in the accounts receivable balance at December 31, 2007 and 2006.

At December 31, 2007, long-term notes receivable consist of non-interest bearing notes receivable from VL Capital, due in 72 monthly installments of $63 beginning April 2008, with a net present value of $3,353, calculated using an imputed interest rate of 5.0% per annum.

Intangible Assets   Net intangible assets are as shown in the following table as of the dates indicated:

	December 31,	
	2007	2006
Deferred stock based compensation	$ 189	$ 394
Fair value of warrants, net	916	1,210
Service agreements and contracts	1,299	—
Customer relationships	560	—
Covenant not to compete	295	—
Trade name	157	—
Loan costs, net	—	37
Intangible assets, net	$ 3,416	$ 1,641

The amortization period of intangible assets are as follows: customer relationships—15 years; covenant not to compete—three years; trade name—two years; service agreements and contracts—six years; deferred stock-based compensation—three years; and fair value of warrants issued to a joint venture partner—five years.

Patent Costs   The Company capitalizes costs of patent applications. As a result of the September 2007 acquisition of MPT, the Company recorded an additional $1,812 representing the fair value of patents acquired. When patents are issued, the Company amortizes the patent cost over the life of the patent, usually 17 years. Future amortization of patent costs at December 31, 2007 is approximately $107 per year for each of the five years ended December 31, 2008 through 2013, and $107 each year thereafter through 2024. If a patent is denied, capitalized patent costs are written off in the period in which a patent application is denied.

Investment in Empire Water Corporation (Empire)   In May 2007, the Company entered into an agreement to acquire certain water rights and related assets. In December 2007, the Company sold its rights to purchase these assets to Empire. As consideration for the sale of these assets, the Company received 6,000,000 shares of Empire common stock, which represents an ownership interest of approximately 32% in Empire as of December 31, 2007.

The Company accounted for the December 2007 transaction under the equity method. Specifically, the Company recorded $2,500 as gain on sale to affiliate upon the receipt of the shares of Empire common stock by estimating the fair value of such stock based upon concurrent sales of Empire common stock to third parties, and reducing the fair value by the Company's ownership interest in Empire. This reduction of approximately $1,900 has been recorded as deferred revenue—affiliate on the balance sheet of the Company at December 31, 2007.

The Company has recorded its investment in Empire at approximately $4,500, while the amount of underlying equity in the net assets of Empire is approximately $3,000. The difference of approximately $1,500 represents the excess of the market value of the Company's investment in Empire over the Company's 32% interest in the net assets of Empire.

The following tables present summarized information concerning the assets, liabilities and results of operations of Empire for the most recent periods for which information is available:

	Dec 31, 2007
Assets	$ 9,460
Liabilities	$ 101

	Six Months Ended Dec 31, 2007	Year Ended June 30, 2007
Revenues	$ —	$ —
Net loss	$ (11)	$ (33)

From BASIN's 10-K 2007 NOTES, Page 27

Note 15: RELATED PARTY TRANSACTIONS

The Company paid legal fees to a legal firm whose partner is a director. The total payments for legal fees to this firm were $315, $192 and $154 for the years ended December 31, 2007, 2006 and 2005, respectively.

The Company also leases office space and equipment from two individuals, one of whom is a director and employee and the other an employee, under month-to-month agreements. The total payments under these related party rental agreements were $57, $54 and $55 for the years ended December 31, 2007, 2006, and 2005, respectively.

In May 2007, the Company entered into an agreement to acquire certain water rights and related assets. In December 2007, the Company sold its rights to purchase these assets to Empire. As consideration for the sale of these assets, the Company received 6,000,000 shares of Empire common stock, which represents an ownership interest of approximately 32% in Empire as of December 31, 2007.

The Company accounted for the December 2007 transaction under the equity method. Specifically, the Company recorded $2,500 as gain on sale to affiliate upon the receipt of the shares of Empire common stock by estimating the fair value of such stock based upon concurrent sales of Empire common stock to third parties, and reducing the fair value by the Company's ownership interest in Empire.

In addition, Empire agreed to purchase one water treatment system from the Company concurrent with the December 2007 closing for a total price of $900. During the year ended December 31, 2007, the Company recorded $653 of system sales revenue and $287 of gross margin on this transaction under the percentage-of-completion method of revenue recognition. The Company has recorded $92 as a charge against other income under the equity method, which represents 32% of the Company's gross margin on this system sale to a related party.

Tall Tales

After studying this chapter, you should be able to:

- Describe Edison Schools' inadequate disclosure in the management discussion and analysis (MD&A) section of its financial statements.
- Recognize Adelphia's failure to disclose related-party transactions and its improper use of non-GAAP transactions.
- Describe BellSouth's improper accounting for foreign payments in violation of the Foreign Corrupt Practices Act (FCPA).
- Identify and explain Krispy Kreme's inappropriate accounting for round-trip transactions.

- Edison Schools, Adelphia, BellSouth, and Krispy Kreme are presented as examples of miscellaneous financial reporting schemes. (Refer to Table 1.1, p. 19.)

CHAPTER OUTLINE

THE EDISON LESSON

Edison Schools, Inc., is presented here as an example of inadequate disclosures in its MD&A.

Taking advantage of problems in public schools throughout the United States, Edison Schools, headquartered in New York City, was founded on the premise that private-sector corporations could run public schools more efficiently and effectively. Edison was listed on NASDAQ in November 1999. In its early years, Edison managed approximately 130 elementary and secondary public schools in about 22 states. It had contracts with public school districts and charter schools to implement its unique curriculum and teaching methods, together with a longer school day, in the contracting schools. The teachers in the Edison-run schools were the original school district teachers. Edison received approximately $6,500 per year for each student enrolled at each school, and the teachers usually received compensation that reflected the extra teaching hours required in the Edison schools.

The company was usually responsible for the costs of running the schools, but the teachers were often paid directly by the school districts and not by Edison. After an investigation into Edison's accounting methods, the U.S. Securities and Exchange Commission (SEC) stated:

> The teacher salaries and non-instruction expenses paid directly by districts (collectively "District-Paid Expenses") comprise a substantial portion of the expense of operating Edison schools. These funds never reach Edison, but are expended by districts directly and then deducted from the district's remittances to Edison. (AAER 1555, 2002)

Publicly traded companies are required to include a **Management Discussion & Analysis (MD&A)** section in their financial filings with the SEC. This section serves to describe the company's financial health and the results of its operations to help users gain a better understanding of the company's financial statements. The MD&A is of particular interest and importance because it shows that the disclosure responsibility regarding financial statements goes beyond a mechanical application of GAAP rules and actually requires an accurate reflection of the company's financial condition and the results of its operations. The SOX Report (2002) stated, "Inadequate disclosure matters may involve situations where the issuer's financial statements are in conformity with GAAP, but fail in some material way to present an accurate picture of the issuer's financial condition."

EDISON'S FICTITIOUS FINANCIAL REPORTING SCHEME VIA INADEQUATE DISCLOSURE

In the case of Edison Schools, Inc., the area of inadequate disclosure did not affect the amount of net income at all. The issue was whether Edison could report the gross amount of the fee per student as its revenues in its income statement and then separately deduct the district-paid expenses or whether it had to report the net payment from the district (i.e., fees minus expenses) as revenues. Although the net income is the same in both cases, the former method could give the impression of a much more active company.

Edison's practice was to record the gross amount as revenues and include the district-paid expenses as its expenses in its income statement. This could present a misleading picture. For example, in the case of one district (District A) in 2001, no cash at all was paid to Edison because, according to the district, the total "Per Pupil Fees" amounted to $7.5 million and the district-paid expenses were $8 million in total. In its income statement, Edison "recorded the entire amount invoiced, $7.5 million, as gross revenue for FY 2001, also recording expenses of $8 million" (AAER 1555, 2002).

In another instance (District B), the SEC alleged that the district "has paid Edison only $400,000 in FY 2002, even though Edison has recorded over $17 million in revenues from District B for the first two quarters of FY 2002, along with over $18 million in expenses" (AAER 1555, 2002). In May 2002, the SEC issued a cease-and-desist order.[1]

Whether a company has zero revenue and zero expense or positive revenue and an equally positive expense—leading to zero net income—can influence an investor's or lender's perception of the company's results and financial position.

In the case of Edison, the SEC alleged: "In its filings with the Commission, Edison has not disclosed the existence and amounts of these District-Paid Expenses. Instead, Edison has inaccurately stated in its Management Discussion and Analysis [MD&A] that it 'receives' all Per Pupil Funding" (AAER 1555, 2002).

It is important to note that the SEC acknowledged that at the time of Edison's accounting treatment of these items in 2001, it was not clear that the revenue in the income statement needed to be reported net of the district-paid expenses for those cases in which Edison was not the primary obligor. (A **primary obligor** is the party that has the ultimate responsibility to pay a vendor or provider of services.) If two or more parties agree with each other that one of them will pay a vendor or provider of services, the party that has the ultimate obligation to the payee for the payment is the primary obligor.

The Emerging Issues Task Force clarified the situation regarding expenses for which a company is responsible but does not pay. Under the guidance of EITF 01-14[2], which became effective in 2002, the Commissioner stated:

> Under this recent accounting guidance, Edison must report revenue on a gross basis to include those District-Paid Expenses for which it is the "primary obligor" for the expense. Where Edison is not the primary obligor for the expenses, Edison must report revenue on a net basis to exclude such expenses. The choice between treatment of revenues on a gross or net basis does not affect net income. (AAER 1555, 2002)

(**Revenue on a gross basis** refers to the amount of revenue an entity earns before the deduction or payment of expenses for which the entity is the primary obligor.)

---

[1] Edison consented to the order and to a settlement without admitting or denying any of the findings contained in the order. As set out in AAER 1555, May 14, 2002.

[2] Current U.S. GAAP has many industry-specific and transaction-specific rules. A new principles-based, converged revenue recognition standard will be adopted, as explained in Chapter 3 of this text. The FASB tentatively requires that the new standard will be effective "for annual reporting periods beginning after December 15, 2016," for public companies (*Revenue Recognition Project*, 2013, p. 15).

The issue was that Edison's financial statements did not accurately and completely "describe the realities of Edison's operations" (AAER 1555, 2002). The SOX Report succinctly stated Edison's situation:

> The Commission did not find that Edison's revenue recognition practices contravene GAAP or that earnings were misstated. However, the Commission nonetheless found that Edison committed violations by failing to provide accurate disclosure, thus showing that technical compliance with GAAP in the financial statements will not insulate an issuer from enforcement action. (p. 24)

EDISON'S CHOICE OF ACCOUNTING TREATMENT

The Edison example involves the *choice* of an accounting treatment and in this case did not have specific signals. However, it is important for users of financial statements to be aware of different reporting methods and to question why one method was chosen rather than another.

The Edison case is particularly interesting because it clearly reveals the basic purpose and ethical considerations at the core of financial reporting. A company is required to release fiscal reports in order to clearly and truthfully reveal its financial condition. It is, therefore, unacceptable for a company to merely abide by the letter of the law if this inadvertently allows for the dissemination of misleading information. In such a case, the spirit of the law must always be communicated.

ARE THEY LIVING HAPPILY EVER AFTER?

- **Edison Schools** now operates under the name "EdisonLearning." According to the EdisonLearning website, the company is working with almost half a million students in over two dozen states and also works with a number of schools overseas (2013).
- In September 2011, former Los Angeles Laker Magic Johnson announced that the Magic Johnson Foundation would be partnering with **EdisonLearning** to develop Bridgescape Learning Centers for at-risk students ("Magic Johnson," 2011).
- **Edison** is no longer listed on the NASDAQ. The company was "taken private" in fall 2003 ("Edison Schools Leaving Publicly Traded Stage," 2003).

THE ADELPHIA ACCOUNT[3]

Adelphia Communications Corporation is presented mainly as an example of:
- **Failure to Disclose Related-Party Transactions and Improper Use of Related-Party Transactions.**
- **Improper use of Non-GAAP Financial Measures.**

Established in 1952 in Coudersport, Pennsylvania, Adelphia grew into one of the largest cable television providers in the United States, operating in 29 states and Puerto Rico. The company, founded by John J. Rigas, was also a provider of local telephone services.

---

[3]Background information in this section is mainly from AAER 1599 (2002), "Adelphia Founder John Rigas Found Guilty" (2004), BR-6413 (2002), and Goldsmith (2005).

In July 2002, the SEC alleged that the Adelphia case involved "one of the most extensive frauds ever to take place at a public company." The frauds centered on **related-party transactions**, which refer to dealings with any party that controls or can significantly influence the operations of a company so as to prevent the company from properly pursuing its own interests. Related-party transactions include dealings with principal shareholders, officers, directors, affiliates, and the relatives of shareholders or management.

In its complaint, the SEC maintained:

- From mid-1999 to the end of 2001, Adelphia excluded "billions of dollars in liabilities from its consolidated financial statements by hiding them in off-balance sheet affiliates."
- During this time, the company "falsified operations statistics and inflated Adelphia's earnings to meet Wall Street's expectations."
- Since 1998 or earlier, the company "concealed rampant self-dealing by the family that founded and controlled Adelphia, the Rigas family." (Quotes from BR-6413, 2002)

The Rigas family allegedly used company funds to purchase costly condominiums, plush holiday accommodation, and luxury cars and even to build a golf course. At his trial in mid-2004, John Rigas was accused of recklessly spending company money. According to examples given by the prosecutor, Rigas used Adelphia's funds to purchase two Christmas trees for $6,000 and to spend $26 million on 3,600 acres of land surrounding his house to ensure that the view would never be obstructed. A witness at the trial described how Adelphia had paid for a lavish family wedding, as well as for a personal trainer and masseur who worked full-time for John Rigas and his sons.

The SEC named six senior Adelphia executives in its civil complaint; four of the six were members of the Rigas family (John Rigas and his three sons); the other two were James Brown and Michael Mulcahey, both vice presidents of the company.

ADELPHIA'S FICTITIOUS FINANCIAL REPORTING SCHEMES

Adelphia's schemes involved abuse of related-party transactions involving members of the Rigas family. In addition to misleading financial statements, Adelphia also disseminated other misleading information.

Scheme #1: Improper Use and Misleading Disclosure of Related-Party Transactions

Adelphia used related-party transactions to hide debt, boost earnings, and loot the company. Most of the offending transactions involved the use of off-balance-sheet partnerships. Highland Holdings, a Rigas family general partnership, and Highland 2000, a Rigas family limited partnership, were two of the "Rigas Entities" used for many of the related-party transactions between Adelphia and the Rigas clan. Dealings between Adelphia, the Rigas Entities, and the Rigas family itself became even more complicated and obscure by the mingling of funds among the various groups. Adelphia, its subsidiaries, and the Rigas Entities all deposited and withdrew cash from a joint cash management system called "Adelphia CMS" that was administered by Adelphia.

A brief examination of some of the major irregularities involving Adelphia's transactions with Rigas Entities, or with members of the Rigas family, will illustrate the need for concern wherever related-party transactions are revealed in a company's financial statements.

Issuing Adelphia Shares Directly to Rigas Entities   A number of direct placements of Adelphia shares were made to Rigas Entities. An examination of these transactions illustrates the dangers of a company transacting with entities owned or controlled by officers or directors of the company. The SEC claimed that, in October 2001 and January 2002, Adelphia made a direct placement to Highland 2000 of $423 million of Adelphia class B shares and notes payable. Adelphia simultaneously transferred over $423 million of debt off its books and created false documentation for its auditors, claiming that Highland 2000 had paid cash for the securities.

The SEC's complaint alleged that the transaction was deceptive mainly for the following reasons:

- The $423,375,076 in debt was not paid down, but instead was shifted to Highland Video.
- Highland 2000 never paid cash for the securities.
- Adelphia remained jointly and severally liable for the debt.
- Highland Video's "assumption" of debt was a sham because it never received any economic benefit from it and was not dealing at arm's length. (BR-6413, 2002)

In addition, the Commissioner maintained that Adelphia engaged in a number of similar transactions in which a Rigas entity received the securities, and as a result, while existing debt was taken off Adelphia's books, new debt was taken on without the new debt being reported on the balance sheet.

Selling Adelphia's Excess Digital Converters to a Rigas Entity   Adelphia had purchased an excess inventory of digital converters. In the last quarter of 2001, it sold $101 million of this inventory to Highland Video. According to the SEC, Highland Video did not operate a cable service and did not need the digital converters. Adelphia accounted for the transaction by reducing its debt by $101 million and crediting inventory by a corresponding amount.

Purchasing Timber Rights from the Rigas Family   According to the Commission, Adelphia purchased certain rights, including timber rights, to 3,656 acres of land owned by the Rigas family in Potter County, Pennsylvania. The family paid under half a million dollars for the land, and Adelphia purchased the timber rights to the land for over $26 million. A highly unusual clause in the contract stated that the timber rights would "revert back to the owner of the underlying land at either the earlier of twenty years or if the percentage of Adelphia stock held by John Rigas fell below 50% of all the outstanding company stock" (BR-6413, 2002). Adelphia's investors were not informed of this contract with the Rigas family.

Self-Dealing Involving a Golf Course, Personal Margin Loans, and the Use of Luxury Condominiums   The SEC claimed that Adelphia used approximately $12.8 million of its funds to construct a golf course on land owned mainly by the Rigas family. Again, this use of company funds for the personal benefit of the Rigas family was not disclosed to investors. In addition, the family had sole use of at least four glamorous condominiums in the United States and Mexico, all courtesy of Adelphia. The company also paid over $241 million in "personal margin loans and other debt of the Rigas family" (BR-6413, 2002).

In the criminal trial of founder John J. Rigas and his son Timothy Rigas, "Prosecutors alleged that the Rigas family siphoned $100 million from Adelphia to pay for personal extravagances, hid $2.3 billion in debt and systematically deceived investors about Adelphia's subscriber growth and its bottom line." Prosecutors at the trial displayed "more than a dozen allegedly false SEC documents signed by various family members and receipts for personal expenses, large and small, including those for 100 pairs of slippers ordered by Timothy Rigas." In fact, the prosecutors accused the family of using Adelphia as a "private ATM." (Quotes from Masters & White, 2004)

Scheme #2: Improper Use of Non-GAAP Financial Measures

Not only are investors interested in information disclosed in the financial statements but they also like to know that a company's customer base is growing and that the technical quality of the plant and products is high. This might explain why Adelphia did not restrict itself to misleading financial information, but misrepresented its performance in non-GAAP financial measures as well. (**Non-GAAP financial measures** are measures that are not included in the income statement, balance sheet, or statement of cash flows from operations that are calculated in accordance with GAAP.) For example, in its 10-Ks for 2000 and 2001, the company was accused of misreporting and overstating the number of its cable subscribers. According to BR-6413, 2002, Adelphia added the following to its list of subscribers:

- 15,000 subscribers of an unconsolidated affiliate located in Brazil.
- 28,000 cable subscribers of an unconsolidated Venezuelan affiliate.
- Customers who received "Powerlink," Adelphia's Internet service.
- 6,000 Adelphia home-security subscribers.

To bump up the numbers even further, apparently Adelphia also added cable subscribers from other Rigas Entities and even included long-distance telephone subscribers as basic cable subscribers.

Furthermore, the SEC maintained that when communicating with investors and financial analysts, Adelphia misrepresented the extent to which it had upgraded its cable plant. The upgrade was initiated to improve the cable plant in two important areas: to increase the plant's ability to transmit signals at greater speeds and to enable the plant to transmit as well as to receive signals from its customers. The phrase that Adelphia liked to use for this upgraded capacity was "two-way cable," but the SEC claimed that the extent of the two-way cable upgrade had been exaggerated. For example, the Commission revealed that in a 1999 presentation to potential investors in a stock offering, Adelphia had used an "overhead slide that contained a pie chart which represented that approximately 50% of Adelphia's cable plant [had been] 'rebuilt.' This claim was fraudulent because Adelphia's cable plant was only approximately 35% rebuilt at the time" (BR-6413, 2002).

SIGNALS OF ADELPHIA'S FICTITIOUS REPORTING SCHEMES

A number of signals could have alerted readers to the schemes that Adelphia was using to present the company in a more positive light.

Signals of Adelphia's Fictitious Reporting Scheme #1—Improper Use and Misleading Disclosure of Related-Party Transactions

Here is an examination of some of the signals indicating that a company may have engaged in improper related-party transactions.

SIGNAL #1: NOTES IN THE FINANCIAL STATEMENTS INDICATING THAT THE COMPANY IS INVOLVED IN BUSINESS TRANSACTIONS WITH RELATED PARTIES Any disclosures in the notes to the financial statements that the company is doing transactions with any major shareholder, officer, or director of the company or any entity owned or controlled by these parties, should alert the reader to be very cautious. These transactions could be used to do any of the following:

- Hide the company's debt.
- Overstate the company's earnings.
- Loot the company's assets in favor of the major shareholders, directors, or officers.

Pay special attention to the related-party transactions note and study all the company's financial statements in search of disclosures of *any* transactions between the company and its major shareholders, directors, or company officers (as well as their families or affiliates). For example, the SEC pointed out that the footnotes in Adelphia's Annual Report for 2000 disclosed the following: "On January 21, 2000, Adelphia closed the previously announced direct placement of 5,901,522 shares of Adelphia Class B common stock with Highland 2000, L.P. a limited partnership owned by the Rigas family." The note then falsely stated that Adelphia had used a portion of this "to repay borrowings under revolving credit facilities." This was misleading because the debt had simply been moved to the Rigas Entities. Even if the information in the notes is misleading, the limited disclosure often alerts the reader to the fact that related-party transactions have occurred. Such transactions are more likely to be manipulated than are **arm's-length transactions**, which are transactions between two parties that do not have a relationship (such as a business or family relationship) with each other. (Quotes from BR-6413, 2002)

SIGNAL #2: MIXING A COMPANY'S ASSETS OR LIABILITIES WITH THOSE OF OTHER PARTIES The intermingling of a company's assets or liabilities with the personal assets or liabilities of its major shareholders, officers, or directors is a signal of poor internal control. This weakness could be exploited to loot a company's assets.

In Adelphia's Annual Report for 2000, a note referred to members of the Rigas family who were "co-borrowers with entities under credit facilities." A disclosure that intermingling occurs among a company's assets and liabilities and those of its directors, officers, or shareholders should be regarded as an alert that more related-party activity may be occurring than is being disclosed. The disclosure may be the tip of the iceberg because it could become very tempting for officers or shareholders to use the company as its own money machine.

ARE THEY LIVING HAPPILY EVER AFTER?

- **James Brown**, former vice president for finance, "pleaded guilty to conspiracy, bank fraud, and wire fraud, [and] was the government's star witness at trial" (Crawford & Dunbar, 2004). In a civil trial in 2012, Brown was sued by Timothy and Michael Rigas who claimed that Brown had never repaid a $400,000 loan. The Rigas family won the civil case against Brown (Hoak, 2013).

- **Michael Mulcahey**, former vice president, was found not guilty of conspiracy and securities fraud ("Status of High-Profile … ," 2005).
- **John J. Rigas**, founder of Adelphia, is now serving a 12-year prison sentence (Gilliland, 2012). In 2005, he was convicted of "conspiracy, bank fraud and securities fraud" ("Status of High-Profile … ," 2005).
- **Timothy Rigas**, son of John Rigas, is now serving a 17-year prison sentence (Gilliland, 2012). He was "found guilty of conspiracy and 15 counts of securities fraud and two counts of bank fraud" (Crawford & Dunbar, 2004).
- **Michael Rigas**, son of John Rigas, entered a guilty plea in November 2005 to "a charge of making a false entry in a financial record" ("Status of High-Profile … ," 2005). In March 2006, Michael Rigas was sentenced to 24 months of probation, which included 10 months of confinement at home (Bray, 2006). The judge in the case remarked that Michael Rigas "stands on an entirely different footing from the two members of his family that were convicted" (Bray, 2006).
- **James Rigas**, son of John Rigas, was not criminally charged.
- **Adelphia** filed for bankruptcy in June 2002. In 2006, the FTC agreed to the acquisition of Adelphia by Time Warner Cable and Comcast ("FTC's Competition Bureau… ," 2006). The company is no longer in existence.
- **Deloitte & Touche LLP.** The SEC instituted public administrative proceedings against Adelphia's auditors and ordered them to pay a "$25 million civil penalty." The auditors agreed to a settlement "without admitting or denying the findings" (AAER 2237, 2005). In addition, the firm paid "another $25 million in an administrative penalty" (Glater, 2005). In 2007, Deloitte & Touche "agreed to pay $167.5 million to settle a case with a trust that was formed after Adelphia Communications Corp. collapsed in 2002" (Johnson, 2007). Deloitte & Touche denied any wrongdoing.

THE BELLSOUTH WARNING

> **BellSouth is presented mainly as an example of Improper Accounting for Foreign Payments in Violation of the Foreign Corrupt Practices Act (FCPA).**

BellSouth is presented mainly as an example of Improper Accounting for Foreign Payments in Violation of the Foreign Corrupt Practices Act (FCPA). BellSouth is a telecommunications corporation headquartered in Atlanta, Georgia. During the 1990s, the company significantly expanded its international operations via acquisitions of telephone companies in as many as 11 different Latin American countries, including Venezuela and Nicaragua. According to the SEC (AAER 1494, 2002), it was in its business dealings with these two countries that BellSouth ran afoul of the FCPA.

The FCPA was passed in 1977 to combat improper dealings by U.S. companies operating in foreign countries, and the act is enforced by both the Department of Justice (DOJ) and the SEC. The FCPA is essentially comprised of two sections: the anti-bribery regulations and the accounting regulations. The consequences of violating any of the provisions of the act may be quite severe and may carry "potential criminal and civil penalties" (SEC v. BellSouth—Update, 2002).

The bribery and accounting provisions frequently overlap because bribery payments are usually misclassified in the accounts, records, and financial statements. The accounting section of the FCPA clearly requires that publicly traded companies operating overseas must "make and keep books, records and accounts, which, in reasonable detail, accurately and fairly reflect their transaction[s] and disposition of assets, and devise and maintain a system of internal accounting controls...." (AAER 1494, 2002). According to the SEC, BellSouth ran into problems with its acquisitions of both Telcel (in Venezuela) and Telefonia (in Nicaragua).[4]

BELLSOUTH'S FICTITIOUS FINANCIAL REPORTING SCHEMES

One of BellSouth's schemes involved the use of fictitious documents. Other schemes included incorrect payments and inaccurate records.

Scheme #1: The Use of Fabricated Invoices at Telcel

BellSouth entered the Venezuelan market in 1991 with its acquisition of a minority interest in Telcel, and in 1997 BellSouth increased its investment in Telcel to a majority holding. By 2002, Telcel had become the largest wireless supplier in Venezuela and was BellSouth's largest revenue earner in Latin America.

The SEC alleged that from 1997 to 2000, "former Telcel senior management authorized payments totaling approximately $10.8 million to six off-shore companies." Furthermore, the Commission stated that "Telcel recorded the disbursements in Telcel's books and records based on fictitious invoices." These fabricated invoices were for "services" rendered to Telcel, although no such services were ever verified and BellSouth was unable to provide any information about these payments or about the location of the money. (Quotes from AAER 1494, 2002)

The strength of the FCPA legislation lies in the requirement that companies keep accurate books and records. Therefore, it is not necessary to first prove illegal intent regarding a payment; a suspicious payment in itself can result in an action. The failure to keep proper records is sufficient cause for an enforcement action.

Scheme #2: The Use of Inappropriate Payments and the Failure to Keep Accurate Records at Telefonia

In 1997, BellSouth had acquired 49 percent of the shares of Telefonia in Nicaragua, as well as an option to acquire another 40 percent. However, there was a problem with the option because Nicaraguan law prohibited foreign companies from holding a majority of the stock in a telecommunications company.

In October 1998, Telefonia hired a lobbyist (at $6,500 per month) who was the wife of a Nicaraguan politician who happened to be the chairman of the telecommunications legislative oversight committee. This committee had "jurisdiction over the foreign ownership restriction," and the chairman's wife worked primarily "on the repeal of the

---

[4] The SEC issued a cease-and-desist order against BellSouth in which the Commissioner found that "BellSouth violated the books and record provisions and internal accounting contract provisions" (AAER 1495, 2002). BellSouth consented to the entry of the order "without admitting or denying the Commissioner's findings." As set out in AAER 1495.

foreign ownership restriction" (AAER 1494, 2002). Although the lobbyist stopped working at Telefonia in May 1999, the movement to revoke the foreign ownership restriction was well under way, and the restriction was repealed in December 1999. By June 2000, BellSouth owned 89 percent of Telefonia. The lobbyist had received a total of $60,000, which included a severance payment.

According to the Commission, BellSouth was well aware that "its payments to the lobbyist could implicate the Foreign Corrupt Practices Act ('FCPA')." Furthermore, the SEC found that:

- Telefonia had "created false books and records" by describing the payments to the lobbyist as "consulting services" and
- BellSouth had neglected "to devise and maintain a system of internal accounting controls at Telefonia sufficient to detect and prevent FCPA violations." (Quotes from AAER 1494, 2002)

IMPROPER ACCOUNTING IN VIOLATION OF THE FCPA

FCPA violations often consist of bribery where the amounts involved are not in themselves material, but the bribery can have serious consequences. Bribery is difficult to identify in financial statements. For information on investigations of suspected bribery or corruption involving a company, search news reports in the U.S. press and the press of the foreign countries in which the company operates.

ARE THEY LIVING HAPPILY EVER AFTER?

- In 2006, **BellSouth** was acquired by AT&T, creating a "telecommunications behemoth ..." (Belson, 2006).

KRISPY KREME[5] AND THE MISSING DOUGH[6]

Krispy Kreme Doughnuts, Inc., is presented mainly as an example of Inappropriate Accounting for Round-Trip Transactions.

The original Krispy Kreme company, founded by Vernon Rudolph in North Carolina in 1937, slowly developed a small string of franchises with what has been described as "an almost legendary product and a loyal customer base" (O'Sullivan, 2005). According to doughnut lore, a fresh Krispy Kreme is the ideal melt-in-your-mouth doughnut, with just the right chewy texture of freshly fried sugary dough drizzled with the perfect glaze. The customers can actually smell the sweet aroma and hear the hot sizzle of doughnuts being cooked to perfection. Krispy Kreme turned the doughnut business into the doughnut experience.

---

[5] The SEC issued a cease-and-desist order against Krispy Kreme in 2009 (AAER 2941). Krispy Kreme consented to the entry of the order "without admitting or denying the findings." As set out in AAER 2941.
[6] The background information for this section is mainly from Brooks (2004), Maremont and Brooks (2005), O'Sullivan (2005), "Scott Livengood, CEO, Krispy Kreme" (2004), and "Summary of Independent Investigation" (2005).

The company was sold to Beatrice Foods in the 1970s, a few years after the original owner died. Many Krispy Kreme devotees were upset by the sale, and several of the franchisees grouped together to repurchase the company in 1982. The business began to grow on the national level as customers all over America lined up to get their first taste of the mouth-watering confection.

The company's business model seemed like a dream come true: a product that needed no introduction and a customer base waiting to sample the merchandise. Scott Livengood, the CEO of Krispy Kreme, took the company public with an initial public offering (IPO) in April 2000 and opened a number of international franchises, with the first European outlet at the Harrods store in London. Livengood was reportedly such an avid fan of the doughnuts that he had a huge cake made entirely of doughnuts when he got married in 2002. Krispy Kreme was constantly mentioned in the media, and even people who had never eaten a doughnut became familiar with the brand.

In the three fiscal-year span from February 2001 to February 2004, the number of stores grew from 58 company-owned stores and 86 franchises to 141 company-owned stores and 216 franchises. During this period, the company usually exceeded Wall Street's expectations, as annual revenue grew from $220 million to $665.6 million. Krispy Kreme's stock price "climbed most dramatically of all, from the IPO price of $5.25 per share to a high of $49.37 per share on August 18, 2003" ("Summary of Independent Investigation," 2005, p. 3).

However, things started to turn sour as Krispy Kreme was accused of having "sweetened results" in its attempts to keep Wall Street happy (Maremont & Brooks, 2005). The corporation was beset with problems that ranged from store closures to rumors about problematic acquisitions and inaccurate accounting practices. In an attempt to shore up the struggling company, Livengood tried to blame Krispy Kreme's problems on the growing popularity of low-carbohydrate diets; so the company announced that it was developing a "sugar-free doughnut" (O'Sullivan, 2005). However, by May 7, 2004, the stock price had dropped to $22.51 per share and kept sliding. The next month, one of several lawsuits was filed against Krispy Kreme, alleging that it had issued "materially false and misleading statements contained in press releases and filings with the Securities and Exchange Commission" (Chimicles & Tikellis LLP, 2004). In October 2004, the SEC informed the company that it was under formal investigation. That same month, the board of directors set up a "special committee" to perform an independent investigation into the business practices of the company.

In the final "Summary of Independent Investigation" (2005), the special committee highlighted a number of problematic areas. In its examination of company management, the committee members stated, "It appears that Livengood was too focused on meeting and exceeding Wall Street expectations and gave too little attention to establishing the appropriate tone from the top" (p. 6). The committee maintained that John Tate, the chief operating officer, was also largely responsible for "failure to set the appropriate managerial tone and environment … " (p. 6).

In addition, the investigation uncovered several accounting errors in Krispy Kreme's financial statements for 2004. Without these errors, the company would not have been able to meet its aggressive sales and earnings estimates as consistently as it did. It is important to note that the special committee did *not* conclude that the accounting errors were intentional, although it noted that "government investigators ... may uncover additional facts that will better illuminate the intent behind various individuals' actions and the underlying events" ("Summary of Independent Investigation," 2005, p. 2). After its investigations, in 2009, the SEC issued an Accounting and Auditing Enforcement Release against Krispy Kreme in which the Commission found: "In each of the second, third and fourth quarters of fiscal 2004, Krispy Kreme engaged in a round-trip transaction in connection with the reacquisition of a franchise" (AAER 2941, 2009). According to the SOX Report (2002), **round-trip transactions** are transactions that "involve simultaneous pre-arranged sales transactions, often of the same product, in order to create a false impression of business activity or revenue" (p. 25).

AN OVERVIEW OF KRISPY KREME'S OPERATIONAL PROBLEMS

Apart from the accounting errors, the company was beset by other problems, which included the following:

- Growth was too rapid, with the addition of too many new franchised stores at the expense of existing franchises.
- Same-store revenue (i.e., revenue of existing franchises) was growing much more slowly than parent-company revenue, which was boosted by the opening of new stores.
- There appeared to be a lack of "controls, procedures and resources adequate for a business experiencing explosive growth" ("Summary of Independent Investigation," 2005, p. 5).
- There appear to have been too few independent outside directors to determine strategy and to control management.
- There were policies favorable to the parent company but detrimental to its franchisees, such as expecting "franchisees to buy equipment and ingredients from headquarters at marked-up prices" (O'Sullivan, 2005).
- The company moved away from its core competency, such as adding new items to the menu and selling doughnuts that were not cooked on-site.

SIGNALS OF KRISPY KREME'S OPERATIONAL PROBLEM OF OPENING TOO MANY FRANCHISES

Although no fraud is involved in these operational issues, they led to the financial problems behind the fictitious financial reporting.

SIGNAL #1: RISE IN FRANCHISE ACQUISITION RIGHTS   An increase in the intangible asset of "franchise acquisition rights" could be an indication that too many franchises have been sold and that some are being repurchased because franchisees are encroaching on each other.

SIGNAL #2: GROWTH OF EXISTING STORE SALES LESS THAN GROWTH IN COMPANY SALES   Another signal of this problem is when growth in company sales is much greater than growth in existing store sales. In the period from the second quarter of

2003 to the second quarter of 2004, Krispy Kreme reported an increase in company revenues of almost 15 percent, while same-store sales increased by less than 1 percent.

AN OVERVIEW OF KRISPY KREME'S FICTITIOUS FINANCIAL REPORTING SCHEMES

An examination of Krispy Kreme's records by its independent investigation, set up by two of its directors, revealed a number of accounting errors, including the following:

1. The recording of round-trip transactions prior to the reacquisition of the franchise in which amounts were added to the reacquisition cost of the franchise. This scheme of misreporting round-trip transactions is examined further below.
2. The recording of early shipments of equipment sales to franchisees, while the equipment remained unused until later periods.
3. The failure to accrue the full amount of incentive compensation expense in accordance with the company's incentive plan.

The Krispy Kreme Scheme of Using Inappropriate Accounting for Round-Trip Transactions

In the case of Krispy Kreme, the "Summary of Independent Investigation" (2005) stated that although the amounts involved were not very large, the "most egregious" accounting errors they uncovered were those involving round-trip transactions with franchise acquisitions (p. 8).

The vehicle that Krispy Kreme used to implement its round-trip transaction stunts was the reacquisition of franchise rights. In three separate repurchases of franchise rights, Krispy Kreme falsely increased the repurchase price of the franchise.

In the first round-trip transaction, Krispy Kreme agreed to pay an extra $800,000 for the repurchase of a franchise in return for the franchisee agreeing to purchase a similar amount of doughnut-making equipment from Krispy Kreme shortly before Krispy Kreme repurchased its franchise. The cash for the extra equipment and the equipment itself went on a "round-trip" to the franchisee and back to Krispy Kreme. Both sales and franchise acquisition rights (an intangible asset) were overstated in the process. According to the SEC, "Krispy Kreme increased the price it paid for the franchise by $800,000, i.e., from $65,000,000 to $65,800,000 in return for the franchise purchasing from Krispy Kreme certain doughnut making equipment" (AAER 2941, 2009).

In the case of the second round-trip transaction, Krispy Kreme inflated its repurchase price "for the franchise by $525,463, which represented an approximation of the total of two disputed amounts that Krispy Kreme claimed it was owed by the franchise" (AAER 2941, 2009).

In the third round-trip transaction, Krispy Kreme paid a distribution to a former franchisee without reducing the repurchase price accordingly. The former franchise holder immediately transferred the amount "back to Krispy Kreme as payment of the management fee" (AAER 2941, 2009). This management fee was an amount that Krispy Kreme had demanded "in consideration for Krispy Kreme's handling of the management duties" since negotiations began for the repurchase of the remaining franchise rights. According to the SEC, "Krispy Kreme booked this fee as income, thereby overstating Krispy Kreme's net income in the fourth quarter by approximately $361,000" (AAER 2941, 2009).

SIGNALS OF KRISPY KREME'S FICTITIOUS REPORTING SCHEME OF MISUSING ROUND-TRIP TRANSACTIONS

SIGNAL #1: ACCOUNTS RECEIVABLE INCREASING AS A PERCENTAGE OF SALES As with any overstatement of sales, accounts receivable increasing as a percentage of sales as measured by, for example, days' sales outstanding (DSO), is a signal of acceleration of fictitious sales.

SIGNAL #2: CFFO LAGGING OPERATING INCOME The cash flow from operations (CFFO) may lag operating income until the "sale" is paid for from the ensuing complementary round-trip transaction payment. If the cash is received in the first part of the trip and repaid in the second part, this signal will be blurred. If the reciprocal payment is supposedly for an investing activity, as in Krispy Kreme's case, this signal will also be obscured.

ARE THEY LIVING HAPPILY EVER AFTER?

- In July 2012, Krispy Kreme celebrated its 75th anniversary. The company currently "has 694 stores across the United States and in 20 foreign countries" ("Krispy Kreme Doughnuts Inc. Celebrates … ," July 1, 2012).
- In 2011, Krispy Kreme posted profits for the first time since 2004 ("Krispy Kreme Doughnuts Inc. Celebrates … " July 1, 2012).
- In June 2005, the special committee decided that "six unnamed company officers should be fired" ("Six Krispy Kreme Execs Ousted," 2005). Shortly thereafter, five of the executives resigned and one retired.
- **Scott Livengood** was removed from his position as CEO in January 2005. Livengood was offered a six-month position as an "interim consultant" (Nowell, 2005).
- **John Tate**, former COO of Krispy Kreme, left the company in August 2004 "to pursue another opportunity" (qtd. in "Krispy Kreme COO Tate Leaving the Company," 2004).
- In the opening months of 2006, Krispy Kreme's stocks were trading in the $5.00–$7.00 per share range—quite a sharp drop from $49.37 per share in August 2003. The company has sold off a number of its franchises. In mid November, 2013, the company's share price was almost $26.00 per share.

Key Terms

Arm's-length transaction
    279

Management Discussion
    and Analysis (MD&A)
    273

Non-GAAP financial
    measures *278*

Primary obligor *274*

Related-party transactions
    276

Revenue on a gross basis
    274

Round-trip transactions
    284

ETHICS AT WORK

Read the extract below from the speech on "Conflicts of Interest and Risk Governance" (2012) by Carlo di Florio, the director of the SEC's Office of Compliance Inspections and Examinations, then respond to the question.

Question:

Carlo di Florio discusses seven elements of an effective compliance and ethics program for corporations. While in the case of Adelphia all seven elements appear to have been neglected, in your opinion, which three of the elements discussed by di Florio would have been most useful in preventing the improper business practices at Adelphia? Explain your answer.

Extract from Speech: Conflicts of Interest and Risk Governance

Carlo V. di Florio
Director, Office of Compliance Inspections and Examinations*
National Society of Compliance Professionals
October 22, 2012

Effective Practices for Managing Conflicts of Interest**.

Turning from how regulators approach conflicts to how firms can assess and mitigate conflicts, I believe that an effective conflicts risk governance framework includes three broad considerations.

1. The first is that there needs to be an effective process, led by a cross-functional leadership team, to identify and understand all conflicts in the business model. These conflicts need to be understood both in terms of their practical business implications as well as in relation to relevant legal standards. This includes a recognition that conflicts are dynamic, and that in addition to continually scanning for new conflicts, each and every conflict that has been identified and addressed needs to be revisited periodically to determine if it is still being appropriately controlled in light of new business circumstances, changing customer profiles, new regulatory obligations, etc. For instance, in our exams of how firms protect material non-public information (MNPI) from inappropriate uses, such as insider trading, we have observed instances where firm programs lagged behind new business strategies that created new sources of MNPI. While the business model evolved, the control framework did not and that exposed these firms to significant risks. It is also important to risk-assess and prioritize which conflicts of interest present the greatest risk to the organization so that resources can be allocated accordingly to mitigate and manage those conflicts effectively both from a compliance risk and reputation risk perspective.

2. The second broad consideration, I believe, is to have a good compliance and ethics program tailored to address the conflicts of interest the firm has identified and

---

* The Securities and Exchange Commission, as a matter of policy, disclaims responsibility for any private statements by its employees.
** Part III of Speech. Obtained from U.S. Securities and Exchange Commission. *www.sec.gov.*

prioritized. [....] Under the securities laws, registrants are expected to have effective written policies and procedures to prevent violations of the securities laws, and to periodically review the adequacy and effectiveness of those policies and procedures. For instance Rule 206(4)-7 under the Investment Advisors Act and Rule 38a-1 under the Investment Company Act establish such requirements for investment advisors and investment companies. Similar requirements also exist for broker-dealers under FINRA rules.[18] In my view in order to be adequate and effective these compliance and supervisory policies and procedures must include processes to identify, assess, mitigate and manage conflicts of interest.

In addition, for reference purposes the U.S. Federal Sentencing Guidelines ("Guidelines") since 2004 have provided helpful guidance on many of the key elements of an effective compliance program. The 2004 and 2010 amendments to the Guidelines, as you know, explicitly require an effective compliance and ethics program as a mitigating factor in determining criminal sentences for corporations. The Guidelines list seven factors that are minimally required. I would like to examine each of these factors in turn, and explain how I believe it relates to effectively managing conflicts of interest. I believe that this analysis is also very germane to whether broker-dealers and investment advisers have met their supervisory obligations under the federal securities laws.

Standards and procedures. The Guidelines look to companies to "establish standards and procedures to prevent and detect criminal conduct." The scope of what this may require depends on the size of the organization, as the commentary to the Guidelines suggests, with larger organizations expected to have more formal operations and resources than smaller ones. However, I believe that for any organization, developing a strong process for identifying and managing conflicts of interest is a key means of preventing and detecting not just criminal conduct, but other behavior that may create regulatory or reputational risks for the business.

Since new conflicts of interest can arise rapidly as a business grows and evolves, and may become apparent to front-line employees before they come to the attention of more senior managers or control functions, communications about these standards and procedures are also an opportunity to emphasize to all employees the importance of their role in recognizing new conflicts of interest, and their responsibility to elevate such conflicts to appropriate control functions. Some firms enhance this process by including conflicts assessment within other processes, such as new product or business approval, conduct customer surveys for potential conflicts, or conduct periodic or ad hoc self-assessments of their business practices.

Oversight. The second factor is that the organization's "governing authority" – typically a board of directors and senior management – is knowledgeable about the content and operation of the compliance and ethics program and exercises reasonable oversight with respect to its implementation and effectiveness. In order to complement this oversight, some firms establish standing committees, composed of senior executives and senior

---

[18] NASD Rules 3010 and 3012, which are incorporated into FINRA's rulebook, contain comparable requirements. In addition, FINRA Rule 3130 requires the CEO of a member firm to certify annually, *inter alia*, that the member has established, reviewed and tested written compliance policies and supervisory procedures reasonably designed to achieve compliance with the federal securities laws. (This is footnote #18 in original speech.)

control personnel, with focused responsibility on conflicts assessment. I believe that, in the financial services world, unremediated conflicts of interest are a leading indicator of the types of problems that a compliance and ethics program is intended to root out. Therefore, I find it difficult to see how the governance structure of a financial services firm can satisfy this factor unless its oversight includes consideration of the effectiveness of the compliance and ethics program in addressing conflicts of interest.

Leadership consistent with effective ethics and compliance program. The third factor is that the organization use reasonable efforts to exclude from any position of leadership any individual who has engaged in conduct inconsistent with an effective compliance and ethics program—in other words, that the fox is not guarding the henhouse. Again, in my view it would be difficult for a financial services firm to satisfy this standard if any of its business unit heads or senior managers has not shown a commitment to proactively identifying and remediating conflicts of interest in the business model of the organization.

Education and Training. The fourth factor is that the organization take reasonable steps to periodically train and otherwise communicate with its leadership, employees and agents about its compliance and ethics program, including its standards and procedures for implementing the program. It follows from what I have already said that, in my view, this training and other communication should include communication about the responsibilities of everyone in the organization regarding identifying, escalating and remediating conflicts of interest. It should be tailored to specific conflicts in the business model and clearly set forth the governance, risk management and compliance procedures to mitigate and manage these conflicts.

Auditing and Monitoring. The fifth factor is to take reasonable steps to ensure that the compliance and ethics program is followed, including monitoring and auditing, as well as periodic testing of the effectiveness of the program, and to have and publicize a system by which employees and agents of the organization can report or seek guidance regarding potential criminal conduct without fear of retaliation. Some firms will discuss with legal and compliance issues prior to a review and then report on issues discovered to any designated conflicts review authority. For financial service firms, this auditing, monitoring and testing should, in my view, encompass testing of the effectiveness of the organization's policies and procedures regarding management of conflicts of interest.

Incentives and discipline. The sixth factor is whether the organization has appropriate incentives to support the compliance and ethics program, and appropriate disciplinary measures for failing to take reasonable steps to prevent or detect criminal conduct. I believe that this factor, especially as it relates to incentives, goes to the heart of many problematic conflicts, since these often may involve incentives that an individual has that are inconsistent with duties that he or she owes to the organization, its clients or his or her customers.

Response and prevention. The final factor is whether the organization takes reasonable steps to respond to any criminal conduct and to prevent its recurrence, including making any necessary modifications to its compliance and ethics program. In the case of a financial institution, I would think that this response would include a consideration of any conflicts of interest that may have incentivized or otherwise facilitated the bad conduct, and consideration of how any such conflicts can more effectively be barred or remediated. Some firms go further, not only analyzing their weaknesses, but also issues identified at other firms so that the same problems do not happen at their establishment.

3. The third consideration, in my view, is that this process for addressing conflicts of interest is fully integrated in the firm's overall risk governance structure. The business is the first line of defense responsible for taking, managing and supervising conflicts of interest, like other risks, effectively and in accordance with laws, regulations and the risk appetite set by the board and senior management of the whole organization. Key risk and control functions, such as compliance, ethics and risk management, are the second line of defense. They need to have adequate resources, independence, standing and authority to implement effective programs and objectively monitor and escalate conflicts of interest and other risk issues. Internal Audit is the third line of defense and is responsible for providing independent verification and assurance that controls are in place and operating effectively to address conflicts of interest. Finally, senior management and the board of directors need to be engaged. This includes considering the risk that conflicts of interest present throughout key business processes, including strategic planning, capital allocation, performance monitoring and evaluation of business units and individual business leaders. Some of the more effective practices I have observed include having key risk and control functions involved in each of these key processes with senior management and the board so they can provide their independent view on how business units and individual business leaders are doing at managing conflicts and promoting a culture of compliance and ethics.

Let me close with a few brief observations for senior managers and independent directors. I believe that your role in conflicts management and ensuring a culture of compliance and ethics is critically important. At the end of the day, managing conflicts is much more than just having a strong compliance program, although that is obviously critical. It also requires establishing a culture that, regardless of regulatory requirements, does not tolerate conduct that casts doubt on the organization's commitment to high ethical standards, and that values the firm's long-term reputation over any possible short-term benefit from exploiting its clients or customers. Former SEC Chairman Richard Breeden said it best when he stated that "[i]t is not an adequate ethical standard to aspire to get through the day without being indicted."[19]

In addition, while it is undoubtedly helpful to have certain individuals or groups who are tasked with specific roles regarding mitigating conflicts, the responsibility of everyone in the organization to identify conflicts and see that they are managed appropriately should always be emphasized. As leaders in your organizations, that responsibility starts with you.

Finally, it is important to think proactively when it comes to conflicts of interest. As I mentioned earlier, in the financial services industry, and likely in other types of organizations as well, conflicts of interest are continually arising in new forms that need to be addressed aggressively and with vision and foresight. Where conflicts of interest are concerned, eternal vigilance and independent oversight are warranted in order to protect an institution's reputation and brand.

---

[19] *Quoted in Business and Professional Ethics for Directors, Executives and Accountants* (2009), available at Google Books. (This is footnote #19 in original speech.)

Assignments

TRUE/FALSE QUESTIONS

Answer the following questions with T for true or F for false for more practice with key terms and concepts from this chapter.

1. The Management Discussion and Analysis (MD&A) section in the SEC filings of publicly traded companies discusses the issuer's financial condition and results of operations to enhance investor understanding of financial statements.

   T   F

2. According to the SEC's AAER 1555, Edison disclosed the existence and amount of its District-Paid Expenses, but did not properly offset them from revenues.

   T   F

3. Technical compliance with GAAP in the financial statements will insulate an issuer of financial statements from enforcement actions by the SEC.

   T   F

4. According to the SEC, Adelphia's improper reporting included inaccurate non-GAAP information.

   T   F

5. One of the signals of the improper use and disclosure of related-party transactions is references in the notes to the financial statements that indicate the intermingling of a company's assets or liabilities with those of its major shareholders, officers, or directors.

   T   F

6. BellSouth is presented in the text as an example of the improper disclosure of non-GAAP information.

   T   F

7. BellSouth properly recorded and disclosed improper payments in its books and records.

   T   F

8. Krispy Kreme's internally appointed independent investigation into its business

practices concluded that the company's accounting errors were intentional.

   T   F

9. In the recording of Krispy Kreme's round-trip transactions, equipment sales were made to a franchisee shortly before the reacquisition of the franchise and the sales price of the equipment was deducted from the reacquisition cost of the franchise.

   T   F

10. Krispy Kreme also failed to accrue the full amount of incentive compensation expense in accordance with the company's incentive plan.

   T   F

FILL-IN-THE-BLANK QUESTIONS

Fill in the blanks with information and concepts from this chapter.

11. In the case of Edison Schools, Inc., its inadequate disclosure did not affect the amount of net _____ it reported.

12. Edison's practice was to report the gross amount of the fee per student as its _____ in its income statement.

13. In the _____ case, the issue was that it did not accurately and completely describe the realities of its operations in its MD & A.

14. The disclosure of related-party transactions should alert the user of financial statements that the transactions could be used to _____ the company's debt, or to _____ its earnings, or to loot the company's assets.

15. According to the SEC, Adelphia purchased land from members of the Rigas family in terms of a contract in which a clause stated that the _____ rights to the land would revert back to the owner after 20 years.

16. The strength of the FCPA legislation lies in the requirement that companies keep accurate _____ and records.

17. According to the SEC, Telcel recorded a disbursement in its books and records based on _____ invoices.

18. The SOX Report defined round-trip transactions as transactions that involve simultaneous pre-_____ sales transactions, often of the same product, to create a false impression of business activity and revenue.

19. An increase in the intangible asset described as "franchise acquisition rights" could be a signal that too many _____ have been sold in the past.

20. Another signal that a company has sold too many franchises is when the growth in total company sales is a much greater percentage than the percentage growth in _____ - _____ sales.

MULTIPLE-CHOICE QUESTIONS

21. Edison Schools is presented in the chapter as an example of:
    (a) Failure to disclose related-party transactions.
    (b) Inadequate disclosures in its Management Discussion and Analysis (MD&A).
    (c) Improper accounting for payments in violation of the Foreign Corrupt Practices Act.
    (d) Inappropriate accounting for round-trip transactions.

22. Which of the following correctly describes the SEC's finding against Edison?
    (a) Edison's revenue recognition practices did not contravene GAAP, but failed to present an accurate picture of the issuer's financial condition.
    (b) Edison's recognition practices contravened GAAP.
    (c) Since the issuance of the guidance of EITF 01-14 in 2002, if a company is the primary obligor for an expense, it must report revenue net of expenses that are deducted from those revenues before payment is made to the entity.
    (d) The net income reported by Edison in its income statement was incorrect.

23. Which of the following is *not* true regarding the SECs allegations against Adelphia?
    (a) The company concealed rampant self-dealing by the family that founded and controlled Adelphia.
    (b) The company falsified operations statistics.
    (c) The company improperly accounted for foreign payments in violation of the Foreign Corrupt Practices Act.
    (d) The company excluded liabilities from its consolidated financial statements.

24. In the text, Signal #1 of improper use of related-party transactions states that any disclosures in the notes to the financial statements that the company is doing transactions with any major shareholder, officer, or director of the company should alert the reader to the fact that these transactions could be used to:
    (a) Hide the company's debt.
    (b) Overstate the company's earnings.
    (c) Loot the company's assets.
    (d) All of the above.

25. Adelphia's overstatement of its number of cable subscribers in its 10-K reports:
    (a) Is an example of a revenue recognition practice that contravenes GAAP.
    (b) Caused it to overstate its earnings.
    (c) Is an example of the failure to properly disclose related-party transactions.
    (d) Is an example of the improper use of non-GAAP measures.

26. According to the SEC, BellSouth's improper accounting for foreign payments in contravention of the Foreign Corrupt Practices Act (FCPA) included all of the following, except:
    (a) The use of fabricated invoices at Telcel.
    (b) Breaking a foreign country's law that prohibited foreign companies from holding a majority of the stock in a telecommunications company.
    (c) The failure to keep accurate records.
    (d) Incorrectly describing payments to a lobbyist as consulting services.

27. The Foreign Corrupt Practices Act is enforced by:
    (a) The Department of Justice.
    (b) The Securities and Exchange Commission.
    (c) The Financial Accounting Standards Board.
    (d) Both (a) and (b).

28. Krispy Kreme is presented in the text as an example of:
    (a) Improper accounting for related-party transactions.

(b) Improper disclosure of non-GAAP financial measures.

(c) Improper disclosure in its Management Discussion and Analysis.

(d) Improper accounting for round-trip transactions.

29. Which of the following regarding Krispy Kreme's round-trip transactions is *not* correct?

(a) Krispy Kreme engaged in contrived equipment sales to franchisees.

(b) The transactions inflated franchise reacquisition purchase prices.

(c) The transactions resulted in the reporting of overstated net income.

(d) The transactions overstated expenses in the income statement.

30. Krispy Kreme's internal investigation revealed each of the following accounting errors *except*:

(a) The misallocation of compensation expenses to franchise reacquisition costs.

(b) The creation of cookie-jar reserves to release into profit in later periods.

(c) The recording of early shipments of equipment sales to franchisees.

(d) The failure to record the full amount of incentive compensation.

FOR DISCUSSION

31. Is the intermingling of a company's assets with those of a major shareholder, director, or company officer illegal? Is it unethical? Or is it both illegal and unethical? Explain your answer.

32. Discuss the improper accounting practices at Adelphia that were similar to the improper accounting practices at Enron. Use specific examples from each company.

SHORT-ANSWER QUESTIONS

33. In the case of Edison Schools, explain why the SEC issued an AAER even though it did not find that Edison's revenue recognition practices did not contravene GAAP.

34. Explain how Adelphia misreported non-GAAP information.

35. Explain why an action can be taken against an issuer of financial statements in terms of the Foreign Corrupt Practices Act in respect of a suspicious payment without proving that the payment was for an illegal activity.

36. Explain what is meant by a "round-trip transaction."

EXERCISES

37. Rhodes Co. manages a school for the Old England School District. In year 1, Rhodes Co.'s first year of operating the school, the school earned per pupil fees of $100,000. Rhodes is responsible for teacher salaries and is considered to be the primary obligor for the salaries. However, the school district paid the teachers' salaries of $70,000 and paid Rhodes the net amount of $30,000 in respect of year 1 operations. Rhodes incurred other administrative expenses of $10,000 for the year (ignoring taxes), which it paid itself.

Required

a. What is the amount of revenue that Rhodes should report in its income statement for year 1 in accordance with EITF 01-14?

b. What is the amount of Rhodes Co.'s net income for year 1?

38. Ruby Company manages the daily operations for the human resources department of Jade Company. In terms of the contract, Ruby receives a fee of $100 per year for each employee on Jade's payroll, less the salary of Jade's bookkeeper, who works full-time on human resource matters. Jade is the "primary obligor" for the bookkeeper's salary.

Last year, Jade had 1,000 employees on its payroll and the bookkeeper's salary (which was paid by Jade) was $40,000. Ruby's other administrative expenses were $10,000.

Required

a. What is the amount of revenue that Ruby Company should report on its income statement for last year in terms of EITF 01-14?

b. What was Ruby's operating income for last year (ignoring taxes)?

39. Crafty Company manufactures and sells printers. On the last day of the first quarter of the year, Crafty contrives with

Tricky Company to sell 100 printers to Tricky Company for $1,000 each. In terms of Crafty's agreement with Tricky, Tricky will sell those 100 printers back to Crafty at the same price of $1,000 each in the second quarter of the year. The cost of each printer that Crafty manufactures is $600. Crafty allocates the full cost of the printers that it purchases from Tricky to inventory.

Examine the following extract from Crafty's income statement, excluding the contrived round-trip transaction:

Income Statement Extract: Crafty Co. First Quarter	
Sales	$200,000
Cost of goods sold	120,000
Gross margin	80,000
Selling and administrative expenses	30,000

Assume that Crafty Company goes ahead with the contrived round-trip transaction with Tricky Company. Prepare Crafty's income statement for the first quarter with the round-trip transaction included. Ignore taxes.

40. Greasy Patties Corporation, a hamburger chain, has 100 stores. In its tenth year of operating, its total sales for year 10 amounted to $100 million. During year 11, Greasy Patties Corporation decides that it would be beneficial to report increased sales for the year, and it opens 50 new stores in year 11. However, the stores competed with each other for sales and same-store sales for old stores decreased by 10 percent in year 11 compared to year 10. The total sales for the new stores that opened in year 11 amounted to $30 million.

Required

How much did total sales for Greasy Patties Corporation increase in year 11 over year 10 in dollars and in percentage?

CASE STUDY

BUCA, Inc.

- **Read** the extracts from the SEC Complaint filed on June 7, 2006, against the former chief financial officer and the former controller of Buca, Inc.
- **Examine** the extracts from the Notes to Buca's Financial Statements (in its 10-Ks) for 2000, 2001, and 2002.
- **Respond** to the following Case Study Questions.

Required

a. **Undisclosed related-party transactions.**

1. Explain the alleged related-party transactions between Buca and High Wire Networks, Inc., as described in paragraphs 21–23 of the SEC Complaint filed in 2006.

2. Read Signal #1 of Adelphia's improper use and misleading disclosure of related-party transactions (in this chapter). Also read the extracts from Buca's related-party transactions notes to its financial statements for years 2000–2002. Explain the similarity, if any, between this signal in Adelphia's notes to its financial statements and the information in Buca's related-party transactions notes to its financial statements.

b. Internal Control Weakness. After reading paragraphs 21 and 22 of the SEC's Complaint filed against Buca, what, if any, internal control weakness do you see that was allegedly present at both Buca and Adelphia and that could have been a signal of allegedly improper use of related-party transactions at both companies?

Extracts from Complaint against Buca, Inc.*

Case 0:06-cv-02320-ADM-AJB Document 1-1 Filed 06/07/2006[7]
UNITED STATES DISTRICT COURT
DISTRICT OF MINNESOTA

UNITED STATES SECURITIES
AND EXCHANGE COMMISSION,

             Plaintiff,

                                     CIVIL ACTION
                                     FILE NO.

v.

GREG A. GADEL and DANIEL J. SKRYPEK,

             Defendants.

PARAGRAPHS 1–13 FROM COMPLAINT:

Plaintiff, United States Securities and Exchange Commission ("Commission") alleges as follows:

NATURE OF THE ACTION

    1. This case concerns fraud and other misconduct by two former officers of Buca, Inc. ("Buca"), a publicly traded, Minneapolis-based Italian restaurant company. Greg A. Gadel ("Gadel"), Buca's former Chief Financial Officer and Daniel J. Skrypek ("Skrypek"), Buca's former Controller, helped preside over a corporate culture at Buca that allowed fraud to flourish. Gadel and Skrypek participated in drafting Buca's proxy statements that materially understated the compensation of both Gadel and Joseph P. Micatrotto, Sr. ("Micatrotto"), Buca's former Chief Executive Officer, President, and Chairman of the Board of Directors. Gadel and Skrypek helped prepare and review financial statements

---

* "Upon the filing of the Commission's complaint, and without admitting or denying the allegations in the complaint, Micatrotto consented to the entry of a final judgment …." (LR 19719, 2006). "The final judgments, entered pursuant to Gadel's and Skrypek's consents, permanently enjoin them from violating Section 17(a) of the Securities Act of 1933 (Securities Act), Sections 10(b), 13(b)(5), and 14(a) of the Securities Exchange Act of 1934 (Exchange Act) and Rules 10b-5, 13b2-1, 13b2-2, 14a-3, and 14a-9 thereunder and from aiding and abetting violations of Sections 13(a), 13(b)(2)(A), and 13(b)(2)(B) of the Exchange Act and Rules 12b-20, 13a-1, and 13a-13 thereunder" (LR 20417, 2007). "Upon the filing of the Commission's complaint, and without admitting or denying the allegations in the complaint, Buca consented to the entry of a final judgment …." (LR 20312, 2007).

---

[7] Obtained from U.S. Securities and Exchange Commission. *www.sec.gov*.

and proxy statements filed with the Commission that failed to disclose a significant related party transaction involving Micatrotto and a series of related party transactions involving Gadel. Finally, Gadel and Skrypek directed the preparation of financial statements that materially overstated Buca's pre-tax income as a result of Gadel's and Skrypek's scheme to meet earnings targets through the improper capitalization of expenses.

2. From 2000 until 2004, Micatrotto, Gadel, and others treated the company as a vehicle through which they could obtain money to pay for personal expenses. Under Gadel and Skrypek's watch, and often with their direct consent, Micatrotto took advantage of Buca's lax accounting culture to improperly obtain reimbursement from Buca for personal expenses totaling nearly $850,000. Gadel and Skrypek approved many of Micatrotto's reimbursement requests, even though they knew, or were reckless in not knowing, that some of the requests contained personal expenses. Although Gadel and Skrypek knew of Micatrotto's improper reimbursements and helped prepare Buca's proxy statements, Buca's proxies never reported the payment of these personal expenses as compensation to Micatrotto for the years 2000 through 2003. As a result of Gadel and Skrypek's failure to ensure disclosure of this information, Buca's proxy statements for the years 2000 through 2003 understated Micatrotto's annual compensation in amounts ranging from 27% to 74%.

3. Gadel improperly charged Buca for such things as family vacations and visits to strip clubs. Skrypek routinely approved Gadel's improper reimbursement requests. From 2000 to 2003, Gadel received more than $96,000 in compensation arising from improper reimbursement requests. As a result, Gadel's compensation, like Micatrotto's, was materially understated in Buca's proxy statements.

4. Micatrotto also participated in a related party transaction that Buca never disclosed in its financial statements or proxy statements, despite Gadel's and Skrypek's knowledge of the transaction. Micatrotto and a Buca vendor bought an Italian villa in 2001 and billed Buca for the purchase and for certain improvements to the villa. Gadel and Skrypek knew of the purchase and approved payments in connection with the purchase of the villa.

5. Likewise, Buca never disclosed a series of related-party transactions involving Gadel in its financial statements or proxy statements. In 2000 and 2001, Gadel was a director and 10% shareholder of a small information technology company that engaged in a series of transactions involving Buca that totaled more than $1 million. Skrypek knew that Gadel had this ownership interest in the information technology company. Nonetheless, neither Gadel nor Skrypek ensured disclosure of these related party transactions in Buca's financial statements or proxy statements for the years 2000 and 2001.

6. Gadel and Skrypek also directed a scheme to meet Buca's earnings targets through the improper capitalization of expenses. Buca disclosed in a 2005 restatement that it had improperly capitalized nearly $12 million in expenses from 2000 until 2004, which had the effect of inflating Buca's reported pre-tax income in amounts ranging between 18.8% and 36.9% per year.

JURISDICTION AND VENUE

7. The Court has jurisdiction over this action pursuant to Section 22(a) of the Securities Act [15 U.S.C. § 77v(a)] and Sections 21(d) and 27 of the Exchange Act [15 U.S.C. §§ 78u(e), 78aa].

8. Venue is proper in this Court pursuant to Section 22(a) of the Securities Act [15 U.S.C. § 77v(a)] and Section 27 of the Exchange Act [15 U.S.C. §78aa].

THE DEFENDANTS

9. Greg A. Gadel is 47 years old and a resident of Eden Prairie, Minnesota. From 1997 until February 2005, Gadel was the CFO and an executive vice president of Buca. Gadel announced his resignation from Buca in December 2004, and left the company in February 2005.

10. Daniel J. Skrypek is 33 years old and a resident of Rosemount, Minnesota. He is a certified public accountant who holds an inactive license to practice in Minnesota. From 1999 until March 2005, Skrypek was Buca's Controller. From 2001 until 2005, he was also a vice president of Buca. In addition, Skrypek was Buca's interim CFO for a short period in 2005. Buca terminated Skrypek's employment in May 2005.

FACTS

11. Buca is a publicly traded company incorporated in Minnesota in 1996 and headquartered in Minneapolis. Buca is the holding company for two restaurant chains, Buca di Beppo and Vinny T's of Boston. Buca conducted an initial public offering of its stock in 1999. Since then, Buca's stock has been traded on NASDAQ. As a public company, Buca is required to file certain documents with the Commission, including annual reports on Forms 10-K, quarterly reports on Forms 10-Q, and proxy statements. From 2000 through 2004, Buca also filed with the Commission several S-8 registration statements in connection with offerings of its securities. These registration statements incorporated by reference Buca's financial statements and certain other Commission filings.

12. Gadel and Skrypek each played a significant role in preparing and ensuring the accuracy of Buca's annual and quarterly reports, financial statements and proxy statements filed with the Commission. Skrypek, as the Controller, created the first working draft of Buca's Commission filings, including consulting with his staff on the accounting numbers contained in those filings. Gadel also reviewed drafts of Buca's quarterly and annual reports, financial statements and proxy statements before they were filed with the Commission. Gadel, along with Micatrotto, had the final authority on the content of Buca's Commission filings. In addition, as an executive officer of Buca, Gadel completed proxy questionnaires each year in connection with the preparation of Buca's proxy statements. Buca used proxy questionnaires as one means of verifying compensation and related party transactions involving its executive officers. Gadel signed all of Buca's quarterly and annual filings with the Commission during his tenure as CFO and certified the accuracy of Buca's Forms 10-K, and the financial statements included in those reports, for the years 2002 and 2003. Additionally, Gadel and Skrypek signed Buca's management representation letters to Buca's independent auditors in connection with their annual audits of Buca's financial statements. Through these management representation letters, Gadel and Skrypek represented, among other things, the accuracy and completeness of Buca's financial statements.

13. Gadel and Micatrotto showed little regard for sound corporate governance and helped create an environment that was conducive to fraud. In addition, Skrypek, as Controller, facilitated the fraudulent conduct that occurred. For example, from 2000

until late 2004, Buca had very few policies regarding billing travel and entertainment expenses ("T&E") to the company. During this time, Gadel, Skrypek, and their subordinates regularly received and approved requests for the reimbursement of personal expenses, including requests accompanied by little or no supporting documentation. Gadel and Micatrotto took full advantage of the lax culture that they had created by regularly billing Buca for a wide variety of personal expenses.

PARAGRAPHS 21-35 FROM COMPLAINT:

Undisclosed Related Party Transactions Between Buca and Vendor in Which Gadel Had Substantial Involvement

21. Gadel had substantial involvement in High Wire Networks, Inc. ("High Wire"), a small information technology company that engaged in a series of transactions involving Buca between 2000 and 2001. High Wire was established in October 2000 by a group that included Gadel and two of the primary owners of EDP, which was one of Buca's major information technology vendors. High Wire provided voice-over internet protocol primarily to companies other than Buca. High Wire ceased operations in late 2001. During the relevant time period, Gadel was a director of High Wire and had a 10% equity interest in the company. Gadel also was one of the two authorized signatories on High Wire's checking account and served as one of High Wire's Buca contacts.

22. Buca essentially funded High Wire's operations, despite the fact that High Wire provided most of its services to companies other than Buca. High Wire had its offices in a portion of Buca's office complex and Buca paid nearly $98,000 to build out the office space occupied by High Wire. Further, EDP billed Buca for salary payments totaling $1,394,775 made to High Wire employees, even though many of these High Wire employees spent little or no time working for Buca.

23. The transactions discussed in the previous paragraph raised suspicions among the more junior members of Buca's accounting staff. A Buca assistant controller discussed with Skrypek that these payments appeared to represent related party transactions requiring disclosure. In fact, the assistant controller later met with Gadel and Skrypek on the issue, and suggested that they contact Buca's auditors. Gadel, however, stated that there was nothing improper with the relationship and Skrypek agreed. Neither Gadel nor Skrypek ever took steps to ensure disclosure of the related-party transactions between Buca and High Wire in Buca's proxy statements or in its Forms 10-K for the years 2000 and 2001.

The Financial Fraud Scheme

Background

24. As a way for Buca to meet analyst earnings estimates, Gadel orchestrated a scheme to inflate income through improper capitalization, which Skrypek helped to execute. Gadel and Skrypek together had the ultimate responsibility at Buca for whether an item should be capitalized. The scheme to inflate Buca's income involved taking ordinary expenses (which should be expensed in the period in which they are incurred) and

treating them as capital expenditures (which may be expensed over time). Beginning in 2000, Gadel and Skrypek would preliminarily assess Buca's financials at the close of each quarter and then determine how much income they needed to "find" in order to meet analysts' earnings estimates for Buca. Gadel and Skrypek found a number of different ways to inflate Buca's income by decreasing expenses through improper capitalization, including the ways detailed in paragraphs 25 through 34 below.

Sham Donations from Vendors Billed Back to the Company

25. Buca improperly capitalized at least $713,000 in expenses incurred in connection with an elaborate bill-back arrangement with certain vendors. The bill-back scheme concerned an annual conference for Buca store managers called the "Paisano Partners Conference." Buca ostensibly funded the Paisano Partners Conference through contributions from its vendors. In reality, certain Buca vendors made contributions to the Paisano Partners Conference with the express understanding that they could bill the contribution amount back to Buca. Gadel focused the bill-back scheme on vendors, such as construction and information technology vendors, that provided goods and services that, under more appropriate circumstances, could be capitalized. Specifically, the Buca vendors involved in the scheme would pay contributions to Buca to help fund the Paisano Partners Conferences. These capital vendors would then bill back the amount of the contribution by burying the contribution amount in a subsequent inflated invoice to Buca. Buca, in turn, would characterize the inflated invoices as capital expenditures. As a result, Buca effectively capitalized the expense of the conference.

26. Gadel orchestrated the bill-back scheme. For example, he directed Buca's construction manager to request that Buca's construction vendors make contributions to the Paisano Partners Conference and then bill back the contribution amount. Construction vendors that participated in the bill-back scheme typically billed for the contribution amount in vaguely worded change orders and invoices, or inflated project bids. Gadel explained to the construction manager that this arrangement would allow Buca to capitalize the vendor's bill-back, and that any Buca vendor with questions about the arrangement could call him directly.

27. Skrypek helped implement this bill-back scheme. Several times, Skrypek instructed employees as to whether certain Paisano Partners contributions should be billed back to Buca through a change order, or whether the amount should be built into the vendor's bid on a Buca project. Although Buca's assistant controller raised with Skrypek concerns about the vague change orders used by vendors making sham donations, Skrypek continued authorizing payment of such orders.

Everyday Repairs and Maintenance

28. Buca improperly capitalized at least $4.67 million in repair and maintenance expenses, as well as general and administrative expenses. Gadel and Skrypek targeted repair and maintenance expenses as a way to make up the difference between analyst earnings expectations and Buca's preliminary financial results. Gadel and Skrypek directed Buca employees at quarter end to review repair and maintenance account invoices over $1,000 to find invoices that could be capitalized in a sufficient quantity to meet an earnings target. Many of the capitalized invoices did not represent properly

capitalizable expenses. Although a Buca assistant controller advised Skrypek that he was uncomfortable with the practice of searching for items to capitalize at the end of each quarter in view of earnings targets, neither Skrypek nor Gadel did anything to change the practice. As the scheme went on, the improper capitalization of repair and maintenance invoices significantly expanded. First, Buca employed a practice of capitalizing most repair and maintenance invoices over $1,000 so that there was no need to review invoices at quarter end for capitalization purposes. Later, at Gadel's direction, Buca set up a capitalization account for invoices under $1,000. Gadel and Skrypek eventually allowed Buca accounting employees to put any small repair or maintenance invoice that the company received into this account, regardless of whether the invoice represented a capital expense.

Invoices from Vendors Related To Buca

29. Gadel and Skrypek also exploited Buca's unusual relationship with High Wire and EDP to improperly capitalize expenses. Buca, through Gadel and Skrypek, improperly capitalized at least $1.5 million worth of invoices submitted as part of an arrangement involving High Wire and EDP. First, EDP billed Buca for salary payments totaling $1,394,775 made to High Wire employees, even though many of these High Wire employees spent little or no time working for Buca. Gadel and Skrypek approved capitalization of these salary payments despite having no documentation supporting such accounting treatment. Second, at Gadel's direction and with Skrypek's knowledge, Buca used an inflated invoice from EDP to improperly capitalize at least $130,000 of ordinary expenses, including Buca's monthly telephone bill. Finally, High Wire occasionally submitted invoices to Buca in the round amount of $100,000 with no description of the goods or services provided. Gadel and Skrypek authorized payment of these vague invoices and approved the capitalization of the invoice payments. They did so even though Buca's assistant controller had raised questions with Skrypek about the nature of various vaguely worded invoices submitted by High Wire and EDP.

30. Because of his close personal involvement in High Wire, Gadel knew, or was reckless in not knowing, that Buca's payments to EDP for High Wire employee salaries and office space were not legitimate capital expenses. Likewise, although Skrypek suspected that Buca might be funding High Wire employees through payments to EDP, he simply authorized payment of EDP's bills and approved the capitalization of those payments. As such, Skrypek knew, or was reckless in not knowing, that EDP's High-Wire-related charges were not genuine capital expenses.

Payments to Independent Contractors

31. Buca, through Gadel and Skrypek, improperly capitalized at least $1 million in payments to independent contractors. The improperly capitalized payments involved both the mischaracterization of certain Buca employees as independent contractors and the mischaracterization of the work of genuine independent contractors as a capital expense.

32. Buca improperly characterized certain employees as independent contractors so that it could capitalize payments to them. For example, in 2002, a portion of the salary of Buca's assistant controller was capitalized. Skrypek told the assistant controller that he would be an independent contractor for his first three months of employment. Since

Buca was in the process of acquiring another restaurant chain at this time, Buca capitalized the assistant controller's salary payments as part of the acquisition.

33. In another example, Buca laid off its vice president of real estate but then immediately hired her as an independent contractor. Gadel instructed the assistant controller to pay the former vice president of real estate a $100,000 "finder's fee" for two leases she had previously negotiated. Paying the vice president this way for the lease negotiations allowed Buca to effectively capitalize her severance payments.

34. Buca also mischaracterized the invoices of genuine independent contractors as capital expenses. For example, Buca, through Gadel and Skrypek, capitalized payments totaling approximately $572,000 made to an independent contractor who provided permitting services for Buca restaurants, despite having no basis to do so. The invoices from this independent contractor contained no itemization of her time or work. The permitting contractor's work mainly concerned the ongoing operations of Buca's restaurants, expenses which are not appropriate for capitalization.

Meeting with Gadel About Accounting Abuses

35. A group of Buca's senior accounting personnel, including the assistant controller, the tax director, and Skrypek, met with Gadel in June 2003 to confront him about some of the accounting abuses identified above. When questioned about the capitalization of expenses, Gadel acknowledged that some of his accounting methods were aggressive, but denied any wrongdoing. When asked specifically about relationships with vendors like High Wire and EDP, Gadel responded that no problems with these relationships existed. Neither Gadel nor Skrypek took any remedial action based on the issues raised at the meeting.

FINANCIAL STATEMENTS

UNITED STATES
SECURITIES AND EXCHANGE COMMISSION
Washington, D.C. 20549

Extracts from FORM 10-K[8]

Annual reports pursuant to Section 13 or 15(d) of the Securities Exchange Act of 1934

For fiscal years 2000–2002

BUCA, INC.

From NOTES to Consolidated Financial Statements 2000: Note 9

9. RELATED-PARTY TRANSACTIONS
Management Agreement—The Company had a management agreement with its former parent company, Parasole Restaurant Holding, Inc. (Parasole), to provide for

---

[8] Extracted from 10-K filings for Buca, Inc. 2000–2002. Obtained from U.S. Securities and Exchange Commission. *www.sec.gov.*

certain management and administrative services. Management fees of approximately $348,000 and $222,500 were charged in 1998 and 1999, respectively. This management agreement terminated during 1999.

In 2000, the Company entered into a management agreement with a member of its Board of Directors to provide for certain management and administrative services. Management fees of approximately $111,000 were charged in 2000.

Purchase of Inventory—The Company has entered into a vendor relationship with Parasole whereby the Company purchases bread products and a majority of the dessert products offered at the Company's Minneapolis-Saint Paul metropolitan area restaurants. The Company purchases the products at rates which management believes approximate market rates. The relationship can terminate at any time at the discretion of the Company; however, the Company expects this relationship to continue. The Company purchased bakery products in the amount of $169,000, $181,000, and $92,000 in 1998, 1999, and 2000, respectively.

Employment Agreement—The Company entered into an employment agreement with one of its officers which requires the payment of annual compensation and certain fringe benefits through 2003 and includes bonus provisions in the form of both stock grants and stock options. In 2000, the Company filed an amendment to the employment agreement that extended the terms of the contract through 2004. (Buca 10-K, 2000; pages F-13, F-14)

From BUCA's 10-K 2001 NOTES: Note 9

---

9. RELATED-PARTY TRANSACTIONS

Management Agreement—The Company had a management agreement with its former parent company, Parasole Restaurant Holding, Inc. (Parasole), to provide for certain management and administrative services.

Management fees of approximately $222,500 were charged in 1999. This management agreement terminated during 1999.

In 2000, the Company entered into a management agreement with a member of its Board of Directors to provide for certain management and administrative services. Management fees of approximately $111,000 and $91,000 were charged in 2000 and 2001, respectively.

Consulting Fees—The Company utilizes the son of one of the board of directors to perform architectural and design related services. Consulting fees of $276,000, $322,000 and $297,000 were charged in 1999, 2000, and 2001, respectively.

Purchase of Inventory—The Company entered into a vendor relationship with Parasole whereby the Company purchases bread products and a majority of the dessert products offered at the Company's Minneapolis-Saint Paul metropolitan area restaurants. The Company purchases the products at rates which management believes

---

[9] Obtained from U.S. Securities and Exchange Commission. *www.sec.gov*.

approximate market rates. The relationship was terminated in 2000. The Company purchased bakery products in the amount of $181,000, and $92,000 in 1999, and 2000, respectively.

Employment Agreement—The Company entered into an employment agreement with one of its officers that requires the payment of annual compensation and certain fringe benefits through 2003 and includes bonus provisions in the form of both stock grants and stock options. In 2000, the Company filed an amendment to the employment agreement that extended the terms of the contract through 2004.

Employee Loan—In March 2001, the Company entered into a $150,000 unsecured loan with one of its officers. The loan accrues interest at a rate of 8 percent per annum with a term of two years. (Buca 10-K 2001; pages F-14,F-15)

From BUCA's 10-K 2002 NOTES: Note 10

---

10. RELATED-PARTY TRANSACTIONS

Management Agreement—In 2000, we entered into a management agreement with a member of our Board of Directors to provide for certain management and administrative services. Management fees of approximately $111,000 in 2000, $91,000 in 2001 and $131,000 in 2002 were paid to such director.

Consulting Fees—The son of a member of our Board of Directors performs architectural and design-related services for us. We paid to him consulting fees of $322,000 in 2000, $297,000 in 2001 and $164,000 in 2002.

Purchase of Inventory—We entered into a vendor relationship with Parasole Restaurant Holdings, Inc., a company owned by two members of our Board, whereby we purchase bread products and a majority of the dessert products offered at our Minneapolis-Saint Paul metropolitan area restaurants. We purchase the products at rates which management believes approximate market rates. The relationship was terminated in 2000. We purchased $92,000 in bakery products in 2000.

Employment Agreements—We entered into an employee agreement with our Chief Executive Officer on July 22, 1996, which was subsequently amended and restated in February 1999, and further amended in September 2000, December 2002, and March 2003. The agreement as amended provides for paying certain salary, fringe benefits and bonus (subject to satisfaction of certain criteria determined by the Compensation Committee of the Board of Directors). The agreement also contains certain confidentiality, non-compete and termination payment provisions, including severance payments of 12 to 24 months. The agreement expires on December 31, 2005.

We entered into employee agreements with both our Executive Vice President and Chief Financial Officer and Chief Operations Officer in December 2002. Each agreement provides for paying certain salary, fringe benefits and bonus (subject to satisfaction of certain criteria determined by the Compensation Committee of the Board of Directors).

---

[10] Obtained from U.S. Securities and Exchange Commission. *www.sec.gov.*

Each agreement also contains certain confidentiality, non-compete and termination payment provisions, including severance payments of 12 to 18 months. The agreements expire on December 31, 2005.

Employee Loan—In March 2001, we entered into a $150,000 unsecured loan with one of our officers. The loan accrued interest at a rate of 8% per annum with a term of two years. The full loan amount and interest were forgiven in 2002 and recorded as a general and administrative expense. (Buca 10-K 2002; pages F-16, F-17)

Mortgage Mayhem

After studying this chapter, you should be able to:

- Explain the role of mortgage-backed securities in the financial meltdown of 2008.
- Identify the role of easy credit in the house price bubble.
- Explain the major public and private sector roles in the dramatic growth of the mortgage lending industry and the securitization of mortgages.
- Identify and describe the major risk factors inherent in subprime loans.
- Identify the increase in the high-risk portion of Countrywide's loans.
- Detect and explain the signals in Countrywide's financial statements that could have alerted readers that Countrywide's allowance for loan losses may have been underestimated.

Countrywide is presented as an example of:

- Inadequate loan disclosures in SEC filings
- Underestimation of allowance for loan losses

CHAPTER OUTLINE

- The Housing Bubble
- Easy Credit: Securitization
- Easy Profit: Tranching
- Easy Banking: Regulations Repealed
- Easy Investing: Credit Default Swaps
- Hard Times
- The Countrywide Story
- Countrywide's Misleading Description of Loans in SEC Filings

THE HOUSING BUBBLE

... [I]t is in the nature of a speculative boom that almost anything can collapse it. Any serious shock to confidence can cause sales by those speculators who have always hoped to get out before the final collapse.... Their pessimism will infect those simpler souls who had thought the market might go up forever.... So the bubble breaks.

J. K. Galbraith, p. 90
The Great Crash 1929

The great American dream of homeownership turned into a nightmare in late 2007, when the housing bubble burst and house prices began to plunge. While many struggling homeowners were victims of unscrupulous mortgage lenders who had sold them seriously flawed loans, some were victims of their own greed and belief in the mistaken myth that the housing market would continue to rise forever. The plunge in house prices marked the beginning of the financial recession and the 2008 Wall Street crash that spread its tentacles into the global economy for years to come.

John Kenneth Galbraith's description of the Great Crash of 1929 is equally true of what happened on Wall Street in 2008. Galbraith explained that during a speculative boom, investors purchase an asset not for the fruits of the asset or the use of it, but for the purpose of selling the asset at a higher price. This leads to a **bubble**, or an inflated price for an asset that is not justified on the grounds of its actual value—for example, a share's price that is not supported by its earnings or a house's price that is not supported by the rents it could earn. Based on this definition of a bubble, house prices in the United States in the early part of the 21st century clearly had foundations of sand—or even quicksand.

Galbraith explained that opportunists begin to ignore the reasons behind rising prices. He wrote that the world before the Great Crash was "a world inhabited not by people who have to be persuaded to believe but by people who want an excuse to believe" (1997, p. 3). With wry humor, Galbraith observed that indispensable aspects of the speculative boom mood include "an inordinate desire to get rich quickly with a minimum of physical effort" (p. 3). He also noted that once the decision has been made to invest in an asset solely for the reason of selling it at a higher price, the investor would be best rewarded in a leveraged transaction if the price does indeed rise. If an investor puts down 20 percent to acquire 100 percent of an asset and the asset increases in price by 100 percent, the investment grows to 1,000 percent of the original outlay. Galbraith thus viewed leveraged transactions as frequent catalysts in boom-bust cycles. Of course, add easy credit—in the form of easy mortgage loans— to this recipe, and you have all the ingredients for a spectacular boom-bust cycle. In addition, throw mortgage-backed securities into the mixture and you have a formula for disaster: the collapse of the bubble that is now known as the financial meltdown of 2008.

In its *Financial Crisis Inquiry Report* of 2011, the Commission on the Causes of the Financial and Economic Crisis explained why the housing bubble was particularly toxic:

> Unlike so many other bubbles—tulip bulbs in Holland in the 1600s, South Sea stocks in the 1700s, Internet stocks in the late 1990s—this one involved not just another commodity but a building block of community and social life and a cornerstone of the economy: the family home. Homes are the foundation upon which many of our social, personal, governmental, and economic structures rest. Children usually go to schools linked to their home addresses; local governments decide how much money they can spend on roads, firehouses, and public safety based on how much property tax revenue they have; house prices are tied to consumer spending. Downturns in the housing industry can cause ripple effects almost everywhere. (p. 4)

EASY CREDIT: SECURITIZATION

The housing boom, like most booms, was fueled by easy credit. Homeownership has long been a part of the American Dream, and as such, it has enjoyed a long history of strong support from the federal government.

In 1938, toward the end of the Great Depression, the Federal National Mortgage Association—or "Fanny Mae"—was established in order to buy up mortgages that were guaranteed by the Federal Housing Administration. After World War II, Fannie Mae bought mortgages that were guaranteed by the Veterans Administration. The original purpose of Fannie Mae was to stimulate the funding and issue of government-insured mortgage loans.

With the 1968 Charter Act, Fannie Mae took the first step in its dramatic evolution: To facilitate affordable housing, its mandate was expanded to include the purchase of regular mortgages that were not government-guaranteed ("Fannie Mae Early History," 2004). Fannie Mae was by now a hybrid entity, being a government enterprise as well as having shareholders.

In 1970, the Federal Home Mortgage Corporation—or "Freddie Mac"—was chartered by Congress to "to keep money flowing to mortgage lenders in support of homeownership and rental housing" ("About Freddie Mac," 2012). Like Fannie Mae, Freddie Mac also accelerated the funding and issue of mortgage loans by buying up loans from mortgage lenders, freeing up these lenders to make further home loans.

This buying up of government-insured loans, as well as uninsured loans, was the beginning of a trend in separating the critical origination of a loan from the continued ownership of that loan. This trend would eventually be destructively expanded and manipulated to bring the U.S. housing market to the brink of disaster because a lender who sold a loan no longer had a direct interest in future principal and interest payments on that loan. With the goal of homeownership being an intrinsic part of the American mentality, government policy did not end at this level of providing capital for home loans or of separating ownership of the loans from the origination of the loans. Even more capital could be freed up to flow into home loans if Fannie Mae were allowed to sell to investors the loans it had purchased from lenders. This process of selling its loans could be accelerated if Fannie Mae were allowed to pool together large quantities of loans and sell interests in those loans to investors in the form of securities in a process known as **securitization**. The 1968 Charter Act gave Fannie Mae the authority to do exactly that ("Fannie Mae Early History, 2004").

In 1970, Fannie Mae issued the first mortgage-backed securities (MBSs) in the United States when it sold securities backed by its FHA and VA loan programs and guaranteed the payment of principal and interest. (A **mortgage-backed security** is a financial instrument that gives the owner an interest in a mortgage loan or a partial interest in a pool of mortgage loans.) Shortly thereafter, Freddie Mac began to sell MBSs backed by regular mortgages. It also guaranteed the principal and interest repayments. Fannie Mae and Freddie Mac's mortgage loans enjoyed the support of explicit government guarantees[1] for their FHA and VA loans and implicit guarantees for other loans on the grounds that they were government-sponsored enterprises (GSEs). GSEs are also at times referred to as government-sponsored *entities*.

There were regulations that prohibited institutional investors, such as pension funds and insurance companies, from investing in mortgage-backed securities that were not backed by GSEs. As a result, investors had little appetite for free-enterprise mortgage-backed securities. In their book examining the history of the financial crisis, McLean and Nocera report: "By June 1983, the government agencies had issued almost $230 billion in mortgage-backed securities, while the purely private sector had issued only $10 billion" (2010, p. 13). The Wall Street firms envied the GSEs' advantage in this lucrative sector and lobbied for what they called "a level playing field." The result of this was the Secondary Mortgage Market Enhancement Act of 1984, which allowed institutional investors, such as pension funds and insurance companies, to invest in non-GSE guaranteed mortgage-backed securities. However, the Act stipulated that such low-risk institutional investors could invest in these non-GSE guaranteed securities only if the securities were rated as eligible for such investments by the rating agencies. This elevated investors' trust in the ability of these rating agencies to accurately grade risk. Later, investors learned that this trust was unwarranted. Nevertheless, GSE loans still dominated the MBS market.

EASY PROFIT: TRANCHING

Once Fannie Mae was given permission to buy conventional mortgages and securitize them, "all kinds of new mortgage companies could be formed—companies that competed with banks and S&Ls [Savings and Loans] for mortgage customers" (McLean & Nocera, 2010, p. 20). At first, these lenders concentrated on making loans that adhered to strict underwriting criteria that were required for the loans to be sold to the GSEs; these loans were known as *GSE conforming loans*. Soon, however, other mortgage lenders

---

[1] Fannie Mae and Freddie Mac, while both public companies, are regarded as having "an implicit government guarantee" (Pickert, 2008). In September 2008, Freddie Mac was placed under a conservatorship to be overseen by the Federal Housing Finance Agency. The Treasury purchased $187.5 billion of shares in Fannie and Freddie so that they would remain solvent (Shenn, 2013).

concentrated on making loans with higher loan-to-value (LTV) ratios and loans to borrowers with lower credit scores or reduced documentation. These loans became known as *subprime loans* that could not be sold to GSEs. **Subprime loans** are loans with a higher risk of default. Originally, the term referred to loans that did not conform to GSE underwriting standards. Over time, the term became vague and generally referred to loans with a higher default risk. In addition, these loans were often second mortgages on the same home, making the LTV ratio even higher and the risk of loss or potential default even greater.

It was in this sector of subprime loans that could not be purchased by the GSEs that Wall Street firms could finally securitize mortgages without competition from the GSEs. Wall Street began working on making securitized subprime bonds more appealing to investors. First, these loans charged borrowers high interest rates to compensate for the higher default risk. Second, the firms began offering letters of credit to guarantee payment to investors in the event of default by borrowers. In this way, investment banks could provide free enterprise lenders with AA or AAA ratings from the now powerful credit-rating firms. This, in turn, allowed the low-risk institutional investors to invest in non-GSE mortgage-backed securities.

To add to the mix, the traders developed the practice of **tranching**, which refers to a process of carving up or separating a pool of mortgages into different classes, or tranches, of securities which absorb different default losses. Using tranching, traders "could divide the securities they sold into several tranches, each with a different level of risk, and of return, for the investor" (Tett, 2009, p. 52). Tranches that absorb the initial or most likely default losses are known as *junior tranches* and usually earn a higher rate of return because of their higher risk. The senior tranches generally earn a lower rate of return. Each of the bonds in a pool of bonds that was securitized had a number of different kinds of risk. For example, there were risks such as interest rate payment default, principal repayment default, or late payment. Furthermore, via tranching traders could create securities that paid interest or principal only or made payments on whatever innovative parts of the loans one could imagine.

Securities backed by seemingly safer parts of the pooled mortgages could earn AA or AAA ratings, even if the underlying mortgages as a whole were of a lower grade. The ratings agencies presumably understood "the intricacies of the hundreds of thousands of mortgages inside each security" (McLean & Nocera, 2010, p. 8). The next decade saw dramatic changes in the mortgage industry: "Subprime loans … increased from $35 billion in 1994 to $160 billion in 1999, accounting for 12.5% of all residential mortgages. By 2003, subprime lending was at $330 billion and going strong" (Pridgen, 2005). Mortgage lenders and investments bankers were making enormous profits selling these loans, and investment banks were making money securitizing them.

EASY BANKING: REGULATIONS REPEALED

Following the Great Crash of 1929, the Glass-Steagall Act of 1933 had separated commercial banking from investment banking, preventing commercial banks from trading in securities. This was intended to keep consumers' deposits safe from being used in riskier investment banking activities and to create a firewall to prevent a financial crisis from spreading through both arms of banking. However, in April 1998, Citicorp, a commercial bank, merged with Travelers Insurance, which owned Smith

Barney, an investment bank. This merger, which was structured to "work around" the Glass-Steagall Act ("The Long Demise," 2003), resulted in a huge and unwieldy "conglomerate … empowered to sell securities, make loans, underwrite stocks, sell insurance" (McDonald & Robinson, 2009, p. 6). By the following year, the banking industry had successfully lobbied Congress to scrap Glass-Steagall, and in November 1999, the Financial Services Modernization Act was passed. An opinion piece in *The Economist* celebrated the repeal of Glass-Steagall:

> It is always good to be rid of bad legislation—and Glass-Steagall was a lousy law from day one. Implemented in the darkest days of the Great Depression, the act played to populist beliefs that banks' securities activities caused the Wall Street crash of 1929 and the economic misery that followed in its wake…. Bankers got the blame. Indeed, they were compared unfavourably [sic] with Al Capone. ("The Wall Falls," 1999)

In hindsight, however, opponents of deregulation often cite the rescinding of Glass-Steagall as the biggest single regulatory cause in creating an environment for the financial meltdown of 2008.

The combination of minimal regulation, easy credit, and loan securitization provided fertile ground for fictitious accounting on a large scale. As the real-estate bubble began to implode, some mortgage lenders, mortgage insurers, and investors in mortgage-backed securities overstated earnings by underestimating and understating the allowance for loan losses.

EASY INVESTING: CREDIT DEFAULT SWAPS

With the repeal of the Glass Steagall Act, the number of new mortgage loans grew dramatically, and the securitization of these loans for trading as MBSs began to skyrocket. Soon, home loans were pooled with other loans, such as car loans, credit card debt, and student loans, then carved into tranches and securitized by the investment banks into what became known as *collateralized debt obligations (CDOs)*.

As the mortgage loans being securitized grew increasingly weighted toward loans with higher loan-to-value ratios, or borrowers with poor credit or second loans on the same houses, the banks grew wary of issuing letters of credit guaranteeing the securitized loans against default. They attempted to hedge their bets. The insurance companies stepped in to offer a different kind of derivative to keep the time bomb ticking. A **derivative financial instrument**, or security, derives its value by reference to an asset or index outside of the instrument itself.

For example, one can invest in a copper derivative security that requires that the holder must be paid an amount determined by reference to the level of a copper price index on a specific date. Insurance companies such as AIG and some investment banks began to write instruments that gave the holder of the instrument the right to be paid if the borrowers of the underlying mortgages backing the MBSs and CDOs defaulted. These derivatives were known as **credit-default swaps (CDSs)**. Wall Street legend has it that the concept of the credit-default swap was developed in 1994 by J.P. Morgan bankers during a company weekend at the luxurious Boca Raton Resort & Club in Florida, according to a *Newsweek* article by Matthew Phillips (2008). Such weekends were allegedly often marked by rowdy festivities, skimpily-clad models, and excessive alcohol. Mark Brickell, a J.P. Morgan employee who attended that particular weekend in Boca Raton later commented: "I've known people who worked on the Manhattan Project … [a]nd for those of us on that trip, there was the same kind of feeling of being present at the creation of something incredibly important." Unfortunately, the credit-default swap would eventually wreak its own kind of havoc and would later be dubbed by *Newsweek* as "The Monster That Ate Wall Street." (Quotes from Philips, 2008)

Part of the problem was that investors could purchase these credit-default swaps whether or not they owned the related MBSs or CDOs. This meant that an investor could effectively take a short position on mortgage bonds. If someone owned CDSs and the related bonds failed, the price of the CDSs would rise. Many of the banks were both underwriters of CDSs as well as investors in CDSs issued by other banks or insurers. If housing prices continued to go up, there would be an asset in the form of the house to back loans of up to 100 percent of the value of the house. In such a scenario, selling CDSs would continue to be very profitable. However, if borrowers defaulted and house prices dropped, the CDSs would represent a gigantic liability for the underwriters. The banks alleged that their risks in loans they had securitized and in CDSs they had written were offset by their investments in CDSs that were underwritten by other banks and insurance companies. The problem was that the banks and insurance companies did not have anywhere near enough cash to make good on the CDSs and insurance policies if house prices dropped and borrowers defaulted.

As the issuance of mortgages, CDSs, MBSs, and CDOs mushroomed during the 1990s, the Commodity Futures Trading Commission (CFTC) increasingly thought that it should oversee the trading of CDSs on the grounds that these derivatives amounted to futures contracts. The banks and insurers lobbied strenuously against this to protect their new, highly lucrative profit stream. In 1996, then-President Bill Clinton appointed attorney Brooksley Born as head of the CFTC. Born started pushing hard to get derivatives under her commission's oversight, but many pushed harder to ensure that derivatives were unregulated. Michael Greenberger, the former director of the CFTC, alleged that he once entered Born's office as she was putting down the phone after speaking to former Assistant Treasury Secretary Larry Summers. She indicated that she had been instructed to stop her efforts to have derivatives regulated (*Inside Job*, 2010, p. 20).

In December 2000, the Commodities Futures Modernization Act was passed, and it specifically excluded the regulation of derivatives by the CFTC. From here on, mortgage loans issued with dubious credit, MBSs, CDOs, and CDSs took off on a steep trajectory. The whole toxic mix was simultaneously fueled by reductions in the cash reserves that banks were required to keep, as well as reductions in interest rates by the Federal Reserve Bank. In April 2008, *The Economist* reported:

> Bankers gathering in Vienna this week for the annual bash of the International Swaps and Derivatives Association (ISDA) had some big numbers to celebrate. The overall market for over-the-counter derivatives shot up to $455 trillion at the end of 2007. Some $62 trillion of that were credit-default swaps (CDSs), whose supercharged growth continues in spite of the crunch. ("Clearing the Fog")

Of course, much of this $62 trillion was backed or covered by subprime loans, and most of the issuers of the CDSs had no hope of being able to pay out the amounts that they had guaranteed if mortgage borrowers defaulted and housing prices dropped.

HARD TIMES

As the mortgage lending industry grew in size and in the direction of engineering and securitizing subprime mortgages, credit-default swaps grew as a tool intended to insure investors against loans that went into default. Investment bankers and AIG, as well as the **monoline insurers** (i.e., insurance companies that insure against only one type of risk), wrote CDSs that "guaranteed" to pay the holders of the swaps in the event of default. However, soon the investment banks and mortgage lenders themselves began to invest in CDSs to hedge against claims against them in the event of default on the bonds they had sold or securitized. Also, the investment bankers often held tranches of the pools of bonds that they purchased and securitized; so they invested in CDSs to hedge against losses due to defaults on bonds underlying the mortgage-backed securities that they had pooled but not sold.

According to the *Financial Crisis Inquiry Report* (2011), AIG's model for its CDSs "did not estimate the market value of the underlying securities" (p. 267). AIG's CDS model focused only on estimating actual payment defaults. The *Report* also pointed out that in 2007, Goldman's demand for AIG to post collateral for the decline in market value on a CDO portfolio covered by a CDS surprised senior AIG executives who believed that payments would be required only in the event of actual losses. Soon, rumors began to spread throughout the MBS and CDO markets that AIG and many of the monoline insurers did not have the capital to make good on their so-called "guarantees." This made it even more difficult for mortgage lenders and investment bankers, including Bear Stearns, Merrill Lynch, and Lehman Brothers, to sell their ownership interests in mortgages and MBSs. Fear that the CDS hedges might fail, and knowledge that house prices and the value of their investments in MBSs were falling, made it impossible for Bear, Merrill, and Lehman to get the short-term financing on which they had relied. On February 28, 2008, AIG "reported a net loss of $5.29 billion, largely due to $11.12 billion in valuation losses related to the super-senior CDO credit default swap exposure and more than $2.6 billion in losses relating to the securities-lending business's mortgage-backed purchases" (*Financial Crisis Report*, pp. 273–274).

The *Financial Crisis Inquiry Report* (2011), explained how Merrill Lynch had been keen on subprime assets until the failure, in late 2006, of two mortgage-loan firms that had received extended credit from Merrill (p. 257). After this, Merrill concentrated on pooling its mortgage investments into CDOs and reselling them. However, the "super-senior" tranches (tranches with high credit ratings and lower returns) were hard to sell, and Merrill had to hold a large portion of them. The situation was about to get worse: "By late 2007, the viability of the monoline insurers from which Merrill had purchased almost $100 million in hedges had come into question" (*Financial Crisis Report*, p. 259).

According to the *Report*, by the end of 2008, Merrill had provided for $13 billion of losses in respect of the monolines and close to another $44 billion on other mortgage-related business losses (p. 259). On September 15, 2008, disaster at Merrill Lynch was averted when it was acquired by Bank of America in a U.S. government-assisted sale (*Financial Crisis Report*, p. 353). Earlier that year, on March 24, 2008, Bear Stearns had been rescued by a government-assisted sale to J.P. Morgan (*Financial Crisis Report*, p. 290). Lehman Brothers was not so fortunate.

In her "Testimony Concerning the Lehman Brother's Examiner's Report" (2010), SEC Chairman Mary Schapiro highlighted how the risk-taking that began in 2006 contributed to Lehman's collapse: "Lehman invested its own capital in assets such as subprime and Alt-A residential mortgages and mortgage-backed securities, commercial real estate, and leveraged lending commitments" (p. 3). Schapiro's testimony pointed out that in June 2008, Lehman posted a $2.8 billion loss, which it attributed "primarily to write-downs on residential and commercial mortgage securities and hedges related to these securities" (p. 4). Lehman's efforts throughout the summer of 2008 to raise capital and sell enough of its assets failed to stem a loss of confidence in its viability. In an apparent attempt to increase confidence in its liquidity, Lehman increased its reliance on what has come to be known as the *Repo 105 Transactions*.

In a typical repurchase transaction (repo), a firm "sells" securities for cash with the understanding that the "buyer" will return the securities for a specified price (usually at a 5 percent discount) at a specified future date. The transaction is made on the grounds that control of the asset has not fully passed to the buyer and such repos are usually accounted for as "financings" rather than "sales." However, Schapiro drew attention to the fact that Lehman "treated repos as sales" for accounting purposes (p. 6). Schapiro cited the conclusion of the *Bankruptcy Examiner's Report* that Lehman's "motive for the transactions was ultimately to reduce its leverage: to temporally remove tens of billions of dollars in assets from its balance sheet at the end of financial reporting periods and use the cash to pay down liabilities as a means to reduce its reported leverage[2]" (p. 6).

The Lehman Bankruptcy Examiner (2010) described Lehman's accounting for Repo 105 transactions as follows:

> Lehman accounted for Repo 105 transactions as "sales" as opposed to financing transactions based upon the overcollateralization or higher than normal haircut in a Repo 105 transaction. By recharacterizing the Repo 105 transaction as a "sale," Lehman removed the inventory from its balance sheet.
>
> Lehman regularly increased its use of Repo 105 transactions in the days prior to reporting periods to reduce its publicly reported net leverage and balance sheet. Lehman's periodic reports did not disclose the cash borrowing from the Repo 105 transaction–*i.e.*, although Lehman had in effect borrowed tens of billions of dollars in these transactions, Lehman did not disclose the known obligation to repay the debt. Lehman used the cash from the Repo 105 transaction to pay down other liabilities, thereby reducing both the total liabilities and the total assets reported on its balance sheet and lowering its leverage ratios. Thus, Lehman's Repo 105 practice consisted of a two-step process: (1) undertaking Repo 105 transactions followed by (2) the use of Repo 105 cash borrowings to pay down liabilities, thereby reducing leverage. A few days after the new quarter began, Lehman would borrow the necessary funds to repay the cash borrowing plus interest, repurchase the securities, and restore the assets to its balance sheet.
>
> Lehman never publicly disclosed its use of Repo 105 transactions, its accounting treatment for these transactions, the considerable escalation of its total Repo 105 usage in late 2007 and into 2008, or the material impact these transactions had on the firm's publicly reported net leverage ratio. (pp. 732–734)

---

[2] Schapiro's "Testimony" cites the Bankruptcy Examiner's Report, pp. 732–734.

It must be emphasized that, in May 2012, the SEC ended their investigation of Lehman and did not recommend any action against them. In addition, the SEC concluded that Lehman had not contravened GAAP. However, post Lehman, accounting rules have been changed. (Gallu, 2012)

According to the *Wall Street Journal*, "no former Lehman top executives, including CEO Richard Fuld, have been charged with any criminal behavior" (Eaglesham & Rappaport, 2011). In fact, it is highly likely that "Lehman Brother's Probably Won't Ever Be Charged With Anything" (Coscarelli, 2012).

According to Schapiro, Lehman was required to furnish growing amounts of security in order to continue doing business but was unable to keep up with these demands because a number of lenders refused to provide even regular loans to the beleaguered investment bank (p. 4). No government-sponsored plan was successfully executed for the sale or rescue of Lehman Brothers, which filed for bankruptcy on September 15, 2008—the same day that Merrill Lynch was acquired by Bank of America (*Financial Crisis Report*, p. 353).

Schapiro (2010) summarized the factors that contributed to both the financial crisis and the demise of Lehman as follows:

- Irresponsible lending practices, which were facilitated by a securitization process that originally was viewed as a risk reduction mechanism;
- Excessive reliance on credit ratings by investors;
- A wide-spread view that markets were almost always self-correcting and an inadequate appreciation of the risks of deregulation that, in some areas, resulted in weaker standards and regulatory gaps;
- The proliferation of complex financial products, including derivatives, with illiquidity and other risk characteristics that were not fully transparent or understood;
- Perverse incentives and asymmetric compensation arrangements that encouraged excessive risk-taking;
- Insufficient risk management and risk oversight by companies involved in marketing and purchasing complex financial products;
- A siloed financial regulatory framework that lacked the ability to monitor and reduce risks flowing across regulated entities and markets; and
- The lack of an adequate statutory framework for the oversight of large investment bank holding companies on a consolidated basis. (p. 1)

THE COUNTRYWIDE STORY[3]

To a large extent, the journey of Countrywide Financial Corporation, from its inception in 1969 to its collapse in 2007 and its purchase by Bank of America in 2008, mirrors the evolution of the mortgage industry. As described earlier in this chapter, once Fannie Mae was given permission to buy conventional mortgages that were not government-guaranteed, the door was opened to the formation of new types of mortgage companies that competed with banks and savings and loans. Many of these lenders followed an evolution that began with making safe, conforming loans to GSEs and then expanding

---

[3] General background information in this section is from *The Financial Crisis Inquiry Report*, 2011; *Friends of Angelo*, 2009; *McLean & Nocera*, 2010; Michaelson, 2009; SEC Complaint June 4, 2009; SEC Complaint Dec. 7, 2009; and *The Subprime Lending Crisis*, 2007.

into high-risk subprime loans. These subprime loans were often pooled and sold to the secondary market as whole loans or as mortgage-backed securities.

According to numerous reports, Angelo Mozilo (cofounder of Countrywide with David Loeb[4]) established Countrywide with the passion of a true believer in the benefits of homeownership. Adam Michaelson (2009), in his book *The Foreclosure of America*, stated that Mozilo and Loeb "had a dream that they could build a new kind of mortgage company and one day be in the position to help all Americans achieve the dream of home ownership" (p. 140). With this goal, the company that later became Countrywide Financial Corporation began in Calabasas, California, as Countrywide Credit Industries.

Mozilo had the vision, the energy, and the charisma to grow Countrywide into the largest mortgage lender in the nation. By 1992, Countrywide was the nation's biggest original lender of single-family mortgages, and the company continued to grow. According to the SEC, Countrywide "originated over $490 billion in mortgage loans in 2005, over $450 billion in 2006, and over $408 billion in 2007" (SEC Complaint, October 24, 2012, par. 3). Wall Street analysts would wait with bated breath to hear what Mozilo had to say about mortgages and the housing market. In fact, by the summer of 2007 (shortly before the mortgage bubble burst), "Mozilo *was* the market" (Muolo & Padilla, 2010, p. 2).

The SEC summed up Countrywide's early business model as follows: "Historically, Countrywide's primary business had been originating prime conforming loans that were saleable to Government Sponsored Entities (GSEs)" (SEC Complaint, June 4, 2009, par. 17). This was a solid business model because in the early days, the GSEs would buy only mortgage loans that conformed to low-risk standards and important attributes such as loan to home-value ratios, borrowers' debt-to-income ratios, and their credit scores. At the time of Countrywide's inception, securitization did not yet exist, and Countrywide depended on selling its low-risk loans to the GSEs in order to obtain further capital to make more loans.

Michaelson (2009), a vice president at Countrywide from 2003–2006, wrote of the high standards instilled in the Countrywide workforce during his early days at the company:

> With a precision and a professionalism I had not seen since the Air Force, the mechanisms of Countrywide processes, procedures, checking and rechecking, and attention to perfect, verifiable detail had to be on a par with or exceeding that of NASA. (p. 111)

However, in the mortgage industry, more and more nonconforming loans were purchased, pooled, and segmented into tranches of different grades of risk and then sold to investors as mortgage-backed securities. Soon, Countrywide had many competitors who concentrated on these precarious, large subprime loans with riskier loan-to-value ratios, debt-to-income ratios, and credit scores, as well as lacking in the documentation of income. To remain competitive, Countrywide jumped on the subprime bandwagon. The nature of the company's transition from prime conforming loans to prime nonconforming loans and subprime loans can be seen in Table 9.1, extracted from the SEC's June 4, 2009, Complaint.

---

[4] Loeb died in July 2003, at the age of 79. He was the retired chairman of IndyMac which, "split off from Countrywide in 1997" (Vincent, 2003).

TABLE 9.1	Countrywide's Move from Prime Mortgage Loans to Subprime, Non-Conforming and Home Equity Loans*					
	2001	**2002**	**2003**	**2004**	**2005**	**2006**
Prime Conforming	50%	59.6%	54.2%	38.2%	32%	31.9%
Prime Non-Conforming	16.5%	24.5%	31.4%	38.7%	47.2%	45.2%
Home Equity	6.8%	4.6%	4.2%	8.5%	9.0%	10.2%
Nonprime (Subprime)	7.8%	3.7%	4.6%	11.0%	8.9%	8.7%
FHA/VA	18.9%	7.6%	5.6%	3.6%	2.1%	2.8%
Commercial	0.0%	0.0%	0.0%	0.0%	0.8%	1.2%

* Obtained from SEC Complaint, June 4, 2009. U.S. Securities and Exchange Commission. Par. 18. *www.sec.gov*.

The SEC Complaint (June 4, 2009) described up Countrywide's dramatic transformation as follows:

> In 2004, Countrywide's reported production of conventional conforming loans dropped to 38.2%, its production of subprime loans had risen to 11%, its production of home equity loans had risen to 8.5%, and its production of conventional non-conforming loans had risen to 38.7%. By 2006, Countrywide had turned its prior business model on its head: a mere 31.9% of its originations were conforming, 45.2% were non-conforming, 8.7% were subprime, and 10.2% were home equity. (par. 19)

As the subprime mortgage lenders lowered underwriting standards, competition to remain the biggest lender may have been one of the forces that drove Countrywide deeper and deeper into high-risk subprime loans. The higher interest rates on subprime loans may also have been a contributing factor.

A 2007 article in the *New York Times* reported, "Last year, for example, the profit margins Countrywide generated on subprime loans that it sold to investors were 1.84 percent, versus 1.07 percent on prime loans." According to former Countrywide employees, "[T]he company's commission structure rewarded sales representatives for making risky, high-cost loans." (Quotes from Morgenson, 2007)

Increased Credit Risk

A particularly risky loan was the 80/20 loan, whereby the borrower took out a loan for 80 percent of the purchase price of the house as well as a second loan for 20 percent of the purchase price, with the result that at the time of purchase, the borrower had no equity in the house. Internal e-mails sent in March and April 2006 show that senior officers at Countrywide were aware of the risks associated with these essentially 100 percent loans, especially when the loans were made under exceptions to underwriting compliance guidelines. In fact, in March 2006, Mozilo stated in an e-mail that the 80/20 subprime loan was "the most dangerous product in existence and there can be nothing more toxic and therefore requires that no devia-tion from guidelines be permitted irrespective of the circumstances" (SEC Complaint, June 4, 2009, par. 48).

Pay-Option ARM Loans

Perhaps the high-risk loan that most dramatically captured public attention during the financial meltdown of 2008 was the **pay-option ARM loan**. These adjustable-rate mort-gage loans allowed for a variety of payments options, one of which was "a minimum payment which was insufficient to cover accruing interest" (SEC Complaint, June 4, 2009, par. 58). Typically, once the unpaid interest on the loan reached 15 percent of the principal amount borrowed, the loan repayment would reset so that future payments would cover both principal and interest. According to the SEC, most of these loans were held for investment as opposed to being sold into the secondary market.

Adam Michaelson (2009) described the meeting at which Countrywide announced the establishment of the pay-option loan, and after the announcement, he asked, "How did you reach the conclusion that home values, and therefore their ability to be refi-nanced, might go up forever?" (p. 21).

Michaelson received the following reply: "Well, forecasting has run the numbers and ... we believe that housing values will continue to rise for the foreseeable future, especially in major metros such as Los Angeles, New York, and others" (p. 20). The speaker continued: "We feel strongly that we have vetted the scenarios, and the risk is offset by the opportunity for market share and revenue gain ..." (p. 21).

Michaelson then followed up with a second question, "Are you ... *nuts*?" It is clear that although Michaelson thought at the time that the pay-option loan was a foolish idea, when he wrote his book, he did not believe that Countrywide and many of the other lenders were "sinister in their intent." He seems have seen Countrywide as hav-ing been impelled by the "forces of the market place." (Quotes from Michaelson, 2009, pp. 21, x, xiv)

Angelo Mozilo was another Countrywide executive who tried to warn the other executives that these pay-option ARM loans could be toxic. According to the SEC, in April 2006, Mozilo wrote in an e-mail, "Since over 70% [of pay-option ARM customers] have opted to make the lower payment it appears that it is just a matter of time that we will be faced with much higher resets and therefore much higher delinquencies" (qtd. in SEC Complaint, June 4, 2009, par. 63). Less than six months later, Mozilo urged Countrywide Bank to "sell all newly originated pay options and begin rolling off the bank balance sheet, in an orderly manner, pay options currently in that port[folio]" (qtd. in SEC Complaint, June 4, 2009, par. 69).

Countrywide was not the first mortgage lender to introduce the risky pay-option ARM loan. However, these risky loans were issued in addition to the risks on other exception loans issued at standards below regular underwriting standards. The com-pany had a particularly toxic mix of these loans. For example, it had loans based on stated income, loans to borrowers with low credit scores or high debt-to-income ratios, loans with high LTV ratios, 80/20 or 100 percent loans, and pay-option ARM loans. This combination of loans made Countrywide's business model unsustainable once property values stopped rising—and the business model was disastrous when home values fell dramatically.

COUNTRYWIDE'S MISLEADING DESCRIPTION OF LOANS IN SEC FILINGS

The SEC Complaint alleged that the description of Countrywide's loans in its 10-Ks was misleading "because its description of 'prime non-conforming' and 'nonprime' loans in its periodic filings were insufficient to inform investors what type of loans were included in these categories" (June 4, 2009, par. 20). For example, the SEC Complaint alleged:

> Nothing … informed investors that Countrywide's "prime non-conforming" category included loan products with increasing amounts of credit risk. While guidance issued by the banking regulators referenced a credit score ("FICO score") at 660 or below as being an indicator of a subprime loan, some within the banking industry drew the distinction at a score of 620 or below. Countrywide, however, did not consider any FICO score to be too low to be categorized within "prime." Nor did Countrywide's definition of "prime" inform investors that its "prime non-conforming" category included so-called "Alt-A" loan products with increasing amounts of credit risk, such as (1) reduced or no documentation loans; (2) stated income loans; and (3) loans with loan to value or combined loan to value ratios of 95% and higher. Finally, it did not disclose that Pay-Option ARM loans, including reduced documentation Pay-Option ARM loans, were included in the category of prime loans. Moreover, to the extent these extremely risky loans were below the loan limits established by the government sponsored entities that purchased these loans ("GSEs"), they would have been reported by Countrywide as prime conforming loans. In 2005 and 2006, Countrywide's Pay-Option ARMs ranged between 17% and 21% of its total loan originations. (June 4, 2009, par. 21)

The SEC Complaint also maintained that Countrywide did not disclose the extent of the changes to its underwriting guidelines. The company used an automated underwriting system known as "CLUES" that analyzed "several variables such as FICO scores, loan to value ratios, documentation type (e.g., full, reduced, stated) and debt-to-income rations" (June 4, 2009, par. 28). However, "The elevated number of exceptions resulted largely from Countrywide's use of exceptions as part of its matching strategy to introduce new guidelines and product changes" (June 4, 2009, par. 29). Apparently, as early as September 2004, Countrywide's own Risk Management department warned the company's senior officers that "several aggressive features of Countrywide's guidelines (e.g., high loan-to-value programs, ARM loans, interest only loans, reduced documentation loans, and loans with layered risk factors) significantly increased Countrywide's credit risk" (SEC Complaint, June 4, 2009, par. 33).

Although the SEC Complaint (June 4, 2009) alleged that the increased risk of the loans was not fully described in the periodic filings, it should be noted that the filings did reveal signals that could have alerted readers to the possibility of loan losses increasing greatly in the future.

COUNTRYWIDE'S UNDERESTIMATION OF ALLOWANCE FOR LOAN LOSSES

Although the SEC alleges that many of the risk factors were not properly disclosed, in Countrywide's filings, the SEC Complaint (June 4, 2009) did not specifically address Countrywide's calculations of its allowance for loans losses in respect of its loans held for investment on its balance sheets in the years leading up to the enormous loan losses in 2007. In addition, the Complaint did not address Countrywide's calculation of the amounts of the allowances for loan losses on loans held for sale in the years leading up to 2007 or the amounts of Countrywide's provision for representations and warranties on loans it had securitized and sold in the years leading up to 2007. The SEC noted that enormous losses were incurred in 2007 in all of these areas. Considering all these aspects together in Form 10-Q for the third quarter of 2007, the SEC stated the following:

> The company's Form 10-Q, filed on November 9, 2007, disclosed that Countrywide had taken a $1 billion impairment loss on its loans held for sale and mortgage backed securities, and had taken $1.9 billion in credit charges related to its allowance for loan losses and its provision for representations and warranties on loans it had securitized and sold. (SEC Complaint, June 4, 2009, par. 106)

While the SEC Complaint (June 4, 2009) alleged that attributes of the loans underwritten were not properly disclosed, it did not make any allegations regarding the fact that the loan losses in 2007 were much greater than the amounts provided for in the allowances for loan losses in the financial statements in the years leading up to 2007. The 10-K filing for 2007 showed loans held for investment net of an allowance for loan losses of approximately $2.4 billion at December 31, whereas the allowance for loans losses at December 31, 2006, was only approximately $0.33 billion. The possible reason that the SEC Complaint (June 4, 2009) did not make an allegation about the fact that the allowances for loan losses before 2007 were so much smaller than the allowances for loan losses in 2007 could be that even with the alleged undisclosed risk in the loan portfolio description and even with the increased delinquencies, Countrywide may not have known of the size of the losses that would occur. Because Countrywide may have believed that the homes that secured the loans could be sold to recover loans of borrowers who defaulted, the size of the impending losses may unwittingly have been underestimated.

Upon default of loans on which the full interest had to be paid monthly, little or no loss would be incurred on foreclosure as long as house prices did not fall. For pay-option loans, or loans of close to 100 percent on which the borrowers chose to pay less than the interest amount, little or no loss would occur on default and foreclosure as long as house prices continued to rise as fast as the unpaid interest.

For loan losses to occur at the alarming rate and extent to which they did, borrowers had to become delinquent on loan repayments and house prices had to fall. It could be argued that leading up to the financial meltdown, many people honestly might not have anticipated the possibility of a sharp drop in the price of houses. Like the period just before the Great Depression of 1929, "those simpler souls who had thought the market might go up forever" (Galbraith, 1997, p. 90) were highly unrealistic. However, they may have really believed this myth and may have had no deliberate intention to deceive.

SIGNALS OF COUNTRYWIDE'S UNDERESTIMATION OF ALLOWANCE FOR LOAN LOSSES

Here is an examination of some of the signals indicating that a company may have understated its allowance for loan losses. A combination of all three of the following signals is particularly alarming.

SIGNAL #1: ALLOWANCE FOR LOAN LOSSES NOT GROWING IN PROPORTION TO THE INCREASE IN RISKIER LOANS   When the allowance for loan losses does not increase in proportion to the increase in the riskier portion of the company's loans, it is a sign that the allowance for loan losses may be understated.

A shift toward riskier loans could be evidenced by disclosure of an increase in the percentage of any of the following:

- High LTV loans
- Pay-option ARM loans
- 80/20 loans
- Undocumented loans
- Nonconforming loans
- Subprime loans

Riskier loans could also be revealed by disclosure of an increase in the percentage of loans made to borrowers with low FICA scores or to borrowers with high debt-to-income ratios.

According to the SEC's Complaint, "Countrywide began originating Pay-Option ARM loans in 2004; by the second quarter of 2005 21% of Countrywide's loan production was 'Pay-Option ARMS.'" Although Countrywide had publicly lauded the product, the SEC's Complaint stated that "several of Countrywide's senior executives, had concluded that the product's risks to the company were severe." (Quotes from SEC Complaint, June 4, 2009, pars. 58, 59)

Indeed, many articles in the business press had alerted readers to the high risks associated with pay-option loans. On December 20, 2006, an article in the *New York Times* cited a report that projected a high foreclosure rate for subprime mortgages. The report examined a number of factors contributing to the increase in subprime mortgage foreclosures—for example, "adjustable rate mortgages with steep built-in rate and payment increases, prepayment penalties, limited income documentation and no escrow for taxes and insurance. The report said that the features caused a higher risk of default regardless of the borrower's credit score" (Nixon, 2006).

As early as January 2003, an article in the *Wall Street Journal* warned that in the subprime sector, the numbers of delinquent loans and foreclosures were much higher than expected (Barta, 2003). In December 2005, the *Washington Post* published an article titled "Mortgage Stress Seen for '06; Delinquencies on Subprime Loans Likely to Spike, Report Says" (Downey). In September 2006, *Business Week* dubbed adjustable ARM loans "Nightmare Mortgages" and pointed out, "The option adjustable rate mortgage (ARM) might be the riskiest and most complicated home loan product ever created" (Der Hovanesian).

For the years ended December 31, 2004, 2005, and 2006, Countrywide's allowance for loan losses as a percentage of loans held for investment did not increase in proportion to the increased risk due to the increase in the pay-option ARM loan portfolio segment of the loans held for investment. In Table 9.2, note that the allowance for loan losses surprisingly dropped from 0.314 percent of all loans held for investment in 2004, to only 0.27 percent in 2005. It then increased to only 0.333 percent in 2006. Meanwhile, as shown in Table 9.3, the pay-option ARM loans increased dramatically: from $4.7 billion in 2004, to $26.12 billion in 2005, to $32.87 billion in 2006.

TABLE 9.2	Calculation of Countrywide's Allowance for Loan Losses as a Percentage of Loans Held for Investment (before Allowance)*		
2007	**2006**	**2005**	**2004**
2.33%	0.333%	0.27%	0.314%

* Table 9.2 is derived from Exhibits 9.1, 9.2, 9.3, and 9.4 which are given after the Tables.

Table 9.4 reveals that Countrywide's risky pay-option ARM loans grew explosively over this time:

- By the end of 2005, the amount of pay-option ARM loans was 556 percent of the amount at the end of 2004, whereas the allowance for loan losses on all loans held for investment was only 151.3 percent of what it was at the end of 2004.
- By the end of 2006, the amount of pay-option ARM loans was 700 percent of the amount at the end of 2004, whereas the amount for the allowance for loan losses on all loans held for investment was only 209 percent of what it was at the end of 2004.

Clearly, each year the allowance for loan losses was not growing nearly as quickly as the high-risk pay-option ARM loans were growing over the same period of time.

TABLE 9.3	Illustration of Loans and Allowance for Loan Losses Derived from Countrywide's 10-Ks (in thousands, except for percentages)*			
	2007	**2006**	**2005**	**2004**
Loans held for investment Net of allowance for loan losses	$ 98,000,713	$78,085,757**	$69,865,447**	$39,661,191
Allowance for loan losses	$ 2,339,491	$ 261,054**	$ 189,201	$ 125,046
Loans held for investment before allowance for loan losses	$100,340,204	$78,346,811	$70,054,648	$39,786,237
Total pay-option ARM loan portfolio held for investment	$ 28,973,498	$32,866,475	$26,122,952	$ 4,701,795
Pay-option loans delinquent:				
• **90 days or more†**	5.71%	0.65%	0.10%	—
• **60 days or more**	—	—	0.22%	0.08%

* Table 9.3 is derived from Exhibits 9.1, 9.2, 9.3, and 9.4 which are given after the Tables.

** For some years, the amounts stated for "loans held for investment" and for "allowance for loan losses" on the face of the balance sheet changed from the amounts in the year originally stated to the amounts shown as comparatives in the following year's 10-K reports, depending on where they disclosed items such as the pool mortgage insurance receivable. The amounts for 2006, in Table 9.3, are the amounts stated in the original 10-K report's balance sheet that was first available to users. The amounts for 2006 changed the most when stated as comparative amounts in the following years' balance sheets.

† After 2005, only loans delinquent for 90 days or more were reported.

TABLE 9.4	Allowances for Loan Losses on All Loans Held for Investment and Amount of Pay-Option ARM Loans Expressed as a Percentage of 2004 Amounts*

	2005 Amount as a Percentage of 2004 Amount	2006 Amount as a Percentage of 2004 Amount
Allowance for loan losses on all loans held for investment	151.3%	209%
Total pay-option ARM loan portfolio held for investment	556%	700%

* Table 9.4 is derived from Exhibits 9.1, 9.2, 9.3, and 9.4 which are given below.

EXHIBIT 9.1	Extracts from Consolidated Balance Sheets Countrywide Financial Corporation 10-K 2005[5]

	December 31	
	2005	2004
	(in thousands, except share data)	
ASSETS		
Cash	$ 1,031,108	$ 751,237
Mortgage loans and mortgage-backed securities held for sale	36,818,688	37,350,149
Trading securities owned, at fair value	10,314,384	10,558,387
Trading securities pledged as collateral, at fair value	668,189	1,303,007
Securities purchased under agreements to resell, securities borrowed and federal funds sold	23,317,361	13,456,448
Loans held for investment, net of allowance for loan losses of $189,201 and $125,046, respectively	70,071,152	39,661,191
Investments in other financial instruments, at fair value	11,455,745	10,091,057
Mortgage servicing rights, net	12,610,839	8,729,929
Premises and equipment, net	1,279,659	985,350
Other assets	7,518,245	5,608,950
Total assets	$175,085,370	$128,495,705

[5] Obtained from U.S. Securities and Exchange Commission. *www.sec.gov*.

EXHIBIT 9.2 Extracts from Consolidated Balance Sheets Countrywide Financial Corporation 10-K 2006[6]

	December 31	
	2006	2005
	(in thousands, except share data)	
ASSETS		
Cash	$ 1,407,000	$ 1,031,108
Mortgage loans held for sale	31,272,630	36,808,185
Trading securities owned, at fair value	20,036,668	10,314,384
Trading securities pledged as collateral, at fair value	1,465,517	668,189
Securities purchased under agreements to resell, securities borrowed and federal funds sold	27,269,897	23,317,361
Loans held for investment, net of allowance for loan losses of $261,054 and $189,201, respectively	78,085,757	69,865,447
Investments in other financial instruments, at fair value	12,769,451	11,260,725
Mortgage servicing rights, at fair value	16,172,064	—
Mortgage servicing rights, net	—	12,610,839
Premises and equipment, net	1,625,456	1,279,659
Other assets	9,841,790	7,929,473
Total assets	$199,946,230	$175,085,370

EXHIBIT 9.3 Extracts from Consolidated Balance Sheets Countrywide Financial Corporation 10-K 2007[7]

	December 31	
	2007	2006
	(in thousands, except share data)	
ASSETS		
Cash	$ 8,810,399	$ 1,407,000
Mortgage loans held for sale	11,681,274	31,272,630
Trading securities owned, at fair value	14,988,780	20,036,668
Trading securities pledged as collateral, at fair value	6,838,044	1,465,517
Securities purchased under agreements to resell, securities borrowed and federal funds sold	9,640,879	27,269,897
Loans held for investment, net of allowance for loan losses of $2,399,491 and $326,817, respectively	98,000,713	78,019,994
Investments in other financial instruments, at fair value	28,173,281	12,769,451
Mortgage servicing rights, at fair value	18,958,180	16,172,064
Premises and equipment, net	1,564,438	1,625,456
Other assets	13,074,073	9,907,553
Total assets	$ 211,730,061	$ 199,946,230

[6] Obtained from U.S. Securities and Exchange Commission. *www.sec.gov*.
[7] Obtained from U.S. Securities and Exchange Commission. *www.sec.gov*.

SIGNAL #2: ALLOWANCE FOR LOAN LOSSES NOT GROWING IN PROPORTION TO THE INCREASE IN TROUBLED LOANS   When the allowance for loan losses does not increase in proportion to the increase in troubled loans, it is a signal that the allowance for loan losses may be understated. One must search the notes to the financial statements for indications of troubled loans. These indications may be found in references to any of the following:

- Loan delinquencies
- Nonperforming loans
- Loans on which interest is no longer being accrued (non-accrual loans)
- Loans with negative amortization
- Troubled debt restructurings

In the Notes to Countrywide's financial statements (see Exhibit 9.4), the increase in loan repayment delinquencies on pay-option ARM loans, as reported in the years leading up to 2007, preceded the massive allowance for loan losses ($2.3 billion) on all loans held for investment in 2007. As shown in Table 9.3, the percentage of pay-option loans delinquent for more than 60 days increased from 0.08 percent in 2004 to 0.22 percent in 2005. This means that the percentage of loans delinquent for 60 days or more were 2.75 times the percentage of such loans in 2004. However, the allowance for loan losses as a percentage of all loans held for investment actually decreased from 0.314 percent at the end of 2004 to 0.27 percent at the end of 2005. The note to the financial statements showed that although delinquencies increased for the risky pay-option loans, the allowance for loan losses as a percentage of all loans held for investment actually *decreased*.

EXHIBIT 9.4	**Extracts from Notes to the Financial Statements Countrywide Financial Corporation 10-K 2005–2007[8]**

Extract from Note 8 (2005):

Following is a summary of pay-option loans held for investment:

	December 31	
	2005	**2004**
	(In thousands)	
Total pay-option loan portfolio	$26,122,952	$4,701,795
Pay-option loans with accumulated negative amortization:		
Principal	$13,973,619	$ 32,818
Accumulated negative amortization (from original loan balance)	$ 142,034	$ 29

(continued)

---

[8] Obtained from U.S. Securities and Exchange Commission. *www.sec.gov*.

	December 31	
	2005	2004
	(In thousands)	
Original loan-to-value ratio (1)	75%	73%
Original combined loan-to-value ratio (2)	78%	75%
Average original FICO score	720	730
Delinquencies (3)	0.22%	0.08%

(1) The ratio of the lower of the appraised value or purchase price of the property to the amount of the loan that is secured by the property.
(2) The ratio of the lower of the appraised value or purchase price of the property to the amount of all loans secured by the property.
(3) Loans delinquent more than 60 days, including non-accrual loans.
Management expects the delinquency rate in the Company's pay-option loan portfolio to increase to a level consistent with the delinquency rate of the rest of the portfolio of loans held for investment as this new product seasons.

Extract from Note 8 (2006):

Following is a summary of pay-option ARM loans held for investment:

	December 31	
	2006	2005
	(in thousands)	
Total pay-option ARM loan portfolio	$32,866,475	$26,122,952
Total principal balance of pay-option ARM loans with accumulated negative amortization	$29,074,810	$13,973,619
Accumulated capitalized interest (from original loan balance)	$ 655,453	$ 74,815
Average original loan-to-value ratio (1)	75%	75%
Average combined original loan-to-value ratio (2)	78%	78%
Average original FICO score (3)	718	720
Loans delinquent 90 days or more	0.65%	0.10%

(1) The ratio of the lower of the amount of the loan that is secured by the property to the original appraised value or purchase price of the property.
(2) The ratio of the lower of the amount of all loans secured by the property to the original appraised value or purchase price of the property.
(3) A FICO score is a measure of borrower creditworthiness determined using a statistical model. FICO scores range from approximately 300 to 850, with a higher score indicating an individual with a more favorable credit profile.
Management expects the delinquency rate in the Company's pay-option ARM loan portfolio to increase as this product seasons.

Extract from Note 8 (2007):

Following is a summary of negatively amortizing ARM loans held for investment:

	December 31	
	2007	2006
	(in thousands)	
Total Pay-Option loan portfolio	$28,973,498	$32,866,475
Total principal balance of Pay-Option loans with accumulated negative amortization	$26,434,496	$29,074,810
Accumulated negative amortization (from original loan balance)	$ 1,233,165	$ 655,453
Unpaid principal balance of Pay-Option loans with supplemental mortgage insurance coverage	$18,374,251	$ 5,729,532
Average original loan-to-value ratio (1)	76%	75%
Average original combined loan-to-value ratio (2)	79%	78%
Average original FICO score (3)	717	718
Loans underwritten with low or no stated income documentation	81%	81%
Borrowers electing to make less than full interest payments	71%	77%
Loans delinquent 90 days or more (4)	5.71%	0.65%

(1) The ratio of the amount of the loan that is secured by the property to the lower of the original appraised value or purchase price of the property.
(2) The ratio of the amount of all loans secured by the property to the lower of the original appraised value or purchase price of the property.
(3) A FICO score is a measure of borrower creditworthiness determined using a statistical model. FICO scores range from approximately 300 to 850, with a higher score indicating an individual with a more favorable credit profile.
(4) Based upon unpaid principal balance.

In the 2006 10-K, there was a change to Note 8 on loans held for investment from reporting delinquencies of more than 60 days, to reporting delinquencies of more than 90 days. As shown in Table 9.3, the percentage of pay-option loans delinquent for 90 days or more, increased from 0.10 percent in 2005 to 0.65 percent in 2006. This means that the percentage of loans delinquent for 90 days or more in 2006 was 6.5 times as high as in 2005. However, the allowance for loan losses for all loans held for investment increased by only 38 percent from the end of 2005 to the end of 2006. The allowance for loan losses on all loans held for investment was not increasing nearly as quickly as the reported delinquencies on the risky pay-option ARM loans were increasing. Allowance for loan losses as a percentage of all loans held for investment actually decreased from 2004 to 2005, whereas loan delinquencies on pay-option ARM loans increased dramatically. In the early years, after the introduction of the pay-option ARM loan product, before many of the loan payments reset, these loans had a lower delinquency rate than the rest of the portfolio. However, this was no prediction of delinquencies in later years, after more of the loans would reset. The rapid increase in delinquencies of pay-option ARM loans from 2004–2006 was a signal of the rapid future increases in delinquencies and loan losses that were likely to occur as the loans reset over time. Of course, one would not expect the allowance for loan losses on all loans held for investment to increase in the exact same proportion as the delinquencies on the pay-option ARM loan section of all loans. However, delinquent pay-option ARM loans are troubled loans, and in the absence of the reporting of other measures of troubled loans in total, one should take it as an alert when the allowance for loan losses as a percentage of all loans held does not increase nearly as significantly as the increase in delinquencies on a significant and high-risk section of the loan portfolio such as pay-option ARM loans.

There were two clear signals in Countrywide's financial statements that loan losses in 2007 could be much greater than the allowance for loan losses at the end of 2006:

1. The allowance for loan losses was not increasing nearly as much as the high-risk pay-option section of the total loans held for investment was growing. (See Signal #1.)
2. The allowance for all loan losses was not increasing nearly as much as the delinquencies on pay-option loans were increasing.

In fact, huge losses became evident in 2007, when the allowance for loan losses on all loans held for investment jumped from $0.261[9] billion in 2006 to $2.34 billion in 2007.

SIGNAL #3: ALLOWANCE FOR LOAN LOSSES NOT INCREASING SIGNIFICANTLY AS HOUSE PRICES FALL

If the allowance for home loan losses does not increase when the value of houses decreases, it is a signal that the company may be understating the allowance for loan losses. The value of the house is the security for the loan if the borrower becomes unable to pay the loan. If the loans become troubled and the price of houses declines, there is an increased likelihood that the lender will suffer a loss on the loan.

In August 2006, *Barron's* published an article by Lon Witter stating that the Commerce Department's estimates indicated that house prices had started to fall and that the price of new homes in the United States had dropped 3 percent since the beginning of the year. The article went on to say, "By any traditional valuation, housing prices at the end of 2005 were 30% to 50% too high." It warned that "a housing crisis approaches" (Witter, 2006). Indeed, the prediction in *Barron's* proved to be correct.

Loans with close to 100 percent loan-to-value ratios and loans on which interest is not being fully paid depend on rising house prices to avoid loan losses when borrowers default. Instructed by the financial meltdown of 2008, we now know that if a lender's allowance for loan losses does not increase significantly when house prices stall or begin to fall, it is a strong signal that the allowance for loan losses is underestimated.

---

[9] In the 2007 10-K, the comparative amount for the 2006 allowance for loan losses on loans held for investment was stated as $0.327 billion. In the 2006 10-K, the allowance for loan losses was stated as $0.261 billion. Either way, there was a dramatic increase from 2006 to 2007.

AN OVERVIEW OF COUNTRYWIDE'S NOTES TO ITS FINANCIAL STATEMENTS

Although the SEC's Complaint (June 4, 2009) alleged that Countrywide did not fully disclose all the risky attributes associated with its loans, note that Countrywide's filings in the years leading up to 2007 did disclose increased delinquencies on loan repayments by its borrowers on pay-option ARM loans held for investment. Countrywide's notes to its financial statements did disclose a large increase pay-option ARM loans as a percentage of its portfolio. The notes also disclosed a significant increase in the pay-option ARM loans with accumulated negative amortization in its loans held for investment. However, the allowance for loan losses in Countrywide's financial statements did not increase in proportion to the increase in the percentage of delinquencies reported on pay-option ARM loans, or in proportion to the increase in the high-risk pay-option ARM loans or the increase in loans with accumulated negative amortization. The relevant notes are presented in Exhibit 9.4.

ACCOUNTING LESSONS FROM THE MORTGAGE CRISIS

Going forward, we can take instruction from the mortgage-backed securities crisis that was at the heart of the financial meltdown of 2008. It is a signal that loan loss provisions in financial statements are probably understated when they do not rise in proportion to delinquencies on loan repayments or other indications of troubled loans. It is an additional signal when house prices begin to decline and provisions for loan losses do not rise in proportion to delinquencies or other signs of troubled loans. It is also an indication that loan losses may be understated when the provision for loan losses does not increase in proportion to the increase in the high-risk loans portion of a lender's loan portfolio.

ARE THEY LIVING HAPPILY EVER AFTER?

- **Countrywide**, once the largest mortgage company in the United States, was acquired by Bank of America in 2008. Countrywide has faced a barrage of lawsuits over the years. In April 2013, Countrywide agreed to pay $500 million in three connected class-action lawsuits "to settle claims that it misrepresented the investment quality of mortgage-backed securities" (Raub, 2013). On October 23, 2013, "Bank of America Corp.'s Countrywide unit was found liable by a jury for selling Fannie Mae and Freddie Mac thousands of defective loans in the first mortgage-fraud case brought by the U.S. government to go to trial" (Hurtado, 2013). The U.S. Attorney's office is requesting fines of up to $848 million.
- **Angelo Mozilo**, former CEO of Countrywide, settled an SEC civil fraud case for $67.5 million in October 2010. Bank of America paid $45 million of this amount. Mozilo did not admit or deny any wrongdoing in respect of this case (Dobuzinskis & Levine, 2010). A criminal investigation against Mozilo was never officially announced and was quietly dropped in February 2011. Federal prosecutors reportedly determined that Mozilo's actions "did not amount to criminal wrongdoing" (Reckard, 2011).
- **David Sambol** (formerly president of Countrywide) **and Eric Sieracki** (formerly CFO of Countrywide) also settled SEC charges in 2010 (Dobuzinskis & Levine, 2010). They agreed to the payment of fines and "neither admitted nor denied the government's charges" (Morgenson, 2010).

Key Terms

ETHICS AT WORK

Read the extract below from the 2011 speech on "The Role of Compliance and Ethics in Risk Management," by Carlo di Florio, Director of the SEC's Office of Compliance Inspections and Examinations; then respond to the following questions.

Questions:

a. Consider some of the ways in which the different links in the chain (from borrowers to mortgage lenders, insurers, and investment bankers) that led to the financial meltdown of 2008 may not have fully disclosed risks to parties with whom they dealt. Specifically, reflect on the Supreme Court statement from almost 50 years ago and discuss how it applies to the crisis of 2008.

b. Do you think that a conflict of interest exists if an investment bank sells mortgage-backed securities (MBSs) to its clients while the bank itself invests in credit-default swaps (CDSs) that essentially bet on the default of the same MBSs that it sells? Explain your answer.

Extract from:

The Role of Compliance and Ethics in Risk Management*

Carlo V. di Florio Director, Office of Compliance Inspections and Examinations[1]
NSCP National Meeting
October 17, 2011

Today I would like to address two related topics that are growing in importance: the heightened role of ethics in an effective regulatory compliance program, and the role of both ethics and compliance in enterprise risk management. The views that I express here today are of course my own and do not necessarily reflect the views of the Commission or of my colleagues on the staff of the Commission.

In the course of discussing these two topics, I would like to explore with you the following propositions:

1. Ethics is fundamental to the securities laws, and I believe ethical culture objectives should be central to an effective regulatory compliance program.

---

*Obtained from U.S. Securities and Exchange Commission. *www.sec.gov.*
[1] The Securities and Exchange Commission, as a matter of policy, disclaims responsibility for any private statements by its employees.

2. Leading standards have recognized the centrality of ethics and have explicitly integrated ethics into the elements of effective compliance and enterprise risk management.

3. Organizations are making meaningful changes to embrace this trend and implement leading practices to make their regulatory compliance and risk management programs more effective.

Ethics and the Federal Securities Laws

The debate about how law and ethics relate to each other traces all the way back to Plato and Aristotle. I am not the Director of the Office of Legal Philosophy, so I won't try to contribute to the received wisdom of the ages on this enormous topic,[2] except to say that for my purposes today, the question really boils down to staying true [to] both the spirit and the letter of the law.

Framed this way, ethics is a topic of enormous significance to anyone whose job it is to seek to promote compliance with the federal securities laws. At their core, the federal securities laws were intended by Congress to be an exercise in applied ethics. As the Supreme Court stated almost five decades ago,

> [a] fundamental purpose, common to [the federal securities] ... statutes, was to substitute a philosophy of full disclosure for the philosophy of caveat emptor and thus to achieve a high standard of business ethics in the securities industry.... "It requires but little appreciation ... of what happened in this country during the 1920's and 1930's to realize how essential it is that the highest ethical standards prevail" in every facet of the securities industry.[3]

Of course, what has happened through the financial crisis I believe is yet another reminder of the fundamental need for stronger ethics, risk management and regulatory compliance practices to prevail. Congress has responded once again, as it did after the Great Depression, with landmark legislation to raise the standards of business ethics in the banking and securities industries.

---

[2] For a deeper plunge into the relationship between law and ethics, a classic exchange on this subject can be found in Positivism and the Separation of Law and Morals, H.L.A. Hart, 71 Harvard L. Rev. 529 (1958) and Positivism and Fidelity to Law: A Reply to Professor Hart, L.L. Fuller, 71 Harvard L. Rev. 630 (1958).
[3] *SEC v. Investment Research Bureau, Inc.*, 375 U.S. 180, 186-87 (1963), quoting *Silver v. New York Stock Exchange*, 373 U.S. 341, 366 (1963).

Assignments

TRUE/FALSE QUESTIONS

Answer the following questions with T for true or F for false for more practice with key terms and concepts from this chapter.

1. Leveraged transactions are frequent catalysts in boom-bust cycles.

   T   F

2. The housing boom was caused by mortgage lenders demanding large down payments from home buyers.

   T   F

3. Fannie Mae and Freddie Mac were established to accelerate the funding and issue of mortgage loans.

   T   F

4. Pooling a number of loans and selling interests in those loans to investors as securities is known as *tranching*.

   T   F

5. As a result of the process of tranching, a ratings agency could give a higher credit rating to a class of securities carved from a pool of loans than would be given to other classes of securities carved from the same pool of loans.

   T   F

6. The term *underwriting standards* refers to the credit risk standards that lenders require to be met before they will grant a loan to a borrower.

   T   F

7. The Glass-Steagall Act of 1933 had separated commercial banking from investment banking, which prevented commercial banks from trading in securities.

   T   F

8. A credit-default swap is a derivative financial instrument that gives only the original lender of the underlying loan the right to payment if the borrower defaults on repayments.

   T   F

9. The 80/20 loan is a mortgage loan whereby the borrower takes out a loan for 80 percent of the purchase price and a second loan for 20 percent of the purchase price, leaving the borrower with no equity in the house at the time of the loan.

   T   F

10. Although the SEC Complaint (June 4, 2009) alleged that Countrywide's description of prime nonconforming and nonprime loans in its 10-K filings was misleading, Countrywide's 10-K filings did reveal that its delinquencies on its pay-option ARM loans were increasing much more rapidly than its allowance for loan losses on all of its loans held for investment.

    T   F

FILL-IN-THE-BLANK QUESTIONS

Fill in the blanks with information and concepts from this chapter.

11. A *bubble* refers to an inflated price for an asset that is not supported by the _____ of the asset.

12. The housing boom, like most booms, was fueled by easy _____.

13. The process in which many loans are pooled together and interests in these pooled loans are sold to investors is known as _____.

14. An MBS is a financial _____ that gives the owner a partial interest in a pool of mortgage loans.

15. In 1970, _____ _____ issued the first MBSs in the United States when it sold securities backed by its FHA and VA loans.

16. Before the passage of the Secondary Mortgage Market Enhancement Act of 1984, there were regulations that prohibited _____ investors from investing in mortgage-backed securities that were not backed by GSEs.

17. Loans that adhered to strict underwriting criteria that were required for the loans to be sold to the GSEs were known as "GSE _____ loans."

18. Tranching is a process of carving up or separating a pool of mortgages into different classes of securities that absorb different _____ losses.

19. The Glass-Steagall Act of 1933 _____ commercial banking from investment banking to prevent consumers' deposits from being used in risky investment banking activities such as trading in securities.

20. A credit-default swap is a financial instrument that gives the holder the right to be paid if the borrowers of the specified loans _____.

MULTIPLE-CHOICE QUESTIONS

21. It is likely that a price bubble exists when:

(a) The price of an asset increases sharply.

(b) The earnings related to an asset increase sharply.

(c) An asset's price and its earnings increase sharply.

(d) An asset's price increases faster than its earnings.

22. The 1968 Charter Act facilitated the granting of mortgage loans by:

(a) Establishing the Federal National Mortgage Association to buy up mortgages that were guaranteed by the Federal Housing Administration (Fannie Mae).

(b) Expanding the mandate of Fannie Mae to include the purchase of mortgages that were not government-guaranteed.

(c) Establishing the Federal Home Mortgage Corporation, or Freddie Mac.

(d) Ending regulations that prohibited institutional investors from investing in mortgage-backed securities that were not backed by GSEs.

23. The Secondary Mortgage Market Enhancement Act of 1984:

(a) Allowed the GSEs (Fannie Mae and Freddie Mac) to sell MBSs (mortgage-backed securities) backed by FHA and VA loans.

(b) Allowed institutional investors such as pension funds and insurance companies to invest in non-GSE guaranteed mortgage-backed securities on the condition that they received appropriate ratings from the ratings agencies.

(c) Stipulated that securities that were backed by a pool of loans had to be categorized into different tranches, or classes, that absorbed different default losses.

(d) Repealed or ended the regulations that had required the separation of investment banking from commercial banking.

24. A credit-default swap:

(a) Is a form of derivative financial instrument.

(b) Is a financial instrument that gives the holder of the instrument the right to receive payment from the writer of the instrument if investments in specified loans suffer defaults or losses.

(c) Could give the holder of the instrument the right to payment on the default of a specified loan even if the holder of the instrument did not have a direct investment in the loan.

(d) All of the above.

25. The Commodities Futures Modernization Act of 2000 and the repeal of the Glass-Steagall Act in 1999:

(a) Effectively ended the separation of commercial banking from investment banking.

(b) Ended the prevention of commercial banks from trading in securities.

(c) Excluded the regulation of derivative financial instruments by the Commodities Futures Trading Commission.

(d) All of the above.

26. Which one of the following statements regarding pay-option ARM loans is *not* correct?

(a) Some borrowers of pay-option ARM loans choose to make monthly payments that are not large enough to cover the interest that accrues on the loans each month.

(b) If a borrower chooses to make monthly payments that do not cover the monthly interest on the loan, the difference between the interest that accrues and the interest that is paid is accrued and added to the loan amount as an asset on the balance sheet.

(c) With pay-option loans, the difference between the interest that accrues each month and the lower amount that borrowers choose to pay is known and reported in financial statements as the "loan delinquency amount."

(d) "Accumulated negative amortization" refers to the accumulated shortfall between the interest that has accrued on a loan and the amount of interest that a borrower has paid.

27. Which one of the following statements does *not* describe the transformation in Countrywide's reported loan portfolio?

(a) In 2004, conventional conforming loans dropped to 38.2 percent.

(b) Subprime loans increased from 2004 to 2006.

(c) By 2006, 31.9% percent of Countrywide's loan originations were conforming.

(d) By 2006, 10.2 percent of Countrywide's loans were home equity loans.

28. The SEC Complaint alleges that the description of Countrywide's loans in its 10-K filings was misleading in which of the following ways?

(a) Its description of prime nonconforming and nonprime loans was insufficient.

(b) It did not disclose the extent of the exceptions to its underwriting guidelines.

(c) It did not disclose that its prime nonconforming category included pay-option ARM loans, including such loans with reduced documentation.

(d) All of the above.

29. Why is an increase in accumulated negative amortization from one year to the next a signal that a decrease in earnings may follow?

(a) This shows that there may have been an increase in a high-risk portion of a lender's loan portfolio.

(b) A loan loss may follow because once the unpaid interest on a pay-option ARM loan reaches a certain percentage of principal borrowed, the loan repayment resets to a higher amount to cover the interest payments, and borrowers may be unable to pay the subsequent higher monthly payment after the payment resets and they may default.

(c) Accumulated negative amortization represents interest that will be earned in future periods but has been paid in the current period.

(d) Both (a) and (b) are correct.

30. Which of the following attributes of loans is *not* an indication of an increased risk of repayment default?

(a) Conforming to GSE underwriting standards.

(b) Having a loan-to-value ratio of 95 percent or higher.

(c) Having reduced documentation or no documentation.

(d) Being a stated income loan.

FOR DISCUSSION

31. Discuss the role of the government sponsored-enterprises (GSEs) in the funding and issuance of mortgage loans.

32. Describe the role of tranching in the granting of easy credit that fueled the housing bubble.

SHORT-ANSWER QUESTIONS

33. As the mortgage industry evolved from making loans that conformed to GSE standards to making and selling subprime loans, what were some of the changes in underwriting standards that occurred?

34. What is meant by *negative amortization*?

35. Explain the "reset" clause in the pay-option ARM loan agreement.

36. What were the main risks of pay-option ARM loans?

37. How were credit-default swaps expected to act as hedges against the risk of investing in mortgage-backed securities?

EXERCISES

38. Murky Mortgage Corp. is a mortgage lender. The following information relates to Murky Mortgage's portfolio of loans held for investment at December 31, 2006:

Principal amount of loans at year end (excluding negative amortization)	$100 million
Interest earned for year	$5 million
Negative amortization accrued during the year	$2 million

Allowance for loan losses at end of year	1% of (loan principal plus accumulated negative amortization)
Accumulated negative amortization at beginning of 2006 (none of this was paid during the year)	$1 million

What is the amount of loans held for investment net of allowance for loan losses on the balance sheet at December 31, 2006?

39. One of the loans included in Sloppy Mortgage Corporation's loans at January 1, 2006, was a pay-option ARM loan of $900,000 taken out on January 1, 2006, when the value of the house was $900,000. The interest earned (or accrued) on this loan for the year was $54,000. The principal repayments during the year amounted to $30,000 ($2,500 per month). The borrower opted to pay principal plus only $1,500 interest per month. The borrower remained current on these repayments for all 12 months of 2006.

On January 1, 2007, the repayment reset to $7,500 per month, and the borrower immediately informed the lender that no future payments would be made on the loan. The house immediately went into foreclosure, and the house quickly sold for $700,000.

What is the amount of the loss that Sloppy Mortgage must recognize in its income statement in 2007 if it has no allowance for loan losses in respect of this loan?

40. Moldy Mortgage Corp. has a loan portfolio with the following loans at December 31, 2013:

Prime conforming loans	$30 billion
Pay-option ARM loans without accumulated negative amortization	$10 billion
Subprime 80/20 loans	$10 billion
Pay-option ARM loans with accumulated negative amortization	$20 billion
	$70 billion

Moldy Mortgage wants to have an allowance for loan losses comprised of the following:

0.1 percent of prime conforming loans

6.0 percent of subprime 80/20 loans

0.5 percent of pay-option ARM loans without negative amortization

10 percent of pay-option ARM loans with accumulated negative amortization

Compute the required balance for the allowance for loan losses at December 31, 2013.

CASE STUDY

TIERONE BANK

- **Read** extracts from the SEC Complaint filed on September 25, 2012, against TierOne Bank.
- **Examine** extracts from TierOne's Financial Statements (10-Ks) for 2005–2008. According to the December 31, 2007, 10-K, "TierOne Corporation ('Company') is a Wisconsin corporation headquartered in Lincoln, Nebraska. TierOne Corporation is the holding company for TierOne Bank ('Bank')" (p. 5).
- **Respond** to the following Case Study Questions.

Required

a. **Underestimation of allowance for loan losses:** In the text, Signal #2 is "Allowance for Loan Losses Not Growing in Proportion to the Increase in Troubled Loans." Read the extracts from TierOne's financial statements and notes to its financial statements for the years 2005–2008. Explain whether you can identify the signal that TierOne's allowance for loan losses may allegedly have been understated. Show supporting calculations for your answer.

b. **Underestimation of allowance for loan losses:** In the text, Signal #3 is "Allowance for Loan Losses Not Increasing Significantly as House Prices Fall." Reread the discussion of Signal #3 in the text, as well as extracts from the SEC Complaint against TierOne. Search online for articles published in late 2008 about falling house prices. Explain how Signal #3 could have alerted users of TierOne's financial statements that its allowance for loan losses at December 2008 may allegedly have been understated.

Extracts from Complaint against TierOne Bank*

Civil Action No. 12-cv-00343 Filed September 25, 2012[10]
IN THE UNITED STATES DISTRICT COURT
FOR THE DISTRICT OF NEBRASKA
Omaha Division

SECURITIES AND EXCHANGE
COMMISSION

PARAGRAPHS 3 and 7:

3. TierOne was a century-old thrift bank that had historically focused on residential and agricultural loans in the Nebraska/Iowa/Kansas region. Beginning in about 2004, TierOne expanded into riskier types of lending in high-growth geographic regions such as Las Vegas, Florida, and Arizona. By the second half of 2008, as a result of the financial crisis and accompanying crash in real estate markets, TierOne was experiencing a significant rise in high-risk problem loans.

7. The full extent of TierOne's loan-related losses did not become publicly known until late 2009, after OTS required TierOne to obtain new appraisals for its impaired loans. TierOne ultimately disclosed over $130 million of additional loan losses. Had TierOne recorded these additional loss provisions in the proper quarters, it would have missed the OTS-required capital ratios as of the end of December 31, 2008, and for each

---

* "Without admitting or denying the allegations in the SEC's complaint," several of the bank executives "agreed to settle the charges against them," while the case against one executive "is ongoing" (LR 22493, 2012).

---

[10] Obtained from U.S. Securities and Exchange Commission. *www.sec.gov*

quarter thereafter. Following the announcements of the additional loss provisions, TierOne's stock price dropped more than 70 percent. TierOne eventually filed for bankruptcy shortly after the bank was shut down by OTS in June 2010.

PARAGRAPHS 24–29

24. Generally Accepted Accounting Principles, or "GAAP," provides that a loan becomes "impaired" when it is probable that the bank will be unable to collect all amounts due under the original loan agreement. In addition, TierOne's written lending policy stated that a loan greater than 90 days past due should be considered impaired.

25. Under GAAP, TierOne was required to assess probable losses associated with its impaired loans and record those losses in its allowance for loan and lease losses ("ALLL"). GAAP permits the impairment to be measured using the fair value of the underlying collateral if the loan is collateral dependent, which is the method that was typically utilized by TierOne.

26. Any increase in ALLL (a balance sheet item) must be accompanied by the recording of a provision for loan losses (an income statement item), thereby increasing reported loss and further eroding the bank's capital, which, in turn, negatively impacted the bank's ability to meet the OTS-required elevated capital ratios.

27. Some of TierOne's real estate loans were eventually foreclosed upon and the underlying collateral became the property of the bank, or OREO. GAAP required TierOne to carry OREO on its books at the lower of the property's book value or fair value, less costs to sell the property.

28. Thus, a key consideration under GAAP regarding the existence and magnitude of losses for impaired loans or OREO is the fair value of the collateral or OREO property. A recent appraisal performed by an independent and certified real estate appraiser is normally the best evidence of a property's fair value. In the absence of a current appraisal, all relevant and current information known at the time must be used. This information includes: the most recent evidence of market declines, broker price opinions ("BPO"), recent comparable sales, internal determinations of value, current project status and offers to purchase or sell.

29. In this case, TierOne intentionally delayed the process of obtaining current appraisals for properties that had declined in value, relying instead on inaccurate data and assumptions.

PARAGRAPHS 60–62

60. In August 2009, OTS directed TierOne to obtain updated appraisals. The new appraisals revealed the actual values of TierOne's collateral for impaired loans and OREO. On October 14, 2009, TierOne filed a Form 8-K reporting an additional $13.9 million in loan loss provisions for the second quarter of 2009. TierOne also announced that it intended to restate its second quarter 2009 financial statements, and that the bank's capital ratios would fall below the levels required by OTS. In the days following this news, TierOne's stock price fell over 17 percent, from approximately $3.27 per share to $2.69 per share.

61. The situation worsened as more OTS-mandated appraisals came in. On November 10, 2009, TierOne filed another Form 8-K reporting an additional loan loss provision of $120.2 million for the third quarter of 2009. TierOne's stock price dropped a further 54 percent over the next three trading days, from approximately $1.71 per share to $0.78 per share.

62. TierOne was shut down by OTS on June 4, 2010, and filed for bankruptcy later that month.

FINANCIAL STATEMENTS

UNITED STATES
SECURITIES AND EXCHANGE COMMISSION
Washington, D.C. 20549

Extracts from FORM 10-K[11]

Annual report pursuant to Section 13 or 15(d) of the Securities Exchange Act of 1934

For the fiscal year ended December 31, 2008

TierOne CORPORATION

Extract from Consolidated Statements of Financial Condition

	At December 31	
	2008	2007
	(Dollars in thousands, except per share data)	
ASSETS		
Cash and due from banks	$ 73,567	$ 79,561
Funds held at Federal Reserve Bank	29,292	—
Federal funds sold	147,000	161,900
Total cash and cash equivalents	249,859	241,461
Investment securities:		
Held to maturity, at cost which approximates fair value	48	70
Available for sale, at fair value	137,664	130,481
Mortgage-backed securities, available for sale, at fair value	3,133	6,689

---

[11] Extracted from 10-K filings for TierOne Corporation. Obtained from U.S. Securities and Exchange Commission. *www.sec.gov*

	At December 31	
	2008	**2007**
	(Dollars in thousands, except per share data)	
Loans receivable:		
Net loans (includes loans held for sale of $13,917 and $9,348 at December 31, 2008 and 2007, respectively)	2,782,220	2,976,129
Allowance for loan losses	(63,220)	(66,540)
Net loans after allowance for loan losses	2,719,000	2,909,589
FHLBank Topeka stock, at cost	47,011	65,837
Premises and equipment, net	35,316	38,028
Accrued interest receivable	16,886	21,248
Other real estate owned and repossessed assets, net	37,236	6,405
Goodwill	—	42,101
Other intangible assets, net	4,722	6,744
Mortgage servicing rights, net	14,806	14,530
Other assets	52,264	54,583
Total assets	$ 3,317,945	$ 3,537,766

From TierOne's 10-K 2008 NOTES: Note 5

Allowance for Loan Losses. The activity in the allowance for loan losses is summarized in the following table:

	Year Ended December 31		
	2008	**2007**	**2006**
	(Dollars in thousands)		
Balance at beginning of year	$ 66,540	$ 33,129	$ 30,870
Provision for loan losses	84,790	65,382	6,053
Charge-offs	(90,398)	(33,037)	(4,107)
Recoveries on loans previously charged-off	2,288	1,066	313
Balance at end of year	$ 63,220	$ 66,540	$ 33,129
Allowance for loan losses as a percentage of net loans	2.27%	2.24%	1.09%

We generally discontinue funding of loans which become nonperforming or are deemed impaired unless additional funding is required to protect our collateral. In addition, due to certain laws and regulations in some states, additional funding may be required. Our reserve for unfunded loan commitments at December 31, 2008 and 2007 was $300,000 and $2.7 million, respectively, which represents potential future losses associated with these unfunded commitments. We did not have a reserve for unfunded loan commitments at December 31, 2006.

Nonperforming Assets and Troubled Debt Restructurings.   Nonperforming assets consist of nonperforming loans, other real estate owned and repossessed assets. Nonperforming loans are loans that are 90 or more days delinquent on which interest recognition has been suspended until realized because of doubts as to the borrower's ability to repay principal and interest. Troubled debt restructurings are loans where the terms have been modified to provide a reduction or deferral of interest or principal because of deterioration in the borrower's financial position. We did not have any accruing loans 90 days or more past due at December 31, 2008 or 2007.

	At December 31	
	2008	2007
	(Dollars in thousands)	
Nonperforming loans (1)	$142,215	$128,490
Other real estate owned and repossessed assets, net (2)	37,236	6,405
Total nonperforming assets	179,451	134,895
Troubled debt restructurings	35,528	19,569
Total nonperforming assets and troubled debt restructurings	$214,979	$154,464

(1) Includes all loans 90 or more days delinquent and all uncollected accrued interest is fully reserved.
(2) Other real estate owned and repossessed asset balances are shown net of related loss allowances.

Extracts from FORM 10-K[12]

For the fiscal year ended December 31, 2006

TierOne CORPORATION

Extract from Consolidated Statements of Financial Condition

	At December 31	
	2006	2005
	(Dollars in thousands, except per share data)	
ASSETS		
Cash and due from banks	$ 86,808	$ 83,534
Federal funds sold	—	4,500
Total cash and cash equivalents	86,808	88,034
Investment securities:		
Held to maturity, at cost which approximates fair value	90	111
Available for sale, at fair value	105,000	102,614
Mortgage-backed securities, available for sale, at fair value	12,272	19,752
Loans receivable:		
Net loans (includes loans held for sale of $19,285 and $8,666 at December 31, 2006 and 2005, respectively)	3,050,160	2,844,670
Allowance for loan losses	(33,129)	(30,870)
Net loans after allowance for loan losses	3,017,031	2,813,800

---

[12] Extracted from 10-K filings for TierOne Corporation. Obtained from U.S. Securities and Exchange Commission. *www.sec.gov.*

From TierOne's 10-K 2006 NOTES: Note 5

Allowance for Loan Losses. The activity in the allowance for loan losses is summarized in the following table:

	Year Ended December 31		
	2006	2005	2004
	(Dollars in thousands)		
Balance at beginning of year	$30,870	$26,831	$19,586
Allowance for loan losses acquired	—	—	4,221
Provision for loan losses	6,053	6,436	4,887
Charge-offs	(4,107)	(3,063)	(2,236)
Recoveries on loans previously charged-off	313	666	373
Balance at end of year	$33,129	$30,870	$26,831
Allowance for loan losses as a percentage of net loans	1.09%	1.09%	1.01%

Nonperforming Assets and Troubled Debt Restructurings. Nonperforming assets consist of nonperforming loans, troubled debt restructurings and real estate owned. Nonperforming loans are loans on which interest recognition has been suspended until realized because of doubts as to the borrower's ability to repay principal and interest. Troubled debt restructurings are loans where the terms have been modified to provide a reduction or deferral of interest or principal because of deterioration in the borrower's financial position.

	At December 31	
	2006	2005
	(Dollars in thousands)	
Nonperforming loans (1)	$30,050	$14,405
Real estate owned, net (2)	5,264	2,446
Total nonperforming assets	35,314	16,851
Troubled debt restructurings	8,904	5,180
Total nonperforming assets and troubled debt restructurings	$44,218	$22,031

(1) Includes all loans 90 or more days delinquent and all uncollected accrued interest is fully reserved.

(2) Real estate owned balances are shown net of related loss allowances.

APPENDIX

The Top Twenty-Five Signals Indicating Possible Fictitious Reporting in Financial Statements

The Top Twenty-Five Signals	The Schemes That a Company May Be Concealing
1. Suspicious track record of top executives, particularly when their previous companies reported swift earnings turnarounds that suddenly evaporated.	May be indicative of any method of overstatement of earnings, or overstatement of cash flow from operations (CFFO), or understatement of debt.
2. Receivables that increase significantly as a percentage of revenues, as measured, for example, by days sales outstanding.	Possible overstatement of revenue via accelerated revenue, or fictitious revenue, or improper valuation of revenue.
3. CFFO that significantly lags behind operating income or net income.	Overstatement of revenue or understatement of expenses.
4. Unusual securitizations or factoring of receivables. (In this case, when testing signals 2 and 3 above, remember to adjust receivables by adding back securitization amounts and to adjust CFFO by deducting securitization amounts.	The need for the securitization itself could be an indication of cash-flow problems. The company could be hiding the CFFO shortfall compared to operating income, and also hiding a buildup in receivables by accelerating a portion of their liquidation into cash.
5. Inventory that increases substantially as a percentage of cost of goods sold as measured, for example, by the inventory-turnover ratio.	Possible overstatement of inventory, or understatement of obsolescence of inventory, or understatement of cost of goods sold.
6. Significant fluctuations in gross margin as a percentage of sales.	Overstatement of ending inventory or of revenues; understatement of purchases or cost of goods manufactured.
7. The creation of large reserves via one-time charges, such as restructuring charges, followed by the drawing down of reserves.	Possible overstatement of reserves to boost later periods' earnings by the release of excess "cookie-jar" reserves back into income.
8. Large amounts allocated to goodwill on the acquisition of other companies, accompanied by the creation of large reserves on acquisition.	Improper use of acquisitions for the overstatement of acquisition reserves, and a corresponding overstatement of goodwill; the possible release of excess cookie-jar reserves into income in future periods, in order to overstate post-acquisition earnings.
9. Large amounts allocated to goodwill on the acquisition of companies that do not have a supernormal return on assets, and the acquisition is not followed by supernormal returns on assets.	Overstatement of goodwill on acquisitions for the purpose of overstating acquisition reserves in order to release the cookie-jar reserves into earnings later on.

(continued)

The Top Twenty-Five Signals	The Schemes That a Company May Be Concealing
10. Adjustments that increase goodwill in a later period with respect to an earlier acquisition.	Overstatement of acquisition reserves for the purpose of overstating later periods' earnings via the later release of the cookie-jar reserves into earnings.
11. A significant decrease in the ratio of sales-to-total-assets (asset-turnover ratio), or a decrease in the ratio of sales to any particular asset such as, for example, property, plant, and equipment (PPE).	This could indicate improper capitalization of expenses; for example, the classification of expenses as PPE. The fictitious asset cannot be used as part of the real infrastructure to produce sales.
12. When an expense that has a fixed-cost component remains a constant percentage of sales revenue, as revenue decreases.	Improper capitalization of an expense as an asset. For example, WorldCom's line-cost expense was misclassified as PPE.
13. Expenses, or a category of expenses, that decline significantly as a percentage of sales.	This could signal understatement of expenses via omitting to record the expenses, or by deferring the expenses, or by improper capitalization of the expenses
14. Current liabilities that decline significantly as a percentage of current assets and sales.	Understatement of expenses via "lack of accrual."
15. Deferred costs or prepaid expenses that increase significantly as a percentage of total assets, or as a percentage of sales.	Understatement of expenses via deferral of expenses.
16. When the development of a product or a program is accompanied by the recording of a significant, intangible asset—such as development costs or start-up costs—and the company hits scheduling problems that are reported in press articles or on the notes to the financial statements, but the intangible asset is not written off.	Failure to record asset impairments.
17. The reserve for bad debts decreases as a percentage of accounts receivable.	Understatement of bad debts expense.
18. When a company has multiple-element contracts and there is a proportional increase in a revenue stream that is more quickly recognized and a decrease in revenue stream that is recognized more slowly.	Acceleration of revenue via improper use of multiple-element contracts through misclassification of revenue streams.
19. Deferred revenue decreases as a percentage of total revenue.	Aggressive recognition of revenue that will be earned only in future periods.
20. A significant decrease in allowances for returns as a percentage of sales.	Allowance for returns may be understated.

(continued)

The Top Twenty-Five Signals	**The Schemes That a Company May Be Concealing**
21. Large increases in investments in unconsolidated affiliates or increases in the assets and liabilities of unconsolidated affiliates especially partnerships, trusts, joint ventures, and company-sponsored corporations as opposed to established independent corporations. This signal becomes stronger if the nature of the entities is vague or their transactions are vaguely described. It becomes stronger still if a significant portion of the company's profit comes from transactions with these entities, or if there are contingent liabilities in respect of these entities.	Overstatement of Earnings and CFFO, and/or understatement of debt via contrived transactions with special purpose entities.
22. Aggressive revenue recognition accounting policies such as, for example, bill and hold sales, or guaranteed or right of return sales (especially when accompanied by increases in discounts as a percentage of sales). Also be wary of percentage of completion method where unbilled sales increase as a percentage of total sales.	Overstatement of sales via channel stuffing or acceleration of revenue recognition or fictitious revenue recognition.
23. Aggressive accounting policies in terms of capitalization of expenses compared to previous periods or compared to other companies in the same industry, for items such as capitalized interest costs, software costs, development costs, or direct response advertising costs.	Improper capitalization of expenses to overstate earnings.
24. Allowance for loan losses not growing in proportion to increases in riskier loans or in proportion to increases in troubled loans. These signals become stronger still if there is simultaneously a decrease in the value of the assets (such as house prices) securing the loans.	Understatement of allowance for loan losses or for losses on investments in securities backed by loans.
25. When the company consistently meets sales or earnings estimates every quarter.	Possible overstatement of earnings via any method of overstatement of revenues or understatement of expenses.

REFERENCES

Chapter 1

"Accounting and Auditing Enforcement Releases." U.S. Securities and Exchange Commission. *www.sec.gov.*

Amato, Neil. July 30, 2012. "Lawmakers Reflect on Sarbanes-Oxley's Effect on Corporate Culture," *Journal of Accountancy. http://journalofaccountancy.com.*

Amended Complaint Charging Five Enron Executives with Fraud and Insider Trading Relating to Enron's Broadband Subsidiary. U.S. Securities and Exchange Commission, May 1, 2003. *www.sec.gov.*

"An Analysis and Summary of SEC Accounting and Auditing Enforcement Releases (AAERs) Issued in 2011/2012." December 5, 2012. AICPA National Conference on Current SEC and PCAOB Developments. *www. aicpaconferencematerials.com.*

Anderson, Sarah, Scott Klinger, and Sam Pizzigati. August 28, 2013. *Executive Excess 2013: Bailed Out, Booted, and Busted,* The Institute for Policy Studies. *www.ips-dc.org.*

Beasley, Mark, Joseph V. Carcello, Dana Hermanson, and Terry L. Neal. May 2010. "Fraudulent Financial Reporting: 1998–2007—An Analysis of U.S. Public Companies," COSO: Committee of Sponsoring Organizations of the Treadway Commission. *www.coso.org.*

Bishop, Toby, and Frank Hydoski. 2009. "Ten Things about Financial Statement Fraud—Third Edition: A Review of SEC Enforcement Releases, 2000–2008," Deloitte Forensic Center. *www.deloitte.com.*

Byrne, John A., Louis Lavelle, Nanette Byrnes, and Marcia Vickers. May 6, 2002. "How to Fix Corporate Governance," *Business Week.* Available online via Academic Search Elite database.

Byrnes, Nanette, Mike McNamee, Diane Brady, Louis Lavelle, and Christopher Palmeri. 2002. "Accounting in Crisis," *Business Week,* January 28. *www. businessweek.com.*

Cohn, Michael. May 30, 2013. "SEC Refocuses on Accounting Fraud," *Accounting Today for the Web CPA. www.accountingtoday.com.*

Croteau, Brian T., Deputy Chief Accountant. December 3, 2012. "Remarks Before the 2012 AICPA National Conference on Current SEC and PCAOB Developments— Audit Policy and Current Auditing and Internal Control Matters." U.S. Securities and Exchange Commission. *www.sec.gov.*

Deterring and Detecting Financial Reporting Fraud: A Platform for Action. October 2010. Center for Audit Quality, Affiliated with the American Institute of CPAs. *www.thecaq.org.*

Dickey, Jonathan C., John H. Sturc, and John D. Van Lobels Sels. 2003. "'Real Time' Enforcement: Recent Trends in SEC Enforcement Actions." Glasser Legalworks Annual Conference on SEC Disclosure, Accounting and Enforcement. May 15–16, San Francisco; May 28–29, New York City. *www.gibsondunn.com.*

Drawbaugh, Kevin, and Dena Aubin. July 29, 2012. "What the Collapse of Peregrine Financial Says about the Sarbanes-Oxley Law," *Huffington Post. www.huffingtonpost. com.*

Dyck, I. J. Alexander, Adair Morse, and Luigi Zingales. February 22, 2013. "How Pervasive Is Corporate Fraud?" Rotman School of Management Working Paper No. 2222608, Social Science Research Network. SSRN. *http://ssrn.com.*

Eaglesham, Jean. March 17, 2013. "Number of Cases Filed by SEC Slows," *Wall Street Journal. http://online.wsj.com/home-page.*

Eaglesham, Jean. May 27, 2013. "Accounting Fraud Targeted: With Crisis-Related Enforcement Ebbing, SEC Is Turning Back to Main Street," *Wall Street Journal. http:// online.wsj.com/home-page.*

"Financial Crimes Report to the Public: Fiscal Years 2010–2011." (October 1, 2009– September 30, 2011)." Federal Bureau of Investigation. *www.fbi.gov.*

The Financial Crisis Inquiry Report: Final Report of the National Commission on the Causes of the Financial and Economic Crisis in the United States. January 2011. Pursuant to Public Law 111-21. *www.gpo.gov.*

First Interim Report of Dick Thornburgh, Bankruptcy Court Examiner. United States Bankruptcy Court Southern District of New York in re: WorldCom Inc. Case No. 02-13533 (AJG), November 4, 2002.

"Fiscal Year 2012 Agency Financial Report." U.S. Securities and Exchange Commission. 2012. *www.sec.gov.*

The Fraud Trial. 2011. Association of Certified Fraud Examiners. *www.acfe.com.*

Gallagher, Daniel M., Chairman. May 10, 2013. "Remarks at the 45th Annual Rocky Mountain Securities Conference." U.S. Securities and Exchange Commission. *www.sec.gov.*

Glassman, Cynthia A. November 17, 2005. "Remarks before the Conference on Listed Companies and Legislators in Dialogue Danish Ministry of Economic and Business Affairs." Speech in Copenhagen, Denmark. U.S. Securities and Exchange Commission. *www.sec.gov.*

Juris, Stephen. March 28, 2013. "Restatements Resurrected?: Accounting Fraud by the Numbers," *Forbes. www.forbes.com.*

"The Laws That Govern the Securities Industry." August 30, 2012. *www.sec.gov.*

Knigge, Michael. September 5, 2010. "Europe, US Take Different Approaches to Whistleblowing," *Deutche Welle. www.dw.de.*

Lawrence, Michael G., and Joseph T. Wells. 2004. "Basic Legal Concepts: Beware Insufficient Knowledge of the Law," *Journal of Accountancy,* October. *http:// journalofaccountancy.com.*

Levitt, Arthur. 2002. *Take on the Street.* New York: Pantheon Books.

Lewis, Craig M. December 13, 2012. "Risk Modeling at the SEC: The Accounting Quality Model." U.S. Securities & Exchange Commission. *www.sec.gov.*

Marcus, David F., and Sara E. Gilley. April 22, 2013. "The Future of SEC Enforcement Actions," Portfolio Media Inc. *www.cornerstone.com.*

Melancon, Barry. February 21, 2012. "Proposed SOX 404(b) Changes Could Add to Investors' Risks," *AICPA Insights. http:// blog.aicpa.org.*

Mueller, Robert S. III, Director, Federal Bureau of Investigation. May 9, 2012. "Statement Before the House Judiciary Committee," Washington D.C. *www.fbi.gov.*

National Hotline Services. "Sarbanes-Oxley Act of 2002: Employee Complaint Procedures."

Noeth, Bryan J. 2011. "Financial Regulation: A Primer on the Dodd-Frank Act," May. *www.research.stlouisfed.org.*

Noked, Noam. March 19, 2013. "SEC Enforcement Focusing on Valuation Issues," *Harvard Law School Forum on Corporate Governance and Financial Regulation. http://blogs.law.harvard.edu.*

Ovide, Shira. October 11, 2011. "MF Global: Likely Among the 10 Biggest Bankruptcies Ever." *Wall Street Journal. http://. onlinewsj.com/home-page.*

"Procedures for the Handling of Retaliation Complaints Under Section 806 of the Sarbanes-Oxley Act of 2002, as Amended." November 3, 2011. United States Department of Labor. Federal Register Vol. 76, No. 213, pp. 68084–68097. *www.osha.gov.*

"The Sarbanes-Oxley Act at 10: Enhancing the Reliability of Financial Reporting and Audit Quality." 2012. Ernst & Young LLP. *www.ey.com.*

Sarno, John, Michael Mueller, and Jennifer Burns. August 12, 2010. "The Final Act: Financial Reporting Implications of the Dodd-Frank Wall Street Reform and Consumer Protection Act." *Heads Up,* Vol. 17, No. 26. Deloitte. *www.deloitte.com.*

Schapiro, Mary L. July 9, 2010. "Speech by SEC Chairman: Remarks at the National Conference of the Society of Corporate Secretaries and Governance Professionals." Chicago, IL. U.S. Securities and Exchange Commission. *www.sec.gov.*

Schapiro, Mary L., Chairman. February 24, 2012. "Speech by SEC Chairman: Remarks at the Practising Law Institute's SEC Speaks." U.S. Securities and Exchange Commission. *www.sec.gov.*

SEC's Enforcement Program Continues to Show Strong Results in Safeguarding Investors and Markets. November 14, 2012. U.S. Securities and Exchange Commission. *www.sec.gov.*

"SEC Awards More Than $14 Million to Whistleblower." 2013. Press Release. U.S. Securities and Exchange Commission. Washington D.C. October 1. *www.sec.gov.*

"SEC Receives More Than 3,000 Whistleblower Tips in FY2012." November 15, 2012. Press Release. U.S. Securities and Exchange Commission. *www.sec.gov.*

SOX Report. 2002. *Report Pursuant to Section 704 of the Sarbanes-Oxley Act of 2002. www.sec.gov.*

Walter, Elisse B., Chairman. May 30, 2013. "Keynote Luncheon Speech." U.S. Securities and Exchange Commission, 32nd Annual SEC and Financial Reporting Institute Conference. *www.sec.gov.*

Weissmann, Jordan. June 27, 2013. "CEOs Now Earn 273 Times the Average Worker's Pay—Should You Be Mad?" *The Atlantic. www.theatlantic.com.*

West, Lawrence A., William A. Baker, and Eric R. Swibel. February 19, 2013. "Dealing with the SEC's Focus on Protecting Whistleblowers from Retaliation." *Client Alert.* Number 1470. Latham & Watkin's Litigation Department. *www.lw.com.*

Whalen, Don, Esq., Mark Cheffers, and Olga Usvyatsky. April 2012. "2011 Financial Restatements—An Eleven Year Comparison." *Audit Analytics. www.auditanalytics.com.*

Wilczynski, Martin S. April 29, 2013. "Making Accounting Enforcement a Priority: The Case for an SEC Financial Accounting Fraud Specialized Unit." *Securities Docket. www.securitiesdocket.com.*

Chapter 2

Arel, Barbara, Cathy A. Beaudoin, and Anna M. Cianci. December 14, 2011. "The Impact of Ethical Leadership, the Internal Audit Function and Moral Intensity on a Financial Reporting Decision," *Journal of Business Ethics. www.springer.com.*

Badaracco, Joseph L. Jr. 2006. "The Discipline of Building Character," *Harvard Business Review,* June. *http://hbr.org.*

Blake, Scott. 2012. "Cecilia Garber." *Miami Today. www.miamitodaynews.com.*

Buchan, Howard F. 2005. "Ethical Decision Making in the Public Accounting Profession: An Extension of Ajzen's Theory of Planned Behavior," *Journal of Business Ethics,* Vol. 61, 165–181.

Buchan, Howard. 2009. "Public Accountants' Perceptions of Ethical Work Climate: An Exploratory Study of the Difference Between Partners and Employees within the Instrumental Dimension," *Open Ethics Journal,* Vol. 3, 1–7. *www.benthamscience.com/open.*

"CGMA Report Reveals Gap in Rhetoric, Reality on Business Ethics," May 21, 2012, AICPA Press Release, www.aicpa.org.

Cohen, Stephen. 2004. The Nature of Moral Reasoning: The Framework and Activities of Ethical Deliberation, Argument, and Decision-Making. New York: Oxford University Press.

Dodd-Frank Wall Street Reform and Consumer Protection Act. 2010. Public Law 111–203—July 21. HR 4173. www.gpo.gov.

Feinberg, Joel. 1993. "Distributive Justice."ed. Thomas I. White. In Business Ethics: A Philosophical Reader. New York: Macmillan.

Finnis, John. 1983. Fundamentals of Ethics. Washington, DC: Georgetown University Press.

Flanagan, Jack, and Kevin Clarke. 2007. "Beyond a Code of Professional Ethics: A Holistic Model of Ethical Decision-Making for Accountants," ABACUS, Vol. 43, No. 4, 488–518. www.ebscohost.com.

Henriques, Dana. June 29, 2009. "Madoff Is Sentenced to 150 Years for Ponzi Scheme," New York Times. www.nytimes.com.

Kellenberger, James. 1995. Relationship Morality. University Park, PA: Pennsylvania State University Press.

Kellenberger, James. December 2004. Personal interview with the author. Northridge, California.

MacIntyre, Alasdair. 2007. After Virtue: A Study in Moral Theory. Notre Dame, IN: University of Notre Dame Press.

Nash, Laura. 2009. "Ethics without the Sermon." Harvard Business Review Classics Series. Boston: Harvard Business Press. Originally published in 1981.

Peluso, Romano. 2012. "Dodd-Frank and the Need for Ethics." ABA Trusts and Investments, July/August. http://magazines.aba.com/timag.

Pincus, Karen. 2002–2003. "Instructor's Notes for Module 2: Management as Users of Accounting Information." In Core Concepts of Accounting Information. Boston: McGraw-Hill/Irwin.

Pratt, Mary K. 2013. "CPAs Are Sexy: Accountants in Demand as Regulatory Climate Tightens," Boston Business Journal, January 14. www.masslive.com/business-news.

Schickel, Joel A. June 18–20, 2009. "Virtue Ethics and Accounting Practice." Eighth International Conference on Catholic Social Thought and Management Education. University of Dayton, Dayton, OH. www.stthomas.edu/cathstudies/cst/conferences/Dayton/Daytonpapers.html.

Singer, Peter. 1993. Practical Ethics. Cambridge University Press. p. 14.

Sinnott-Armstrong, Walter. 2012. "Consequen-tialism." ed. Edward N. Zalta. Stanford Encyclopedia of Philosophy. Winter. http://plato.stanford.edu.

Tidrick, Donald E. May 2013. "Examining the Ethics Process: A Conversation with PEEC Chair Wes Williams," CPA Journal, www.cpajournal.com.

Van Voris, Bob, and David Glovin. December 20, 2012. "Peter Madoff Gets 10 Years for His Role in Brother's Ponzi Fraud," Bloomberg. www.bloomberg.com

Chapter 3

AAER 1393. U.S. Securities and Exchange Commission Accounting and Auditing Enforcement Release. May 15, 2001. www.sec.gov.

AAER 1394. U.S. Securities and Exchange Commission Accounting and Auditing Enforcement Release. May 15, 2001. www.sec.gov.

AAER 2884. U.S. Securities and Exchange Commission Accounting and Auditing Enforcement Release. September 24, 2008. www.sec.gov.

Beazer Homes USA, Inc. Selected Financial Statements 2004-2007. U.S. Securities and Exchange Commission. www.sec.gov.

Byrne, John A. 2003. (Quotes courtesy of Harper Collins.) *Chainsaw: The Notorious Career of Al Dunlap in the Era of Profit-at-Any-Price.* New York: Harper Business.

Byron, Christopher. 2004. *Testosterone Inc. Tales of CEOs Gone Wild.* Hoboken, NJ: Wiley.

Canedy, Dana. March 18, 1998a. "A Warning by Sunbeam Stuns Wall St." *New York Times.* Available online via ProQuest database.

_____. May 7, 1998b. "A Big Sales Gain for Sunbeam Proves Costly to Investor," *New York Times.* Available online via ProQuest database.

_____. May 12, 1998c. "Amid Big Losses, Sunbeam Plans to Cut 6,400 Jobs and 8 Plants," *New York Times.* Available online via ProQuest database.

Cullinan, Charles P., and Gail B. Wright. 2003. *Cases from the SEC Files: Topics in Auditing.* Upper Saddle River, NJ: Pearson Education.

Dunlap, Albert J., with Bob Andelman. 1997. *Mean Business: How I Save Bad Companies and Make Good Companies Great.* New York: Fireside.

Florian, Ellen, and M. Adamo. November 15, 2010. "Tough-Guy CEO Al Dunlap is Getting in Touch with His Cuddly Side," *Fortune.* Available online via EBSCOhost.

Frank, Robert, and Joann S. Lublin. November 13, 1996. "Dunlap's Ax Falls—6,000 Times—At Sunbeam," *Wall Street Journal.* Available online via ProQuest database.

Jarden Corporation. January 24, 2005. "Jarden Complete Acquisition of American Household, Inc." News Release. *www.jarden.com.*

Jenkins, Carri P. 1997. "Downsizing or Dumbsizing?" *BYU Magazine Online.* Brigham Young University, Spring. *http://magazine.byu.edu.*

Laing, Jonathan. June 16, 1997."High Noon at Sunbeam," *Barron's.* Available online via ProQuest database.

_____. March 9, 1998a. "Into the Maw," *Barron's.* Available online via ProQuest database.

_____. June 8, 1998b. "Dangerous Games," *Barron's.* Available online via ProQuest database.

LR 17001. *U.S. Securities and Exchange Commission* Litigation Release. May 15, 2001. *www.sec.gov.*

LR 17710. *U.S. Securities and Exchange Commission* Litigation Release. September 4, 2002. *www.sec.gov.*

Lublin, Joann S., and Oscar Suris. April 9, 1997. "'Chainsaw Al' Now Aspires to be 'Al the Builder,'" *Wall Street Journal.* Available online via ProQuest database.

"Morgan Stanley Told to Pay $850 Million." May 18, 2005. *MSNBC.com. ww.nbcnews.com.*

"Munroe Foundation Receives Largest Single Gift: Al and Judy Dunlap Give $5 Million to Munroe Pediatrics." July 26, 2005. *Munroe Foundation: Munroe Regional Medical Center. www.munroefoundaton.com.*

Murphy, Franklin D., and Barry Ray. August 2006. "Dunlap gift to help students bridge college/career gap." *Florida State Times. www.unicomm.fsu.edu/Florida-State-Times.*

Porter, Jane, and Alina Dizik. September 11, 2007. "Make That 'Dr. Chainsaw.'" *BloombergBusinessweek. www.businessweek.com.*

Portfolio's Worst American CEOs of All Time. CNBC, April 30, 2009. *www.cnbc.com.ChristianScience Monitor,*

Scherer, Ron. November 8, 1996. "Towns Dread Job Cuts But Investors Applaud the Role of 'Chainsaw,'"

Schifrin, Matthew. May 4, 1998. "The Unkindest Cut," *Forbes.* Available online via ProQuest database.

SOX Report. 2002. *SEC Report Pursuant to Section 704 of the Sarbanes-Oxley Act of 2002.* U.S. Securities and Exchange Commission. *www.sec.gov.*

Statement of Financial Accounting Standards No. 48. Financial Accounting Standards Board. *www.fasb.org.*

"Sunbeam's Cloudy Outlook: Chairman Al Warns on Profits." March 20, 1998. *New York Post.*

Thomas Jr., Landon. March 24, 2007. "Five Days: Smiles at Morgan Stanley," *New York Times.* Available online via EBSCOHost.

Williams, Pamela. July 21, 2001. "Al Dunlap's Disgrace," *Australian Financial Review. www.newsstore.fairfax.com.au.*

Chapter 4

AAER 1017. Securities and Exchange Commission Accounting and Auditing Enforcement Release, March 25, 1998. *www.sec.gov.*

AAER 1020. Securities and Exchange Commission Accounting and Auditing Enforcement Release, March 25, 1998. *www.sec.gov.*

AAER 1027. Securities and Exchange Commission Accounting and Auditing Enforcement Release, April 27, 1998. *www.sec.gov.*

AAER 1133. Securities and Exchange Commission Accounting and Auditing Enforcement Release, May 17, 1999. *www.sec.gov.*

AAER 1275. Securities and Exchange Commission Accounting and Auditing Enforcement Release, June 14, 2000. *www.sec.gov.*

AAER 1542. Securities and Exchange Commission Accounting and Auditing Enforcement Release, April 11, 2002. *www.sec.gov.*

AAER 2234. Securities and Exchange Commission Accounting and Auditing Enforcement Release, April 19, 2005. *www.sec.gov.*

"Another Cendant Hung Jury." February 10, 2006. *Los Angeles Times.*

Burns, Greg. January 2, 2006. "Enron Case Big Test of the 'Idiot Defense': Ex-Chief Vows to Say He Was Blind to Crimes," *Chicago Tribune.* Available online via InfoTrac OneFile (Gale).

"Community Foundation Honors Two Local Residents at Annual 'Celebration of Philanthropy' Event." January 24, 2003. *Community Foundation for Palm Beach and Martin Counties. www.yourcommunityfoundation.org.*

Complaint 18919. Case No. 04 CV 2002 JAH (RBB). October 5, 2004. *www.sec.gov.*

"E. Kirk Shelton Is Guilty on All Counts of Accounting Fraud." January 5, 2005. *RISMedia. www.rismedia.com.*

"Ex-Cendant Chairman Sentenced for Fraud." January 18, 2007. *New York Times. www.nytimes.com.*

Farrell, Greg. November 23, 2006. "Cendant Conviction Upheld," *USA Today. www.usatoday.com.*

Graebner, Lynn. January 17, 2006. "Insignia Solutions Keeps Nasdaq Listing," *San Francisco Business Times. www.bizjournals.com/sanfrancisco.*

Graubert et al. vs. Insignia Solutions. April 20, 1998. Defendant's Memorandum in Support of Settlement, *United States District Court Northern District of California, San Jose Division. www.securities.stanford.edu/1009/INSGY97/006.html.*

Haigh, Susan. August 4, 2005. "Cendant Official Must Pay Back $3.27 Billion." *Washingtonpost.com.*

Insignia Solutions, PLC. Form 8-K. 2009. Securities and Exchange Commission. *www.sec.gov.*

Kershaw, Sarah. September 16, 2010. "Walter Forbes Connecticut Mansion Sells for $7 Million." *New York Times. www.nytimes.com.*

Levitt, Arthur. September 28, 1998. "The Numbers Game: Remarks at NYU Center for Law and Business." *www.sec.gov.*

LR 16919; AAER 1372. *Securities and Exchange Commission* Litigation Release, February 28, 2001. *www.sec.gov.*

LR 17465. Securities and Exchange Commission v. Xerox Corporation Litigation Release, April 11, 2002. *www.sec.gov.*

LR 18711; AAER 2014. *Securities and Exchange Commission* Litigation Release, May 14, 2004. *www.sec.gov.*

LR 19191. Securities and Exchange Commission v. KPMG LL1 et al. Litigation Release, April 19, 2005. *www.sec.gov.*

LR 21548. Securities and Exchange Commission Litigation Release, June 3, 2010. *www.sec.gov.*

Mills, Jane, and David Voreacos. November 17, 2005." Ex-Cendant Chief at Retrial Denies Inflating Income; Forbes Testifies Subordinates Handled Books," *The Record* (Bergen County, NJ). Available online via LexisNexis database.

Norris, Floyd, and Diana B. Henriques. June 15, 2000. "3 Admit Guilt in Falsifying CUC's Books." *New York Times. www.nytimes.com.*

"NSU to Honor Ron and Kathy Assaf with President's Community Award at its Celebration of Excellence." January 12, 2012.News Release. Nova Southeastern University. *http://nsunews.nova.edu.*

NYSE. November 9, 2001. *New York Stock Exchange Press Release. www.nyse.com.*

SEC Press Release. June 5, 2003. *Securities and Exchange Commission News Release.* "Six Former Senior Executives of Xerox Settle SEC Enforcement Action Charging Them With Fraud." *www.sec.gov.*

"SEC Complaint Reveals What Caused It to Sue KPMG." February 23, 2003. *The Accountant.* Available online via LexisNexis database.

SOX Report. 2002. *Report Pursuant to Section 704 of the Sarbanes-Oxley Act of 2002. www.sec.gov.*

"Status of High-Profile Corporate Scandals." November 23, 2005. *Washingtonpost.com, Associated Press. wwvv.washingtonpost.com.*

Taub, Stephen. January 29, 2007. "Former Cendant Controller Gets Probation." *CFO. com. www.cfo.com.*

Taub, Stephen. January 30, 2007. "Ex-Cendant CFO Avoids Prison." *CFO.com. www.cfo.com.*

Taub, Stephen. March 27, 2008. "Xerox, KPMG Settle Investor Suit." *CFO.com. www.cfo.com/article.cfm/10942620.*

Whiteman, Lou. July 14, 2003. "No Cause for Alarm," *The Daily Deal.* Available online via InfoTrac OneFile (Gale).

"Xerox Cleared in Criminal Investigation." October 20, 2004.*United Press International.* Available online via LexisNexis database.

Chapter 5

AAER 1585. U.S. Securities and Exchange Commission Accounting and Auditing Enforcement Release, June 27, 2002. *www.sec.gov.*

AAER 1678. U.S. Securities and Exchange Commission Accounting and Auditing Enforcement Release, November 26, 2002. *www.sec.gov.*

AAER 1966. U.S. Securities and Exchange Commission Accounting and Auditing Enforcement Release, March 2, 2004. *www.sec.gov.*

AAER 1977. U.S. Securities and Exchange Commission Accounting and Auditing Enforcement Release, March 17, 2004. *www.sec.gov.*

"An Appeals Court Is Urged to Uphold Ebbers Conviction." November 12, 2005. *New York Times. www.nytimes.com.*

Bureau of Prisons Website. October 18, 2005. *www.bop.gov.*

Clough, Alexandra. August 2, 2009. "Ex-WorldCom Exec Out of Prison, Back in Area," *Palm Beach Post. www.palmbeachpost.com.*

Crawford, Krysten. March 15, 2005. "Ex-WorldCom CEO Ebbers Guilty." *CNN Money. www.money.cnn.com.*

"*Ebbers' Wife Files for Divorce.*" April 24, 2008. *Tulsa World, www.tulsaworld.com.*

"*Enron Trial to Highlight 2006 Corporate Scandal Cases.*" December 26, 2005. *Chicago Sun Times,* Available online via ProQuest database.

"*Ex-WorldCom Exec Gets a Year in Prison.*" August 9, 2005. *Associated Press. www.nbcnews.com.*

"*Ex-WorldCom Executive Sentenced to Prison.*" August 5, 2005. *Reuters. www.nbcnews.com.*

Faber, David. September 9, 2003. "The Big Lie: Inside the Rise and Fraud of WorldCom," *CNBC News Transcripts.* Available online via LexisNexis database.

First Interim Report of Dick Thornburgh, Bankruptcy Court Examiner. November 4, 2002. United States Bankruptcy Court Southern District of New York in re:WorldCom, Inc. Case No. 02-13533 (AJG).

Guyon, Janet. May 16, 2005. "Jack Grubman Is Back. Just Ask Him."*Fortune. www. money.cnn.com/magazines/fortune.*

Jeter, Lynne W. 2003. *Disconnected: Deceit and Betrayal at WorldCom.* Hoboken, NJ: John Wiley & Sons.

Krim, Jonathan. August 29, 2002. "Fast and Loose at WorldCom: Lack of Controls, Pressure to Grow Set Stage for Financial Deceptions," *Washington Post. www. washingtonpost.com.*

LR 17753. *U.S. Securities and Exchange Commission* Litigation Release. September 26, 2002. *www.sec.gov.*

LR 17829. *U.S. Securities and Exchange Commission* Litigation Release. November 1, 2002. *www.sec.gov.*

LR 18277. *U.S. Securities and Exchange Commission* Litigation Release. August 7, 2003. *www.sec.gov.*

LR 18605. *U.S. Securities and Exchange Commission* Litigation Release. March 2, 2004. *www.sec.gov.*

LR 19657. *U.S. Securities and Exchange Commission* Litigation Release. April 17, 2006. *www.sec.gov.*

Malik, Om. 2003. *Broadbandits: Inside the $750 Billion Telecom Heist.* Hoboken, NJ: John Wiley & Sons.

McCafferty, Joseph. September 1, 1998. "Scott Sullivan-WorldCom, Inc.," *CFO Magazine. www3.cfo.com.*

"*New York Judge Grants Ebbers Bail.*" September 7, 2005. *Associated Press. www.nbcnews.com.*

Pulliam, Susan. March 24, 2005. "Crossing the Line: At Center of Fraud, WorldCom Official Sees Life Unravel," *Wall Street Journal. http://online.wsj.com.*

Pulliam, Susan, and Deborah Solomon. October 30, 2002. "Uncooking the Books," *Wall Street Journal.* Available online via ProQuest database.

Reaves, Gail. May 16, 2002. "Accounting for Anguish," *Fort Worth Weekly Online. www.fwweekly.com.*

Second Interim Report of Dick Thornburgh, Bankruptcy Court Examiner. June 9, 2003. United States Bankruptcy Court Southern District of New York in re:WorldCom Inc. Case No. 02-13533 (AJG).

Securities and Exchange Commission v. Tyco International, Ltd. Complaint. April 13, 2006. United States District Court, Southern District of New York. *www.sec.gov.*

"*Sullivan Gets Five Years for WorldCom Fraud,*" August 11, 2005. *Associated Press. www.nbcnews.com.*

Third and Final Report of Dick Thornburgh, Bankruptcy Court Examiner. January 26, 2004. United States Bankruptcy

Court Southern District of New York in re:WorldCom Inc. Case No. 02-13533 (AJG).

Tkaczyk, Christopher. November 1, 2009. "The 10 Largest U.S. Bankruptcies," *CNNMoney. www.money.cnn.com.*

Tyco International, Ltd. Financial Statements, 1998–2002. U.S. Securities and Exchange Commission. *www.sec.gov.*

United States of America v. Bernard J. Ebbers, Indictment S3 02 Cr. 1144 (BUS). March 4, 2005. *www.justice.gov.*

United States of America v. Scott D. Sullivan and Buford Yates, Jr., Indictment 02 Cr. August 28, 2002. *www.justice.gov.*

"Verizon Business." January 23, 2006. News Release. *http://newscenter.verizon.com.*

"WorldCom Ex-Controller Gets a Year in Prison." August 10, 2005. *Associated Press. www.nbcnews.com.*

"WorldCom's Finance Chief Says He Lied." Los Angeles Times. February 20, 2005.

Chapter 6

"8-Year Sentence for Rite Aid Exec." May 27, 2004. *CBSNEWS.com. www.cbsnews.com.*

AAER 1095. January 13, 1999. *U.S. Securities and Exchange Commission* Accounting and Auditing Enforcement Release. *www.sec.gov.*

AAER 1283. U.S. Securities and Exchange Commission Accounting and Auditing Enforcement Release, June 30, 2000. *www.sec.gov.*

AAER 1579. U.S. Securities and Exchange Commission Accounting and Auditing Enforcement Release, June 21, 2002. *www.sec.gov.*

AAER 3165. U.S. Securities and Exchange Commission Accounting and Auditing Enforcement Release, August 5, 2010. *www.sec.gov.*

Becker, C. September 2, 2002. "No Contest for Ex-AHERF Chief: Sherif Abdelhak Defends Himself, Stating He Intended to Keep the Healthcare System Open for Patients." *www.ncbi.nlm.nih.gov.*

Becker, Cinda. February 3, 2003. "Early Release: Abdelhak Wins Parole after Serving 3 Months." *Modern Healthcare. www.modernhealthcare.com.*

Berner, Robert, and Mark Maremont. October 20, 1999. "Lost Heir," *Wall Street Journal* (Eastern edition). Available online via ProQuest database.

Bowling, Brian. April 24, 2013. "Creditors of Defunct AHERF to Receive Undisclosed Settlement from Accounting Firm," *Triblive. http://triblive.com.*

Dobby, Christine. May 4, 2011. "Crown Defends Trial Judge in Livent Appeal," *Financial Post. www.business.financialpost.com.*

Federwisch, Anne. 2007. "Exploring Ethical Lapses During the Rite Aid Crisis," *Markkula Center for Applied Ethics.* Santa Clara University. *www.scu.edu/ethics.*

Fitzpatrick, Dan. November 4, 2007. "AHERF's Ex-chief Bitter about His Fall," *Pittsburgh Post-Gazette. www.post-gazette.com.*

"Flying by Their Seats." July 29, 1985. *Wall Street Journal.* Available online via ProQuest database.

"Fortune 500." 2013. CNNMoney. *www.money.cnn.com.*

Heinzl, Mark. October 27, 2005. "Slow Canada: Fraud Cases Can Drag On," *Wall Street Journal.* Available online via ProQuest database.

Jones, Kenneth. March 29, 2012. "Convicted Producer Garth Drabinsky's Appeal Won't Be Heard by Canadian Supreme Court," *Playbill.com. www.playbill.com.*

Levitt, Arthur. September 28, 1998. "The Numbers Game." Remarks at NYU Center for Law and Business, New York.

"Lockheed L-1011 TriStar," Airliners. net. *www.airliners.net/aircraft-data/stats. main?id=271.*

"Lockheed L-1011 TriStar History." August 25, 2003. *GlobalSecurity.org.* *www.globalsecurity.org.*

Lockheed Martin Website. *www.lockheedmartin.com.*

Madhusudanan, Sindhu. July 9, 2013. "Lockheed Martin Is Only Maryland Company on 2013 Fortune 500 List." *http:// baltimore.citybizlist.com.*

Massey, Steve. January 17, 1999. "Anatomy of a Bankruptcy. Part I: Wake Up to Break Up," *Post-gazette.com.* *www.postgazette.com.*

Miller, Matt. December 1, 2011. "Ex-Rite Aid Executives Face Off in Federal Court." *The Patriot-News.* *www.pennlive.com.*

Mondout, Patrick. "Lockheed L-1011," *Super70s.com.* *www.super70s.com.*

Mulford, Charles W., and Eugene E. Comiskey. 2002. *The Financial Numbers Game: Detecting Creative Accounting Practices.* New York: John Wiley & Sons.

Navistar International Corporation. Statement of Income 2002–2003. U.S. Securities and Exchange Commission. *www.sec.gov.*

"Pennsylvania Attorney General Fisher: Former AHERF Official Pleads to Raiding Endowments; CEO Sentenced to 11 1 /2–23 Months." August 29, 2002. *www.thefreelibrary.com.*

Reisinger, Sue. October 24, 2012. "Ex-Rite Aid GC Loses Yet Another Case." *Corporate Council.* *www.law.com.*

Shecter, Barbara. February 13, 2013. "Curtain to Rise Again for Livent at OSC." *Financial Post.* *www.business.financialpost.com.*

Schilit, Howard. 2002. *Financial Shenanigans.* 2nd edition. New York: McGraw Hill.

Scolforo, Mark. October 15, 2004. "Former Rite Aid Vice Chairman Sentenced to 10 Years in Fraud Case," *The Daily Item.* *www.dailyitem.com.*

Scolforo, Mark. August 11, 2005. "Judge Cuts a Year from Rite Aid Chief Grass'

Sentence," *San Diego Union Tribune.* *www.signonsandiego.com.*

Simon, Bernard. October 23, 2002. "Theater Founders Are Charged with Fraud," *New York Times* (Late edition East Coast). Available online via ProQuest database.

SOX Report. 2002. *Report Pursuant to Section 704 of the Sarbanes-Oxley Act of 2002.* *www.sec.gov.*

Tillson, Tamsen. February 10, 2005. "Legit Plot Twist: Judge Rules Livent Duo Must Pay 23 Mil," *Daily Variety.* Available online via InfoTrac database.

Weinstein, Stephen. August 1, 2000. "Understanding AHERF: Observations of the Recent Settlements Involving Allegheny Health, Education and Research Foundation." Speech before the AICPA National Healthcare Industry Conference, Washington, D.C.

Willatt, Norris. December 21, 1970. "Out of the Spin?" *Barron's National Business and Financial Weekly.* Available online via ProQuest database.

Chapter 7

"Annual Partnership Meeting." October 26, 2000. *LJM Investments.* *http://smartmoney.com.*

Bajaj, Vikas. March 22, 2010. "India's Woes Reflected in Bid to Restart Old Enron Plant." *New York Times.* *www.nytimes.com.*

Bankruptcy Report #1: First Interim Report of Neal Batson, Court-Appointed Examiner. September 21, 2002. U.S. Bankruptcy Court Southern District of New York. Chapter 11, Case No. 01-16034 (AJG).

Bankruptcy Report #2: Second Interim Report of Neal Batson, Court-Appointed Examiner. January 21, 2003. U.S. Bankruptcy Court Southern District of New York. Chapter 11, Case No. 01-16034 (AJG).

Bankruptcy Report #3: Third Interim Report of Neal Batson, Court-Appointed Examiner. June 30, 2003. U.S. Bankruptcy Court

Southern District of New York. Chapter 11, Case No. 01-16034 (AJG).

Basin Water Inc. Selected Financial Statements 2006–2007. *www.sec.gov*.

Berthelsen, Christian, and Mark Martin. February 5, 2003. "Energy Trader Admits His Guilt," *San Francisco Chronicle*. Available online via ProQuest database.

"Breakdown of Charges against Lay, Skilling." January 20, 2006. *Associated Press*. *www.nbcnews.com*.

Brooks, Nancy Rivera. December 9, 2002. "Settlement Reveals Another Enron Strategy," *Los Angeles Times*. Available online via ProQuest database.

Bryce, Robert. 2002. *Pipe Dreams: Greed, Ego, and the Death of Enron*. New York: Public Affairs.

Byrnes, Nanette, Mike McNamee, Diane Brady, Louis Lavelle, and Christopher Palmeri. January 28, 2002. "Accounting in Crisis," *Business Week*, Special Report, 44, 5p, 1c. Available online via EBSCOhost database.

Cohn, Scott. February 8, 2011. "Former Enron CEO Denied Release to Attend Son's Funeral," *CNBC*. *www.cnbc.com*.

Complaint. United States District Court, Central District of California. Securities and Exchange Commission v. P. L. Jenson and T.C. Tekulve. Case No. CV11-05316 R(AGRX). June 24, 2011. *www.sec.gov*.

Davis, Michael. October 22, 2002. "The Energy Trading Flop," *Houston Chronicle*. *www. dukeemployees.com/deregulation2402.shtml*.

"The Defendants of the Enron Era." November 25, 2011. *Houston Chronicle*. *www.chron.com*.

Douglass, Elizabeth. March 20, 2004. "Tapes Bolster Electricity Claims," *Los Angeles Times*, C1. Available online via ProQuest database.

Eichenwald, Kurt. 2005. *Conspiracy of Fools: A True Story*. New York: Broadway Books.

Eichenwald, Kurt, and Matt Richtel. October 18, 2002. "Enron Trader Pleads Guilty to Conspiracy," *New York Times*. *www.nytimes.com*.

Emshwiller, John R. January 4, 2006. "Executives on Trial: Enron Prosecutors, after Plea Bargain, Can Reduce Technical Jargon in Trial," *Wall Street Journal*. Available online via ProQuest database.

"Enron Defendants Not Guilty for Charges," *Economic Times Online*. July 21, 2005. Bennett, Coleman and Co. *http://economictimes.com*.

"Enron Timeline." December 13, 2005. *Houston Chronicle*. *www.chron.com*

FASB Summary of Statement No. 167, 2009. *www.fasb.org*

"Fastow and His Wife Plead Guilty." January 14, 2004. *CNNMoney.com*. *www.cnnmoney.com*.

Feeley, Jef, and Laurel Brubaker Calkins. May 25, 2006. "Enron's Skilling Convicted of Conspiracy; Lay Verdict Next," *Bloomberg. com*. *www.bloomberg.com*.

Fisher, Daniel. January 7, 2002. "Shell Game," *Forbes Magazine*. *www.forbes.com*.

Flood, Mary. April 28, 2005. "Key Witness in Enron Trial Makes a Few Concessions," *Houston Chronicle*. *www.chron.com*.

Flood, Mary. July 21, 2005. "Broadband Trial: The Outcome," *CBS News*. *www.cbsnews.com*.

Flood, Mary, and Tom Fowler. February 5, 2003. "The Fall of Enron," *Houston Chronicle*. Available online via ProQuest database.

Gruley, Bryan, and Rebecca Smith. April 26, 2002. "Anatomy of a Fall: Keys to Success Left Kenneth Lay Open to Disaster," *Wall Street Journal*. *http://online. wsj.com/home-page*.

Harden, Blaine. March 1, 2005. "Utility Exposes Enron Green at Its Core," *Washington Post*. *www.washingtonpost.com*.

Hays, Kristen, and Anna Driver. June 21, 2013. "Former Enron CEO Skilling's Sentence Cut to 14 Years," *Reuters. www.reuters.com.*

Hays, Kristen. January 5, 2006. "Enron Defense Argues Houston Too Hot to Be Fair: Lawyers Cite Anger Shown in Jury Pool Questionnaires," *Chicago Sun-Times.* Available online via ProQuest database.

Hiltzik, Michael. July 18, 2012. "Manipulation of California Energy Market Gives Consumers a Jolt." *Los Angeles Times. www.latimes.com.*

Inmate Locator. *Federal Bureau of Prisons. www.bop.gov/iloc2/LocateInmate.jsp.*

Jaffe, Mark. March 19, 2012. "Fastow Draws on Enron Failure in Speech on Ethics at CU," *Denver Post. www.denverpost.com.*

Jore, Dharmendra. March 4, 2013. "Dabhol Power Plant Shuts Down as Gas Supply Stops Indefinitely," *Hindustan Times. www.hindustantimes.com.*

Kardashian, Kirk. October 10, 2012. "Andrew Fastow, Former Enron CFO, Talks Ethics With Students." Tuck School of Business at Dartmouth. *http://www.tuck.dartmouth.edu.*

Lattman, Peter. April 16, 2012. "Supreme Court Rejects Former Enron Chief's Latest Appeal," *DealBook. www.dealbook.nytimes.com.*

Lavelle, Marianne. April 25, 2005. "Rebecca Mark-Jusbasche," *U.S. News & World Report. www.usnews.com/usnews/biztech/articles/050425/25eewhere.htm.*

LR 17692. U.S. Securities and Exchange Commission Litigation Release. August 21, 2002. *www.sec.gov.*

LR 18543. U.S. Securities and Exchange Commission Litigation Release. January 14, 2004. *www.sec.gov.*

LR 17762. U.S. Securities and Exchange Commission Litigation Release. October 2, 2002. *www.sec.gov.*

LR 22014. U.S. Securities and Exchange Commission Litigation Release. June 27, 2011. *www.sec.gov.*

Malik, Om. 2003. *Broadbandits: Inside the $750 Billion Telecom Heist.* Hoboken, NJ: John Wiley & Sons.

McLean, Bethany, and Peter Elkind. 2004. *The Smartest Guys in the Room: The Amazing Rise and Scandalous Fall of Enron.* New York: Portfolio.

Mulligan, Thomas S. March 15, 2006. "Enron Witness Tells of Transfer," *Los Angeles Times.*

Mulligan, Thomas S. May 26, 2006. "Enron's Top Executives Are Convicted of Fraud," *Los Angeles Times.*

Oppel, Richard A. March 27, 2003. "Panel Finds Manipulation by Energy Companies," *New York Times* (Late edition), A14. Available online via ProQuest database.

Ovide, Shira. October 31, 2011. "MF Global: Likely Among the 10 Biggest Bankruptcies Ever." *http://blogs.wsj.com.*

Partington, Richard. July 14, 2012. "The Enron Cast: Where Are They Now?" *Financial News. www.efinancialnews.com.*

Pasha, Shaheen. July 5, 2006. "Enron Founder Ken Lay Dies," *CNN Money.* money.cnn.com.

"Payments to Date." May 2, 2011. *Enron Creditors Recovery Corp. www.enron.com.*

Peterson, Jonathon. July 16, 2005. "Enron Settles Claim of Price Gouging," *Los Angeles Times*, C1. Available online via ProQuest database.

Powers Report. February 1, 2002. *Report of Investigation by the Special Investigative Committee of the Board of Directors of Enron Corp.* William C. Powers, Jr., Chair, with Raymond S. Troubh and Herbert S. Winokur, Jr. *www.sec.gov.*

Roberts, Johnny, and Evan Thomas. March 11, 2002. "Enron's Dirty Laundry," *Newsweek.*

"SEC Charges Kenneth L. Lay, Enron's Former Chairman and Chief Executive Officer, with Fraud and Insider Trading," *U.S. Securities and Exchange Commission, 2004-94,* July 8, 2004. *www.sec.gov.*

"SEC Files Amended Complaint Charging Five Enron Executives with Fraud and Insider Trading Relating to Enron's Broadband Subsidiary," *U.S. Securities and Exchange Commission, 2003-58,* May 1, 2003. *www.sec.gov.*

Smith, Doug, and Nancy Rivera Brooks. March 29, 2003. "Glendale Abetted Enron in Energy Ploys, Papers Imply," *Los Angeles Times.* Available online via *ProQuest* database.

Smith, Randall. August 3, 2005. "CIBC to Pay $2.4 Billion over Enron," *Wall Street Journal. www.onlinewsj.com/home-page.*

Smith, Rebecca and Arron Lucchetti. August 28, 2000. "Rebecca Mark's Exit Leaves Azurix Treading Deep Water." *Wall Street Journal. online.wsj.com*

Smith, Rebecca, and John R. Wilke. October 18, 2002. "Enron Trader Admits to Fraud in California Crisis," *Wall Street Journal* (Eastern edition). Available online via ProQuest database.

Soroosh, Jalal, and Jack T. Ciesielski. July 2004. "Accounting for Special Purpose Entities Revised: FASB Interpretation 46(R)," *CPA Journal. www.cpajournal.com.*

SOX Report. 2002. *Report Pursuant to Section 704 of the Sarbanes-Oxley Act of 2002. www.sec.gov.*

"Status of High-Profile Corporate Scandals." November 23, 2005. *Associated Press Financial Wire.* Available online via LexisNexis database.

Stinebaker, Joe. January 3, 2007. "Former Enron Exec Causey in Prison." *Washington Post. www.washingtonpost.com.*

Swartz, Mimi, with Sherron Watkins. 2003. *Power Failure: The Inside Story of the Collapse of Enron.* New York: Doubleday-Random House.

"Two Enron Traders Avoid Prison." February 15, 2007. *New York Times. www.nytimes.com.*

"UC Reaches $168-Million Settlement with Enron Directors in Securities Fraud Case." January 7, 2005. *University of California Office of the President: News Release. www. universityofcalifornia.edu/news.*

Wilke, John, and Robert Gavin. October 22, 2002. "Deregulation," *Wall Street Journal. http://online.wsj.com/home-page.*

Chapter 8

AAER 1494. *U.S. Securities and Exchange Commission* Accounting and Auditing Enforcement Release. January 15, 2002. *www.sec.gov.*

AAER 1495. *U.S. Securities and Exchange Commission* Accounting and Auditing Enforcement Release. Litigation Release No. 17310. January 15, 2002. *www. sec.gov.*

AAER 1555. *U.S. Securities and Exchange Commission* Accounting and Auditing Enforcement Release. May 14, 2002. *www.sec.gov.*

AAER 1599. *U.S. Securities and Exchange Commission* Accounting and Auditing Enforcement Release. Litigation Release No. 17627. July 24, 2002. *www.sec.gov.*

AAER 1664. *U.S. Securities and Exchange Commission* Accounting and Auditing Enforcement Release. Litigation Release No. 17837. November 14, 2002. *www.sec.gov.*

AAER 2237. *U.S. Securities and Exchange Commission* Accounting and Auditing Enforcement Release. April 26, 2005. *www.sec.gov.*

AAER No. 2764. U.S. Securities and Exchange Commission Accounting and Auditing Enforcement Release. January 3, 2008. *www.sec.gov.*

AAER No. 2765. U.S. Securities and Exchange Commission Accounting and Auditing Enforcement Release. January 3, 2008. *www.sec.gov.*

AAER 2941. U.S. Securities and Exchange Commission Accounting and Auditing Enforcement Release. March 4, 2009. www.sec.gov.

"Adelphia Founder John Rigas Found Guilty." July 8, 2004. *Associated Press. www.nbcnews.com.*

"BellSouth Profit Up on Wireless Growth." January 25, 2006. *Reuters. www. news.com/BellSouth.*

Belson, Ken. March 5, 2006. "AT&T to Buy BellSouth, Creating Telecom Giant," *New York Times. www.nytimes.com.*

BR-6413. U.S. Securities and Exchange Commission Complaint against Adelphia Communications Corp., John Rigas, Timothy Rigas, Michael Rigas, James Rigas, James Brown, and Michael Mulcahey. Release No. 17627. July 24, 2002. *www.sec.gov.*

Bray, Chad. November 25, 2005. "Moving the Market: Adelphia Ex-Officer Admits to Filing False Report," *Wall Street Journal.* Available online via ProQuest database.

Bray, Chad. March 3, 2006. "Ex-Adelphia Executive Michael Rigas Avoids Jail Time for Role in Fraud," *Wall Street Journal. http://online.wsj.com/home-page.*

Brooks, Rick. October 11, 2004. "SEC Commences a Formal Probe of Krispy Kreme," *Wall Street Journal.* Available online via ProQuest database.

Buca, Inc. Financial Statements. 2000, 2001, 2002. U.S. Securities and Exchange Commission. *www.sec.gov.*

Chimicles & Tikellis LLP. June 22, 2004. "Class Action Lawsuit against Krispy Kreme Doughnuts Inc." *www.chimicles.com.*

Complaint. United States District Court, Minnesota. U.S. Securities and Exchange Commission vs. Greg A. Gadel and Daniel J. Skrypek. Case 0:06-cv-02320-ADM-AJB, Document 1-1. Filed 06/07/2006. *www.sec.gov.*

Crawford, Krysten, and Winnie Dunbar. July 8, 2004. "John Rigas Guilty of Conspiracy: Adelphia Founder, Son, Found Guilty on Some Charges That They Looted Cable Company," CNN/Money. *http:// money.cnn.com.*

di Florio, Carlo V. October 22, 2012. "Conflicts of Interest and Risk Governance." U.S. Securities and Exchange Commission. Speech. *www.sec.gov.*

"Dial a Deal." March 5, 2006. *Wall Street Journal. http://online.wsj.com/home-page.*

EdisonLearning, Inc. Website. http://edisonlearning.com.

"Edison Schools Leaving Publicly Traded Stage." July 14, 2003. *TheStreet.com. www. thestreet.com.*

"FTC's Competition Bureau Closes Investigation into Comcast, Time Warner Cable and Adelphia Communications Transactions," January 31, 2006. Federal Trade Commission. *www.ftc.gov.*

Gilliland, Donald. March 27, 2012. "10 Years Later, Two Members of the Rigas Family That Founded Adelphia Maintain Their Innocence," *The Patriot News. www.pennlive.com.*

Glater, Jonathan D. April 27, 2005. "Adelphia Auditor Agrees to Pay $50 Million Into Investors' Fund," *New York Times. www.nytimes.com.*

Goldsmith, Jill. March 28, 2005. "Perk Parade Hits a Slump: 'Will Adelphia Indulgences Jerk Benefits for Hollywood?'" *Variety.com. www.variety.com.*

Grant, Peter. April 19, 2006. "Adelphia's Sale Plan Suffers a Blow," *Wall Street Journal.*

Hoak, Kimberley. May 1, 2013. "Judge Rules Brown Owes Rigas Family over $400,000," *Potter Leader-Enterprise. www.potterleaderenterprise.com.*

Johnson, Sarah. August 6, 2007. "Deloitte to Pay $167.5M in Adelphia Case." *www.cfo.com.*

"Krispy Kreme COO Tate Leaving the Company." August 16, 2004. *The Business Journal. www.bizjournals.com.*

"Krispy Kreme Doughnuts Inc. Celebrates 75 Years." July 1, 2012. *Winston-Salem Journal. www.journalnow.com.*

"Krispy Kreme Names CEO: Shares Jump." March 8, 2006. *Los Angeles Times.*

LR 19719. U.S. Securities and Exchange Commission Litigation Release. June 7, 2006. *www.sec.gov.*

LR 19720. U.S. Securities and Exchange Commission Litigation Release. June 7, 2006. *www.sec.gov.*

LR 20312. U.S. Securities and Exchange Commission Litigation Release. September 28, 2007. *www.sec.gov.*

LR 20417. U.S. Securities and Exchange Commission Litigation Release. December 27, 2007. *www.sec.gov.*

"Magic Johnson Reforming Education in LA." September 14, 2011. *Huffington Post. www.huffingtonpost.com.*

Maremont, Mark, and Rick Brooks. August 11, 2005. "Report Shows How Krispy Kreme Sweetened Results; Panel Says Doughnut Maker Used 'Egregious' Practices, Blames Ex-CEO, Directors," *Wall Street Journal.* Available online via ProQuest database.

Martin, Dan. October 10, 2005. "Edison Schools Are Only Average," *Honolulu Star-Bulletin. http://archives.starbulletin.com.*

Masters, Brooke A., and Ben White. July 9, 2004. "Adelphia Founder, Son Convicted of Fraud," *Washington Post. www.washingtonpost.com.*

Nowell, Paul. January 19, 2005. "Krispy Kreme Ousts CEO in Turnaround Bid," *Washington Post. www.washingtonpost.com.*

O'Sullivan, Kate. June 1, 2005 "Kreamed! The Rise and Fall of Krispy Kreme Is a Cautionary Tale of Ambition, Greed, and Inexperience," *CFO Magazine. www.cfo.com.*

Revenue Recognition Project Updated July 2013. July 24, 2013. Financial Accounting Standards Board. *www.fasb.org.*

"Rigas, Brown Case in Judge's Hands." June 23, 2012. *Endeavor News. www.endeavornews.com.*

"Scott Livengood, CEO, Krispy Kreme." June 22, 2004. *CNN.com. www.cnn.com.*

Searcey, Dionne et al. March 5, 2006. "AT&T Nears $65 Billion Deal to Buy BellSouth," *Wall Street Journal. http://online.wsj.com/home-page.*

"SEC Charges Adelphia and Rips Family with Massive Financial Fraud." June 24, 2002. SEC Press Release. *www.sec.gov.*

SEC v. BellSouth-Update. March 16, 2002. *Foley FCPA Enforcement:* SEC and DOJ Enforcement Actions and Opinions. *www.foley.com/fcpa-anti-corruption.*

"Six Krispy Kreme Execs Ousted." June 21, 2005. *Associated Press. www.nbcnews.com.*

SOX Report. 2002. *Report Pursuant to Section 704 of the Sarbanes-Oxley Act of 2002. www.sec.gov.*

Snider, Shane. January 15, 2002. "SEC Settles Action with BellSouth," *Triangle Business Journal. www.bizjournals.com/nashville.*

"Status of High-Profile Corporate Scandals." November 23, 2005. *Associated Press.* Available online via LexisNexis database.

"Summary of Independent Investigation" by the Special Committee of the Board of Directors of Krispy Kreme Doughnuts, Inc. Published on the Securities and Exchange Commission website. August 10, 2005. *www.sec.gov.*

Woodward, Tali. June 20, 2002. "Edison's Failing Grade," *CorpWatch. http://corpwatch.org.*

Chapter 9

"About Freddie Mac." 2012. Company Profile. *www.freddiemac.com.*

Andrews, Suzanna. April 2010. "Larry Fink's $12 Trillion Shadow," *Vanity Fair. www.vanityfair.com.*

Balive, Marcelo, with Javier Castano and Plinio Garrido. March 18, 2011. "Losing Home—Immigrant Families' Path Through Foreclosure and Beyond," *New America Media. http://newamericamedia.org.*

Bankruptcy Report of Anton R. Valukas, Examiner. 2010. U.S. Bankruptcy Court Southern District of New York. Lehman Brothers Holdings Inc. Chapter 11, Case No. 08-13555. March 11.

Barta, Patrick. January 8, 2003. "Mortgage Delinquencies Fall, But Foreclosures Show Gains," *Wall Street Journal. online.wsj.com/ home-page.*

Browne, John. July 24, 2008. "No Bottom Yet for Flailing Financials." *321Gold.com. http://321gold.com.*

Christie, Les. December 30, 2008. "Home Prices Post Record 18% Drop: The 20-City S&P Case-Shiller Index Has Posted Losses for a Staggering 27 Months in a Row," *CNNMoney. www.CNNMoney.com.*

"Clearing the Fog." April 17, 2008. *The Economist. www.economist.com.*

Coscarelli, Joe. May 24, 2012. "Lehman Brother's Probably Won't Ever Be Charged With Anything," *New York Magazine. www.nymag.com.*

Countrywide Financial Corporation 10-Ks. 2004–2007. *www.sec.gov.*

Der Hovanesian, Mara. September 10, 2006. "Nightmare Mortgages," *Business Week. www.businessweek.com.*

Doubuzinskis, Alex, and Dan Levine. October 15, 2010. "Mozilo Settles Countrywide Fraud Case at $67.5 Million," *Reuters. www.reuters.com.*

Downey, Kirstin. December 7, 2005. "Mortgage Stress Seen for '06; Delinquencies on Subprime Loans Likely to Spike, Report Says," *Washington Post. www.washingtonpost.com.*

Eaglesham, Jean, and Liz Rappaport. March 12, 2011. "Lehman Probe Stalls; Chance of No Charges," *Wall Street Journal. http://online.wsj.com/home-page.*

"Fannie Mae Early History." 2004. *Alliemae. www.alliemae.org.*

The Financial Crisis Inquiry Report: Final Report of the National Commission on the Causes of the Financial and Economic Crisis in the United States. January 2011. Pursuant to Public Law 111-21. *www.gpo.gov.*

Friends of Angelo: Countrywide's Systematic and Successful Effort to Buy Influence and Block Reform. March 19, 2009. Staff Report, U.S. House of Representatives, 111th Congress, Committee on Oversight and Government Reform. Darrell Issa, Ranking Member. *www.oversight.house.gov.*

Galbraith, John Kenneth. 1997. *The Great Crash 1929.* New York: Mariner Books/Houghton Mifflin. Reprint.

Gallu, Joshua. May 24, 2012. "SEC Staff Ends Probe of Lehman Without Finding Fraud," *Bloomberg. www.bloomberg.com.*

Gittelsohn, John, and Ronald Campbell. July 12, 2007. "Street of Broken Dreams," *Orange County Register. www.ocregister.com.*

Gittelsohn, John, and Matthew Padilla. April 15, 2007. "Cutting-Edge Company Becomes a Cautionary Tale," *Orange County Register. www.ocregister.com.*

_____. May 4, 2007. "More Bad News for Lender," *Orange County Register.* Available online via ProQuest database.

Haddad, Annette. October 12, 2004. "State Dominates Subprime Mortgage Lending in U.S.," *Los Angeles Times. www.latimes.com.*

Healy, Beth. June 25, 2010. "Mass. Wins $102m in Subprime Loan Case," *Boston Globe. www.boston.com.*

Hurtado, Patricia. October 24, 2013. "BofA's Countrywide Found Liable for Defrauding Fannie Mae." *Bloomberg.* *www.bloomberg.com.*

Inside Job. 2010. Documentary. Sony Pictures Transcript. September. *www.sonyclassics.com.*

LR. 21068A. U.S. Securities and Exchange Commission Litigation Release. June 4, 2009. *www.sec.gov.*

LR. 21327. U.S. Securities and Exchange Commission Litigation Release. December 7, 2009. *www.sec.gov.*

LR. 21609. U.S. Securities and Exchange Commission Litigation Release. July 30, 2010. *www.sec.gov.*

McDonald, Lawrence G., with Patrick Robinson. 2009. *A Colossal Failure of Common Sense: The Inside Story of the Collapse of Lehman Brothers.* New York: Crown Publishing/Random House.

McLean, Bethany, and Joe Nocera. 2010. *All the Devils Are Here: The Hidden History of the Financial Crisis.* New York: Portfolio/Penguin.

Michaelson, Adam. 2009. *The Foreclosure of America: The Inside Story of the Rise and Fall of Countrywide Home Loans, the Mortgage Crisis, and the Default of the American Dream.* New York: Berkley Books.

Morgenson, Gretchen. August 26, 2007. "Inside the Countrywide Lending Spree," *New York Times. www.nytimes.com.*

Morgenson, Gretchen. October 15, 2010. "Lending Magnate Settles Fraud Case," *New York Times. www.nytimes.com.*

Muola, Paul, and Mathew Padilla. 2010. *Chain of Blame: How Wall Street Caused the Mortgage and Credit Crisis.* Hoboken, NJ: John Wiley & Sons.

Nixon, Ron. December 20, 2006. "Study Predicts Foreclosure for 1 in 5 Subprime Loans," *New York Times. www.nytimes.com.*

Philips, Matthew. September 26, 2008. "The Monster That Ate Wall Street," *Newsweek. www.thedailybeast.com/newsweek.*

Pickert, Kate. July 14, 2008. "A Brief History of Fannie Mae and Freddie Mac," *Time. www.time.com.*

Pridgen, Dee. 2005. "Predatory Lending: The Hidden Scourge of the Housing Market." Wyoming Lawyer. October/Vol. XXVIII, No. 5. *www.wyomingbar.org.*

Raub, Timothy. April 17, 2013. "Countrywide Financial Corp. Reaches $500 Million Settlement In 3 Mortgage-Backed Securities Class Actions." Litigation Resource Community. *www.lexisnexis.com.*

Reckard, E. Scott. February 18, 2011. "U.S. Drops Criminal Probe of Former Countrywide Chief Angelo Mozilo." *Los Angeles Times. www.latimes.com.*

Ritholtz, Barry. August 4, 2012. "Repeal of Glass-Steagall: Not a Cause, but a Multiplier," *Washington Post. www.washingtonpost.com.*

SEC Complaint. June 4, 2009. *Securities and Exchange Commission* Complaint for Violation of the Federal Securities Laws vs. Angelo Mozilo, David Sambol, and Eric Sieracki.SACV09–03994. United States District Court, Central District of California. *www.sec.gov.*

SEC Complaint. December 7, 2009. *Securities and Exchange Commission* Complaint for Violation of the Federal Securities Laws vs. Morrice, et al. SACV09-01426. United States District Court, Central District of California. *www.sec.gov.*

SEC Complaint. October 24, 2012. *Securities and Exchange Commission* Complaint-in-Intervention of the United States of America vs. Bank of America Corporation, successor to Countrywide Financial Corporation, Countrywide Home Loans, Inc., and Full Spectrum Lending. 12 Civ. 1422 (JSR). United States District Court, Southern District of New York. *www.justice.gov.*

SEC Complaint. September 25, 2012. *Securities and Exchange Commission* Complaint vs. G. Lundstrom, J. Laphen, and T. Lundstrom of TierOne Bank. Civil Action No. 12-cv-00343. United States District Court, District of Nebraska: Omaha Division. *www.sec.gov.*

Schapiro, Mary L. April 20, 2010. "Testimony Concerning the Lehman Brothers Examiner's Report," U.S. Securities and Exchange Commission. *www.sec.gov.*

Shenn, Jody. March 15, 2013. "Fannie Mae Preferred Stock Soars to High Since Bailout Month," *Bloomberg. www.bloomberg.com.*

Smythe, Christie. August 27, 2013. "Bank of America Must Face Mortgage Fraud Trial: Judge," *Bloomberg. www.bloomberg.com.*

Sorkin, Andrew Ross. 2010. *Too Big to Fail.* New York: Penguin Books.

TierOne Corporation. Extracts from selected financial statements. U.S. Securities and Exchange Commission. *www.sec.gov.*

The Subprime Lending Crisis: The Economic Impact on Wealth, Property, Values and Tax Revenues, and How We Got Here. October 2007. Report and Recommendations by the Majority Staff of the Joint Economic Committee. Senator Charles E. Schumer, Chairman. Rep. Carolyn B. Maloney, Vice Chair. *www.jec.senate.gov.*

Tett, Gillain. 2009. *Fool's Gold.* New York: Free Press/Simon & Schuster.

"The Wall Falls." October 28, 1999. *The Economist. www.economist.com.*

Vincent, Roger. July 3, 2003. "David Loeb, 79; Founded Mortgage Banking Firms," *Los Angeles Times. www.latimes.com.*

Witter, Lon. 2006. "The No-Money-Down Disaster," *Barron's*, August 21. *www.dowjones.com/factiva.*

"Who Is Fannie Mae Today?" 2012. Company Overview. *www.fanniemae.com.*

GLOSSARY/SUBJECT INDEX

Boom-bust cycles, 302–303
Borget, Louis, 206
Born, Brooksley, 307
Boston Business Journal, 24
Boynton, Richard, 53
Brazil, Cuiábá Power Plant in, 233–235
Bribery, 277, 278
Brickell, Mark, 307
British Telecom, 131
Brown, Franklin, C., 180
Brown, James, 275–276
Brown, Karen, 180
Brown, William, 240
Bubble, 302–303
    An inflated price for an asset that
    is not justified on the grounds of
    its actual value.
Buca, Inc., 290–300
Buckley, Robert, 46–47
Bundled contracts, 99
Business ethics, 24
Business schools, 11
Business world, ethical decision-making
    in, 29–34
Byrne, John, 50, 53, 65
Byron, Christopher, 48

C

California electricity fiasco, 220–223
California Public Employees Retirement
    System (CALPERS), 226
California Public Utilities Commission
    (CPUC), 220
Cameron, Kim S., 52
Capitalization of costs, 149–150, 174
Capitalization policy, 174
Carrot-and-stick approach, 52–56
Case studies
  Basin Water, Inc., 260–267

Beazer Homes USA, Inc., 77–92
Buca, Inc., 290–300
Navistar International Corporation,
    191–201
Peregrine Systems, Inc., 111–119
Peter Madoff, 40–44
TierOne Bank, 330–336
Tyco International, 155–166
Cash flow from operations (CFFO), 64,
    67, 69, 71, 98, 100–101, 104, 107,
    146, 179, 182, 246, 248–250, 282
    The amount of cash generated
    from the company's main
    operating activities, such as
    sales, services rendered, or
    other operating activities. (Cash
    flow from operations may also
    be referred to as *cash flow from
    operating activities.*)
Categorical imperative, 27
    As conceived by Kant, it is a
    binding moral obligation that
    must be universal, rational, and
    impartial.
Causey, Richard, 253
CDO (collateralized debt obligation),
    210, 306
CDS (credit-default swap), 306–308
Cendant Corporation, 150
Center for Audit Quality, 3
CFFO (cash flow from operations)
CFTC (Commodity Futures Trading
    Commission), 17, 307
CFTF (Corporate Fraud Task Force), 16
Channel stuffing, 59
    Persuading customers to place
    a later period's orders in the
    current period. The seller
    "stuffs" more inventory into the
    customer's warehouse than the
    customer currently needs.

with the act that produces the greatest amount of pleasure.

Hedonist's paradox, 26

Hirko, Joe, 218

Holding books open, 95–96
Keeping the current period's books and records open for a few extra days after the close of a reporting period to record additional sales.

Homeownership, 303–304, 311

Housing bubble, 302–310, 323

Housing market, 14

Houston Natural Gas (HNG), 203, 204–205

Hudspeth, Robert, 121, 133

Human rights, 33–34

I

IDB Communications, Inc., 126

IFRS (international financial reporting standards), 11

Impaired asset, 183
An asset whose carrying value is less than its fair or recoverable value.

Improper accounting of foreign payments, 276–278

Improper capitalization of expenses, 137–138, 146–150, 171, 174
The improper categorization of expenses as assets.

Improper deferral of expenses, 168, 169, 170–171, 173
Any technique that avoids the recording of an expense in the current period by shifting the recognition of the expense to a later period's financial statements.

Improper expense recognition, 168–174
The omission of expenses or movement of expenses from the financial statements in the period in which they should be recorded to an earlier or later period.

Improper revenue recognition, 93–107
Incorrectly recording a transaction in the financial statements, indicating that the conditions have been met for the earning of revenue.
definition of, 95
fictitious revenue, 102–105
improper timing, 98–101
premature revenue recognition, 97
at Sensormatic, 95–98

Improper timing of revenue recognition, 56–60, 66–70, 95–96, 98–101
The process of formally recording a revenue item in the financial statements in an earlier or later period than the period in which the item should have been recorded.

Improper use of restructuring reserves, 60–61, 70–71

Improper valuation of revenue, 105–107

Inadequate allowances for returns, 106
The amount that the company has set aside in the income statement to allow for customer returns is insufficient.

Inadequate disclosure, 269–271

India, Dabhol Power Project in, 213–214

Initial public offerings (IPOs), 143–144

In persona rights, 32

In rem rights, 32

Inside directors, 8–9

J

K

L

M

tethered to any truth claims; right action and the good are wholly dependent on, and relative to, the situation, actors, culture, group, or time period.

Morgan Stanley, 62–63, 72

Morse, Gene, 140–141

Mortgage-backed securities (MBSs), 303, 304, 308
Financial instruments that give the owners an interest in a mortgage loan or a partial interest in a pool of mortgage loans.

Mozilo, Angelo, 311, 312–313, 324

Muckleroy, Mike, 206

Mulcahey, Michael, 276

Multiple-element contracts, 99

Mutual Series Investment Fund, 47

Myers, David, 142, 150

N

NASDAQ (National Association of Securities Dealers Automated Quotations stock market), 11

National Association of Securities Dealers Automated Quotations (NASDAQ), 11

National Commission on the Causes of the Financial and Economic Crisis in the United States, 15, 303

National Westminster Bank, 235

Navistar International Corporation, 191–201

Net accounts receivable, 181

Net asset value, 145
The net amount of the fair value of a business entity's assets less the value of its liabilities and reserves.

Net income, 100–101

New York Stock Exchange (NYSE), 11

NI (net income), 100–101

Nitec Paper Corp., 49

Nonconforming loans, 311–312
See also Subprime loans

Non-consolidation rule, 241

Non-GAAP financial measures, 274
Measures that are not included in the income statement, balance sheet, or statement of cash flows from operations that are calculated in accordance with GAAP.

Nonperforming assets, 334–335, 336

Noonan, Timothy J., 180, 185–188

Normand, Troy, 142

Normative ethics, 24, 25–29
A branch of ethics that offers guidelines or norms on how to distinguish between right actions and wrong actions.

Notes receivable, 265–266

NYSE (New York Stock Exchange), 11

O

Obama, Barack, 15

Occupational Safety and Health Administration (OSHA), 16, 17n

Odlyzko, Andrew, 127

Off-balance-sheet entities, 225, 242, 247
See also Special purpose entities (SPEs)

O'Hara, Paul, 53

One-time charges, 71, 146

Operating income, 98, 100–101, 104, 107, 179, 182, 248–250, 282

Operational problems, 280–281

Osprey Trust, 235, 237–239

Outside directors, 8–9

Overseas Private Investment Corporation (OPIC), 213

Overstated earnings, 60–61, 70–71
by Enron, 211, 241–248
signals of, 241–248
by Sunbeam, 70–71

V

Variable costs, 52, 149
Variable interest entities (VIEs), 242
Vendor rebates, 176–177, 193–194
Vendors, on accounts payable list, 173
VIE (variable interest entity), 242
Vinson, Betty, 141, 142, 150
Virtue ethics, 25, 27–29
> An agent-centered normative ethical theory that uses virtuous character as the criterion for right action.

Virtues, 27–29
Volcker Rule, 17

W

Waldron, Murray, 122
Walker, Richard, 102
Wal-Mart, 55
Warranty reserve, 194–196
Water privatization, 214
Watkins, Sherron, 254
Weather derivative, 212
Whalley, Greg, 217
Whistleblowing, 6, 11, 16–17
White, Mary Jo, 4
White, Newt, 55–56
Whitewing Associates, 237–239

WilTel, 126
WorldCom, 6–7, 9, 10, 12, 120–151
> acquisitions by, 125–132, 142–143
> adjustments, 136*t*
> collapse of, 138–142
> failures at, 142–145
> fictitious financial reporting schemes, 134–138
> outcomes for, 151
> problems at, 132–134
> quarterly statements and balance sheets, 148*t*
> ratios, 147*t*
> signals of fraud at, 145–150
> wizards of, 121–125

X

Xerox, 98–101, 247

Y

Yates, Buford, 141, 142, 151

Z

Zisman, Stuart, 236